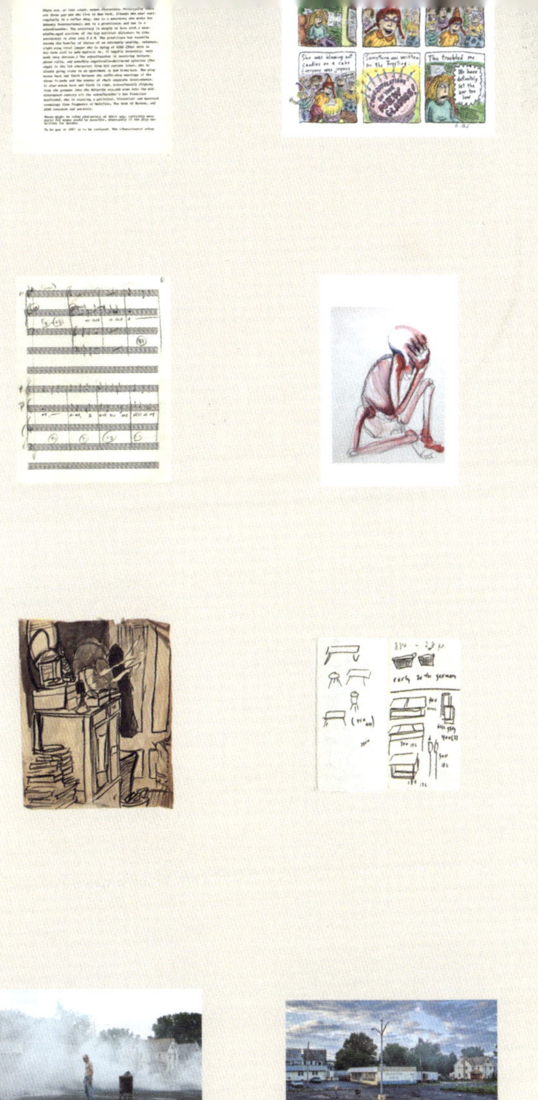

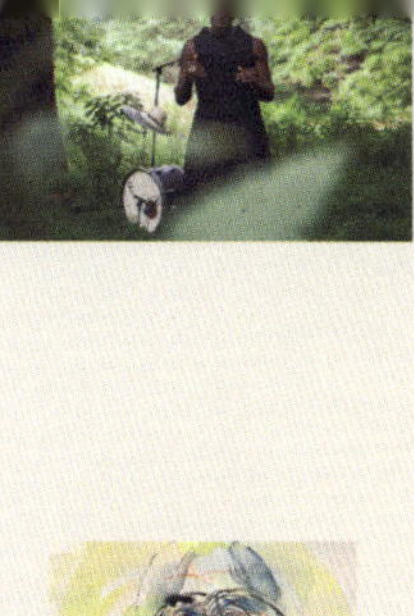

I0818996

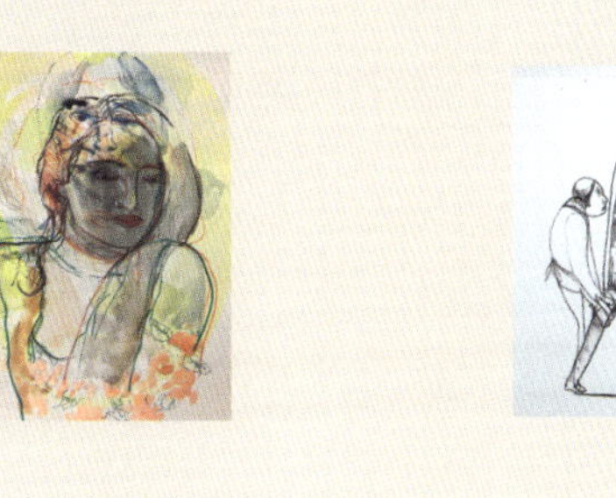

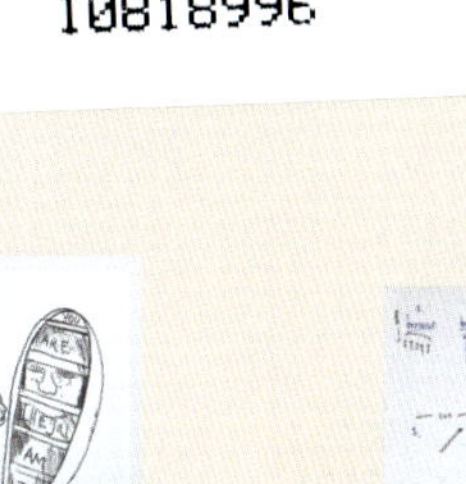

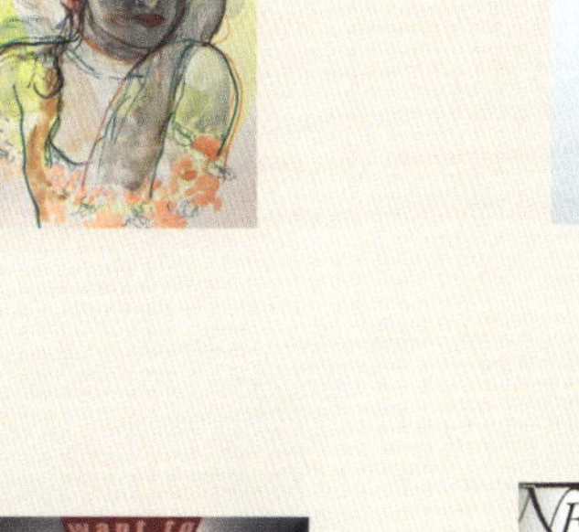

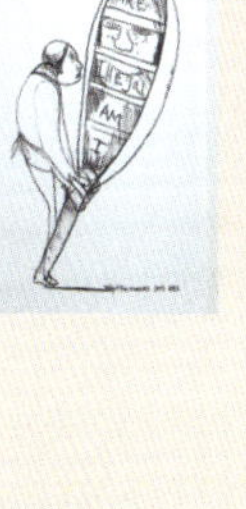

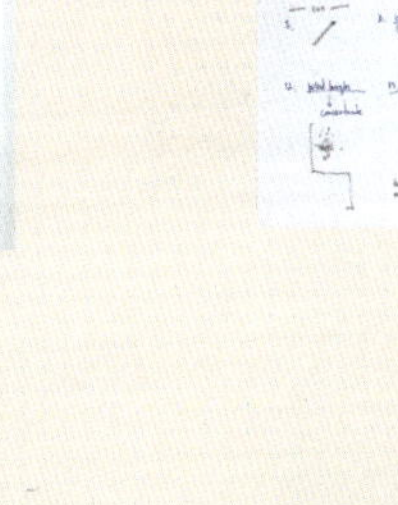

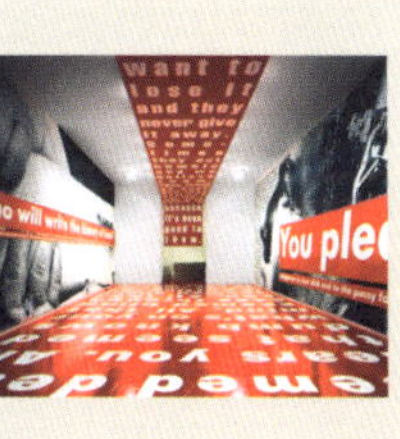

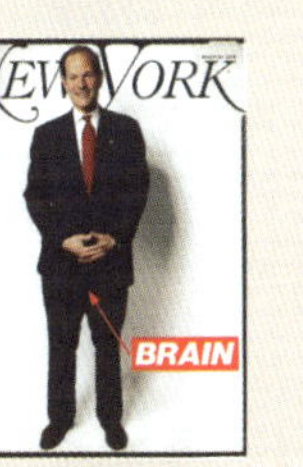
NEW YORK
BRAIN

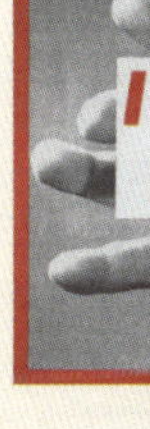

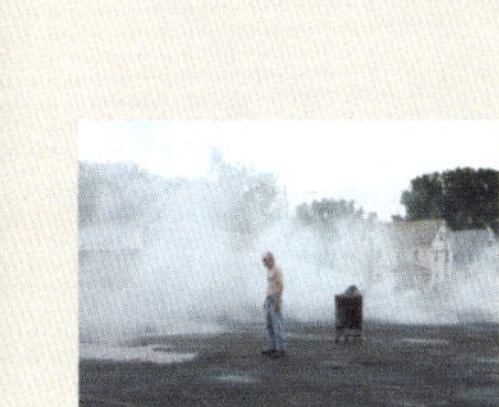

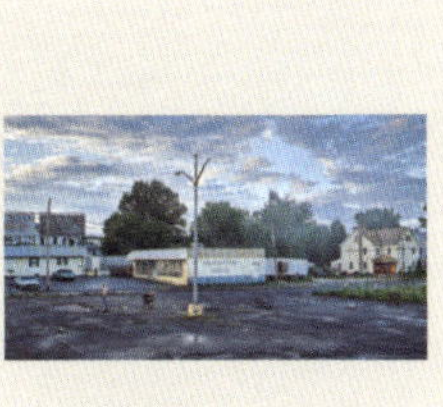

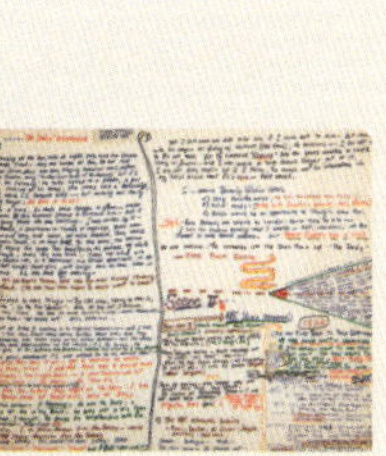

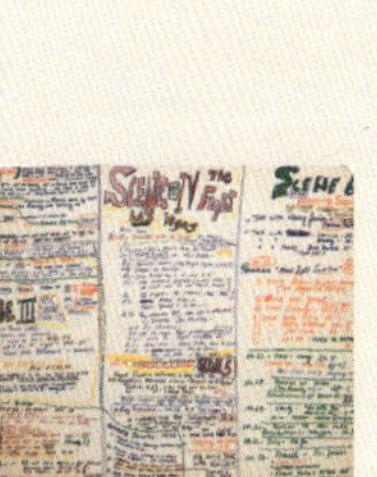

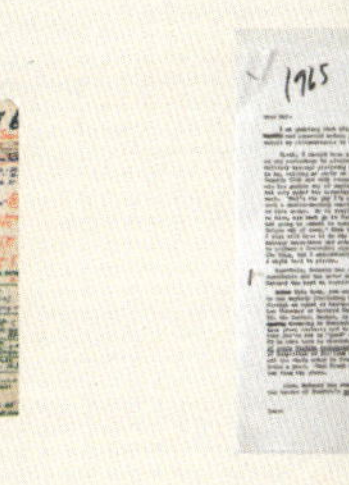

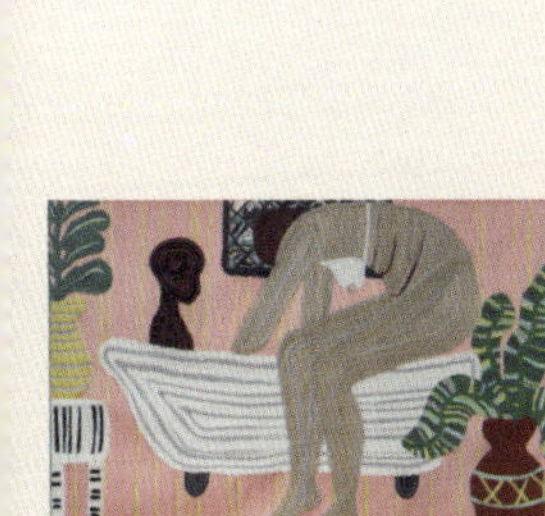

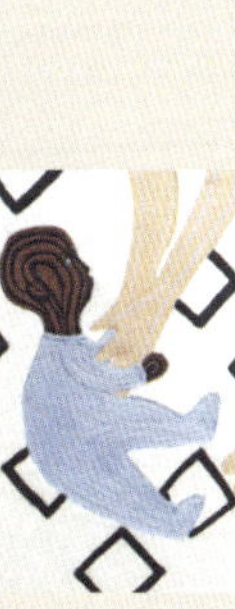

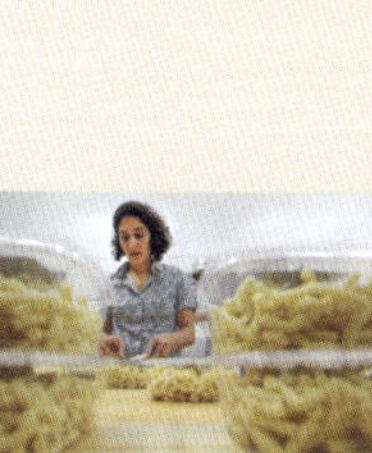

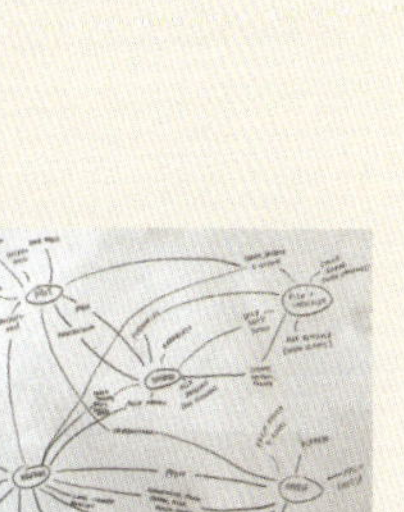

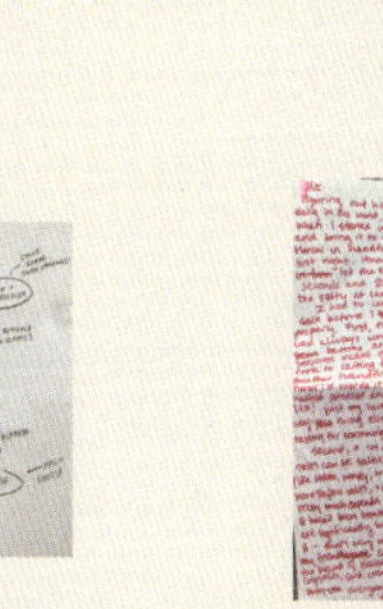

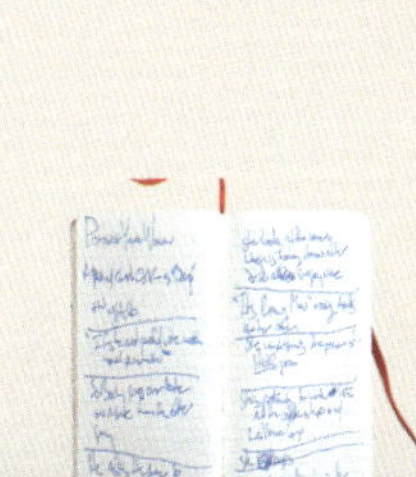

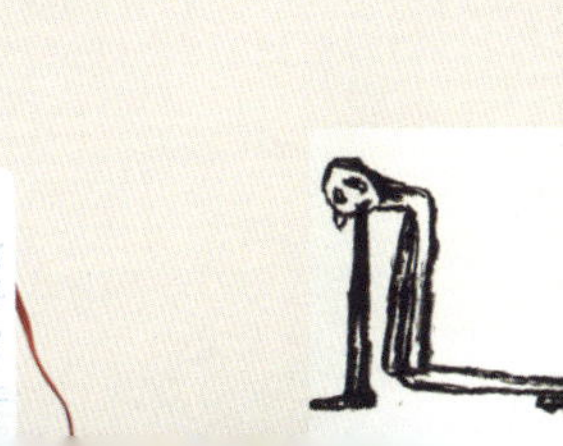

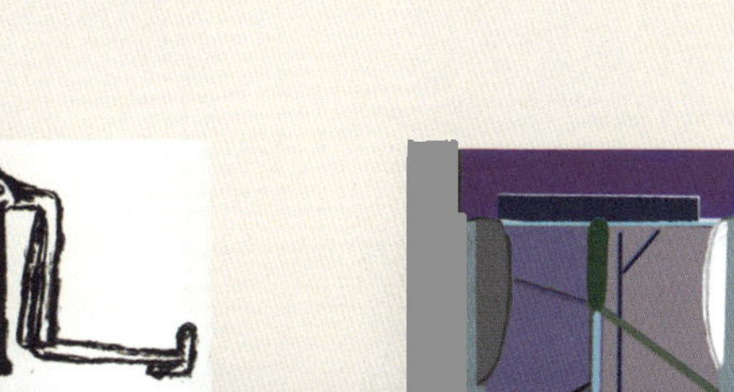

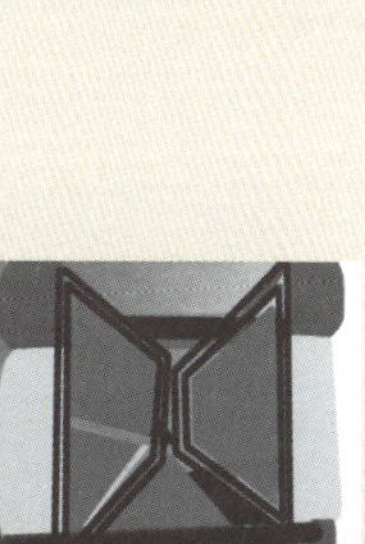

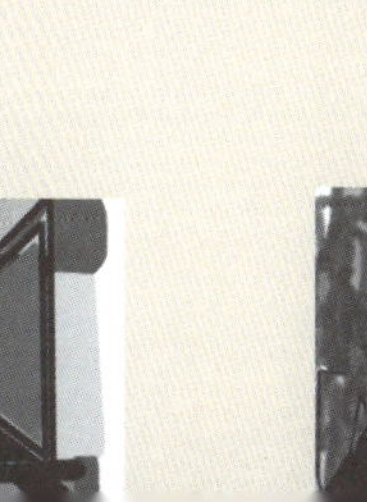

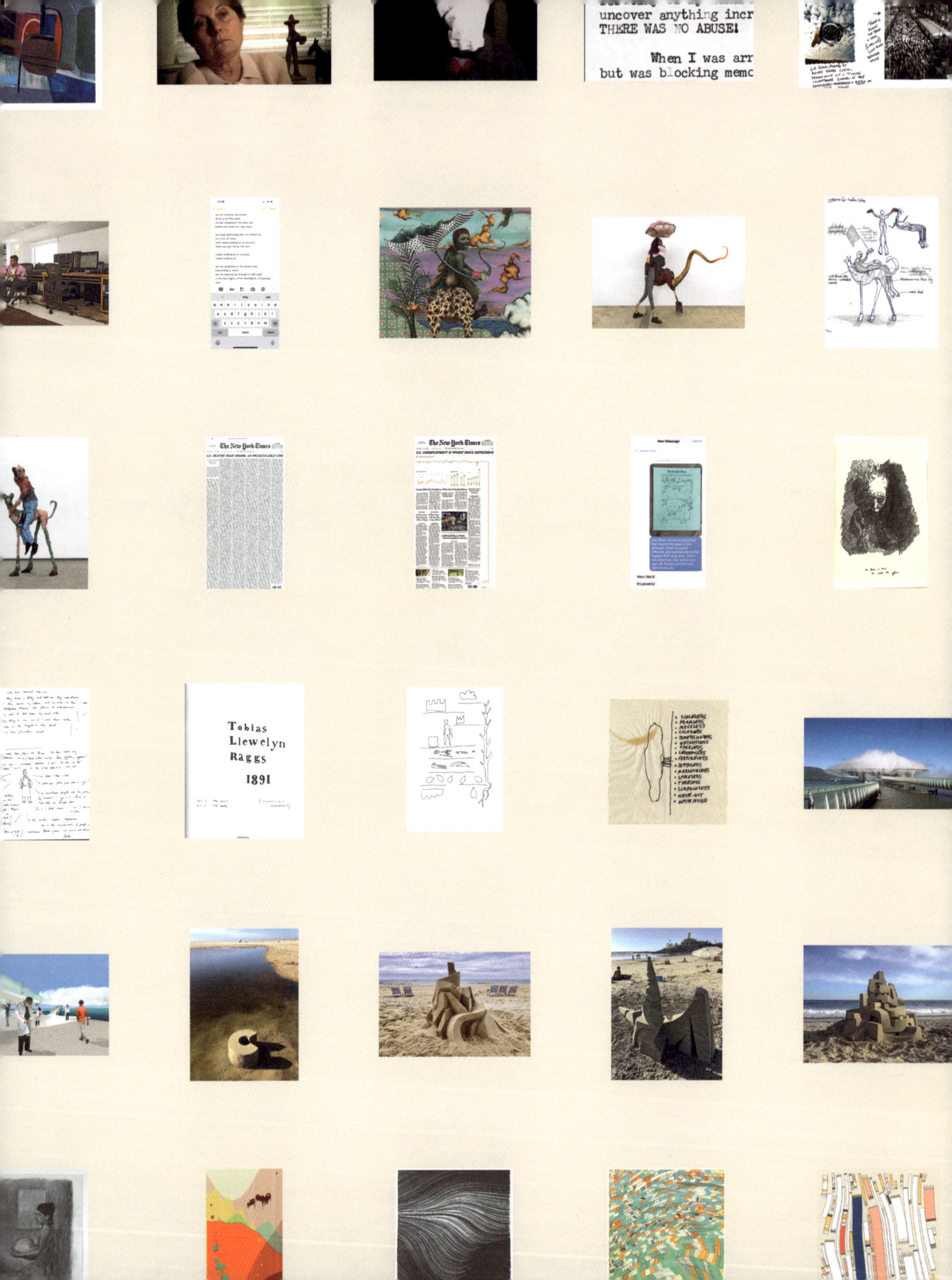
uncover anything incr
THERE WAS NO ABUSE!
When I was arr
but was blocking memc
The New York Times
The New York Times
Tobias
Llewelyn
Raggs
1891

The Work

of Art

ADAM MOSS was the editor of *New York* magazine, *The New York Times Magazine*, and *7 Days*. As editor of *New York*, he also oversaw the creation of five digital magazines: *Vulture*, *The Cut*, *Daily Intelligencer*, *Grub Street*, and *The Strategist*. He was elected to the Magazine Editors' Hall of Fame in 2019.

ALSO BY ADAM MOSS

"New York" Look Book: A Gallery of Street Fashion (co-edited); *"New York" Stories: Landmark Writing from Four Decades of "New York" Magazine* (co-edited); *My First New York: Early Adventures in the Big City (As Remembered by Actors, Artists, Athletes, Chefs, Comedians, Filmmakers, Mayors, Models, Moguls, Porn Stars, Rockers, Writers, and Others)* (co-edited); *In Season: More Than 150 Fresh and Simple Recipes from "New York" Magazine Inspired by Farmers' Market Ingredients* (co-edited); *Highbrow, Lowbrow, Brilliant, Despicable: 50 Years of "New York"* (co-edited)

Penguin Press, New York, 2024

The Work of Art

How something comes from nothing

ADAM MOSS

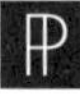

PENGUIN PRESS
An imprint of Penguin Random House LLC
penguinrandomhouse.com

Pages 422–424 constitute an extension of this copyright page.

ISBN 9780593297582 (hardcover)
ISBN 9780593297599 (ebook)

Printed in China
10 9 8 7 6 5 4

DESIGNED BY PENTAGRAM
Design and cover by Luke Hayman, Rob Hewitt, Patrick Crowley, and Anna LaGrone.
Cover background image: Marcel Proust, *Manuscript of In Search of Lost Time*, Bibliothèque nationale de France

MARDEE GOFF, PROJECT MANAGER

For Daniel

Contents

INTRODUCTION 1

You, Where Are You?
1 **KARA WALKER**
A Subtlety, or the Marvelous Sugar Baby 20

Bread Crumbs
2 **TONY KUSHNER**
Angels in America 33

The Child's Way
3 **ROZ CHAST**
"Gifts from the House of Low Goals" 48

Will Your Hand Do the Thing Your Mind Wants?
4 **MICHAEL CUNNINGHAM**
The Hours 55

God Flows Through Him
5 **MOSES SUMNEY**
"Doomed" 64

Later You'll Understand
6 **SOFIA COPPOLA**
Lost in Translation; Marie Antoinette 73

And There It Was
7 **SUSAN MEISELAS**
Carnival Strippers 80

A Puzzle
8 **STEPHEN SONDHEIM**
"Getting Married Today" 91

Waiting
9 **LOUISE GLÜCK**
"Song" 100

You're Never Going to Be Someone Else
10 **MARIA de LOS ANGELES**
True North 109

Tribe
11 **NICO MUHLY**
Reliable Sources 118

Disappearing Himself
12 **THOMAS BARTLETT**
Harvest/"Out on the Weekend" 126

The Sperm Bank and the Scroll
13 **TWYLA THARP**
"Commentaries on the Floating World"; *Twyla Now* 138

What Did You Do When You Were a Kid?
14 **JOHN DERIAN**
Decoupage 148

Enough About Me / What About Me?
15 **BARBARA KRUGER**
A Life's Work 157

What If Dr. Seuss Fucked Maya Angelou?
16 **DAVID MANDEL**
Veep; Two Jokes 164

There's Only One Way It Could Possibly Be
17 **GREGORY CREWDSON**
Redemption Center 174

The Unconscious Is Waiting to See If You Mean It
18 **MARIE HOWE**
"The Singularity" 182

What the Hell Could You Ask Sinatra?
19 **GAY TALESE**
"Frank Sinatra Has a Cold" 188

A Kind of Derangement
20 **CHERYL POPE**
Mother and Child on Blue Mat 198

With Beginner's Eyes
21 **SAMIN NOSRAT**
Salt, Fat, Acid, Heat 208

Brain, Hand, Pencil, Paper
22 **JOANNA QUINN & LES MILLS**
Beryl 216

Writing in the Dark
23 **WESLEY MORRIS**
The Notebooks 224

There, I've Killed It
24 **AMY SILLMAN**
Miss Gleason 232

Conjurer Extraordinaire
25 **ANDREW JARECKI**
Capturing the Friedmans 251

The Song on His Phone
26 **ROSTAM**
"In a River" 262

Laugh Here
27 **IRA GLASS**
This American Life 266

I Am a Portal
28 **SIMPHIWE NDZUBE**
Hunter 272

A "Rothko" on A1
29 **DEAN BAQUET & TOM BODKIN**
New York Times front page, May 24, 2020 280

Itchy Little Breakthroughs
30 **MAX PORTER**
Tobias Llewelyn Raggs 1891 (:Unconscious Throughout) 291

Theory and Fog
31 **ELIZABETH DILLER**
The Blur Building 298

Here Today, Gone Today
32 **IAN ADELMAN, CALVIN SEIBERT**
Todos Santos Castle 304

The Computer Has a Hand Too
33 **TYLER HOBBS**
Fidenza 312

It Is *Always* Harder
34 **MARC JACOBS**
Striped Jersey Dress 319

Alter Ego
35 **GRADY WEST**
Dina Martina 326

The Brain Is a Slide Carousel
36 **WILL SHORTZ**
"Driving Around" 332

A Map of Her Mind
37 **SHEILA HETI**
How Should a Person Be? 338

I Am Begrudgingly on the Wall
38 **GERALD LOVELL**
Chameleon 347

Stay Simple
39 **JODY WILLIAMS & RITA SODI**
Svizzerina 354

Don't Hold Back
40 **TAYLOR MAC & MACHINE DAZZLE**
A 24-Decade History of Popular Music 358

Arguing
41 **DAVID SIMON**
The Wire, Season 2 368

It's Your Book, You Can Do Whatever You Want
42 **GEORGE SAUNDERS**
Lincoln in the Bardo 376

How Great Thou Art
43 **SUZAN-LORI PARKS**
Plays for the Plague Year 388

AFTERWORD 400

APPENDIX 406

ACKNOWLEDGMENTS 420

CREDITS 422

Introduction

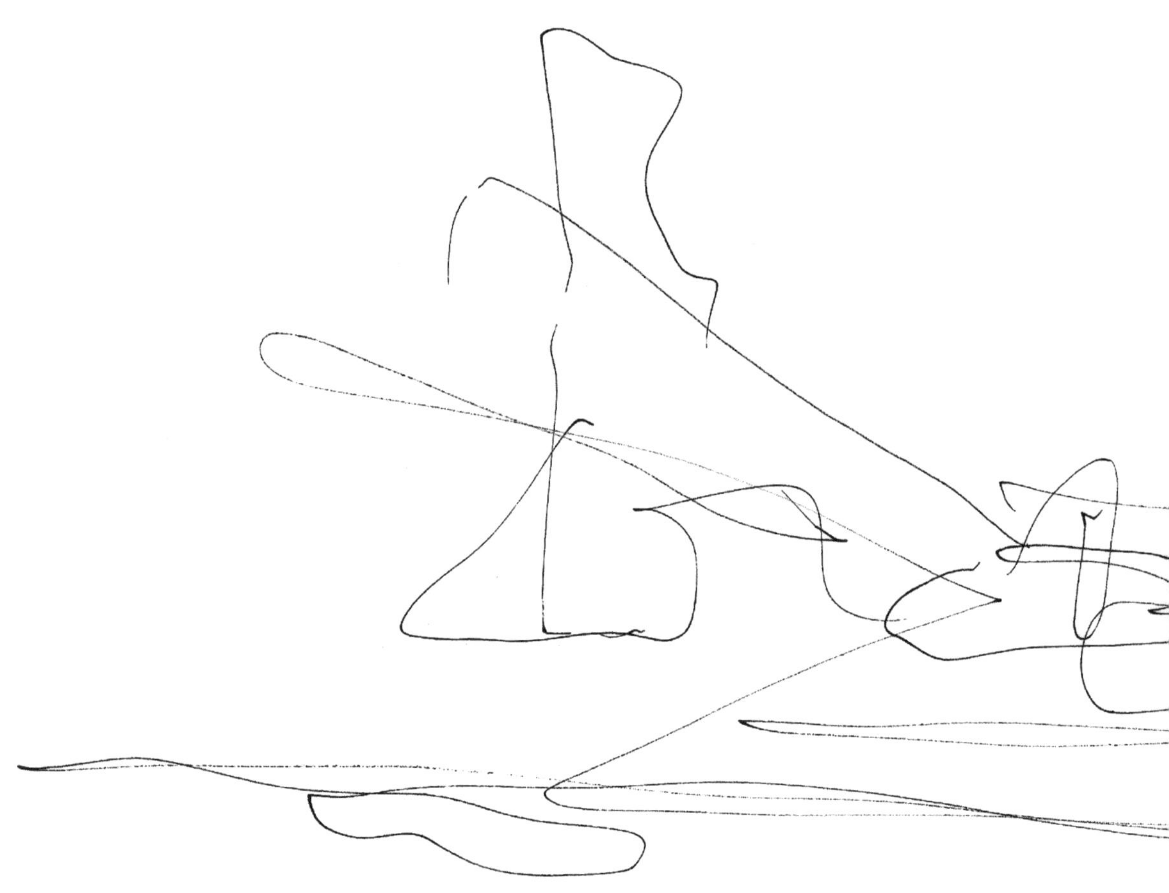

HOW DOES THIS

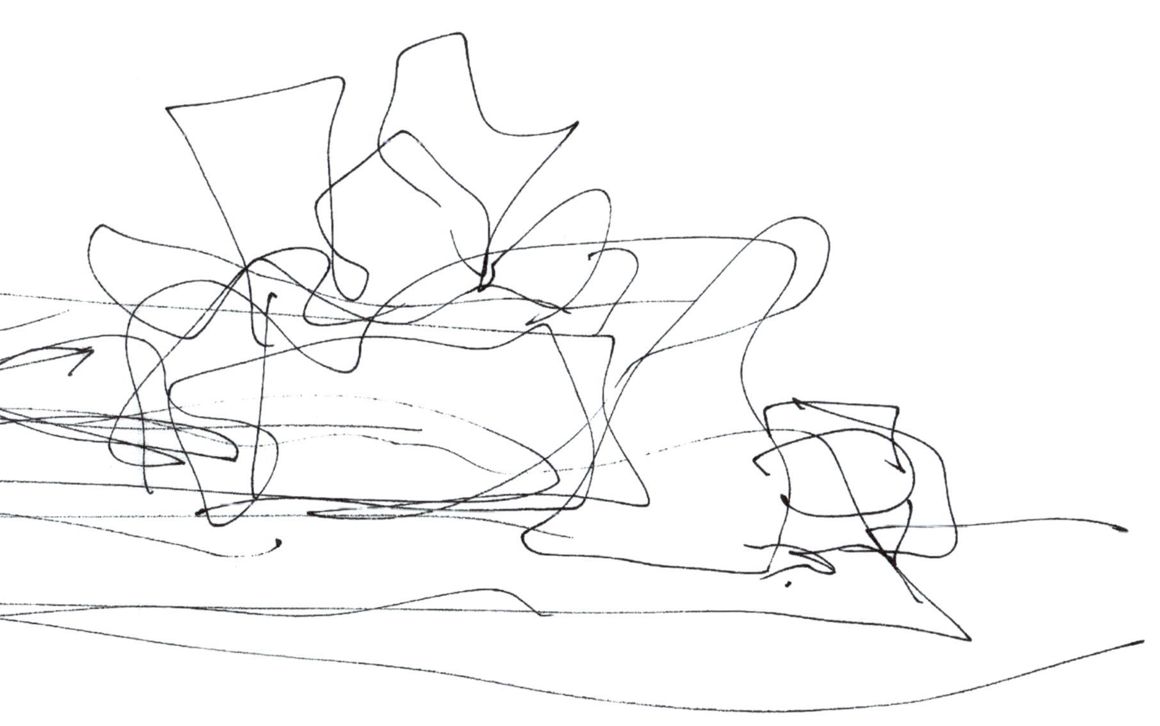

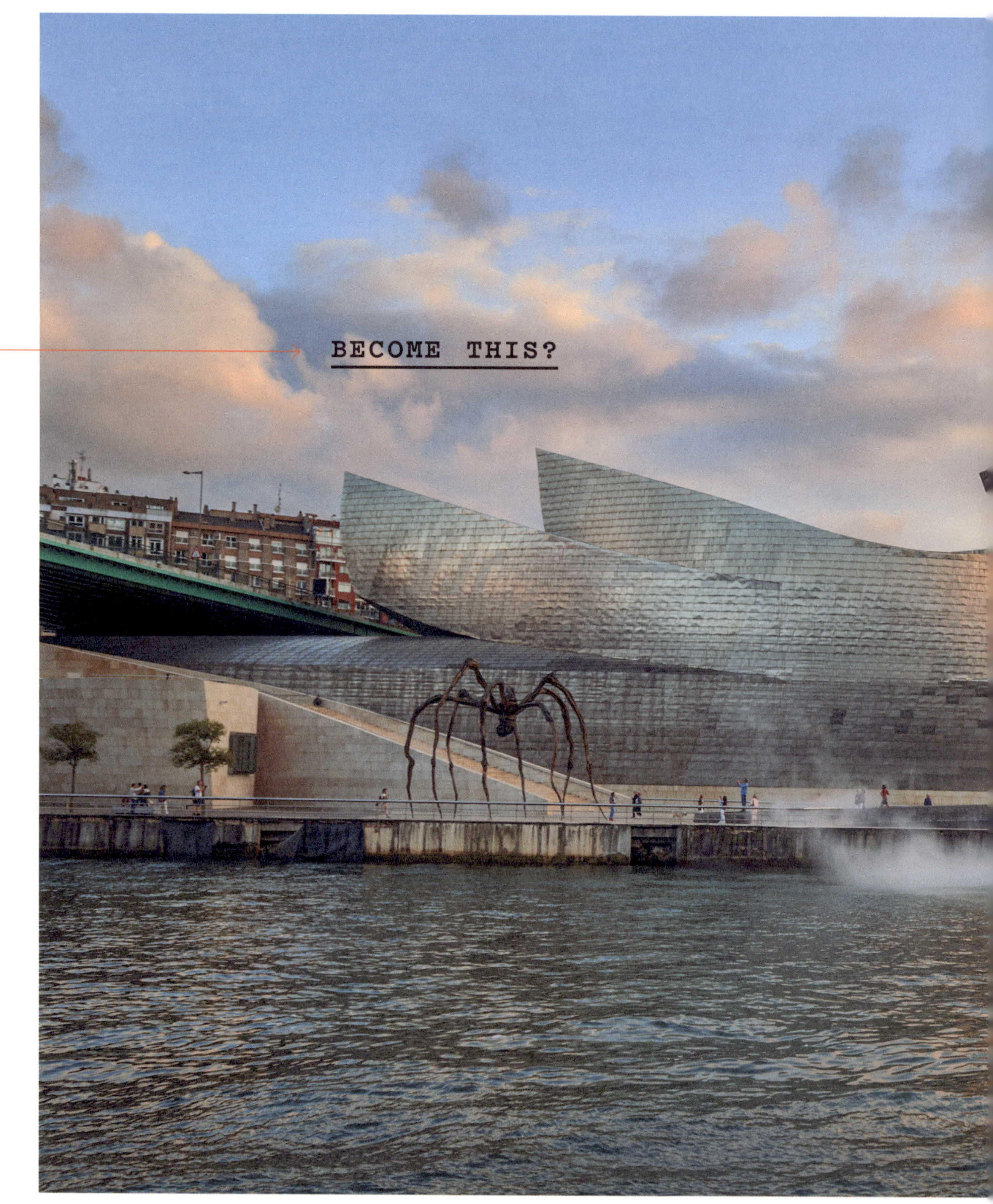
BECOME THIS?

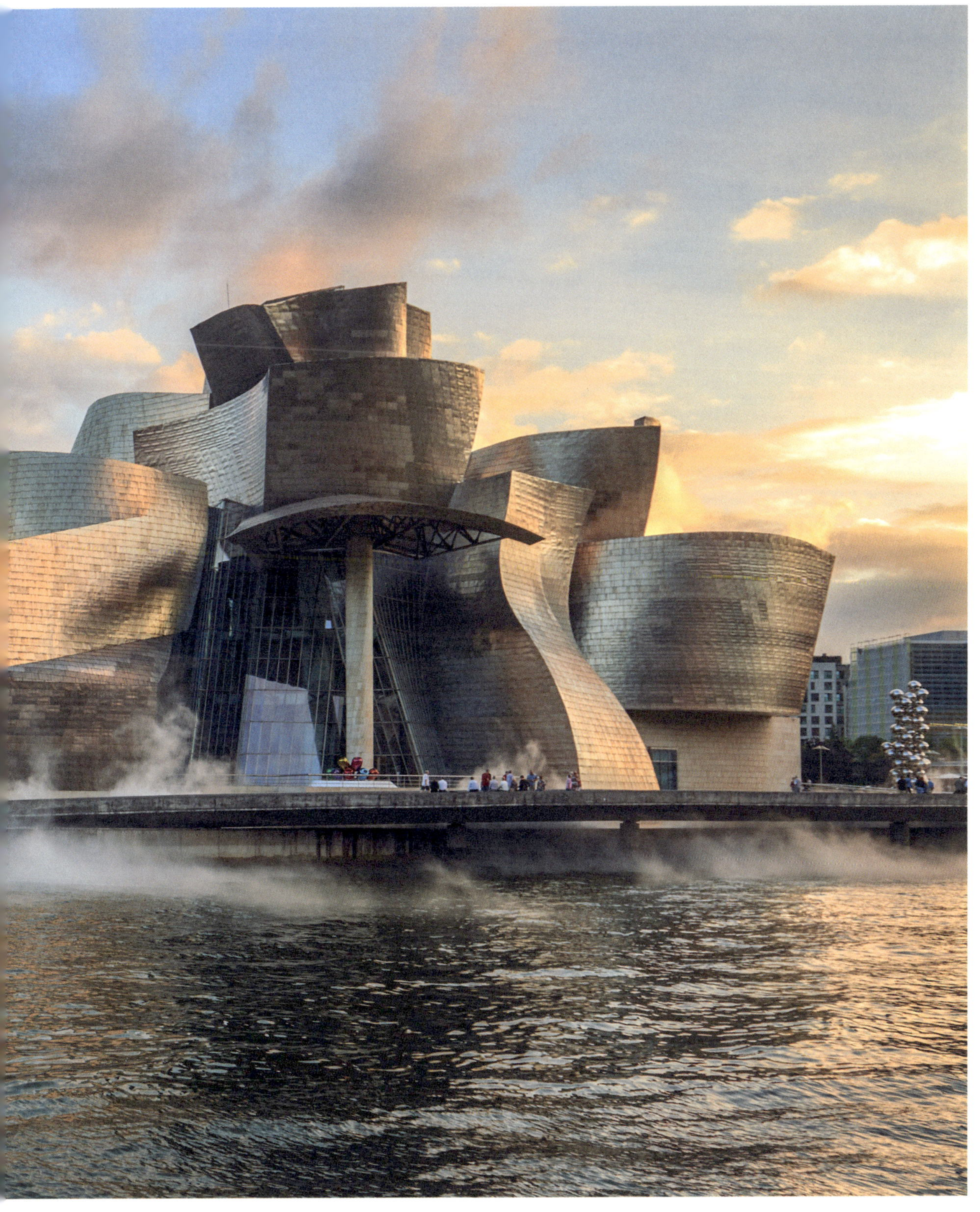

I WAS STANDING in the gift shop of the Guggenheim in Bilbao, Spain, flipping through the book *Gehry Draws*, when I came across the scribble you just passed a couple of pages back. It was more or less the first intimation the building's architect, Frank Gehry, had of the museum, which became an architectural icon the moment it was built; it's been compared with a boat, a fish, an artichoke, and Marilyn Monroe. I happen to love a doodle, and the scribble was a compelling little doodle in its own right, but what was so striking to me was how much it resembled the cockamamie (and extraordinary) structure I had come to Bilbao to see.

As I looked at the scribble and at the walls, and then back again at the drawing, an image out of a Pixar short popped into my head: the doodle shimmied to life to become the building it imagined, which now surrounded me. Gehry talks about these scribbles (his word for them—and there are many, just like this one) as his way of "thinking aloud." And for a brief moment, I was right there with him when he had that first electric thought envisioning the place. It was one of those fleeting associations you hardly register. I moved on.

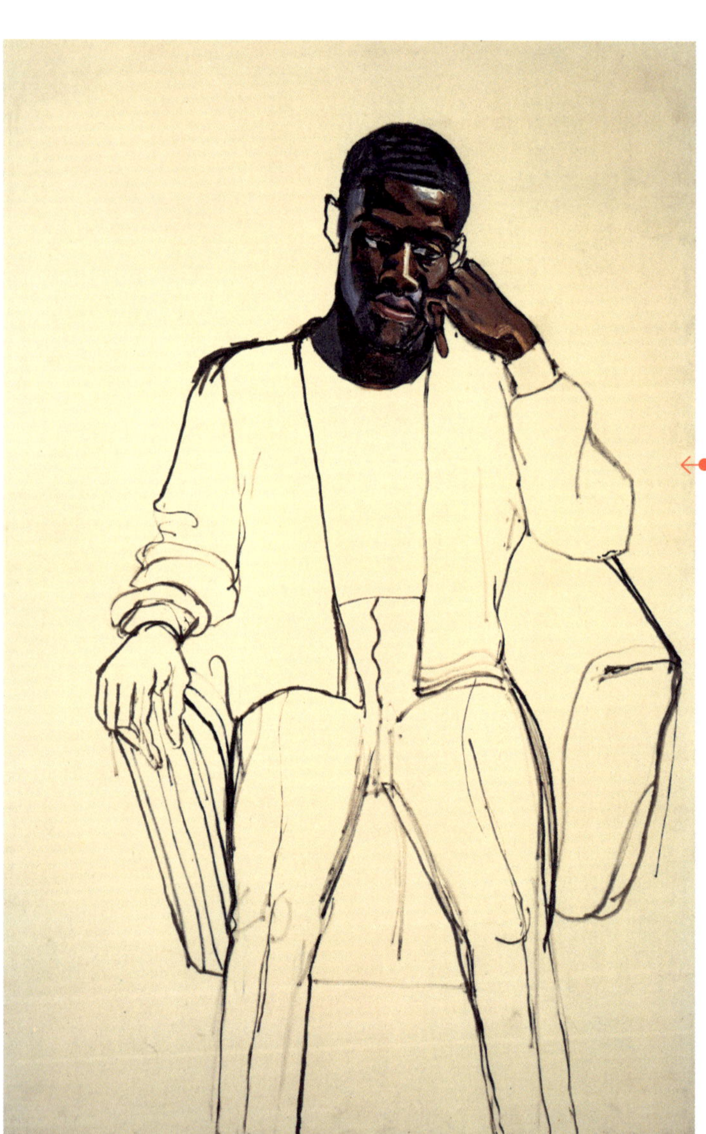

And yet I'd had a similar experience while I was still upstairs in the museum, at an exhibit of Alice Neel paintings that had been traveling around the world. Among them was a picture of a man named James Hunter, called *Black Draftee (James Hunter)*.

As the story goes, Hunter came for a sitting, then went to Vietnam; he never returned to her studio. Neel looked at what she had applied to the canvas in that one meeting and declared the painting finished. I'm nuts about a lot of her work, but on that day as I was tooling around the galleries, I kept circling back to this painting. I was stuck on it. The interrupted portrait of Hunter was haunting, but what really got to me was the implied portrait—of Neel the artist, painting the picture. So there I was with her, too, experiencing the sitting as she experienced it.

And then it happened again. A day or so later I was in Madrid at the

Prado museum, and I saw this painting by Velázquez, one of the many court portraits of Philip IV.

It's hardly the most interesting of his works, but see where you can make out a trace of where it looks like the artist initially posed the king's leg before fixing it? Standing by the painting, staring down the flaw, I felt as if I'd discovered a secret. It came as a gift to view Velázquez as mortal, making a decision and then thinking better of it.[1]

1. That's what I *thought* I was seeing. As I learned later, scholars have determined that in this painting, the leg was the vestige of an earlier work he had painted over. Still, it happens also to be true that Velázquez frequently left marks from his mistakes and second thoughts on the canvas. He's well-known for it.

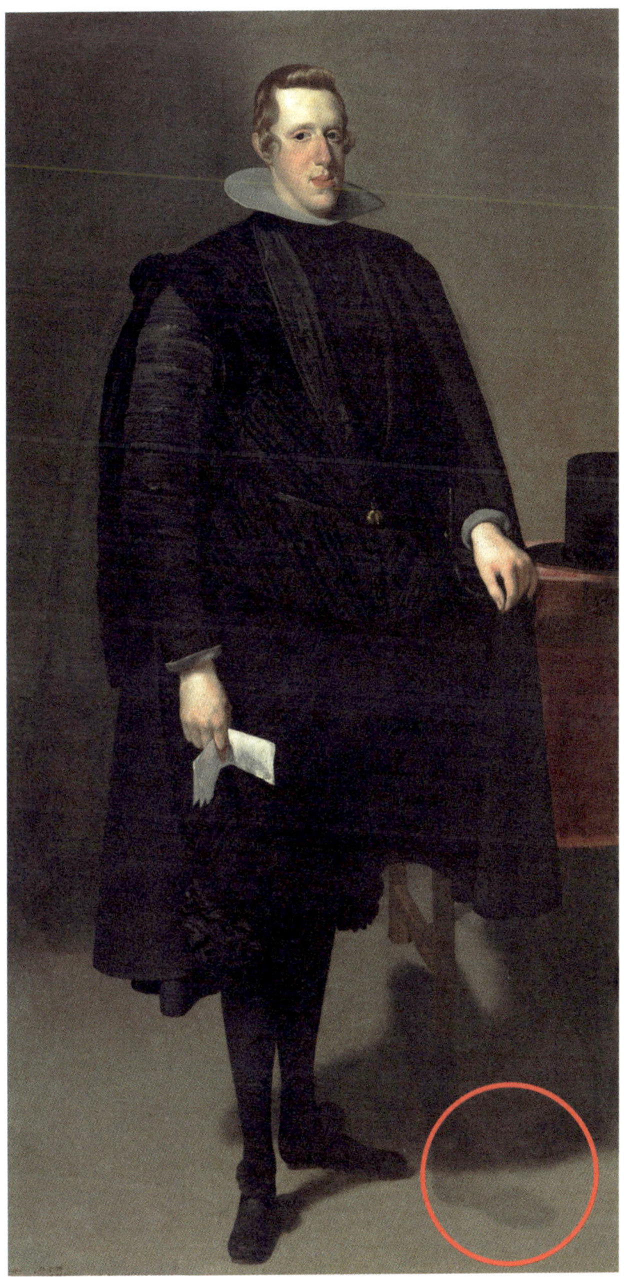

I've long been attracted to this sort of artifact—of artists caught in the act of making art. If you look around, you can find them in corners of the internet: academic websites, auction house offerings, fanzines. They show up in the occasional exhibit, or as a sideshow in museum retrospectives. There are many types: tossed-off sketches and more-considered studies, unfinished work, meandering notes to self, scribbled lyric fragments, marked-up text, mad outlines. I find them almost inexplicably beautiful in all their genres.

Some of my interest is aesthetic. I appreciate a crude hand; I can see the artist in it. I respect the honesty of the specimens, knowing they were not meant for me to see. They're forensically interesting, often revealing stages of thinking. But I suppose what I find most satisfying about them is the way they seem to embody anticipation. They're full of portent, more verb than noun. Also, poring over them gives me the same charge I get from reading the letters and journals of famous people. There's a nosy pleasure in that, and I've often thought, in passing, that someone ought to put these kinds of documents in a book. So, to begin with, that's what you're holding right now.

But that's not really what this book is about. The true value of unbaked scrawls and sketches and whatnot is as a window to an artist's process. *Process* is an ugly-sounding word—pedestrian jargon for the inherently wondrous act of creation—but it describes a method by which a thing evolves, which has always had a hold on me. For over forty

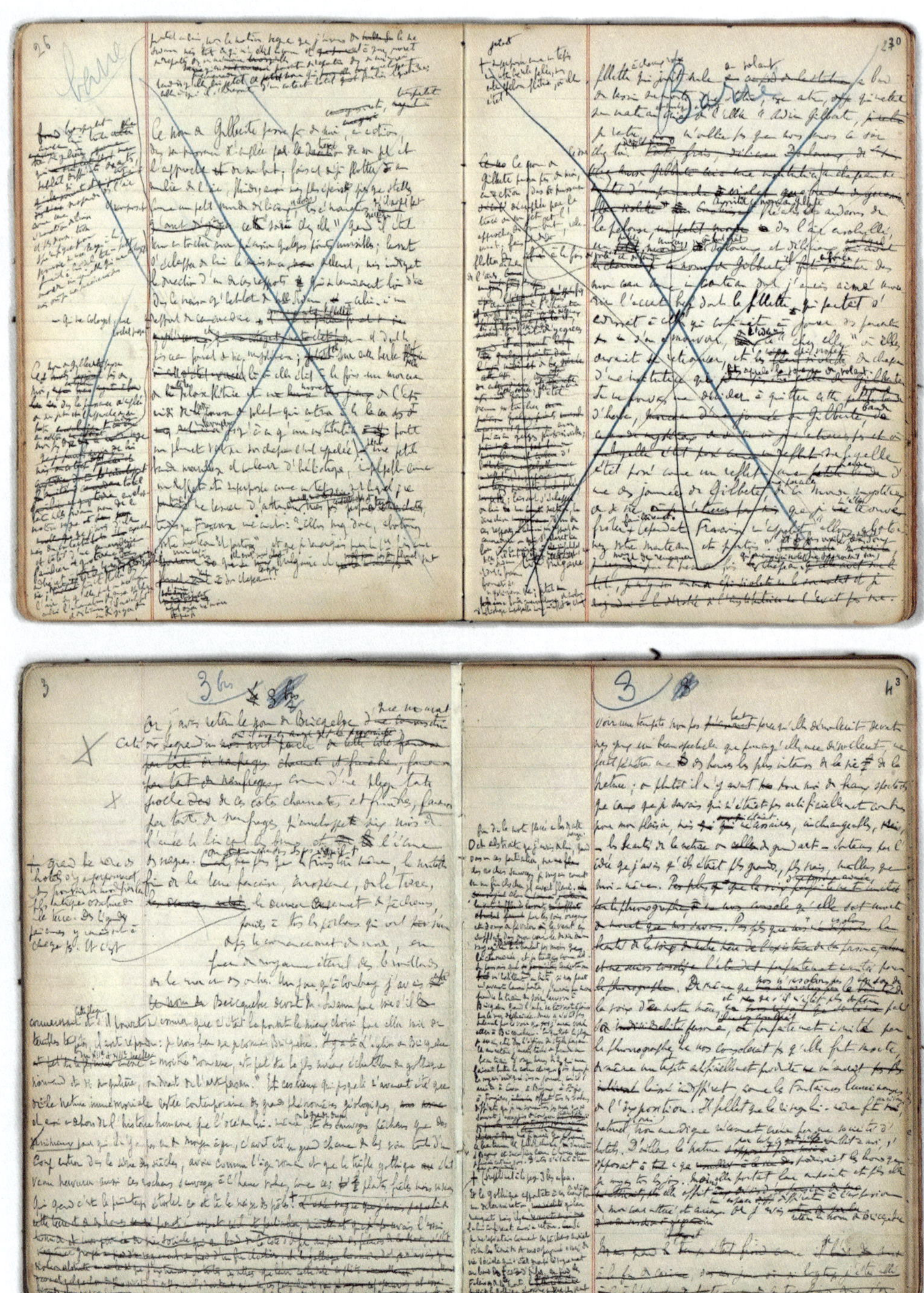

Here are two: Proust's markings on a manuscript of *In Search of Lost Time/Remembrance of Things Past*. There are thousands of pages like this....

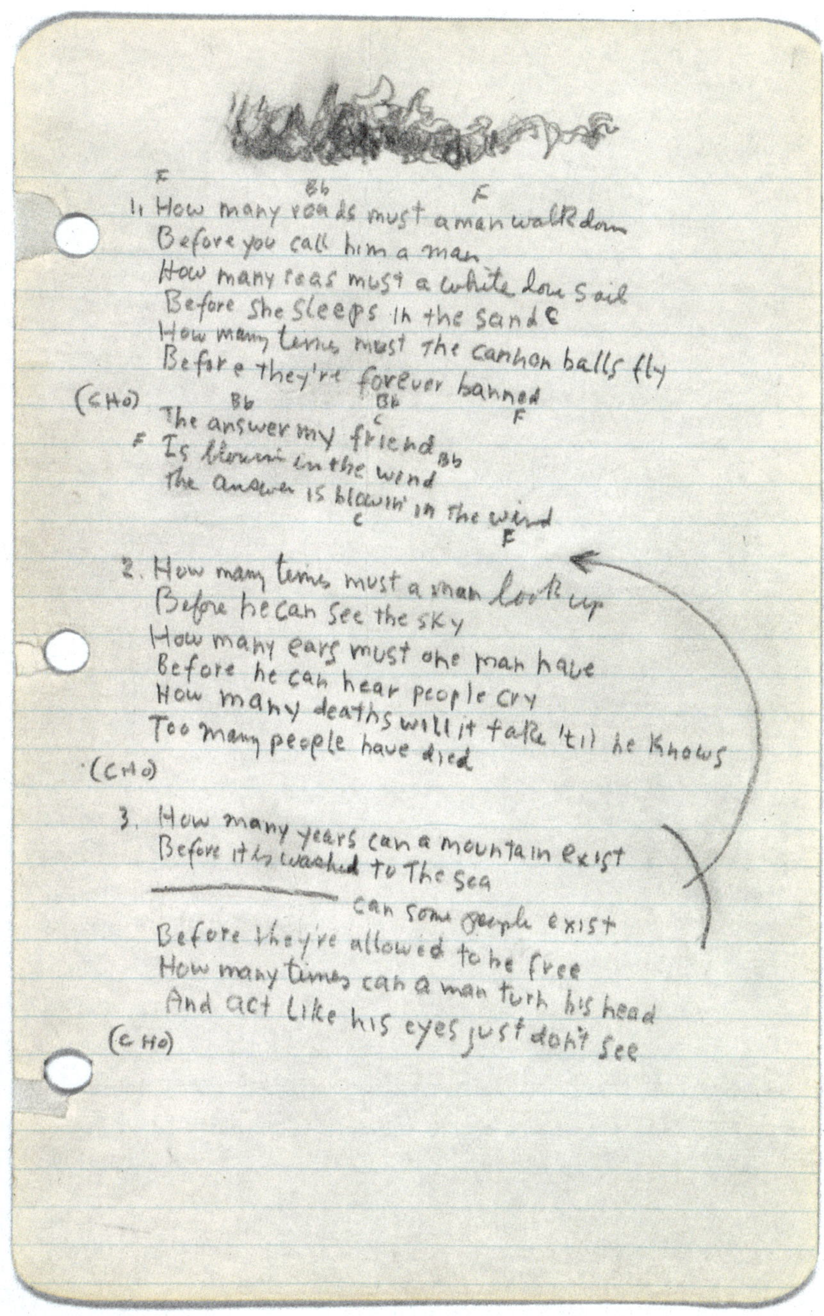

1. How many roads must a man walk down
Before you call him a man
How many seas must a white dove sail
Before she sleeps in the sand
How many times must the cannon balls fly
Before they're forever banned
(CHO) The answer my friend
Is blowin' in the wind
The answer is blowin' in the wind

2. How many times must a man look up
Before he can see the sky
How many ears must one man have
Before he can hear people cry
How many deaths will it take 'til he knows
Too many people have died
(CHO)

3. How many years can a mountain exist
Before it's washed to the sea
________ can some people exist
Before they're allowed to be free
How many times can a man turn his head
And act like his eyes just don't see
(CHO)

And this: Bob Dylan still working out "Blowin' in the Wind" in 1962, about a month after he first wrote the song (which he said took about thirty minutes). In the final version, the two stanzas were shifted as his arrow indicates. I find lyric scrawls (often on hotel stationery) especially vivid evidence of artists in mid-thought. For more artifacts like this, see the Appendix.

years I was an editor, of magazines mostly: *New York* most recently, *The New York Times Magazine* before that, and also a short-lived weekly called *7 Days*. Particularly in the kinds of general-interest magazines I was editing, you could follow your curiosities any old place (that was the job description), and mine was often the *how* of anything. While a childlike interest perhaps—naive and open-ended, each *how* toppling into another—it was also opportunistic. I published a lot of what is known as process journalism, origin stories especially, which could then be fashioned into narrative.

As an editor, what I liked about these stories (beyond their answers to my questions) was the classic structure of them—each inherently dramatic, starting with nothing and ending with something. Cultural procedurals were especially good material. Years ago I assigned a story on Stephen Sondheim in which he explained, in thousands of words, how he wrote a single song. That was pretty great. I published the story on the Guggenheim Museum in Bilbao that compared the building with Marilyn Monroe. I traced the evolutions of songs and novels and soap opera arcs. As an editor and as a reader, I found the story of how creators create irresistible.

And that interest wasn't restricted to the page. When I could get a closer look, I took advantage of opportunities that came my way. One day I was invited to visit the set of the HBO political satire *Veep*. There I watched David Mandel, who ran the show, tune a joke. Its punchline was a Jewish holiday. He kept barking out variations, landing the joke on different holidays—Yom Kippur or Simchat Torah, which is funnier?—improving it steadily until one turn fell flat. That's when he knew he had gone too far. All that for a throwaway joke? I was mesmerized.

You'll see I talk to Mandel about that later on. But I mention it here to say that I've always been a freak for the zealous pursuit of the better, especially where culture is concerned. I love the story of it, and also the motive. So that, too, is what this book is—a celebration of the art that happens when instinct meets rigor. But it isn't only that either.

I'm a painter. I feel ridiculous saying that. But when I quit my magazine job sometime before that trip to Spain, I decided to try my hand as an artist. It wasn't entirely abrupt: in my work I always found it satisfying telling stories in photographs and graphics and drawings, and in spare moments—a whim at first—I picked up a paintbrush to try making images myself. I have no background in art at all, but I liked it, and I dabbled. Then I left my job, and I began to paint more seriously. That was the beginning of my torment: I just wasn't very good.

After I learned a few skills, I could paint all right—basic stuff. My drawing got better, I knew my way around a color wheel, I could represent in a primitive way. And representation was what I was after—mainly because I didn't have the courage to be more adventurous. If I were to try to describe what sort of painter I was, I guess you could say I was a figure painter with a distorting style (much like Alice Neel in my fantasies), but the distortion wasn't always exactly deliberate. I just couldn't do any better. Decent paintings sometimes emerged, but they seemed almost by accident. And they were accidents I couldn't necessarily re-create. I was conservative—if one part of a painting showed promise, I would protect it and put the rest of the painting at risk. Sometimes I could get something going, and then tentatively feel emboldened to try something new (my paintings weren't loose enough; I kept trying new ways to break the bad habits I was already picking up as a new painter), and then fall back, and that would scare me—so I would retreat to what I knew, which meant resuming the bad habits. As a result I made the same painting over and over again. I got frustrated easily and gave up easily, never knowing when to persevere or surrender. I had no faith that I could make the painting I wanted. If I stopped midway, that ideal painting could at least remain intact—in my mind. If I painted it, and painted poorly, I'd be crushed. You can see that these are all problems more of the head than of the hand (though there were plenty of technique issues as well). Basically, it all seemed impossible.

And yet though it sounds horrible, it wasn't entirely. It was like a bad affair. I loved it even as it tortured me. And at least it consumed me. In spite of my troubles, I kept painting. Though I pretended otherwise, I really was ambitious. I wanted to be good. And when I was at my most exasperated, I found myself asking the same question I had asked as an editor: How does anybody make art?

Only now, my professional interest had become personal. The problems I am describing were ones of editorial self-scrutiny run amok, as if I had an overeager immune system that was sabotaging me. Editing[2] is deliberating—choosing a word or a thought, dismissing or advancing; it comes up often in this book as a way to describe artistic decision-making. And in my journalism career, editing had served me well. My temperament was well suited to it. I always had trouble writing—I was too self-conscious (you can see a pattern). And I couldn't bear working alone. But I thrived in a group and in *response*: I could corral ideas, and sharpen them. And I enjoyed thinking of the magazine itself as a canvas, playing with new ways to use it. In the various magazines I ran, we were forever trying to invent original story forms, and those attempts got even more interesting (we could invent whole new magazines on the fly) as the digital age kept offering up new toys to work with. But the emphasis here is on the *we*. There was safety in numbers. It was as part of a community that I was most successful.

But that was in the past. Now I was on my own wanting to be a painter—and I was vain enough to hope that I could even, maybe, make something interesting. Because why else do it? I didn't dare express that hope out loud, because serious art making seemed so far out of reach.

I was staring at a canvas, in a room all by myself, and getting—not nowhere, but not far enough. I took to YouTube for tutorials, but realized it wasn't practical help I was seeking—in fact, the inevitably contradictory guidance often confused me. And anyway, I figured skills would just come with more practice. I went to see a lot of art. And I read a lot about painting. In one book, a monograph about the figurative artist Eric Fischl (*Eric Fischl:*

2. While the term *editing* came up to describe almost any aspect of conscious creative work, the subjects mostly used it to describe subtraction: dismissing an idea, whittling down a stanza. It's a very pliant term—invoked in decorating or dressing or even speech (editing your own thoughts before you utter them), beyond the more traditional use that I employed for forty years. Originally this book was called *Editing*, but it was ultimately too limiting a term for what I was attempting to describe.

1970–2007) I came across this passage in which he described the making of one of his more famous paintings, called *Bad Boy*.

Here's the picture.

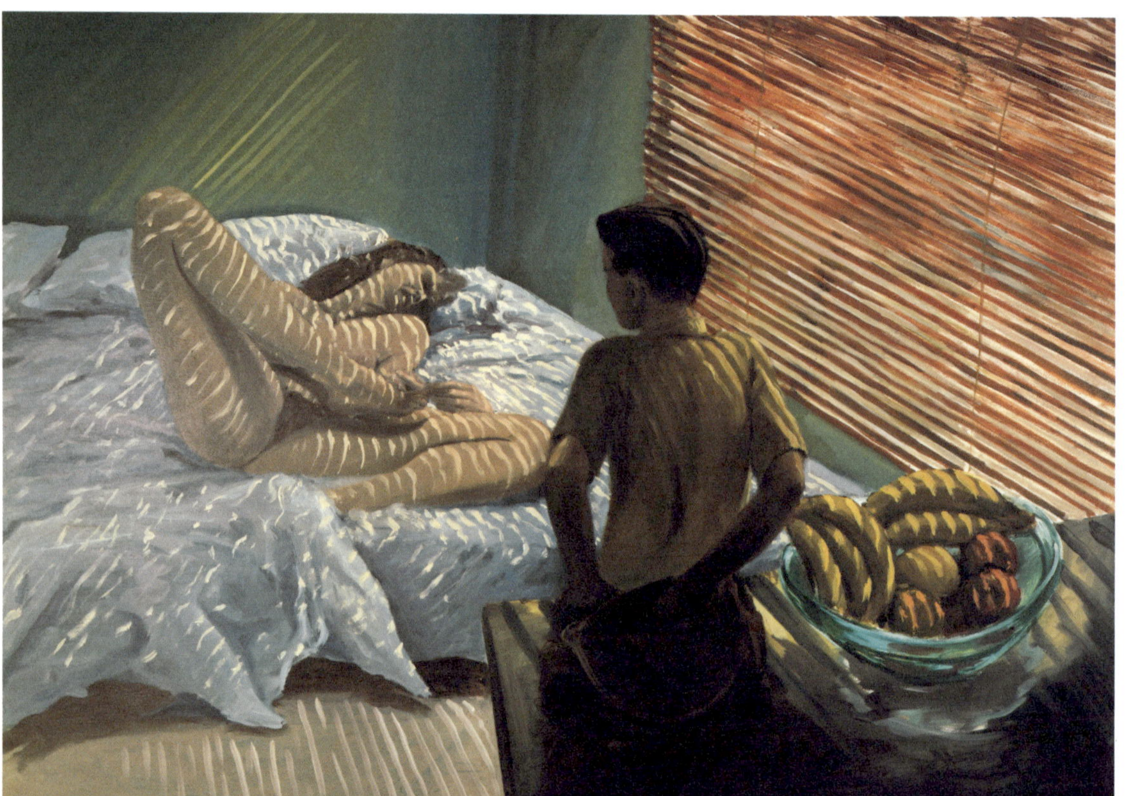

Here's what Fischl had to say about it:

[Bad Boy] *was an extremely meaningful painting for me to paint, not only because of what it ultimately came to mean to my career, but also because of how I got to it. . . . I was so lost in that picture that I actually had no idea what I was looking for. . . . I started out just wanting to paint a bowl of fruit. I went from painting that bowl of fruit to constructing the room that the fruit could be in, to finding who might be in that room and what time of day it was. Who I first thought was in the room wasn't there. People came and went. The twelve-year-old boy stealing money from the purse started out as an infant, lying next to the woman; then became a five-year-old sitting on the edge of the bed. . . . He literally grew up in that room. . . . I just kept following it, [trying] things that didn't work. I just painted things in, and painted things out.*

Reading this account, I felt some of my torture starting to lift. I appreciated Fischl's willingness to allow me into his mind as he stumbled through the work. His struggle was comforting—and illuminating. It gave me the beginnings of an idea.

When artists speak, they generally focus on what their work means. They think up a spiel they can repeat over and over, and I guess it's what most people want to hear. I have listened to and even published countless words on artists' missions, their purposes, their *projects*. Some of it is interesting. A lot of times it's just gassy.

In any case, I realized it's not what I want to know. My curiosity is earthbound: Where do they begin, and what do they do next, and when do they know they are finished? And more crucially: What do they do when they lose faith? *Do* they lose faith?

In other words, how do artists think? As I considered my flailing artistic efforts, I realized I was begging for entrance into the artist's head. At least one big problem I was having, underlying all the others, is that I just couldn't *see* it, couldn't envision how it might work if it were working. That was why I'd noticed what I'd noticed on that Spain trip, at a moment when my frustrations were most acute, and my hunt for creative entrails had become increasingly compulsive. This is a book about following associations—and about how they cohere into something tangible. And, in retrospect, this string (how my mind was looking to put something together before I was aware of it) was this book's genesis: If I could somehow make the process legible, I might find making art myself less intimidating and begin to make headway. And maybe what was true for me might also be true for a reader.

So, no meaning, no magic, just the work of it:

The work of art.

As I am writing this, I find myself constantly tempted to use the word *miracle* to describe the wonderful thing that art is. It's such a ready description: a hardwired cliché. But I resist, because I am trying to describe art making to mean its exact opposite.

The urge to invest creation with mysticism is almost as old as humankind. In her TED talk on the subject, Elizabeth Gilbert speaks about how in ancient Greece and Rome, "people believed that creativity was this divine attendant spirit that came to human beings from some distant and unknowable source for distant and unknowable reasons." Plato wrote about "the madness of those who are possessed by the Muses." And "when he receives the inspired word, either his intelligence is enthralled in sleep, or he is demented by some distemper or possession." That's how it went: Creativity came from without, consumed the artist in a trance. The work just appeared.

As legend has it, that all ended with the Age of Reason, and eventually Freud. People got wise to the idea of internal forces, to the subconscious. The spiritual hogwash was banished.

Except it wasn't. The preoccupation with the mystical is stubborn.[3] A tiny sampling:

"The artist's mind is a copy of the divine mind," said Leonardo da Vinci during the Renaissance.

Jump ahead:

"Art is a collaboration between God and the artist, and the less the artist does the better," said André Gide, four-hundred-odd years later.

3. A corollary to this trope is the notion that making art is, necessarily, torture. Quote attributed to Hemingway: "There is nothing to writing. All you do is sit down at the typewriter and bleed." Better, by Charles Bukowski: "Don't ever write a novel unless it hurts like a hot turd coming out." From these descriptions, of all artist groups, writers would appear to be in the most agony. Or maybe they're just the most articulate about the bleeding.

Then:

"How does a person create a song?" asked Joni Mitchell. "A lot of it is being . . . in touch with the miraculous. . . . The muse has got to be there. You throw a question up to the muse, and maybe they drop something back on you."

A song by Tupac Shakur (2Pac) goes like this:

If I upset you don't stress never forget
That God isn't finished with me yet
I feel his hand on my brain
When I write rhymes, I go blind and let the Lord do his thing

Even artists less inclined to view the process in supernatural terms still grapple with an essential mystery. "There are a few things I've written that I'm really proud of," Tony Kushner told me while I was talking to him for this book. "And I always think, where did that come from? How did that happen?"

Many artists don't dare wonder—or at the very least want to talk about it. This is deliberate. As Joan Didion noted, "Whether they are painters or photographers or composers or choreographers or for that matter writers, people whose work it is to make something out of nothing do not much like to talk about what they do or how they do it. . . . Superstition prevails." This was true for her as well. "In dreams we do not analyze the action, or it vanishes," she wrote. "I once knew I 'had' a novel when it presented itself to me as an oil slick, with an iridescent surface; during the several years it took me to finish the novel I mentioned the oil slick to no one, afraid the talismanic hold the image had on me would fade. . . ."

The allure of this way of thinking is not difficult to appreciate.[4] Where art comes from *is* mysterious. I talked to a lot of very rational artists for this book, and to the one, they went fuzzy when trying to describe a cathartic moment, as if they'd gone under anesthesia when the big idea came. It's weird—the mind is weird.

And a mystical frame also happens to be functional. It satisfies the grandiosity that makes it possible to do something that hard. It gives a ready out to the struggling. It makes the whole business more glamorous. (I want to be magical too!) But I don't think it's really the best way to understand how an artist works.

My ambition for this book is secular—to try to capture the artist's process in all its mundanity. If that sounds like a buzzkill, it isn't: it's an exploration of the human, not the godly, with its own more interesting drama.[5] My aim is to render the *experience* of creativity—that is, the frustration, elation, regret, first glimmers, second thoughts, distress, and triumph that lead to works of art. The thought when I began was, if I can strip creation of its romance, and break it down into discrete and concrete parts, could that help me (and you) to see art as a product of *work*, a structured mental process? And in that sense, to offer a way forward? Then as I was

4. And then there's God, the original Creator. One midrash (Torah interpretation) sent by a friend seemed relevant to this project: "In the beginning God created the heavens and the earth." But it's not as if he got it right the first time. Said Rabbi Abbahu: "Hence we learn that the Holy One, blessed be He, went on creating worlds and destroying them until he created [heaven and earth] and then He said, 'These please me. Those did not please me.'" The Creator editing his work.

5. From Elena Ferrante: "I would prefer that we definitively stop making the alphabet sacred, that we complete the secularization of literature, that we stop feeling we're just below the gods and directly inspired by them." That's kind of the idea here.

putting the book together, Peter Jackson's documentary series on the making of the Beatles' *Let It Be* aired, and any number of viewers noted the shivers they felt while seeing Paul McCartney spontaneously riff the first chords to the song "Get Back." It was striking because it was so rare: How often do you have a chance to witness the moment of emergence? And those few minutes in the documentary clarified my intent. If I couldn't capture such a moment in this two-dimensional form, maybe I could summon it and take it apart, rendering it less and yet more miraculous at the same time.

One of my first conversations for this project was with Stephen Sondheim. He told me he had an idea for a novella. "What I wanted to do," he said, "was to [construct] an absolute stream of consciousness of how I arrive at, let's say, a given line or lyric or the birth of a rhyme. I would write every single thought that came into my head, like Molly Bloom's monologue in *Ulysses*."

Sondheim never wrote that book, but he did write two books examining his own creative process. In them he included the original pages of his lyrics written out in longhand as he was noodling with them, alternate rhymes off to the side.

I first read those books years ago. I found myself lost in his pencil scrawls, playing along with him as he went about writing his songs, comparing his rhyme choices with ones I came up with. I go back to those yellow legal-pad pages all the time.

This book is composed of more than forty case studies, conversations, little biographies. I asked artists to walk me through, in as much detail as they could muster, the evolution of a novel, a painting, a photograph, a movie, a joke, a song, and to supply physical documentation of their process as a map of their thinking or as a prompt to help them remember. In the end, I was fortunate to find an astonishingly accomplished array of creators to participate, winners of every possible prize, though that's the least of it. I am grateful to them for jinxing the muse and exposing themselves, engaging in a dialogue that sometimes felt (as they kept telling me) like creative therapy.

The group spans genres: painters, novelists, filmmakers, songwriters. And because of my own background, I cast a wide net—you'll find some journalists in here because I am interested in the way that journalism can function as art, as well as food makers and sandcastle builders. Mostly I was interested in art making as a solo activity. In a couple of instances, I interviewed collaborators together. Some chapters touch on how creativity works in institutions. I talked to innovators of narrative forms and a critic rethinking what criticism could be. I thought an edited crossword puzzle would be cool to look at (and it was), so I included it. It's not all art in the way we usually talk about art, but I see no particular value in purity.

I took some of the subjects from my friend group[6] because I love their work, have always been mystified by what they do, and thought they might feel comfortable enough to be candid, which I feared most artists here wouldn't be—I was kind of panicked at the beginning. But for the most part, my fears were

6. You'll see that I go back and forth between referring to these artists by their first and last names in the chapters. I feel I ought to explain, though there's no particular logic to it (except in the cases of those I already knew, who it felt ridiculous to call by a last name). It's just that sometimes the exchange felt like a first name sort of encounter and sometimes not. I wasn't going to refer to Stephen Sondheim as Steve, even if that would have been perfectly okay with him.

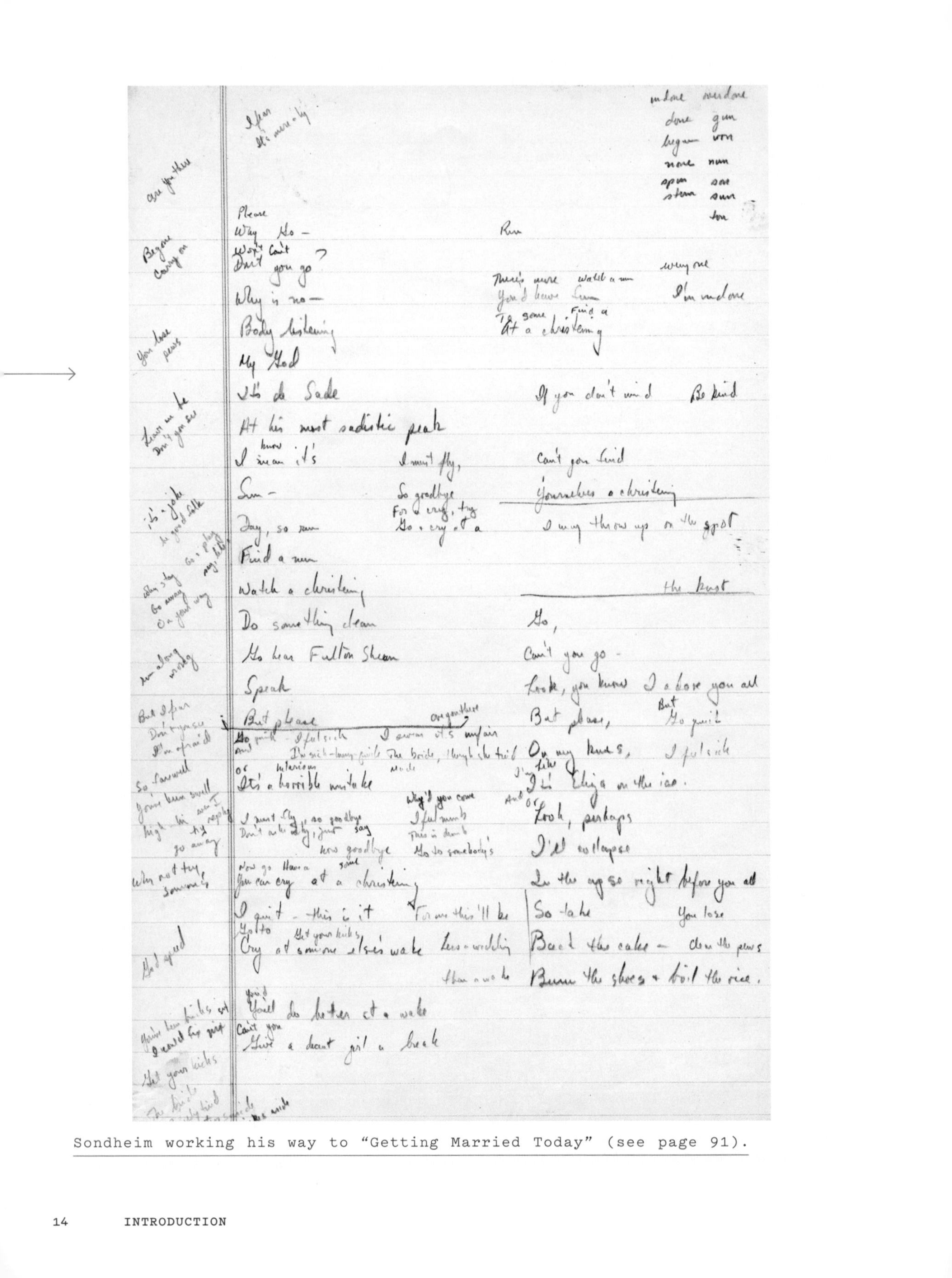

Sondheim working his way to “Getting Married Today” (see page 91).

unfounded. I went to many of my art crushes—Sondheim, Kara Walker, Moses Sumney—and was overjoyed when they agreed to join in. Some of the book's subjects were suggested by others to fill genres I thought good to have in the book, or paths that seemed helpful. I included them when I also felt struck by the work, and they often turned out to be among my favorite entries. You'll see that some of the works discussed here are famous, while others have never seen the light of day. It's an eclectic collection, all told. I hope that's a virtue.

I had in mind a rolling montage sequence, one aha after another. That's not always what I got. The book's subject is *becoming*—where works come from, but also artists. And it pokes around at some hopeless questions I couldn't let go of, the origin of sensibility (voice / style / artistic imprint) and even of talent. So while most of the chapters chart the path of a given work, in some cases, they are more like creative bildungsromans, exploring all kinds of artistic comings-of-age. At the heart of it all is the artist as protagonist and often antagonist as well, battling obstacles before victory. It's a book of happy endings.

What makes an artist? That's a big question, bigger than this book can answer. But do the people I talked to for this book have anything in common? Many of the artists themselves asked me that question. I take a stab at answering it in the afterword. More broadly, the book's proposition, and, in a sense, one of its findings, is that regardless of genres, creative paths look similar.

As I was talking to the subjects, there were two quotes I kept in mind—a couple of literary masters implicitly duking it out in roughly the same time period. One was by W. H. Auden. "When a successful author," Auden wrote, and here I think you can include all artist types, "analyzes the reasons for his success, he generally underestimates the talent he was born with, and overestimates his skill in employing it." James Baldwin thought otherwise: "Talent is insignificant. . . . Beyond talent lie all the usual words: discipline, love, luck, but most of all, endurance."[7]

I didn't take sides in this argument (though I came to feel that they're both right). There are capacities one is born with, no question, but where do you go from there? That is, successful artists have talent, but talent for what?

The literature on creativity tells a pretty consistent story.[8] Art requires access to the imagination, a notoriously difficult place to visit. The imagination fuels an idea. The artist acts urgently, often impulsively, on that idea but brings conscious rigor to the evaluation of what the imagination has spewed. Ultimately, experience, intellect, insight, and drive enable them to shape the work and then to edit it over and over, until that idea has been turned into a finished work. Each stage—the imagining, judging, and shaping—is important; one way or another, each entered these conversations.

There were patterns: in their training (often early and rigorous, even if they were training themselves) and the way drives emerge, and in how influences are

7. Another party heard from: "Being an artist is much more like being a carpenter than like being God . . ." said the theater composer John Kander (he made this comment when he was ninety-six, so he'd had a long time to think about it). "What we do is a craft. I mean you can have a great inner talent and a lot of people do, but without craft it's very hard for the talent to emerge."

8. One way or another, most readings of creative activity come to the same place—a seesaw, though analogies vary. The writer Ocean Vuong talks about the Eastern understanding of creativity in terms of yin and yang. "Yin is the mode where . . . you wait and accrue knowledge propelled by curiosity," Vuong said. "The metaphor I often use is yin is akin to fishing with a large net, casting your net wide and waiting for the bounty to fill. And yang is the decisive moment when decisions are made and order happens."

absorbed and thrown over, how constraints and circumstances (timing, luck, allies) create structures that allow accidents to happen. Along the way, there is making and destroying, self-sabotage, doubt and despair, but the unifying fact of this book is that successful creators do not give up, even when the thwarting seems insurmountable. If this book has a plot, overcoming these thwarts was it. (How stubborn they all were! And, fundamentally, though they would rarely admit it, optimistic—deep down they believed the work would emerge, even if it would require a lot of torture to get there.)

Art requires a strong ego, that was clear. With enough perseverance, they would arrive at what Max Porter called the "itchy little breakthrough"—a phrase I loved the instant he said it.

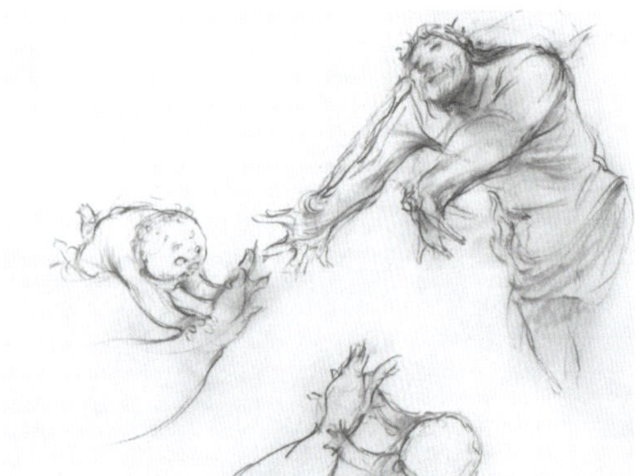

Like this one by animator Joanna Quinn (page 216). Seems apt somehow: Jesus yearning.

Of course, all artists are different as well—very different. The particulars are the meat of it. Mostly I've tried to stay out of the way and let the artists tell their creation story in their own words. Some of the chapters are rendered in dialogue, others as an artist's monologue or a simple account of the conversations. Most of the time I let the artists choose the project; sometimes I offered a preference. I conducted many of these conversations during the worst of COVID, so the pandemic enters into it. And some accounts are fleshier than others: not everyone is equally introspective about their work. I was really surprised that anybody was.

I've tried to separate genres and story types and put them in a sequence that made sense to me, but read these chapters in any order you like (you will anyway).[9] The book is not meant to be linear, though I hope it adds up. As I came across some of the patterns, I delicately noted them, made a little tally, sometimes in the text but more often in the footnotes, as if I were reading the book myself and jotting in the margins of each entry, much the way I used to make comments on a manuscript as an editor. The notes reflect some of my own dunderheaded wonderings as I was making my way from conversation to conversation, trying on different analogies (were artists like athletes? Mathematicians? Games-players? Why did the conversations keep veering into religious territory?) in order to make some sense of what they were telling me about how creative alchemy worked for them. The footnotes also include occasional trace memories from my own experience when I thought they were relevant, and some of my own feelings (envy, mystification, disbelief) as I was listening. And they perform their usual function, to decipher references when I didn't want to interrupt the subject's speech.

Central to this project are the exhibits—those process artifacts. I love drawings especially, and included

9. Also obviously true: you'll know some of these works, others not. I've tried to describe the work sufficiently for those who are unfamiliar with it, but if I haven't (and description—my powers of it anyway—only goes so far), go find the book, stream the song, check out the work online, and then read the chapter again. It's not the goal of this book, but maybe I'll turn you on to work you'll love too. Hope so.

10. FWIW, as I talked to these artists, I kept hearing their conversations reduced to the same self-help-y three Fs: focus, fanaticism, and faith. My overly slick magazine training at work, I'm sure, but it was also kind of true.

as many as would fit. Beyond the beauty of line, I am moved by what they reveal: mind to hand, without mediation. Generally, while recollection could get hazy, or became more straightforward in memory or through my prodding, or was distorted by subjects for their own self-serving reasons, I trusted the specimens of the process: They were done in real time. They couldn't lie or misremember.

I relied on pack rats, journal writers, and record keepers, which a lot of very talented people aren't (and it never occurred to some to think that their detritus might someday have worth to someone). Sometimes I came up dry and did the best I could, if I thought the conversations were valuable even without them. The exhibits (mostly) tumble from the text or are pointed to by red arrows. I am always irritated by books that force you to hunt for the illustrations, so I've tried to minimize your wandering.

The subjects' accounts of a work's evolution, their stray thoughts on what goes into creative decision-making, their notes to self, contact sheets, outlines, doodles—are meant to work like passes to the artists' interior. Which may be useful to you, if guidance is what you're looking for. This book isn't self-help, but I find there are plenty of lessons within it.[10] If you're a fan of anyone here in particular, I hope the conversations with them will feed your fandom—that was certainly my experience. And if you're just a culture-curious person, I'd like to think there's plenty for you here as well: the journey from a thought to a work is a gripping saga.

As for me, the project did help answer my own vexing questions. The artists' reconstructions, practical and psychological, made the creative act lucid to me, which was my great hope. The origin stories and artifacts they shared, replete with their evidence of struggle, rendered the artists vulnerable. Every scrawl indicating a second thought demonstrated that they were fallible.

Over the course of the two-plus years I made my way from one artist to another, I sometimes viewed the project as my own version of the children's book *Are You My Mother?* I was looking for something, which I didn't find in quite the way I was seeking, but that I found nevertheless.

As Virginia Woolf wrote in this killer description of creative turmoil, "anyone moderately familiar with the rigours of composition will not need to be told the story in detail; how he wrote and it seemed good; read and it seemed vile; corrected and tore up; cut out; put in; was in ecstasy; in despair; had his good nights and bad mornings; snatched at ideas and lost them; saw his book plain before him and it vanished; acted his people's parts as he ate; mouthed them as he walked; now cried; now laughed; vacillated between this style and that; now preferred the heroic and pompous; next the plain and simple; now the vales of Tempe; then the fields of Kent or Cornwall; and could not decide whether he was the divinest genius or the greatest fool in the world."

In other words, making art is an ordeal. You may wonder what sort of person would put herself through it.

In the pages that follow, you'll find forty-three-plus answers to that question.

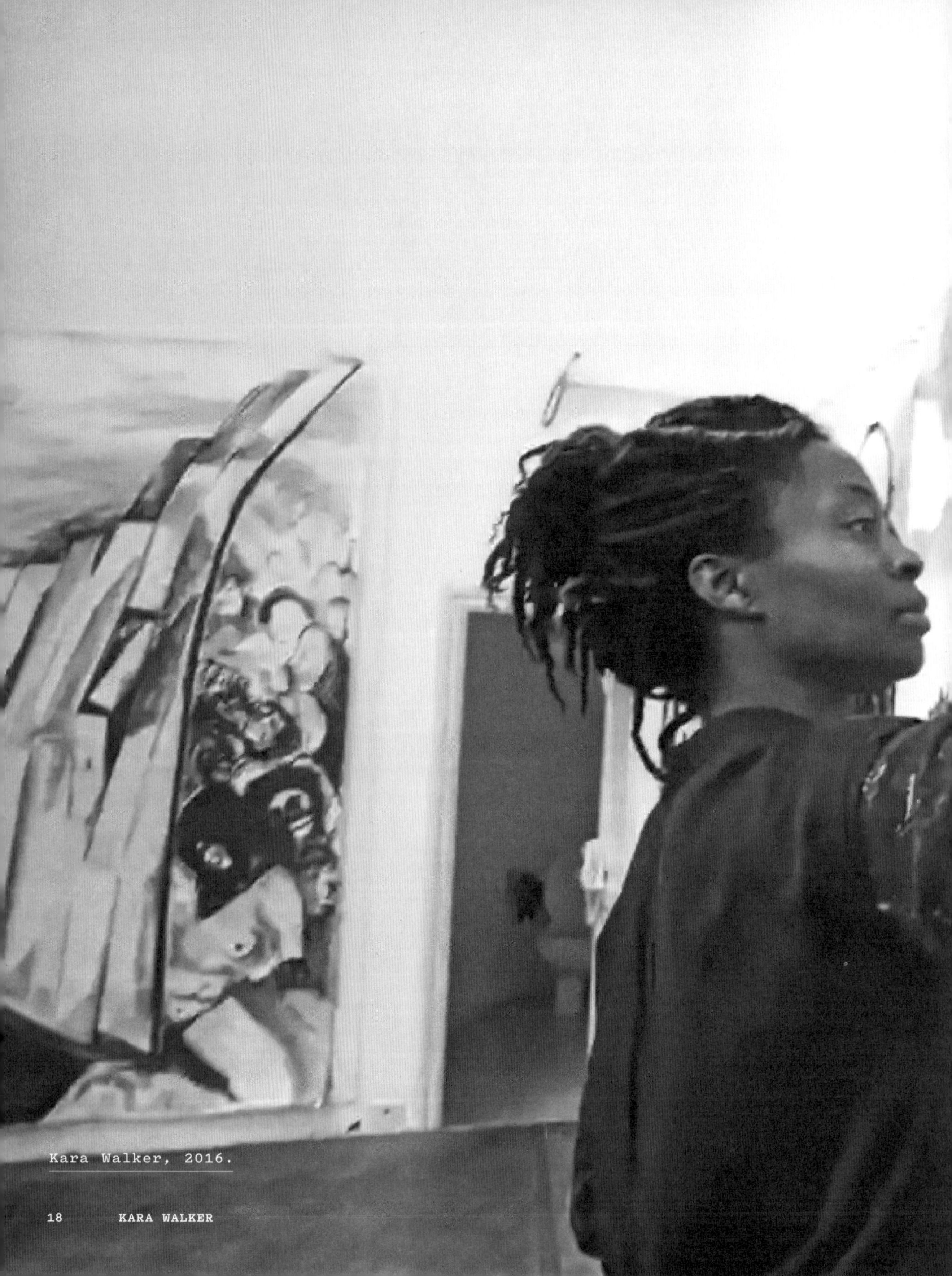

Kara Walker, 2016.

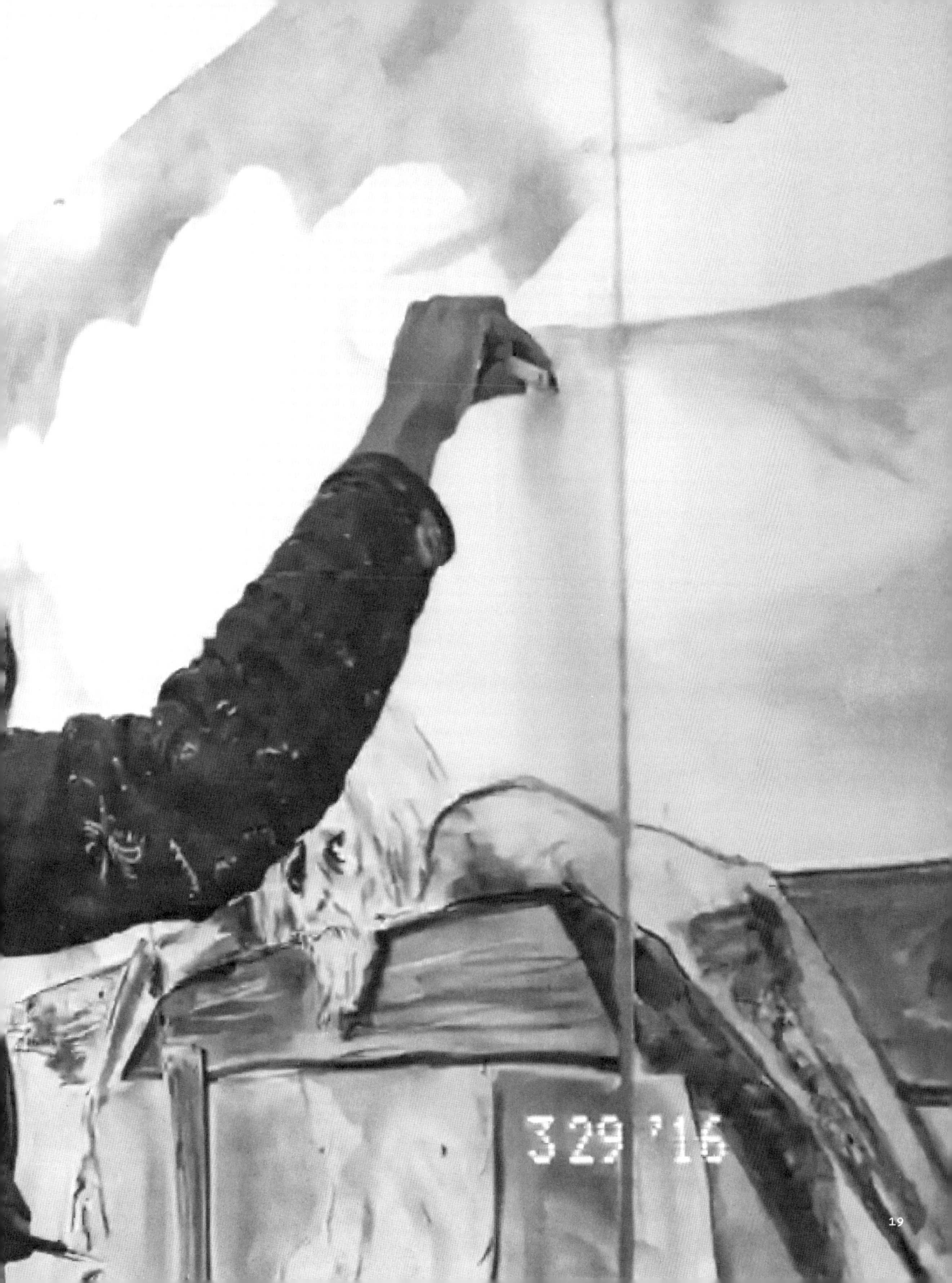
3 29 '16

I

KARA WALKER

You, Where Are You?

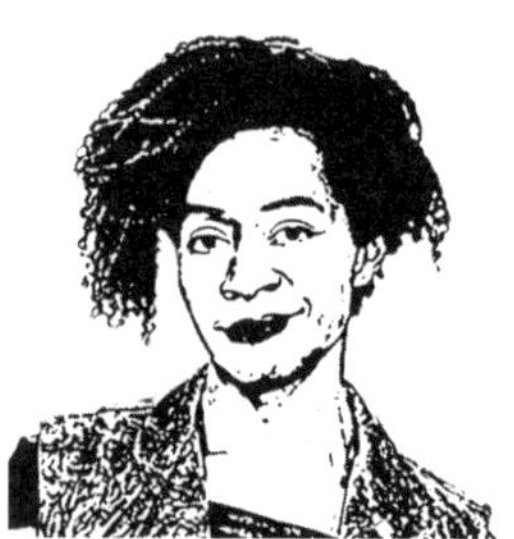

OCCUPATION: Visual Artist

WORK DISCUSSED: *A Subtlety, or the Marvelous Sugar Baby* (2014)

BORN: 1969

I'D READ ABOUT Kara Walker's sculpture *A Subtlety, or the Marvelous Sugar Baby*—or as it was commonly referred to, the Sphinx—but I can't say I was really prepared for it. I had biked to where it was being displayed, in the old Domino Sugar Refinery right by the Williamsburg Bridge. The factory was on the verge of being destroyed, which was why Creative Time, an arts organization devoted to public works,[1] had approached Walker in the first place, inviting her to make a piece of art among the sugar ruins.

I entered the building, and if I remember correctly, it was a little twisty to get to the right place. You walked past deserted rooms, until suddenly you were in a vast cavernous space. And there, standing before you, was the giant face of a "mammy" figure, perched forward with two giant breasts, sphinxlike. Her body extended behind her. She was immense—seventy-five feet long, thirty-five feet high—and surrounding her were more life-size figurines, boys with baskets. The Sphinx was white. She was covered in refined sugar—in fact, she appeared to have been made entirely of sugar. *The Marvelous Sugar Baby* was at first almost comical to me but then very quickly became horrifying. Later, I learned that was the frequent reaction—laughter/horror—to the sculpture, which was actually a set of sculptures: the Sphinx and the statues of boys with baskets. You could smell the sugar, smell the molasses; it was already (and this was the beginning of its run) a little rancid. I wandered back, taking in her whole length, until I was face-to-face with her exposed vulva. People, including several families, mostly white, were studying her, some taking pictures, some chattering, some agog. I went home and found myself thinking about her a lot. Several weeks later, I went back. The figurines had largely melted. The stench was vile. The spectators were now mostly Black.

Walker was one of the first artists I spoke to for this book. I didn't know yet how to express what I was looking for, but she

1. Creative Time is a nonprofit that supports public art—with a particular focus on spaces with historical resonance.

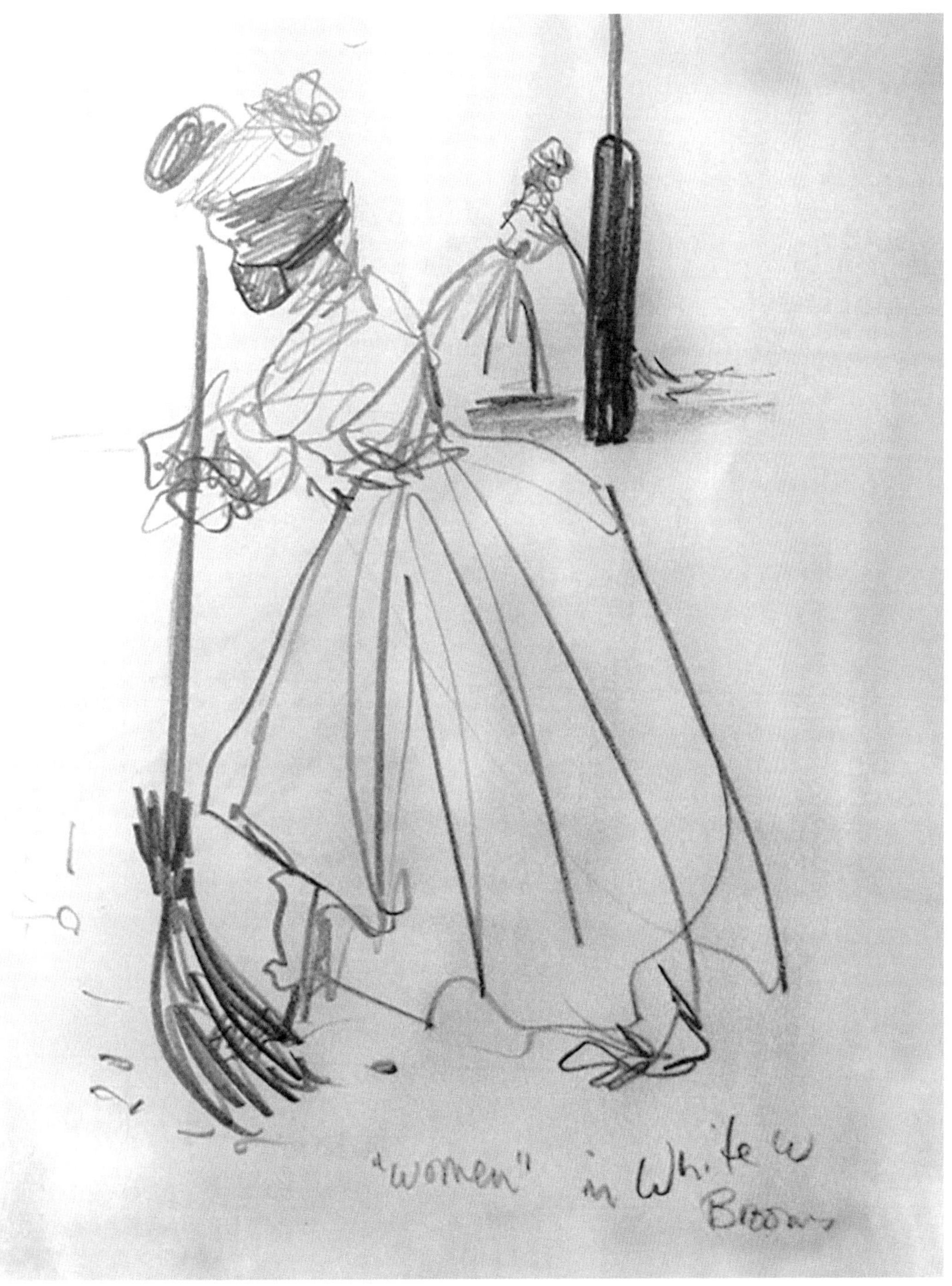

Walker sent me this note shortly after we spoke:
Re: First Thoughts from 2013 about Domino
I found an email that I sent to Anne Pasternak (the director of Creative Time) of the space after the initial visit. See below. K.
She attached several sketches/jottings, including the one above and the three on the following page.

seemed to know. I could sense she was curious as well, that she wanted to know where this monumental sculpture had come from. When we first met, she described a current work she was struggling with, one that was meant to respond to the January 6 insurrection. "I was feeling very frustrated," she said. "I had been making a piece about white nationalism, or the origins of it, and I just started making a drawing with my feet because I had sat down to make a drawing, and I was like, *I can't trust this hand not to make something very obvious, that we already know*. So I took a cue from Trisha Brown,[2] put some paper on the floor, and just let my body do the work.[3] And I thought, *Well, that's better*. It's just a fucking mess, but it totally fit the mood."

Eventually we got to the unusual creation story of *A Subtlety*, in which a PowerPoint and an epiphany on the Q train were pivotal to her making of the sculptures. It wasn't at all what I expected. You'll see that the path that led to *A Subtlety* is a cascading series of associations, but Walker approached it like a research project. I was really surprised at how methodical her thinking was, maybe because some romantic, stubborn part of me believed that artists are all instinct.

A Subtlety, or the Marvelous Sugar Baby took over a year to take shape, from Walker's first visit to the site until its opening on May 10, 2014. When she was first approached by Creative Time with the open-ended invitation to do whatever she liked in the vast, historically fraught factory, Walker—who had become well known for her art, mostly about the Antebellum South and mostly comprising black-and-white silhouette cutouts of enslaved people—was emerging from a fallow period artistically. She'd been looking to move away from the silhouettes, but hadn't settled yet into a new project, or even a desired medium. She had never done a piece of public sculpture before, and the site intimidated her, but she found it difficult to resist.

KARA WALKER: I have to go back in time to, what was it, early spring, late winter of 2013? In 2011 I had two shows that opened at the same time in Manhattan. I did a whole bunch of drawings and prints—big, sort of block letter text pieces. And a shadow puppet film. I was trying to shift some focus away from the silhouette work into drawing and other material, trying to create a space for illustration, drawings of hidden moments, as if they could be book covers for all the possible dissertations on Black life and Black culture from,

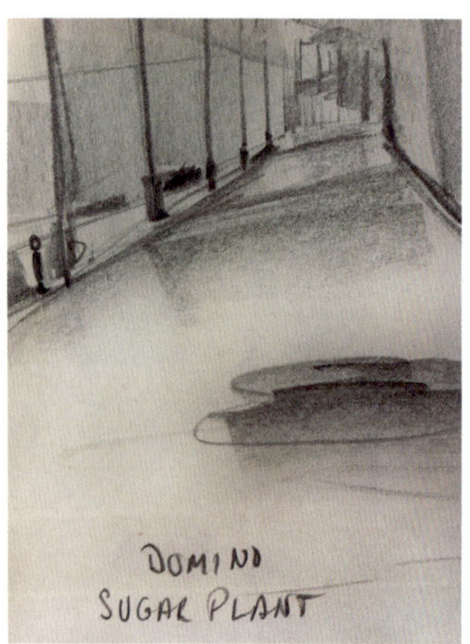

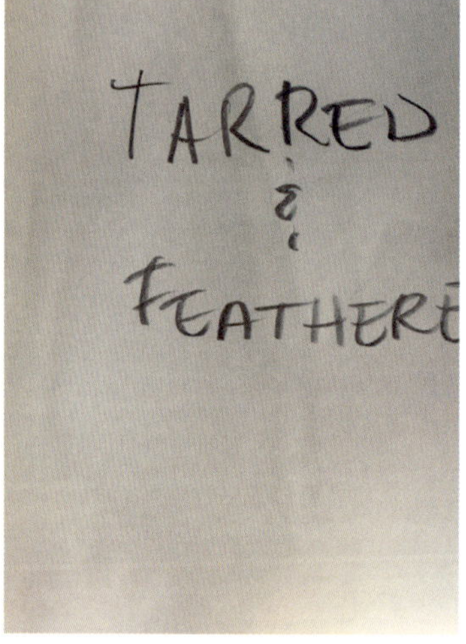

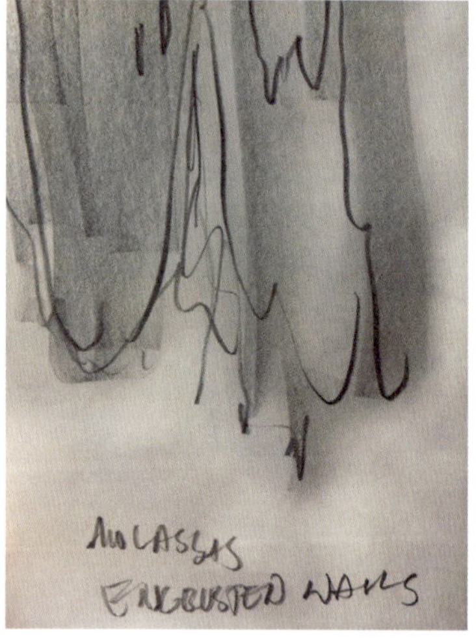

More immediate associations on visiting the Domino space.

like, Reconstruction forward.

But what happened is I bought a house, and so from 2012 to 2013, all I was doing was the house. I did not make anything. There was a year where I did a bunch of little cartoon drawings, like scrolls, but really it was like: *Why am I not working?* I didn't understand. It was the weirdest experience not to feel productive.

By 2013, I finally had a feeling of being settled. And that's when Creative Time approached. You know, I'm sort of inclined to keep saying no to things, but then I just thought, why not, I'll look. We went to the Domino refinery, and I was pretty floored. I felt I kind of got it, it felt kind of perfect. So saying yes was one thing.

And then—I was trying to think of an analogy earlier. It was like flood gates opened, *dadada*, but I can't swim. It ushered in this huge flood of possibility. And then I was tumbling around in that, trying to conjure magical sort-of-inflatables in order to survive.

What About This? Creative Time didn't say anything about what they were looking for. So I had a sketchbook, and I kept asking myself, *What about this, or this, or this?* That was what it was like for three months. I was hardly even drawing. *How do I think about the volume of this space?* And then, *How do I think about the history of this location?* And then, *How do I think about the history of what this location has been processing?* I was overwhelmed. For a couple of those months, I couldn't figure out how to begin.

They weren't really ideas, just sort of little bubbles, kind of like, how to traverse the space very quickly? Something that moves? Machinery? Image, video, multimedia? You can envision all kinds of things. It could be a group happening, for instance. And when I was sitting in my studio or my room, it was hard to really picture the volume that I was going to be working with for real. It was like smashing your head over and over because everything seems like a possibility. I'd see something on TV, and I'm like, *What about that?* I was sketching people on roller skates! No, really. Stupid shit.

And then I finally said to myself, *You, where are you?*[4] You know, like looking in the mirror, like, *Who* are *you, Kara? Stop sketching stuff!* And the deadline for presenting my idea was fast approaching.

One of the lovely things about Creative Time was that they were at my beck and call. If I wanted to research something, they would say yes. So, for a while, I was thinking of some kind of conveyor, one material transforming to another material. And chickens. I don't know why, but I was thinking about chickens. And then I also was thinking about waste products, the effect of the sugar on the Domino plant, the heavy molasses smell—caked onto every surface was a kind of molasses. And about oil and other by-products and the overreliance we have on things that are bad for us. And they did some research for me into chicken processing, slaughterhouses. And I thought, *What if I do this? I won't import raw coke or whatever and put it in this space . . . that's the wrong direction*. But then I thought, *Wait, what is the right direction?*

A PowerPoint So I put together this PowerPoint, which confused everybody at Creative Time. But the PowerPoint was the only sketch I approved of. I couldn't trust my hand to draw the thing I was trying to articulate, because it just wants to make things cute.

It's funny. The PowerPoint was like my office life. It was a way of synthesizing material,

2. Trisha Brown was a choreographer who was also a visual artist. She made drawings with her hands—and feet.

3. Walker drawing with different parts of her body, because she is afraid her hands will try to draw too "cute," is a classic hack. Artists' hacks are plentiful, and sometimes very odd. For their book *Sketchbook with Voices*, Eric Fischl and the art critic Jerry Saltz interviewed artists. "What I found so compelling was to hear how artists got themselves out of their dead spots," Fischl wrote me. "Richard Artschwager was overworking a painting. He decided to watch TV and only go into his studio to paint during commercials. That gave him about two minutes at a time to work. He said it took him most of the afternoon soaps but eventually he got past whatever it was that was holding him back." There's a fun book on the subject by Mason Currey called *Daily Rituals*. Among its findings: When Igor Stravinsky was blocked, he stood on his head. W. H. Auden would take a benzedrine every morning. John Cheever would get dressed in a suit, take the elevator to a room in the basement, and then strip to his boxers to work (not a hack really, but too nutty not to include).

4. Though Walker is expressing general impatience with herself here, I think she is also alluding to the thing that makes her *her*. She was trying to move away from her silhouettes, but toward something that still felt particular to her. As you read this book, you'll notice that artists have different attitudes about their signature—or whatever you want to call it: a style of expression that is them as surely as is a fingerprint, or the way they sign their name. Some run away from it, some toward it. In making *A Subtlety*, Kara Walker did both.

THE POWERPOINT

Excerpts. Not so legible (and crudely reconstructed) but you get the idea. A PowerPoint!

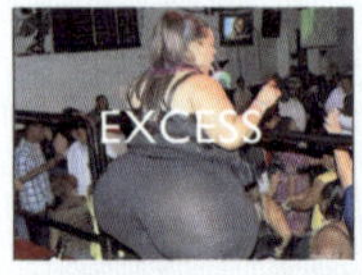

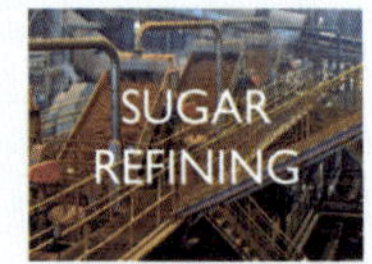

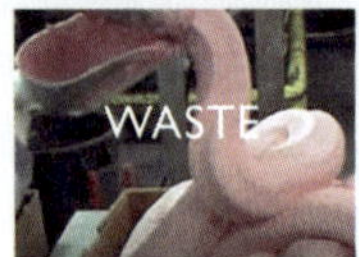

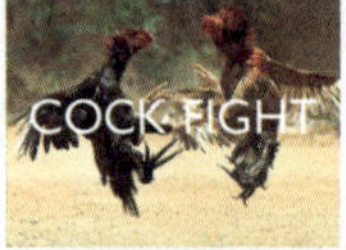

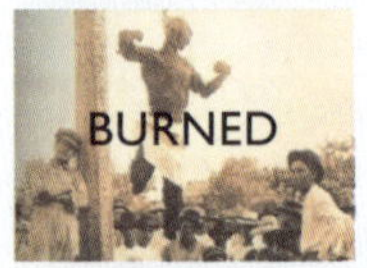

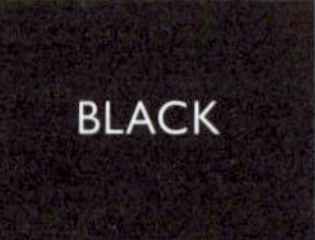

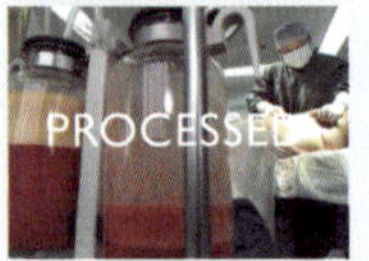

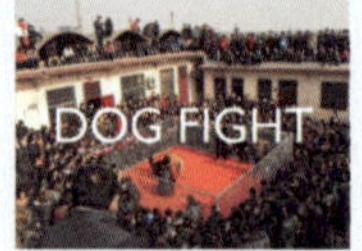

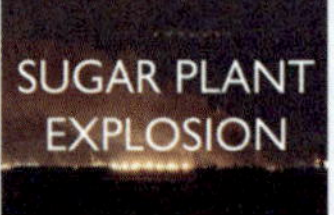

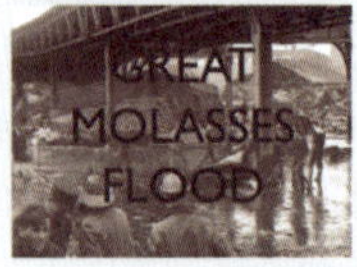

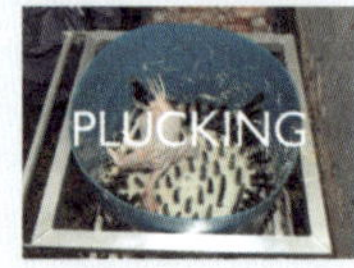

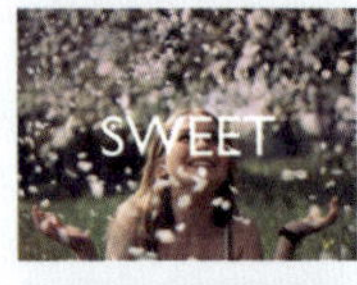

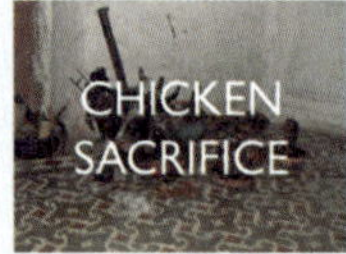

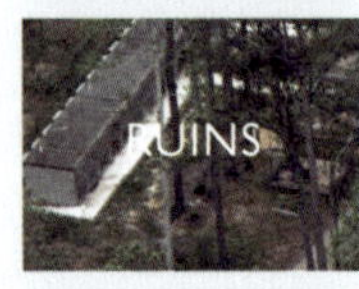

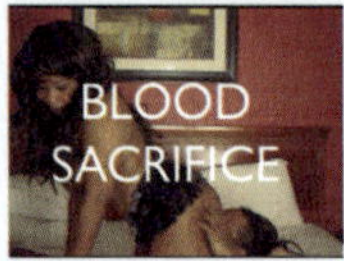

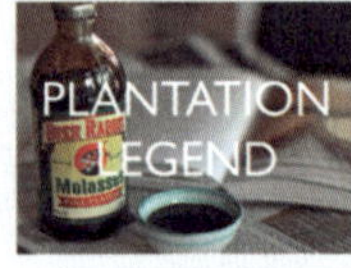

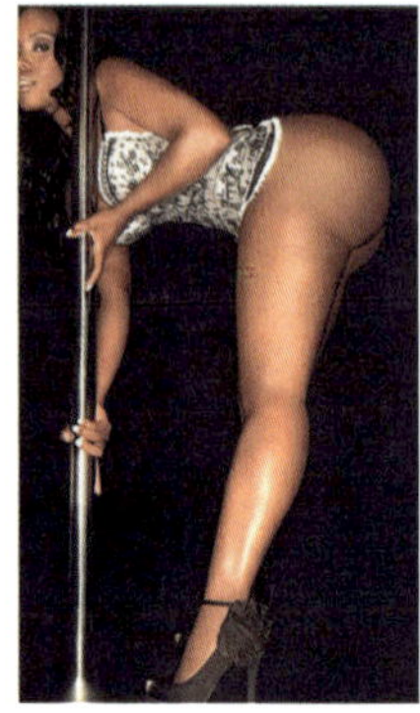

but it also has a rhythm and poetry to it. I was gathering images that included the chickens but then went into voodoo and rum and sugar and the transatlantic slave trade. I started to read about the process of sugar refining, and that it's not a given that sugar should exist in the world.[5] I started to think about my role as the artist in relation to doing a big public art project. I got interested in men like [the Domino sugar magnate] Henry Osborne Havemeyer.[6] Those are the gods of Industry. That's really what I have to imagine myself to be.

We had a meeting scheduled for December 2013. I was trying to get a little thesis going. And I'm not talking to anybody about it. It's sitting in my head. I don't usually have people that I talk to about what I'm doing. I'm too secretive sometimes—but especially this one because it was top secret. So I'm jotting things down, scattered notes. But the one thing that really changed everything was Sidney Mintz's[7] book on the history of sugar.

I mean, I had been getting there, because the last piece of the PowerPoint involved text and images with words on them, started with sugar and brown sugar, and then I added a pole dancer.

And it sort of ends with ruins—a sugar

5. As Walker was describing creating *A Subtlety*, her preoccupation was about getting the idea of it right, which the PowerPoint helped her figure out. And she was concerned with technical problems regarding its physical construction. But listening to her, you might think it were a building project rather than an artwork: at no point did she seem concerned with how to give it its visual power, which to me was such an important factor in its impact. This is true of many of the accounts in this book, and it kept surprising me. Is it experience that seems to give them faith that once they solve the intellectual problem at hand, the expression of it—*the art part*?—will take care of itself?

6. Henry Osborne Havemeyer was president of the American Sugar Refining Company—which was once the owner of the Domino Sugar Refinery.

7. *The New York Times* called Sidney Mintz the father of food anthropology. He wrote extensively on the link between sugar and slavery.

8. She's talking about the Rolling Stones song "Brown Sugar."

refinery explosion in Savannah that I remember happening. And that was entirely caused by sugar crystals in the air.

Anyway, what to do with ruins? We romanticize them. We celebrate them. We go on vacation in them. We make them a public sort of entertainment.

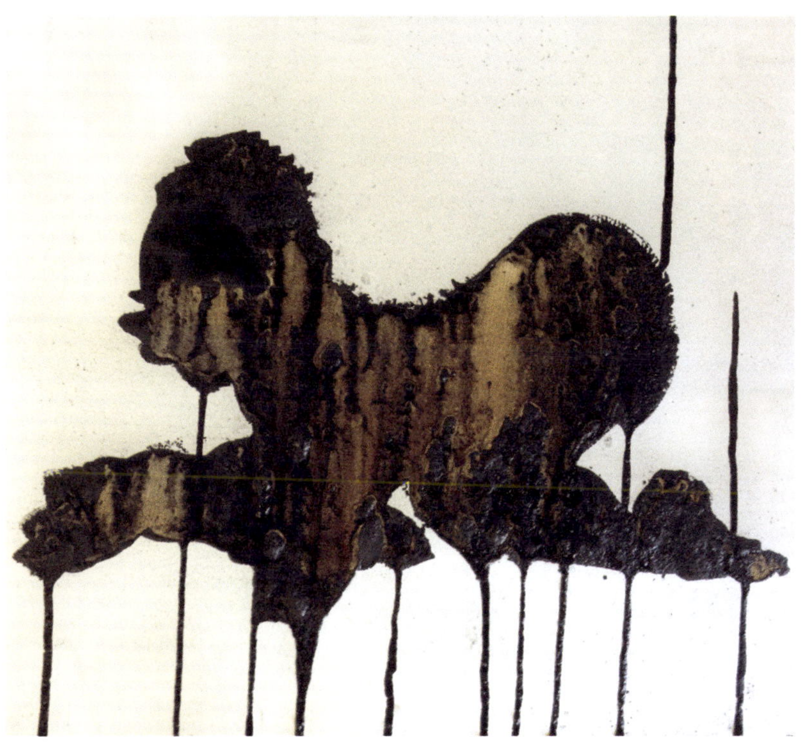

Sex and Sugar The sexuality of sugar was already in my head. I free-associate with brown sugar being a nickname for Black female sexuality, and the Rolling Stones song.[8] Plus, the liquid stickiness of it just seemed really potent as a sexual symbol.

But the Mintz book put the exclamation point on the fact that sugar has been about desire, since it was refined. Before sugar, you got sweetness from fruit or honey. The sugar high is a real high, like gold, like a spice worth its weight in gold. So only the powerful had access to it. And the quest for that particular sweetness, it generated my history, it generated the transatlantic slave trade. You get the triangle trade, sugar and rum, Africa and the Caribbean and England—and molasses was the by-product.

And so the PowerPoint is what I gave Creative Time. I said, "I think I'm getting closer." And they were like, "What is it, exactly? Is it going to be a slideshow?" And I said, "No, no, this isn't the piece!"

I don't know how to explain the magic process—maybe it's not magic but something that switches. I thought, *You know, Kara, you're an artist. You're kind of a distiller yourself. You have to take all of this information, those impulses and make some sort of icon, whether it's like the silhouette or . . . it just has to fuse into one thing. And it has to be something like you have no choice about. The time for playing is over.*

And I'm feeling, now I know what the material is. I *feel* the material. It's not just an intellectual pursuit. It lives in my body.

Revelation on the Q Train And here's what happened: I was on the Q train. And I was reading the Sidney Mintz book. And there's a section where he talks about the "subtleties"—these special decorative [sugar ornaments] exclusively for kings, for the celebration of weddings . . . and you know, we're so used to fucking sugar we don't even realize how special sugar is. . . .

And I was just like, *Oh, it's a sugar sculpture!*

And I realized the Sphinx was the perfect sort of ruin. And that was the big moment. From that point on, the drawings are drawn with molasses, stuck together.

And I thought, *It can't just be a Sphinx, because then it only reads on that one note. We have to open it up to all these other sorts of desires that sugar exploits and represents.* And our covetousness for sugar is not unlike sexualized

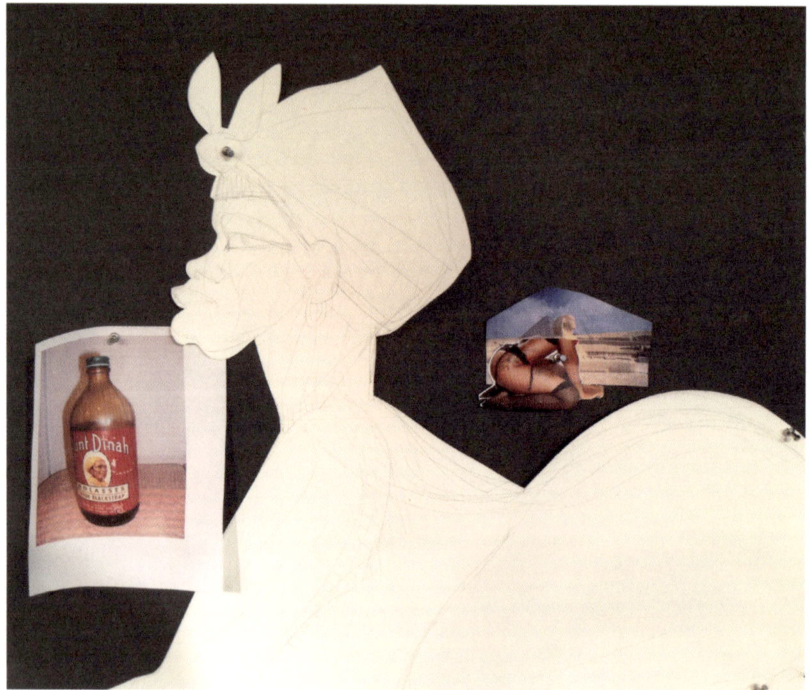

Like this one.

covetousness. The power is hard to quantify. So it had to be a female, larger-than-life queen figure with everything open and bare and bare breasted.

A Mammy Sculpture I'm not sure exactly when I got the idea to do the sculpture as a mammy figure. Mammy-like figures existed so much in my work already. Michael Jenkins from my gallery [Sikkema Jenkins & Co.] found a drawing of mine from the late nineties or something with a mammy Sphinx on it. And there's one sketch that was also kind of instrumental, it was a collage with the back end of her butt in the air.

And so now I had to build a sculpture, and that was terrible. The first iteration at my studio, I was so embarrassed. I don't know how to do sculpture. So let me just make a table-sized one, of papier-mâché. And the first one collapsed. That kind of thing can be a big setback when you think you know how to do other *things*.

I felt, *I don't know how to do anything. Who do you think you are?*

So then I made a smaller little clay Sphinx figure, just kind of modeled on the Sphinx. And I took a little snapshot with the refinery behind it. And I had a model of the space, like a little foam-core model.

Creative Time helped me facilitate how it could get made, I just knew it should be an object, monumental, something grand. I started looking stuff up, and I found these little sugar boys sculptures online—candy dishes. And I thought, these are appalling. I don't know how I found those boys. My studio was in the Garment District for so long, so I always happened to pass by shops that had tchotchkes in the window, like African queen kind of figurines. And I thought, *These are kind of strange, why are these being made. Who buys them—besides me apparently?*

Logistics So the Sphinx was going to be the main sculpture. And the challenge for me was how to make it solid. And finally it was just, settle on a face or something, settle on a kind of body and then work with a model maker to make a figure that was a passing resemblance to the sketch.

And then I thought these boys could be attendant figures.

I wanted them made as candy sculptures, made of sugar. I'm thinking everything is going to be made of sugar. And basically it became, What is possible, what is not possible? What is achievable in the time frame? What is achievable financially? In physics? At a certain point everything was achievable. We just had to say what it was. So it was this giant sugar sculpture and these candy figurines at a human scale.

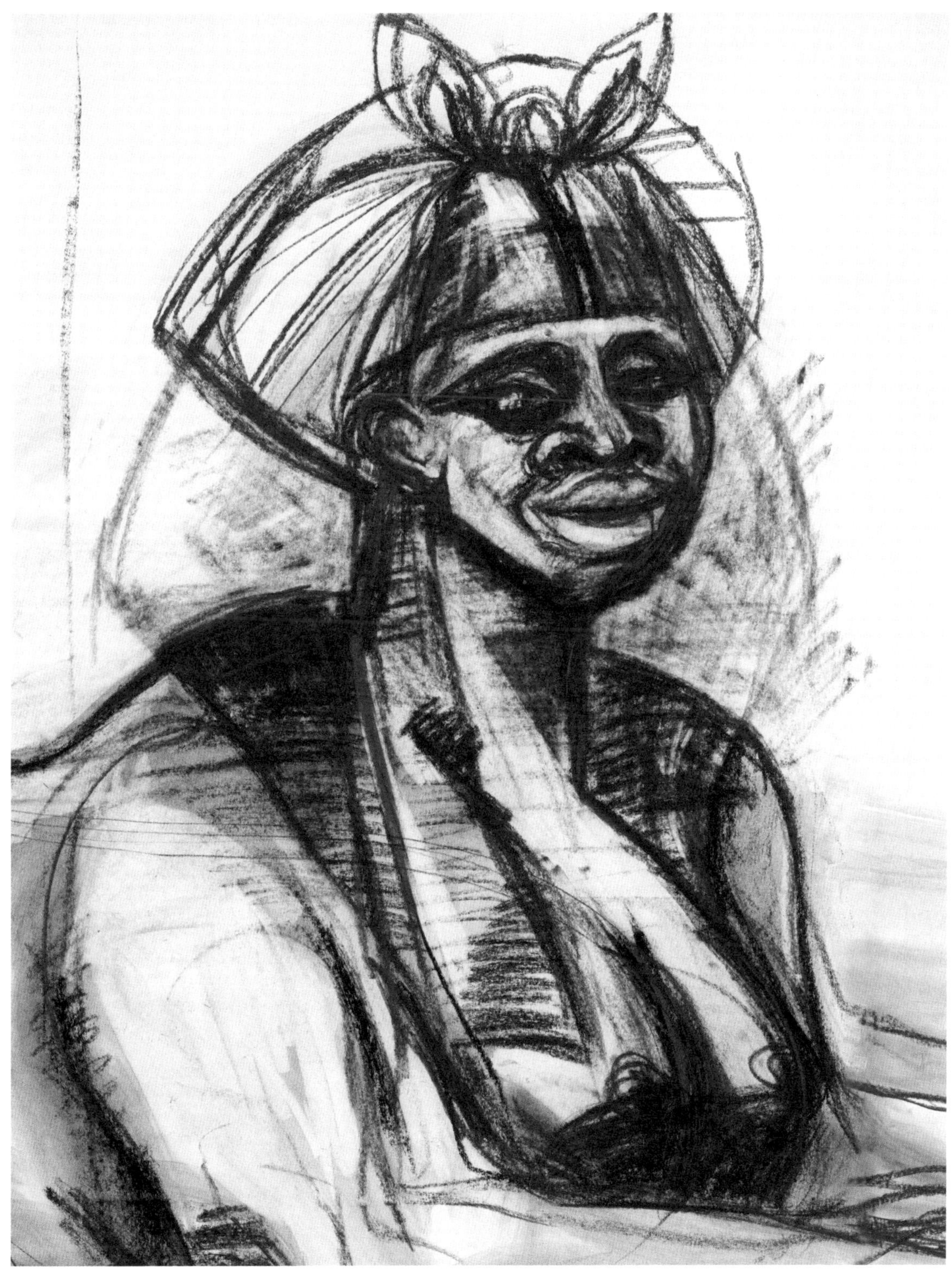

The Marvelous Sugar Baby, in two dimensions above and, on the next page, in three.

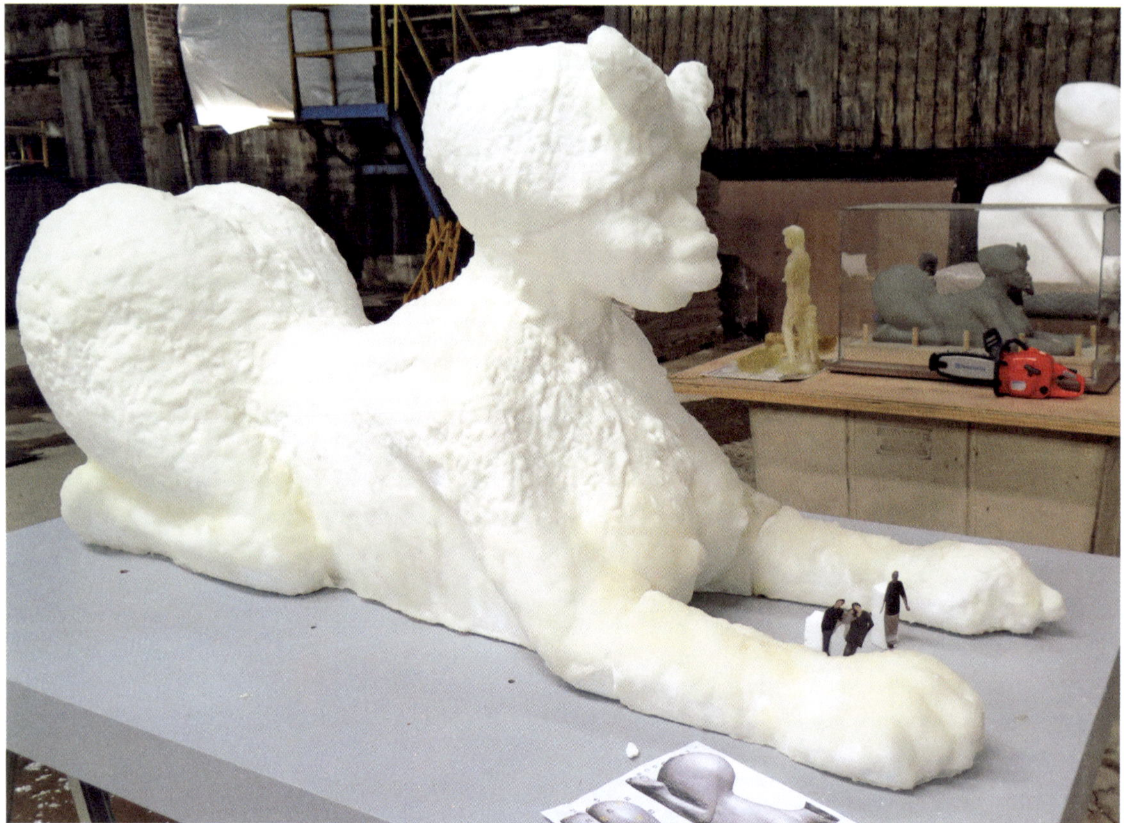

I didn't ever have the specific notion that it would melt. That just sort of came with it. I knew it would be an unstable object. But we didn't really know how unstable until we started making them.

It was all trial and error because nobody had ever done it. People had made smaller sugar sculptures, and there were people in the candy business, of course, and bakers. But when we started asking around for how to do this, no one wanted to touch it. They said, it's not going to work. The first one, when we made the molds—well, let me first explain that it's easy to make candy, it's sugar and water and temperature. It just has to reach the hard ball stage, when you can pour it into the mold and let it sit. But for us, the molds were so big and the temperature was so hot, it never cooled in the interior. So the first one, we took it out of the mold, and at about six o'clock that evening, it was a puddle.

Compromise Eventually, we thought maybe we have to do some of these in resin, some in resin and some in candy. Okay, compromise. Don't love it, but maybe it will create the effect.

So we made as many of these sugar boys as we could. And then the day before the opening, a truck backed into one of them, maybe two of them got knocked over. Oh my God, that was bad. I don't know if you remember, but some of the figures have figures inside their baskets. I just picked up the broken pieces of the ones that had fallen and put them in the baskets of the ones who were standing.

The building process, when that actually started, that was amazing. I'd have fits of giggles because I just couldn't believe we're doing this. The development was interesting, all of that was interesting, but just stepping into the space . . . I don't know how to describe it really. It was intimidating. It was, is this mine?

I had to go back in there and figure out how to make it mine.

There were some things I literally couldn't do. I wasn't really capable of moving giant blocks of polystyrene. So I would go over there regularly and talk with the team who was shaping everything. It wasn't until the last phase of it, the last four weeks, that I felt I was really doing something.

A Deadline We're on a time frame that was very tight. It was kind of clockworkish.

We decided to open early May, and then we just started an eight-week run. So things are going to fall into place, or not. I had done what I could do.

On May 10 it opened. My daughter went to see it a couple of days before. And there's a picture of her when she first gets into the space, laughing, which resonated for me because it reminded me so much of my first experience when I presented the work. There was the *not seeing* of it. People walked into the factory and they were like, "Wow, wow, wow, look at all the sugar boys." People walking and walking and walking, and then suddenly it was there. And they didn't know there would be a big thing there. They were just like, *Oh my God*. And I found that very satisfying. So, my daughter walked in there—she's a teenager and she's looking around—and I sort of pointed to it. We were standing in front of it, just looking. It wasn't just, "Oh, the breasts, oh, the sugar, it's made of what?" You walk around the sculpture, and it keeps changing shape and meaning in the viewer's eye and mind—I mean hopefully. And maybe it sort of elicits some of those harder feelings that I was thinking about as I was making it—I hope so.

All I can say is, I was trying to materialize and manifest the feeling of the histories I wanted to talk about. I had ingested that. I had done something that affected me, and I knew what it was. I knew the effect I wanted it to have. And that was it.

I don't know about anything, really. I always feel like I'm a novice and I'm just starting out and even if I have to make work similar to work I've already made, cut paper or something, it's a lot like starting from zero.

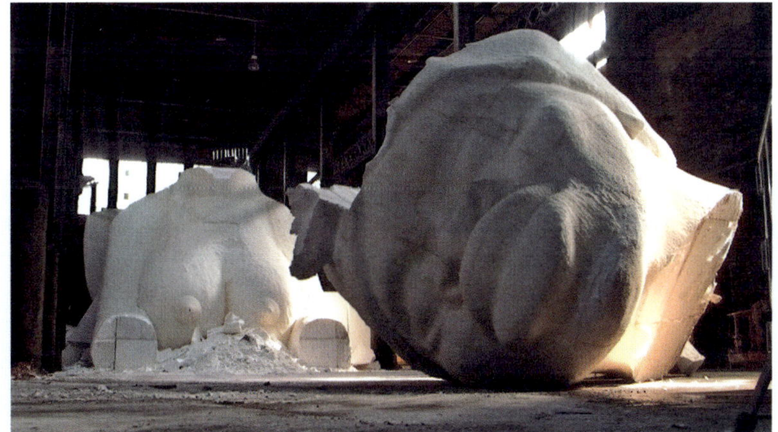

DESTROYED

Because I was very taken with the ephemerality of the project—not just its melting but the fact that whatever was left after its exhibition at Domino was deliberately destroyed—I asked Walker why she would destroy a work she had given so much of herself to, and with such astonishing effect.

"Well, what is the purpose of a monumental sculpture on a grand scale but to be destroyed?" she answered. "I had my moments when I thought, *Well, maybe I shouldn't*, but I felt ickier holding on to it than letting it go. I felt I was playing some sort of game with it. I had promised it, you're going to come and then you're going to go. And that's just how it has to be."

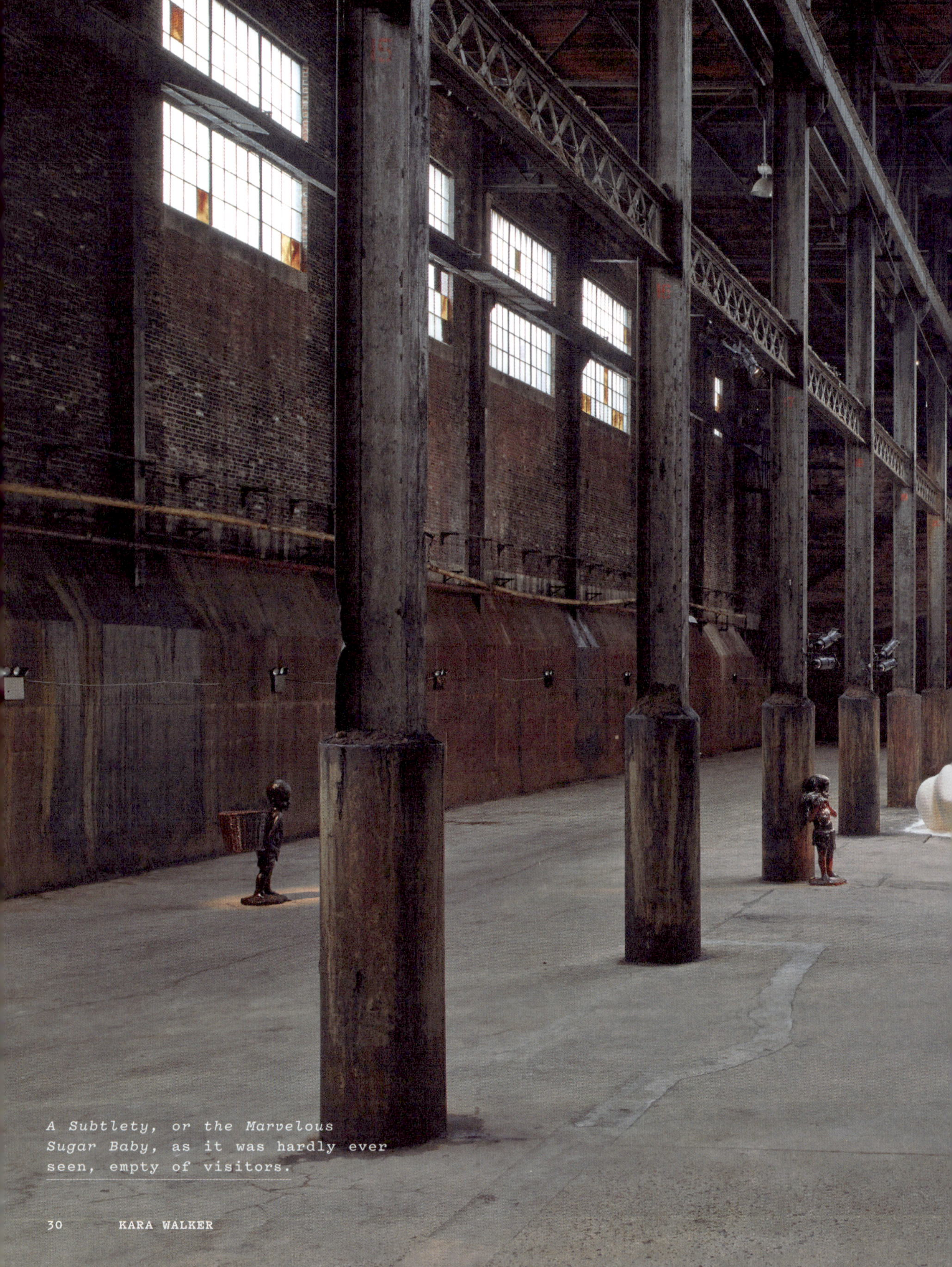

A Subtlety, or the Marvelous Sugar Baby, as it was hardly ever seen, empty of visitors.

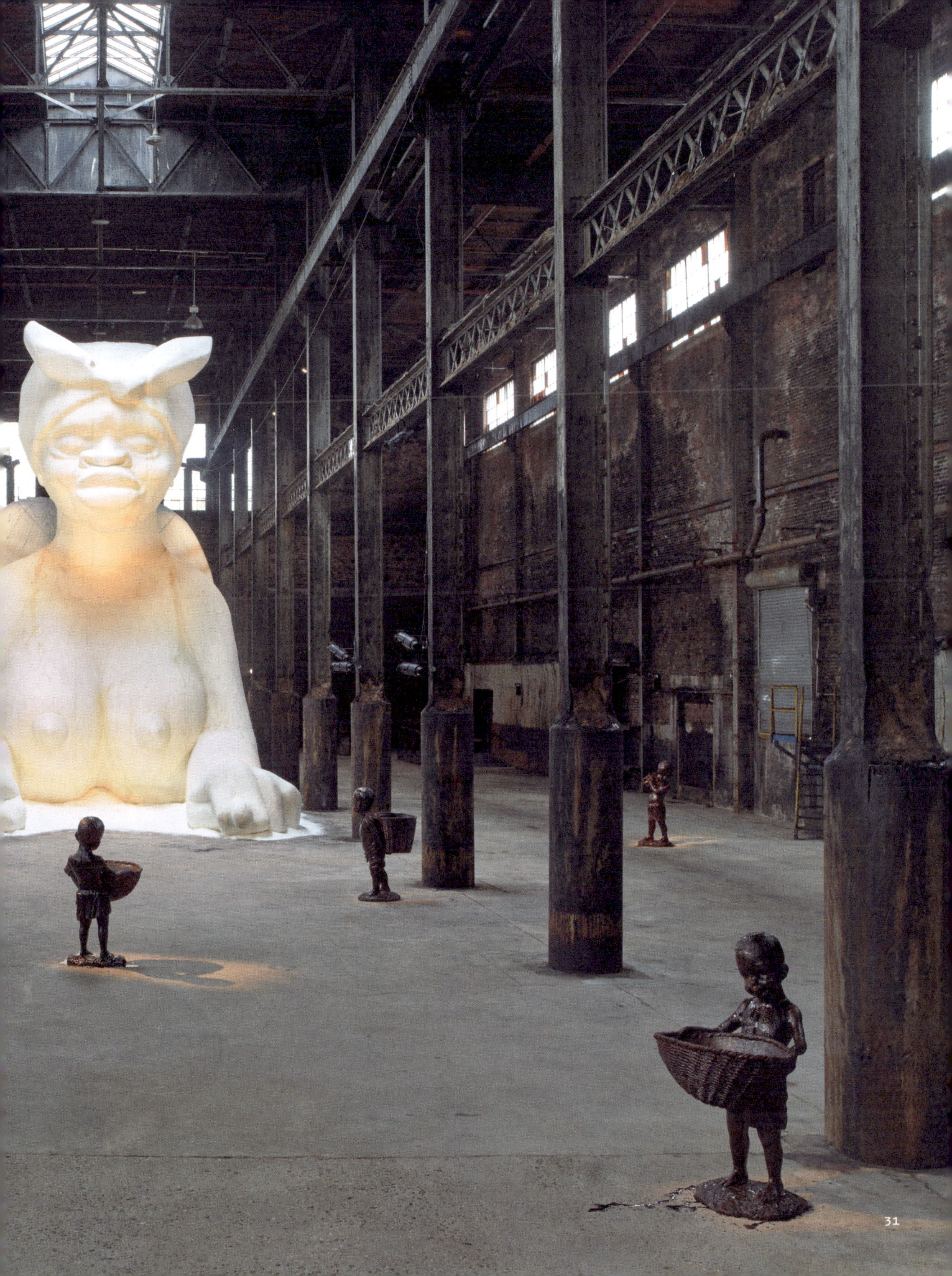

I wish I was an octopus. A fucking octopus.

Sit and wait. It'll be a minute. You want a...

Suzy? He's gonna do it. No, I mean he really is. Yep, yep, yep, yep, really, no, Look I gotta... waitaminnit.

Look, I gotta -- you want to call me, when, ~~tomorrow~~? Tomorrow I... hey. No. Fuck no. Wait. ~~I don't~~... Oh Christ - no, wait, here, yep - hold - (Shithead) -- sorry, sorry, no -.

I... who? Aw, Jeez, Harry, the fuck you do that for? Buncha fuckin paranoiac freaks is all, wait - no, Harry Judge John Francis Grimes, Manhattan Family -- oh fuck, wait - hold -

Hello? Judge ~~[illegible]~~ Diekmann? Mrs. Diekmann? Oh. Sorry. Deep voice. You got - tickets, oh right, Tickets yeah hold -

what? WHAT?

Suzy? So look I can't tell you that, I not really! Le Cirque or something, today -- Whattaya mean, how do I know? I'm his goddam lawyer! Oh yeah, right, confidential. So... So baby darling, call the Maitre D' - I can't, this isn't my job, you get paid - what, so what, I'll call the fucking Post, they love me there -- hold.

I SAID I FUCKING PROMISED

touch him, Harry. How?

Susan -

Out of his head: Roy Cohn, beginning of "octopus" speech, first try, above. (Pure monologue.) As it evolved, on the right.

2

TONY KUSHNER

Bread Crumbs

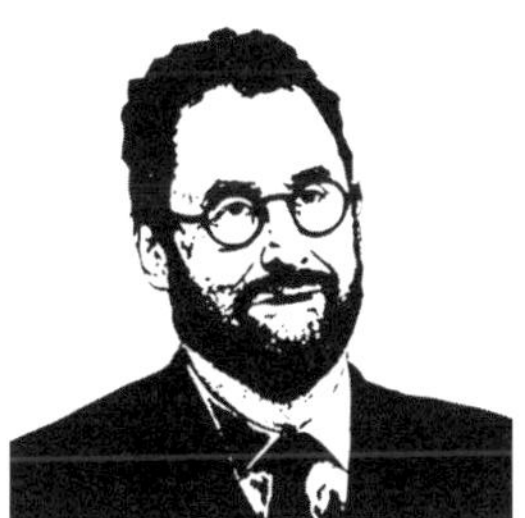

OCCUPATION: Playwright/Screenwriter
WORK DISCUSSED: *Angels in America* (1991/1992)
BORN: 1956

I ARRIVED AT TONY KUSHNER'S house in Provincetown and was greeted by his husband, Mark Harris, a friend and colleague, and their dog, Loofah. Mark took off and Loofah found a spot on the floor. Tony and I settled in his living room, curled on the couches for a long conversation. It was summer, early COVID. The release of Steven Spielberg's *West Side Story*, for which Tony had written the script, was still months away, even though the movie was finished a while ago. A revival of the musical Tony wrote, *Caroline, or Change* (an excellent musical too—evidence of the broad nature of Tony's talent, as if some were needed), was also in suspended animation; it had been set to open just as the pandemic began. But Tony was hardly idle; he was furiously writing another movie with Spielberg,[1] and the speed with which it was coming surprised him, since he is very invested in his identity as a procrastinator. I told him the obvious, that he seemed plenty productive.

"I'm not, though. It's pathetic," Tony said. "Todd Haynes[2] called me a while back and said, 'Would you do this series with me, about Freud?' It was so much up my alley I said yes immediately. And I never heard back from him. And then I saw him later, and I said, 'What are you working on?' And he said, 'A miniseries about Freud with this British playwright.' And I was aghast. I tried not to have a reaction, but I couldn't resist. I said, 'Fuck, what happened to me?' He said, 'Oh, I'm sorry, I forgot. I wanted to hire you. But Christine [Vachon, the producer][3] said absolutely not. If you hire him, you're never going to get the script." I laughed. "Spielberg for some reason has been the soul of patience with me.

ROY COHN, OCTOPUS BEGINNING, FINAL

Roy (Hitting a button): Hold. (To Joe) I wish I was an octopus, a fucking octopus. Eight loving arms and all those suckers. Know what I mean?
Joe: No, I . . .
Roy (Gesturing to a deli platter of little sandwiches on his desk): You want lunch?
Joe: No, that's OK really I just . . .
Roy (Hitting a button): Ailene? Roy Cohn. Now what kind of greeting is . . . I thought we were friends, Ali. . . . Look, Mrs. Soffer, you don't have to get . . . You're upset. You're yelling. You'll aggravate your condition, you shouldn't yell, you'll pop little blood vessels in your face if you yell. . . . No, that was a joke, Mrs. Soffer, I was joking. . . . I already apologized sixteen times for that, Mrs. Soffer, you . . . (While she's fulminating, Roy covers the mouthpiece with his hand and talks to Joe.) This'll take a minute, eat already, what is this tasty sandwich here it's— (He takes a bite of a sandwich.) Mmmmm, liver or some . . . Here.

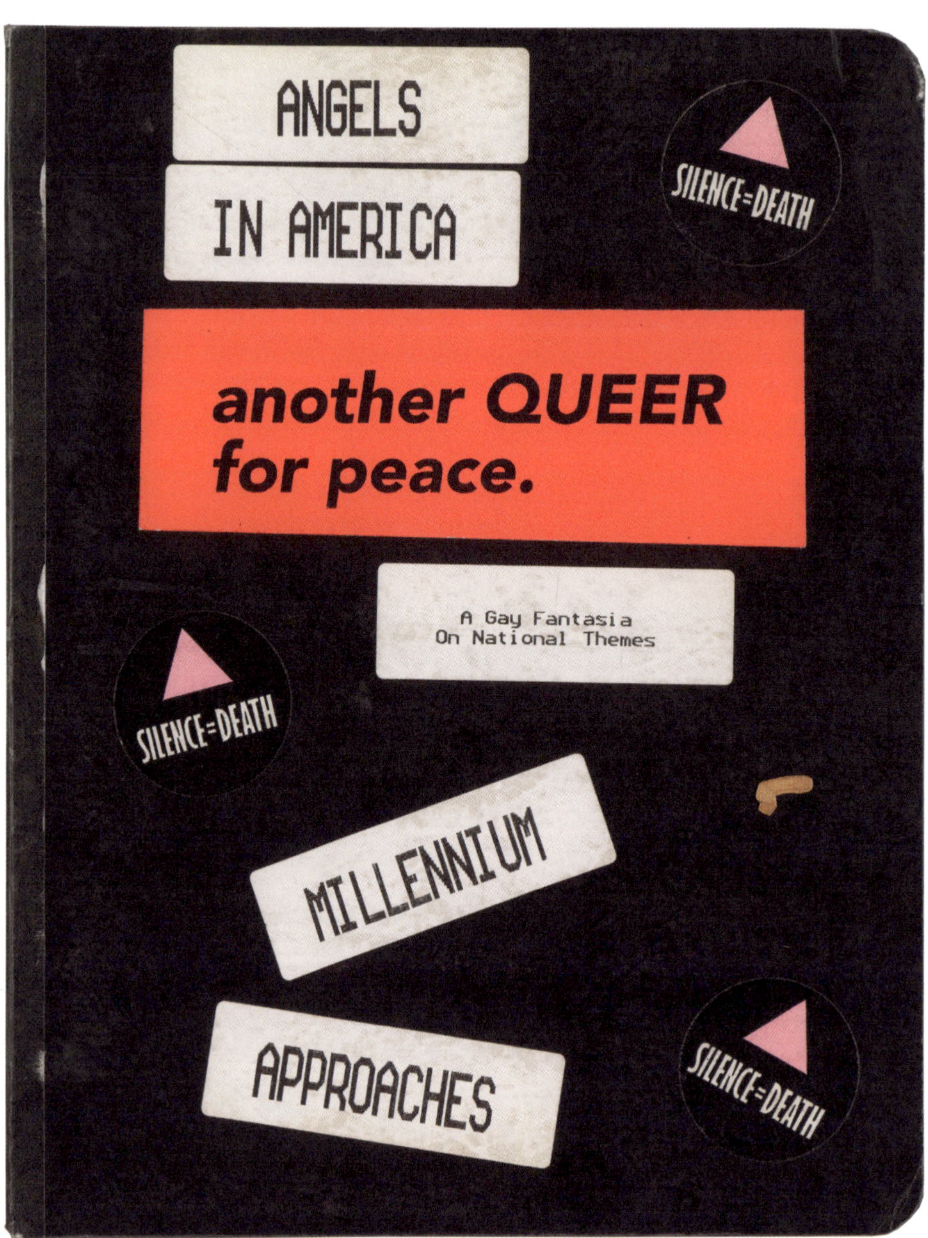

Angels in America notebook, cover and inside. Speaks for itself.

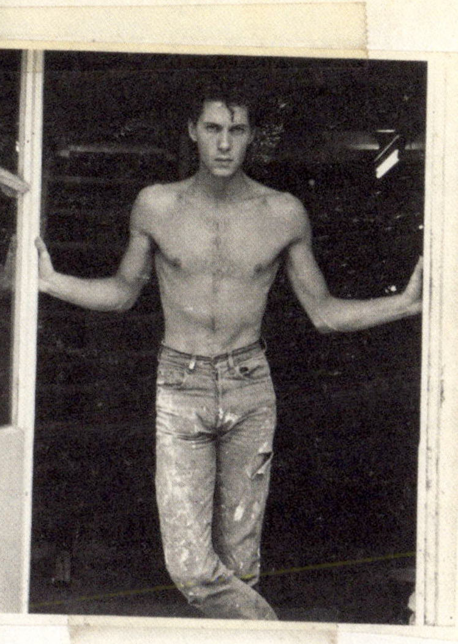

...n me, O Democracy, to serve you
...nme!
I am trilling these songs.
For you O Democracy
Walt Whitman

K • 5¼ IN. x 7½ IN.

RULING
COLLEGE RULED & MARGIN
COLLEGE RULED & MARGIN & PAGED
COLLEGE RULED & MARGIN

N.J. 07208 MADE IN U.S.A.

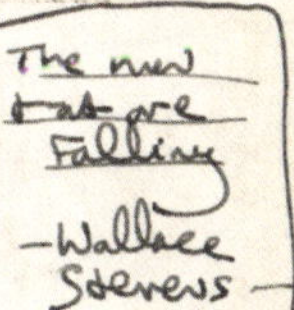

ANGELS IN AMERICA

With silence only as their benediction
God's angels come
Where, in the shadow of a great affliction,
The soul sits dumb.
J. G. Whittier

The Fear of sexuality parallels the
fear of germs. Erotic desires are
experienced as a chaos within—
Cindy Patton
Sex & Germs

People like us
Are gonna make it because
We don't want freedom
We don't want justice
We just want
Someone to love.
David Byrne.

I always have seven hundred reasons why I mustn't start working right now: I don't trust my instrument, I think I'm not really good."

Freud hovered over our talk, which concerns Kushner's masterwork *Angels in America*, and how it came together, a story in which the subconscious, in the shape of a dream, plays a central part. I probably don't have to explain how good it is, since it's widely considered the most accomplished play of the last chunk of the twentieth century at least; it's the winner of Tonys and the Pulitzer and all that. Just to give you some orientation though, it's actually two plays—*Millennium Approaches* and *Perestroika*, written in succession but usually performed together. Its hero is a gay man named Prior, who is struck with AIDS and has hallucinations, but it is also a thickly plotted epic involving the Mormon church, Ethel Rosenberg, and the trajectory of history. Prior has a boyfriend named Louis, who abandons him. Louis then has an affair with Joe, a Mormon and a closeted gay man. Joe has a wife named Harper, who is addicted to pills and also has hallucinations. Joe's mother, Hannah Pitt, comes to visit and works at the Mormon Visitors' Center. The counterpoint to Prior is the notorious real-life lawyer Roy Cohn, who also has AIDS and who has designs on Joe.

Rounding out the characters is Belize, a friend of Prior's who becomes Roy's nurse; and, most crucially, an angel who has descended from heaven through Prior's ceiling to take him back with her, because he is, she tells him, a prophet who is destined to rescue the otherworld, which by the way is in tatters because it has been abandoned by God. Does that make sense? It is a complex construction, but proceeds, when you see it, with inexorable forward motion, as if every decision were obvious. Which of course it wasn't. You might want to refer to this paragraph if you're unfamiliar with the play—and then, if your appetite is whetted enough, watch the very good HBO miniseries Mike Nichols made of it—since my conversation with Tony is a piece-by-piece account of how the epic emerged.

We got to the story of *Angels* in a winding way that suggests the labyrinth of Tony's mind, which is as funny and thoughtful as his plays. But let's just pick it up at how he became a playwright in the first place.

Experience Does Teach You "I think I really always wanted to be a writer," he said, "but I've always found writing scary. I have ADHD[4] or something, I don't know what it is. In any case, I didn't actually know what I wanted to

THE UNCONSCIOUS HAS IT ALL FIGURED OUT

As Tony was considering the sort of play he might want to write, he found himself attracted to the possibilities of epic theater, thinking particularly about Shakespeare. "Shakespeare makes you want to come in and do what most people don't know they have to do with works of art, which is, you are as capable of failing it as it is of failing you," Tony said. "You have to bring yourself to it. And somehow Shakespeare just makes that the thing you want to do.

"I love big, long, discursive things. I loved *Moby-Dick*. I just became obsessed with Melville, rejecting the idea that you had to exclude things. One of Brecht's friends, Walter Benjamin, said that beneath the surface there are these tunnels constantly being made that connect things. I loved that idea, and because I'm Freudian and have been in analysis forever, I really believe in the unconscious as a schematic.

"It sort of became my method of construction. I just had some vague intuition that there might be some way to join these things. I would write them down in a notebook and keep playing with them until I figured out how they join."

do. I came from this tiny town in Louisiana. Both my parents were musicians. My father was very erudite—a great reader of poetry. My father, who was a Juilliard-trained clarinetist, lived for art—music and poetry especially, and had a kind of eidetic memory, could recite *Endymion* by heart and Robert Burns and Shakespeare. He really loved language and loved words. He wasn't a mean person, but he couldn't read a book that was badly written. It just made him angry. And it was sort of, if you weren't a genius, if you weren't Keats, what was the point? He and I clashed badly on my bar mitzvah sermon. I was just young enough for him to stomp on it—he took it away and wrote his own version of it. And that's what I delivered."

"It makes sense to me that that might make it terrifying to be a writer," I said.

Tony gave me a slightly pained look. "But part of it about writing also is that I'm an emotional coward, I become a little disarranged by having to go into painful places. So I have to trick myself[5] into doing what you're supposed to do, which is to get into difficult emotional terrain. And the more I've come to understand my writing, the harder it's gotten, which I think is probably true of any kind of anxiety-based art. Experience does teach you. One, you start to realize what human beings are actually capable of, what a great work of art is really—I mean if you were an earthworm, you'd probably be able to figure out that *Hamlet* is a great play. But the more times you see *Hamlet*, the more you realize this impossibly great thing lies so far beyond your capabilities. One starts to assume a proper level of awe for what a truly great work of art is, and how many shortcomings you bring to this enterprise."

Tony's modesty, his default stance, alternated with pride. It didn't feel insincere, even if he is pretty hard on himself.

"The few times you've stumbled into something good," Tony said, "you think, *How did that happen? What if I had gone down this other road instead? Would I have ever gotten to this thing that I've accidentally come across?* I mean, there are a few things I've written, moments in some of the things I've written, that I'm really rather proud of. Where did that come from?"

"That's what this conversation is about," I told him. "Also this book."

"Good luck." He laughed.

The early years in a biography are often the dullest, but in Tony's own account of his chronology, you can see how the strands—intellectual and otherwise—start to weave. He went to Columbia. "In my junior year I took Edward Tayler's[6] class in Shakespeare—and his maxim was to really understand Shakespeare, you have to be able to count to two, because everything was dyads and dialectics and antinomies. And I read Marx for the first time. And I was taking a modern drama class, reading Brecht—the theory as well as the plays. And I was a medieval studies major—"

"Why that?"

"Because I was a Jew and gay and the glory of the church and all that I am . . . am I just babbling?"

I assured him that he wasn't, but he sped up and fast-forwarded to NYU.

A Beautiful Boy Named Bill "I was a graduate student at NYU's theater acting program. I was a directing student, not a playwriting student. Directing was sort of a way of getting into writing through the back door, because I was terrified to own the identity of being a writer." He met Stephen Spinella, an acting student, there—a friendship that would become essential. The drama program often did collaborations with the dance department—that was crucial too. "One of the first things I wrote was for

---

1. The movie he was writing with Steven Spielberg was *The Fabelmans*. Previously he'd written *Lincoln* and *Munich* for Spielberg as well.

2. Todd Haynes is the director of *Safe* and *Far from Heaven*, among other movies.

3. Christine Vachon is a well-known producer, mostly of independent movies.

4. You'll see that ADHD comes up often in these conversations, which I guess makes sense. It makes one distractible, which might help the mind hopscotch around—a useful tool to stir up the imagination. But another symptom is an ability to hyperfocus on a single thing, intense focus being equally essential to the act of making anything. The two functions—distraction and focus—need each other. "ADHD is not necessarily a deficit of attention," reads an entry on Healthline, "but rather a problem with regulating one's attention span. . . . So, while mundane tasks may be difficult to focus on, others may be completely absorbing." This back-and-forth between wandering and bearing down is kind of the whole story.

5. As I went from one encounter to another, people kept referring to all the ways they had to delude themselves. We all delude ourselves, sure, but these guys were masters at it, and knew exactly what they were doing. It was one of the first things I noticed.

6. Edward Tayler was a noted literary scholar.

one of these collaborations." But also: "There was a dancer there named Bill who was unbelievably beautiful. I saw him once dancing in a studio without his shirt on, and I was faint."

Tony started to explore the cruising aspects of gay life of New York—situations that he would later integrate into *Angels*. And he wrote more. In 1985, his first play, *A Bright Room Called Day*, was produced at a theater on Twenty-Second Street. A friend knew Oskar Eustis, who now runs the Public Theater, but was even then a formidable figure, running an avant-garde theater company in San Francisco called the Eureka [Theater Company]. "Oskar was this hot kind of red diaper baby guy. He spoke German, he had actually read Marx, unlike most everybody else, and really had theories. He was legendary. This friend brought Oskar to see the first performance. And Oskar asked to see the script afterwards. He read the script, liked it, and then he [went] back to the Eureka."

The Eureka would go on to produce *Bright Room* in San Francisco. "And when the play closed [in 1987] Oskar and I went out to the Embarcadero for hot dogs. The play hadn't been particularly successful, but Oskar said, 'We are really excited about your writing. We want to do a thing with you.' They had a standing company of three straight women and one straight man. I had come out of the closet between 1982 and 1984, at a point when the epidemic was really starting to make its way through the community in that terrifying way—and you know, Reagan and all that stuff. So I decided that since it was for San Francisco, I should really write about being gay. And so that's what I told Oskar. We both scratched our heads a little bit over the fact that if we got a grant for it [which Eustis was proposing], it was going to be for these four straight actors. And I said I needed to think about it."

A Dream Before we get to what happened next, though, we need to go back in time for a moment:

"Remember the dancer Bill I was telling you about?" Tony said. "I was in St. Louis on an NEA directing fellowship. And I heard that Bill was sick. He was the first person I knew fairly well who had gotten sick. Then I got a phone call from a mutual friend who said that Bill had died. I was in a weird little house, some rich drunk lady's house in St. Louis I had rented. And I dreamt that Bill was in this room, in his pajamas. And he was screaming in terror and looking up at the ceiling. The ceiling was starting to bulge like in a horror movie. The lights were flickering, he was cowering in the bed, screaming, and then the ceiling collapsed and fell on the bed and covered him in plaster. And this angel came through the hole in the ceiling."

Tony had dreamed "what turned out to be the punch line to the end of *Millennium Approaches*."

Two Mormons on the Street "I went back to New York, there were two adorable Mormon guys on Carroll Street in Brooklyn," Tony continued. "They were missionaries and not getting a lot of attention from angry Brooklynites on their way to work. I asked one of them if I could have a copy of the Book of Mormon, which I'd read before. One of them was seriously hot, so there was a level of erotic obsession. And I had been doing a lot of driving back and forth in St. Louis. Bruce Springsteen's *Born in the USA* had just come out, I'd listen to the tape over and over again, thinking about Springsteen's butt. And as I said, I was a medieval studies major and we were fifteen years from the millennium, which is a very big deal if you're a medieval studies major. And as I say, I was thinking about America, *Born in the USA*. The Mormon angel Moroni is the only real homespun American angel. But he didn't have wings. My angel had wings. And was a woman. Or Bill's angel, I guess I should say.

"I went back to St. Louis, I was still thinking about this dream. And then I wrote a poem, which nobody's ever seen except for me. It was an attempt to fake my way through the epidemic and this dream about Bill and these

There are, at last count, seven characters. Principally there are three gay men who live in New York, friends who meet semi-regularly in a coffee shop. One is a secretary who works for Amnesty International; one is a prostitute; and one is a schoolteacher. The secretary is deeply in love with a near-middle-aged survivor of the Gay Activist Alliance; he (the secretary) is also into S & M. The prostitute has recently become the hustler of choice of an extremely wealthy, infamous, right-wing trial lawyer who is dying of AIDS (That this is Roy Cohn will be made explicit or, if legally necessary, only made very obvious.) The schoolteacher is receiving letters, phone calls, and possibly angelically-delivered epistles (The angel is the 7th character) from his current lover, who is slowly going crazy in an apartment in San Francisco. The play moves back and forth between the coffe-shop meetings of the three friends and the events of their separate involvements. It also moves back and forth in time, occassionally slipping from the present into the McCarthy era,and even into the mid-nineteenth century via the schoolteacher's San Francisco boyfriend, who is creating a political, historical and mystical cosmology from fragments of Melville, The Book Of Mormon, and AIDS research and paranoia.

There might be other characters on their way; certainly more parts for women would be possible, especially if the play was written for Eureka.

Angels, very early imagining. The play, as first described in what was probably a grant proposal. The only character that made it to the finish was Roy Cohn.

boys and the angel, and whatever else I stuffed in there. I'm not a poet—I've always had the good taste to know that—so I put it away."

And Roy Cohn After Eustis suggested working together, Tony thought back to his dream, and the poem he'd written about it. In fact, he'd filled notebooks writing about his dream. He gave it a title. "I called it *Angels in America*," he said.

"I guess probably a year before that, Roy Cohn had died. I had been interested in him since I was ten. I heard these terrifying stories about the McCarthy era from my parents, and the Rosenbergs, and all the stuff that one has heard about if you were born in 1956. My father had given me a copy of Fred Cook's *The Nightmare Decade* to read, in which Cohn looms significantly as one of the great villains, as he should. Cook talks about him and David Schine[7] chasing each other naked through the Ritz in Paris and snapping each other's butts with towels. I was this little closeted gay boy, and I picked up all the signifiers."

As Tony got older, his interest in Cohn grew. "When I came to Columbia, at the beginning of Studio 54 [where Cohn was a regular], I was disgusted that this horrible man suddenly was in the *New York Post* every day with Liza Minnelli and Halston. Then we all saw that bizarre Mike Wallace interview where he's saying, 'I don't have AIDS.' So he's really beginning to loom for me as a gay Jewish man."

When Cohn died, Tony found himself feeling some sympathy. He was particularly upset

7. David Schine was a hotel heir, vehement anti-communist, and crony of Roy Cohn's.

American Prophet tonight you become
American Eye that pierceth Night;
American Heart all hot for truth
The true great vocalist; the knowing Mind
Tongue-of-the-Land, Seer-Head

I can't find the right voice for the Angel. It's either monotonously bombastically Whitmanian or its Cranky/crotchety Poundian -- one dull, the other comical, neither sounding like much more than a 3rd rate literary conceit. Ugh. And of course what's happening on stage is funny but it isn't, shouldn't *ever* be cute or artsy.

Maybe I should junk all the show-offy poesy and make the Angel NewEngland Plain. Crystal clear speech. I don't know if that'd work.

I'm used to my free-verse Arias giving my best and deepest thoughts expression. Maybe in this play that's not right. Hard, hard to give that up. But . . .

The rant on the page reading very good. Maybe that's the way.

Notebook 1: Finding the angel's voice.

about an article in *The Nation* by Robert Sherrill, "one of the great old lions of the Left. He wrote this really venomous piece [building on] what Jack Anderson[8] had written about Cohn, about his body's condition at the end, talking about the number of lesions around his anus. I mean, it was ugly. And this was quoted rather gleefully by Sherrill, who then also resorted to the old bromide that there's something about homosexuality that seems to have a natural affinity for fascism, and the lavender mafia around Ronald and Nancy Reagan. It was infuriating and enraging. I felt angry on his behalf. And I felt that meant I really should start to think about writing something."

In the meantime, Tony and the Eureka had gotten their grant from the NEA, which Tony called "a command."[9]

"So now you had to write it," I said.

"Well, it was a command to write *something*, but because of the watermark on the check, it was the people of the United States of America—the federal government—who had commissioned this play. I'm in my own way a very patriotic person. I have a belief that a combination of action on the street and representation in the halls of power would bring about transformation

8. Jack Anderson was another lefty journalist.

9. It might be the coincidence of this particular collection of subjects, but many of the projects in this book started out as commissions—or invitations of some sort. Commissions jump-start projects and often define them. The dreaded blank page isn't blank if it has a prompt on it. (Kara Walker's sugar sculpture was the result of an open-ended invitation. Marie Howe's was more of a poke. Louise Glück's was a kind of game between friends.)

Problems to Solve

1) There's the overall problem of the play as a unified concerted event rather than as a series of solutions to the problems of MILLENNIUM — or as a long narrative but, for no very clear reason & towards no perceptible goal.

What's it Meant:

One idea that has begun to move me is the relationship of forgiveness to change.

That if the past is forgiveable it must be related somehow to our changing ourselves — if we are to be forgiven.

By our deeds shall we be known.

Changing is giving the future due acknowledging that there is

2: Searching for the play's meaning.

for everybody. And what Reagan was doing at that point . . . it just felt terrifying. And I'm sure that's where *A Gay Fantasia on National Themes* [the play's subtitle] came from."

Preaching to the Converted "The impulse," said Tony, "is always, what do you feel most confused about and most unsure about. You can assume that others like you are having similar doubts. As I've always said, your job is to preach to the converted. That's what preachers are supposed to talk about. It's not the things we know are true, but the things we're worried might not be true, that contravene our faith. That's the place to go. Anything good comes from a place of unknowing.

"I pulled out the poem from a filing cabinet, and I said, 'Oskar. I think I have a title.' And I thought, *Why am I saying it to him, it's a terrible title*. And he said, 'Right the fuck on'—when Oskar likes something, you really can tell. So butch and manly and just a daddy guy.

"I wrote, with very little trouble, sixty pages, which is an hour onstage. Oskar made me sign a contract—he wanted the play to be two hours because *Bright Room* had been three. I said I wanted to have songs. Jazz with songs. And I did write lyrics, and a couple of the lines from them wound up in the play. But needless to say, it didn't turn into a musical."

The sixty pages began to have a shape.

The Upside of Constraint Tony considered the company, the three straight women actors and the fourth, a man. Because he wanted to write about AIDS and being gay in America, it wasn't obvious how to do that with these particular actors. But he began to build the play around their specific attributes.[10]

"Jeff King, the man in the company, was six foot two and looks like a linebacker," Tony said. "I thought, *There's gonna be a Mormon guy. And he'd be a great closet case. What if he could be a Mormon missionary?*

"So I made Jeff King Joe [the Mormon] and I made Lorri [Holt] his wife [Harper, the woman addicted to pills] because she was small and in her early thirties and a little bit nuts. I needed to figure out something for [another woman in the troupe]. She was really sort of a rough-hewn person. So I thought maybe Joe would have a mother who was a Mormon also. At first I thought, *I'm going to make the angel a man because it would be hotter and whatever*. Then I thought, *No, I can't: in the dream the angel was female*. So I said, *Let's make it female*, and I made it Sigrid [Wurschmidt]." That took care of the Eureka company.

"It [took me a while to] come up with a gay couple, I wanted to write a gay couple. Also my friend Kimberly[11] had had a terrible accident. I was taking care of somebody who was catastrophically ill. That really fed into Louis." Louis would do the opposite—run from taking care of his very ill boyfriend, Prior—but he was the character with whom Tony would most identify.

Prior, around whom the play would eventually revolve, would be played by Stephen Spinella, the actor Tony had so admired at NYU. "At this point, I knew anything I wrote needed to have Stephen Spinella in it." Prior was, in a sense, written for him. "There was just no actor on earth who has a better command than Stephen. He had already become sort of my avatar."

He said, "I knew I wanted Roy Cohn in there somewhere," in some sort of father-son thing with Joe. Tony had read a lot about Cohn and his relationship with Joe McCarthy. "It started off as a paternal thing. Kind of S-M. Daddy and his boy. I will admit that I was somewhat attracted to those power dynamics."

He understood that their stories would have to intertwine, even as he wasn't sure yet exactly how. "I've always loved chamber music. And if you listen to chamber music, if you're paying attention, you can start to understand how the music is constructed. I began very much in these terms. I thought of Roy as a kind of continuum, a line that went down the middle, and then the two couples would weave. And I knew Joe would connect to Roy and then Joe would connect to Louis.

"I think the play originally started with Harper's monologue about when you look at the world from a spaceship. I had written it sitting on the Bethesda Fountain[12] on a January day. And then I just put it away, I said, *Maybe I'll use that, that's pretty good*. I think she opened the play first, and then the rabbi [a character who appears only once, delivering a eulogy for Louis's grandmother that introduces the theme of migration], and then Roy. But I switched them around. Roy was in the first place at some points and then the rabbi became permanently first."

One thing he absolutely knew was that at the turn of the play, which he had at first thought was the end of act I, the angel would appear. ("I always start with an outline. The outline said the angel arrives by intermission.") But she hadn't at the end of the sixty pages he typed up. ("I write in longhand. And then I type it. I always do that. So that my first draft is really my second draft. And if anybody looks at your 'first' draft, it's not going

10. You might note the number of times limitations imposed by circumstances come up in the pages that follow. It always appears as a good thing, at least in retrospect, if the project succeeds.

11. Tony has called Kimberly Flynn, a dramaturge, his closest friend.

12. Central Park's Bethesda Fountain is central to *Angels*. The last scene is set there, and the fountain's angel is the centerpiece of the gorgeous last monologue.

13. Longhand before typing = permission to vomit. A recurring theme.

14. What is it about movement? Many of the book's subjects—Gregory Crewdson, Cheryl Pope—mentioned feeling more creative when in motion. Swimming, boxing, walking, riding trains. For what it's worth (maybe not much), there's some research that supports that.

15. While I'm tracing patterns, I would be remiss in not pointing out that Melville is cited over and over and over in this book. *Billy Budd*. *Moby-Dick*. The number-one influence, if you're counting.

to be as bad as your first. It gives you permission to be a terrible stupid idiot.[13])

"I thought this is some sort of dumb soap opera," Tony said of that first effort, which he gave to Oskar Eustis to read. "I kind of loved it but I also thought it was kind of horrible. I sent it to Oskar, and he clearly wasn't nuts about it. He'll deny that. He said, 'There's great stuff, comrade, and we'll just keep going. And we'll edit.' And this was clearly a lie."

Even if Eustis wasn't wild about the play, he gave Tony useful insight about how to understand what seemed to be pouring forth. "Oskar said, 'You know what you're showing is that under really unbearable pressure, reality is going to start to crack. And that is in a sense the action of *Millennium Approaches*.'"

Tony understood exactly what Eustis was saying. The play he seemed to be writing was fantastical; strange things kept happening. They were having a cumulative effect. "I read comic books when I was a kid, and I learned how to construct the science fiction fantasy thing. The reason the angel works is the escalation of supernatural events that happen to Prior in the first act. The play gets crazier and crazier. It really moves in on you, until you know something is going to happen. And as Coleridge said about Shakespeare, his genius was that he always preferred expectation to surprise."

All the while, Tony was unlocking, combining. He hadn't meant for Prior's and Harper's stories to converge, but once he figured out how to do that, through their mutual hallucinations, "that was a big liberation."

Writing on Vehicles He began to write act 2. "Still, the angel wasn't showing up. But I had more scenes that I thought were worth including." Among these was another that felt like giving birth. The first scene of the act involved Prior collapsing in his apartment—"which is probably the hardest thing I ever had to write. I got on the subway. I always write on the subways and airplanes really well.[14] I went out towards Coney Island and I said, 'I'm not getting off this fucking train until I write this,' because I couldn't go into the second act without it. I knew what the scene was. I was just such a chicken about it, because it's about somebody having a psychotic break.

"I got the second act done, and that's when Oskar called and said, 'Okay, we're now really late. And you're in breach of contract, and why don't you come out and we'll do a reading of the play.' I got on the plane and there was one other scene—I knew that I wanted the ghosts to start showing up, so I wrote really quickly on the plane. I thought, *There's only one other thing I know is going to happen—Ethel Rosenberg*

WRITING ROY

Tony said that a particularly tough part of these first pages was writing a scene he knew he needed: the conversation between Roy and the doctor when the doctor tells him he has AIDS.

"The last thing I wrote in act 1 was Roy and his doctor, because I knew that's how I wanted to end act 1. The scene didn't work. I struggled for weeks. Then, for some reason, I reread *Billy Budd*.[15] And I came across this line about Claggart: he had perfected the use of the rationale as an ambidextrous instrument for effecting the irrational. In other words, a great order is a disorder and a great disorder is an order, these things are one. It made me realize what I was getting at with Cohn, which is true of right-wing thinking in general—that reality is an activity of the imagination. They're fundamentally idealists, they believe that the idea precedes matter.

They reject the notion that you begin with material reality. You just demand that reality obey your fantasies. "Then I called my friend Kimberly and said, 'I think I've just written the best scene that I've ever written.'"

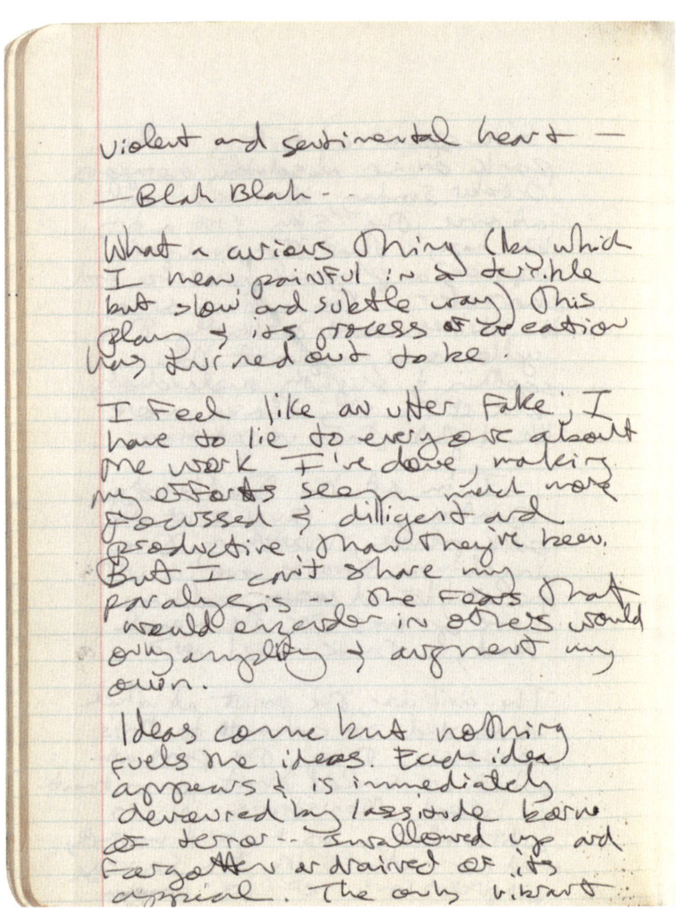

violent and sentimental heart —

—Blah Blah..

What a curious thing (by which I mean painful in a terrible but slow and subtle way) this play & its process of creation has turned out to be.

I feel like an utter fake; I have to lie to everyone about the work I've done, making my efforts seem much more focussed & dilligent and productive than they've been. But I can't share my paralysis -- the fears that would engender in others would only amplify & augment my own.

Ideas come but nothing fuels the ideas. Each idea appears & is immediately devoured by lassitude born of terror -- swallowed up and forgotten or drained of its appeal. The only vibrant

3: Deep doubt.

is going to show up. So I quickly typed that out. And we did a reading of that.

"In the reading, we got to Roy and Joe and Ethel, and then the play just stopped. I didn't have anything else, but we had already been reading for two hours and forty-five minutes. And it had not been boring. It was working in this kind of exhilarating way—so good that Oskar now thought it could be a two-and-a-half-hour play! I went out walking with Sigrid, and she said, 'What else are you thinking?' and I said, 'I don't know, all this stuff. I've written tons of notes and one monologue na, na, na. And it's Harper's and I don't know when she would even say it.' It was Harper's night flight to San Francisco. [That's the one he wrote sitting at Bethesda Fountain.] Sigrid read it and then she handed it back to me, and she says, 'You know, I think you should make this two plays.'"

A Conversation with Louis Which of course is what came to pass. But meanwhile, the play was long—very long. "I became panicked that I didn't know how I was going to cut the play down. The characters wouldn't do the thing that they're supposed to do in the outline. So I just had to ask a character. And the character I was closest with was Louis, and I said, you know, 'What's this play about?' And I felt like I was sort of taking dictation. . . .

"So Louis started talking, and I realized that

he was very nervous while he was talking, correcting himself a lot, especially when it comes to politically correct things. And I thought, *Oh, he's talking to someone else*, and I started to see Belize [who, in addition to being Prior's friend and Roy's nurse, also has some wonderfully spiky political arguments with Louis]. So I put Belize in there, and then I started really having fun. By the time I was done, I had this massive stack of paper. But the purpose of the writing was to make the thing shorter!"

Eventually he finished the first play, *Millennium Approaches*. Finally, the angel appeared through the ceiling. But even as the play began actual performances, he wasn't done writing. "The show went well," said Tony. "The audience got it, and they were waiting for something to happen. They were watching and waiting. I call them 'penny drop' moments—when the audience starts having a singular experience and everybody bonds. And the energy that those moments can create is astonishing. There are some really good plays without them, including *Perestroika*, which I think may be a better play than *Millennium*, but it doesn't have that moment."

How Do You Write an Epistle? There was another play to go, *Perestroika*, which would have its own struggles, most of which I won't go into here. But there was one particular part of *Perestroika* I did want to talk to Tony about, because it was a part he has felt he never got right—the angel's "epistle," which is a crucial scene in the second play: it is the angel's own nervous breakdown, her description of how heaven has been devastated by the disappearance of the Creator. To make matters more difficult, it is relayed by Prior as he's talking to Belize, so it is acted out and described, back and forth. The epistle delivers pivotal exposition, but the angel also needs to seem broken, while at the same time delivering a very funny speech. That balance makes it impossible to play. But when Tony and I first started talking, he had seen a version on Zoom for a benefit that he thought might have worked, so he'd been thinking about it. He set up the epistle for me.

"I had gone up to Russian River and in ten days wrote hundreds of pages. And then I drove back with this gigantic stack of legal paper and turned on the car radio driving back from Napa Valley. The first thing that came on—I'm not making this up—was Mozart's Bassoon Concerto, which was one of my mother's big practice pieces. Then it went right from that to Mozart's Clarinet Concerto, one of my father's big practice pieces! And then the Black Crowes song—she talks to angels, she would sing with angels, something, like, about angels. I finally got scared and I turned off the radio.[16]

"Okay, so the angel crashes through the ceiling. I knew she was going to crash into the ceiling because that happened in my dream. And when *Millennium* was done, people in the audience were devastated at the end because they thought [the angel's arrival] meant Prior was dead. I had even thought for a moment that Prior was dead.

"But some people were exhilarated because—this is exactly what you used to say in the Middle Ages—the kingdom of God is both the day of judgment and the day of wrath, it's the end of history, the end of suffering and the beginning of the kingdom of God. . . ."

"So you started to realize that had dramatic possibilities?" I asked.

"Well, I accidentally stumbled on it," he answered. But it set up *Perestroika*'s themes, how it would deal with what might happen if God just couldn't hack the pressure.

Tony realized the second play would involve, in a sense, the exchanging of partners—Belize becomes Roy's nurse, Prior is rescued by Hannah after he collapses in the visitors' center.[17] And then the angel, who's experiencing a

16. Tony kept alternating between Freudian and mystical explanations for the connections he kept making on the page. More dialectic, I guess.

17. Playwriting (novel writing, TV writing) sometimes seems reducible to a logic equation—a series of hypotheticals: If I want to connect *X* character with *Y* character, what would happen? I know it's not as schematic as all that . . . but maybe a little bit? As I was listening to Suzan-Lori Parks (see the last chapter) particularly, I kept thinking of dramatic construction as a what-if math problem: add this, subtract that, change the variables—but then I kept looking for ways to reduce the mysterious to something a little more straightforward.

This brings me to the very point of the problem with my politics, and I feel that I could better end the play if I were a better person, or if i were in better faith. because I don't understand the politics of change, in my own life, I've experienced very little of that, of change, just occasionally I can manage something a little better than before because I've gotten older, more tired of waging the same stupid battles the same stupid ways, or I'm feeling more expansive, good-hearted and generous because I have more success, more money, more security-- feeling less pinched in my own life and so able to give more to others. or in some ways I'm smarter than I used to be, I know more, and I understand more deeply (but Oh! The things I have forgotten!) None of this really feels like it adds up to change.

Mama's death has changed me. It's made me sadder. It hurts a lot, anyway, I'll cry several times a day. Is that change? There is some sort of glacier-slow alteration, some adjustment being made to the staggering fact of her absence, for I will never see her again on this earth.

Harper with Joe--is trying to slip the bonds of having loved the wrong person. All the avenues her life might have gone down, some terrible and some perhaps much better than where she landed, and all those possibilities foreclosed around going down the road with him a ways. But they've reached a dead end, and she has paid a lot for believing in the wrong person, for loving the wrong person too much-- it has lessened her, and she has to get away.

Prior gets sicker all through act 4. He spends act 3 trying to find some comfort, I guess, I'm a little worried that I have ~~him~~ just running about like a plot function, but... he's ~~searching~~ for a way to live, and there's the fact of the disease that catches up with him. And at the same time he meets Hannah. And she helps him, but how? That's a weakness. She is supposed to give him strengthm but I'm not at all sure she's actually done that. the cold embrace of god speech is perhaps something she tell him before the angels arrives. I don't know-- it might be an idea. that sometimes one has to resign oneself to he tragic. She could sound a lutlle like daddy there-- the sounding-like-daddy I sometimes feel when I hear Kim go on and on and on about her problems. A hard stoicism. She could maybe give prior that.

4: The personal and strategic.

truly existential crisis, would beseech Prior to ascend to heaven to clean up the mess.

"I began to really play with this idea of the angel as a kind of [agent of] failed revelations. I thought a lot about the prophet that rejects the vision, then complains about it."

The confluence of the millennium and what was happening in the disintegrating Soviet Union—perestroika, glasnost, even Chernobyl ("I thought that was apocalyptic and millennial")—compelled him to create a bravura end-time speech for the angel, a spectacular aria of disintegration that would be the pivot of the second play. That was the epistle. He wrote it, and has kept rewriting it, long after the play was finished and performed.

"I've learned so much about being a playwright," Tony said. "There's this glob of text that I rewrite and rewrite, but it never gets all that much easier. And in a certain sense, I've made my peace with it. The play's doing fine. So I don't worry too much about it.

"I've seen a couple of people get close to really nailing her," he said about the angel, and we talked a bit about the Zoom version he'd recently seen, which altered his text some and in which the angel was played by four actresses, spookily layering parts of the speech on top of each other.

"It's hard to perform a being who is not human. And it's important that she not be human. And some of what she says is meant to be confusing to Prior. You want to make it idiotproof, or when people read it, they think it's a joke. If you do that, it guts the experience, and the speech comes out as gobbledygook."

Seeking Magic That led to talking about various productions and some aspects of the play he still thinks haven't been realized. "When the angel pierces through the ceiling, nobody's done what I really want. It's to see what I saw in the dream—a heavenly visitation in plaster and lath debris. She doesn't appear in the room, she just punches through the membrane. That speaks to me in all these—" He stopped. "And then what's always bothered me, is that nobody vanishes. Harper vanishes, but she doesn't—she just walks offstage, and this is theater, so people understand the convention. I want the *zhuzh* of it, the magic trick. But also—these things have deeper meanings. And this is a play about AIDS—there one day and gone the next."

"So you were linking Harper's disappearance with AIDS?"

"That took me decades."

"Do you find yourself understanding your subconscious by looking at your plays in retrospect, seeing things you were working out that you didn't realize at the time?"

We'd circled back to our trickster psyches again and again. Earlier, he had talked about the mind's own wit, the way it cracks itself up while you wait to get the joke. "It's a thing your brain does all the time," he'd said. "The unconscious is leaving little puns and little jokes. Bread crumb traces is what I call them.

"There are themes that you come back to over and over again,"[18] Tony said. "There are specific things about myself that I've always been unhappy about: I put them onstage to try and figure them out. I have to be careful, because I tend to be very unsympathetic to those characters, and they can get beaten up a lot. That's why Louis is hauled over the coals in a terrible way.

"I've never been one of those people—like Mann and O'Neill, I think—who don't want to be analyzed because they thought their magic will be taken away. I feel I got great value from being in analysis for myself. But I don't know that I have ever really thought I could cure anything in myself in writing plays. I don't think my plays, or my movies, will cure anything. You put these questions and visions in the world, and then you don't know what is going to be made of them."

All Art Fails Eventually, inevitably, we got around to talking about failure. It had been a long conversation, and it would soon be time to go. Tony was so forgiving of himself—and others. I couldn't help but think that his analysis had worked.

"All art fails," he said, "because all art is essentially Orpheus. All art is meant to resurrect the dead, and it will not succeed in doing that. The great model for all artists is Orpheus, and in his greatest work he bombed. He didn't get her out.

"Almost all playwrights are like physicists—we do our work from our late teens to about thirty-three. And then we're kind of garbage. We may generate some interesting things after that, but for some reason it seems to go that way.

"There are flaws and problems and failures in every work that I love. A lot of people feel that the epistle is the big mistake in *Angels*. [The critic] Michael Feingold just vomited all over it, but then Robert Altman [who at one point had wanted to film *Angels*] said he thought *Millennium* was just this kind of piffle, what you have to get through to get to the meat of the matter, which was *Perestroika*."

Art, Tony said, "is always endurance. I don't think you should ever feel like a failure unless you catch yourself in the habit of lying about something, telling yourself that you have to do this for money or safety. If you've really made peace with dishonesty within yourself, only then have you failed."

We got up to face our afternoons, Tony to a scene he was dreading writing, me to a painting I couldn't figure out, the dog padding optimistically behind us.

18. Whether you feel trapped or empowered by the recurrence of themes you're fated to noodle over endlessly seems to vary widely by artist.

3

ROZ CHAST

The Child's Way

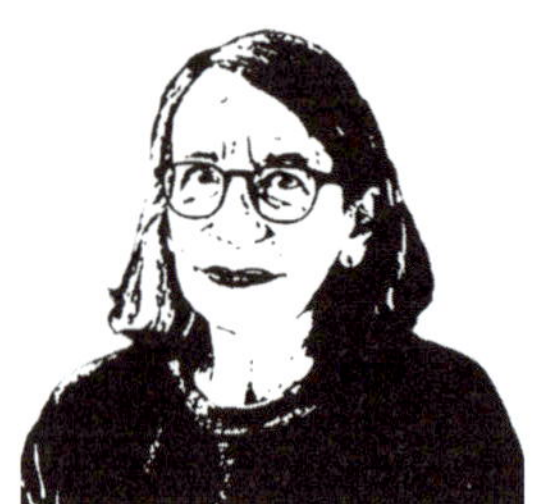

OCCUPATION: Cartoonist

WORK DISCUSSED: "Gifts from the House of Low Goals" (1998)

BORN: 1954

ROZ CHAST'S HOUSE is in suburban Connecticut. I don't why I found that strange; she just seems so urban, angsty, and neurotic, but I guess we are all angsty everywhere; that's why her work has such universal power. She answered the door, looking very much like the cartoon self she frequently draws, and gave me a house tour, her walls like a museum of cartooning, with framed cartoons of her own and of the fellow cartoonists, present and past, she clearly considers extended family.[1] She showed me a Charles Addams scarf she'd just gotten, which she described as her white whale. (She is a collector of cartoon-printed scarves—she had many; who knew there was such a thing?) After a quick visit with her birds, who have their own room, she led me to her studio. Strewn throughout the room are piles of rejected cartoons, and of cut-up cartoons, parts of which she might use someday, just piles and piles of hundreds of cartoon ideas in some stage of development.

I love Roz's work, but then who doesn't? Her demented cartoons appear regularly in *The New Yorker*, to which she has contributed for over forty years. She's also written or illustrated over a dozen books, including the National Book Critics Circle award winner *Can't We Talk About Something More Pleasant?*, a soulful cartoon memoir of taking care of her aging parents. In it you see the more "grown-up" artist she might have been, not only because of the book's depth but also because, interestingly to me, you see some glimpses of a drawing style that looks (and was) art trained. Which isn't to say that her cartoons are un-grown-up. Far from it. (She was elected to the American Philosophical Society, which seems apt.) But she has very emphatically embraced a jubilant, juvenile voice she calls "the child's way."

A mammoth sculpture, an epic play—those are projects of long gestation. A cartoon takes minutes. But how

1. In talking to the collection of artists for this book, I soon started to see that who they identified as their kin—what particular community or tradition they felt a part of—was central to how they made their work. This "family" (ancestors, contemporaries) taught them what values were important, inspired them, hectored them. Like any family, really.

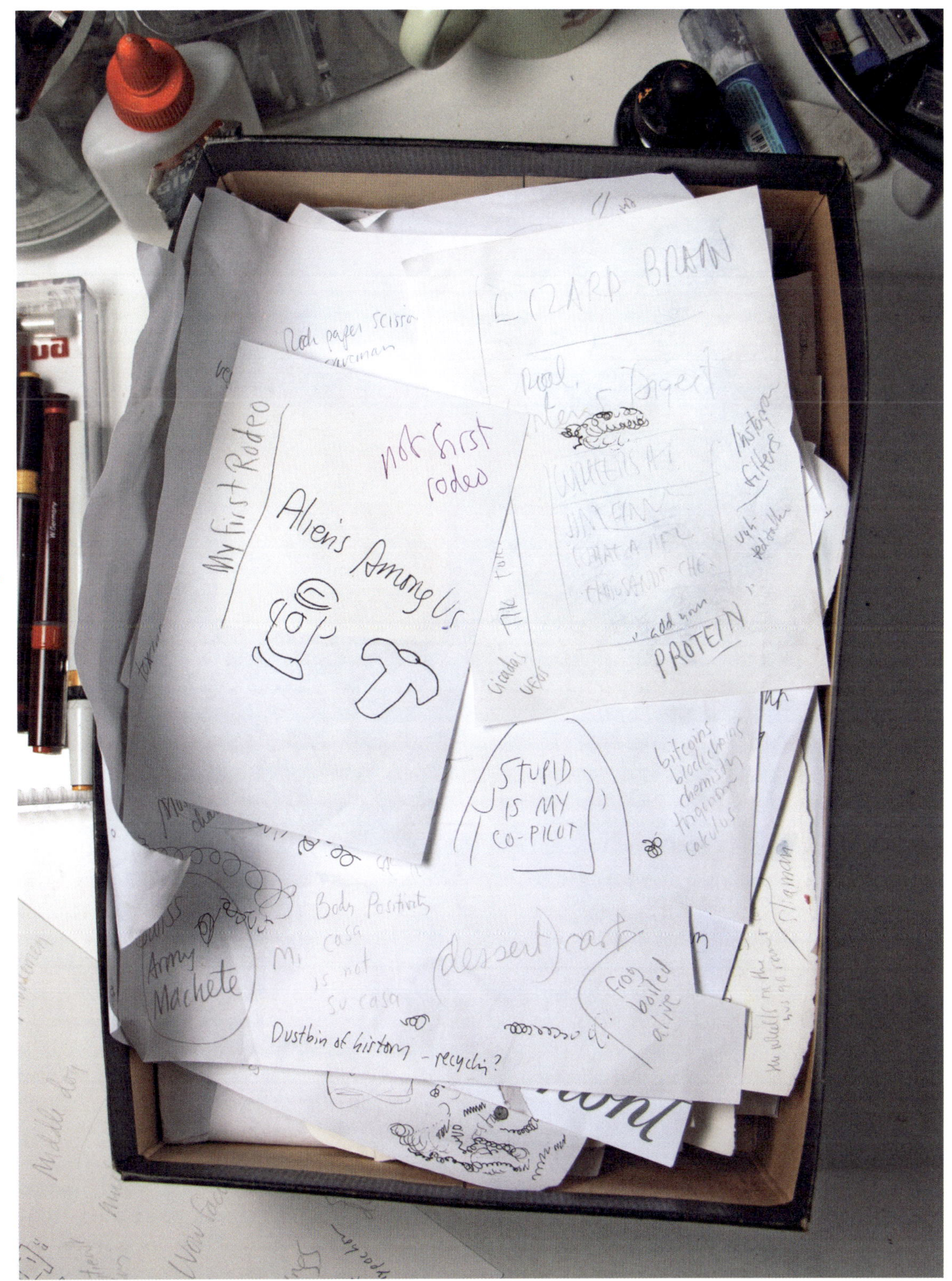

Idea germs. A shoebox full of them, which gets emptied out out when it's full.

different is it really?[2] I went to Roz to understand. We first spoke on Zoom. She very kindly followed up on that conversation by choosing a cartoon at random and drawing me another cartoon to show me how it was made, called "Gifts from the House of Low Goals." The two cartoons are side by side on the right.

She also let me look in the box into which she throws her idea bits. That's the box you saw on the preceding page. Associations are associations; hers are just a bit wackier than most. Turns out, the distance between her cartoon persona and her actual self is pretty tiny, maybe nonexistent.

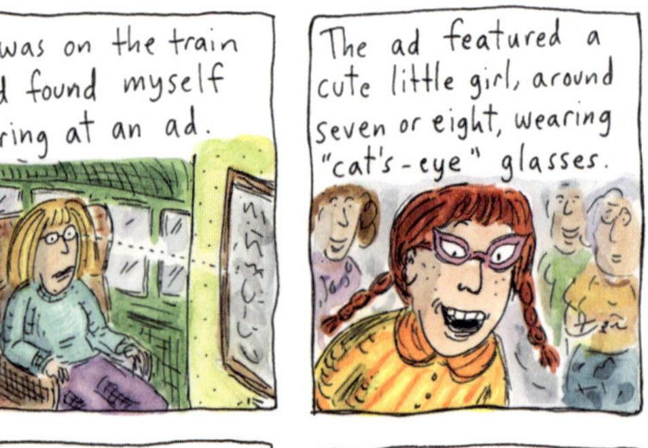

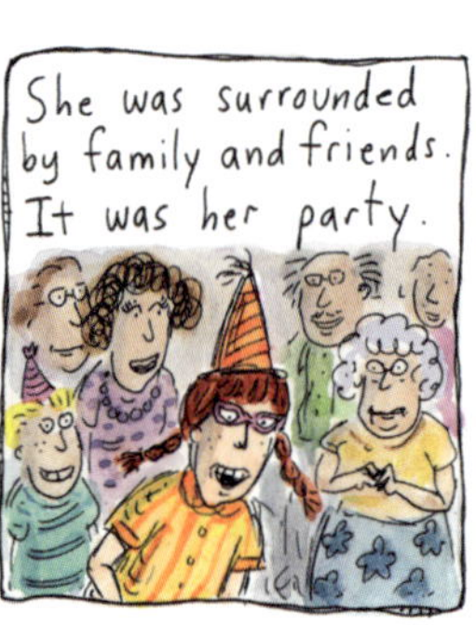

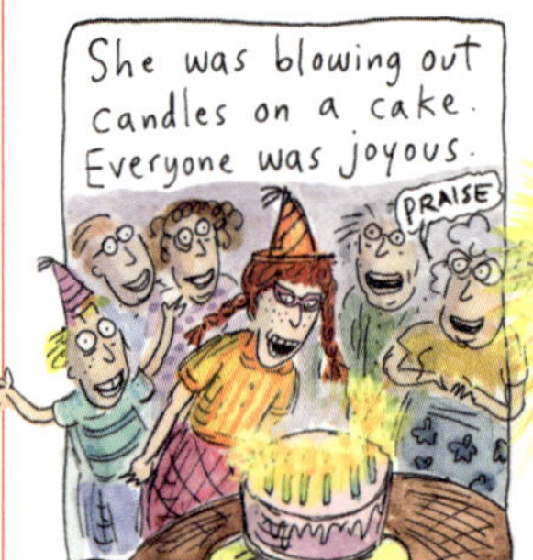

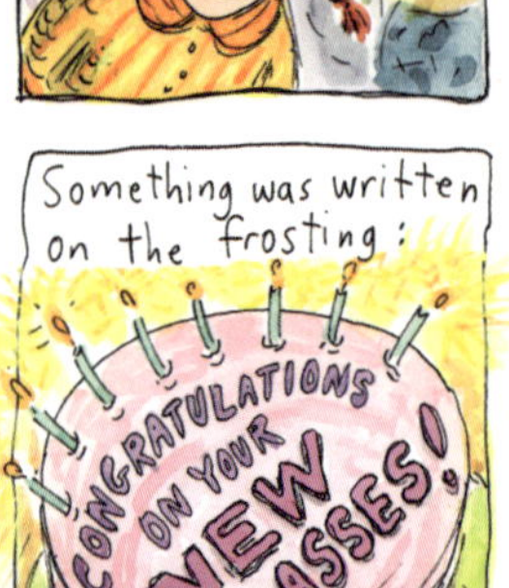

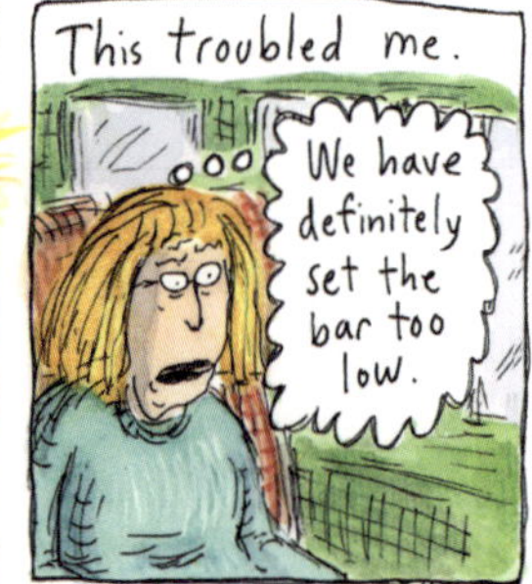

Roz sent this...

The Beginnings of an Idea

Roz Chast: I can give you a couple of examples of where cartoon ideas came from. There was a cartoon I did years ago, when my son was about sixteen and doing homework in the living room. There was a boom box with music going. And if you've been around teenagers, you know that there's nothing more disgusting in the eyes of a teenager than to watch a grown-up dancing. I hate to dance, but I wanted to see if he was paying any attention. So I'm like doing my mom dance and it was, "Mom, stop. You're hurting me." And it made me laugh. So I asked if I could use that in a cartoon.

Another time I'm on Metro-North, and there was an ad for—maybe it was Carvel—and there was a little girl, she's wearing these cute cat-eye glasses, and she has a party hat on. She's blowing out the candles on the cake, and on the cake it says, "Congratulations on your new glasses." And I just thought, *We have set the bar low!* So I had all these things, like "Congratulations on your new armchair" and "I'm so glad you're not an arsonist."

Adam Moss: *Do these cartoons come to you fully blown? Or are you constantly revising these things once you've set them down?*

RC: Depends. There are times—like when I saw an "end of the world" guy. And I just wanted to draw one of those guys. So I did, and I thought, *Oh, he needs a wife.* So he has his THE END IS NEAR sign and she is next to him, looking like the female version of him. And she is carrying a sign that says, YOU WISH.

AM: *Do you keep these observations in a notebook?*

RC: I'm not organized enough to keep a notebook. But I have slips of paper in an idea box. There are like thousands of them. A whole box of "Nope," "Slow-pour coffee," "Choose-Your-Own-Adventure." The entire box is nonsensical. [She pours a bunch of notes out on her desk.] Here, I'll read you: Okay, "Concierge." This is circled and underlined like five times. "Hacks." "Semi-heirloom tomatoes." "Bitcoin fairy."

GIFTS FROM THE HOUSE OF LOW GOALS

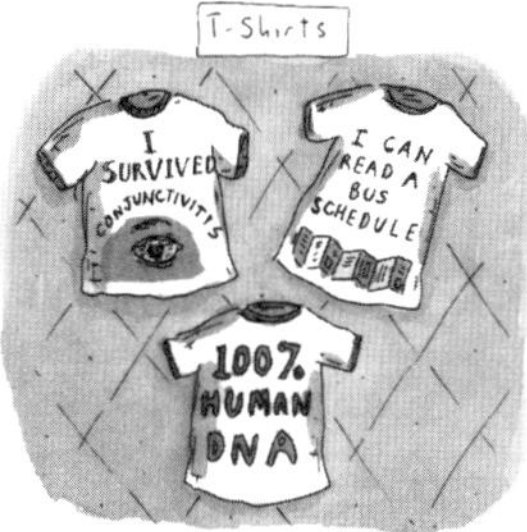

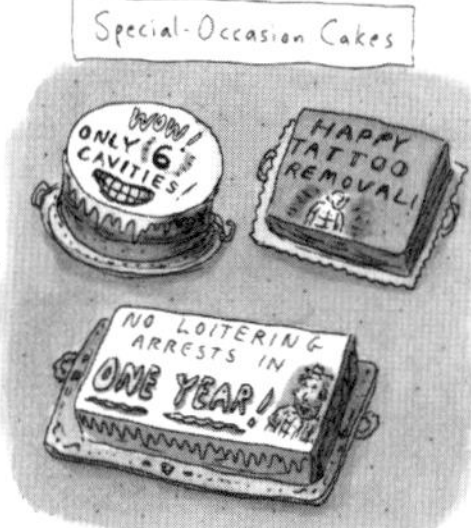

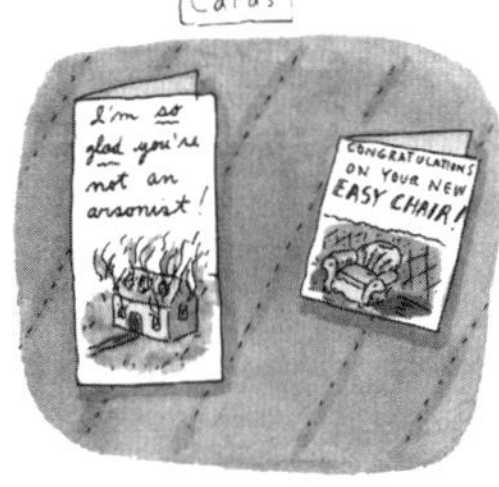

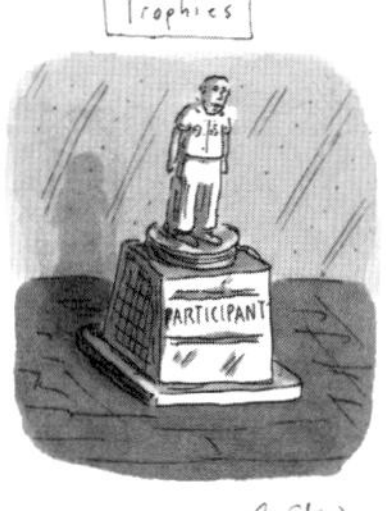

...to explain this.

This one just says "Podiatrist." Hmm. "Niche audience." "Big hair." I did sell a cartoon with that idea. Little Red Riding Hood is visiting her grandmother in bed. And I had just been in Texas, where the women had helmet heads. And the grandmother has this giant hairstyle, and Little Red Riding Hood says, "Um, what big hair you have. . . ."

Let's see: "Uber." "Compassion fatigue." "Chief Happiness Officer."

AM: *When you go back to these things, do you know what you were thinking about?*

RC: Sometimes yes, sometimes no. A lot of the ideas happen when I'm actually working. When I'm at my desk. The ideas begin to percolate.

AM: *So you sit down. And one of your scraps says "Concierge."*

RC: It made sense at the time. But now it . . .

AM: *So what do you do, do you run through different scenarios in your head, are you working out language, are you starting to draw?*

RC: It all happens simultaneously. Once I decided that the end of the world guy needed a wife, I knew what was going to be on the sign. Boom, done. But that's rare. Most times, I draw, I write, I figure it out. I'm kind of immersed in it. One time I was chewing gum and I forgot, and the gum just actually fell out of my mouth. That's really kind of a moment that lives on in time for me.

Cut

RC: Anyway, then a lot of what I do is cut.[3] If I can say something in ten words as opposed to fifty, it helps the joke.

Comedy has a lot to do with rhythm and how you tell a story. I'm not the most analytical person about this, I'm usually feeling my way blindly through something, but you see something, it seems better, sometimes you realize the other version was better, but you just look it over and decide—I'm going to go with that, you know.

AM: *Because you're generating a lot of these?*

RC: At *The New Yorker*, we submit a group of cartoons a week, batches we call them—for me, that's usually six or seven. So a lot of stuff I do just gets shoved aside. But if something gets rejected that I think is a good idea, I'll resubmit it multiple times.[4]

AM: *Altered?*

RC: Sure. If I think there's an idea there I'm going to see if I can find a better way to tell the story. It's kind of like if you were telling somebody a story and their attention wandered, you'd go into the time machine and try to tell it a better way. A lot of times, if I think something's funny, I'll just keep at it.[5] Being a cartoonist really involves stubbornness coupled with a kind of stupidity.

Child Is Good

AM: *Do you have rules that help you?*

2. Jokes too. How different is cracking a joke from writing a novel? Not much, if you really squint.

3. Is there a context in which cutting $\neq$ improving, across all these genres? Yes, but not many.

4. If just one cartoon in that batch gets published, she considers it a success. One tenth of her published cartoons are reworkings of rejected cartoons. "Revisions of idea, drawing, language, all of it. If I like an idea, if I really think there's a cartoon there, I feel like the rejection is my fault, and I have to figure out a way to say it better and draw it better. Or, aagh, the third panel has to be second."

5. She is redrawing the same cartoon over and over as she is fixing it. Which seems like it could get exhausting, but no. "It's like writing but drawing, it's editing, editing, editing. When I redraw something, it's very hard for me to do it exactly the same way I just did, because I think, 'This could be better.'" Also, on the subject of revision—"Sometimes I think there's a word that's funnier. It's a word that will suddenly pop into my head that I just like—*dainty*! I forgot about *dainty*! So I have to figure out how I can use it."

RC: I have a friend whose kid is an artist, and she told me something that her kid once said. She was trying to show her daughter how to do something, and her daughter said, "I want you to do it the child way." And that's how I feel about work. I want to do it the child way.

I'm bad at stuff like cartoon lettering. I'm bad at straight lines. I'm bad at, like, do a drawing and have a gag line.

AM: *But you can actually draw very well. I was looking at your book* Can't We Talk About Something More Pleasant? *and there are some really sophisticated drawings of your mother. And it occurred to me that the visual style that you describe as clunky is a kind of construct. When did that begin?*

RC: Hmm, well, when I was like twelve or thirteen, I started to feel my way toward something like how I draw now. That's when I started to think, *I'm going to be a cartoonist*.

AM: *But then you went to art school. And I presume that they were teaching you all sorts of ways to draw "better." Was it hard to hold on to this more primitive style of expression?*

RC: Well before going to RISD [Rhode Island School of Design], I went to the Art Students League, where you have a giant sketch pad and a box of charcoal and draw from the model. So art school wasn't the first time I had exposure to classical drawings, but RISD *was* the first time I had exposure to people who had actual contempt for cartoons. There were so many things about RISD that made me anxious. But I don't know. For me, it was just that I really liked drawing the child's way.

And so I was trying to hang on to my style. It was just so depressing. For a couple of years I kind of lost the thread, I felt shitty about cartoons and myself. And then by my senior year, it was like, *I will do the assignments. But for myself, I'm going to draw the child's way.*

AM: *The world you create is so specifically singular. Did that just happen organically?*

RC: It really is a weird combination of stubbornness and stupidity. I haven't ever been able to figure out what people want from me, even though I've tried.

I think if you talk to a lot of cartoonists, you'll find that most of us did not have particularly happy childhoods. So maybe if you feel that you're not going to make people happy no matter how hard you tried, you might as well do what you want to do, because they're not going to be happy anyway. For me, it's like, I don't want to be bored.

There's a vacuum cleaner going. Do you hear it? Somebody's vacuuming, just some random person came into our house, vacuuming. In

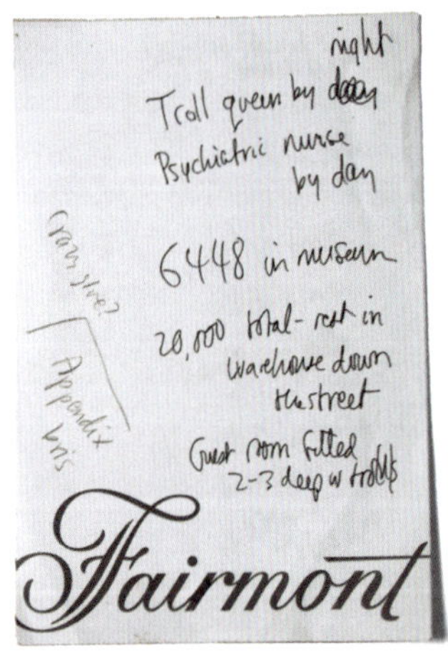

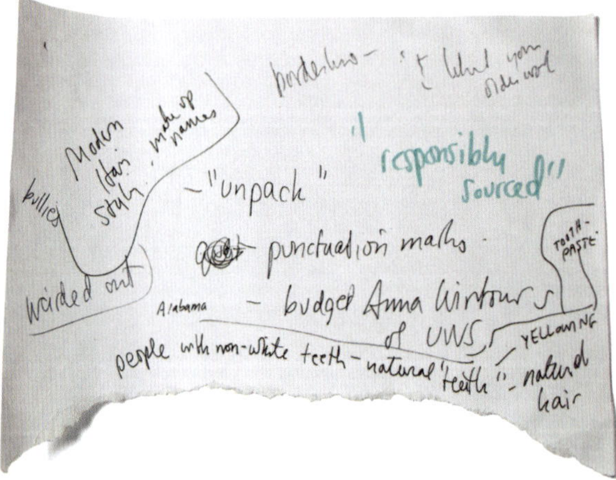

Idea-scrap close-ups. Not that they make much sense even to her.

Connecticut, that happens sometimes.

The Same Thing, Over and Over

AM: *Are there some themes you keep coming back to?*

RC: Oh, that's everything. There's an aspect where I'm always basically drawing the same thing over and over because I've got to figure it out. It might just be something stupid like, Why was I born? Why do I feel compelled to do this? Why is somebody vacuuming in my house?

AM: *You've written a few books. Is that process any different? What about* Can't We Talk About Something More Pleasant?

RC: Well, actually, that was very different at the beginning. Because I had never done a project like that. It was like one big cartoon and it was impossible. I knew where it began and where it ended. I was just going to tell the story of taking care of my parents and realizing I had to be more involved with their lives, which for some reason came as a complete shock to me. I was going kind of batty about it. And I talked to my shrink about it and he suggested, uh, chapters. You know, books have chapters! That helped. I had a complicated relationship with my parents, and I had to put it into context.

AM: *Did you write it and then draw, or were you doing it at the same time?*

RC: I sort of felt my way through it. I did it the child's way! It's such a good way of expressing it really.

AM: *I know you're learning to play the ukulele. Child's way too?*

RC: Well, I'm just learning to play the chords. It's an instrument, but it's halfway between a real instrument and a toy. It's a little bit of a cartoon instrument.

AM: *Do you ever work stuff out when you're sleeping?*

RC: I absolutely have cartoon dreams![6] I had one dream where these two guys were arguing about a jar of mustard, whether it was Gulden's or French's. If there is a dream that has less meaning than that, I don't think I've found it. I have another one that's still in the bank, that *The New Yorker* hasn't used. The dream was the doctor telling me that I had this fatal disease, but the name of it was completely nonsensical. I've had dreams where I woke up and I thought it was so, so funny. One was about swans square dancing, and in the dream it was called squawn dancing. And then I woke up, and it was like, *No, that's not really funny. It's ridiculous.*

6. In fact, she was just finishing a book called *I Must Be Dreaming*. We were talking about reaching the ends of books, and she introduced me to a great German phrase: *Torschlusspanik*. She translated it as "door-shutting panic."

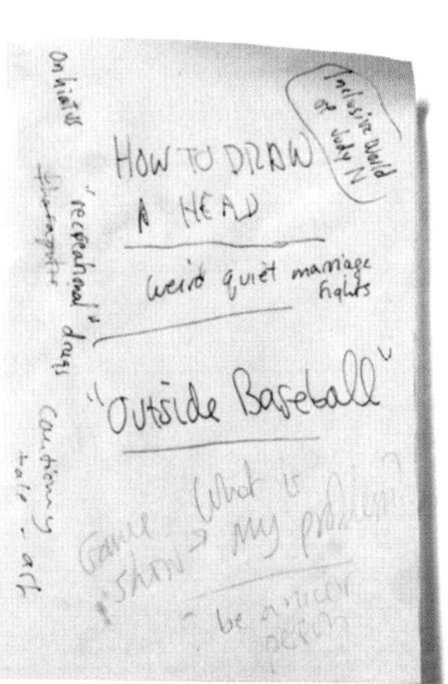

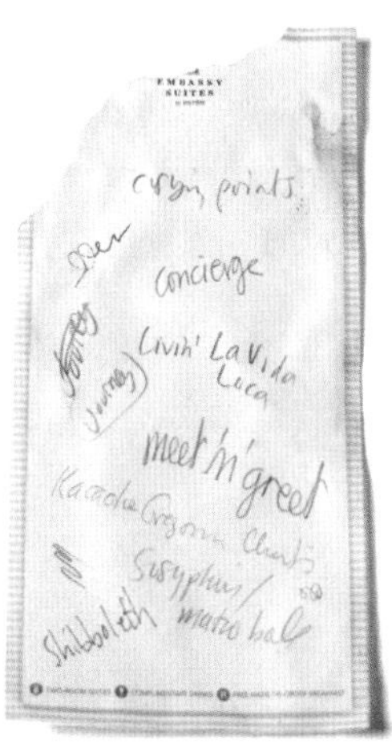

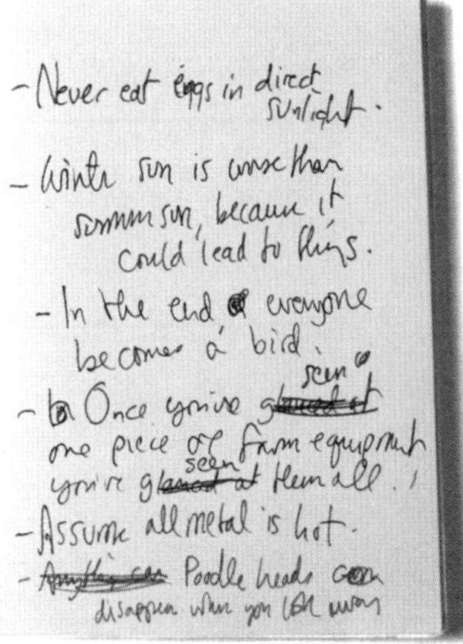

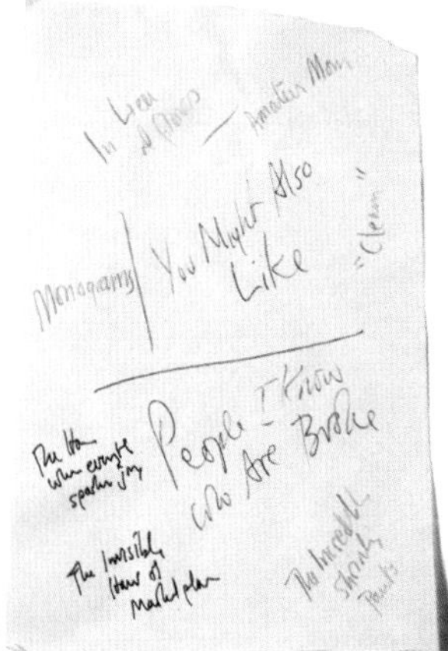

but we are alive, you and I, right now.

change his name to Mr. Dalloway? change Dryden to Woolf?

Mr. Brother (as a title for something)

Call it Mr. Woolf?

remember the problem of first names

be sure to work in Virginia's envy of Vanessa, her feeling that Vanessa is the truly fulfilled and creative one because she has had children.

change Dryden to Woolf to Septimus Smith?

make Mr. Dalloway's first memory the same as mine, either flour being sifted or something else that could be common to both?

call it The Hours?

maybe end Virginia's section with her conviction that Vanessa will live on through her children while she herself will be a mere footnote, a spinster-ish writer who produced only minor, tinselly works

maybe my mother lives on to a happy, slightly boozy old age

or maybe thre are two versions of the mother story, offered simultneously--in one, she kills herself, and in the other she survives, gets a divorce, and lives on to a happy...

toward the end--a scene between the young Mr. Dalloway and the young Septimus, like in Wellfleet--maybe an altered version of the scene written long ago, in which they kiss and go for a walk around the pond

Virginia's tea with Vanessa coincides with Septimus' funeral

What they're all moving toward:

Virginia, at tea with Vanessa, believes Vanessa will live on

Call it *The Hours*? Random note page, undated. This is midway in his thinking, with a Mr. Dalloway (who will later disappear from the drafts) but also a Virginia Woolf.

4

MICHAEL CUNNINGHAM

Will Your Hand Do the Thing Your Mind Wants?

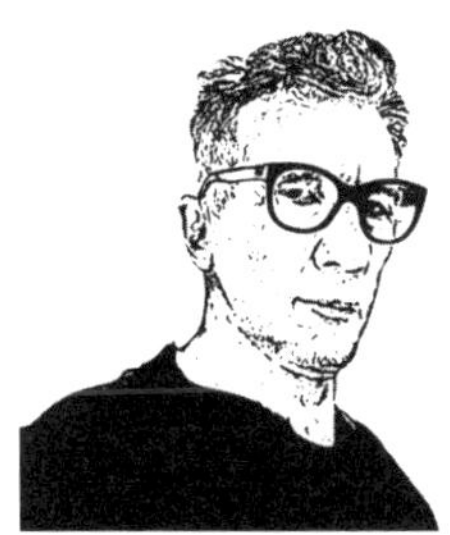

OCCUPATION: Writer

WORK DISCUSSED: *The Hours* (1998)

BORN: 1952

ONE AFTERNOON I was sitting with Michael Cunningham in his writing studio, ransacking bags of old documents and opening countless files, looking for evidence of the origins of his novel *The Hours*. I'm going back in time a bit: Michael is a close friend, and I was leaning on our friendship for an experiment. I had been thinking about writing this book, and I wanted to see if my conceit would work—that the artifacts of something's beginnings might yield insight into how an artist's mind works. He was game, though he warned me he wasn't sure what he'd saved—the record of his work was kind of a mess. But he remembered his early thinking about the book (which, for reference, is three interweaving stories related to Virginia Woolf's *Mrs. Dalloway*—Virginia Woolf writing it, a homemaker reading it, a present-day "Clarissa," nicknamed after it). He explained:

"Everything about *The Hours* was a surprise to me. Originally it was going to be a contemporary version of *Mrs. Dalloway*, set in New York City among gay men. At the time I started writing, there was a kind of gay Chelsea society that felt disconcertingly like the London society in which Clarissa Dalloway lived. Clarissa was fifty-two, I think, and I thought, *Okay, this book will be about a gay party boy who turns fifty-two, the age in which you are not considered young when viewed through any possible lens. Mrs. Dalloway* is quite specifically set after World War I—subtly but clearly, it is about the war. And so maybe my book would be set against the AIDS epidemic. [Which is why the character Richard, the poet in the finished book, is a casualty of AIDS. Richard, incidentally, was originally a woman.] Anyway, eventually I realized this wasn't a necessary book; it was a riff on a great book. It was a kind of trick, just taking an existing book, a book greater than I ever hoped to write myself, and just setting it in that milieu. And who needs that? Why in the world would anyone need my gay *Mrs. Dalloway* when we've got the original goods? I might have that original draft somewhere. You lose track of how many drafts you go through.

"I decided it just had to be a story about a woman, a contemporary version of *Mrs. Dalloway*, in which Mrs. Dalloway has many more options than she did in Woolf's time. But that too felt more like an idea for a book than a book. So I toyed with bringing Virginia Woolf into it somehow. There was a while when I thought the right-hand pages were going to be the contemporary version of *Mrs. Dalloway* and on the left side was going to be the story of Virginia Woolf writing *Mrs. Dalloway*.

"But all that wasn't coming together; it felt academic and insufficiently alive and I was really about to give it up. I remember sitting in my studio ready to abandon the book. But I had put a year into it. So I gave it another shot. I tried to figure out what it was about Mrs. Dalloway that was so compelling to me, and my mother drifted into my head. And I realized eventually that my mother, as a homemaker, has always seemed to me to be trapped in a life that was too small for her. If you look at it like this: two women, my mother and Virginia Woolf, who each in their way were trying to do more than was possible—Virginia Woolf writing *Mrs. Dalloway* and my mother baking a cake—then my mother gets to be in the book just as surely as does Virginia Woolf. And that's when the book started to come to be what it was."

Michael and I went hunting through garbage bags and boxes of paper in a small closet, looking for the traces of *The Hours'* origins. We found just about everything else. But then, somewhere in his computer drive, he found the "gay" draft he wasn't sure existed. Here is how the book once began.

And here is what that turned into.

THE HOURS

(It was the morning of the day Mr. Dalloway would end his life.)

Mr. Dalloway had forgotten to buy the flowers. That's what he told Richard. In fact, he had meant not to buy flowers at all. Flowers were so expected, so drearily sentimental. If Septimus were still alive, if he could somehow be involved in the planning of his own service, Mr. Dalloway felt certain he would not want flowers. Septimus would have held up one large, languid hand (it had been said that his hands were more articulate than some men's faces); his dark eyes would have assumed a pained and humorous expression (he believed everything in the world was profound and at least a little bit funny); and he'd have said something like, 'Flowers at a funeral are for grandmothers or gangsters, please let me fade away with whatever's left of my dignity.' He'd have had another idea, and there Mr. Dalloway felt the limits of his own imagination, like the end of a leash. Instead of flowers, what? Nothing at all? That didn't sound right. It seemed there should be something in the room, and it seemed further that Septimus would have known exactly what.

The opening of a Mr. Dalloway version of *The Hours*.

Michael was surprised to see the gay draft. Even he didn't remember much about this early version of what would become a Pulitzer Prize–winning book, an opera starring Renée Fleming, a Dutch play, and a Hollywood movie for which Nicole Kidman would win an Oscar for playing a part that wasn't even present at the start.[I] It's impossible to imagine *The Hours* without Virginia Woolf. But there you have it.

Incidentally, we also found in our rummaging a list of notes to himself midway between the gay draft and the finished book—a particularly clear glimpse of a novelist's constantly revising mind at work. That's what you saw opposite the opening of this chapter.

Persistence, endurance—much of the work we love wouldn't exist if the artist hadn't been spectacularly tenacious; I am certain pretty much anybody else would have moved on when Michael didn't. But as I was listening to him and reading over his notes, I was struck by another quality as well: a Martian-like ability to be outside and inside himself at the same time. To look at his own work not defensively but critically; to say, nah, this is crap, but somehow (and this is what seemed impossible to me) not to annihilate himself in the process.

On Not Giving Up A year or so later I went to visit Michael again, tape recorder in hand. I wanted particularly to talk to him about giving up, or not—a quandary very close to my quitter's heart. It was an artificial conversation for us, since we see each other often, though never on the record. The little red light of the tape gave structure to our usual meanderings.

This time we were in the apartment he shares with his husband, the psychologist and writer Ken Corbett. Michael had written a new novel[2] he had just given to Kenny to read. Kenny was visiting his mother, so Michael was alone to fret. Michael often says that Kenny is his best reader, and he hadn't shown this version of the novel to him (or anyone) for the years he'd been writing it. "I don't worry, as I do with many people, that Kenny will read something bad and realize anything else I did was just a fluke, and this is terrible. It's just, 'God, I hope he doesn't effectively convince me that I have to rewrite the entire final third of it.' But he might."

I reminded him of an afternoon two, three summers ago; he had just had a conversation with his agent about an earlier draft he'd given her to read. It was the same novel he'd just given to Kenny, but only sort of—this one has taken a long time and gone through entire rethinks; in many ways he'd written several books searching for the right one. At that point, he had written the book in two parts, one set years after the other. On that afternoon, he'd just gotten off the phone with the agent. "She thought the second half of the book was just wrong," he reported at the time, a little dazed. She told him he ought to junk it and start over. We were sitting on a beach. "Oh no," I said, or something like that. I was devastated for him. But he took it in stride. "She was right," he said, without a trace of self-pity. I was pretty sure that my response would have been to throw myself into the ocean.

"Yeah, it's not what you want to hear," he said, recalling that conversation we had on the beach. "But for me, my fear of hearing 'you have to throw out the whole second half' is so overshadowed by the fear that no one will tell me it's not working until it's out in the world, because, you know, most books just aren't very good. I don't feel very precious about it. I figure, well, there's always more where that came from."[3]

I had known Michael for the sweep of his very accomplished career—I'd met him when he was a struggling-ish writer (he did already have a published first novel he didn't talk much about because he didn't like it enough), celebrated with him when *The*

PROLOGUE

She hurries from the house, wearing a coat too heavy for the weather. It is 1941. Another war has begun. She has left a note for Leonard, and another for Vanessa. She walks purposefully toward the river, certain of what she'll do, but even now she is almost distracted by the sight of the downs, the church, and a scattering of sheep, incandescent, tinged with a faint hint of sulfur, grazing under a darkening sky. She pauses, watching the sheep and the sky, then walks on. The voices murmur behind her; combers drone in the sky, though she looks for the planes and can't see them. She walks past one of the farm workers (is his name John?), a robust, small-headed man wearing a potato-colored vest, cleaning the ditch that runs through the osier bed. He looks up at her, looks down again into the brown water.

The opening of *The Hours*, as published. The decision to make Virginia Woolf's suicide the prologue came late (and at the outset Virginia Woolf wasn't in the novel at all).

1. The opera *The Hours* opened at the Met pretty much simultaneously with the play version of the novel, which had been mounted by Ivo van Hove's theater company in the Netherlands. This was twenty-four years after the book (1998), and twenty years after the movie. What was it about *The Hours* that made it so inviting for adaptation? Michael was always generous in letting other creators take a whack at his work, but when *The Hours* kept bobbing up in so many new forms, Michael was, I think, genuinely puzzled.

2. The novel *Day* was published in 2023.

3. The definition of faith, in a single offhand remark.

New Yorker published his remarkable short story "White Angel" and then again when that story became part of the much-loved book about a trio of friends called *A Home at the End of the World*, and again when he published his epic family novel *Flesh and Blood*, and especially when he won the Pulitzer Prize for *The Hours*.[4] And then I'd tried to console him when the Pulitzer actually threw him into a funk. ("I was happy for three days and then depressed about it—for a long time. Which I've never fully understood, only, you know, it's only downhill from here. I was surprised how bad I felt about it, and then I just came out of it. It's obviously nice to win a Pulitzer, even if you do have some bad days about it.")

4. There were other books, of course—*Specimen Days* being one I especially loved—and screenplays and television scripts. And he taught writing at Yale.

The Freedom of Low Expectations We were sitting in his Brooklyn loft, eating burritos. I returned to *The Hours*. "My memory of your state of mind before you set out to write *The Hours* was that you had just written *Flesh and Blood* with the thought that it might be popular," I began. "And then when it wasn't in the way you'd imagined, it kind of freed you up to write a personal, and—you thought—little book."

"Yes, that's right," Michael said. "I mean, *Flesh and Blood* was the book that I wanted to write. But it was my impression—and the impression of the publisher—that it would also be my big book. The thought was that *Home at the End of the World* was my solid midlist book and then this family saga was gonna really sell. I don't think anyone ever really knows why a book sells or doesn't. But it didn't. So I thought, *Well, I'm not gonna be a best-selling writer*. Which was disappointing and liberating at the same time. So when I wrote *The Hours*, I thought, *This will be a little arty book. It will sell a few copies, then march with*

A ROUTINE

I find I'm just as interested in writing habits as many people seem to be (people kept asking me what I was learning about that) so I asked Michael to describe his.

"I need to write first thing in the morning," he said. "I need to segue from sleep and dreams directly into this invented world of mine because part of the deal is maintaining, for several years, your belief in this world, and if I were to even run a few errands before I got to work, I'd get derailed. I'd get so lost in the realness of the real world that when I turned on the computer and looked at what I'd been writing, I'd think, 'Well, this isn't as deep as the dry cleaner'—or the drugstore, or wherever else I've just been.

"I write for about four, five hours, after which there's nothing there anymore. But I also learned that for me it was going to be much more helpful to think in terms of time spent, as opposed to page limit—because if you just have to produce words and you write too much of what you know isn't working—and there are those days—then you are in danger of losing faith in your book. But if I am in my chair, ready to write whatever arrives—ten pages or one sentence—I've fulfilled my commitment. The next day I read what I wrote, catch up with myself. For me it's as much about the language as it is about the story, and I find myself needing a solid sentence to stand on in order to move forward. I usually have some idea of what I'm going to write that day. Although we have complicated feelings about Ernest Hemingway, he said a great thing that I read early on: always stop writing for the day when you feel you have more to write, so you're eager to get back to it. I try to do that.

"As for writing environment, I have a studio that's not where I live that I go to every day. I'm not one of those delicate creatures where if a dog barks that's it, but I do need to be in a fairly familiar place so the background sort of fades away. I can't write in a coffeehouse, for instance. I just need to be in a space capsule."

whatever dignity it can muster to the remainders table. Which was an opinion shared by the publisher."

"All your many initial versions of *The Hours* involved *Mrs. Dalloway* in some fashion," I said. "You jettisoned one way to respond to the book after another, but you never departed from your intention to work off *Mrs. Dalloway.* What was so important to you about *Mrs. Dalloway*?"

"Well, *Mrs. Dalloway* was one of the first great books I read as a kid. Some girl I liked sort of urged me to read Virginia Woolf. I'm not even sure I finished the book, because I couldn't figure it out. I wasn't particularly bookish as a kid. What really struck me about it was the language. I had never seen language like that before. I had never seen sentences so . . . ambitious and graceful and surprising, all at the same time. I had never seen so many parentheticals and semicolons before. I didn't know you could do that with a sentence. It was like you've grown up on the songs they sing in your village, and then someone takes you to a concert and they're playing Beethoven, and you just think, *What the fuck?*"

"In high school, were you dabbling with writing at all?"

"No, I was more of a visual arts kid."

I said, "I remember from when we took a drawing class together that you were pretty good."

"I guess," he said. "But it didn't turn out to be a sufficiently driving passion. When I got to college, thinking I was going to study art, there were some people in the classes I took who were not only really gifted but who were bottomlessly interested in the fundamental proposition of trying to produce something that was alive. They were indefatigable. And I just wasn't as indefatigable as they were. I would get discouraged and give up. The girl next to me would get discouraged and start over again."

"Were you intimidated by their levels of prowess?" I asked. "Was it that they were just more talented than you were at drawing and painting?"

Interest, Not Talent "I think it's really hard to comfortably separate talent from this unquenchable interest in the problem presented by the task," he said. I hadn't thought about it that way—as interest rather than talent. Michael continued, "Like they never got tired of trying to paint. And I started writing and realized that I felt that way about writing. That the fundamental question, Can you do some sort of justice to life using only words and ink? was endlessly interesting to me. But then, sure, some people are able to produce unthinkingly a squiggle that has a kind of life. That, I couldn't do. There's a question of—I guess I'll call it athleticism. Will your hand actually do the thing that you have in your mind? So I'm starting to write, and at the same time beginning to wonder if I really possess what a serious visual artist possesses."

"And writing came easier to you?"

"I didn't feel instantly brilliant at it. I was pretty good. I was good with language. It took me quite a while to understand that in order to be serious and good, a story did not need to come to some huge explosive conclusion. You know, I just didn't read enough Chekhov." He laughed. "My sense of my ability to write still comes and goes. It depends on the day. But I don't know if I've ever in all these years lost that fundamental interest in the proposition: here's ink, paper, words in a dictionary."

Getting Stuck We returned to *The Hours.* He'd made a lot of notes, a bit of which you've just seen. And he didn't really mention his idea to anyone, including Kenny, "for the practical reason that no matter how intimate the person you might talk to about it, you need to maintain your faith in the story you are about to spend God knows how long writing, and there's no surer way that I know to lose faith than by summing it up too soon. 'It's about a guy, a whale bit off his leg, he's really mad.'" Michael laughs in the big bellowing way he does.

"So we talked before about cycling through various versions," I said. He'd just mentioned another one, where his version of a day in

Mrs. Dalloway's life would be accompanied by notes to himself, another device he soon realized "was pretentious and uninteresting."

"So many false tries," I said. We finally got around to the question. "Why didn't you just give the book up?"

"You know, just this endless determination. By then I had written enough to know that most of the time you get to a certain point in a book you want to give it up.[5] And to write another book that won't cause me the same trouble. And it does. You just end up stuck all over again. So you might as well stay with the thing."

"And you always get stuck?"

"It took me a while to realize that if a novel is any good, it's going to defeat what little idea that took you into it in the first place. It's going to become something else, and your experience of that as a writer is, *Oh it's just not working out*. When actually it's going in a direction that's more interesting and complicated than what got you there. And I suppose that's what happened here. I realized it was really a book about women, and I just felt like, lose the gay man thing, and then what we talked about before, about my mother's labors set against Virginia Woolf's."

We got into a discussion of the novel's particulars, which I was especially interested in because I had just reread the book before coming over. For instance, Michael put Virginia Woolf's decision to end her life at the beginning, which he'd told me was a late decision he made so her eventual suicide (which he felt was necessary to include) wouldn't hang over the book. I asked him about another one (I suppose this requires a spoiler alert), a surprise plot device Michael employs at the end of his book that ties together two of the threads: the son of the homemaker character in one of the intertwined stories is revealed to be, grown-up, the suicidal poet in the contemporary story. I'd read the book maybe three times and seen the movie, but it still startled me when I read the book again—and I wondered how that simple, spectacularly effective narrative move came about.

"That came late too. I felt for the longest time like, I don't know how these strands are going to meet. And one day I just saw this, and I thought, *Hmmm*. Then it was, you know, let's give it a shot, even though I was sure everyone was going to see it coming. And I was surprised as anybody that people were surprised by it."

"When you come up with a solution like that, are you elated? I mean, emotionally, does it feel satisfying?"

"Oh, certainly not elation. An element of relief. But throughout this book—I always feel this, but maybe more so with this one—I thought, *This is probably terrible*. And I showed it to a lot of people, waiting for someone to say, 'This is just a contraption with an obvious ending. Don't publish this.' And people kept not saying that."

"What were you so worried about? Was it this twist?"

"Oh, you know, I find it easiest just to worry about everything. That I had Virginia Woolf wrong," he continued. "That, you know, how dare I as a man. . . . But also, the time it takes to write a novel inevitably requires a level of familiarity with it that makes it almost impossible to imagine that it could be interesting to anybody. Going over it the hundredth time, you can't possibly know what it would be like reading it the first time."

"And it is inevitable that a book will start to bore you?"

"No, that's not it. I haven't had a novel begin to bore me. And that's probably because I keep thinking I will find a way to make it better. But you know it's also true that you don't want to take forever to write a novel because you

5. Of course, nobody gave up on any of the works covered here in this book—that's the nature of a retrospective study of success. Still, a predilection not to give up seems about as core a prerequisite for an artist as any I can imagine.

6. A similar thought about the difference between what one envisions and what one can actually summon, by Gustave Flaubert: "I am irritated by my own writing. I am like a violinist whose ear is true, but whose fingers refuse to reproduce precisely the sound he hears within."

7. It was true: the question of what talent is—or why some people seem to have it and others don't—dogged me every step of the way, no doubt a desperate stab at understanding whether I had any, or whether there might be some trick to acquire it. Pretty much everyone I talked to thought the question was ridiculous. I was a little embarrassed about it. It was like wondering why the sky is blue (though there *is* an answer to that)—people had a talent for something or they didn't, right? Was this question naive? Was the answer knowable? Regardless, I kept asking. Michael was one of the people willing to give me an answer I could publish.

don't want to get to the point where the book ceases to be—I guess, you just don't want to outgrow it."

The Better Book in Your Head "I was really struck, as I was rereading the book," I said, "how much you underscore the theme of having something in your head that is impossible to realize on the page. It comes up in a couple of contexts." I wondered if that gulf was particularly frustrating to him as he was writing this book.

"You *always* have a better book in mind than you're able to write. And one of the things you have to be able to do, if you're going to write novels, is survive that discrepancy between the book you were able to write and the better book you imagined."[6]

"Is there a mood you're in that feels to you the most productive—or the most doomed, for that matter?"

"There are better days and lesser days. What varies the most is the degree to which the aperture is open or closed."

"What do you mean 'the aperture'?"

"Whatever is coming through is either coming through in gushes or dribbles. But the dribbles are about as good as the gushes."

"Let's go back to what you called athleticism before." In all my conversations with the artists for this book, I kept trying to understand where talent comes from, to no avail.[7] I thought maybe Michael, who is fond of what he calls "crackpot theories," might offer one. "You want to take a stab and describe what you think talent is, or where it comes from?" I asked. But he didn't really bite.

"As I mentioned before, it's hard to separate talent from the almost spectrum-y degree of endless interest in something."

"All your years of teaching haven't led to any theories as to why certain people have facility and others don't?"

"Honestly, my sense based on all the writers I've worked with is that the aliens aimed a beam of light at some of you, and I don't know why," he said. "And I think the actual, visceral experience of a lot of people who have some kind of gift is, 'What, everybody can't do that?' "

I wanted to talk about age, since he'd mentioned it before in relation to Clarissa, and he and I talk about the subject a lot in every possible context. "Do you feel anything gets different for you in your work as you age?"

"So far, I don't feel a significant difference. I feel it lies ahead. It's so difficult to separate aging from the passage of time. I find I'm a little less interested in lyricism, for instance."

"So it's just changing taste, then?" I asked him. "What about experience? Is experience always good— "

"Like do you sacrifice a kind of reckless—"

"Exactly. Are there things that come to you when you don't know better?"

"Sometimes. And sometimes you're writing pretentious shit. But take Walt Whitman. He spent all his life rewriting *Leaves of Grass*. And the first edition is, on the one hand, not as accomplished as the final edition. And yet the first edition has a kind of vigor that's not in the ninth edition. I don't know how you can fail not to be a little nervous about that. One of the reasons I love Philip Roth is those later books are some of the best stuff he's written. It's the work of a mature writer."

I told him I was struck with the number of times in all our conversations about writing that he swatted away any admission of satisfaction with his work. Didn't he have *any*? "Do you ever experience happiness in what you write?" I asked.

"I think if you didn't, why would you do it?" he said. "No, absolutely, the good moments range from 'that's a really good line' to when you're walking around, you think of something and you have to get back home to write it down."

So much of happiness, it turned out, is anticipation.

"Because the best times," he said, "are while you're working on it, you're still imagining what it might be. And it feels like it could be anything."

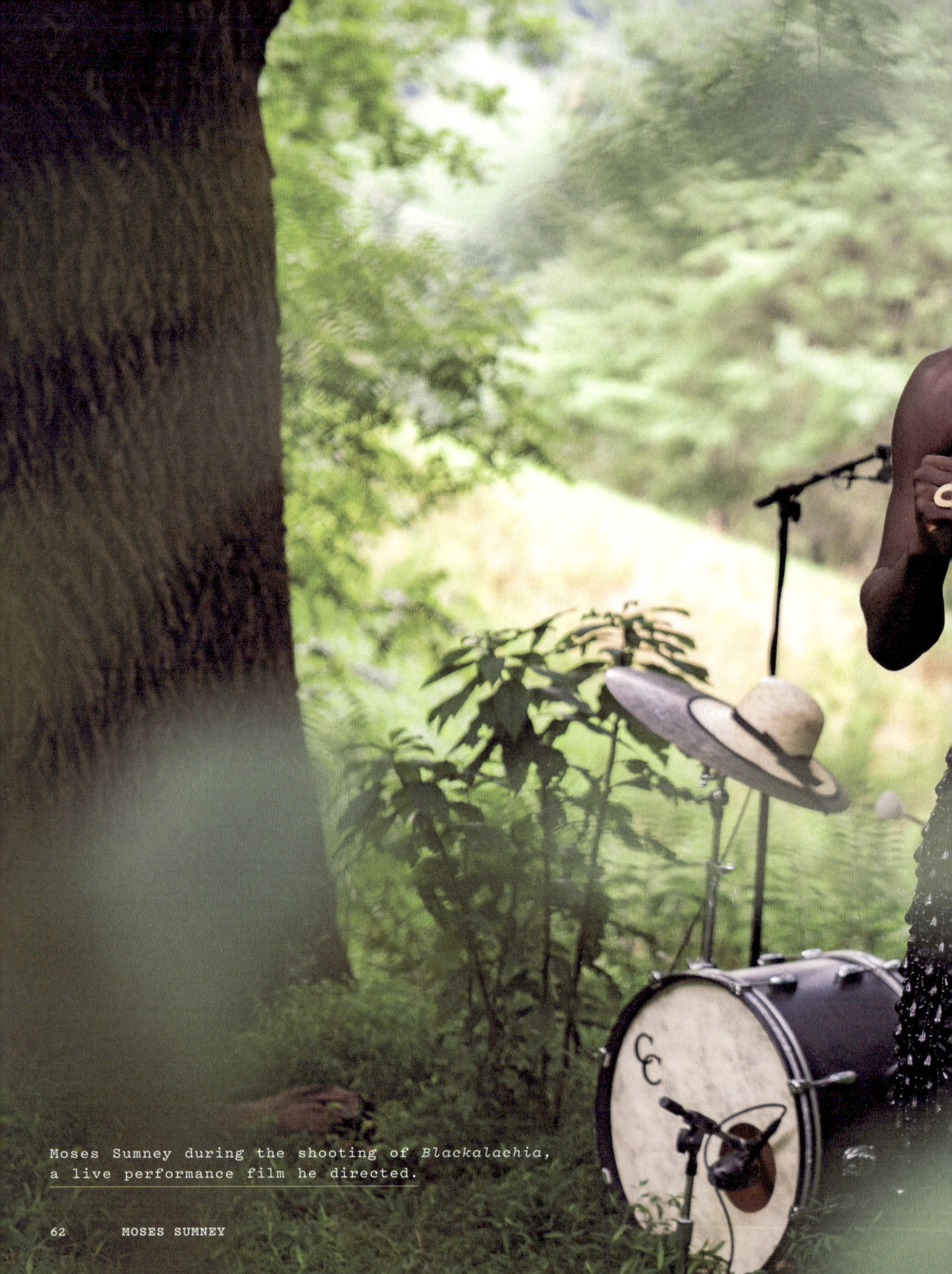

Moses Sumney during the shooting of *Blackalachia*, a live performance film he directed.

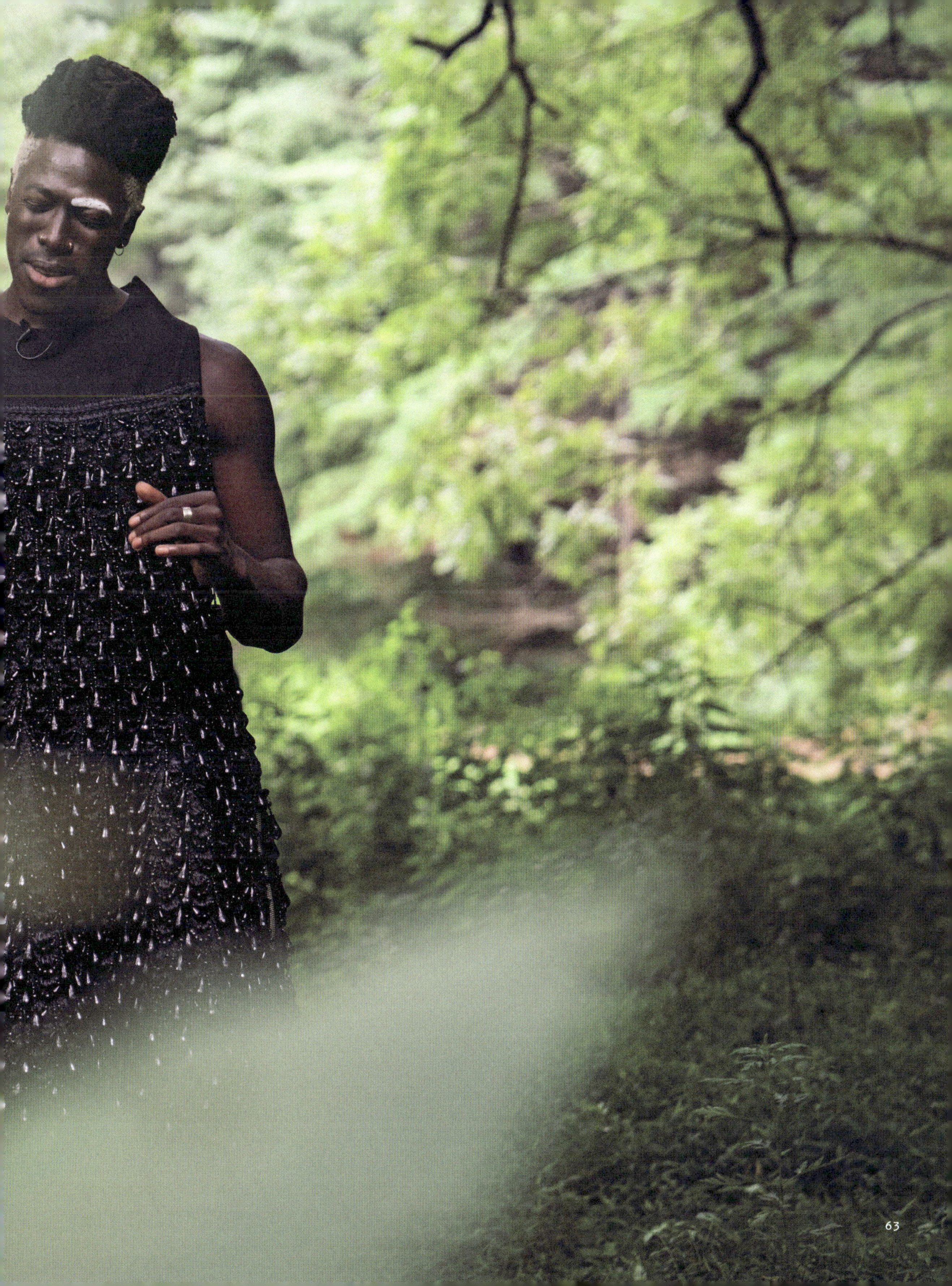

5

MOSES SUMNEY

God Flows Through Him

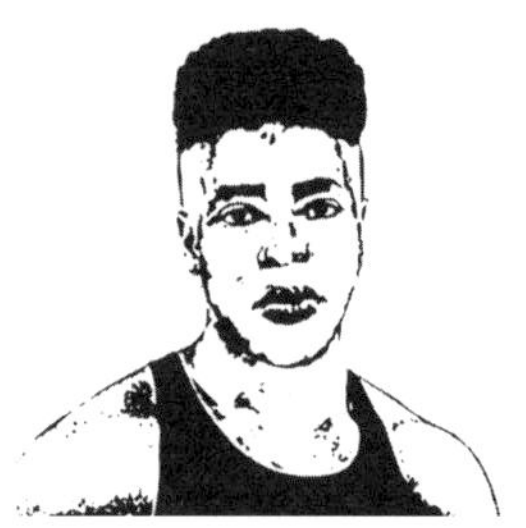

OCCUPATION: Musician

WORK DISCUSSED: "Doomed" (2017)

BORN: 1992

AT SOME POINT in every one of these conversations, as a matter of habit and curiosity, I would ask the artist where they thought inspiration came from. I kept bringing it up, even though who could know? And most people would say the unconscious, or something like that. But every once in a while, someone would mention God. "It comes from God absolutely," Moses Sumney explained, a little surprised by the question. "It feels like it's floating through."

Sumney is a singer/songwriter with an ethereal falsetto voice who blurs genres—indie, soul, a little pop, art rock, some jazz inflection, maybe gospel. But even with the divine lilt of his sound, I'd always found him pretty secular, since most of his subject matter is earthly, and I (along with everybody else) find him corporeal and alluring, an indie sexpot. It wasn't until I listened to the tape of our conversation over and over that I began to hear how spiritual he really is, how God seeps into almost every utterance, especially about making music. He talked about how, as an adolescent, when he was afraid of losing his falsetto, he prayed and prayed to God to hold on to it. God apparently answered.

Anyway, I shouldn't have been surprised. Sumney is the son of two pastors from Ghana. He started singing in a choir. The song he chose to trace, from his first full-length album, *Aromanticism*, addressing his inability to love, is called "Doomed"—as in, "Am I doomed?" a plaintive question he asks of God.

MOSES SUMNEY: In the church growing up, where my parents were pastors, there was a lot of gospel music. There were a few African gospel songs, too, because my parents were Ghanaian, and they ran a kind of Ghanaian-ish church in San Bernardino. In the house they played gospel and reggae, which was not my flavor. My sister listened to a lot of pop music and R & B—Destiny's Child and Usher, whatever the music of the day was. And I was somehow very into country music. I exclusively listened to country radio as a child. Martina McBride, Tim McGraw, and

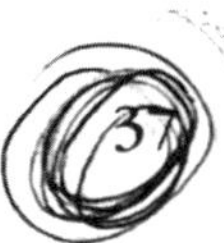

Hollow one
With inverted tongue
From whence (once) does (my) (your) fulfillment come?

All this life
Shadows of night
Hung above in place of sun

If I feel you
And nobody else
Well, am I a friend

I feel you
But nobody else
Though you're somebody
And you say nothing
Of To the stoic suffering
~~That (coldly) stirs inside of me~~
That stirs lukewarm inside of me
If Loveles

If lovelessness
Is Godlessness
~~Will my soul fall to the wayside~~
Will you cast me to the wayside
Maybe these feelings
Of painted ceilings
Only happen on the outside
Maybe the feeling
Of sky-painted ceilings
Will reveal the covering of
I can't see a gray sky

Maybe the feeling
Of sky-painted

"Doomed." Trying out lyrics, most of which ended up in the finished song.

of course Shania Twain.

I was a very introspective, quiet child, and I didn't really have any friends.[1] So I would just listen to country music in my bedroom. My first memory of wanting to be a singer was from one day when we were at church—we went to church every day, because that's where my parents worked from, day care was the back of the church—my father had a tape machine there. And my dad let me and my sister record our voices. I remember [Sumney sings a brief note; it's lovely, of course] I just recorded my voice. In the car, my dad let us listen to the tape. And hearing my voice back on tape, I had the realization that that's what I wanted to do forever. And then I started to mess around with writing songs. Privately, in my bedroom. I never fantasized about being a country singer. It must have crossed my mind, because that's what I was listening to. But I do remember telling my dad I was going to be a singer, and him laughing and saying, "Are you going to be like the first Black country singer?" I think that was my first concept of having genre presented as a problem.

His First Songs I've always just made up melodies. One day, I must have been around seven, I wrote a song called "One-Night Stand." The lyrics were something like "a one-night stand for a one-night man." You know, I truly had no clue what it meant. I held it very closely. I thought, *Oh God, this is my first song.* So I would take it with me everywhere. I went to a private Christian school. And one day I left [the lyrics] at the lunch table. One of the older kids found it, and told on me. I was a really good kid, I was probably the most well-behaved child you ever met. The teacher came up to me and said, "I know this isn't you. We're gonna just throw it away. I'm not gonna tell, just don't do that again."

And then again at the lunch table, I remember finding a poem. Someone had written it and left it there. It was called "Nobody." It was really sad. It went something like, "Nobody loves me. Nobody cares. Nobody brings me peaches and pears. Nobody listens and laughs at my jokes. Nobody brings me hope." I haven't actually tried to recall it since I was a kid. But I remember feeling like I related to it because I was such a loner. I was like, *This is a bit dramatic, but I can get into it.* I put music to it, and in my head, that was my song too. I would sing it to myself all the time. I never sang it for anyone else, ever.

That was when I was seven, and then I went on a hiatus after that. Took a five-year break. You know, I needed to step away. [*laughs*] We moved to Ghana, and I had a best friend who knew that I wanted to be a singer. One day he came to school with a song he had handwritten. He said, "Check out this song I wrote," singing it to me, reading it to me. And I was, huh, "*You* don't write songs. *I* write them. I'm the songwriter." I was very offended. Then I thought, *Wait, I haven't been writing songs, for years.* And I went home and started to write. Instantly a song came out. It was called "Mesmerizing Eyes." Genre-wise, it was an R & B pop song, like late nineties Boyz II Men. A love song. "I'm looking into a girl's mesmerizing eyes." What did I know about mesmerizing eyes? I showed it to my friend, said, "Check this out." He said, "You're still on that? I lied to you. I didn't write that song, that was a Westlife song."[2]

So I really learned, you don't tell people you want to be a singer. Because that's silly. I devised this plan where I thought, *I'm just gonna write songs. I'm going to practice singing. I'm going to make beats. And I'm going to do it all privately.*

I bought a notebook, and I gave myself a quota.[3] I had to write at least three or four songs a month. Nothing crazy. I didn't record them. I didn't play any instruments, so they were all a cappella. But I had an incredible memory for melody, still do. I can hear something once and recall

1. Many of the subjects here described isolated childhoods (e.g., Roz Chast, earlier). I've found that most people say their childhoods were lonely, whether they really were or not—loneliness is the state they remember. Still, maybe there's something there. Aloneness gives one the room and the incentive to make art—and gets you in the habit of talking to yourself.

2. Westlife is an Irish pop band.

3. A quota is a deal you make with yourself, a self-negotiation—one of many in this book. See George Saunders. Also Amy Sillman.

4. "Brown Skin" is an early, very popular song by the singer India.Arie.

39

"I want to know about the meaning of love beyond the realm of fantasy — beyond what we imagine can happen. I want to know love's truths as we live them."

"Lovelessness is more common than love." xxvii

"Wedded to lovelessness"

Love is like God. Unseen but felt. We long for it though we've never truly known it. Love is God. God is love.

Cathexis

We cannot be whole human beings without knowing how to love. To be human is to love. Removing loved ones from your life depletes you of humanity.

"to yearn for love even as we doubt it exists" (18)

I've lived a loveless life. Have I lived at all?

A journal entry as Sumney was writing "Doomed": "When I really have something to write about, I'll journal, do a period of freewriting," Sumney said. "When I'm working on a record, I journal a lot more, trying to think about a song, what is this about, what is this title trying to say. Then I'll write my way around finding it. But I try not to think about it too much."

it, years later. I wrote in my bedroom and on the way to school, which was about an hour and a half away from my home. I would sit in my corner in the back of the bus with my little notebook and just write. I'd hear melodies in my head, and I'd write some words down so I could remember—maybe I'd write a title. Over the course of the month—because I have my quota!—I would come back to the songs. *This sounds like a verse, this sounds like a bridge, this sounds like a chorus.* If I got to the end of the month and I had only two, I'd think, *All right, gotta write another one.* And I'd bang it out.

In the early days I was taking my cues from pop music. Most of my songs were love songs. And it wasn't until I discovered the music of India.Arie at around fourteen[4] that I completely changed my approach to songwriting. That was the first time I had ever heard someone write about something deeper. She had a song called "Brown Skin." I remember an interview with her. I had never heard anyone talking about brown skin and celebrating it. I was dark-skinned; I had never felt attractive, and I knew that was connected to how dark my skin was. I remember her talking about how music was a tool for healing, and I realized my purpose as a songwriter is to talk about stuff, to write meaningfully. Whatever it needs to be, it needs to be deep.

There was one song—I probably shouldn't tell this story, but oh, I don't care—called "Little Girl" that was inspired by my sister, who was . . . let's call her grown for her age. She was a gorgeous teenager, and she would hang out with the older men, and I could see how detrimental this was to her spiritually. I wrote the song about the culture of young women who were wooed by older rich men. I think I can remember it: "Little girl, little girl, she gets all the diamonds and pearls, she acts way too big in the world, little girl." The bridge was something like "but look at this other life you could have." And "you're so beautiful and wonderful, don't lose it all."

His Voice I was not aware of the voice that people know me for now until I was well into my twenties. I was a bass. I sang bass in the choir—this register you hear me speaking in. The falsetto developed because when I was a child, I had a really high voice, a really high singing voice. And I could sing whistle notes at that age. Mind you, this is all me alone in my bedroom being like [*sings a note*]; I think that's a high note—am I crazy? When I hit puberty—I was quite late, it didn't really happen until I was like fifteen or sixteen—I was really afraid I would lose my upper register. Because I knew that was something unique about me. I started praying, like actually praying to God, please don't let me lose my falsetto. My voice dropped really low. And so I obsessively practiced singing in falsetto so that I wouldn't lose it.

Because I was so introverted in my process, I perfected singing quietly. And when you go to sing quietly, singing in falsetto makes the most sense because it's the quietest part of your voice. I practiced for years, but I wasn't performing. I had no real gauge if I was a good singer or not. I had a feeling. And I had faith and hope. Later when I was in college and singing solo for the first time, I started to sing falsetto publicly. Singing in my chest voice was always kind of hard and scary. Falsetto was a comfort zone, because I had rehearsed it so much.

FINAL

"DOOMED"

Hollow one
With inverted tongue
From whence does fulfillment come?
When I expel
From this mortal shell
Will I die for living numb?
Am I vital
If my heart is idle?
Am I doomed?
Am I vital
If my heart is idle?
Am I doomed?
I feel you
But nobody else
Though you're someone I can't see
Yet you say nothing
Of the stoic suffering
That stirs lukewarm in me
If lovelessness is godlessness
Will you cast me to the wayside?
Well, I feel the peeling
Of half-painted ceilings
Reveal the covering of a blank sky
Am I vital
If my heart is idle?
Am I doomed?
Cradle me
So I can see
If I'm doomed
Am I vital
If my heart is idle?
Am I doomed?
Cradle me
So I can see
If I'm doomed
Am I vital
If my heart is idle
Am I doomed?

Am I Doomed? I named the album *Aromanticism* before I started to write it. I knew that was what I wanted to talk about. It became a thesis. With every song I wrote, I would ask myself, *How does this relate to the theme?* I had written probably about thirty songs. Then after thirteen or so months, I got the initial

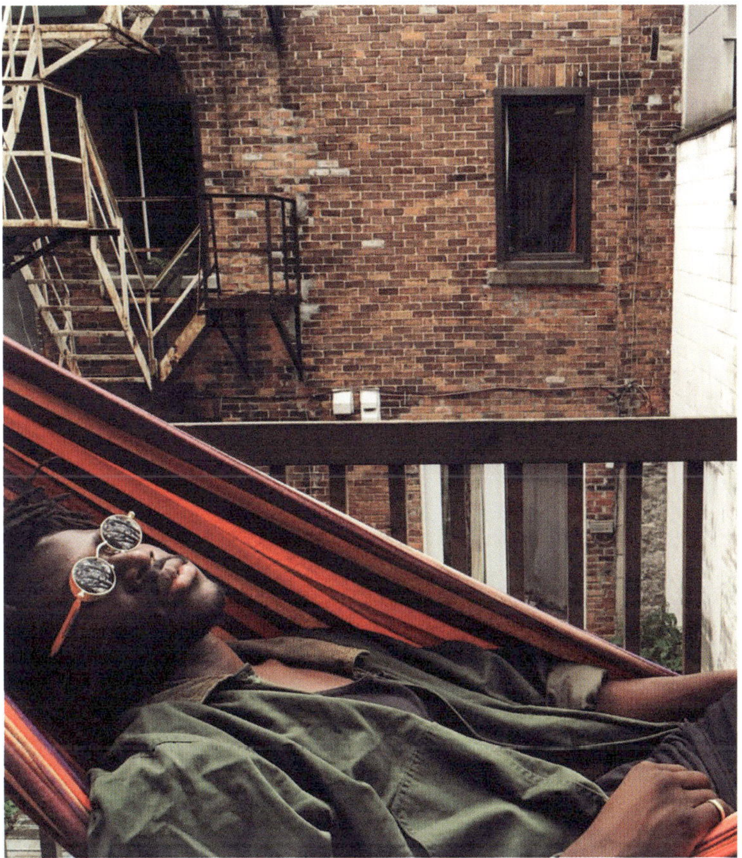

A picture Sumney said was taken in the courtyard where he was writing the song. "This is where it started raining after I did a first pass of the vocal."

idea for "Doomed."

Most of the songs were guitar based, because I had learned guitar and that's what I could play on my own. I wanted to write something hymnal that felt meditative and melodically unlinear—I remember listening specifically to "Dust and Water" by Antony and the Johnsons, which doesn't come back a lot melodically. And it was meditative and beautiful. I was working with a producer named Matt Otto, and I brought him all these inspiration songs. I told him, "I want to do something simple, just synth and a voice. And I don't know what it's going to be about, but let's find it."

My music up to this point was so complex, chord-wise; I was always writing jazz chords and these sevens and trying to be really musical. I think I realized that all those years of not being able to play an instrument gave me a little bit of a complex, so when I learned the guitar, I thought music had to be complicated. Earlier that year, I had been opening for Sufjan Stevens. In sound check one day, he came over to me and said, "Why do your songs have so many jazz chords?" And I was actually horrified by the question. He just walked away. Clearly it stuck with me. I said to Matt, "I need a song that's just four chords, triads, C, A, F, G." I call them basic bitch chords.

And I said, "No minor chords, and I'm gonna make it sad as hell." And the challenge is to make a major chord sound really sad—like *saccharine* sadness. We edited down this loop of four chords. Most of my songs come about singing gibberish,[5] trying to access this plane where it flows, and see what comes out. I did this like six-minute pass of the song. And held that [*sings*] *doooooom* note. We'd opened the door of the studio, it was the only way to get air in. And as I finished the note, the sky opened, and it started to pour. The sun was shining, but it was pouring. And that just felt like a sign from God that I had found it. That was one pass. Usually it's like fifty passes, trying to figure out the melody.

I didn't write the lyrics until about a year later. In the meantime, I was thinking about it every day. Some songs you write quickly—the next song on the record, "Indulge Me," top to bottom, including recording the vocals, took about thirty

5. 100% of the songwriters in this book write gibberish before, or while, they write lyrics. Professional tip.

minutes. But for "Doomed," I didn't know what it was about, but I could feel it. And it also felt hefty; those lyrics had to be damn good. So what I did was to start performing it. I probably performed it for a year without words. People came up to me and said, "'Doomed,' that was my favorite song, I couldn't stop crying." I'm like, "The one with the wordless mumbles?" Someone said, "I think you could work on your diction a little bit." I said, "I was legitimately singing mumbles, so don't worry."

We performed a lot of different versions of it, with a three-part horn section and a guitarist, and then I did an orchestral version, and then one based on vocal loops. It was interesting to see that it could survive all these iterations and still hold weight as a song. As much as the lyrics are important to that song, the feeling mattered more. What's really beautiful is seeing how, spiritually, you know what something is about without being told. That's an incredible thing to learn about human nature, or the ear, or the mind, whatever it was. But the lyric writing was always going to have to be the most introspective lyric writing I've ever done, and I think to date it still is.

I think I felt it was about God from day one. The hymnal quality. And those thundershowers. All right, God, I'll make this about you. You want attention so bad. Of course, I knew that I was addressing aromanticism as a concept, so putting those two together was really interesting. What does it mean to feel lovelessness but still feel God, or the concept of God? Like if you can't love your brother, how can you love God? That was scary to me because at the time I was like, *Oh yeah, I love God. I don't know about you other hoes, but I love God.* But the first phrase that really came to me is, "Am I doomed?" Quite the existential question.

I sat with that for a really long time. There's this meditation center called Self-Realization Fellowship in LA, which is like an open park.[6] I would kind of walk there, in the mountains, and read, and think about this song. I really wanted it to be honest. Whenever I tried to push it lyrically, it would just be too much, too weighty, too *woe is me* or *eternal damnation*. And finally I got to that phrase, "If lovelessness is godlessness will you cast me to the wayside?" Although it's not the last lyric of the song, it was the missing piece. Vocally, we weren't going to add much. At one point I asked, *Is there a string arrangement? A horn arrangement?* And then there was the realization that oh, no. It was just two tracks, which for my music is crazy. Seeing how minimal it could be was a light bulb. And I think finishing "Doomed" was the realization that the record was worthy of being heard.

6. "Big cities don't really work for me," Sumney said. "I've got to go off to the mountains, I've got to be alone. Sometimes I have to be alone for days before the clarity presents itself. Really, it's just kind of sitting there waiting for the inspiration to strike. Waiting is so central. And when it comes it's just *fwoosh*." For more on waiting, see Louise Glück.

7. You've got to be at least a little good at something to keep going. If you just plain suck, you're going to give it up.

ONE MEDIUM INFORMS ANOTHER

Sumney is also a photographer. "I think I'm only interested in learning things that I've showed natural affinity for, because I like being good at stuff,"[7] he said. "So I might not try woodworking, because I'm not confident I'll feel good about the results. With photography, I've always thought visually, and when I started directing my music videos, a director I respected advised that if I wanted to be a better director, I should start photographing. And it came at the right time because I felt I needed a break from music. I never left my schedule that I set for myself at thirteen, my quota, until 2020, when I thought I needed to explore something that I loved that wasn't a job. I still take pictures a lot. I have a self-portraiture practice especially. My music and songwriting definitely inform photography. All mediums inform each other.

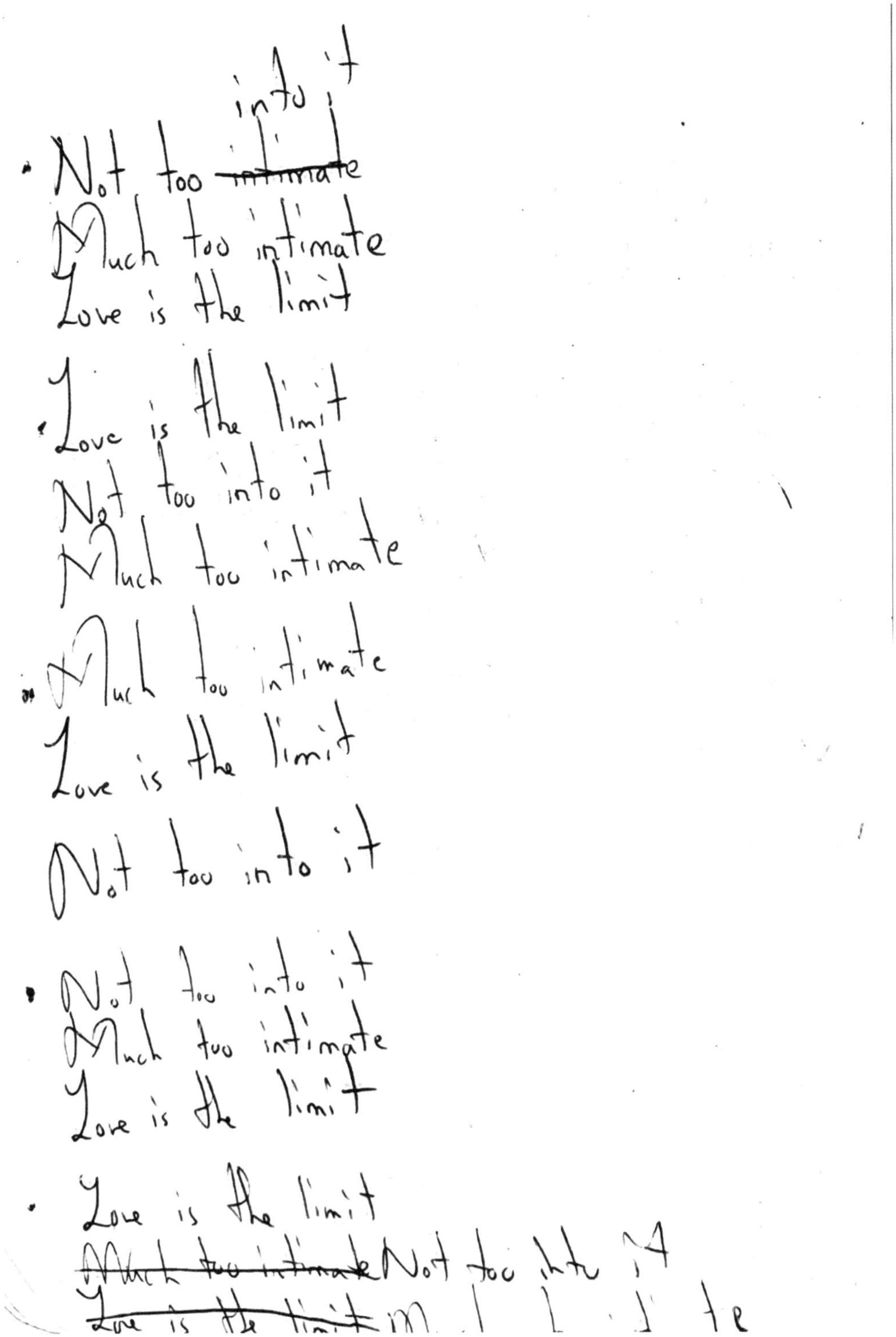

into it

- Not too ~~intimate~~
Much too intimate
Love is the limit

- Love is the limit
Not too into it
Much too intimate

- Much too intimate
Love is the limit

Not too into it

- Not too into it
Much too intimate
Love is the limit

- Love is the limit
~~Much too intimate~~ Not too into it
~~Love is the limit~~ Much too intimate

Almost: Lyrics for "Doomed" that ended up being repurposed into another song, "The Limit," which was never released.

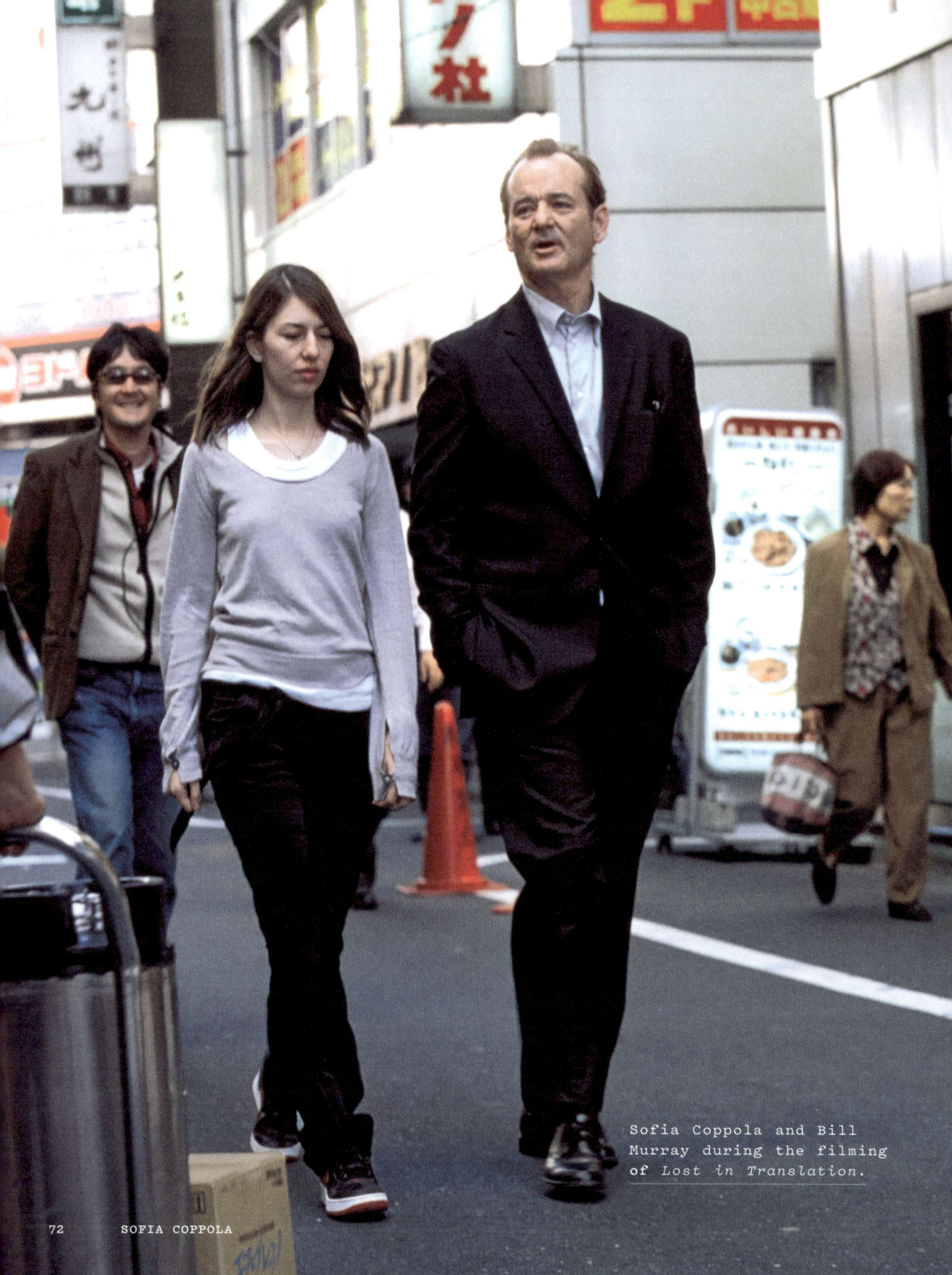

Sofia Coppola and Bill Murray during the filming of *Lost in Translation*.

6

SOFIA COPPOLA

Later You'll Understand

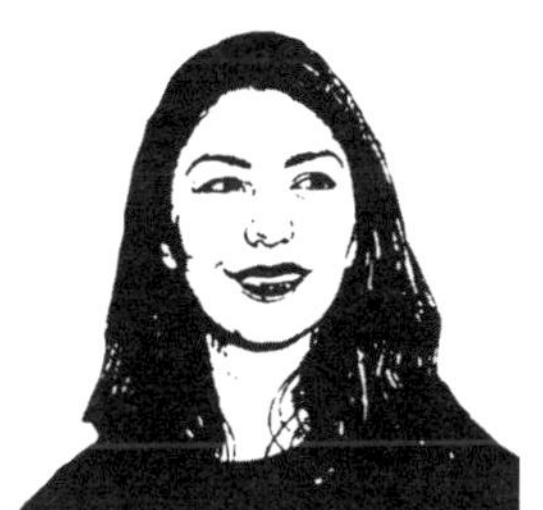

OCCUPATION: Filmmaker

WORK DISCUSSED: *Lost in Translation* (2003); *Marie Antoinette* (2006)

BORN: 1971

I'D INTERVIEWED SOFIA COPPOLA once before, in Los Angeles for a *New York* event. She was lovely, demure but forthright, just as she was when we Zoomed for this conversation. When I reached her, she was in Belize, I think, shrouded in fronds.

Sofia, who is the daughter of Francis Ford Coppola, had a childhood of privilege, which only makes her emergence as a major filmmaker that much more impressive to me, though no one's young years are simple, and God knows plenty of people raised in comfort have become serious artists. She acted in her father's movies, but was chased out of life in front of a camera after the negative reaction to her role in *The Godfather Part III*, which she has always said she took just to help her father out. She made music videos, did various projects with famous friends, and became a kind of muse to Marc Jacobs (page 319).

It certainly seemed like a charmed life, but she was attracted to work, and in her twenties tried her hand at directing movies, her father's business. To her own surprise, she was very good at it. She had a gorgeous eye, an intuition for when to be restrained and when to go all out, a feel for how to integrate pop music and style into serious moviemaking in a way that felt new. After making *The Virgin Suicides*, she embarked on two projects simultaneously, *Lost in Translation*, which emerged out of her own experience as a foreigner in Tokyo, and *Marie Antoinette*, which she adapted from a biography by Antonia Fraser, and in which, it seems from her description below, she recognized aspects of herself. She fused the story of Marie and Louis XVI with the music of her own youth; the attitude of the movie is joltingly contemporary, which involved enormous artistic risk. But she was unflinching. Although she lacks the persona of one, she is a very courageous filmmaker; her recessive manner is deceptive. Since writing the two movies side by side and filming them in sequence, she's made many more (*Somewhere*, *The Bling Ring*, *The Beguiled*, *On the Rocks*), as well as some visually adventurous

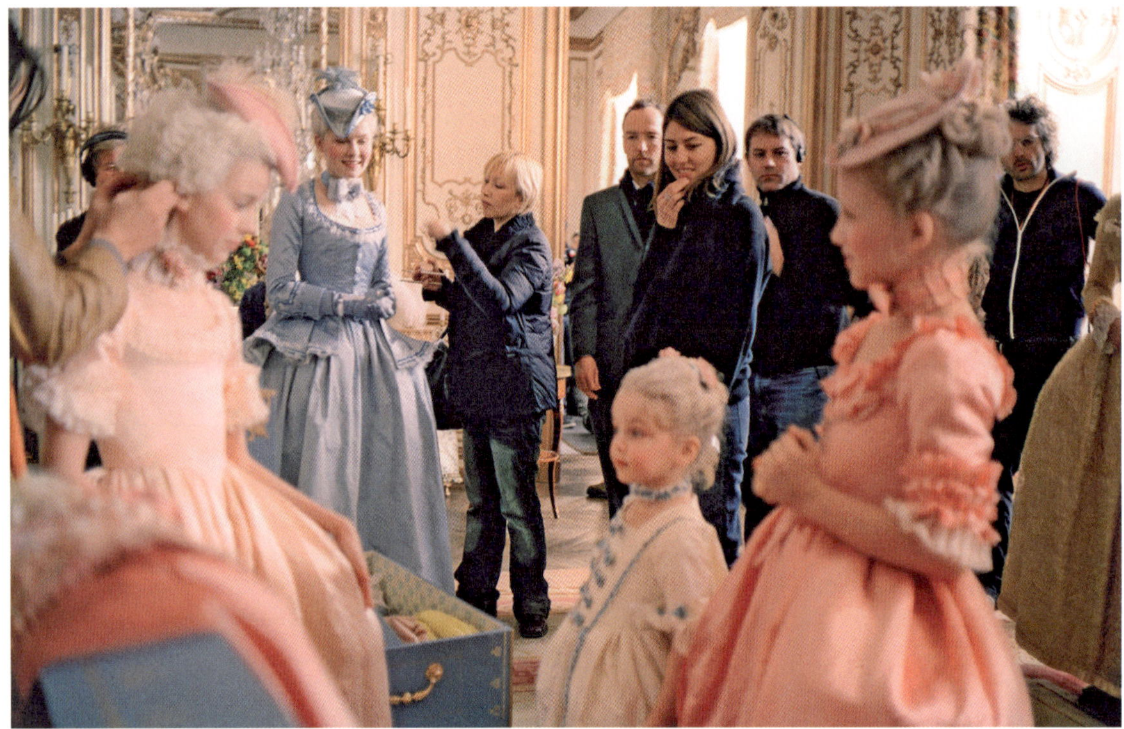

On the set of *Marie Antoinette* with Kirsten Dunst (and others).

commercials, music videos, and shorts with the same distinctive voice. In our conversation, though, we focused on the period when, fresh from the success of her first movie, she turned to *Marie Antoinette* and *Lost in Translation*. The first got a middling reception but has only grown in reputation, and the second became an instant classic and won her an Academy Award for its screenplay.

SOFIA COPPOLA: I wasn't ever planning on being a film director. And then I made *Virgin Suicides*, and I enjoyed it and it turned out I knew how to do it, strangely enough. I was like twenty-nine. Throughout my twenties I spent a lot of time going to Tokyo with my friends. I had a little clothing line—Kim Gordon was doing X-girl,[1] and I helped do fashion shows for them. And the world was more separate back then [around 1999]—like, did the internet exist? It was another planet. So I had this idea in my head that I wanted to do something about what it feels like to be in Tokyo as a foreigner. It was very abstract. I started collecting images and writing little notes for scenes.

At the same time, I was thinking about Marie Antoinette. I would get stuck on one project, then I would go to work on the other, and when that got stuck I'd go back again, back and forth. I'd heard about Antonia Fraser's take on Marie Antoinette,[2] and it intrigued me. I loved that Antonia was more sympathetic to her; the book imagined her point of view as a fourteen-year-old girl being handed over to the French, them taking away her underwear and her dog. The period was appealing to me. I was a teenager during the New Romantic period,[3] Galliano did a collection around it; I always liked the decadence of that time. I was reading the book and I visited Versailles, and they took me on a tour of her private apartments. The scale was small and very human. Marie Antoinette is a famous villain, but she was also a young girl who was trying to please everyone. I thought Kirsten Dunst, who I worked with on *Virgin Suicides*, could play her, could *be* her as a teenager—she has an adorable side that would help. Also, I'm very motivated by visuals, and seeing Versailles was inspiring.

So I was going back and forth. When you're writing, you have bursts of excitement and then moments of being really down, and it's terrible. But instead of just sitting in despair, I would go to the other project. *Lost in Translation* was an original screenplay. And for me, that's much, much harder because you have nowhere to look, no road map. I just gathered little moments—the script is really a series of little moments. My inspiration was Richard Brautigan,[4] whose poems were little moments—my brother and I called writing the script this way "Brautigan style." It was kind of like "Charlotte and Bob[5] meet for shabu-shabu and it doesn't go well, and then here's one line that they say." As I say, moments.

It really just started with Tokyo. I was newly married when I would go over there, and I was not feeling connected in my marriage. So I was lonely and drifting, and it was just sort of a fantasy that Bill Murray would show up at the bar. And I mean, really Bill Murray. I wrote it for him and I wasn't going to make it without him. I find actors really motivating, like visuals—picturing the actor. So there I was, in LA where I didn't feel connected, and then with my friends in Tokyo, where we were having a really interesting time—I was trying to understand it. I think for a lot of creative people, they're just trying to figure out what they're going through. I started thinking about Bill Murray because you meet different travelers insulated in a hotel, and I could just see him in a kimono and being too tall in this small world. I had known people having midlife crises in their forties or whatever, and I just combined them, two people having crises together. But I had never written an original screenplay. I remember having a moment where, like, I don't know what happens next! And then I was walking, I tripped and broke my toe, and I was like, that's it. I'll just put that in the script: she breaks her toe and he has to take her to the hospital. You think you're faking it, making stuff up out of the air, and then it becomes the story.[6]

But mostly when I didn't know what would happen next, I would turn to Marie Antoinette—which was more like . . . homework. I'm not a good reader, but Antonia Fraser was really friendly to me, so I would talk to her about it. I'd ask, "Do you really think she had an affair with Axel von Fersen?"[7] And Antonia would say, "I hope she did!" Antonia's a really fun spirit. I didn't want to make a historical film. Some people interpreted that as if I were being vapid, but you know, Marie Antoinette was interested in beauty and friends and her children and nature, and I was really trying to make it from her point of view. The parts I struggled with most were the small scenes I had to have with some official people talking about what was going on. I just felt like it's not my thing. I tried to write through to Marie Antoinette at the Conciergerie[8] later—what's touching about her is that she really does grow into herself as a dignified person in the last part of her life, when her son is taken away. It's so sad. But I didn't want to film in a prison cell—it just felt like a whole other movie. So I decided to end her story when they leave Versailles. It became clear to me that the movie was a coming-of-age story, about her transition from girl to woman.

And so, in the end, the party's over, her bedroom is trashed after the revolution, and it's like the room is *really* trashed. They were living in their fantasy world as the world outside was falling apart. I always find those kinds

1. Kim Gordon was in the band Sonic Youth and cofounded X-girl, a clothing line.

2. Antonia Fraser wrote the biography *Marie Antoinette: The Journey*.

3. New Romantics refers to a 1980s youth movement that grew out of New Wave music and was characterized by over-the-top fashion and androgyny.

4. Richard Brautigan was a poet and novelist.

5. Charlotte, the new wife of a celebrity photographer, and Bob, an aging movie star in a troubled marriage, are played by Scarlett Johansson and Bill Murray.

6. Can it ever be as straightforward as this? Break your toe, break your character's toe, see what high jinks ensue? I guess so. In any case, the broken toe leads to a poignant scene in the movie. See Suzan-Lori Parks and Sheila Heti for more drama straight from life.

7. Axel von Fersen was a Swedish count who may or may not have had an affair with Marie Antoinette.

8. The Conciergerie was a prison during the French Revolution.

of stories—this kind of decadence is fascinating to me.

Throughout, what that room looked like was incredibly important. I look at photos when I'm starting a project. I remember going to the Metropolitan Museum of Art's Costume Institute and Andrew Bolton[9] showing me some dresses from that period. I was struck by how the colors were so much brighter than you would expect. And the music. I could tap into my teen childhood imagination and do the movie as if it was like a video for one of those bands I listened to as a teenager. I knew it was obnoxious. I knew the French would probably have problems with it—and with an American girl tackling French history.

I just did not want to do it like *Masterpiece Theatre*. I was probably overcompensating. I didn't want big master shots. I wanted the camera close to her, intimate with her. I felt I was going to show her side of it, and it had to be done in an audacious way. It was about finding your identity and role, which is something I can relate to. You know—you're born into a certain circumstance, and what you make out of it is who you are.

I remember in the handoff scene,[10] I was really focused on trying to make Marie look young because Kirsten needed to age during the story. Her hair was small, and it just grows bigger and bigger as the story goes. The scene where she's on a little balcony and it zooms out really wide? Do you know the movie *Darling*, with Julie Christie? It has a balcony scene, and when I was writing the script, I was like, *How do I show the feeling of being small in a big, big place? Oh, I'll do the* Darling *shot*. The red Converses that pop up briefly came, in a way, from the Ken Russell movie *Lisztomania*.[11] Roman [Sofia's brother] showed it to me—it was set in the nineteenth century, but they had like paparazzi cameras. I wanted a little bit of that in *Marie Antoinette*—at one point we had a Rolls-Royce parked outside, but we didn't end up using that.

When I'm adapting something, the first thing is I'll go through the book and highlight anything that interests me, then try to string the things together. I don't really outline. I don't like being too organized. I like being in a state where you can listen to your subconscious. I'm always struggling to get to ninety pages. My scripts are sparse because I'm directing it. It's not a book; it's not meant to be read. They're really just notes to yourself. I mean, except for the dialogue—you want to choose the right word.

You ask about writing dialogue. Well, in general, I like expressing as much visually as I can. I think in life, people don't express themselves and talk about their feelings. They have mannerisms. They show their feelings.

At the end of *Lost in Translation*, Bill Murray whispers something privately to Scarlett [Johansson]. And that happened because when I was writing the script, I could never sum up their experience together. It felt so cheesy for him to say, you meant something to me. And when we were shooting it, we were still trying to figure that out. I thought, *Okay, we'll do what the Italians do. Just whisper in her ear. And then we'll add the dialogue later.*

It actually was the last day of shooting. I think it helps to film in order as much as you can. We were all exhausted, and Scarlett was leaving to go on to her next thing. So it was just really touching when we filmed it. In the edit, we watched the scene, and it was clear that the whisper was so much better than dialogue. It didn't matter what he was saying. It's just between the two of them. But it was really kind of an accident. I never thought it would become a moment.[12]

Eventually I'd end up making *Lost in Translation* before *Marie Antoinette*. Which was a good thing because the French seemed to like *Lost in Translation*, and that's why they let us film *Marie Antoinette* in Versailles.

9. Andrew Bolton is the head curator of the Anna Wintour Costume Center at the Metropolitan Museum of Art.

10. The handoff is a lengthy scene that takes place on the border of Austria and France, where a very young Marie is actually handed off to Louis XVI.

11. *Lisztomania* is a flamboyant 1975 film by Ken Russell that imagines Franz Liszt as a classical pop idol.

12. That whisper became something of a sensation, inviting rampant speculation of what Murray might have said. It's also a great moment in the movie. Withholding is a powerful tool in art (sometimes a cruel one in life).

1330 Ross Street**Petaluma, CA
Web site: officehelper.com

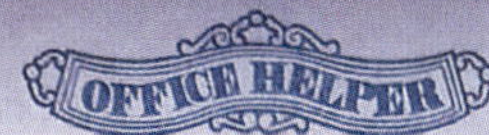

Phone 800-862-4963**Fax 800-933-7964
E-mail: oh@officehelper.com

manchild - herbie hancock
Tom tom club - new
- " girls of love "

BOB ARRIVES IN TOKYO

PARK HYATT greeted at elevator, ~~GARDEN LOBBY ROOM~~

ALONE IN ROOM

PARK HYATT BAR

COMMERCIAL SHOOT

BAR

HOTEL ROOM - HOOKER

BREAKFAST ALONE (see charlotte & john)

ELEVATOR - SEES CHARLOTTE

C at temple?

TALK SHOW - IRON CHEF

HOTEL ROOM - fax from wife, can't sleep

C can't sleep

SWIMS LAPS

Day in tokyo

- a
B - can't sleep
C

→ Bar - they meet

natalie love

nov. SC 18 MAPS

Notes for *Lost in Translation.*

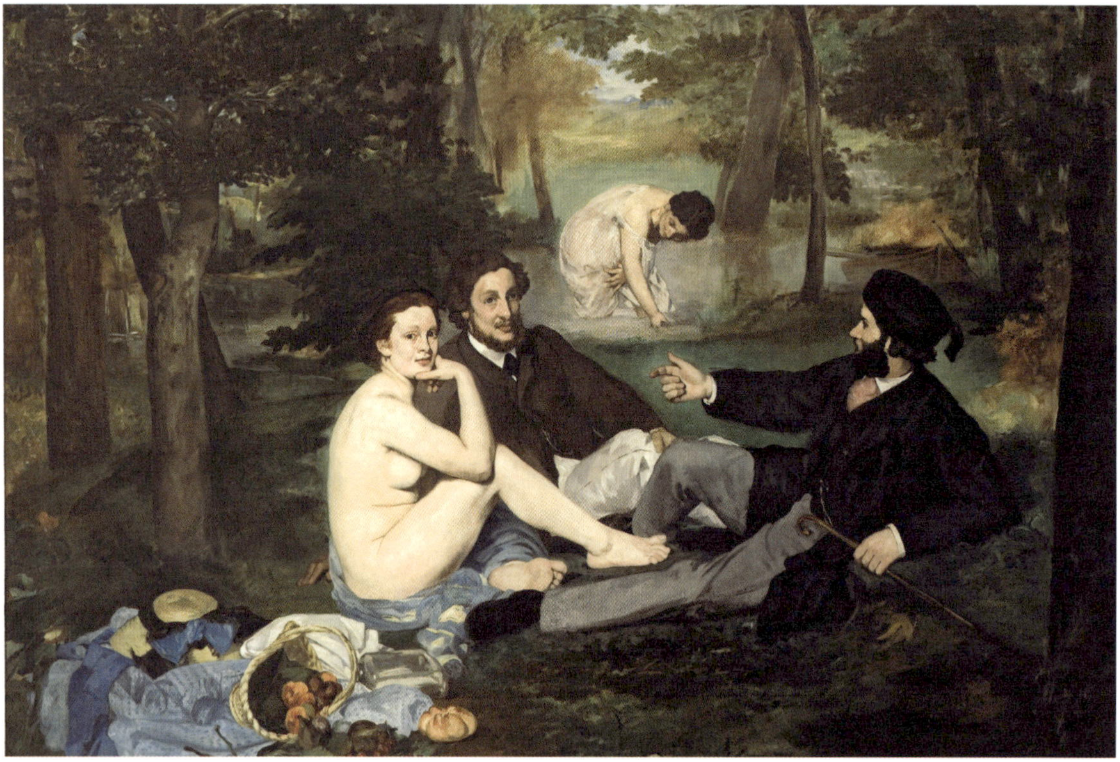

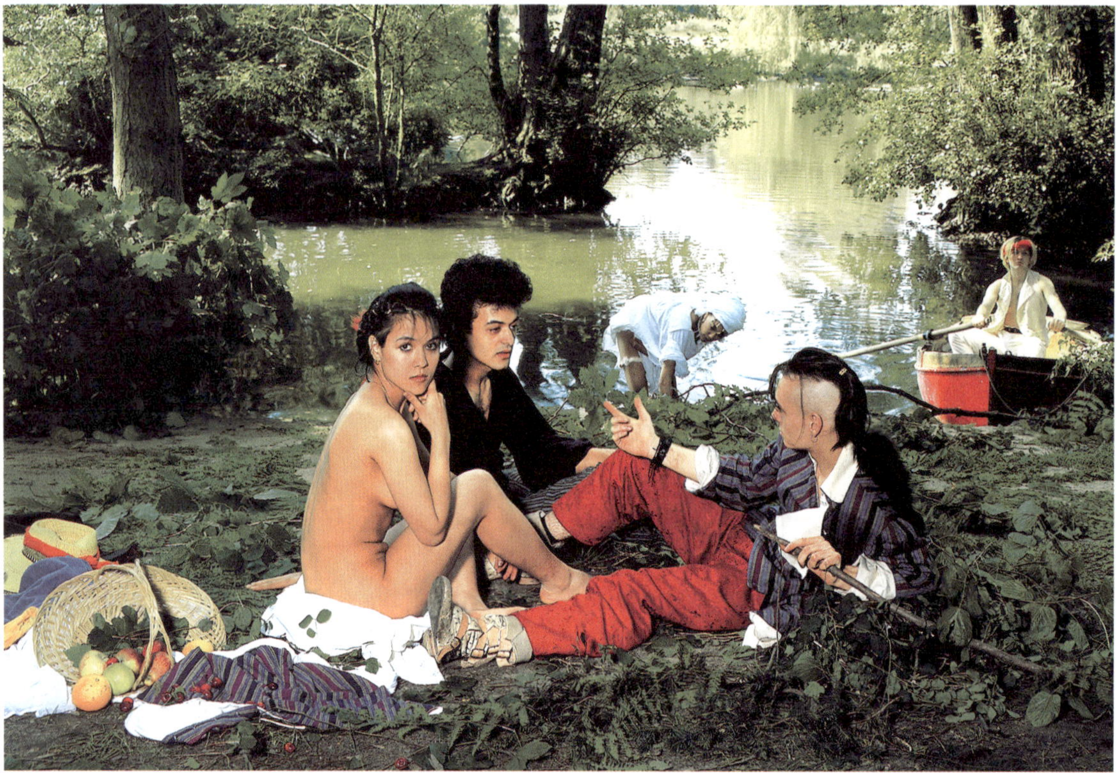

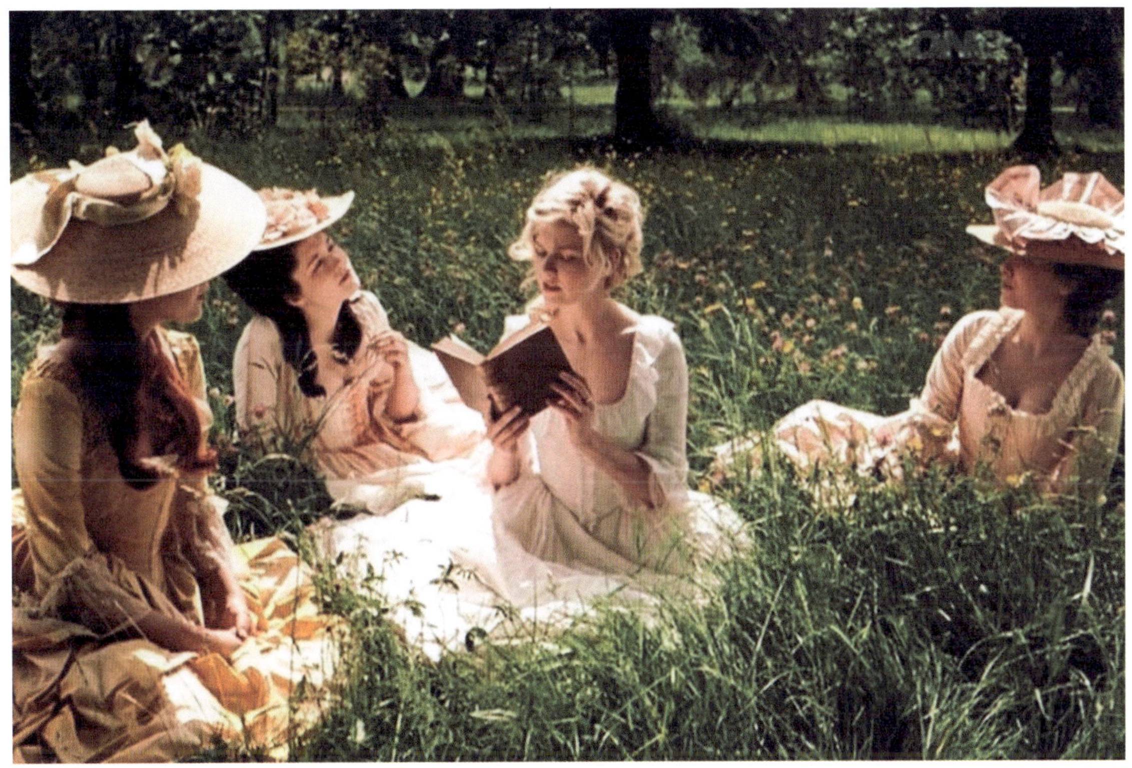

From *Marie Antoinette*, the evolution of a shot. *Le Déjeuner sur l'herbe*, painting by Édouard Manet, 1863. Bow Wow Wow, *See Jungle! See Jungle! Go Join Your Gang Yeah, City All Over! Go Ape Crazy!*, record cover, 1981. *Marie Antoinette*, film still, 2006.

I'm working on a new project now, an adaptation of Edith Wharton's *The Custom of the Country*.[13] When I'm writing, I try not to look at what I'm doing, I just keep going until the end, because as a writer you can just get overcome with doubt. I try not to show it to anyone. My brother is the first person I show things to because I trust him; he knows me enough that his feedback is not going to interfere. When I was editing *Marie Antoinette*, my dad, who obviously always has great advice, said, "You need to see more of Louis." And I said, it's not about him. But he was looking at it from a male point of view.

When you're working, there's so much self-loathing. Everyone feels like their stuff is awful. When I was at CalArts I was studying painting—I'm a terrible painter—but I remember there's a stage of a painting that just looks like a mess and then all of a sudden it becomes a painting. Movies are like that too. Magically it starts to take shape. Now I have faith, because I've done it enough I don't despair too much. I think, *We'll get through it. I'll turn it into* something.

When I was starting out, I would have an instinct to change something, wouldn't do it, and then in edit I would say, *I wish I had changed that*. And so now I've learned that when you have an instinct to do something, you shouldn't doubt yourself—go with it. Later you'll understand.

13. Coppola's next project turned out to be a movie biography of Priscilla Presley. *The Custom of the Country* was announced as an Apple television series and, as of this writing, was delayed, perhaps indefinitely. So it goes.

7

SUSAN MEISELAS

And There It Was

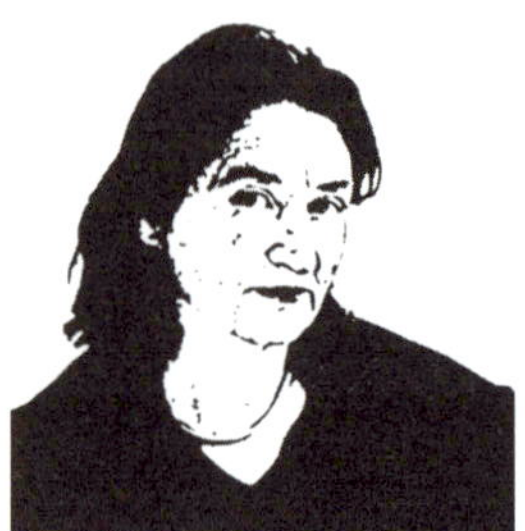

OCCUPATION: Photographer

WORK DISCUSSED: *Carnival Strippers* (1976)

BORN: 1948

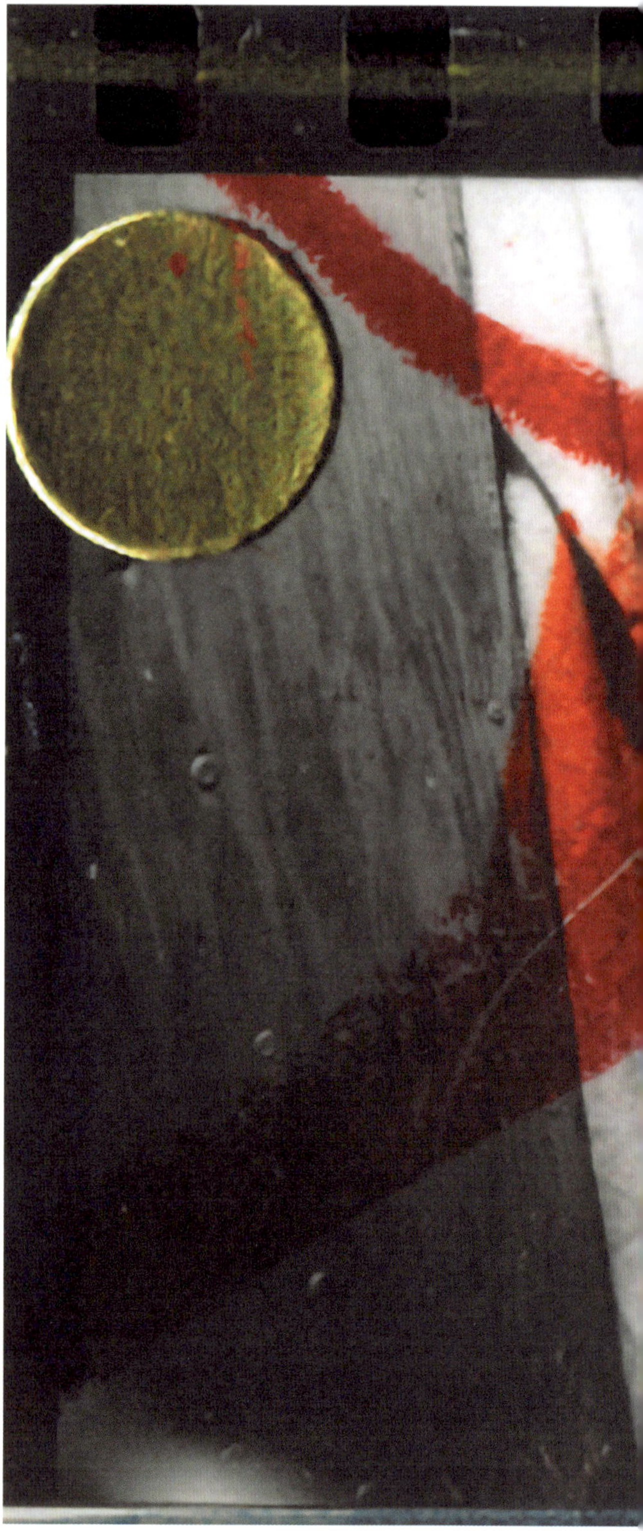

Carnival Strippers.

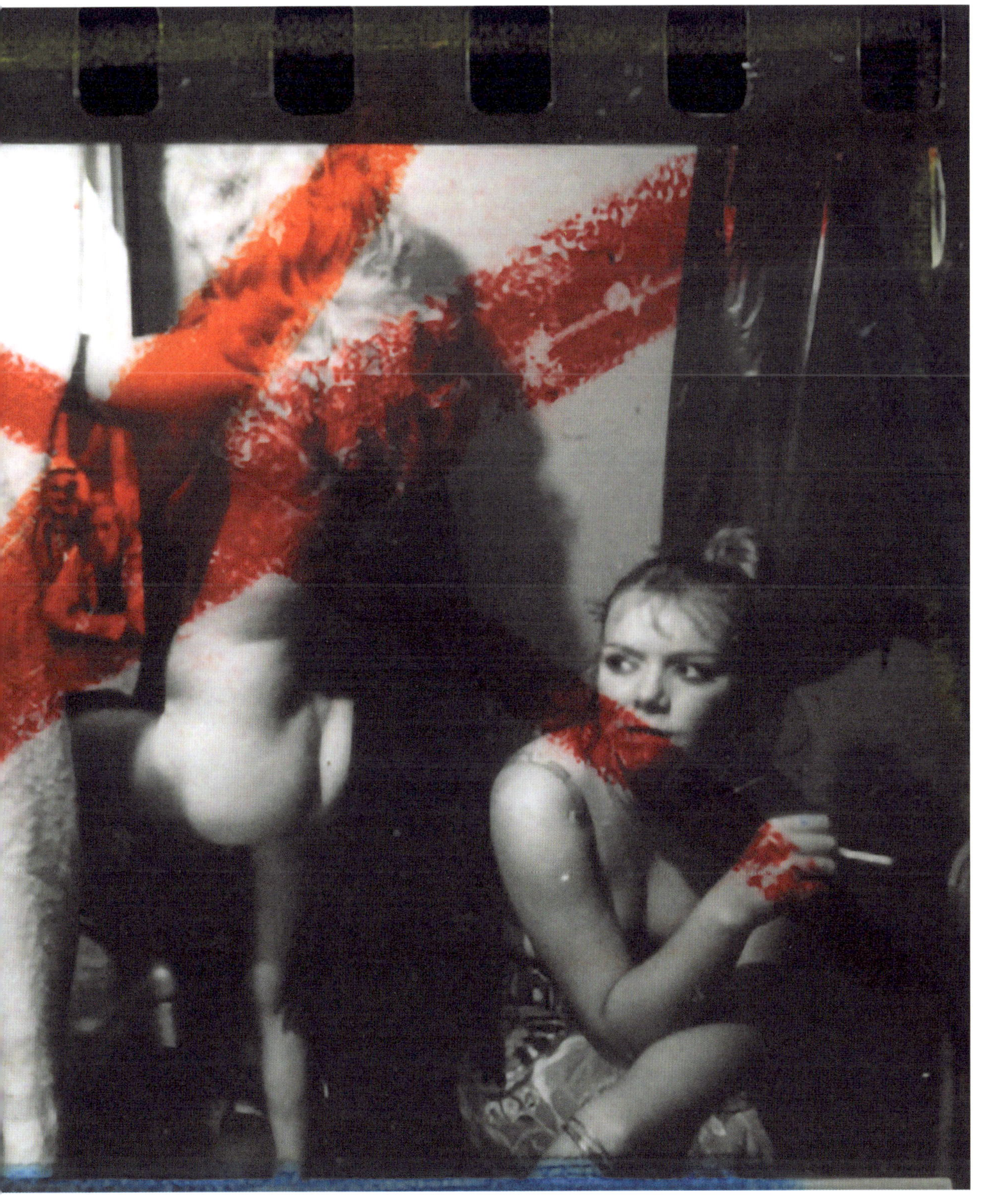

"YOU KEEP ASKING—when am I gonna say I'm a photographer?"

It's true, I was. I was looking for an aha moment, but I wasn't getting an answer.

I knew Susan Meiselas as a fearless and artful conflict photographer. But I had come to her place in Soho to talk about the very different sort of project that launched her, a book of pictures that she'd made in her twenties without any formal photographic education, called *Carnival Strippers*. For three-plus years she'd documented The Girl Show,[1] a strip show on fairgrounds up and down the East Coast. Her subjects were the girls, the managers, and the leering men who came to see them. A few particular women became her principal cast. She photographed them and interviewed them extensively, their voices a crucial part of the project.

Carnival Strippers is a strikingly confident piece of work that has had many iterations—several book editions, a show at the Whitney Museum, a couple of plays. It's a classic of book-length photojournalism, up there in my view with Robert Frank's *The Americans* or Walker Evans's *Let Us Now Praise Famous Men*. And yet, when Meiselas made *Carnival Strippers*, she didn't consider herself a photographer. She had just been following her curiosity into an unfamiliar world, a strip show, making use of an instrument (a camera) and an art form (documentary pictures) that she knew next to nothing about. "These days people are very intentional about what their motivation or purpose is," she said. Most of the other origin stories on these pages have some degree of intention—but by her account, she stumbled into this project, and only in retrospect would she realize that perhaps, sometime in the making of it, she had become a photographer. It unspools like happenstance, but of course it never is just happenstance.

Maybe it starts here: "When I was a child, my father gave me a camera. Why did he do that? I don't know. When I saw my cousin Elsa"—who was a professional family photographer—"I loved her independent spirit, I saw her as a free spirit and camera aligned." And so "I was beginning to take pictures. I was beginning to see the world in pictures."

As Susan grew up, her main interests were early education and anthropology. "I would say my whole life was influenced by John Dewey. Montessori." She went to the Harvard Graduate School of Education, and while there took a photography course and got a job with Frederick Wiseman, the legendary documentary filmmaker. "Fred was mostly a sound artist, when you really think about him. So I learned to hear, maybe. I am much more comfortable listening to someone before I look."

She went to teach in the South Bronx. "I built a darkroom, I took the kids out on the street," Susan said. "How do we understand what's happening in the visual world? I was very attracted to that conceptually. The kids would meet their local neighbors. They would start to do interviews. I'd say, 'You come back with a photograph and you tell me what's in that photograph.' Very simple concepts.

"People have said to me, 'Oh, then you just started doing what you were teaching kids to do.' I said, 'That's right.'

"I met Dick Rogers, he was a photographer becoming a filmmaker. Dick and I became involved in the summer of '71, he went on a road trip and left me behind, which was infuriating. . . .

"*Carnival Strippers* came into my life at a critical moment."

Just Curious The moment: It was the early seventies. If she had a consuming interest, it was anthropology. If she had developed some photography skills along the way, she didn't recognize them. She was pissed that her photographer boyfriend was going off without her. She was a teacher. She had summers off. "And the next summer I say, 'I'm going on the

1. Sometimes also referred to as The Girls Show.

2. The interviews she did with the girls were, to her mind, immensely important, as important as the photographs. Her mother, back in Long Island, helped her transcribe the stripper accounts—an unusual mother-daughter project that Susan said fascinated her mother. Apropos of not much, Susan grew up in the same town I did, as did Louise Glück (page 100).

3. A motordrome is a track for car and motorcycle racing.

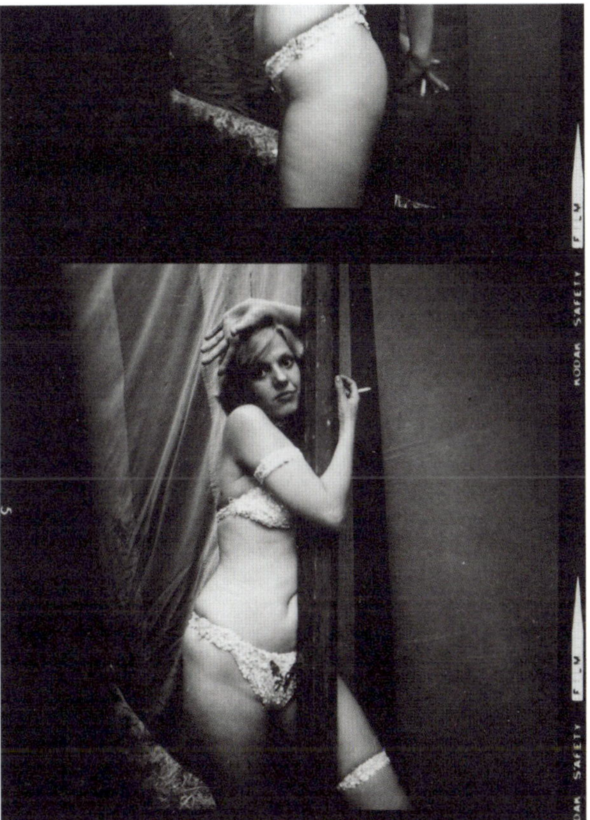

Lena. Also, the curtain as metaphor.

next road trip.' "

"In the summer of '72, we decide we're gonna look at state fairs and small circuses. We head west. I'm photographing the environment of the state fairs. By the time we get back east, I see this thing called The Girl Show, and it's the end of the summer.

"It propels me to want to go back. I'd gotten a little hint. I've met a couple of girls who define themselves as strippers. I'm taping. Right from the beginning, I'm taping with a clunky cassette recorder.[2]

"I have a very early interview, and it's fascinating. How they talk about what it means to do this thing. You have to remember, it's the beginning of the women's movement: Do we dress to attract men? How do we see our bodies? *Our Bodies, Ourselves*."

After the summer, she returned to teaching. When the school year was over, she went back on the road. The girls were sirens.

"I see this world, but I don't engage with it. The important thing about the step towards an immersion, and what immersion opens—it means to commit. I have not yet committed.

"You're not on assignment, nobody's paying you to do anything, you're on your own, it's your own free summer. You're not yet defined as a photographer even, except you're carrying a camera. And you're curious.

"I don't think I meet any of the women from '72 into '73. In '73 I see a manager who recognizes me from '72. He's a very important piece of the puzzle, allowing me to hang around as much as I would. Remember, women like me didn't get to go into the dressing room, didn't even get to go into the tent."

That summer—'73—she met Lena. Lena would become the centerpiece of the project, but Susan didn't know that yet. "I have tape of this girl, who I meet in maybe Bangor, Maine. You hear me recording her ask for a job. She's literally saying, 'I need a job.' She's leaving her husband. She says she can dance. And [the manager] says that's great. This unfolds in two minutes. And I think this was the bridge to making the photographs. Feeling like I want to follow this girl into this life.

"I'm there with Lena, who's with a garbage bag of her clothes, telling me the story of her husband taking four wheels off her car. She escapes to the carnival. That's her story. "I had an instinct: gotta follow this girl."

Following Lena "As we're moving from one traveling show to another," Susan said, "Dick and I are sleeping on the campgrounds of the fair, and he's doing his own project on the crazy motordrome guys.[3] We're watching Lena fall in love with Dave, the star of the motordrome. And I'm fascinated. The girls, the guys—the guys that are looking at these women.

"I'm taking up the tensions amongst the girls and the managers, the girls and themselves, the girls and their boyfriends. It's very chaotic. It's not like you meet these girls and stay with them the whole summer. Each site leads to a different kind of configuration. Somebody's always falling in love and leaving, or having a fight with someone else, or needs money. Town to town, it's shifting." But Lena, and another girl, Shortie, became central.

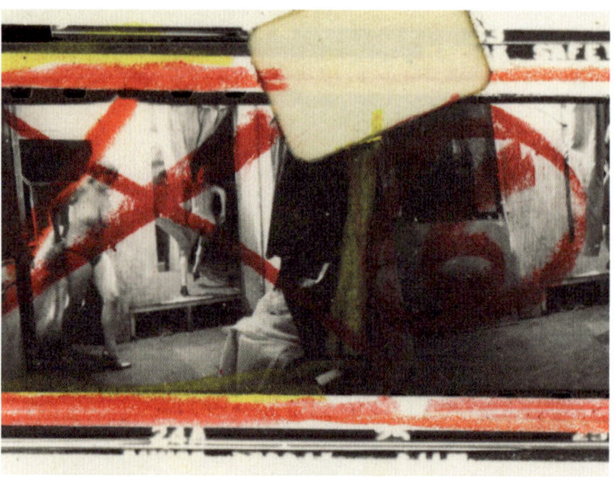

Contact sheet, curtains. The red *X* meant "use," not "reject."

Finally, Susan was committed. "When I start to work that summer in '73, I'm processing Monday, Tuesday, making contact sheets, making prints. I'm processing the film from every weekend, I'm shooting, I'm coming back. I bring the contact sheets back to show the women." She wanted to invite their participation, having recognized the problematic nature of her own kind of looking. Some of them were still there the next weekend in the next town.

"I begin a conversation. They don't get what I'm doing. They say, 'Why are you so interested in what we're doing?' "

But Art? As Susan was telling the story, her focus was on her anthropological immersion in the project.[4] There was not a moment when she talked about the photography itself, which puzzled me, because the pictures themselves are extraordinary—the *art* of the pictures, not just their content. I recognized her reticence as almost an ideology. "The tension is in being an artist just on your own, versus feeling responsible to a subject or a community."

Susan did not see herself as an artist, and still does not. The focus of her work is her subjects, not herself. That may sound axiomatic, but it isn't. It's not the same with other photographers, or almost anyone else in this book, who are more focused on the imposition of what they bring to the work.

I asked her to talk about how her use of the camera itself developed—she'd had so little training, and yet the framing of the pictures, the intimacy, seemed the work of experience. She tried to answer but really couldn't. "I was learning to look at how I was seeing, and trying to understand what I was seeing." It was a slow, unfolding process, she said, but not a particularly deliberate one. I'd imagined that as she was reviewing the contact sheets every week, she must have at least been teaching herself to make adjustments. But no: She just followed what was, with every passing week, a more intense interest in what she was seeing, and intuitively maneuvered herself into better position to capture it. She followed her body, not her mind.

Letting Others See Gradually she had amassed an immense body of work—many hundreds of pictures, tapes, manuscripts. Bit by bit, she began to exhibit it. "In '74, I think, there was a show in a little museum in Brockton [Massachusetts] that we did—Dick and I—which was just the story of Lena and Dave." Susan also attended an anthropology conference where she stuck some *Carnival Strippers* pictures up on the walls. From that conference, she was invited to show the work in a gallery in Buffalo, "four little rooms, with the sound from the exterior, the dressing room, and

4. In a sense, I was asking the same question I asked Kara Walker. They each created a structure to figure something out. But where does the *art* assert itself? Am I making too much of the distinction? For each, the art followed the research project.

5. It would be disingenuous not to acknowledge the role connections play in art careers. Susan's book might still have been published without her sister's guidance, but it surely helped.

6. The use of color would figure heavily in Susan's career. Her color photographs from Nicaragua were pioneering, and polarizing. "I got a lot of criticism for the Nicaragua color when it came out. Because people thought it was beautifying war," she said. "Those early reviews were painful because I wasn't thinking about what people were going to say. I was just doing what I felt was right. Even Cartier-Bresson criticized me. He said, 'You can't do color.' Cartier-Bresson really loved *Carnival Strippers*, and told me that, it meant a lot to me. And you can imagine, I'm young, just turning thirty, and he's seeing this work and telling me, you shouldn't be doing this. Like, who was he to tell me that? It was like God had spoken. I just feel lucky that I was stubborn enough. I remember it as just doing what I was doing."

the exit. That was really important because it was sound. That was Fred [Wiseman]'s training. I loved the visuals. But I think the innovation really was to value the sound."

In 1975, she finally quit her job as a teacher. "And I'm starting to think this project might be a book." But still she could not name the work she was doing. "The genealogy is very visible to me now," she said. "I knew I wasn't Diane Arbus. I didn't feel I was like Lee Friedlander. I wasn't a street photographer. I didn't like just passing through, making my pictures and moving on. I tried it—it didn't hold me."

Her sister, who worked as an assistant editor at Farrar, Straus and Giroux, told her the publishing house wanted to start a line of photography books.[5] Susan brought in her contact sheets from the Girl Shows, along with the transcripts, and Farrar, Straus published *Carnival Strippers*.

"The book was very shitty quality. But it was gritty. It sold out. And then it went dormant." *Carnival Strippers* was still noticed from time to time. Someone wrote a play centered on Lena. There was a fuss in some circles, and then the attention dissipated. "My life went on."

In 2001 a curator at the Whitney Museum, who had worked with Susan on another project, mounted a show of the work. *Carnival Strippers*' reputation kept ascending. And with each iteration, Susan had another opportunity to consider what she'd made. "I didn't really look back until the Whitney ran the show in 2001 and they decided to reprint the book. The book had been out of print for twenty years." For that new edition, she made many changes to correct what she felt the first book had done wrong. That book went out of print as well.

In 2022, the book was reprinted again. A gallery showed color pictures[6] she'd been surprised to find in the extensive archive she'd kept of the project. To accompany the new edition, she constructed a "making of" account. Each dive back into the work brought new revelations for her about this youthful project, which was still, I got the sense, a bit of a mystery to her.

Who Was She? One day we sat in her Mott Street studio poring through the "archeology" of the contact sheets in the 2021 book. For her, contact sheets are memory. "What I remember," she said, "is what I recovered."

Before we got the contact sheets, we looked at her notebooks. They are copious. "What's interesting is when I went back into this box and found these notes, there was a structure to my thinking," she said.

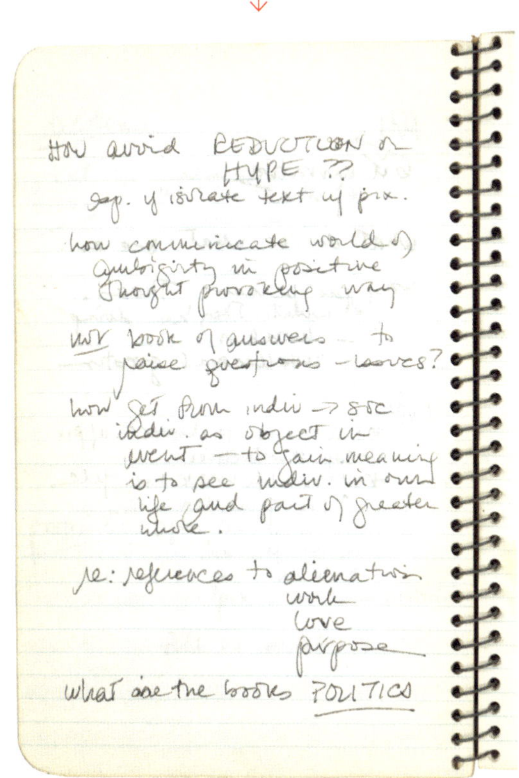

"The feminists are saying there's an exploitation of women. And I'm saying, 'Well, wait a minute. Listen to what they're saying.'" She remembered that she'd offered the project to the then new *Ms.* magazine, and they refused it, which vexed her. But she was bucking the orthodoxy of the time. She also recalled a thought she'd had at one point to make this a history—the road from early burlesque to the Girl Show. But her interest was anthropological, even cinematic, not historical.

Still fixated on the art of it, when we got to the contact sheets, I asked her to reconstruct her

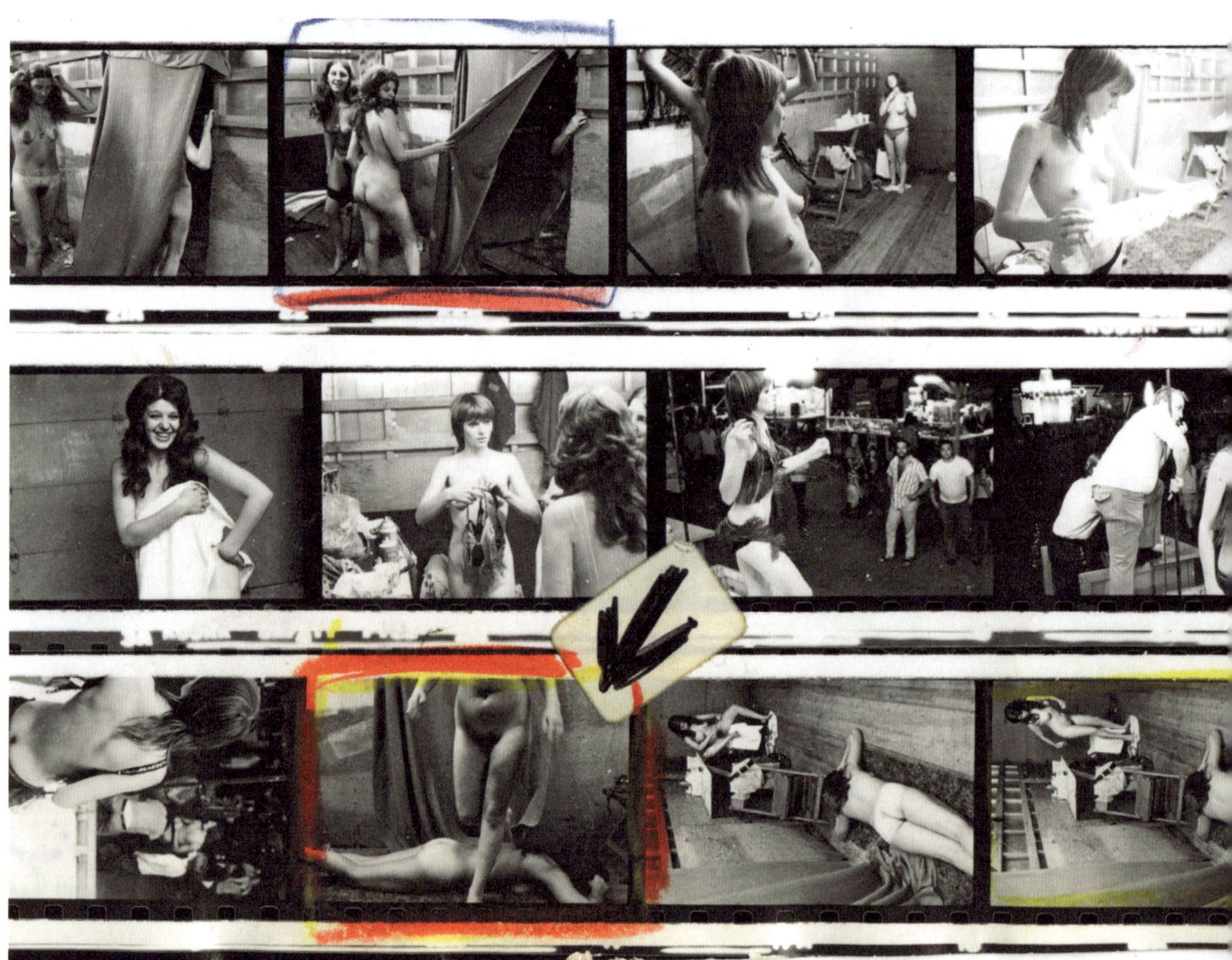

shooting decisions as best she can remember.

"Looking through the boxes was a rediscovery of my own process, frame by frame. There's something about being in a small space that leads to a different kind of framing. I'm probably moving my body more than changing any other factor as I'm struggling with problems of light, which is why color diminishes—there's one light bulb, you can't shoot Kodachrome. You can see me starting to dissect the visual culture I'm observing. My eye is just looking to get something. I'm very attentive to specific detail."

As we moved through the book, she focused on the curtain that appears in so many of the images and became one of her central metaphors.[7] "Just a gesture of their going in and out of space, out of the curtain. The curtain is the transition. The way it protects them and is also their point of exposure."

7. Metaphor not imposed, but recognized. Seen.

The Crucial Photograph She Didn't Realize She'd Taken She stopped on one page. "I looked at these contacts and thought suddenly, *Wow, I can't believe this, there's only one frame of this*. It's not like I took ten and this is the best one." She drew my attention to one isolated picture on the contact sheet.

"In this shot, she's coming back from the

stage. The other girl was wiped out. And it became the symbolic picture of the whole book, one of my most important images. But there was only one frame. I didn't see it. When I processed the film in the week that followed, *that's* when I saw it.

"I mean, there it was."

Strippers to War After the publication of *Carnival Strippers*, she joined Magnum, a vaunted photo agency, and got a few assignments. But, she said, "I don't find myself very marketable in the world of so-called photojournalism. I'm the quirky girl that just did *Carnival Strippers*, what does she know? You're not going to send her to war."

Ultimately, she sent herself to war, went on her own dime to Nicaragua, and eventually became one of the more celebrated conflict photographers of the late twentieth century.

"But when do I say I'm a photographer? I don't know. I mean, I probably tried to say it a few times. But when did I believe it?

"If I'd had an iPhone back then," she said, "I'm sure *Carnival Strippers* would have been a movie, not stills."

"And then," I said, "your whole life would have been different."

"Yeah," she replied. "Wouldn't that have been fun?"

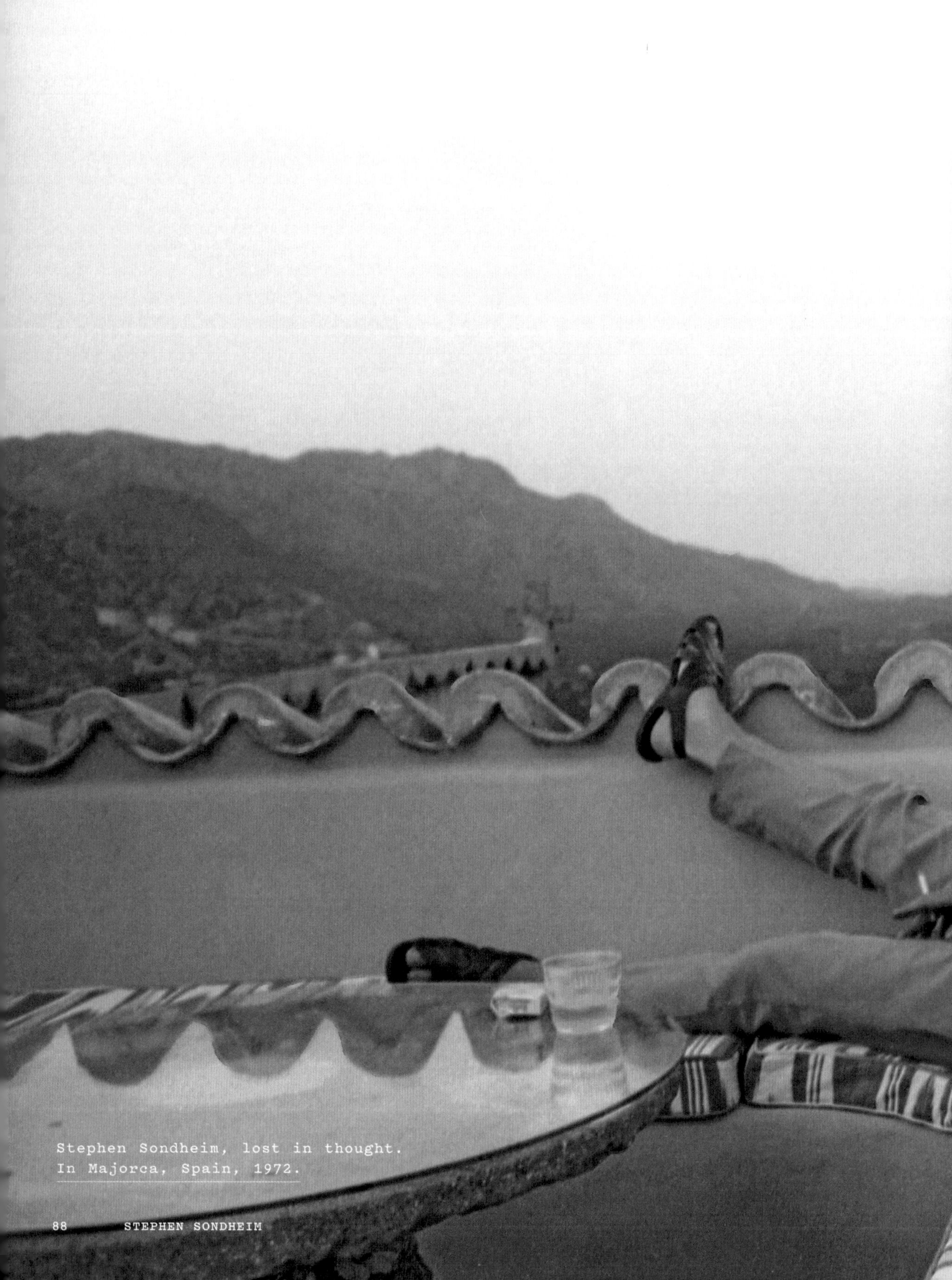

Stephen Sondheim, lost in thought.
In Majorca, Spain, 1972.

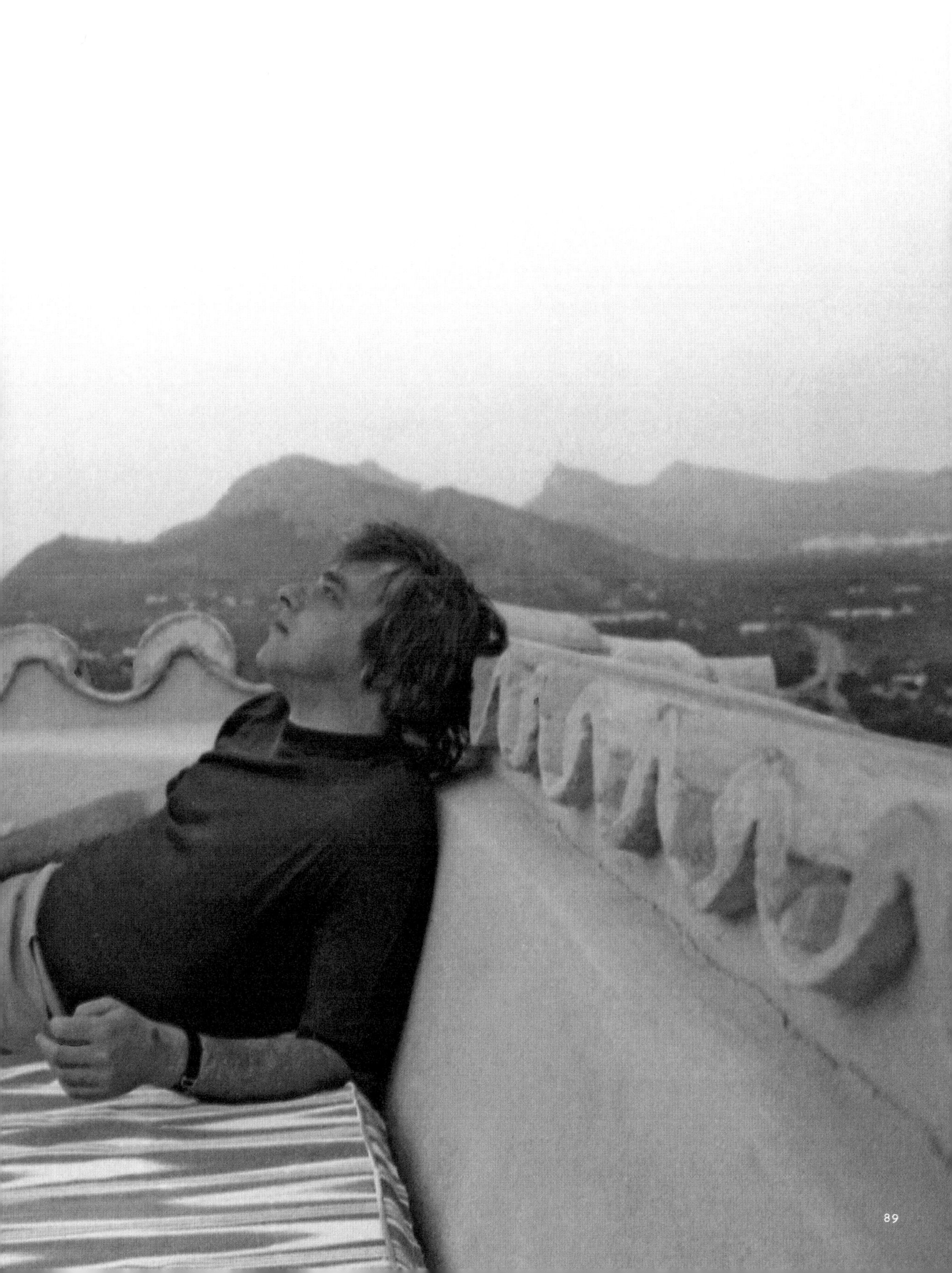

SCENE SIX

A woman in a white choir robe appears as lights come up on Jamie's kitchen. The woman is accompanied by a choir of guests. Jamie is shining a pair of men's black shoes.

WOMAN:

Bless this day, finally it's true,
He can marry you.
The heart leaps up to behold
This golden day.

(Paul appears in dress shirt, shorts and socks)

PAUL: Jamie, I can't find my shoes any –

Today is for Jamie.
Jamie, the best man that I've ever known –
I'll cherish and I'll keep you,
I'll honour you forever.
Today is for Jamie,
My husband – and mine all alone.

(Spoken) Jamie, we're really getting married!

(Paul exits; Jamie shakes his head "yes" and it becomes "no")

JAMIE:

Pardon me, is everybody there?
Because if everybody's there
I want to thank you all for coming to the wedding.
I'd appreciate your going even more,
I mean, you must have lots of better things to do,
And not a word of it to Paul. Remember Paul?
You know, the man I'm going to marry,
But I'm not because I wouldn't ruin
Anyone as wonderful as he is –

But I thank you all
For the gifts and the flowers.
Thank you all,
Now it's back to the showers.
Don't tell Paul,
But I'm not getting married today.

WOMAN:

Bless this day, suddenly it's true:
He can marry you.
The heart sinks down and feels dead,
This dreadful day.

(Bobbie appears dressed as the Maid of Honour)

49

"Getting Married Today," gender flip. An early alteration of the lyrics, turning Amy into Jamie. In the end, Sondheim's changes to the original lyrics were fewer than he appeared to initially imagine he'd need.

8

STEPHEN SONDHEIM

A Puzzle

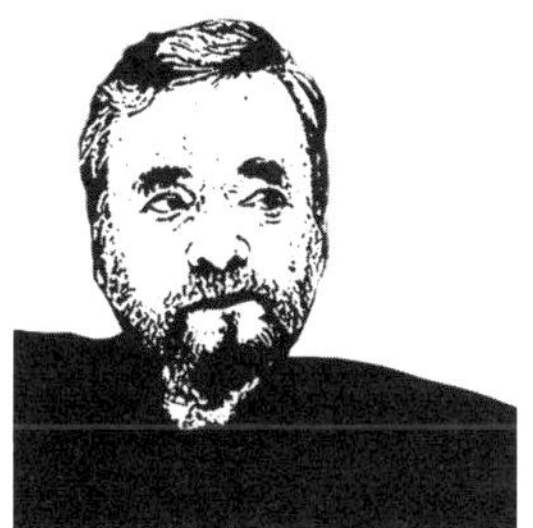

OCCUPATION: Composer

WORK DISCUSSED: "Getting Married Today" (1970/2018)

BORN: 1930; DIED: 2021

MY MOTHER TOOK me to see *Company* when I was thirteen years old. I didn't understand much of it. The musical wonders what's the point of marriage and is pretty cynical about adult relationships generally—it isn't exactly *Peter Pan*. *Company* was a weird show for a mother to take a son to, especially when the mother is in a difficult marriage and the son kind of knows that, but I loved it anyway. The story, such as it is, is about Bobby, a guy who just can't make up his mind about whether to get married. Bobby's story made no sense to me, but somehow Stephen Sondheim's music did. *Company* is the musical that prompted Sondheim's reputation for coldness, because it's so clever it can come across as arch. Yet beneath the complex and sophisticated wordplay about experiences way beyond my own, there were powerful feelings gurgling just under the surface. Fear, yearning, anxiety—Sondheim tapped into a deep neurotic well. And even with my voice just beginning to crack, I felt it.

Some fifty years later, I was talking to Sondheim about how he worked, about *Company*, and about one song in particular. Sondheim was ninety at the time. He died a year later.

It was a freighted conversation for me because I am such a fanboy. From that *Company* performance forward, I have seen everything Sondheim ever wrote, most multiple times. I have felt sometimes, and ridiculously, that much of what I've learned from life I learned from his songs, and that I wanted to know him, as I believed he knew me. And yet he was a puzzle. His songs are carefully composed, elaborate, heady. There's enormous pleasure in their design, but their impact is also powerfully emotional, sometimes even primitive. As I was talking to him, I found myself thinking a lot about the parallel planes of his work: How to reconcile the meticulous exterior with the roiling interior? I came to this conversation with the preposterous hope that I might come to understand where the depth of feeling in his work comes from; also, perhaps generally, that I might gain insight into the relationship between craft and its effect, for in Sondheim that chasm seems particularly wide.

I was nervous, but it helped that he was interested in this project. As I mentioned earlier, he wrote two books of his own creative introspection, *Finishing the Hat* and *Look, I Made a Hat*, both titles playing off a song from his musical *Sunday in the Park with George* about overwhelming creative drive, its ecstasy and its consequences. The books, candid and funny and almost epically precise, provide the backstory and explanation for his choices, song by song, throughout his career.

Sondheim was a remarkably astute observer of human psychology, and I've wondered if his interest in his own process was also an interest in his psyche, but I sort of doubt it. I get the feeling it was the more disinterested stance of a technician, marveling at how elements come together to make something work. In any case, in this conversation we discussed *Company*, because it contained his most recent work[1]—altered lyrics for a fairly radical reinterpretation of the show, in which Bobby the man becomes Bobbie a woman with an implied ticking biological clock, recast as a hallucination with heavy *Alice in Wonderland* overtones.

This was not the first attempt to reimagine *Company*. It turns out it wasn't only a thirteen-year-old me who couldn't understand Bobby; pretty much no one could. Bobby is, by general consensus, a beige hole at the center of the show, a passive bystander. Theater fans (mostly theater "queens," to be sure) have feverishly searched for clues in the text to prove he must be a closeted gay man. Many have speculated that the show was autobiographical, a reading Sondheim vehemently denied (he also refused to allow a gay *Company* to proceed when it was presented to him). In one revival, Bobby was bisexual, providing, tepidly, at least a possible motivation for his anguish.

This new gender-flipped version offered another solution. What did Sondheim know about a thirtysomething woman facing down her dwindling fertility? Nothing, but when he wrote the show, by his own admission, he didn't really know much about marriage, either, and had never been in a serious relationship. Over the years, Sondheim would go on to write about a murderous barber, Japanese samurai, and several presidential assassins, subjects he didn't know much about, either, though he imbued all of these with his central (and autobiographical) themes: loneliness, the crushing disappointment of life, and ambivalence above all.

How did Sondheim write songs? Well, the first thing to know is they rarely started with Sondheim—they usually began in the mind of a playwright (or "book writer" as they're called in musicals). The book writer plotted the show, sketched out some scenes, and then Sondheim plucked the material—appropriating them from monologues or situations in the text, often borrowing language to work with. *Company* originated with a set of short plays by George Furth,[2] in which various third wheels witness a series of teetering marriages. In creating the musical, Sondheim, Furth, and the director Harold Prince turned all the third-wheel characters into a single third wheel, who, Sondheim explained, they then made into a protagonist—without perhaps succeeding in figuring out who he was. (That was Sondheim's diagnosis of the problem, though he also didn't think there was much of a problem.)

I wanted to discuss a song called "Getting Married Today" with Sondheim, because it is one of my favorites—dazzling, intricate, and hilarious, sung at warp speed. (Also, I was intrigued because it is a replacement song for one he had to junk, and I wanted to talk about that too.) I have seen "Getting Married Today" described as the fastest song in all of musical theater, and one of the most difficult to sing, and both are probably true. But even more than that, the song on its own does something incredible. In the original version of the show, the song takes place in the head of a woman at the altar, terrified of tying the

1. After Sondheim's death, the theater world learned that during his last days he'd completed a musical he'd long been working on. *Here We Are* was staged in New York in 2023.

2. George Furth wrote eleven one-act plays that were never produced. They found their way to Harold Prince, a producer as well as director, who thought they would work better as a musical.

knot. It goes on to conjure a full-blown anxiety attack, ambivalence gone haywire. It's funny, but it's not a novelty song—it's deceptively deep. And structurally it's self-sufficient—it's like a one-act play in itself.

Fantasies Called Songs In our conversation, Sondheim was kind and generous with me and clearly still had all of his marbles. I've let him wander a bit here to give you a sense of how he talked, and to share how methodical he was in his thinking as he talked me through the song.

"Well to start, the song's original purpose is to introduce Amy," he said, "a character George [Furth] had imagined, based on someone he knew—a hysterical girl who is hysterical because she is afraid to commit herself to marriage. It's all there in George's script. Here's how I look at it: If you think about writing a speech for a character, what would happen? Many times, what I do is act the character. Then it's, how do I make this clear, dramatic, amusing . . . ? And of course, what do I want to say? So much more important than how do you want to say it.

"Usually the decision about what gets sung out of the book comes out of endless discussions with the book writer about where songs will function best. When is it best to speak a scene, when to sing it. And that's a matter of playwriting structure, because the structure of a musical is exactly like the structure of a play. Except there are moments that are almost like fantasies, which are called songs.

"I remember for example when I was working with [writer and director James] Lapine on *Sunday in the Park with George*, and he's a poetic writer, and he started, and we were talking about where the songs should go. And I said, 'You know, James, I don't think this should be a musical. What you're doing is so poetic and atmospheric that if anybody sings a song, they're going to tear the fabric in two.' I said, 'Why don't I just write some incidental music.' And he said, 'Oh stop it,' so I stopped. But there are times where there should be no song."

In the case of *Company*, George Furth wrote the scene of Amy's crack-up as a monologue. It's worth taking a moment to compare it with the song Sondheim wrote from it because he lifted so much of the spirit of Furth's monologue—and yet Sondheim's transmutation is so completely, recognizably his own.

In our conversation, Sondheim gave me

AMY

Oh, my, you are here...I wanted to reach you so you wouldn't waste an hour hanging around waiting for us, who aren't even coming...don't tell Paul. I mean, he doesn't know yet that we aren't coming. I wanted to tell him, since I've known it ever since I felt this knawing, twisting, harrowing agony at the pit of my stomach. I should've...I wouldn've...but I couldn'tve. Just couldn'tve. I will.Of course, I will. I just haven't. He is so unerringly right and noble and moral and thrilling how could I? He"d be shocked to know -- to learn -- that there are people like me. People that think this whole ritual is barbaric and the whole ceremony is stupid and the whole process is outmoded....not to mention the terror in the hearts of those like me who feel almost insanity at the thought of actually doing it. I mean, I'm not a virgin or anything. I do have some sense of sophistication. And I also know, beyond a shadow, that Paul will take a mistress probably on our very honeymoon he'll get so bored and feel so tied down and loath me so. That is fact. Our relationship has been so wonderously perfect that I cannot allow it all to change. Paul says it will only grow deeper and more solid and stuff that he knows he doesn't mean. He means 'let's see' is probably what he means...and I say 'why see'? If everyone just left everything alone then everything would stay as it is. Well, even if it wouldn't it wouldn't be put to the SUPREME test of permanence. Oh that word is so enduring, so non-ending, so puky. When we had the a lecture in musical structure. The song, he said, wasn't introduced by dialogue, as many songs are. "George is the only author I worked with who was completely unmusical. In fact, when I met him, he was in his forties and had never listened to music. He didn't even own a phonograph. So you'll notice that the songs in *Company* are never in the middle of scenes in the Rodgers and Hammerstein way. They're either at the beginning or end of the scene, or somebody comments on what's going on. That goes against everything I was ever trained to do by Oscar. . . ."

Oscar was Oscar Hammerstein. His son was Sondheim's friend when they were children. The legendary lyricist became Sondheim's teacher.

"Oscar taught me that you carry the dialogue forward in a song, and not against it. But none of George's dialogue is good for leading into song. So every song is either a commentary or an internal monologue."

"Getting Married Today" is an internal monologue.

First Attempt "We have to see Amy in the middle of her hysteria," continued Sondheim. "And so I wrote a song called 'The Wedding Is Off.' It's a very jagged song because it's about a lady who's falling apart. And the trouble with the song is that it fell into a pit that I often fall into—too many words. Well, that's not right—more like too many words that are juxtaposed in such a way that it might be difficult for the listener to understand. And we decided, before we went to Boston [to try out the show] that it had to go." The decision was made by Sondheim, the director Harold Prince, and the actress who was playing Amy, Beth Howland. "Beth had sung it in rehearsals in New York. And it wasn't her fault; it was my fault—the song was virtually unintelligible."

And the Second "And so just before leaving New York, I wrote a new song: I thought, I don't want to lose the hysteria. So I decided on this sort of rhythm, express train stream

FINAL

GETTING MARRIED TODAY (EXCERPTED)

(Church Lady and Paul sing, oblivious to Amy's crisis. Then . . .)

AMY
Pardon me, is everybody here?
Because if everybody's here
I want to thank you all for coming to the wedding.
I'd appreciate your going even more,
I mean, you must have lots of better things to do,
And not a word of it to Paul.
Remember Paul? You know, the man I'm gonna marry.
But I'm not, because I wouldn't ruin
Anyone as wonderful as he is—
But I thank you all / For the gifts and the flowers.
Thank you all, / Now it's back to the showers.
Don't tell Paul, / But I'm not getting married today.
(Church Lady sings. Then back to Amy.)
Listen, everybody,
Look, I don't know what you're waiting for.
A wedding, what's a wedding?
It's a prehistoric ritual
Where everybody promises fidelity forever,
Which is maybe the most horrifying word I've ever heard,
And which is followed by a honeymoon
Where suddenly he'll realize
He's saddled with a nut
And want to kill me, which he should.
So listen,
Thanks a bunch, / But I'm not getting married.
Go have lunch, / 'Cause I'm not getting married.
You've been grand / But I'm not getting married.
Don't just stand
There, I'm not getting married!
And don't tell Paul,
But I'm not getting married today.
Go! / Can't you go?
Why is no- / Body listening?
Goodbye! / Go and cry
At another person's wake.
If you're quick, / For a kick
You could pick / Up a christening,
But please, / On my knees,
There's a human life at stake!

(And that's just half the song . . .)

THE WEDDING IS OFF (EXCERPTED)

(Choir sings, similar to in "Getting Married Today." Then. . .)

AMY
The music is swelling.
The guests are inside.
The parents are kvelling,
And look at the bride:
Beautiful gown, even at retail—
Lamp the veil, folks, notice the coif.
And another fabulous detail:
The wedding is off!
(The choir sings again, then—)
The choir is singing,
The preacher's been paid,
The bells go on ringing—
I hope it's a raid.
Staggering gifts, dazzling flowers,
Picturewise, the show is a boff—
Thanks a heap, now back to the showers,
The wedding is off!
Hey, chaps,
You can clear the apse.
And you on the keys,
Please
Play "Taps."
Be nice,
Kindly strike the rice.
I'm cutting the act, ankling the pact
Chickening out, and as a matter of fact—
(Choir sings again)
I know it's been rough, gang,
To come all this way.
Can't thank you enough, gang—
I wish I could stay.
Gotta cut out, due at the shrinker,
Plus I have this terrible cough—
Futurewise, the show is a stinker—
(Another choir section)
Look, who's the musician?
Is this an audition?
No, something is odd—
Will those who hear me, nod?
Look, I really don't mind it,
But who is behind it,
The Marquis de Sade?
(I'm only kidding, God!). . .

of consciousness. And the words are intelligible because I made the rhythm very steady."

Looking at the lyrics to "The Wedding Is Off," it is identical in intent to "Getting Married Today"—a song imagining a bride telling all her wedding congregants to get lost—but Sondheim rewrote nearly every line when he set out to replace the song. And it isn't just the lyrics themselves that he shifted; he took a bulldozer to the rhyme scheme. "The Wedding Is Off" is very rhymey right from the get-go; "Getting Married Today" builds to its rhymes. You wouldn't notice it at first, but it's a dramatic difference. When we were talking, I hadn't yet heard "The Wedding Is Off," I'd only read the lyrics. I asked Sondheim whether the new song sounded, musically, like the old song. He was surprisingly emphatic (count the noes in his answer), and I think that was because of the pride he felt in how he had solved his problem.

"Oh, not at all," he said. "No, no, no, no. Not at all. Not the least bit similar, because this [new] melody is almost 'monody,' if you know that musical term, meaning just one voice going, very steady—unlike 'Wedding Is Off.' 'Getting Married Today' is monotonous in rhythm. Where there are breaks in the rhythm, it lets the audience relax for a second, but mostly it's a genuine stream of consciousness, and the key word is *stream*. It flows." (After our conversation, Sondheim sent me a tape of himself singing the song in his charming, scratchy voice. And it's true that "The Wedding Is Off" juts this way and that; it's a little hard to listen to. "Getting Married Today" is less dissonant.)

"By the time I wrote the song, I knew what I wanted. It wasn't as difficult to write as 'The Wedding Is Off' because I knew the territory. And of course, once you set up a pattern like that, it's really a matter of filling it out. It's much easier to write than something with changes in rhythm. She just babbles, which implies steady rhythm. When you babble, you babble like this [he starts to sing], you babble like that. She can't shut up.

1.

"Getting Married Today," original version. 1. Lyric scratchings on his typical yellow legal pad. 2. The score. 3. Draft with most of the bottom two stanzas (circled) altered in the final. Kept *listening/christening* but many inspired rhyming lyrics were tossed right in the bin.

"When I write songs, usually I start with trying to find a so-called refrain line, a center pole for the song, so there's some kind of home base. But in this song, there really isn't any. That's because she's spinning her wheels."

To fully appreciate just how deliberate Sondheim was in his method, consider this dissection of "Getting Married Today" from *Finishing the Hat*: "The patter sections may seem difficult to sing in one breath as they ought to be sung, but in fact they're calculated to alternate vowel and consonant sounds in such a way as to make them easy for the tongue, teeth and breath to articulate. . . . In the best rapid patter songs, the faster you sing, the easier it is." Also: "If I had rhymed the lines in the patter, it would have implied an organized control of Amy's thought processes, when in fact disorder is the essence of hysteria. Simply avoiding rhymes, however, would not have been a satisfying solution; to give unrhymed lines full value . . . you have to keep the sounds of the accented words as different from each other as possible. [But] a completely unrhymed song would have been monotonous and shapeless, which is why Amy suddenly starts to rhyme with a vengeance. . . ."

You just don't get more exacting than that.

"Getting Married Today" took less than a week to write. Partly this was because Sondheim knew he was writing for Howland—or Amy as played by Howland. "Boy, does that make it easier. One doesn't often get a chance to do that"—because most songs are written before a show is cast—"unless you're out of town and you're changing something. And that's why some of the most famous or successful songs in shows have been written out of town."

There were few changes once he'd set the song down. The show opened. Howland's maniacal performance of the song is enshrined in Broadway legend. All well. But I wondered out loud to Sondheim whether it was difficult to kill, as he did with "The Wedding Is Off," songs over which he'd labored so hard.

Mistake, Erase. "No, nope, and I'll tell you why," he said. "Oscar taught it not by speech but by example. When *Oklahoma!* opened in New Haven, when it was called *Away We Go!*, there was a song that he and Dick [Richard Rodgers] wrote called 'Boys and Girls Like

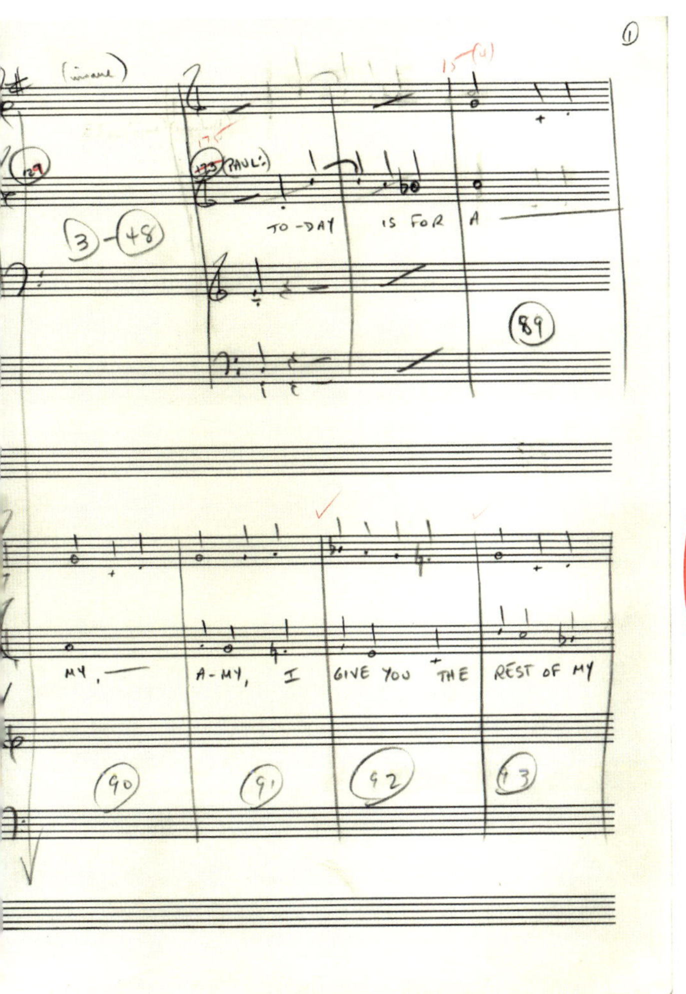

AMY (cont'd)

THANKS A HEAP,
BUT I'M NOT GETTING MARRIED -
GET SOME SLEEP,
'CAUSE I'M NOT GETTING MARRIED -
AND DON'T TELL PAUL,
BUT I'M NOT GETTING MARRIED TODAY!

GO -
CAN'T YOU GO?
WHY IS NO-
BODY LISTENING?
MY GOD,
IT'S DE SADE
AT HIS MOST SADISTIC PEAK.
I MEAN IT'S SUN-
DAY, SO RUN,
FIND A NUN
OR A CHRISTENING -
DO SOMETHING CLEAN,
GO HEAR FULTON SHEAN
SPEAK.
I KNOW THIS

IS A VERY PRETTY LITTLE
CHAPEL HERE, WELL ACTUALLY WE
THOUGHT OF PRESBYTERIAN BUT
PAUL YOU KNOW IS JEWISH AND MY
MOTHER IS A CATHOLIC SO
SYNAGOGUES WERE OUT WHICH IS BE-
SIDE THE POINT SINCE ANYWAY THE
WHOLE THING IS RIDICULOUS, CON-
SIDERING WE'VE LIVED TOGETHER
NEARLY SEVEN YEARS I WISH YOU'D
LEAVE BECAUSE I THINK I'M COMING
DOWN WITH HEPATITIS, YOU CAN
COOK THE RICE
'CAUSE I'M NOT GETTING MARRIED -
HE'S TOO NICE,
SO I'M NOT GETTING MARRIED -
YOU"VE BEEN GRAND,
BUT I'M NOT GETTING MARRIED -
DON'T JUST STAND XHEKEX
THERE, I'M NOT GETTING MARRIED
TODAY!

CHOIR

BLESS THIS DAY....(insane, etc.)...

2.

3.

You and Me.' It was the show's big tune—capital BT. You remember that big, big hit songs came out of musicals, right? And this was going to be it. It was in the overture and entr'acte, and then there was a reprise in the second act. And it went in for exactly, I think, one performance in New Haven, and Oscar said, 'Out. It doesn't work, it's holding up the show, blah blah.' I saw this guy throw out what he and his partner thought was the most valuable song in the show. And without qualm, what counts is the show. Anything, no matter how attractive, that holds up or distorts or confuses must go. No tears." He paused. "Oh, sometimes I think, *Oh God, I would love everybody to have heard that rhyme*. But no. It's called Mistake, Erase.'"

We briefly digressed to another song he had to toss, some years later, which reminded him of the "Wedding Is Off" problem: "There was a song I wrote for *A Little Night Music* that never got past the first rehearsal, because when I heard the girl playing Charlotte [the embittered wife of a flagrantly adulterous count], I thought, *No, it's not working*. It suffered from exactly the same thing. It was a song called 'My Husband the Pig.' She's buttering her toast and railing, but it's a different kind of hysteria than Amy's—it's a hysteria of rage. Which makes you yell one minute and then soften."

The Gender Switch We finally got to the new *Company*, the version we were ostensibly meant to talk about. In this production, "Getting Married Today" is sung by a gay man named Jamie, and is set before the wedding rather than at it. Like in the original, it stops the show. I had wanted to discuss the changes Sondheim had to make to the song to accommodate the switch, but in fact they were few. Basically he just had to solve two key rhymes from the original to eliminate the word *wife*: *Pinnacle of life* becomes *pinnacle of joy* so he could rhyme *boy unites with boy*. And originally, Amy's soon-to-be-husband sings, "Amy I give you the rest of my life . . . Today is for Amy / my happily / soon-to-be / wife." But again, no wife for Jamie. So Sondheim completed the stanza with "Today is for Jamie, my lover, my partner, my life." Not the most felicitous Sondheim lyric, but it got the job done.

What else? Well, *lunch* becomes *brunch* at one point. But that's about it. As you compare the gender-switched *Company* with the original, you see that though there were some jokes he had to lose, rearrangements of who sang what songs, and some surgical interventions that were necessary here and there, the musical core of the show was pretty nearly exactly as he wrote it, even with such a drastic reinterpretation. In a sense (and maybe, as a wild Sondheim fan, I am overstating this), Sondheim's work is as durable as Shakespeare's. Its emotional power is so strong it can withstand manipulation (sometimes wrongheaded, sometimes illuminating) by even the most ambitious of directors.

Solving Problems I was reminded of my early encounter with the music, and the way it worked for me even divorced from its context. And I kept thinking about his method. His songs were written to animate a situation the book writer created, so why should they work independently of it?[3] The playwright posed a riddle. Sondheim nailed an answer. That was the gist.

As I listened to him, I could almost see him work, jumping from piano to couch—number two pencil in his hand—solving problems. That's how he had set the scene for me. Sondheim was famously, fiercely attracted to puzzles of all kinds, and was very good at them. As it happens, he was *New York* magazine's first puzzle constructor, a piece of trivia I've always marveled at. He loved a game (at an early age, he even flirted with becoming a magician). For a game to be satisfying to him, its problems had to be complicated, but still with an available solution. He used puzzles as a metaphor for art making. He was fascinated by the "puzzle of music," he said; once immersed in the music, the "puzzle takes over."

Sondheim described himself as a great mimic, and he was. He was brilliant at pastiche, adaptive, an expert technician. But how did he translate those skills into feeling? How did the adept arrangement of language and notes transmute into the very powerful something that "come[s] through," to borrow one of his *Company* lyrics?

This question had been bugging me. Artists solve problems, of course. People solve problems. It's what they do. But in this conversation, the very cool way Sondheim described his work was at such a distance from the psychological intensity of the music itself. I found myself wondering, *Does the right brain know what the left brain is doing? Does it have to?* By Sondheim's account, he solved the equation he'd settled on for the song, and if he had done it correctly, he seemed to trust that he would unleash what was underneath. "'Art' in itself is an attempt to bring order out of chaos," he has said. But with him, the disconnect between the order and chaos seemed especially pronounced.

What was especially striking to me about Sondheim was how he twinned his meticulous precision with a remarkable flexibility. He was open and not defensive about his work, whether subjecting it to his own scrutiny or the shaping of others. In the case of this new production of *Company*, he was approached by the director Marianne Elliott, whose previous work he'd admired. "I said, 'All right, I don't know if this will work,' and she said, 'I'll tell you what: let me do a little workshop of the piece.' And in the audience was a woman of about Bobbie's age that I know well, a producer. I just wanted to get her reaction, and she said, 'I absolutely get it, And I think it's a swell idea.' And then Marianne told me that at the workshop, there was a guy running the camera, who didn't know the show. And when he was packing up, he said to her, 'Tell me about this show,' and he said, 'You mean it worked with a guy?' "

3. Of course, this is true for the many songs from musicals that became standards, sung on their own. Many of Sondheim's songs became standards as well—"Send in the Clowns" from *A Little Night Music*, "Being Alive" from *Company*. Whole cabaret acts—entire theater revues—have been built around Sondheim's decontextualized songs.

And so Sondheim was in. In the new version, "Getting Married Today" was particularly successful, played as farce but with the heart of it intact. The London Jamie won an Olivier; the New York Jamie won a Tony. "The Amy scene," said Sondheim, "you have to be carried out. What more can you ask?"

He was genuinely excited to see his work played with: "How can you write for the theater and not? What keeps theater alive is that it can be reinterpreted. I've often said the problem with movies is the performances are perfect, but always the same." He was an easy audience. He was thrilled with plenty of imaginative (sometimes overly imaginative) versions of his work: "I've never been appalled."

Textbook So here you have an almost platonic model of a creative person, as described by the creativity theorists: an otherworldly access to his imagination; a rigor with his own method, hard on himself but not punishing; with a contortionist's flexibility.

If you know something about his biography, you might push the point even further. He had a monstrous mother, both seductive and mean—she wrote an often-quoted letter to him at one point saying her only regret was giving birth to him. His father left his mother (and, to some extent, him) when he was ten. He described himself as growing up without parents. The divorce was when he developed his passion for games—for problems with solutions. He was a precocious pianist. He liked the structure of music. He sought order from the chaos of his life.

And into this virtual orphanhood stepped Oscar Hammerstein. The grown-up famous lyricist taught the vulnerable and eager child what he knew. Hammerstein gave the young Sondheim a near-perfect vehicle to redirect his pain. Eventually, the protégé's power would exceed his mentor's.

It's a creativity fairy tale (which might, by the way, make a pretty good Sondheim musical), and an armchair psychologist might say it explains a lot.

But is it fair? Foolish? Why even try to figure out how he could do what he did? I am drawn to his biography because in a way it lives out my own fantasy. Yet maybe it's impossible to account for his powers, to solve Sondheim's own puzzle. Whatever his makeup, it worked. Even to his last days, he was writing new material. And even after having accomplished everything anyone could hope to accomplish, he didn't need directors to reimagine his work—he was constantly fiddling with it himself. I asked him whether he returned to old songs he had trouble solving, years later. "It happens all the time. I'm walking around and I say, *I've got it.* If you're trying, it doesn't work. But if you're doing something else, you suddenly think, *Oh, I know what that should have been. That would have been much better.*"

And with that, we were done. It had been a hilarious conversation because it was interrupted over and over by my technological fumbles with the tape and, because he was an old man on a diuretic, by his persistent need to excuse himself to pee. At one point, we reconnected, and he said,

"I'm still here."

I cracked up. If you're a Sondheim fan, you know why. But now it makes me sad.

9
LOUISE GLÜCK
Waiting

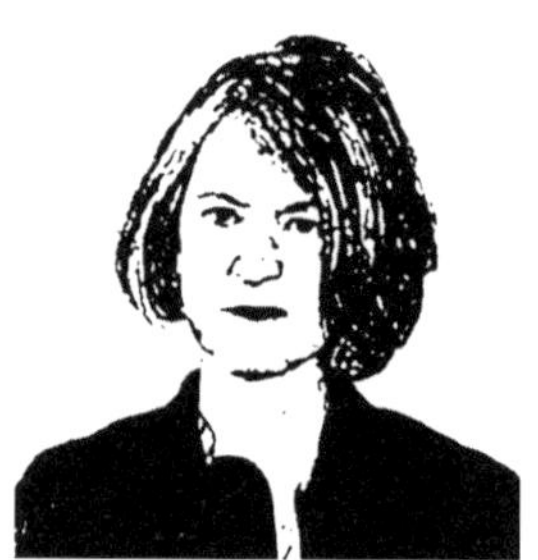

OCCUPATION: Poet

WORK DISCUSSED: "Song" (2020)

BORN: 1943; DIED: 2023

WHEN LOUISE GLÜCK won the 2020 Nobel Prize in Literature, fellow poet Dan Chiasson described in *The New Yorker* the general exaltation that greeted the news. "The reasons for the widespread joy are both simple and deep," he said. "Simple, because Louise Glück is a great writer who deserves the prize. Her work is thrilling and surprising; it's both intimate and grand; she appeals to people who read only poetry and to people who read almost no poetry. . . . Her poems are anathema to easy comfort, and often seem to ban or forbid the going and conventional emotional logic. And yet people read them to know the contours of their own inner lives." I'm in the category of people who read little poetry. Yet I respond to her directness, her astringent, surprising language turns, and also her humor; and like Chiasson says, they help me understand myself better. Her poems feel effortless—and I wanted to understand the effort that makes them so.

Louise Glück was born in 1943 and died some time after we spoke. Her father was a businessman and, according to her obituary, a frustrated poet. She grew up in the Long Island cluster of villages known as the Five Towns, where I also grew up—a nouveau-riche suburb that always reminded me of the setting of Philip Roth's *Goodbye, Columbus*. Louise described the place beautifully to me as full of people "with that profound ignorance that expresses itself as contentment." It is hard to believe such a sensitive artist could emerge from such a place.[1]

Her parents—mother especially—encouraged her artistic interests, which showed up early. She was, she says in her introspective essay "Education of the Poet," "encouraged in every gift. If we hummed we got music lessons. If we skipped, dance. And so on." She wrote poetry and painted. Before long, she quit painting. "As a painter I could see the limits of my talent," she said to me. "And I could see that I was only going to do

1. I know I'm a little tough on my hometown, but the context of an artist's upbringing does affect her development, doesn't it? How could Louise Glück have grown up in the Five Towns? For her biographer to ponder.

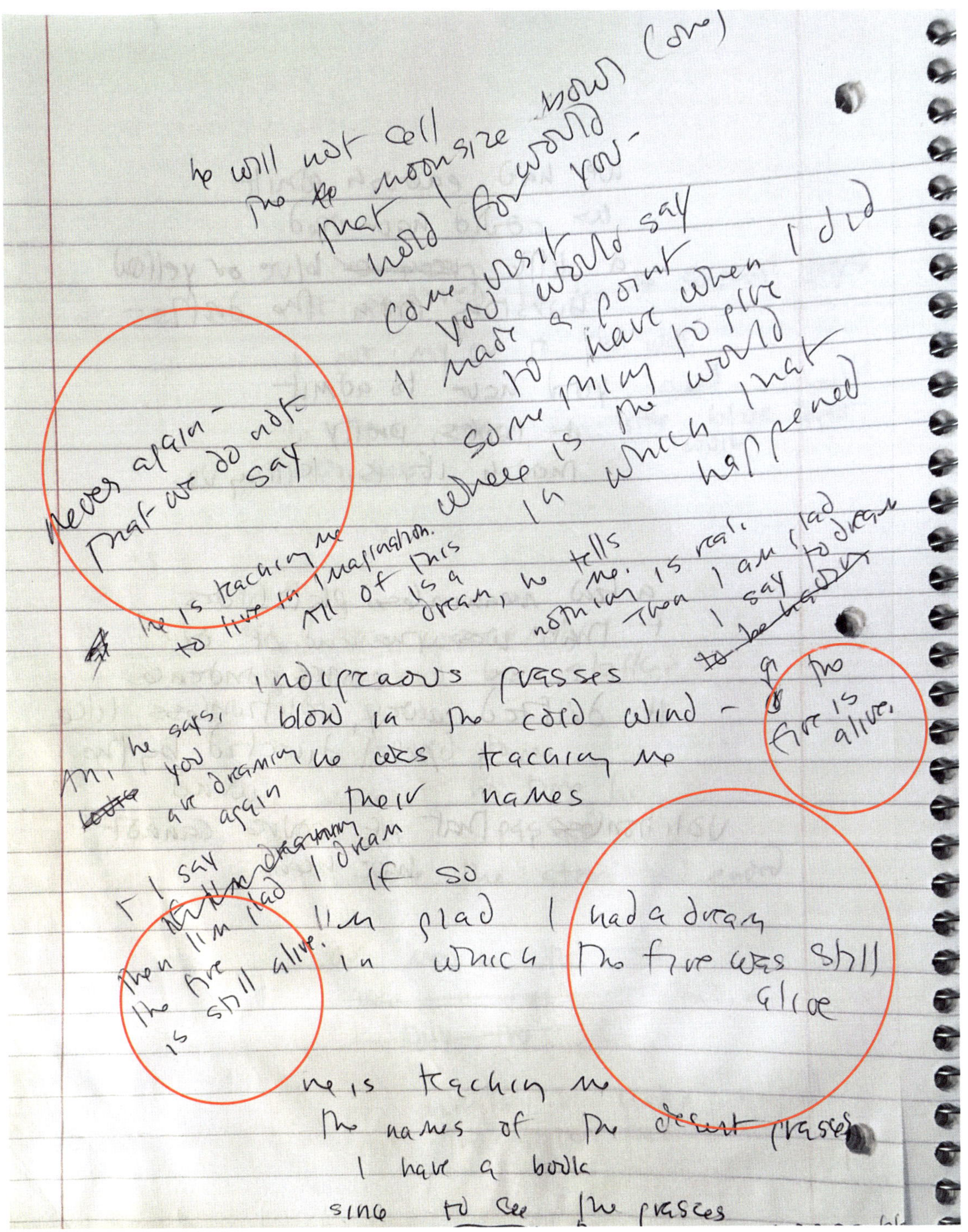

Rehearsing lines for "Song," including the crucial "never again-that we do not say," which became "Never again: that is what we do not say" in the poem itself, and the poem's concluding line, "the fire is still alive"-with the "still" coming and going in her notes.

conventional work. And somehow with writing, I didn't see the limit. Once you see the limit of your gift, it's very hard to work. The thing you want is out of the question; it's been removed from the equation." From "Education of the Poet": "Writing answered all sorts of needs. I wanted to make something. I wanted to finish my own sentences. And I was sufficiently addicted to my mother's approval to want to shine at something she held in high esteem. When I wrote, our wishes coincided."

When writing, she felt confident. There are many other contexts in which she didn't. A crucial part of her life story involves the acute anorexia she experienced as an adolescent, which caused her to leave high school before she was finished. She underwent intense psychoanalysis and chose Sarah Lawrence to go to school because it was close enough to her analyst that she could still lie on the couch four times a week. "And then I just started starving myself so I would be taken out of school," she said to me. "It worked like a charm." She was eager to get going. She published her debut volume of poems, *Firstborn*, in 1968, when she was twenty-five.

For our conversation, she chose "Song," from her book *Winter Recipes from the Collective*, the poem she described as having unlocked the volume and a poem she also happened to like quite a bit. She sent me some fragments that showed her working out the poems on shreds of paper and in her notebook. We looked at them as we spoke. I was intimidated to talk to her, because of the sternness of the voice in many of her poems (and in our correspondence. This was at a point in the pandemic when most communication was on Zoom. I offered a link. The response: "No. Zoom. Ever." She agreed to speak to me only if she could rewrite passages of her own speech that didn't meet her precise standards). Also, I happen to know a lot of people who were afraid of her. But she was quick to disabuse the idea that she is as forbidding as many think, and in fact I found her delightful. We talked about "Song," and—mostly, as I reflect on our conversation—about waiting.

A Line in a Dream

Adam Moss: *Let's just start chronologically. How did this poem begin for you?*

Louise Glück: I didn't remember until I looked at those pages I sent you. But then I did recall something about its origins. There's that piece of paper in the notebook that says, "Leo Cruz has white bowls, I think I must get some to you." Those lines appeared to me in a dream. I remember waking up and writing them down and thinking, *This is a gold mine*. Though there's nothing distinguished about the sentence. The language is very plainspoken. And of course it was altered in the final version. But I had a sense when I woke up that day that I had something on the line—some very large fish was toying with me under the water.

AM: *Do you know why?*

LG: I think that it was partly the proper name.[2] I know no one by that name. Nobody knows who Leo Cruz is. And if no one knows who he is, no one knows where to find him. So there was that sense of something—or someone—who exists, but you can't get to him, you can't find him. And obviously this is a poem written during COVID, with all the terror and longing of that time. But I didn't want to write a poem that was explicit; I wanted more of a parable. And I saw something in those two lines about what the last year and a half has been. And the poem developed from them. There were a lot of false leads. But you write them all down because you don't know what will, despite its present clumsiness, actually be the most important element of the poem. So that's how it began. And early on I got the last line. It had to do with the kiln—the fire's still alive. I was very excited about that line too. So then I had two pieces.

AM: *And at that point you knew what the poem was about?*

2. As she was talking to me, I noticed that a line in her notebook (you can see it) identifies the character as Lucas Cruz, not Leo. "Is Leo the one that came to you in the dream?" I asked. "No, I must have changed it," replied Louise. I asked why. She thought for a moment. "I think I wanted something that would sound more Southwestern, or Spanish. And Lucas Cruz? The *s* and *z* repeated each other. And Leo doesn't sound as arbitrarily named. Not that I went through that laborious thought process."

LG: Most people who have talked about this book talk about its gloom, its grimness. But that to me is not what it is at all. It's a survival manual: *The fire is still alive.* It isn't about survival as in trudging up a slow incline, hopelessly. It's about survival as a kind of triumph, which is how I see it.

AM: *You had written all the other poems in the book before this, right?*

LG: All but one. The very last poem added was the poem called "Second Wind," which is a smaller poem, an afterthought. As I was putting the book together, I felt that it had a contribution to make. But "Song" was the poem that let me see that I had a book. Until I wrote it, I just had poems that sort of went together.

AM: *What was it about "Song" that made the rest of it make sense to you?*

LG: It made a turn; it was tonally different from the existing poems. It complicated them. Initially I used punctuation because I like punctuation. But the effect here was wrong. Without punctuation the lines somehow released into the air. They float. They linger.

AM: *My experience of "Song" is that it's the most hopeful in the book—the fire of the imagination in its glory. Was that your sense too?*

LG: Oh, absolutely. I mean, despite everything in the dream, the fire is still alive. The belief in the fire survives all of these impossibilities: you can't see Leo Cruz again, you can't have white bowls, you can't see the desert grasses. But you have a book and can live in imagination. And that's not nothing.

AM: *The power of imagination shows up in several other poems in the volume.*

LG: I think so too. And that's why I think of this book as not a dirge. [I laugh.]

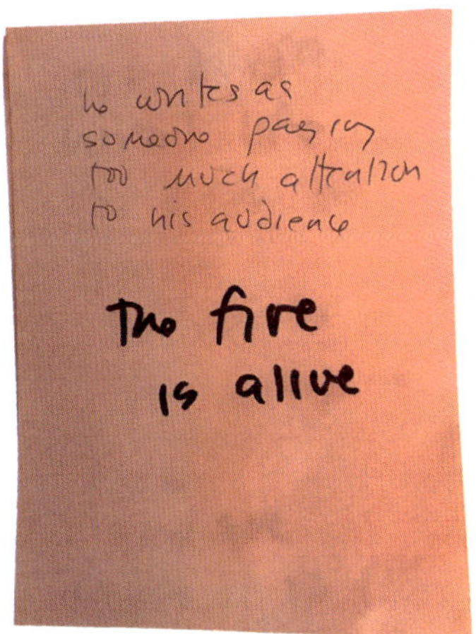

Again: "The fire is alive," scrawled on a note she was writing during a faculty meeting.

Fragment Before Sequence

AM: *Let's go back to the writing of "Song." You had the first line after you woke up from the dream, and then soon after you had the last line. Did you start making practical steps toward turning it into a poem?*

LG: I don't do it like that.

AM: *Okay.*

LG: I have to have a lot of points in the—call it for want of a better word—narrative line before I can sit down and try to play out the progression, the sequence in which things occur. And even then, once I have a draft, that sequence might change. But at the very beginning, when I have only a fragment of language or even two pieces that seem related, I just, in a sense, ignore them. But the ignoring allows for a kind of haunting. And so I was haunted by them in that period. Because I couldn't go to the gym and I was taking long walks every day. So strange, Jesus, what a year . . .

I would take my walks and I would almost hum the poem in my head. I had worked out a different version for the opening line: "Leo Cruz makes the most beautiful white bowls." I can hardly explain to you why I so love that line. But I love it. If you recited it to someone they'd say, "What?" but to me it was one of the most beautiful lines I had ever written in my life. Partly it was because I saw things in it that had not been realized. I could see them, feel them, even if I didn't know how to give them form. So as I was walking, other phrases began to occur that would flesh out the poem.

I tried writing in my head elaborations of the bowls, what they looked like, but that was just talking. When you do that, you're sort of waiting to write a good line, and then you can actually erase all the intervening lines. You're looking for momentum. And somewhere along the line, I wrote, "never again, that is what we do not say," and it was pivotal. The "never again" absolute is balanced by "that is what we do not say." The idea of "never again" hovers in the air, but the refusal to say it is an unwillingness to capitulate to the absolute. As long as life continues anywhere, life continues.

AM: *It seems to me looking at the notebook pages that one of the things you were working out is how explicit to be at the point Leo Cruz explains the purpose of imagination. In the notes, there's a line "because intention is more moving than effortless splendor."*

LG: Oh God, that's pretty bad. [*laughs*] That became "the things man makes / are more beautiful / than what exists in nature."

AM: *Earlier it was "the things God makes." You substituted nature for God at some point.*

LG: The rhythm of the sentence remained. But initially the sweeping statement (once it was cured of God) was the poem's pronouncement. "Leo thinks" was added later. But as soon as that happened, the theory becomes one person's conviction or wish, one side of an intimate argument. This change showed me how to do the poem as a back-and-forth. Someone is wandering across the desert with a book of grasses, and Leo is somewhere making white bowls. And somehow there is a conversation between them that's either remembered or invented because it is obviously not occurring within the space of the poem. . . .

I liked that the future exists in the poem—we make plans to walk the hills together, or whatever I ended up saying—that was the last bit I figured out. I had a lot of really bad plans.

AM: *Right.*

LG: And I had the whole poem. But I had that clunker in the middle.

AM: *But you knew its function in the poem, right?*

LG: I knew that in order to do the "never again," there had to be a plan. At some point it was "I make plans," or "I plan," or "I tell him I'm going to. . . ." These were all variants. . . .

And then on your long walk—the same walk every day like a prisoner—you repeat these phrases, and sooner or later they get fixed. But you don't feel as though you fixed them; something in your head fixes them.

AM: *I like that.*

LG: And when you get the thing right, you begin to see the shape emerge. And the more the shape emerges, the faster you can work. I begin to see where there are gaps that need filling. I like electric transitions, I don't like charged silence to be filled in with narrative to get you from point A to point B. This poem was written pretty rapidly but for that recalcitrant stanza.

The Assignment

AM: *How rapidly is rapidly?*

LG: Really rapid is a half hour. This was about a week and a half, two weeks. It came, I should say, from an assignment. I had written some poems that summer I thought were very good, like "A Children's Story," and I began to be hopeful about this manuscript. But I felt it needed a tonal element that was not in the book yet. I was in the habit of having iced coffee in the afternoon on my terrace with a very good friend, Sandra Lim, who is an extraordinary poet. So I asked her to give me assignments, because I like them. I like having a task. It takes your mind off having to write. And one part of her assignment that excited me was, write a poem that contains an invitation. And when I got the Leo Cruz line in my dream, it connected right away to Sandra's assignment.

AM: *In what sense?*

LG: I thought, *This is the assignment poem*. The invitation in this poem is the one that can't be made. He can't say, "Come visit me," he can't say, "I want to show you my new bowl." And the other—well, not quite an invitation—is the smoke rising from the desert. It could be ominous but it isn't. It's like signals people make who are lost. *Find me.* That's a kind of invitation.

AM: *These pages that we're looking at, when you take these walks, do you come back to your house and just scribble?*

LG: Sometimes I write things down on the walks. It's important to me not to carry a notebook. If you carry a notebook, the walk becomes too purposeful. I take this magical thinking very seriously.

I was taken out of high school in my senior year because I was acutely anorexic. When I stopped starving myself, I started exercising; I walked all day, literally, every day. I'd stop in at the bakery and borrow a pen and piece of paper. Well, I kept the paper. Because carrying supplies seemed to me dangerous. A jinx. Now I carry a pen. But no notebook. If I write something down, I write on a receipt. When I was eighteen, I could count on remembering. Now I need backup. But I still believe the really good lines will return when they are part of something. There's something in your head that doesn't forget.

AM: *Weeds out the bad and selects the good.*

LG: Well, we like to think so.

AM: *That's a very hopeful idea itself.*

LG: Well, I'm actually very hopeful. I know most of the people who read my poems think I'm not. I mean, I have a very tragic vision of human life but I'm very optimistic in the short term. And I like to have a good time. No one would believe this. But it's true. [I laugh.]

On these walks, I would try different ways of using the desert grasses. I really wanted to use the word *indigenous*. But I couldn't figure out how. And so that didn't get in the poem.

AM: *Why that word?*

LG: I thought it was precise, elegant. I like directness. I'm not interested in opulence.

AM: *What you described, getting a first line and a last line and filling in the middle, is that typical?*

LG: It's not uncommon. When I was very young, I used to have the end always. And I had no idea where to begin to get to it. Then I realized you could take a last line and make it a first line. So that gave me another strategy. I do tend to write a lot of last lines. But the other thing that would happen to me commonly is that I would write a couple of stanzas and then I'd hit a wall. And it was clear something new had entered the poem, but I could not find what I needed. And then sometimes

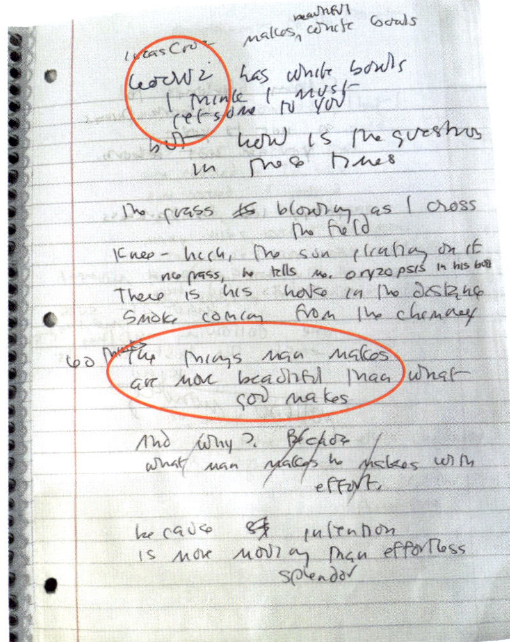

More notes for "Song," toggling between Lucas and Leo. Down the page, "God" was eventually banished.

other people can help. They can say, "Try this."

AM: *Do you show people fragments of a poem?*

LG: Never fragments. But if I get to an impasse on something that seems sufficiently developed, then I would show it to someone.

AM: *You have confidantes who help you in this way? Allies?*

LG: I've always had—*allies* is a nice word for it.

AM: *I recently read "Education of the Poet," which is a really beautiful essay. Can I ask you to elaborate on a couple of paragraphs from that essay?*

LG: We can try.

Two-Year Wait

AM: *Okay, when you describe how a poem begins, you say, "Always there seems something ahead, the next poem or story, visible at least apprehensible, but unreachable. To perceive it at all is to be haunted by it; some sound, some tone becomes a torment." Let's start there.*

LG: That essay was written a really long time ago, but it's still true for me. One example would be the opening lines of "The Wild Iris": "At the end of my suffering / there was a door." That line came to me like Leo Cruz—just there it was. And it was so potent, and so beautiful. And it was a period when I wasn't writing at all. There are many periods like that. But this was pretty early on. Initially I was enthralled, euphoric. I thought, *What a gorgeous line, what an amazing poem this is going to be*. But then I didn't know what the condition was out of which the line was spoken. It had a kind of finality that precluded development. So my euphoria turned into torment. It took me two years to begin to write the poem, of which that is the first line. And during those two years I would wake up in the morning, and the first thing in my head would be "at the end of my suffering / there was a door." And then I would try to get away from it, because it had become a taunt. Here I am, but you can't find me. And then the last moment before I went to sleep I'd hear it again. There was about a year and a half of utter misery because I felt I had a vein of gold and I didn't know how to get to it. And then I started writing the poems that became "The Wild Iris."[3] And I suddenly knew how to do something that might work for that line.

AM: *The essay continues with "That's my sense of the poem's beginnings. What follows is a period of more concentrated work, so-called because as long as one is working the thing itself is wrong or unfinished: a failure. Still, this engagement is absorbing as nothing else I have ever in my life known." Is absorbing the same as happy making?*

LG: No. But it's kind of better. The whole of the self is utterly engaged in something that seems more important than anything in the world.

AM: *And is that—*

LG: One of my former husbands remarked that when I had a good day writing, I looked like a Catholic who had seen the pope.

AM: [*laughs*]

LG: So.

AM: *Can we fill this in? You write these things on scraps of paper or in your notebook. There must be some point when you sit down and make a formal draft.*

LG: No, it doesn't go like that. Because every poem is written differently. Some elements recur. But every poem has its own story. Some

FINAL

SONG

Leo Cruz makes the most beautiful white bowls;
I think I must get some to you
but how is the question
in these times

He is teaching me
the names of the desert grasses;
I have a book
since to see the grasses is impossible

Leo thinks the things man makes
are more beautiful
than what exists in nature

and I say no.
And Leo says
wait and see.

We make plans
to walk the trails together.
When, I ask him,
when? Never again:
that is what we do not say.

He is teaching me
to live in imagination:

a cold wind
blows as I cross the desert;
I can see his house in the distance;
smoke is coming from the chimney

That is the kiln, I think;
only Leo makes porcelain in the desert

Ah, he says, you are dreaming again

And I say then I'm glad I dream
the fire is still alive

poems are written in ten minutes; with those, there are no distinctions among stages. And those poems are usually the best—they have seamlessness and a wildness usually. You try to make the others sound like that. But I only make a draft when I've got the tone in my head. And a sense of key transitions. It's different every time, but it usually involves at some point the moving of a stanza or stanzas so that things that occur at the beginning get moved to the end or the middle. . . .

AM: *Is there a phase where you encounter a recurring difficulty? Something that trips you up over and over?*

LG: No, the only recurring thing is that sense of frustration when I have no idea what to do next.

AM: *What do you do in that moment to help yourself?*

LG: I just wait. For me, the really hard thing about writing is how much patience you need to have. I mean, you can will things, but whenever I've tried to do that, the poem just goes to hell. Becomes a contrivance. An arrangement made with a mind instead of a discovery. If you want a discovery that will surprise you, too, you just have to wait.

AM: *Most people I've talked to describe that dormant period as torture. But you seem more accepting. Is that correct?*

LG: No, it's not. The discovery of the line is thrilling. The period of waiting is not. I am despondent and tormented. And I feel doomed. It's terrible. But I don't react to those feelings by trying to eliminate them through diligence or intelligence, because what's needed is not diligence or intelligence. What's needed is an intervention of something outside yourself, better than yourself, but with access to yourself.

AM: *You think of it as otherworldly.*

LG: I do.

AM: *That's interesting to me because you've spent so many years in psychoanalysis*[4] *and yet you don't think of it as uncovering something in your subconscious, as I would have thought. In your writings you sometimes use the word* gift. *How do you understand that gift—divine, luck, something your parents gave you?*

LG: Well, it's so intermittent that it certainly doesn't seem like something I have. The gift I have is stubbornness. And patience. And kind of good taste, I guess you could say.

Backward and Forward

AM: *How do you use notebooks generally—as a way to work out your thoughts?*

LG: It's more peculiar than that. I never kept diaries. Twenty years ago, I had a whiplash injury. And at that time I had a physical trainer. And she said, "Get a notebook and write in it every day. And you'll discover that you're not in as much pain as you think." But that wasn't the case. I discovered that things were worse than I knew. And so I started this journal, which was a long sustained wail about the body. And after I'd done this for a year, strange things started to happen. In the early years of my whiplash anguish, I wasn't writing at all. And then I found that when I was up at night writing in my pain journal, I would get a line for a poem. But I didn't want it to get mixed up in the text of the journal. So the journal would begin [from the front]. But the poem lines, I would start on the last page. And the two things met in the middle. And it made writing the poems very peculiar because as you were working forward in time you were actually turning pages backward.

AM: *Do you still work your notebook backwards?*

LG: Yes. Because it's the only way I know to keep the two separate. I never knew when I was writing lines how fertile a period it was going to be. Last summer, when I wrote the book really fast, in three weeks, my notebook has only about five pages of complaint, and the rest of it is writing.

AM: *Do you consider that progress?*

LG: I consider that a miracle.

3. *The Wild Iris* is one of her more celebrated volumes. "A lot of the lines in *The Wild Iris* came from my teenage poems, they were just reclaimed," she said. "In high school, I wrote things with gorgeous lines," she said. "But the poems were idiotic. I think the first thing I ever wrote where I could see I'd made a leap was a poem called 'Cottonmouth Country.' It's really the only good poem in *Firstborn*."

4. Since she was so well versed in psychoanalysis, and Freud seems to come up so often in these conversations, I asked if she would describe writing poetry as a product of free association. She said it was just the opposite. "Free association is a plummet. The more you do it, the worse it gets. But when writing is happening rapidly, you're climbing to heaven. You're in paradise."

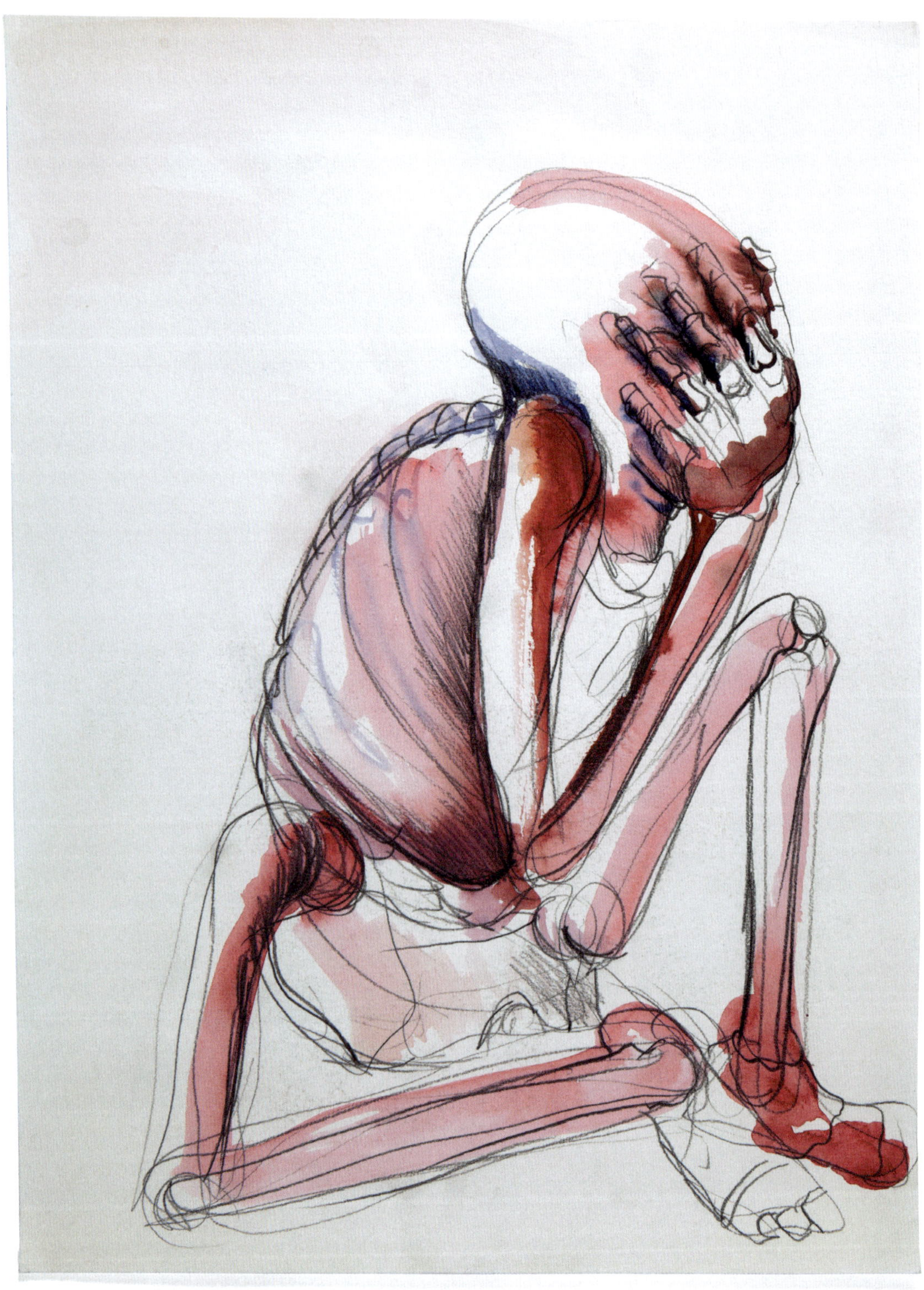

One of the larger drawings (18 × 24 in.) from *True North*.
It hangs in my living room.

10

MARIA de LOS ANGELES

You're Never Going to Be Someone Else

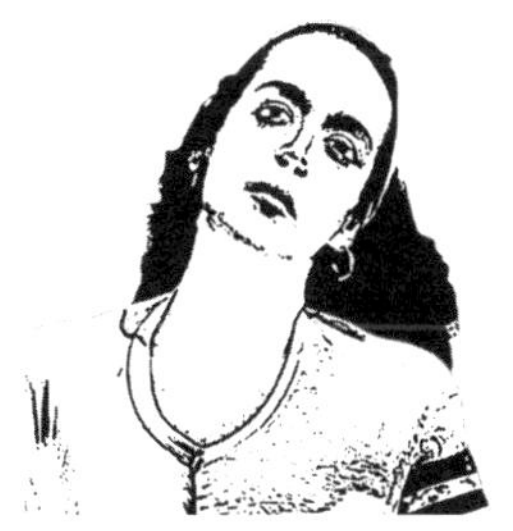

OCCUPATION: Visual Artist

WORK DISCUSSED: *True North*

BORN: 1988

WHEN MARIA DE LOS ANGELES was around eleven, her mother brought her and her siblings to Tijuana, Mexico, where they waited for a stranger in a minivan. Eventually, a woman arrived. Maria and her sisters were drugged. They crossed the border passed out in the back of the van, impersonating the woman's children, who had papers. Maria's mother followed, after a border crossing in the desert on foot with a smuggler.

As an artist, Maria has grappled with how to tell her story—or, more generally, its larger context: the story of illegal migration from Mexico to the United States. The way forward has not always been clear to her and has been mixed up with her own evolution in which art itself has played such an extraordinary role, as a language she could speak when she knew little English, and a buoy to hold on to in scary waters. Maria is also my teacher and friend. I have known her since she graduated from the Yale School of Art and was looking for students. She is wiry, with long black hair draping her slender frame—frenetic and resolutely upbeat. She frequently texts me, asks me how my art is going, shows me pictures of whatever she's making. Her personality has always been a mystery to me—she's one of the kindest people I know, but she has a steely, relentless determination. One day, we were sitting in her basement studio talking about her anguish over this migration work she just couldn't make. I'd pressed her about it—how an artist wrestles with frustration was something we talked about a lot, and it is one of the themes I kept circling back to in these visits because I felt so crippled by it.[1] On this day, she thought she had maybe finally found a solution she wanted to show me, so that's what we were doing, sorting through hundreds of drawings she had yanked from boxes.

Very few of the drawings referenced her personal history specifically, but in a sense they all did. Upon arrival in the US, the family

1. Because she is my teacher and I'm obsessed with figuring out how to motor through my own feelings of failure, I fear I may have dragged her into these conversations about frustration. I *think* these feelings are also real for her, and she wasn't just trying to be nice by identifying with me. But she is so generous that I'm not sure.

made its way up the coast of California, ending up in Santa Rosa. They'd done all right in Mexico, but the US pulled at them as it has for so many, and they pushed north. They worked the fields as migrants; her father eventually found work in construction. Maria spoke only Spanish, and was enrolled in the seventh grade, though she had never made it past the second grade in the small towns in Mexico where she had grown up. The school in California was full of other migrant kids, but also some Hispanic children who had been born in the United States and who resented newcomers like her. The school was rough, with gang violence; she was beaten up. But she drew pictures constantly, as she had drawn in Mexico, and drawing gave her pleasure. It was also a way to communicate, a common language others would understand before she could find the English words. She drew flowers mostly, and made marionettes. One of her teachers bought a drawing, she sold a string puppet, and then, Maria said, "I started to make things that other people would want."

As she got a little older, she'd copy cholo-style images from *Lowrider* magazine. "And then," Maria said, "people would see my sketches, and say, 'Oh this is nice, would you make one for me?' I started making little drawings for people, and people liked me because I was drawing. You know, if someone tried to beat me up, they would be like, 'Don't beat Maria up, she does art. She draws really cool, she's our friend.' I think I saw how people saw me as somebody who drew." And she sold pictures. "I really didn't think about it as talent. I thought of it as, *Oh, I can make fifty bucks*. I didn't have papers, I couldn't have a job."

She felt trapped in a kind of purgatory ("I was upset because there was no way out of my situation"). But she was resourceful and headstrong. She took her own life into her hands. Without even telling her parents, she maneuvered into a wealthier high school with an art program. She saw art as the way out, but it was also, she realized, who she was. She had no formal skills, but people were kind—someone bought her an easel, which she still has. They were moved by her drive[2] and gentle nature and wanted to help. "It was difficult for the teachers because I was so far behind. But one teacher started to teach me—how to use materials, basic painting and stuff." She had no money, but as the other kids went to college, her teachers steered her to Santa Rosa Junior College, a school with a good art department, where she could keep moving. She stretched a two-year program into four, "lingering because I was undocumented" and didn't know where to go. She pushed herself forward. Summers she picked grapes.

She got a job assisting an architect-designer couple who were untroubled by her lack of documentation, and moved into their house. "They helped me a lot," Maria said. "They believed there was such a thing as raw talent, which they didn't think I had. But they said, 'You could fake it.' The wife, who was the designer, showed me how to paint, she taught me about Matisse and Cézanne."

"I applied to schools. I had no money, didn't have any idea how I could pay for it. I got into [the art school] Pratt." A sympathetic financial aid officer to whom she confessed her status promised her money, but not enough. "She made it happen, she got me like twenty-two grand. And I happened to have met this art collector, and he said, 'Maybe we could do a fundraiser.' So I did an art sale, sold my work from Santa Rosa. I sold it all."

Maria thrived at Pratt, and afterward was accepted at the very elite Yale School of Art. But she felt like she was failing. "I thought I was doing bad, got really upset over the critiques. In my years at school, I was really concerned with technical stuff, like is it any good?" She didn't think she was very good. Also, what she was doing felt wrong. "I was being an abstract expressionist, and I guess I wanted to be that, but I wasn't saying what I wanted to say. I just felt burdened by my education."

There was a kind of painting she wanted

2. I was not able to witness the real working habits of most of the book's subjects. But hers, I could: she has a studio near where she lives in Jersey City, and she works *all* the time. I mean constantly, day and night.

to make—political but painterly, Mexican inflected; symbolic but also cartoonlike—that was a direct expression of who she was, with both her fury and childlike spirit. She has a hard time describing it, but she knew what she wanted to create and couldn't do it. At Yale, she made paintings—in her mind, terrible paintings. She didn't have the skills, the

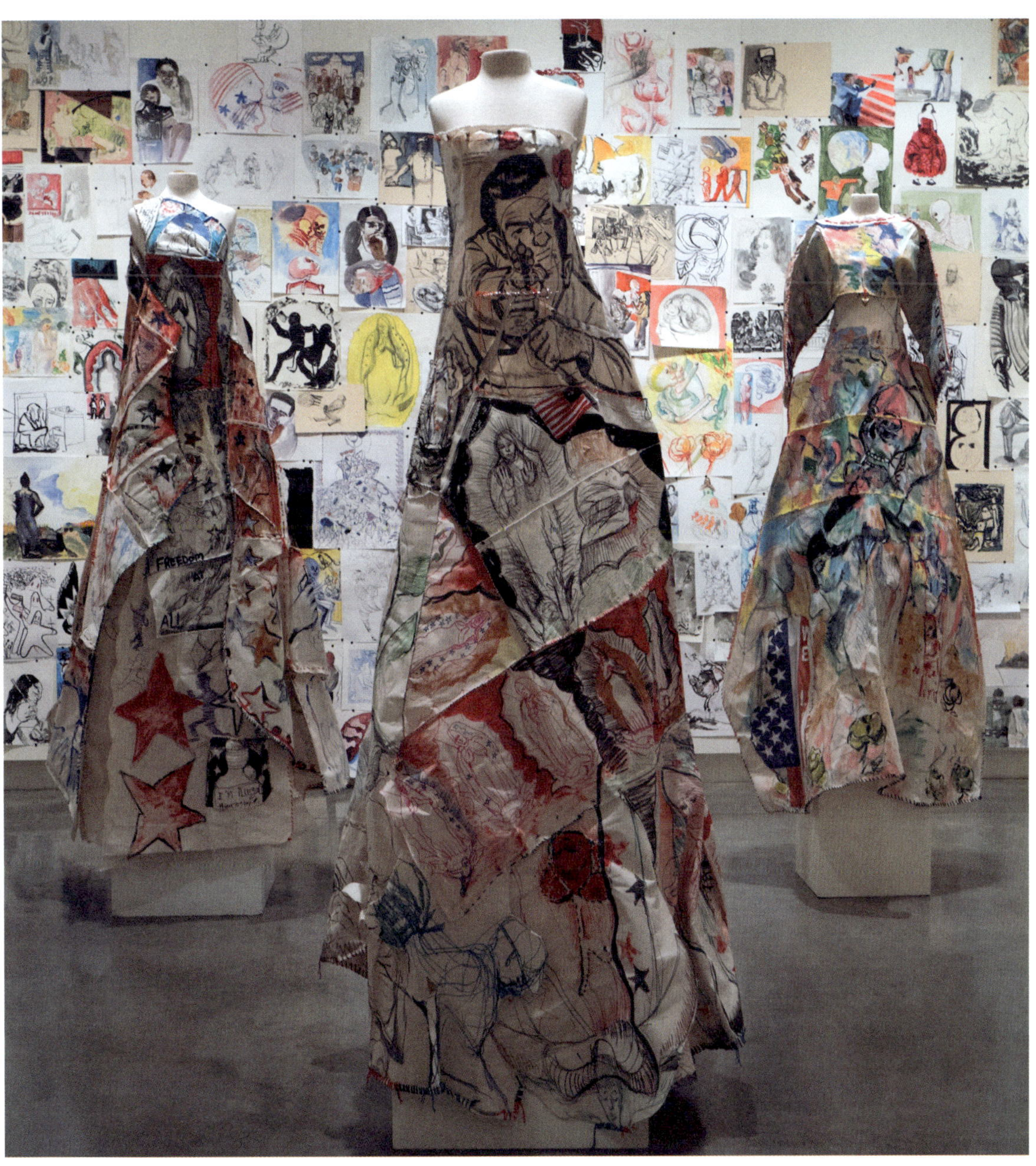

The dresses. Alongside her works on paper at the Schneider Museum of Art in 2018 was this installation of her dresses–what she calls "mixed media identity garment sculptures"–that combine drawing, painting, and collage materials (flags, papers, and metals).

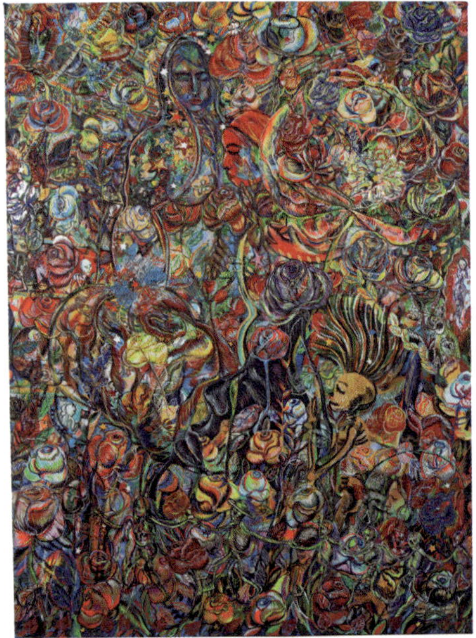

The florals. *Guadalupe y Juan Diego*, 2015-2022, 56 × 76 in.

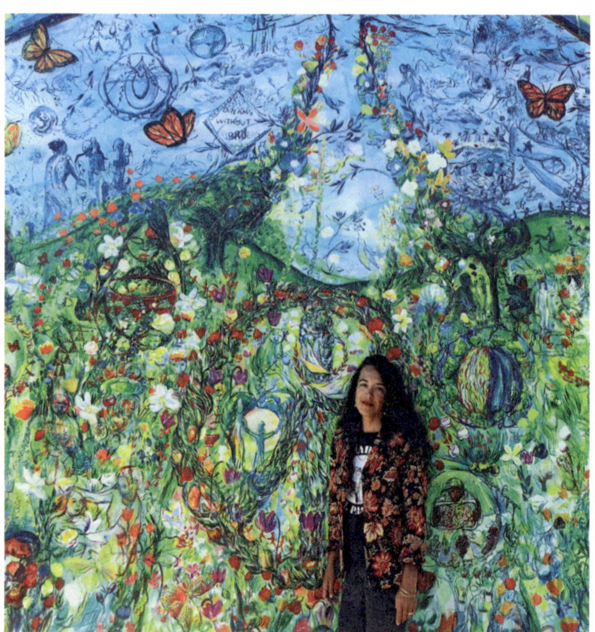

The murals. Maria in front of *Valley of Dreams*, 2021, 12 × 12 ft.

clarity, or the confidence. "I was struggling with so much—how I want to organize the color, how I want the pigment to be layered, whether they're too symbolic, or not direct enough. They just felt so muffled."

At one point, she said, a friend "who was a photography student wanted to do portraits of me of how I saw myself—that was her project—so I dressed myself in textiles from Mexico. I looked like a Frida Kahlo impersonator." But it gave Maria an idea: "I said to her, 'If my work is the closest thing to who I am, why don't I make something to wear for the photo?' And so I just made myself a dress from my work."

The work was a mural she was making, an abstract collage of images dealing with Mexican themes. She took the canvas from the wall and just wore it—fashioned it into a dress for the photograph. And then she made another dress in the same vein on paper.

The dresses were amazing—wearable murals with hand drawings, mostly telling stories in the mural tradition, stretched to reach around and hug the body that's in it. You can see some of her dresses on page 111.

The dresses were just a kind of a lark, an accident. And in the meantime, she was still struggling with her painting.

She was a teaching assistant for a professor she came to think of as a mentor.[3] "I told him I was having a really hard time telling my story. I had to tell him that I grew up undocumented, kind of hiding, in secret. I wrote the whole storyline of my family. I couldn't make a painting. I failed every time. I had these cloud-like people appearing from the sky, but I wasn't able to take it farther than that. He told me I should stop trying to summarize it as a painting, and start drawing."

Since childhood, Maria had

3. It's worth noting how much the kindness of strangers plays into this account. Maria is the sort of person you just want to help, which is, in and of itself, helpful.

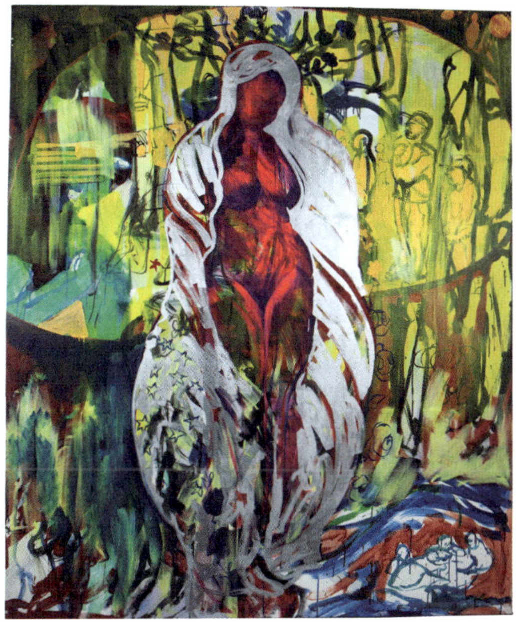

“I am just so embarrassed by it.” This is the Yale painting she regarded as a failure, though she subsequently painted over it and likes it okay now.

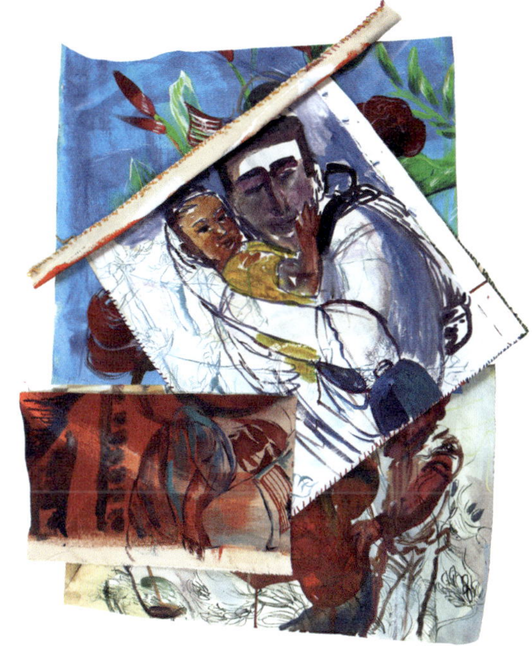

Destroy, create. A work in progress from the shards of her old Yale paintings.

always felt freest when she drew; the images tumbled from her without inhibition. So she followed his advice and drew at a frenzied pace. She couldn’t imagine what to do with the work that resulted.

The Paintings She Couldn’t Paint Maria is a stampede. Her affect is vulnerable and at times insecure, but her optimism propels her forward at a furious clip.

She graduated from Yale. She continued to make the drawings. She found a painting style that worked for her, but they still were not the paintings she said she was trying to paint—these were bright, exploding with color, very rich, gorgeous, floral paintings.

The paintings interested collectors. Her work started to sell. They showed in museums. She got commissions for paintings and giant murals at schools and public places.

And she returned to the dresses. The dresses were helping her get closer to the story she wanted to tell. I happen to love the dresses especially. At the time I became her student, she was hard at work on them, and they have continued to progress. “Eventually I incorporated trim that looks like lace, and now it has evolved into incorporating other objects—found objects like American flags, not just hand-painted on them. And I began to add words. I moved from canvas to recycled materials, and these days I’m wanting to make more on paper—do it as a paper-making project, bring out my etching press, then create etchings and prints that become the dress. Like single images.”

You might expect that she’d just settle into these two forms—paintings saturated with color that collectors coveted (and, it should be said, that she liked too), dress-murals that were unique, powerful, and very beautiful; dresses gaining traction in the world, bought by museums, that at one time I thought might be her life's work. But that was not the case. Perhaps everyone has a work that seems, for now, beyond one's grasp, but it particularly tugged at Maria, wouldn't let go. It's hard not to see an immigrant's drive—or need—in her. That might be too easy an analogy in this case, but it seems apt. She has a propulsive energy, as all artists seem to. With her, it is everything.

"At the end of the day, before painting is intellectual, it's physical," she said. "If I'm not drawing or painting, I get really depressed. And I've tried to trick myself around feeling stuck. Being stuck, it's like feeling you cannot really be anything. Painting is an act of faith."

As I moved between artists, I heard this sentiment over and over—deep down, you had to believe you could make the work that eluded you, otherwise you couldn't work. And for all her frustration, Maria believed it.

Attacking Her Work I traced Maria's progress over many months, which makes this something like a sketch of an artist in real time. Progress is straightforward only in retrospect; in the moment it lurches and retreats, tacking several directions at once. One day at her studio—she was thirty-four, and it was now seven years since she graduated—she was shuffling stuff around to make room to lay out her work for me to look at, and she moved a giant canvas out into the hall. But it was facing backward; she wasn't letting me see it. As nicely as I could, I forced her to show it to me. It was one of those Yale paintings she considered a failure. "I am just so embarrassed by it," she said.

The painting was in the studio because she was revisiting the Yale work, or more accurately, she had recently hauled out all the Yale work and sliced the paintings to bits with a knife. "I have rolls and rolls of it. I just cut 'em up."

Plenty of artists destroy what they don't like; almost all painters paint over old canvases or over one mark and then another (I recently heard the artist Tracey Emin describing continually chasing after canvases with a brush as they're physically being removed to her dealer because there's something in them she can't stand), but it impressed me how unsentimental and ruthless Maria was with her own work, attacking it not with anger, but with a sense that destruction leads to creation, eventually.

"That pile of Yale paintings was my struggle with telling a story," she said. She is now married and legal, but the urgency of telling that story has not diminished. "There's a huge disconnect between my drawings and paintings." The drawings were political and personal at the same time—spontaneous and alive. "I've always been secretive about them. They're not made to be sold or anything. They're sort of made for me."

A Book of Drawings At the same time Maria was slicing up her paintings, she was once again circling her trove of drawings. She'd made thousands of pictures, quick five-minute pictures she'd draw on the subway, more complex ones when she had a particular notion. She'd sold all the Santa Rosa pictures to pay for college, and pictures she'd made at Pratt had burned in a fire. But she still had maybe two thousand drawings. She stared them down. Maybe she had devalued them. Were they too easy for her?

In any case, she considered: What if this more private, personal work wasn't just for herself? She wondered, what if she retrieved the drawings from the boxes and tried to turn them into a unique artwork, a handmade book made up of the drawings themselves? And then maybe a limited edition of prints from them—before, perhaps, a bound book that could be reproduced? Would that work? She'd envisioned herself as a painter, but why? Was this the artwork she'd had bottled up inside her?

Drawings were her life, after all. And without trying, she had united the drawings with a common language: skeletons for migrants, a border like a stage set, law enforcement represented by a range of satirical figures. They were coherent. She began wrestling with various considerations—how literal the storytelling ought to be, how symbolic or violent or funny. (She was afraid of letting the project get too dark, but maybe that was wrong—maybe she should allow herself to get more violent?) You can see some of the images, with her thinking, on page 116.

That was the project we had set out to talk about when we were first sitting down for this book. At the time she described this book of drawings, this epic impressionistic migrant saga, as maybe her true passion project. But that focus didn't last long.

When I came back to her studio another day, she had tacked again, back to painting. I've never understood why the distinction between paintings and drawings was so important to her, but it was. Maybe it was because paintings are traditionally valued more than drawings, or maybe it was just that she refused to give up. She's always been stubborn, a colossus of determination in a small body. It's one of the things I love about her.

Now she was thinking that the trick to make that Holy Grail painting that was still in her mind could be found in the freedom she was allowing herself in the drawings. The new paintings she showed me were her first stab at thinking that way—you could see the hand working a little differently—and they were nice.

Then, a couple of weeks later, she texted me yet more paintings, and these she was even more enthusiastic about. These new paintings were made, as it turned out, from the shards of her old Yale paintings. She'd recombined them, collaged them, painted over them. "By the time you come over next week, I should have three or four more of them," she told me. "I'm quite excited about it."

They were interesting too—you could see where she was going. During this period of watching her closely, I could actually see her work sharpen. She was getting braver but also clearer. I had just been in a class she taught where I watched this growth happen in my fellow students.[4] But it was thrilling to see it in the teacher as well.

All of the Above Then on another day, some months later, she was talking about the book again. In the meantime, she had gotten a prestigious teaching gig back at Yale (apparently they didn't think her old work was so terrible) and—here's where circumstances factor in—she was using their print studio to make prints of the drawings. She really liked what was happening. She had even given the book a name—*True North*. And while this renewed enthusiasm was pushing the painting aside, she'd return to it, she said. And to the dresses as well.

This seemed to me a pretty good illustration of the way an artist—any artist—thinks, one idea firing the next, shifting thoughts, conditions, setbacks, leaps, all feeling the way to some elusive destination. By the time anyone reads this, there will no doubt be more efforts on Maria's part to summon the work that lives in her mind's eye. I'm sure each will be interesting, some will be sublime, and together they will get her closer to her vision. But they won't get her there entirely; they can't. She said so herself.

"You're never going to be someone else," she said. I had been expressing impatience with my art again, and she was giving me some advice, but it was also obvious she was talking about herself as well. "There are two people you are. You are the person that you currently are. And then there is the person that you imagine yourself to be.

"As you get older, maybe that other version becomes more distant, and you settle into who you are, maybe not. I'm always in there—sometimes clearly, sometimes muffled. Your struggle is to get clearer. But I don't know that any artist really understands themselves."

4. One day in her studio, I asked her to make a taxonomy of the kinds of students she sees. Obligingly, she broke them into three struggling groups: (1) "those who have a vision of what they want, and their unhappiness is because they're not able to physically achieve that idea—their skills haven't caught up with their ambition; (2) students who do not know what they want, but they're in touch with their feelings and play, even though they don't know where their experiments are going—as a teacher I have to pressure them to deliver their idea and (3) those who are always questioning, and for them it's more about confidence." I found this breakdown helpful, and asked what kind of student I am. She copped out and said, "Oh my God, all of them." At that point her husband, Ryan, who is a photographer and serious skateboarder, entered the room. He joined the conversation as I asked my usual question: What do artists who succeed have in common? "They're driven," said Ryan, looking at his wife. "They're *really* driven."

"When I was in school, I wanted to make a mural of my drawings," said Maria. "I plastered the walls of my studio with them. I liked how they were not in order—a person could choose the order. Once you put them on the wall, then they come down, and that's it. So that's how eventually I got to the book.

"The overall story of the two thousand drawings is migration. It's made of family clusters, spiritual guides, Lady Liberty, Lady Guadalupe, symbolic people. On the opposite side is the law—border patrol, cops, politicians. People walk in and out of the frame. Some tend to be more violent, and I want some of them to be kind of cute. I collage pieces of paper, create mini storylines.

"I thought about the border as a line. The skeletons aren't morbid—they're more of the Mexican kind, waiting, always crossing, and getting kind of lost. I rejected human features—they're too real. Too traumatizing, I guess.

"I just draw what comes to mind. There are real moments and there are imagined moments. Sometimes I'll get an idea and it'll just be there. And then sometimes I'll try to draw it a few times until I get it."

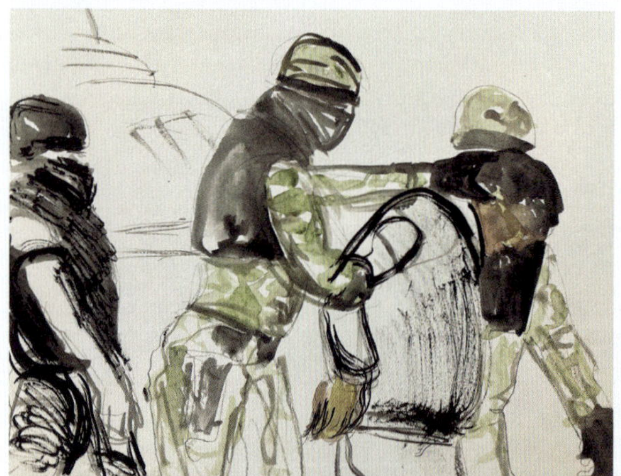

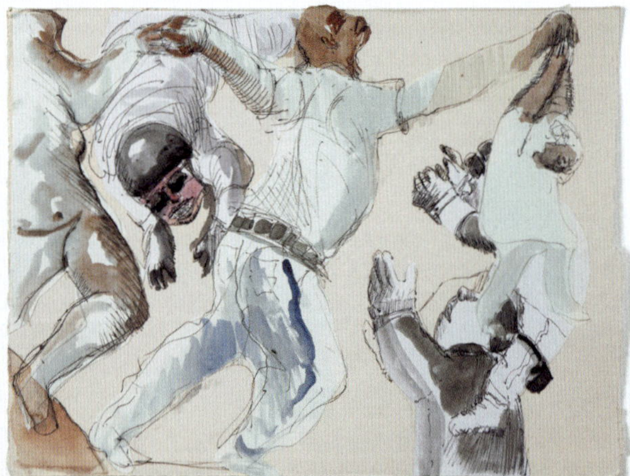

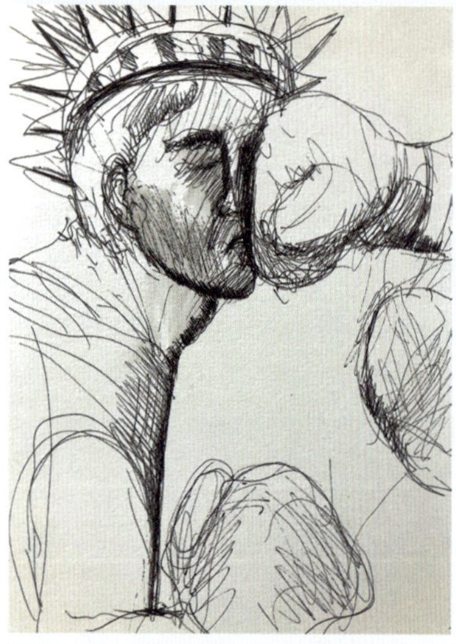

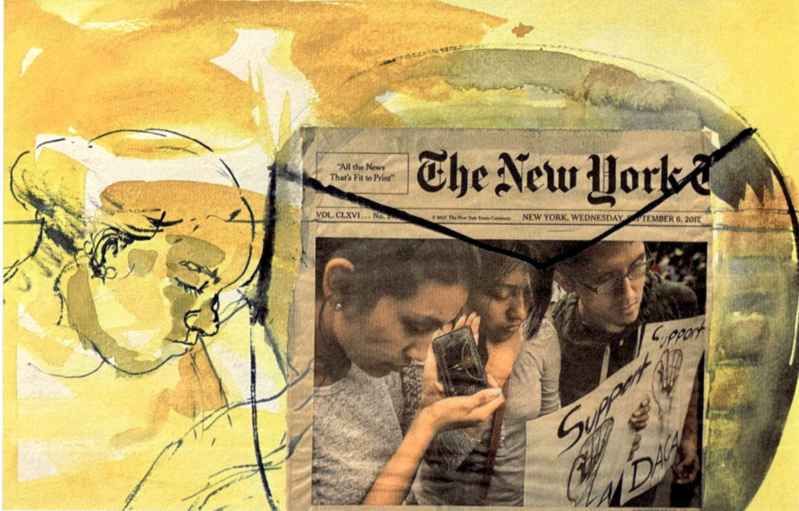

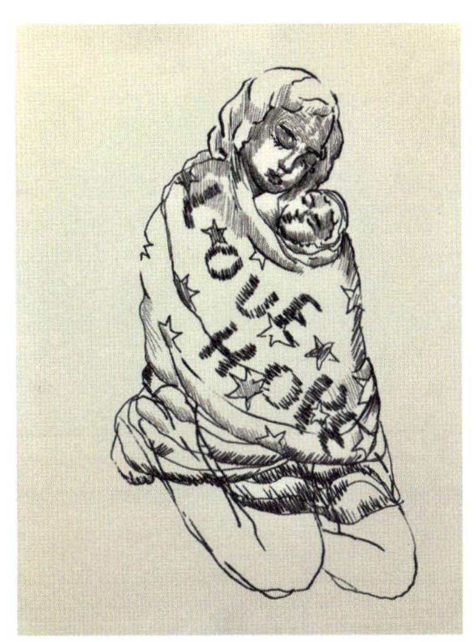
LOVE
HOPE

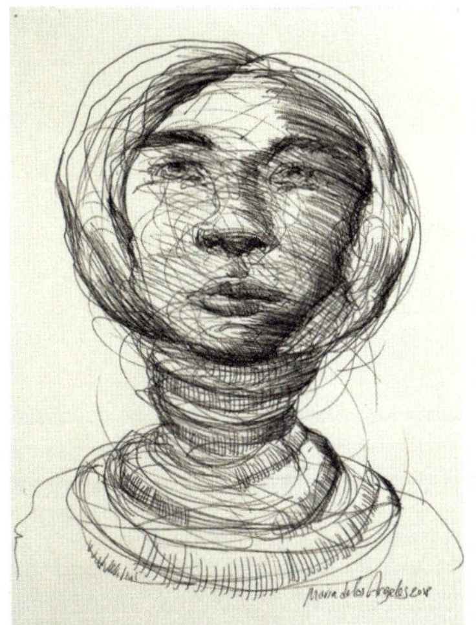

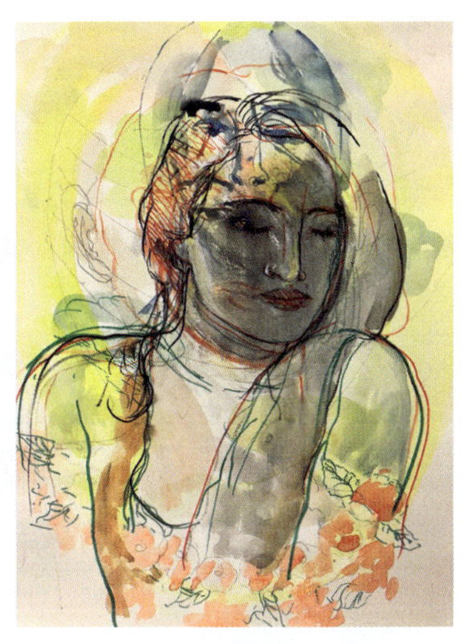

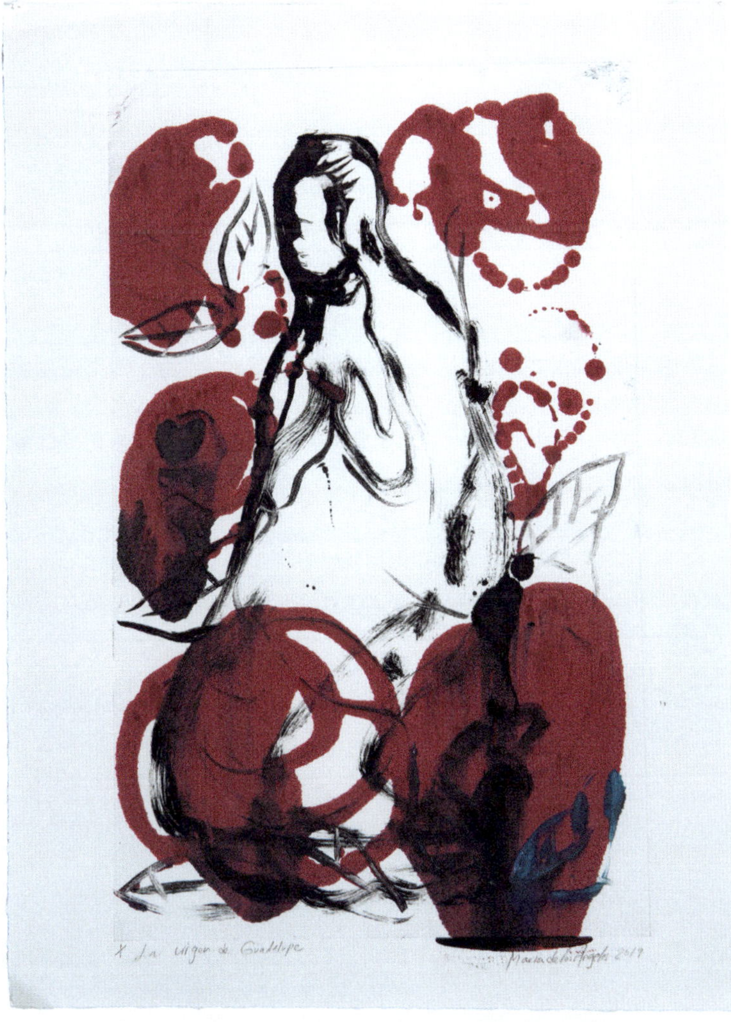
X La Virgen de Guadalupe

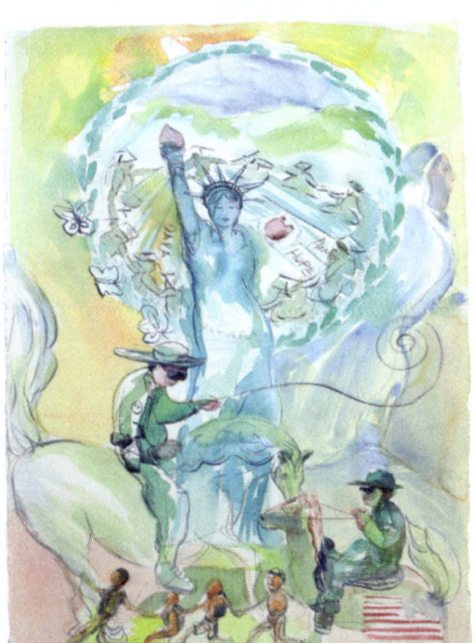

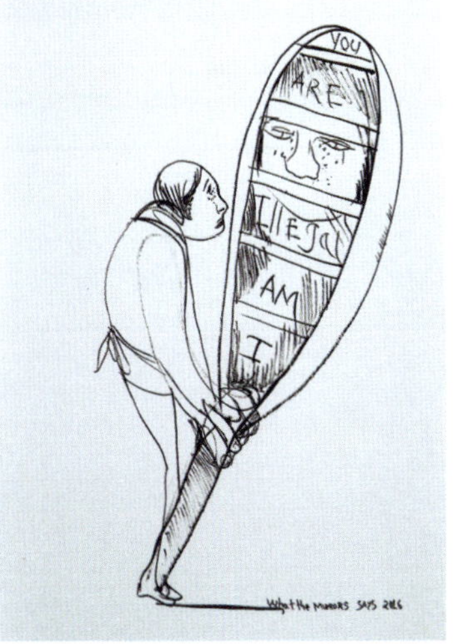
YOU
ARE
AM
I
What the Mirrors Says 2016

II

NICO MUHLY

Tribe

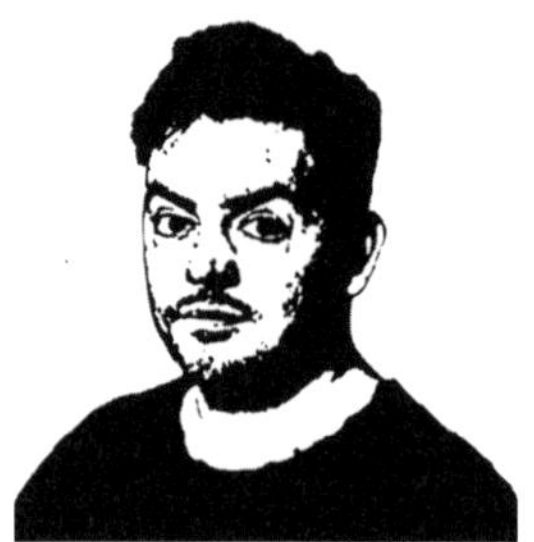

OCCUPATION: Composer

WORK DISCUSSED: *Reliable Sources* (2018)

BORN: 1981

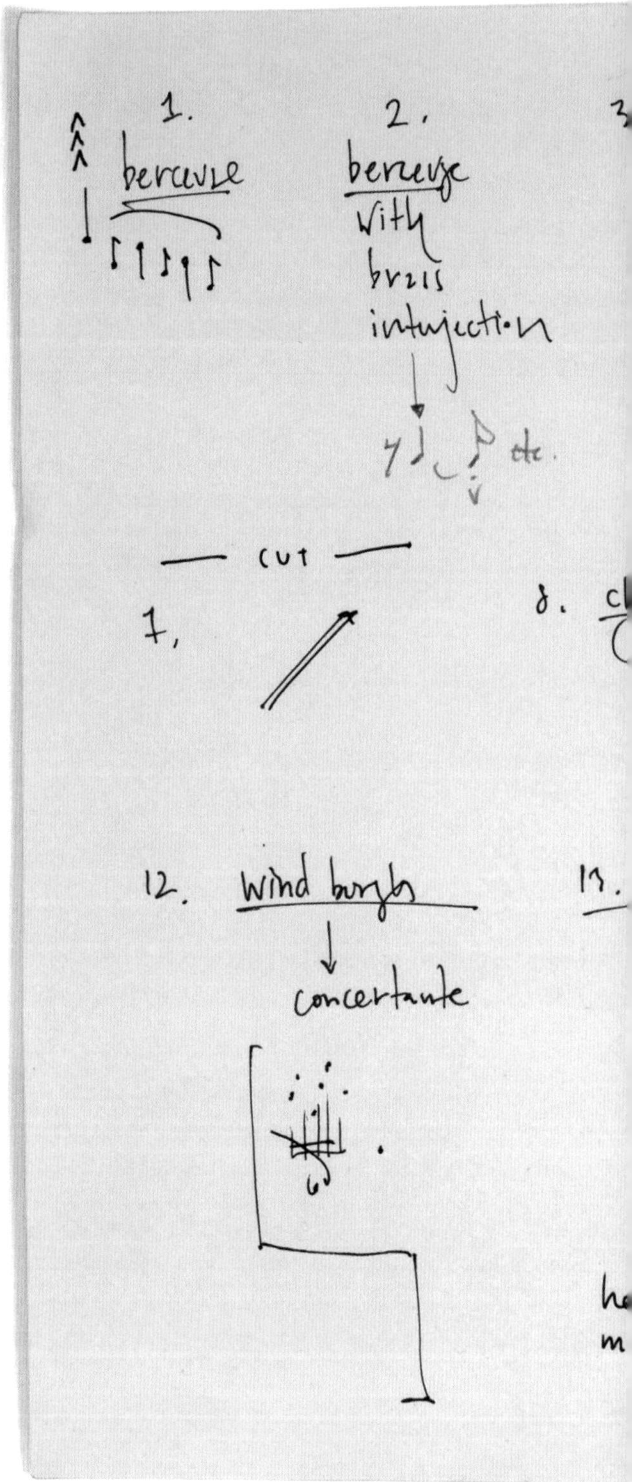

Reliable Sources, mapped out in about twenty minutes.

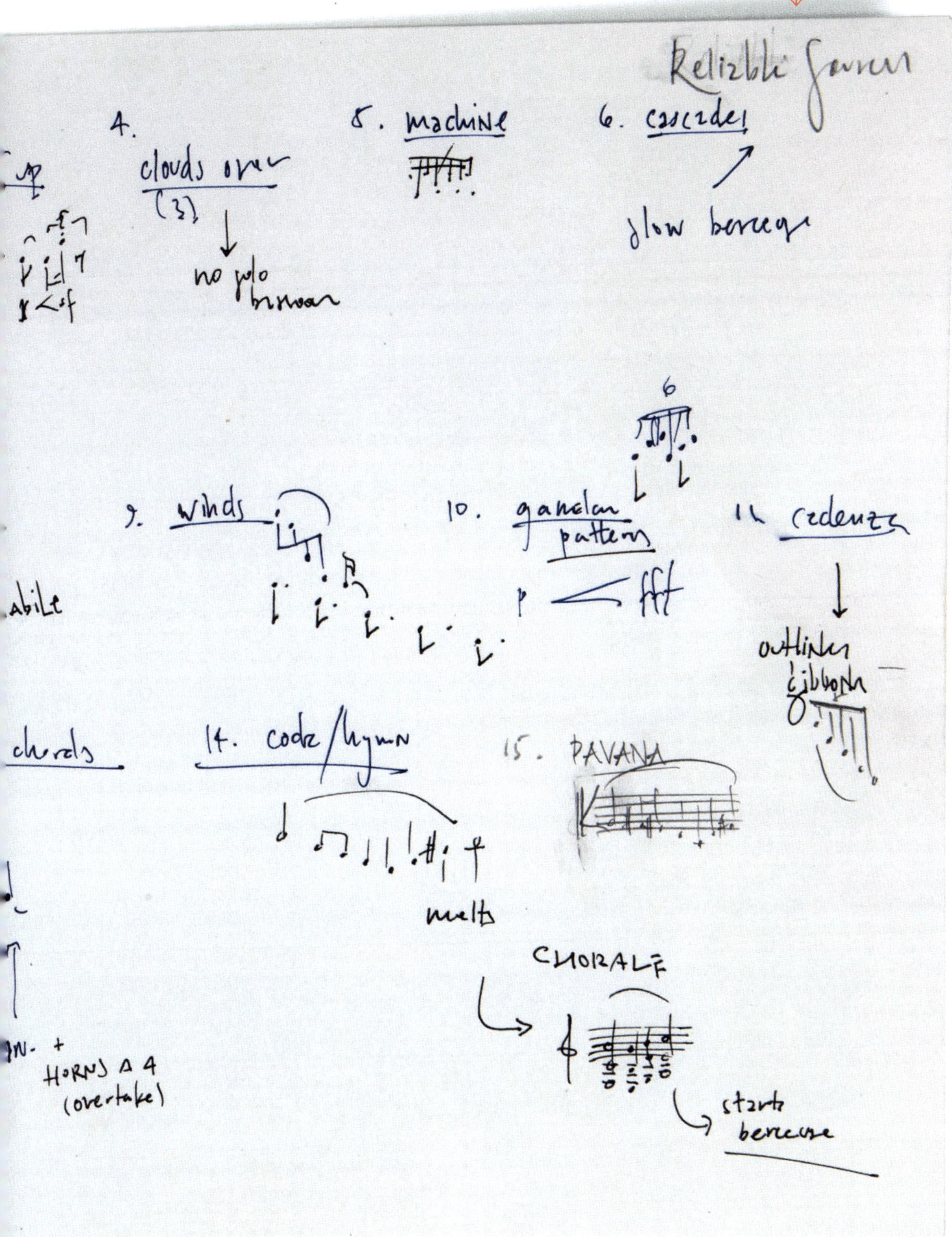
4.
clouds over
5. machine
6. cascades
slow berceuse
9. winds
10. gamelan pattern
11. cadenza
14. coda/hymn
15. PAVANA
melts
CHORALE
starts berceuse
HORNS a 4
(overtake)

"THE PHONE RINGS. It's Mike Harley, head of the bassoon department at the University of South Carolina."

Nico Muhly was taking me through how he came to write *Reliable Sources*, a piece he chose as emblematic of the way he writes music. Nico is a composer of contemporary classical music, tons and tons of it. He is a spinning top of highbrow cool, frequently collaborating with indie popular music musicians like Björk, Sufjan Stevens, Anohni (formerly Antony) of Antony and the Johnsons, and young choreographers like Justin Peck. He has written ballets, film scores—and two full-scale operas for the Met. He was the subject of a full-length *New Yorker* profile when he was twenty-six. I know him a little bit because he is a close friend and studio-mate of my friend Thomas Bartlett (page 126)—they form the nucleus of a Rat Pack of aesthetes, which I mean in the best and most envious way. From afar, I've always been dazzled by Nico's puckish manner and the motor in his brain, which you can almost hear whirring in his speech.

We were sitting in his tiny studio space, surrounded by a keyboard and electronic equipment, some plants, a neater setup than I might have imagined for such an oversize "Artist" personality, but then I suppose I was just determined to see him like that. "Mike says, 'I want to commission a bassoon concerto,'" Nico recalled. "And I was like, *Hmmm*—difficult—because there aren't many of them. The bassoon is a funny one. Of the woodwinds it's got a pretty severe range. Oftentimes it's just the base of the chord and can be sort of boring."

So the work would be challenging, which is a kind of a prerequisite. But also, crucially, it was going to be commissioned by several schools at once, which meant it would have a life—many pieces of contemporary classical music get performed once, and never again, which is the way these things go in Nico's line of work, but also a little crushing: "You can feel like you make this thing and they bury you inside a pyramid."

When Harley called, Nico had just finished writing an opera—*Marnie*, which had been commissioned by the Metropolitan Opera. *Marnie* exhausted him.

But while opera is usually narrative, this bassoon piece could be more of a study, which appealed to him. Also, Nico tends to say yes when asked to do something because he thrives in motion. He fired back questions to Harley. "What's fun to play, what do you hate to play? What's easy, what's hard? Because I think for a concerto you want to make something hard but worth it." He got back answers that interested him, and agreed.

"And then," Nico said to me, "you know you have the tyranny of, *What am I going to do?*" There were the usual questions he asked himself: "What can I do that hasn't been done before? How can I write something meaningful and not just, like, show off shit?"

He had ideas. He'd been marinating in Orlando Gibbons, an early music composer he'd been enamored of as a young chorister and who doesn't get much contemporary airtime. "I've been doing a long project on the music of Orlando Gibbons," Nico told me, referring not to a specific work but to a consuming interest. "It's kind of like a memory project, which is music that's incredibly important to me but is virtually unknown in an orchestral context. [Gibbons] was one of the boxes unlocking when I was a boy that turned me into a composer. It goes in and out of emotional abstraction. I wrote an organ concerto based on one of his pieces. I had been wanting to see if there was a way to embed the Gibbons music into my own language in a way that was mysterious and secret."

He had a notion of a piece in which he would hide the Gibbons in a complex deconstruction of Gibbons chords, with different parts of the orchestra functioning like "windup toys," repetitively doing their thing at different tempos. And then, eventually, the Gibbons would emerge. "Can I sustain a piece of music that has chords all derived from the older material that you don't really see until the end?" Nico wondered. "And how long can it be, without it feeling like a set of variations? The challenge of having to occupy a single chord for a relatively long amount of time and then switch to another one, and then another, without it feeling like *Oh shit, here we are again*. It's been my lifelong work to learn how to erect secret scaffolding."

He shared the Gibbons idea with Harley. Harley was enthusiastic.

"So, the first thing I did was plan out the big architecture of the piece," Nico explained. "I knew what I wanted. Let's imagine the whole orchestra is a series of machines, each with its own set of rules. . . ."

Then he launched into a mesmerizing monologue, very little of which I understood. I'll give you a taste of it, but first I want to explain his method. Nico pointed to a little piece of paper, on which he had written something like a score, but not. That's what you see on pages 118–119. "So this is an outline," he said. "There's barely rhythm, it's more shape. You notate a gesture, abstractly. You figure out the notes later. It's the topography. I really want to get this under control right away. Because otherwise you feel like you're wandering. At no point did I have notes when I was playing this out, by the way. If I zoom too far into the notes, I'll get lost in it. And it's counterproductive. Whereas saving that stuff for later is a treat."

Even if topographic, the map I was looking at seemed like it might have taken a very long time to work out. It didn't. He plotted out the entire twenty-minute piece, more or less in the same amount of time it takes to play it.[1] While he explained, generally, that "I'll change it as I go along," this piece in particular didn't change very much: "At a certain point you just start to see it."

I asked him if he simply hears the whole thing in his head, or figures it out as he goes along, and how he knows how it will sound. I realize these are dumb questions, but I am astounded by how much appeared in first imagining. He said the hearing/figuring-out thing is about fifty-fifty; as for knowing how it will sound, he said simply, "That's what you go to school for, you learn how to reverse engineer." And I suppose that makes sense, but I just can't take in how it's possible to process this level of complexity and at this speed.

Nico at the MIDI As we sat in his little studio, he brought the piece up on his computer. The software he uses is called MIDI, and it plays the score as written, like a player piano. So as his gorgeous music filled the tiny room, he explained, "I wanted to create a really cataclysmic black hole of lack of information out of which would emerge the original Gibbons."

I listened, and nodded as if I understood, but I didn't really.

Here is Nico, narrating:

The rules are: each set of variations is going to have the orchestra doing tasks, repetitive gestures for the duration . . . the bassoon would do the opposite, or something like the opposite . . . each variation will feel like a different kind of game surface. Each game surface will always be made of the same chords, all of which will relate to Gibbons in some way. . . . So you have ten vessels that contain similar objects, but the way that each object moves is different in each one. . . . And then is this moment of reveal when we see it's been this seventeenth-century thing the whole time! . . .

So the first unit looks like these little staccato dots, right? Let's see who's participating in those! OHHH [under his breath, he's now playing the MIDI] . . . *ohhh, that chord, that's the second chord . . . and then, this is our FAVORITE chord. . . . I'm going to play you everything that's not a bassoon. . . . Then we get the second variation, and here again it's everything*

1. This is a book about struggle, isn't it? Not always. Reliable Sources in its full shape just sort of materialized from Nico. I think this was nothing special—it's more or less how he works—but when stories of art that kind of poured out (see Suzan-Lori Parks's account of the writing of *Topdog/Underdog* on page 399) were recounted to me during some of these conversations, I couldn't quite believe it. Works that came of strife—at least with those I could make sense of their construction. Where I am as I am writing this footnote—in Oaxaca, Mexico, on Christmas Eve—the impossibly infectious "Feliz Navidad" is blasting from the street. José Feliciano wrote the song in ten minutes. Does the speed, or the ease, of a work's origin have any relation to its quality? For what it's worth, Bob Dylan insisted his best songs came quickest, before he could get bogged down. Nico doesn't write quite that fast, but his method here—plotting the trajectory in full, details later—is another way to subvert the bogging. His quickly plotted topography is a musical outline, and it's lovely.

but the bassoon. . . . So this is primary texture inside the secondary texture. This is like three clarinets playing this part. . . . If you listen to everything but that, you get the secondary texture, which are these things that start quiet and get loud . . . and then our favorite chord comes in piano. . . . So . . . listen to this. That's a big NASTY cluster of stuff. . . ."

He paused, wanting to show me a Stravinsky piece that is similar, but he couldn't find it on Apple Music and . . .

UGH, it's like it's truly deranged here that they won't show me . . . they're pieces of shit. . . . DERANGED! . . . Ahh, there . . . just listen to this texture . . . why won't it show me fucking Stravinsky? . . . COCKSUCKERS . . . this is like the dumbest way to prove a point here. . . . Okay, here's a swarm, which is like very, very fast. It's basically a bunch of woodwinds playing at different times, like insects. . . ."

Then he went looking for another piece for illustration purposes, one he wrote, but he couldn't find that either. . . .

It's like, I wrote the fucking piece, ummm, sorry. . . . It's so frustrating . . . ahh . . . OH NO . . . I just want to play you what it actually is . . . because the MIDI is like a piece of shit . . . ugh . . . okay. . . . So once I had this whole situation, then I was thinking about what to do with the bassoon, right? I was always thinking . . . not the opposite, but different . . . so the magic trick here is that I have the English horn playing exactly what the bassoon played the first time . . . inside the second variation there's been like this permeability . . . so check this out . . . ummm . . . they're going down while he's going up in a totally different rhythm and you'll recognize. . . . Damn this MIDI. . . . It's almost like the bassoon is cutting through all this stuff . . . when it's like THISSSSS . . . this kind of completely metronomic sound. . . . The bassoon is doing this whole other . . . it's 1-2-3, he's going 2-3-4-5-6-7, 1-2-3 like that . . . just completely against the time, so just check this out, it's like 1-2-3-4-5-6-7, 1-2-3-4-5-6-7, I wouldn't expect the listener to get there, but you get a sense that there's this displacement . . . and here's like . . . I need a break from this fucking chord . . . and then we're back."

And on like that. He was lost in the music, and referring to the page in front of us, and watching the MIDI screen: a blur of movement. But the important point is, he got the gist of this worked out in his mind the first moment he set it down.

"Once I fill in the architecture, it's all intuition," he said. But it's worth also emphasizing that the architecture establishes the rules the piece will be governed by—"This is the big structure, this is the hungry little animal that needs to be fed structure, and then these are all the delicious ingredients for the fucker."[2]

Regarding what he had just shown me, perhaps sensing my bafflement, he said, "But you don't need to know any of this to have a good time." He then gave me a droll grin, if such a thing is possible.

I kept pressing him on what changed from his original plan, thinking there would have to be something.

"If I'm being totally honest," he said, "I'm pretty sure that I didn't have this [beginning]. I'm pretty sure I originally started here. And then I probably just ended big like this. . . . I was going to end with this dreamy ghost. But then I got to the end and I didn't like it, it sucks. I had been trying to think of it like a little memory bell, but it wasn't working."

So he made some adjustments, but dismissed their significance. "I honestly think it was actually the equivalent of wiping off the edge of a plate or something, where the work was done but there was one fucked-up thing: just wipe the edge of the plate."

What is complicated for him is his schedule. He is madly peripatetic, working on any number of projects at once, each with its own timetable. "Let's see. I started thinking about it in August 2017. I started writing like ten months later, I had this whole opera at the Met, and some of this shit in England and Singapore. I'd just peek at it occasionally and be like, *Here's an idea.*" He filled it in in little

2. Structure = everything? No, but quite a lot.

EMAIL SNIPPETS FROM HARLEY TO NICO

October 31, 2014, Mike Harley to Nico Muhly
NICO!
Let me get right to the point.
I . . . have been given the opportunity by our wind ensemble director to ask pretty much anyone I'd like to write a concerto for bassoon with wind ensemble or chamber winds. You are one of my favorite composers in all the world, and I'd be honored if you would take this on . . . Why might you be interested in writing such a piece? Well, not to state the obvious, but it's the bassoon for Christ's sake!!! :-)
. . .

July 17, 2018, Nico Muhly to Mike Harley
IGNORE all the rehearsal marks this is just for my own weird harmony process nonsense.
IGNORE the fact that this is all in bass clef, I will fix all that
With this situation, what I'm looking for is places to breathe that aren't right before a barline. So it might be about sneaking breaths in, but I've always found that if I try to estimate where that is, that I get it wrong.
FOR INSTANCE
in this situation, how far do you reckon you could get? Could you get all the way to the last few beats of rehearsal mark 4 (or "bar" 6) and breathe before that low B?

July 17, 2018, Mike Harley to Nico Muhly
Yes, I can make it all the way through the end of rehearsal 4 / beginning of 5 on a single breath . . . honestly it can be hard to predict where comfortable breaths will need to occur; players will most likely just breathe where they think it makes the most sense for comfort and phrasing.
:-) . . .

August 21, 2018. Nico Muhly to Mike Harley
hey boo.
q = 104 - 112ish, all articulated notes . . . how does this settle? Also what will your eyebrows look like

Aug 22, 2018. Mike Harley to Nico Muhly
That's OK! Twill take a little work to get up up to tempo but it lies well.
My eyebrows will raise and lower rapidly as I try desperately to play in tune, hopefully with a modicum of success.

August 22, 2018. Nico Muhly to Mike Harley
Cool!!!! So close to having a full draft of this hoe. What I want to do is send you a draft. . . . and then
we can go back and forth if there is ANYTHING that could be easier or harder or fun or whatever.

increments when he found a spare moment, often on the road, which he is constantly.

But he manages. He looked back on the pile of documents showing iterations of the composition. "Okay, let's see how far I got in this draft. This is actually pretty decent. That means in a single day I sketched, sketched, sketched in six minutes of it."

And all the while, as he went along, he sent little bits of the piece to Harley, asking if this is what he wanted, making sure it was playable. He said he is deliberately casual in these notes to allow his correspondent to object or demur if he wants to. Harley was a yes from beginning to end.

It took Nico about fifteen months, from that first call to the premiere, to complete the piece. And true to his hope, *Reliable Sources* has been played at universities across the country.

His Own Origin Story There aren't many children who would embrace the early sacramental music of Orlando Gibbons, and Nico was certainly an unusual child. But he was not by his own description a prodigy, at least not in the way we tend to think of them.

"My mother is a painter, my father is a documentary filmmaker. There was music in my house, but not a striking amount of it. My mother listens to music obsessively when she paints, but it was the usual kind of NPR-plus diet—you kind of absorb it. We lived in Providence, we moved into a house with a kind of super-jacked-up piano in the basement, we brought it upstairs, and it was decided that I should kind of maybe take lessons, and I'm nine at this point, which is very old. I didn't take to piano particularly well. Like clearly I was in some way talented, but I wasn't a prodigy. I was an only child. I didn't play sports. Oftentimes I was jealous of people who had the kind of camaraderie you have in sports, and piano was an incredibly solitary thing. Someone in school was like, 'I've been singing in the boy choir, you should check it out.' With the choir, you're on a team, and I really liked it. And you're learning a new language because like half of it was in Latin, and the music was from the sixteenth century, and I loved it. And then I was like eleven, and it just kind of clicked, and suddenly I was good at both things—piano and choir. It was over just a couple of months. I think it's mysterious about why that happened. It was just that something required these two different muscles to work together. And at the time, I thought, well, what if I tried to write music? Just to see what that feels like. I wrote a little thing for the choir, and they did that.

"So it was a perfect storm, involving parents who were their version of supportive.[3] It's really an anti-romantic origin story about music making. It's just sort of accretion, which is compositionally how my music functions.

"I became very technically facile on the piano, which helps because it's easy to see what's going on. If you're playing Bach, it's like *That's cool, let me try that chord*—you can imitate it.

"Then I switched to a fancy private school, with a better music program. And oh—right—then I went to Rome. My mother went to the American Academy in Rome, and it was decreed I would go with her. And then, a series of really serendipitous things occurred. For one, there was an empty composer's studio there with a piano, and they were like, 'Sure, take it.' And there was a concert pianist who agreed to teach me. At this point I'm thirteen, and suddenly I'm in Rome alone basically, and I have all this time. And I'm furious at my mom, who had dragged me to Rome. But when I was there, I started writing a lot of music just for fun. So Rome was kind of miraculous."

Nico came back to the US and entered a program near Tanglewood, the music festival in the Berkshires in Massachusetts, where he first met others like him. "Like whoa, here are ten other kid composers. Suddenly you're surrounded by people who are doing what they're meant to be doing and doing it really well. I would write up there, like a piece a week, and there were moments of *This sounds like stuff that I like by other people, only by me. That's cool."*

And at that point, "it started to turn into this total maniac relationship to it that has basically continued unbroken since that time. In hindsight, I must have been really difficult to be around."

Though he had less formal training than his peers, Nico entered the Juilliard School of Music (while also attending Columbia University in a dual-degree program). "Looking at some of the students there, I recognized something very dark, which is: What happens if you sacrifice your childhood on the pyre of your talent? I'd see these haunted violin players with sunken faces who had done unspeakable things to their sanity, people you know who came out of their mom's vagina with the violin. I thought, I don't know if that's my vibe." He began to write music for his fellow students to play. "My friend Nadia[4] asked me to write a piece for a recital and I was, 'Well, okay.' So I write it, and I realize it's the only contemporary piece in the program. And it's next to Bach. And people start calling you and saying, 'Write something for my recital.'"

As he was getting a master's at Juilliard, it all started to happen: commissions, a valuable apprenticeship/assistantship with Philip Glass, his first record in 2006. Not long after, he had achieved white-hot fame not just as a wunderkind but also as an unusually charismatic artist, more like a pop star than many pop stars.

3. This is in response to a question I kept pressing—Who was supporting their artistic interests as a child?—believing that there is always someone in everybody's story. Which there is.

4. Nadia Sirota, who became a well-known violinist.

Well and Unwell Nico was now in his early forties, and it's not like he let up in the period between Juilliard and *Reliable Sources*, or after. It is a relentless life—manic by his own admission. Nico has many talents; a surprising one to me is what a good writer he is, introspective and candid. He has a blog that he writes now and then. One of his short essays is called "Thoughts on Being Well," and it starts like this:

"I have been, it turns out, unwell for a long time" he wrote. "I felt empty, or invisible. This physical manifestation of the work wasn't something I'd made; it was something that was happening around me to which I was a passive and silent witness." He feels better now, having altered his medical regimen, but I thought this being unwell was worth talking about, especially given the links people make between creative expression and, well, madness.

"I know people have these romantic notions of, like, Mozart must have been mad, but you shouldn't romanticize it ever," he said. "It's horrible. It is not a gift. I want to treat it like diabetes, where it's this constant pain-in-the-ass thing that you just try and keep under control—something that exists and that's dangerous and to a certain extent wants you dead, but you just have to deal with it. I check in with myself about my meds, I try to figure out if there are any external stressors."

The stressors tend to be the kinds of irritants most people take in stride, but the wiring that makes him so productive is fragile. Is there a cause and effect here? It would be impossible to know. "Very rarely is it work that does it," he said. "Oftentimes the stressors are bizarre—really random things like *The New York Times* does one of those article roundups like three easy things to cook this weekend and the order of the articles is different from the headline. Or how Apple Music works, the frustration I had earlier.

"The contract I make with the universe every day is that I'm going to do the best that I can, and in return I would like the fucking web editors to do the same. It can register as anal and meticulous, but it's not that, it really is this contract: *do the work well*. It's not about things not necessarily working, it's about the effort. Because my mania gets triggered when I start to feel like my sense of reality and other people's sense of reality are different."

This strikes me as crucial. The remark takes us back to his own origins. It seemed that an important aspect of what pushed him forward was a need for a kind of companionship, a search to find others who were like him—other similar creatures with unusual talents, but also drive and idiosyncratic brains that perform best in the higher atmosphere, which describes Nico's friend group and his matrix of collaborators. Happy ending: he found his own planet.

It's a planet most people will never live on. But I find it perhaps useful to note that in Nico's mind, what distinguishes this tribe is not the result but the effort.

He talked about one kid in the orchestra for the original *Reliable Sources* premiere. "At a certain point, because I'm old, I don't care if people play my music badly," he said. "It's kind of, like, cool. There was this solo being played by a super-eager boy—and he completely shat the bed in the performance! And I was like, *This is good*. This is what you want: *I have fucked up onstage, in ways that fixed the problem that made me fuck up.*

"Had I just always not fucked up, but been nervous in that way, it would have eventually led to a serious disaster. That happens to everyone, always. Compositionally for me, the death is if something's too long. And you literally cannot know this until the premiere. Even in rehearsals, you might think, *Oh, it's a little long, but the energy of the premiere will fix it, not a problem*. And then there you are in a roomful of one thousand people, and you just feel everyone taking a breath in this fucking part I should have cut eight months ago. Opera is the absolute worst for this. It will 100 percent happen."

But "if you make a mistake that's done with energy and commitment, even if it's a chaotic feeling, it changes you. In a way that a lazy mistake doesn't.

"You really do just have to fuck up."

12

THOMAS BARTLETT

Disappearing Himself

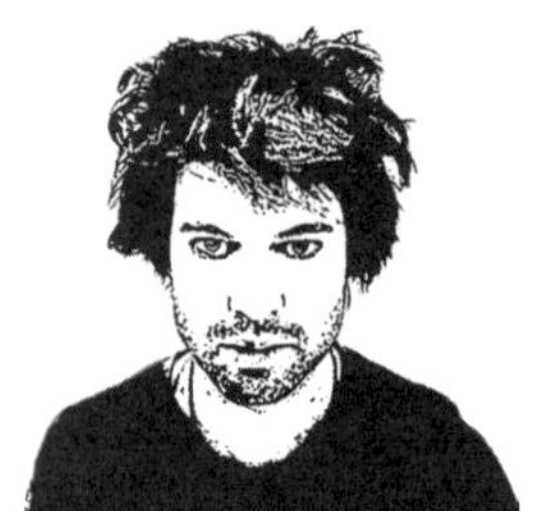

OCCUPATION: Musician/Producer

WORK DISCUSSED: *Harvest/* "Out on the Weekend"

BORN: 1981

NEXT DOOR TO NICO MUHLY, in the studio they share, is Thomas Bartlett. They have a great deal in common: they often work together; they are devoted to their tribes, which overlap; they spin on similar aesthetic axes. Thomas is chiefly a music producer, which is more a musician than a film producer is a filmmaker—he makes the work happen, but as creative partner usually rather than enabler. Like Nico, he is working on a thousand projects at once, often with members of what I think of as his repertory company, which includes Norah Jones, Martha Wainwright, Justin Vivian Bond, David Stith, Justin Vernon of Bon Iver, and Glen Hansard, the Irish singer-songwriter who won an Oscar for the movie *Once*.

These musicians constitute the principal cast of the project we sat down to talk about, a reimagining of Neil Young's *Harvest*, with each musician in his troupe assigned a different song by Thomas.[1] Thomas offered to take me through the rethinking he had to do of the song he had Glen Hansard sing, "Out on the Weekend," which was the opening track. The record label Nonesuch, which was releasing the album, liked the sense of sadness that permeated the new record but thought it was missing from the Hansard track the first go-round. So Thomas and Hansard went at it again. Thomas thought the reworking of the song might give a good picture of how a producer works, because the variables (the song, the singer) were otherwise the same.

But the other reason I wanted to talk to Thomas is that Thomas, very unusually, abdicated from the career as the performing artist he might have had. Before I knew him (he is now a good friend), I had listened to him. He was a singer-songwriter who went by the name Doveman. His music—beautiful, delicate, and intelligent—didn't make him famous, but he had his passionate fans, and he easily could have kept going, especially as he was learning what he was capable of more and more with each record. Thomas was the musical prodigy Nico wasn't. He was making records at thirteen, and his path upward illustrates the ways in which early talent can be nurtured. Relationships matter—with his teachers, who were crucial to him; with one boy, Sam Amidon, who was his early musical partner and who later became a formidable musical artist in his own right; with a network of musicians who were also his friends. And also, of course, here as everywhere else, there was the matter of ambition. Thomas wanted to be a star.

But then, gradually, he just gave it up. He realized he hated performing, hated the attention he had been actively seeking—and had the self-awareness to realize that what he really loved was melding minds with other musicians, advancing their work while rendering his own invisible.[2] He deliberately never released his favorite Doveman record; it is a secret or, at the least, a private pleasure. That seemed pretty extraordinary to me (running counter to most people's dreams of fame). His wasn't the usual artist's mind, but his refusal of a talent available to him made his brain an interesting one to pick.

Thomas is a deeply tender person, wickedly smart, his boyish face usually marked by a trace of eye makeup. His loyalties are fierce—especially to his family and to his girlfriend, Ella Hunt, an actress and singer, whose music he is also helping to cultivate (his intensely close, bohemian-ish family hosts a magical dinner most weeks for all their artist friends). "When I met Thomas," said Glen Hansard, "I met New York. It's a connoisseur's world and it's absolutely intoxicating." Thomas's whole life is a kind of hothouse, and perhaps because of that, beautiful things grow out of it.

Establishing Terms

Adam Moss: *So what is a producer?*

Thomas Bartlett: That is a very confusing thing at this point. It used to be so clear. Very often it would be the person who not only chose the singer, but the whole band, the material. It was very much an auteur director. The singer was like an actor. That changed. The range of different ways that a producer can be involved in a project is vast. There are instances when the artist has basically made a complete thing and brought it to me, and I say I prefer this version, maybe take out that verse, nothing else. And there can be times when as a producer I'm writing every song, starting every idea, really working from the very beginning, very much like a total creative partner.

AM: *Which do you prefer?*

TB: I like both, a lot. Sometimes, with producers, you hear their work and you know it's their work, right? And I'm very much not that sort of producer. My emotional fetish, and the thing that I love most in the world, is to get into somebody's head and make them feel, oh my God, how is this person understanding my most inexpressible thoughts? That makes me feel so good. And that's my goal at all times. Sometimes that means starting from scratch, sometimes that means being a sounding board. It's also that just on a technical level, things have changed a lot. Now it's possible to make full records in a room like this [we are speaking in a tiny studio, with a big microphone, piano, computer equipment], which just was not the case. For a long time, producers would have nothing to do with engineering. At this point, 90 percent of what I do is just in here, with the singer singing into that microphone, and I'm engineering everything here.

AM: *In the projects you're doing now, what role are you playing?*

TB: Okay, let's see. I'm making a record with Bebel Gilberto that's bossa nova, songs that her dad[3] sang. She picked the material; I don't know the material. There's a thing I'm doing for her that's hard for me to see. Like I genuinely feel I'm useless, and yet she feels like it cannot happen without me. But then David Stith, who records as DM Stith—I'm a huge fan of his, and I felt I would wreck what he did because I can tell his work is the product of many small decisions, each

1. This record was made in 2015 and was meant at one point to be released for *Harvest*'s fiftieth anniversary in 2022, but didn't make it. As of this writing it has still not been released.

2. There is a kind of editor, a very sensitive writer's editor, that this description perfectly captures. I wasn't that kind (I was more of a bigger-picture editor), but when I worked with one, I was in awe of their ability to lose themselves in somebody else's work, and very much envied the writer they were serving. It's a remarkably selfless activity.

3. Bebel Gilberto's father was João Gilberto, often considered the father of bossa nova.

of which I would never make. He dismissed my concern. He brought me songs at an early enough stage that I thought, *Oh wait, I hear how I could be useful.* We would get together every couple months for four or five days, over the last two years. We've ended up with a twelve-song record. There's a way in which I'm aesthetically intimidated by David. I feel nervous working with almost anybody usually, but I felt continually nervous with David. He tends to like things that are a little more abrasive, or wilder. He makes me feel boring. I have a bag of tricks that I can do, ninety-nine people out of one hundred would say, "Ooh, that's exactly right." And with David, I have no clue. So what that meant was that I became very inventive in trying to come up with ideas that excite him. It made me generate all these new ideas that I've now added to my bag of tricks.

AM: *Were these ideas to simplify his wildness?*

TB: Absolutely. It was like, *How can I translate for all the people for whom his work feels less dazzling—how can I make them hear it?* The main thing I've done is to spotlight his voice, and to make him relax and revel in his voice, let that be enough sometimes. I really love recording voices; it's kind of my thing. I find it useful to do it in this room. I have to be totally concentrated on the singer. It reminds me—when I'm doing it well—of my first really great piano teacher. Sometimes she wouldn't even give me feedback, she would just say, "Okay, play it again." And I could feel her concentrating on me. It feels more psychic than anything else.

An Old Record Made New

AM: *Let's talk about the* Harvest *project.*

TB: Okay, at one point Steve Salett,[4] who owns this studio, suggested we do a covers record of *Harvest*. And I had been doing these shows called the Burgundy Stain, that was maybe before I knew you. They were at Le Poisson Rouge, it was like Doveman and friends. I would ask four or so friends to come, we had sort of a house band, and I would pick songs that I wanted them to sing. It was kind of a variety show, everybody playing everybody else's songs. It was a testing ground for production ideas. Glen [Hansard] was one of the people in it, and he so completely loved the way the band played that the next day we started recording with that band. That was his first solo record. And he was by far the biggest artist I had produced at that point. And then there had been these Hal Willner[5] shows—he really changed my life when I was fifteen, I think, and living in London studying with a piano teacher there. Hal had put together a show of lots of different singers doing versions of *Anthology of American Folk Music* songs. I went: there was Nick Cave and Kate and Anna McGarrigle, Rufus and Martha Wainwright, Jarvis Cocker, Beth Orton, probably twenty different singers. I remember sitting in the audience, just thinking, like, *Oh, I found my tribe. These are my people.*

Now, twenty years later, I've played with pretty much everyone who was there. It really *was* my tribe. And that was the inspiration for

4. Steve Salett is a composer and producer and performs as The Poison Tree.

5. Hal Willner was a music producer who specialized in this sort of thing—events and records with lots of performers. He died during COVID.

WHAT FOCUS IS

"What I think of when I'm doing really well, it just feels like an intensity of concentration that I don't see other people have," Thomas said. "Literally just on how a note will sound. My piano teacher would refer to it as the core of tone. She would push my attention around to make sure it was really doing the job. When I work with a singer, all I'm doing is focusing on them. I have this quasi-mystical feeling that the singers will get the best vocals by me being right there with them."

Burgundy Stain. Anyway, Steve had an idea about doing a whole series of recontextualizing albums, revisiting old albums. In theory, we're still going to do it, but seven years later, this *Harvest* record is what we've done. I thought of different friends who would be really good singing these songs, I started texting people, and pretty much everybody said yes. So we had my dream lineup come in and record over the course of two days. Bon Iver. Viv [Justin

THOMAS BARTLETT/GLEN HANSARD: Producing "Out on the Weekend" through text.

Mon, Nov 22, 7:41 PM

glen! a question for you. do you remember the harvest covers thing that I did *way* way back? (it was something like 2013). it has languished for years, just because getting all the permissions/legal stuff sorted for it was such a headache, and we sort of just gave up at a certain point...but now we've released that next year is the 50th anniversary of harvest, and some people are interested—met with nonesuch last week, and they seemed very enthusiastic about the possibility of them releasing it.
I hadn't really thought about the record in ages, and have been pleasantly surprised... it's really good!! ha.
here's a soundcloud:

but in listening through, the dominant tone is so much kind of spooky/pretty/sad, and I really love that, and I was wondering if there's any chance you would be open to us trying (remotely), a spooky creaky piano version of "out on the weekend"? I'm just feeling like there's so much delicacy up at the top of the record, and I would love to save the real full band thing for later in it? and that you and I could make such a beautiful striking thing out of "on the weekend", make it more like a hymn or something...I've got some piano ideas for it, if that's something you would consider! let me know! and sending so much love and barrels of missing you!!

Mon, Nov 22, 11:17 PM

Thomas, great to hear from you! Yes! Let's follow your instinct in this snd you can send me piano and I'll sing along! Sounds perfect!
I'd love another shot at it.
I think of you so much, it'll be brilliant to collaborate again!

yay!! I'll send you a couple of options tomorrow! (I have an idea for reharmonizing, but it might be too much, so maybe I should stick with original chords...and then also can't decide if the instrumental parts should be just piano, with me playing sort of his harmonica line, or if it should be you playing harmonica over the piano) anyways, I'll send you some options, and see if anything speaks to you. and if not, it's no worries, because the existing track is kind of perfect, I'm just interested to push the whole record one click spookier. love you so!!!

Tue, Nov 23, 1:35 AM

Let's go as deep and spooky as you feel, if you do go the reharmonized toute maybe give me some pointers on the beginnings of verses etc?
I love this idea Thomas.
Love you!!
Gx

Tue, Nov 23, 7:43 PM

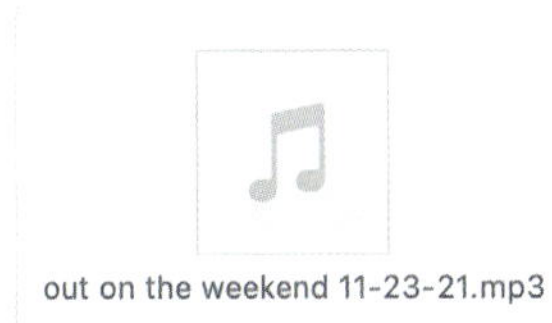
out on the weekend 11-23-21.mp3

hi! so here's a first thought, but totally just take this as a jumping off point—I'm liking the reharmonizing, but I'm not attached to it if it's not feeling right to you...and I do think that having you play harmonica at the top, instead of piano doing the melody, would be cooler (although I almost wonder about not doing the intro, and just having think that having you play harmonica at the top, instead of piano doing the melody, would be cooler (although I almost wonder about not doing the intro, and just having sort of the riff I'm playing under the verse be the start?)...anyways, just a first bash through an idea, let me know what you think!!

Tue, Nov 23, 10:31 PM

Thomas! I love it!
I sang it 3 times in a row without thinking..
I'll send a link now.
Let me know what works or what doesn't! I love it just as it is!
You can comp a vocal, or I'll try more.
Gxx

ooh yay, I'm excited to hear!!

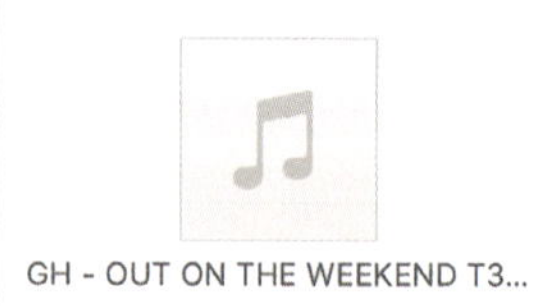

GH - OUT ON THE WEEKEND T3...

oooh I *love* this!! yay!!!

2 quick questions:
1. I kind of unthinkingly kept it in the original key, but you're so correct to drop down the octave instead of singing it in the normal spot. but wondering, would it be better if I pushed the key up a few steps? I'll send you just a quick bit of it to check what it feels like to sing a little bit up (unless you feel like this key is definitely the way to go, in which case I'm sold)
2. I do think that harmonica at the beginning could be a gorgeous thing, so, once we sort out the key, maybe I could make a version of the intro where I'm not playing the melody, and you could do a little harmonica?

I'd be happy to try harmonica Thomas, but I don't have one here.. I'm on lake Como in Italy. I have to say I love how low the key is. I've been sing down low a lot more recently and feel very comfortable in this range. But I'll let you decide. And I love your intro.. it immediately identifies the song.

ooh lake como!! nice! and just for you to check for a sec, here it is a few steps up, just sing a moment, and if you think it's better in the original, I'm sold!

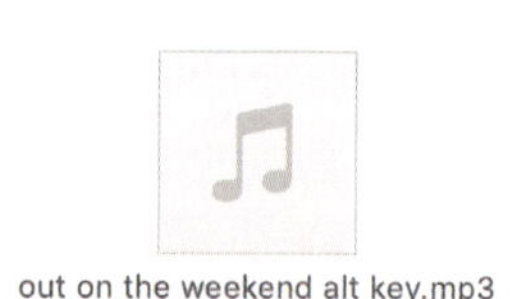

out on the weekend alt key.mp3

Ok give me a few mins!

okay cool! that's not the full song, just a snippet for you to try. and thank you *so* much! I love making things with, it's been so much too long!!

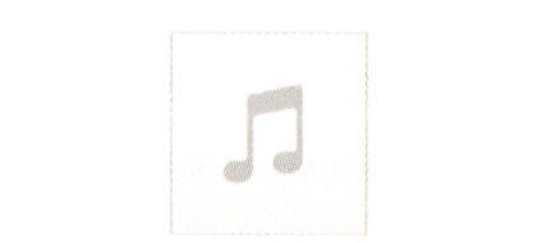

GH - OUT ON THE WEEKEND Alt...

I might prefer the lower key, but it sounds more like me in the higher key. Your call!

agh, I'm really torn!! the lower key is kind of gutting, I love it. but there's something so beautiful about how the chorus feels in this higher key (where in the lower one, you sort of have to change the melody to give it any sense of rise, you know?)...

Ok! Send me a full one in the higher key and let's see if I can do it justice.

okay amazing!! if you don't mind, then let me do that, and then we can always go back to the lower if it's just better. coming at you shortly! thank you thank you!!

Ok perfect!!

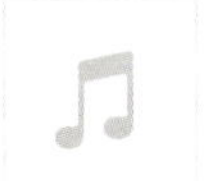

out on the weekend alt key 11-23...

Great! I'm on it now..

yay thank you!!

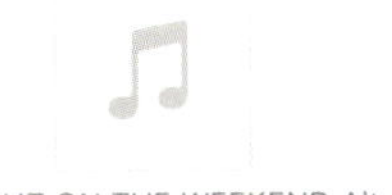

GH - OUT ON THE WEEKEND Alt...

this is gorgeous!! (halfway through now)...are you happy with it, or definitely feeling the other one more?

oh wow, just hit the 2nd chorus, that's fucking gorgeous

Ah great! Now I think I prefer this key! Was nice to sing!

okay great!! yeah, this is really special!! still has the brokenness/loneliness that I love, but it just sits so comfortably and gorgeously in your voice. I'm gonna play around with adding just some very subtle little things, just like windy op-1 that you can barely feel or something...but will keep it pretty bare...will send you something a little later for thoughts.

thank you SO much!! god you're incredible

Oh Thomas I'm so so happy to have sang it again in this way.. it's really beautiful! Go Op-1 !!

Wed, Nov 24, 1:34 AM

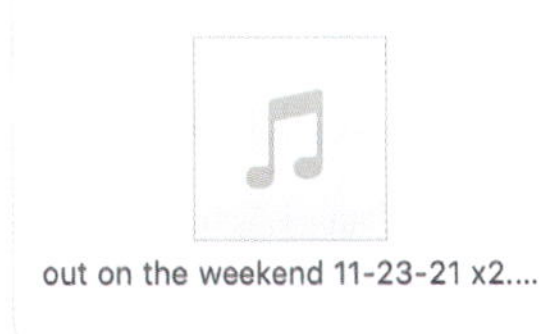

out on the weekend 11-23-21 x2....

I love this! did some very minimal comping, but vast majority your first vocal. and just some little bits of wind and stuff. let me know if you're okay with it!

It's absolutely magic Thomas!!! Thank you for including me! I really love it!!!!

Vivian Bond]. Martha [Wainwright]. Sam [Amidon]. Trixie Whitley. Norah Jones. It felt very much like one of the Burgundy Stain things, where we're hanging out backstage and I'm saying, "Would you sing harmony vocals on this?" Martha, I had given her the song "Old Man" to sing, partly just so I could hear it in her voice. I knew it would sound great, and she and her dad[6] have a complicated enough relationship; I thought that was fun. Bon Iver had meant to come and record in person, and then he got sick one day. And he was really apologetic. I said, "If you're still up for it, you could just send me vocals." I must have sent a simple accompaniment. When we put his three vocal tracks together, it was like, *Oh, that's the sound of Bon Iver*. For Sam, Trixie, and Norah, I think they all thought they were doing absolutely straight covers of their songs. And their songs are so distinctively each of those three people.

You Can't Escape Yourself

AM: *Stop there. So each had a particular imprint.[7] Do you think that's a developed thing?*

TB: Or innate? That is a conundrum. I lean towards thinking it's innate. We are blind to our own essence, you know? And one of the things I try to do as a producer is to get people to do what comes to them the most naturally, because people underestimate that thing about themselves. Like the thing that feels like breathing is not that interesting, you know? I certainly experience that sometimes when I try to rip something off. And then I realize I was in good faith trying to copy a thing. But it just sounds like me.

AM: *And the Glen Hansard track?*

TB: Well, it was just him and a harmonica, and it was really good. But you can see why Nonesuch had the reaction they did: it just feels like it's coming from a different record. Most of the other versions feel sadder than the original. So I went back to Glen—my thought was let's just make his sadder, let's spookify it. Actually, my first thought was, What if I made it sort of a hymn? I texted him and he said sure.

This was their exchange.

AM: *As you were working with the song, what were you thinking?*

TB: The basic thing was, What happens if I take this into minor instead of major? As I was playing it and looking at the lyrics, it was, How do I acknowledge the shift in lyric? And the decision to hold off the chorus, that was a big one. When I'm trying to make something as bare as this work, these tiny inflections are everything. Then as you're taking it to this mode, it becomes necessary, at least in my mind, to give it this other harmonic narrative. I think in the second verse I made it major. It was more harmonic language for the sake of harmony than response to the lyric. Then if at the very end we resolve it to minor, we still get the feeling of arrival. That was the logic of it. I sent it to Glen and he was delighted, but then I missed the harmonica. Eventually, I rerecorded the piano so I'm not playing melody anymore, I'm just playing chords. I wanted it to start with just the harmonica. I reversed the piano, stripping away the chord version, and then I started fading back in. That's world-building right there.

A Ukulele at Three

AM: *What was your earliest experience with music?*

TB: When I was at day care, I used to strum on a wooden block. And then eventually my parents got me a ukulele. So that was my first instrument.

AM: *And you were . . .*

TB: Three. When I was four, I wanted piano lessons and I was very determined. Mom said I could have lessons if I called the teacher. She had to dial for me.

AM: *Were your parents musical?*

TB: Not at all. But I was just obsessed with music from very young. I saw *Stop Making Sense* and David Byrne became my hero. I would run around the house in Dad's jacket to look like David at the end.

AM: *What were you responding to?*

TB: The physicality, I think. It's mystifying to

me now, because I don't feel as drawn to music as much as I do to literature or food. I don't recognize myself in that anymore.

I had a piano teacher who was a local folk musician. And through him, I met Sam [Amidon], we were six. The teacher decided to have all of his little students form a band. I played piano, Sam played the fiddle. Soon Sam and I were just kind of more advanced, and we got into playing contra dance music, which is a New England tradition that borrows from Southern square dancing and Irish line dancing. We played every Friday night, four hundred people in an old garage dancing. I was eight or nine. At eleven we were on *All Things Considered*, little prodigy kids playing contra dances.

With contra music, it's totally taught by ear. I had really good ear skills. A lot of the fun in it for me was taking these standard contra tunes and reharmonizing in a way that felt different. And then a lot of the time I would write tunes that built the subversion into them. I was just constantly writing tunes.

After a year spent in London with a very serious teacher, we had, I think, put out four records. And I was getting bored of the strictures of contra dance.

I remember feeling, for all my piano training, I didn't want a career as a classical pianist. When I did play recitals, it just felt—I would get sick to my stomach. I got back to New York, I started at Columbia, I was maybe seventeen, I got into a fancy competition, and I did not get far. I very much felt like, *Oh my God, this is not my world. I really hate this*. And by then I was writing songs. I had started writing songs tentatively a couple of years before—the songs that eventually became Doveman songs. I sang. My voice was really quiet and weird, but I couldn't imagine singing any other way. I recorded some of them with Sam. It was very self-directed; I recorded a CD and burned one thousand copies of it. And called myself Doveman because my brother had made this postcard collage at some point with my head on a dove's body.

I booked a few Doveman shows. We played at CBGB, which is a weird one, and Mercury Lounge. I'd send in the CDs, and if they liked the music enough, they would give you the least desirable slot possible—like Tuesday at seven. Sam was also starting to sing and record, and we lived in Harlem, in the same apartment. He and I started to go to Joe's Pub every Sunday night because Chocolate Genius [a band and music collective] had a residency there. I was obsessed, we were just superfans. One week, there was a piano player there who I thought was terrible. And most offensively to me, though Joe's Pub had a piano, he was playing on a digital keyboard. So I went backstage after the show, introduced myself to Marc Anthony Thompson,[8] and said, "I hated your keyboardist this

6. Martha Wainwright's father is Loudon Wainwright III. By both of their accounts, their relationship has been testy.

7. This question of musical imprint is similar to questions I kept asking about "voice" in writing or a particular style in visual art. Where does it come from? My own paintings have my imprint, whether I like it or not. My editing style did too. The magazines I edited all were, I was told, recognizably my work, though not through any intention of my own. Is a style, in any of these contexts, cultivated or does it just happen?

8. Marc Anthony Thompson, a singer-songwriter, started Chocolate Genius, a musical collective.

WHAT A TEACHER CAN DO

"I started to work with a teacher who completely opened the world to me," Thomas said. "She introduced me to the concept of art: this is a thing to take seriously. I remember the first Bach that she had me play and a feeling of discovery, as I was reading through it, that was electric. It wasn't just fun, it had connection to a grand tradition—a lineage of scholars. You could devote your life to this thing. I was her most gifted student. I remember pretty early there was a Bach prelude and fugue that she had me play. I brought it in and played it, and she was almost in tears afterward. And then she showed me how it would normally be played. She said, 'You showed me another way.'"

week, I hated the digital piano." He said, "Do you play?" I said yes, he took my number and called me and said, "Do you want to play?" I said, "Of course, yes." He said, "What gear do you have?" and I didn't have any, but I'm googling as I'm on the phone, there was a Wurlitzer for $1,000 at Rogue Music. So I said, "I have a Wurlitzer." I bought one on the way to rehearsal. I knew the songs inside and out. This was a bunch of musicians I totally revered, and they were super impressed with me. I played the show that night. So because of my contra skills and really crazy technical technique, I could outplay any of them. And everything can be traced to that show. Pat [Dillet] and Dougie [Bowne] were in the audience. Dougie became the Doveman drummer. Pat produced all the Doveman records. David Byrne was in the audience. And Oren Bloedow was playing, that's how I started playing with Elysian Fields. So I started to play with Chocolate Genius, I went on tour with Elysian Fields, in Europe. Dropped out of Columbia. And never stopped.

How Doveman Was Born

TB: I wanted to be an indie rock star. I totally did. It's just so horrifying to think about, but the National somehow found me, and invited me to record with them as a session musician. Then they invited me to start playing with them when they were playing live, and I said, "I will, if I can open." I was always trying to leverage Doveman into things. My initial impulse was, I can't get that many people to come to a Doveman show, but if I do a Doveman show with Glen and Norah, people are gonna come and hear me sing.

AM: *Did it give you pleasure at that point? Or was it just the abstract idea of indie fame?*

TB: It was the abstract idea of it. I was so uncomfortable with being onstage, I would always be off in a corner, as hidden as possible. Sam, who played banjo, would be center stage. I had Sam do all the talking, chatting and making surreal jokes. I didn't get huge pleasure out of performing the songs I don't think, and I always knew it was a little wispy to grab people's attention. But somehow I still held on to the idea. I thought, *I'm going to make this music and I'll bring people around to my aesthetic eventually.*

AM: *As opposed to trying to refine the music into something that was more . . .*

TB: Palatable. Or popular.

AM: *But the writing of the songs you liked.*

TB: Very much. And I realized this recently. For probably ten years I had a running internal dialogue in my head, just thinking about lyrics. Just trying to write. All the time. Like when I was going to sleep, that was the only thing I was thinking about.

A SOFT PLACE

GLEN HANSARD: Thomas's whole thing is intimacy. Every artist wants to be seen, wants to be loved. Making records is a complicated and difficult endeavor, because you're putting so much on the line—you want it to sound one way one minute, completely the opposite the next, your vulnerabilities are all exposed. And in this area, Thomas is a soft place. He knows exactly how to push. He knows how to tell you it's not good enough. He creates an intimate atmosphere where you're allowed to fail. Being around people like Thomas Bartlett makes you want to be better. My friendship with him—I wanted that sound on my record. Basically, when we first did this song, we just kind of wandered into the studio. My version was quite straight. If I like a song, I usually just sing it. I don't ever really plan to make it my own. It was a pretty nice version, but I remember feeling it was too on the nose. I was absolutely delighted when he got back to me and said, "Look, let's try this." Thomas came back with this version; I just melted.

AM: *Lyrics, not musical phrases?*
TB: Very often I would have the outline of a song and know musically more or less what was going to happen, but only have a few words. I remember there was a show that in retrospect couldn't have been more perfect, but at the time, it was like, *Oh God, what am I doing wrong?* A Doveman show at Joe's Pub. But the entirety of the audience was Lou Reed, Laurie Anderson, David Byrne, Antony, and my parents. They were the only people in the room.
AM: *That's quite a collection of fans.*
TB: Yeah, and it felt great. But there's only so far you can take that particular kind of niche cult appeal. Somewhere along there—I guess it had to do with Glen deciding that he wanted me to produce his record—slowly but surely, the ambition and feeling of where I'm focused started to shift from Doveman into making music for other people. Being a gatherer of talent. Then it was hard for me to even conceive of having wanted to be sitting onstage, singing my songs.

The Abdication

AM: *Was there a particular moment you decided to, essentially, give Doveman up?*
TB: It was very gradual. By the time I put out the last Doveman record, which I thought had all the elements lined up—like, I had changed the aesthetic just a little to be more popular, and I had famous friends lined up behind me. The National is the backing band for half the record, Glen is singing on it, Norah is singing on it, Martha is singing. Maybe this was a reaction to the disappointment that it didn't do what I expected—but in my head I was already moving away from even wanting it that much.
AM: *But it seems you could have continued to write and record music and not perform it.*
TB: And that's in fact what I'm doing. I made a Doveman record a couple of years ago that I think is very clearly the best Doveman record, by leaps and bounds. And I'm not going to release it. I'd made it after this revelation I had—that I was getting all this work as a sideman, as a session musician, and I had found I was really good at finding little instrumental hooks, making things catchy, doing flashy things that bring a burst. But it was unthinkable to use any of that on my own music. It was somehow impure. If you listen to a Doveman record, you would have no way of knowing that I'm a good piano player. None at all. Somehow that felt admirable to me—that I had this really beautiful aesthetic restraint. But this record wasn't like that; I treated it as if I were producing myself for the first time. I thought, *I really am capable of this thing that I like.* I'm so often as a producer telling people to stop overcomplicating things, stop getting in their own way. In the past I might have chewed it over and over. On this one, gesturally, I thought, *Just go with it.*
AM: *So why not release it?*
TB: Well, one of the reasons is how much I hate performing, and there would have been pressure to do at least a few shows. I had this realization that the record had been happier to me as a thing that just existed, that friends heard in a room, than it was as a thing out in the world. You know? I've played it for people I love, and I've tried to imagine a way that releasing it would make me feel better, and I've not been able to come up with one that seems in any way possible.
AM: *Is there just a kind of erasure that you're seeking?*
TB: Totally. I like the feeling of being invisible. It feels kind of glamorous to have made this thing and not let people hear it. I like that.
AM: *The arc of your career has such a poetic shape to it. Like a crescendo of self and talent, which you then pulled back into its disappearance.*
TB: Absolutely.
AM: *And its reanimation in others.*
TB: As a producer, I am able to do this thing I could not do as a performer. I look back on myself with a huge amount of mystification. I have these ambitions and then I'm making art that telegraphs in every way, "Don't look at me." I was intensely divided and didn't know it. I'm baffled by that.

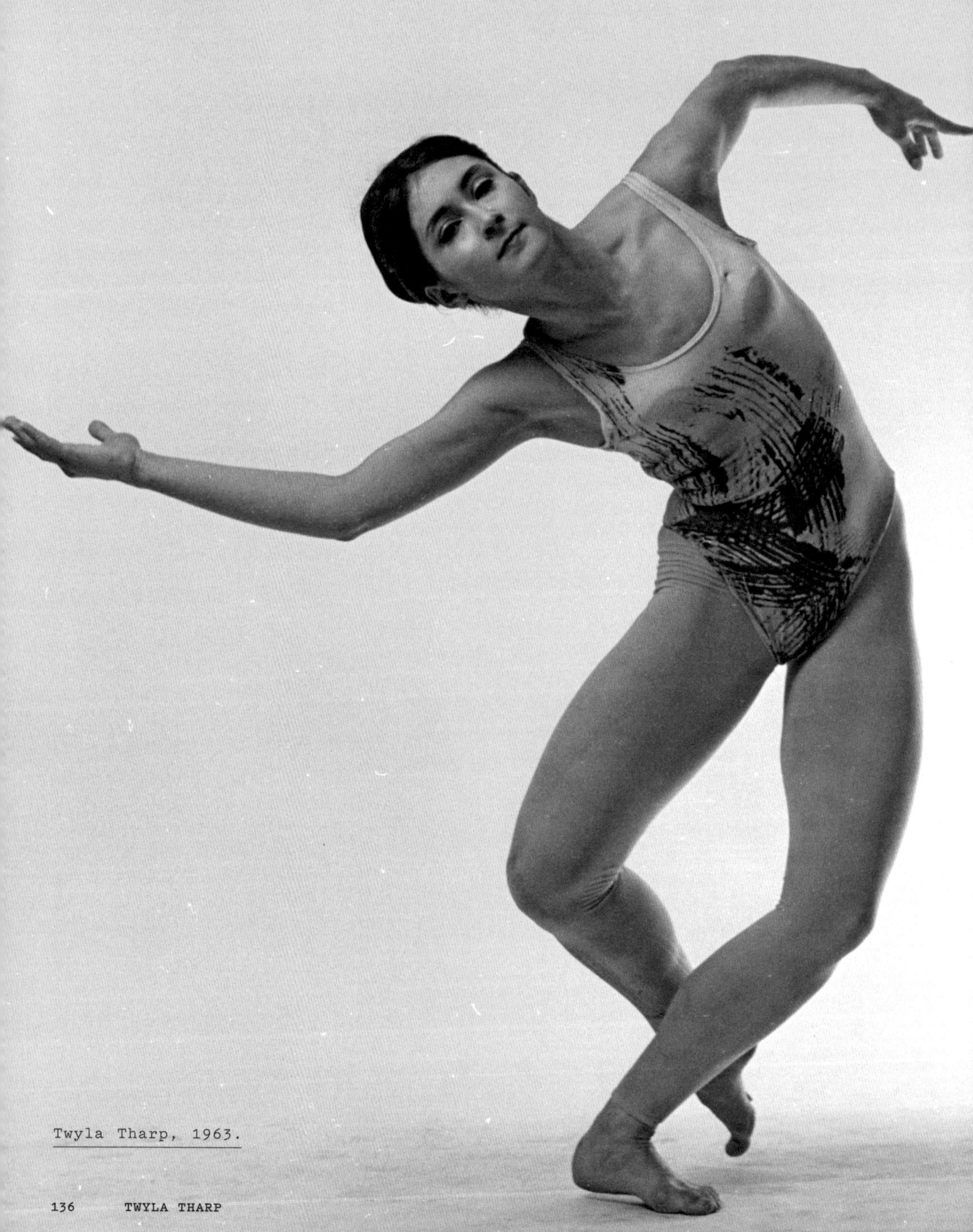

Twyla Tharp, 1963.

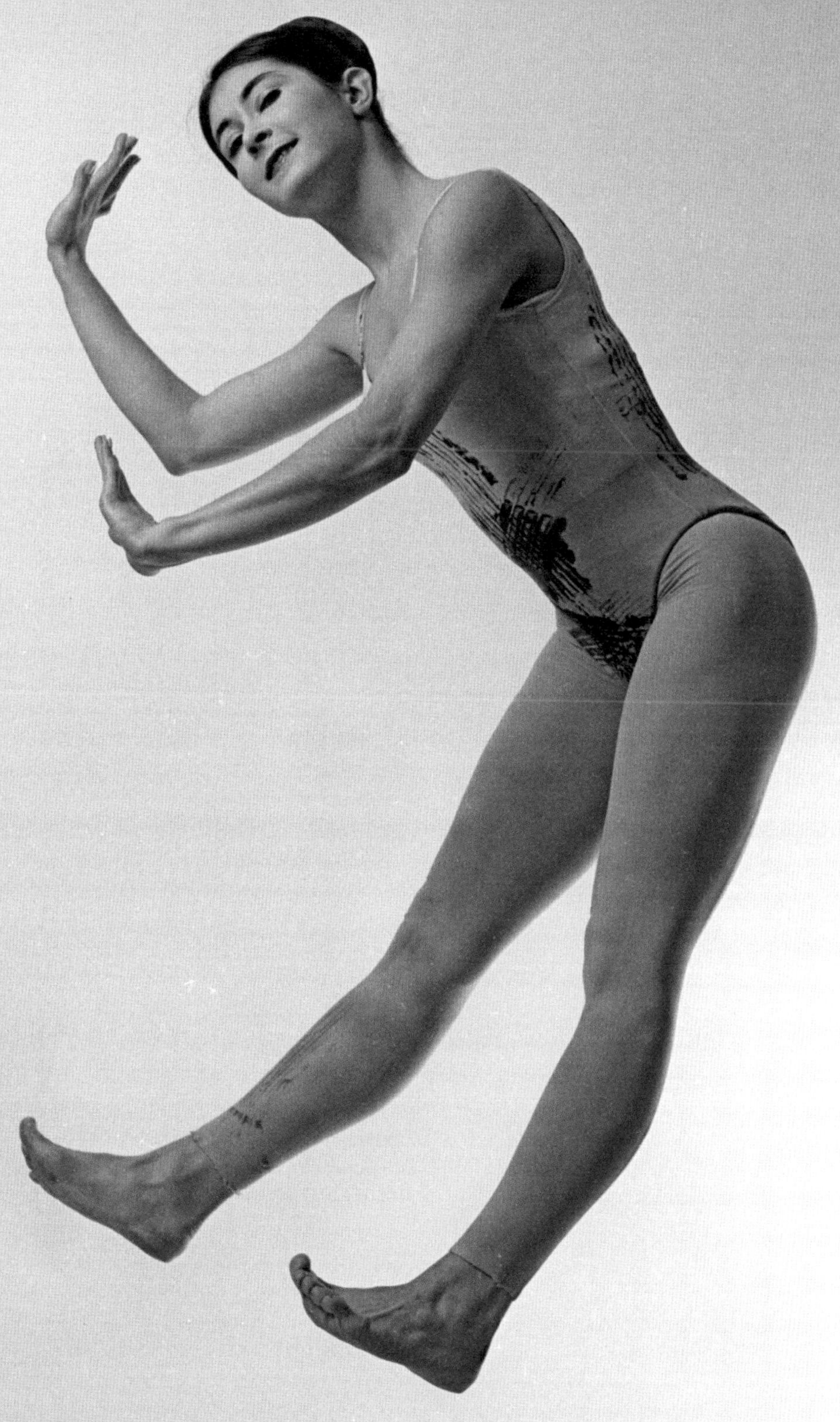

13
TWYLA THARP
The Sperm Bank and the Scroll

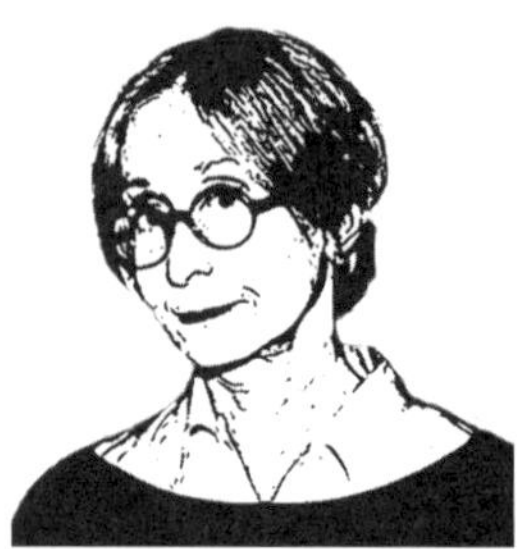

OCCUPATION: Choreographer

WORK DISCUSSED: "Commentaries on the Floating World"; *Twyla Now* (2021)

BORN: 1941

I WAS AT TWYLA THARP'S HOUSE, which is also her studio. It's up in the sky on Central Park West, a penthouse. When you enter, there's a large, empty, light-soaked room, with a wood floor like you see in rehearsal spaces, because that's what it is. This space takes up most of her apartment. There's a tiny bed tucked in the back, separated by pretty versions of hospital curtains, a Northern California bathroom, an elegant bourgeois kitchen, everything immaculate. But that's it. It's otherwise a giant temple to dance—a gleaming wood blank slate and a busy cluster of cameras to the side, light pouring in from the skylight. I described the setup to a friend, who immediately said, "Oh, she's an art monk," which fit.

Tharp is also charming and a big flirt. We were sitting in the kitchen, discussing the work she was about to make, "In C." COVID had just arrived, but she was madly busy. "Okay, here's the thing, the body to those of us who are dance people, we give precedence to it over the mind. For example, I'll find myself on the street, and I'll be a little cold and waiting in a line, and I'll start to [she makes a little movement], and I go, *Oh that was good*. I say to myself, *Remember, we can use that.* It's like, *Okay, brain, catch up with the body.*"

I asked how she captures these movements she makes on the street.

"Are you ready?" she said. She told me to follow her.

We entered the main room, where I saw a giant scroll of paper unspooled on the floor from one end of a part of the room to the other, maybe fourteen feet long and two feet wide. This, it turns out, is her notebook.

We squatted to look at the beginning of the scroll and tried to make it out. "I started to work on a piece called 'In C,' which is Terry Riley," she said, naming the composer. "Do you know that piece of music?" I said no. "Well, you should," she said sternly. Also impishly. It was a little bit of a performance.

"Terry Riley was given credit for having distorted music into what we call minimalism." Tharp first heard the piece in the sixties

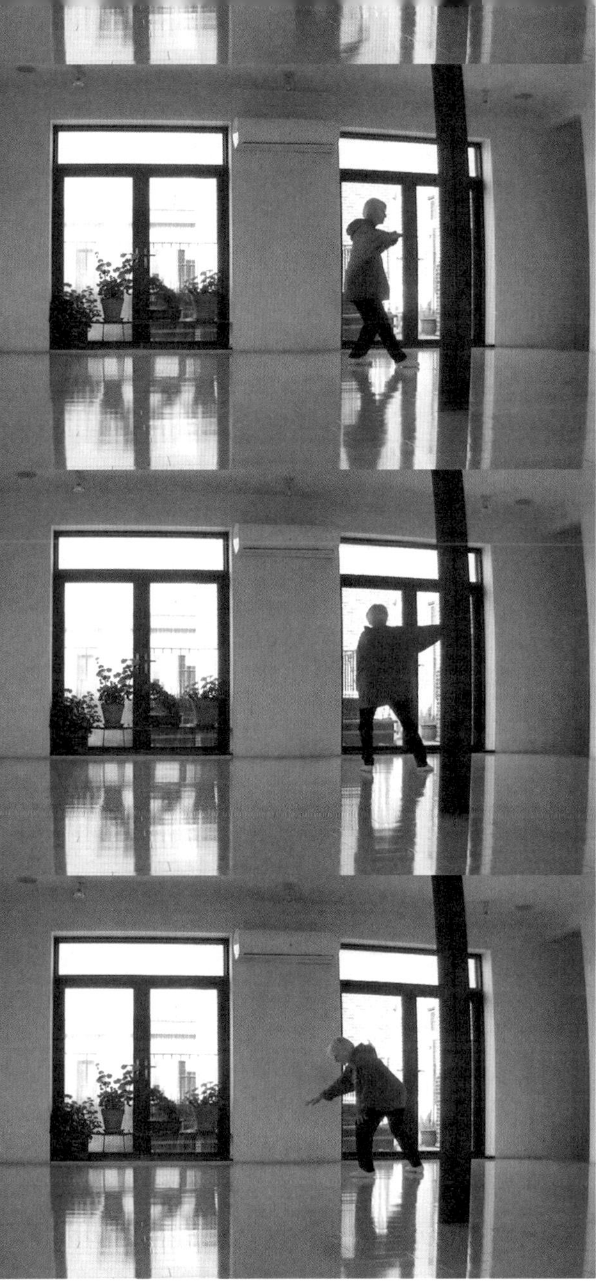

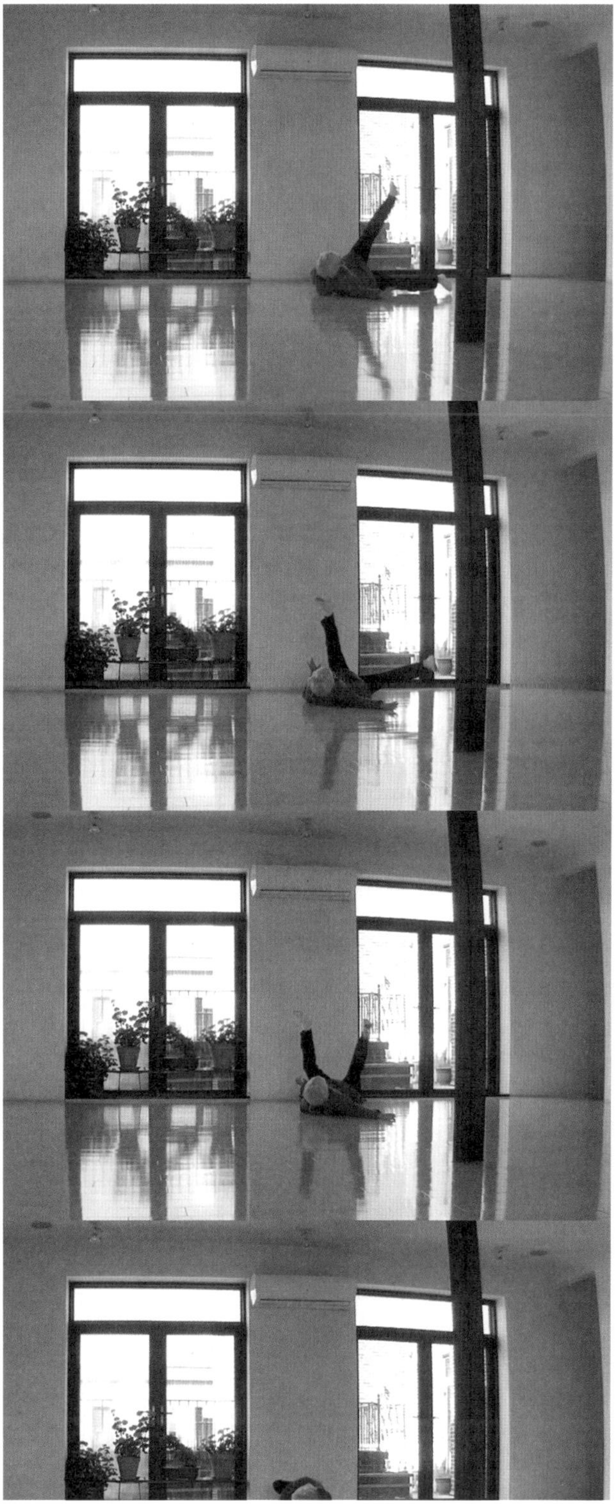

From the sperm bank. One move, broken down. She has thousands of hours of these tapes.

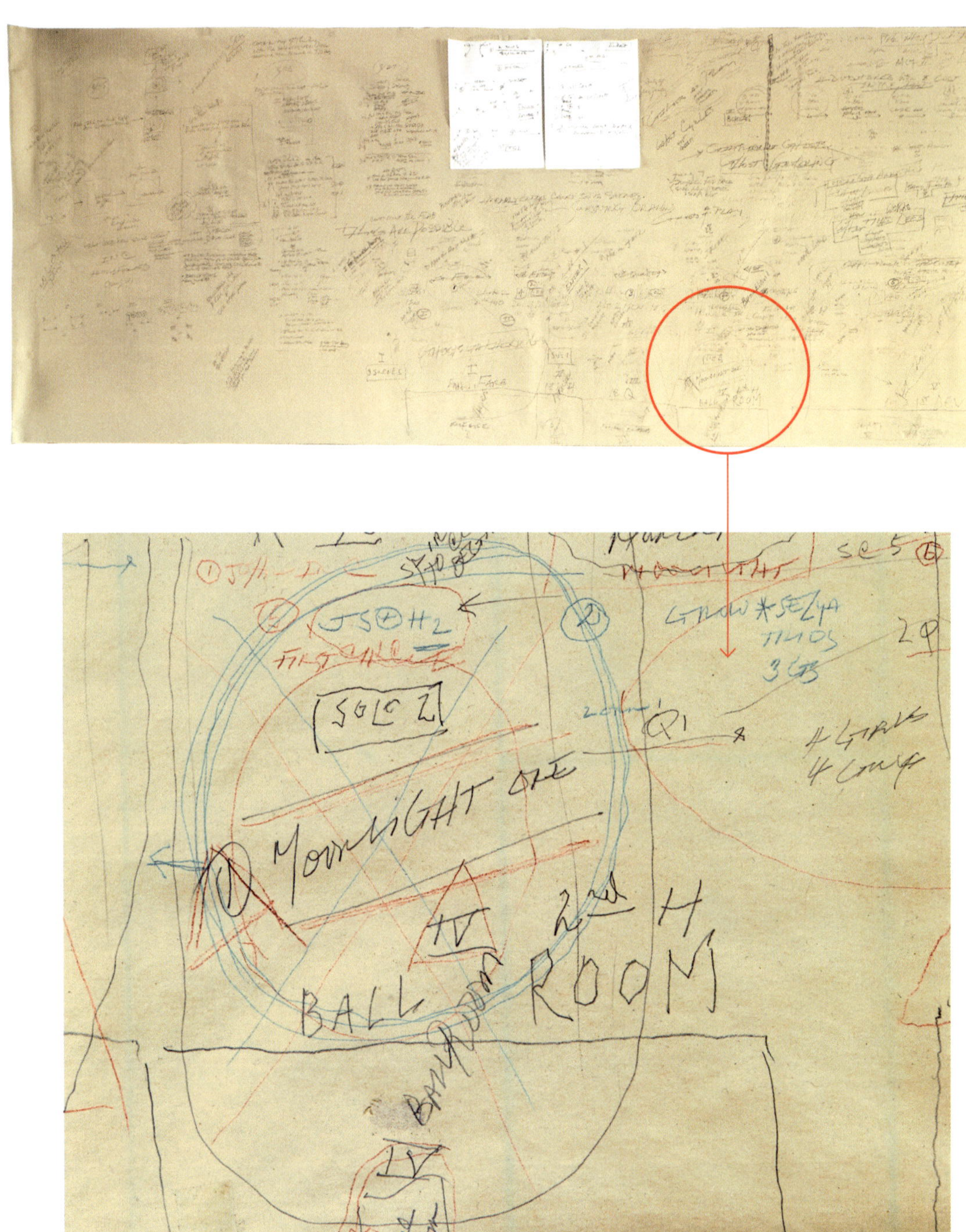

The scroll and (below) a detail: "The scrolls are a relatively recent development," she said. "The scrolls are like the subconscious. They're rough ideas. Vague. And I can do proportions on them. As I move along, I can do timing–all of which you can't do on pieces of paper. And then it becomes about the structure of the thing."

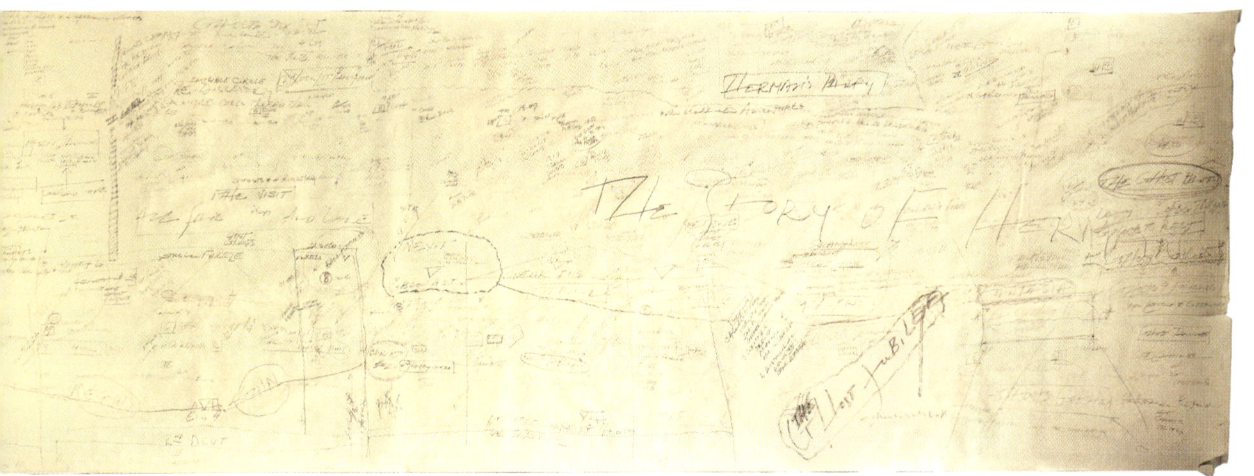

and had been mulling making dance to it ever since. "It has no melodic element, no kind of build, no structural development. It's chance operative, in that its form can be any number of instruments coming in at any time, as long as they play these fifty-three units—for any length of time they want until they're done." In other words, it is a seemingly impossible piece of music to set dance to, which was why she'd always wanted to tackle it.[1] "It has truth in it," she said.

She pointed to the scroll and began narrating what she was seeing on it, which all looked like hieroglyphics to me. "We'll go like this and then we'll go like that. *Bodyee* or *yupboteat* or *eeup* or *up*." I was mystified, but the scroll is just for her; no one else is supposed to understand it. "I got this scroll out," she explained, "because I was invited to do a Zoom project and I said what the hell am I going to do. So I thought, 'In C.' It's just that every time I start 'In C,' something gets in the way. It's such a difficult, unpleasant piece. I must have started it eight or ten times."

The scroll was a record of initial working out of the piece—like notes she's jotting down as she figures it out.

"Opposition, snap, attitude front, weight on right, alt left. Open attitude, pirouette, right and right. Flic flac over under, transfer weight left."

Tharp was recovering from a meniscus tear in her leg and limping around the apartment a bit, but still able to demonstrate, dragging me in as a partner. I was hopeless. She was amused. I asked her if what she's written on the scroll was her own language. "Well, it's bastardized like dialect—some of it is ballet. Flic Flac is in the ballet, but snap is not. Snap is like a snap."

The scroll notes were from the last time she was trying to make this dance—for an American Ballet Theatre commission. She'd abandoned it because she learned that her commission was going to premiere at a gala. "I thought, *Oh dear, these people are paying $25,000 a table and then they see 'In C' and it drags on and goes nowhere? I don't think so.*" She gave them a Brahms quintet instead, for a piece that ended up being called "A Gathering of Ghosts." She is not above pleasing her audience—far from it.

But when she recently got another commission from a ballet company in Düsseldorf to make anything she wanted, she thought, okay, she's going to do it this time—make "In C," finally. Because of the pandemic, she will

1. Challenge motivates, as opposed to terrifies, or in spite of terrifies, over and over on these pages. If challenge was not a goad for you, you probably wouldn't be in this line of work.

make it by Zoom. She pointed to two more scrolls, which were empty now but eventually will be filled with markings, plotting out the entire ballet. "That'll allow me to stand back and look at the whole piece and see if I move along with it, the drama, the non-drama. See what's flat, fix that." And it'll tell her where every dancer is onstage.

"At this point I probably have four and a half, five hours of material on 'In C.' So I will go back and edit that." She had devised a system to create order within the relative anarchy of the piece, which she described as "doing it on the clock." While the musicians will play as they're intended to play (start and finish more or less whenever they want), the dancers will always be in sync with the clock. I'm not going to describe how that works exactly (I'm not sure I even understand it), but it creates structure, which makes the dance possible. "The basic part is called the pulse," Tharp said, "and it's really boring and just starts with something simple. The idea is, this person is on the whole time, and they will evolve their movements, so you never see them shift, but you never see them static either." She knows at this point that she is going to work in a piece of movement that appears at the beginning of the scroll. Then another section will be something she created in another context, which she calls Savannah because she originally choreographed it for a dancer named Savannah Lowery. And then also another she calls Sam & Mary, which she originally created for a lecture she gave.

Savannah and Sam & Mary are taken from an enormous digital vault she keeps of her ideas, which she refers to as her "sperm bank." It's like an overstuffed trunk of dance phrases, movements, set pieces. To the side of the rehearsal space is a thicket of video equipment that's crucial to her process. Video is how she records her ideas, which she dances out herself. And it's also how she communicates with her dancers.

In the case of "In C," her dancers were in Germany, and so the equipment was vital. She was choreographing the ballet virtually from her apartment, teaching the steps with her video camera by dancing all the parts herself, which is crazy because most of the ballet is performed in duets and groups, big swaths in unison. But she uses the camera even when she choreographs locally. She generally does all the moves herself, with no one around to help demonstrate.

That's because it's clear she is absolutely certain no one can do it like she can. Tharp doesn't even try to fake the creative humility you see in many artists—no one I talked to was more brazenly confident, more willing to own the narcissism it takes to make art.[2] But she was disarming about it, and it was refreshing. "I know exactly what it's supposed to be like, I don't have to explain what it is. I do it." And then Tharp broke into dialogue, arguing with herself: "I say, 'Well that's not what I want.' I say, 'No because it's better.' I say, 'You're right, I was wrong, excuse me.'" She cracked herself up.

As she talked about what she wanted to put in the ballet, she free-associated. "Circles—circles are very interesting. Clockwise, counterclockwise, inside, outside, the juxtaposition of circles going into a single point, the spiral." She got around to the Korean boy band BTS. "I think they're great. They've managed to do the ideal thing, being singular in growth so you feel their individualness, but also their unity. The more you can bring differences to the table and yet reconcile, that's power."

Like all choreographers, she creates dances for specific dancers. She'd spent some time getting to know the dancers in Germany virtually, assessing what they can do and can't do, evaluating their talent and also, in some cases dismissively, their attitude. She wanted dancers who were devoted to the project.

After she determined who can do what, "I'll have them in the room, if they can't do it, I'll change it so they can make it work." And in some sense, they are collaborators: "They know their bodies better than you do. You

2. I don't mean narcissism pejoratively. Not in this context. I envy it, if anything.

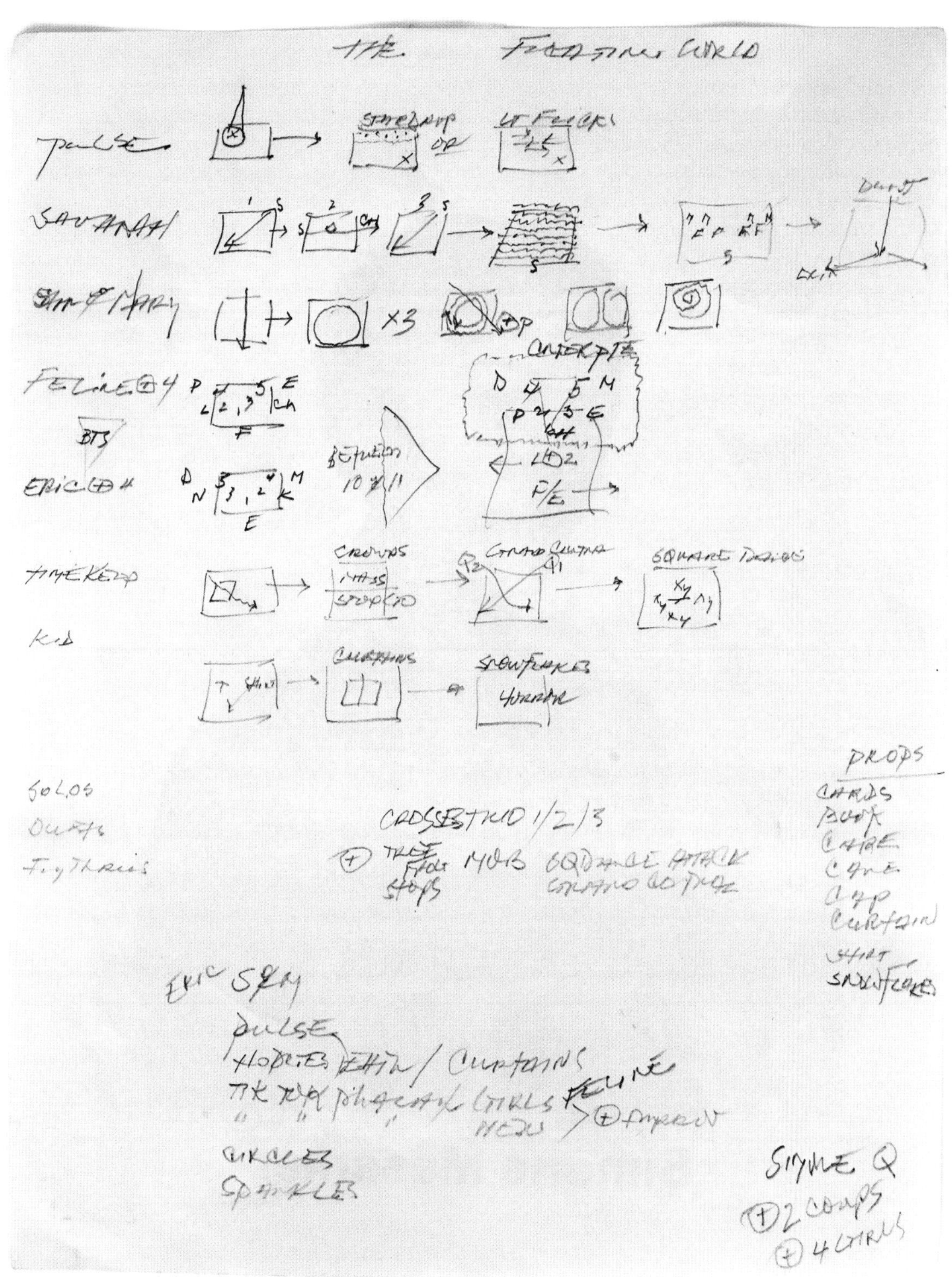

Notebook notations (an actual notebook) for “In C” (later “Commentaries on the Floating World”).

listen to them, right?" I asked if she allows for their suggestions. Tharp said, "If they're clever, they don't ask. They just do it and hope you won't notice . . . but you do. And you say, 'Well, that actually is a good idea!' Because you have to keep them around. . . ."

But whatever alteration happens during the rehearsal period, it happens fast. "You have two weeks to do it, because if you aren't done by the end of two weeks, they're brain dead. They're fried. They can't take in any more information."

She had three months from our conversation until those rehearsals—she had to have the whole piece pretty much worked out, which involves, beyond creative expression, a certain amount of train trafficking, knowing where the dancers go in and out, making sure she hasn't created something so reckless it'll result in broken limbs. Even with the difficulty of choreographing from 3,700 miles away, she was characteristically undaunted, eager to figure it out.

We went back to the kitchen, and I asked her to start at the beginning:

Twyla Tharp: I started making dances when I was six. I had twin brothers and a younger sister. And when the babysitter was there, I had a quartet. We did some swinging around.

My mother blessed everything, she was a concert pianist. She started all four of her kids on ear training while we were still tiny babies. By the time I was two years old, I was practicing like two hours a day. I continued in that way until I went to college. I was studying counterpoint when I was a kid. Without that exposure at that age, I [couldn't have done it]. Only a child's mind works that way.[3] It binds everything to the rhythm and the love of music. That's just who children are. It made me capable of a focus.

Adam Moss: *Did your siblings grow up the same way?*

TT: They didn't. My mother couldn't maintain it. My brothers were twins. They developed their own language, a private language. They had accents. By the time they went to first grade, they still couldn't speak English. My mother couldn't get to them the way she could get to me.

AM: *Do you think it was your mother's intensity that fueled your creative drive?*[4]

TT: Apart from the lessons, the thing that was most valuable in my childhood was working at a drive-in. And seeing how those films, even without sound, communicated and bound the audience together.

AM: *Do you make dances with audiences in mind?*

TT: There are movements that an audience will feel, and there are movements that will push them back in their seats; they'll be in awe. You have that kind of control. When I started making pieces for a bigger market, suddenly you have to take into account, how do people think? How do they feel?. . .

You know when we were doing the so-called avant-garde,[5] and the audiences got bored, that was their problem. But then it became my problem. And I knew how to keep the audience from getting bored. It changed me. The avant-garde is basically, fuck you. It's icy and isolated and very privileged in its attitude. Just because it's inaccessible, is it better art? I don't know about that.

AM: *When you work out little movements, like the sort you said you did on the street, are you trying to solve a problem? Do you say, I have six minutes here, let me just . . .*

TT: No, I like it to sneak up on me. I like to be surprised. I'm a restless child.[6]

AM: *So it's always movement first, not mind first?*

TT: Well, if I see a necessity—how to get them in, how to get them out, that's a different deal. Or if you're dealing with narrative and you

3. Another early start, when the plasticity of a child's mind just makes it all go down so easy.

4. Maybe here's the place to say that Tharp has written a quite good, very successful, much-passed-around creativity book herself, called *The Creative Habit*.

5. Tharp began in the avant-garde before moving into ballet, but it's ballet that integrates modern dance, jazz, hip-hop, and anything else—popular, classical—that interests her. This mixture of styles was considered revolutionary.

6. Tharp is hardly the only subject in this book to describe herself as a child.

7. This line about needing to disassociate from yourself in order to be sufficiently ruthless with your work, uttered early in these conversations, followed me through every one that followed.

8. The context of this remark was something she said to me earlier, off the cuff, dismissing dancers who only started to choreograph when they'd retired. Twyla had made a career out of choreography. The arrivistes made her mad.

have a narrative problem. But that's usually more thinking, *Oh, I've done something like this before, I'll bet I could use it.* I mean, if I get up against the wall, I'm not above pulling in something I know will work because I've already done it that way.

AM: *Do you find yourself dreaming solutions?*

TT: On occasion when I'm on deadline and my neck is really on the line, I will realize my situation is so dire that I must have a solution in the morning. I can do that. I can will myself to dream it. Also, every now and then I'll wake up with a certain kind of feeling, and it will be enough to send me into a different way of thinking. Maybe because I was injured, in the night recently I was feeling water, water, water, and I'm going, *Yeah.* Water. No stoppage, nothing abrupt.

AM: *In general, do you have to see the whole thing, or can you build a dance part by part?*

TT: By part. I used to get nervous about either the ending or the beginning, but then I realized the ending is just another part like the middle. There's a Chekhov story I love. He had a nephew who came to him with his little book; he's studying writing. He says, "Uncle Chekhov, where do I start my story?" And Chekhov says, "Take your blue book, tear it in half, and start there." Often I go back and redo the beginning, because though you may think you know where you're going, it's probably going to end up differently. And I find that it's valuable to let it evolve and then go back and take off that fake beginning.

AM: *How important is the beginning?*

TT: You have thirty seconds. Thirty seconds before people are either bored or they love you. You can win them later, but it's going to be harder.

AM: *Is that thirty seconds the hardest part?*

TT: No, I'm pretty good at that part.

AM: *How do you think about editing your work?*

TT: Editing means, how much objectivity do you have really? How much can you disassociate from your own bias? How much can you disassociate yourself from the wish fulfillment component that is involved in work of all sorts? You've got to become not you.[7]

AM: *What kinds of dancers make the best choreographers?*

TT: Young ones.[8]

AM: *Is worrying what your dancers can handle a big part of your thinking as you work through a piece?*

TT: Always. It's always what's reasonable and then push a little beyond that. Not too far.

AM: *You've been doing this a long time. What do you know now that you didn't when you started?*

TT: I've learned it's more rewarding for me to be empathetic.

AM: *Is experience ever a detriment—does it ever inhibit you creatively, knowing what hasn't worked before?*

TT: You have to forget it didn't work. It's different now. Who knows?

AM: *When you finish a piece, are you still toying with it years later?*

TT: Noooooo. I am done with it, and if I am not saying at the end of that, *I'm never making another piece ever again in my whole life, I've put it all out there*—if I don't accomplish that, the piece is no good.

And that seemed the right place to stop.

Six months later In May 2021, I was back in her apartment. We were photographing the scroll and her notebooks. I didn't have to be there, but I came anyway because I sort of fell in love with her the first time. She was in an even feistier mood.

This time, we took our seats and stared at her computer together. Tomorrow, she would enter a rehearsal studio for the first time since COVID to start putting together a new show at City Center. She was eager to show me what she was planning. But first, I asked her how "In C" went. Indulging me, she searched for a video. The piece had been renamed "Commentaries on the Floating World" and shot as a recording but not, at that point, performed live.

For the next couple of hours, I watched her watch the screen, narrating. First up was this piece.

"See this. Seventeen dancers, forty minutes in three weeks. Running two studios simultaneously with four assistants. Here we go—"

As she watched, she was impressed with what she was seeing. "Actually, it's a good piece." She pointed out phrases she liked especially. As she was making the piece from afar, she'd dug them out of her archive. "You don't have time to come up with this many ideas in three weeks, believe me. You have to stockpile it. The material is being used so quickly. I fed whole phrases in, which ordinarily you can't do."

In our earlier conversation, she'd talked about a male dancer whose attitude she didn't like. Without prompting, she brought him up again: "There was one guy in there that was so fucked-up, I said don't go there. Attitude, moved weird, was a little aggressive. He's not—nobody is worth it. I kept watching, and I'm saying to myself, *Don't do it*. And he turned out to be fabulous."

When I asked her how the dancers accommodated the complicated demands of the music that's always changing, I realized that, of all Tharp's traits, resilience is maybe the most striking one. In our last conversation, we'd spent so much time talking about how important the radical nature of Riley's music was to the piece. Now, she casually mentioned she'd abandoned the entire scheme. All those random variations—out.

"It had to be set. Because they're German. They could not accommodate the notion of spontaneity. But it's okay. It basically set itself. It's not like Brahms, you can't dick around with Brahms."

Later, I asked her about the frustration she'd exhibited in one portion of an *American Masters* documentary I'd just seen (in it, she fretted over the difficulty of choreographing on Zoom), and she told me that she'd faked her frustration, or at least amped it up, so the filmmakers would have some tension to work with.[9] She says she simply doesn't get frustrated: "It doesn't happen to me. If something turns a corner, I turn a corner."

Anyway, she didn't really want to talk about "In C" / "Commentaries on the Floating World." She was onto the next thing. She found a grainy seven-year-old video of the New York City Ballet dancer Tiler Peck working out a piece with her fellow dancer Robbie Fairchild. This duet will be the first dance in the City Center program she was going to start rehearsing tomorrow, which was called *Twyla Now*.

The video is from when Tharp had lured Peck and Fairchild up to a Harlem dance studio for a piece she wanted to make. "It was done," she said, "because these two dancers who are very talented and who were bored to tears at the City Ballet and it's snowing outside and the poor little things, their boots leak. So they come up to Harlem, they're rehearsing, and they cut *Nutcracker* rehearsals in order to just come in and dance. And I made the whole thing very fast. I'm very fast. These are very talented, sophisticated dancers. Tiler Peck is faster than the shit. So it's like bang bang, okay, speed. We'll use speed."

Peck and Fairchild returned to Harlem over and over to make the dance with Tharp. She was seductive and they were hungry. "I mean genuinely, they were freezing to death. If one of them had been injured, that would have been it, I had no insurance. Nobody was paying them. Nobody knew we were working there." On the screen, she was watching Peck. "Tiler has this. It'll be interesting to see the dancer she is six or seven years later. . . . Okay, now, already you see Robbie, who's a very good dancer, freeze. It's probably the third time they've done this. He didn't know what he was doing—"

Tharp was staring into her computer, loving this. "It's a very unusual adagio. And it's not easy to find a new adagio, because there have been hundreds of thousands of adagios done. So that's what I'm looking for."

Peck, whom Tharp describes as "a charmer and will get out there and sell it to death," will perform the piece with a different dancer at City Center.

9. Her helping the documentarians wasn't a fluke. I noticed how invested she seemed to be in others' success. Dancers, writers: she talked about the whole wide world of creative types as if it were one family, and she was its mom. Just one more reason to love her.

Fairchild will be there, too, but in a different piece, dancing Tharp's part in a piece she did with Mikhail Baryshnikov for a show they took on tour. (Baryshnikov's part will be done by the City Ballet star Sara Mearns.) She finds footage of that show in her archive.

"Our tour was the highest grossing tour in dance. We beat Fonteyn and Nureyev." I asked if making a work for Baryshnikov intimidated her, but I already knew the answer. "You're a modern dancer from the Midwest. He's a superstar. You go, *Okay, I can do this. Let's see* you *do this.* And then pretty soon, there's a respect that gets developed. He was handed that [his talent] on a silver platter. He was instantly a great dancer. And what do I have to do? I have to construct an entire vocabulary, make dances, and still people are baffled."

Finally, we got to the finale of the dance, which she watched intently, pointing to a particularly triumphant last gesture she makes. "Oh, I love that part. That part is so good! You'd pay money to see that, right? I always give myself the last word. After all, I was the choreographer."

Sandwiched between these two pieces will be a world premiere, which was developed out of improvisations she did years ago and deposited in her "sperm bank." This video vault is another kind of notebook.

"Okay," she said, opening the video vault, "here is the historic sperm bank. These are historic documents." She started recording herself playing around in 1968, and has made, she said, thousands of hours of tape, sometimes bringing in others to play around with her. "I started making phrases I could lift whole cloth, take off James Brown, put on Brahms if the material is good. This is me evolving a phrase, actually. This is how a phrase gets solidified. It's like you have a rough piece of wood and you're carving it into a form and then you polish it and so forth—"

As she was looking for the tape she had decided to adapt for this new piece, she stopped at one faded tape of her dancing with a male partner. "Ah, this is a guy I picked up in the gym, I started working on it with him. . . . Okay, here's the duet—"

It's from 1991. You can see a younger Tharp trying out all sorts of moves in an empty studio, some lyrical, some athletic, many very difficult. I was spellbound. Tharp was too: "Okay, this is the duet I will start to rehearse tomorrow. The trick will be setting it on two dancers so it looks improvised. . . . I'm going to have to look at this in slow motion to figure out what the hell he's doing here. It's a flip in the half."

She was watching closely, thinking about tomorrow. "It's gonna be very hard to get dancers to be able to do that. The problem is, as you can see, I'm very strong. Most women don't have that kind of strength. They can't hold their own weight this way. And dancers are taught to make it look easy. Hello, people, it was not easy."

We wandered through tape after tape; she was in a reverie. "Ah, this is one of these improv sessions that is not making it into anything, which is really kinda too bad because it's a hoot. . . . Here's a good one. I like this one quite a bit. You have to watch it closely. Be patient. Let this finish. . . . Oh, I was a very good dancer. Very accurate. Very unmannered. Very sophisticated dancer . . ."

I asked, somewhat delicately, how it felt not to be able to perform anymore. She bristled, maybe joking, but with her, you can't really tell.

"What do you mean I can't perform anymore? Like I might die?"

It was getting late. Tomorrow her exile will be over. "I haven't been working with dancers in the studio for whatever—a year," she said. She was nearly eighty, and so excited she practically jumped out of her chair.

Six months later I went to see *Twyla Now* at City Center. It was in many ways a culmination of her life's work, and it was beautiful. But I didn't know what was more impressive—what was happening on the stage, or what was happening in the row to my left. I was sitting near her. I watched Twyla Tharp watch Twyla Tharp. She was rapt.

14

JOHN DERIAN

What Did You Do When You Were a Kid?

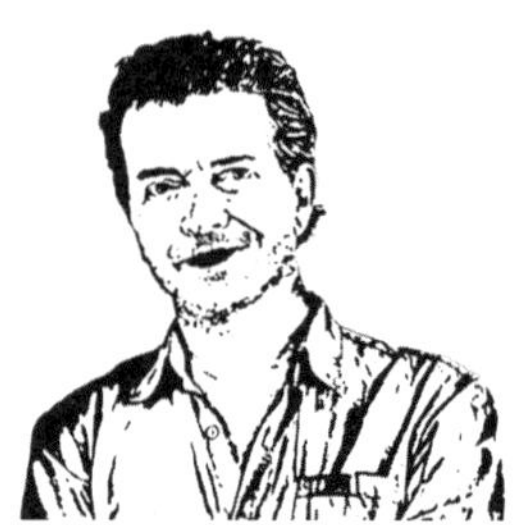

OCCUPATION: Artist/Designer
WORK DISCUSSED: Decoupage
BORN: 1962

JOHN DERIAN HAS THE most specific taste of anyone I know, and he's built an empire around it. He is a one-man brand with five stores selling objets of various kinds to others who share his particular sense of the beautiful: bowls, furniture, puzzles, wallpaper, and especially his John Derian decoupage, decorative plates and such with antiquey-curio prints behind glass that are wildly popular and sell all over the world. What's surprising about all that is that his taste is not at all conventional, though he's almost single-handedly made it more so—it's proven to be very commercial. In any case, it's his, and it's genuine. He doesn't bend to the market. He lives what he sells. He's a friend, and I spend a fair amount of time in his various ramshackle environments, where I see his wonderland in action.

I would define that taste (which I happen to love) as bohemian disrepair, with a vulnerable beauty and a sly Edward Gorey type of wit. Everything seems exquisitely poised between joy and ruin. For his house in Provincetown, he spent a ton of money to preserve the flaking wallpaper and chipping paint—when pictures of the home appeared in a lifestyle blog, the comments flipped between "God, this is heaven" and "How could you live like that?" He defines it more simply: "I like old things. I sort of live in the past. I like the simplicity of it all. I'm kind of eclectic, but not a hoarder. I remember that book *Pentimento* by Lillian Hellman. I just like the idea of layers of stuff behind stuff."

John is funny and disarming and seems as puzzled by himself as everyone else is. He insists he doesn't have any idea how to run a business, though that's clearly not true. But it's certainly not the essence of him. For this chapter, I sat down to assemble what I was thinking of as an aesthetic biography. But really I wanted to talk to him about taste, and how one's taste develops. We sat in his studio on Second Street in the East Village, down the block from three of his stores, a hidden first-floor version of his grandmother's attic overflowing with "ephemera," the catchall phrase

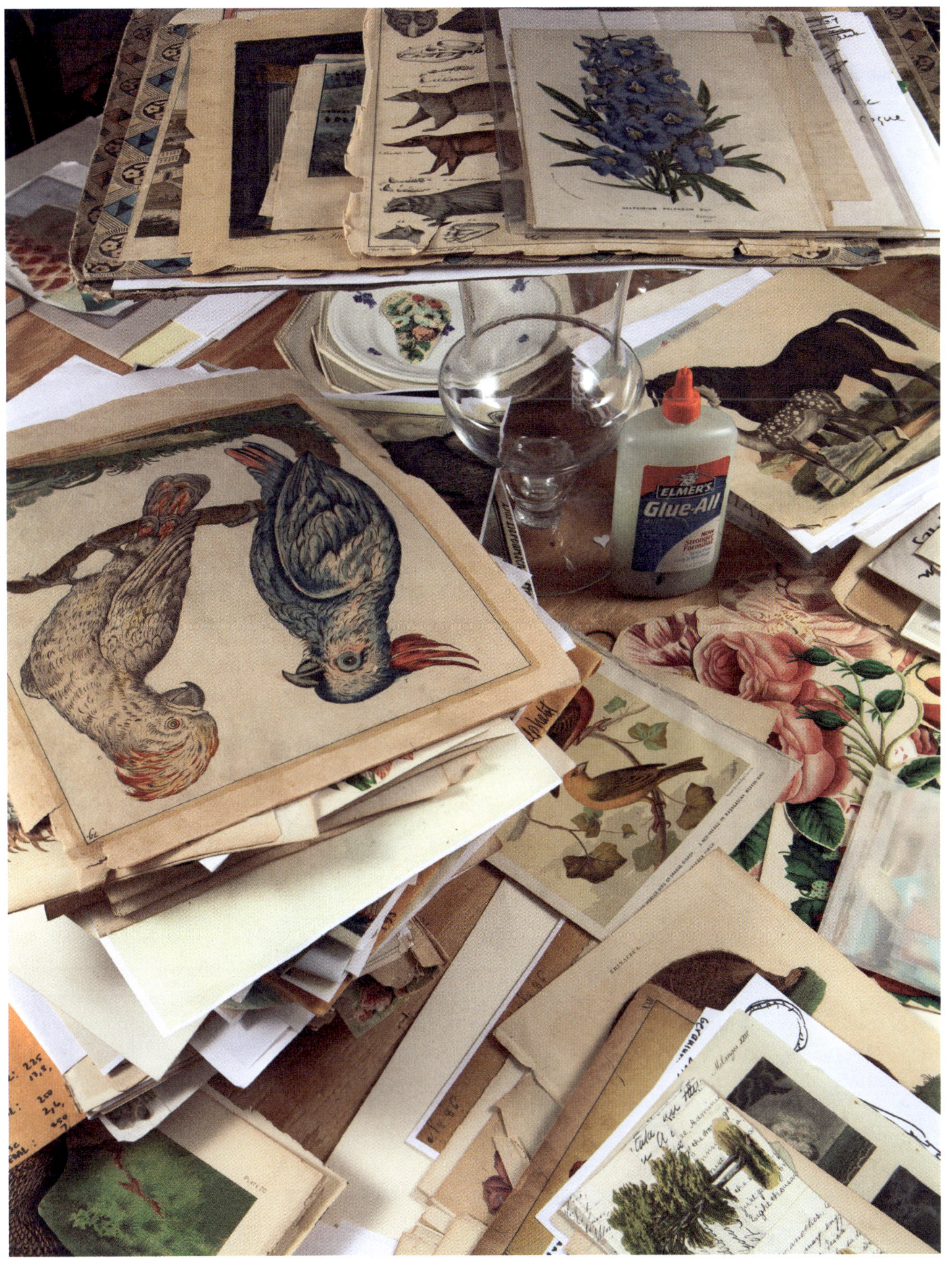

John Derian's desk. Ephemera on the way to the glue factory for decoupage. Also, the glue.

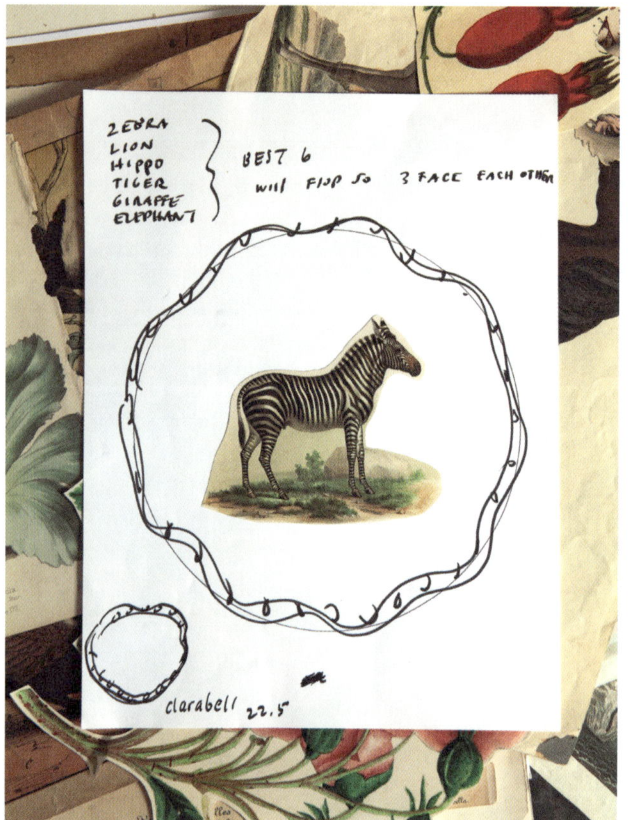

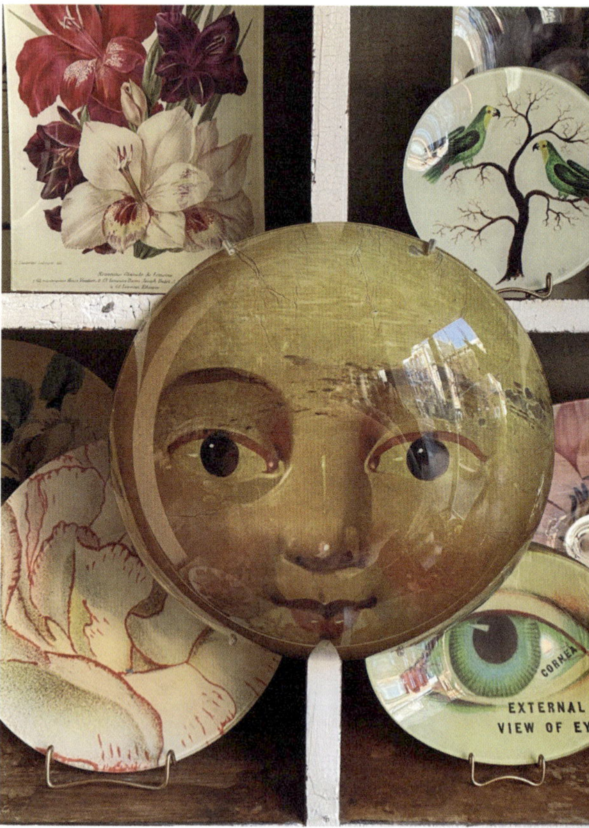

Print to plate. And paperweight. His decoupage knows few bounds.

for the prints that are on their way to becoming decoupage. It is an enchanted room that looks as if it had been mummified just before the invention of the light bulb.

Adam Moss: *With respect to the way you look at the world, how much can you trace back to the beginning of your life?*
John Derian: It's funny—I've had a few occasions where people wanted to meet me to talk about their businesses, as if I had advice. I just say, "What did you do when you were a kid?" Because I feel like I trace everything back to my childhood. I made forts. I created environments, under porches and in trees, and in attics. I was always exploring and always dirty. I remember a tenant in our house threw a bunch of pillows in the trash, and I took the pillows, I put them in the bushes, and made a room. And I'm still making rooms. I was always just moving things around to create a space in the dirt. And I would play in the attic.[1] I had a nephew and niece. My nephew's four and a half years younger than I am, and my niece about seven, and so I would babysit them. In the attic, we had these time machines that I made, and I would push them in a closet and change the whole room around. Then they'd come out of the closet and I'd pretend that they'd traveled somewhere. Even now, they'll tell you that they still believe it.
AM: *Tell me about the attic.*
JD: Well, my grandmother bought the house. It was in Watertown, Mass. She was a really strong, independent woman. Had not the best success with marriage, her husband—my

grandfather—ended up dying in prison—I don't really know why. I think it was sexual abuse. My mother's father was in jail for other things.

AM: *What other things?*

JD: I think alcoholism. But my grandmother was the one in charge. They had a little grocery store. The attic was where I'd play my imaginary games. I'd draw a picture, move furniture around. And playact.

AM: *Was your family concerned with the look of things?*

JD: It was all very basic. When my grandmother died, I was ten, and then my dad took over the whole thing and he basically ripped out all the molding, lowered the ceilings, and paneled the walls. It was the seventies. I was horrified. My grandmother's eyeglasses were just on the walkway, like, fallen. And it seemed awful. I mean, later when I tried to sort of reconnect with him, I found myself helping him do those things to the house, like, building walls or putting up Sheetrock.

AM: *I'd imagine that for you in particular, that would have been painful.*

JD: I just thought that I had to make an effort, because we had such a terrible relationship. I was a creative person in a noncreative family. He was like, *What do I do with this kid?* Which filled me with fear.

AM: *So not much encouragement for your creative pursuits.*

JD: But then in seventh grade, I had an art teacher,[2] and when I told him I did paint by numbers, he just got . . .

AM: *Excited.*

JD: Hostile.

AM: *Oh.*

JD: And yelled. And then threw brushes and watercolors and paper at me. "Don't ever paint by number again." So I started drawing—waterfalls, and painting flowers.

AM: *Did you have talent?*

JD: I didn't really—not at painting. But I was making things too. And collecting things. I was making mobiles and drawing people. Drawing things, cutting them out, stenciling them onto glass and mirrors.

AM: *All right, well, so that's the beginning.*

JD: You know, it is funny when I think about it now. Basically, I would do a drawing of a tree, but then I would cut out the whole thing. And put it on top of the mirror. And then stipple the paint in it and peel it off, and it would leave the design. When I had it framed in the Watertown Mall, people said, "You should sell this." I was so embarrassed. I didn't think it was any good, I just was framing it because I was giving it as a gift. I was pushing away any thought that there was something here.

AM: *When you were making these early decoupage-like constructions—were you modeling something you saw, or making it up as you went along?*

JD: I'm not sure. But I remember working with old objects. My sister turned me on to yard sales and trash picking. And when I was twenty I met this guy Chris at MassArt. We went to Marblehead, Mass., and looked at antiques. And there was a flea market in Salem where I went to buy and ask questions. You get an idea of what things are, and what period. And there was a guy who was selling out his father's antique shop, so every week he'd have boxes of old books—books that were all broken up. And then at some point later I was laying them out on my bed and drawing on them.

AM: *Drawing on the books.*

JD: On book pages. I'd peel off one of the pages and draw on them.[3]

AM: *Was that because you liked the way the drawing looked on the book?*

JD: I just didn't like working on white paper. It was intimidating. It helped to have something on it.

AM: *How did you end up in college?*

JD: I really didn't have any idea what I was doing. I was a mystery to my family. I didn't have any drive. I didn't know what to do.

AM: *You really make it seem like you were an idiot. Which I know is not true.*

---

1. I feel I should say—because maybe it's relevant?—that, as an adult, John is consumed with playing games. Anagrams, charades, cards. I do not know a single person more into games, of any sort. Is there some connection between the game mind and the creation mind? I found myself asking that question a lot (see Sondheim, Shortz).

2. Again: your parents may not have your artistic back, but there is always someone.

3. He wasn't the only person who said they drew in books. (See Max Porter. And for the same reason, to avoid the white page. The terror of it.)

JD: No, I wasn't an idiot. But things just sort of happened. I went to this place called Salem State College. I barely went to class. But I did hang out with kids doing, you know, black beauties and stuff. That was fun. And after a semester I used the art I made at Salem State to transfer to Mass. Where I met that guy Chris who took me antiquing. He became my boyfriend.

AM: *Was there a point in here where you thought,* Okay, I'm going to be an artist?

JD: I didn't really know. What I was really feeling was, *Am I already failing?* It seemed like I was never gonna start and finish anything 'cause I was so bad at—I just never understood school. Basically, for whatever reason, all my teachers were alcoholics. In Watertown, no one had any ambition.

AM: *You may not have had ambition, though that's kind of hard to believe, but you had a pretty specific taste, even then. Where do you think you got that?*

JD: None of us had it growing up. But one thing I did with my brothers was to explore a lot of abandoned buildings, because we were near the BFGoodrich, in Watertown, so we would climb in at night and explore. And I remember loving it—and making forts in those places too.

AM: *And movies? Books? School?*

JD: Movies, I watched a lot as a teenager. I would hide from my family on weekends. In a dark place, I definitely escaped. I would find old report cards: "Doesn't pay attention. Stares out the window." I remember being in class, my hair being pulled and pinched and ears being yanked. I had a lot of screaming nightmares as a kid, one recurring dream about witches—and hedges, for some reason.

AM: *Was there a moment you remember when you began to view the constructions you'd been making as a serious grown-up pursuit?*

JD: When I met Chris, I learned about antiques. And that box of books that had the pages that I would rip out and paint on—that's kind of what led me to start to find old printed ephemera. Chris's mother had a flower shop, so that was another world I was able to explore. We had all kind of materials in the house, which I would use to make things. He introduced me to a glue gun. I made some wreaths, they were covered in green moss. And I put Elmer's glue on them and dipped them in potpourri. And someone asked to buy a wreath. That was my first sale. It's how I began my business career, selling and making things like that. I was around twenty at the time.

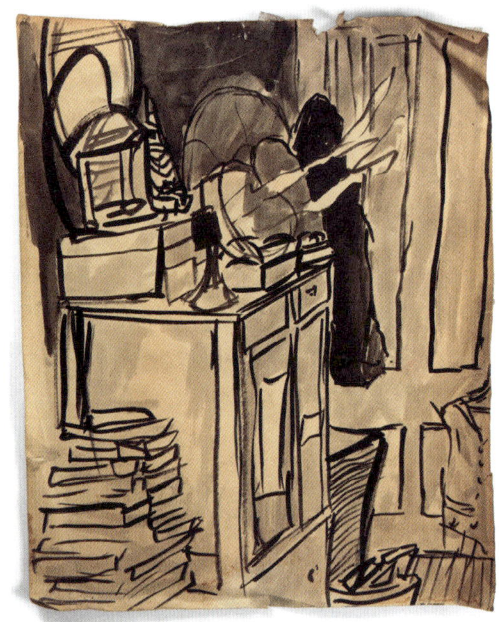

A drawing John made of the first room he felt was really "his."

AM: *You clearly had a knack.*

JD: It's kind of a mystery. I did have a psychic tell me that things speak to me, and I do have a connection to them. But that's kind of weird to say. You know when you see something—it triggers something in you. I think going to that flea market every Sunday with Chris in Salem, I would just come back with more and more things. After we broke up, I eventually moved to an apartment. I moved into a nicely painted room with piles of things that I just collected, and it suddenly seemed that there was my aesthetic, right there.

AM: *There's not a single room I've ever seen of yours that isn't actually thought through, every*

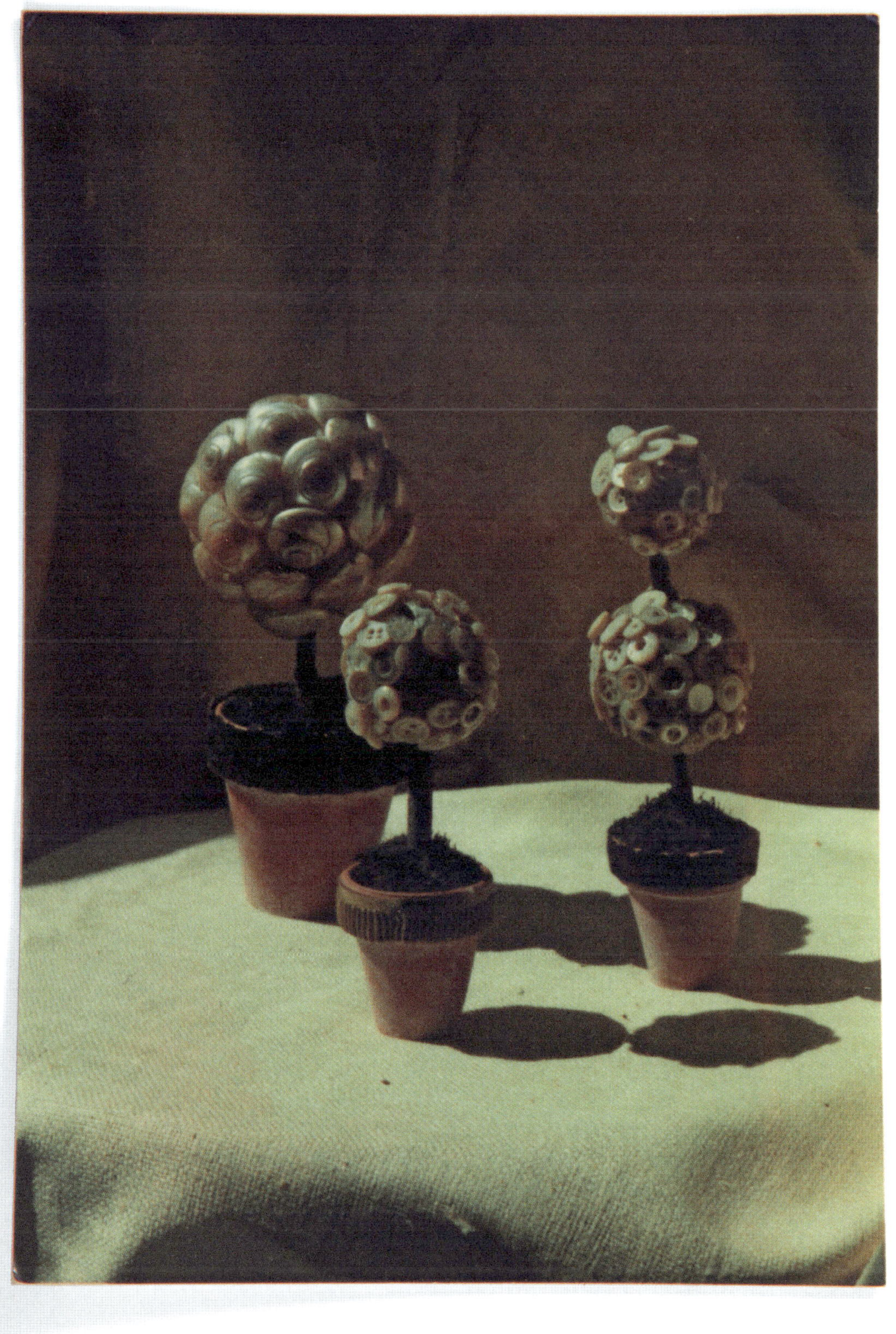

inch of the room. I don't know how deliberate it is, but the effect is strong. So, was this the first room you ever made like that?

JD: Yes. I always say that was my favorite time of my life. I had three jobs. I worked in the Brattle Theatre. I worked as a waiter. And I worked one day a week in a shop in Boston, on Sundays.

AM: *What kind of shop was that?*

JD: A little home store. Gift shop kind of thing. Then I quit and I started making all these one-of-a-kind items. And painting furniture, kind of like Bloomsbury.

AM: *And the decoupage?*

JD: Well, back at the flower shop, the owner asked me to make things, and I just made things out of my brain. I've always been especially drawn to things about nature—to branches, or things that were sculptural that weren't necessarily sculptures. I started making trees. I had an obsession with buttons, so I started making trees out of buttons—button topiaries.

That's what I would sell at that shop where I worked. I would cover boxes with old prints. Because I had now amassed ephemera. And I learned about painted finishes, so I was gluing paper images onto boxes.

AM: *The box of books was the beginning of that.*

JD: That was the beginning. Because of that, I started noticing more of those colorful images, and when I could find them and buy them, I would. I painted on anything I could—tables, chairs, whatever. I had an old chenille bedspread that I found at this place called Dollar A Pound or something, and I would cut it up and glue it onto lampshades, and I sold the lampshades. I made little collage-y things, like greeting cards, and I would paint things and add ribbons. I did it all in my basement. The shop had other decorative things. There was a woman who painted furniture too. And so she came in one day with some clear glass plates and said, "Oh, you should try making some plates out of these, I don't have the time, but you kind of work on the back of them." I took them to my studio and . . .

AM: *So, decoupage.*

JD: Yeah. She just said, "You glue things under it." And that's all she said. So I went and I experimented with the glue consistencies. I only made two plates. Sold them. Then I went to New York, in 1990 I think, for the summer, and I thought, *Maybe I'll make those plates.* I got a job at a start-up magazine in production. I was in charge of the Xerox machine. I realized one day that I could glue on the Xerox paper and it looked great, and it didn't crumble, and it didn't stain the old things. Then it was, *Oh, eureka, I can actually reproduce something.* Because until that moment, everything I'd made had been one of a kind. Someone then said to me there's a guy at Bergdorf that makes plates, so I went to Bergdorf to see what he was doing. . . .

AM: *But had you never heard of decoupage before?*

JD: No. Nor had I ever seen a plate made that way. I just kind of guessed.[4] This Bergdorf guy, his things were cool, he would fill the plates with sand. He created pockets and things. That helped guide me to how the backs should be more finished, 'cause mine were just, like, painted.

So I added a felt and made it so you could put it on a table and not scratch your table. I basically made a collection of seven. I tried Barneys; that didn't work. Then the woman who owned the Boston gift store said she had friends that had a shop uptown. They said, "We're gonna take this $20 plate and we're gonna sell it for $40, and people are gonna sell it in their stores for $80." And I was like, okay. Then three days later I got $30,000 worth of business.

AM: *Wow.*

JD: When I went back to Cambridge, that's all I did. Just had friends helping me cut and glue. I moved to New York in '92. I did everything out of my apartment. My apartment got too small, or my business got too big. And my friend Chris, the same Chris, said, "Oh, there's

4. So many stumble into a tradition they never knew about and that they then go on to change.

5. When you are out in nature with John, you see the same quality with him that you see when you're in a store—not just a keen eye, taking in everything, but a remarkably quick one, instantly isolating the beautiful thing, no matter how hidden away, it takes me many minutes to notice. Attention plus speed, not a usual combination.

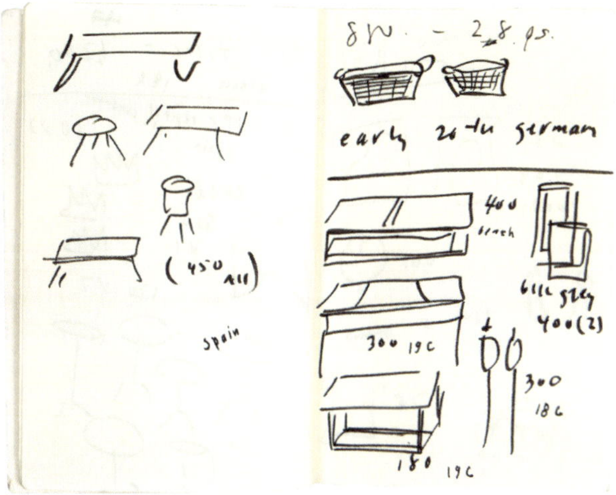

JD: When I go to the flea markets in France, I draw all the things I buy. Like in a second. So I'll know that from this dealer I bought four mirrors, and these are the prices that I paid. This is the Spanish dealer and I bought these tables, this is a German guy that I bought all these baskets from.

AM: *I went to an antique bazaar with you once and watched as you ripped through it, saying, "I'll take this and this," speeding around like a cartoon character. I just stared, amazed. How are you able to do it that fast?*

JD: I go through a space and watch what things I react to.[5] I look for big things first and then small. But I'm also buying to fill needs. Like I know that people like side tables. It's amazing what you can do in half an hour.

AM: *When you see something, do you immediately figure out what you can sell it for?*

JD: I try to buy things that I know I can double the price. If I can't double it, I won't do it. I just got this set of plates when I was in France—ceramic plates that have fruits attached to them, from the sixties. I bought a bunch. It was one of those things I wasn't sure about how much to price it for, and if I did my regular markup, it seemed like everything was way too expensive. And then I had the plates in the store for a day, at a lower price, and we sold four. I put the price back up to what I normally charge, and we sold almost all of it.

AM: *How much do you trust your instincts at this point?*

JD: A lot. I might sell six of something, but I've never not sold anything.

a place for rent on Second Street." I saw the space and thought, *There's a storefront, maybe I can do a little store in the front, where I could sell the decoupage, and then in the back could be the studio.*

AM: *All you sold was the decoupage.*

JD: Well, it was some decoupage and some antiques, and then I went to Paris and discovered people that do a white pottery. And a bedding line. Then there was a *New York Times* thing on me. Which was helpful. And then a few years later, Anna Wintour came in my store, and kind of changed things, too, because suddenly I had things that she wanted and liked. She did a whole "best shop in New York" thing—six pages of models in my store in *Vogue*, and that was huge. At that point I started selling the decoupage to other stores.

AM: *Okay, how do you make decoupage?*

JD: I'm basically inspired by the imagery that I find. Here's six fruits with the same background and you can hang them in a group, you know. Mostly at first for decorators. I started doing single images. I started printing things that were stained and broken and ripped. I would have something on my wall and be like, *Oh, I wonder if anyone would like that?* And then that became the most popular thing. Which would surprise me—

AM: *Because it was too distressed?*

JD: Yeah. So then I realized . . .

AM: *So then you realized there were other people who had the same taste you did.*

JD: Yes.

1960s

Barbara Kruger began her career as a pasteup artist and graphic designer in the 1960s. Her work included designing small box-shaped advertisements for mail-order products, like this, with headlines over images. Maybe that was the beginning.

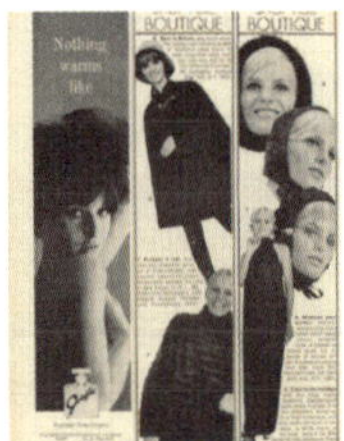

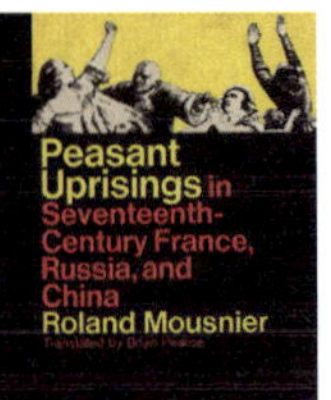

1970s

By the early seventies, she was designing book jackets, text over image.

1978

In the late seventies, she made a book called *Pictures/Readings*, which included text and images, but were separated.

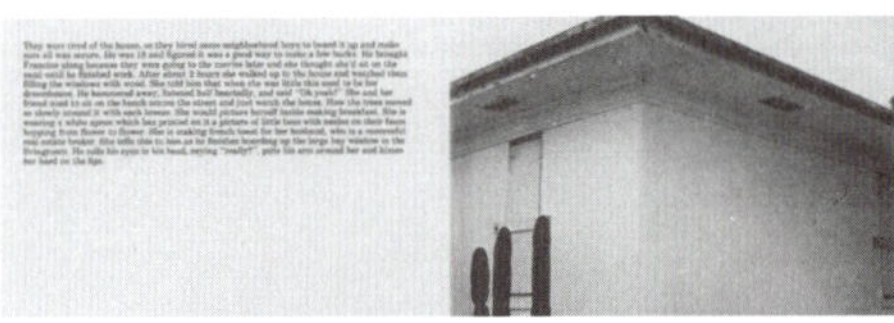

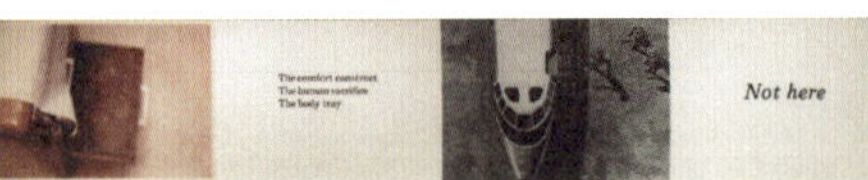

Over the next few years, text and images were still separated in her work, but the language was getting more blunt.

1981

The incorporation of media: *Pictures and Promises: A Display of Advertising, Slogans, and Interventions*, curated by Barbara Kruger.

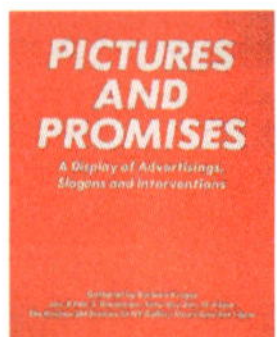

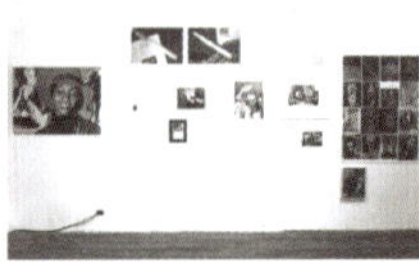

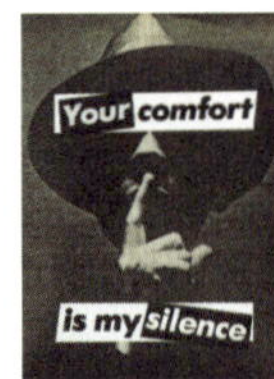

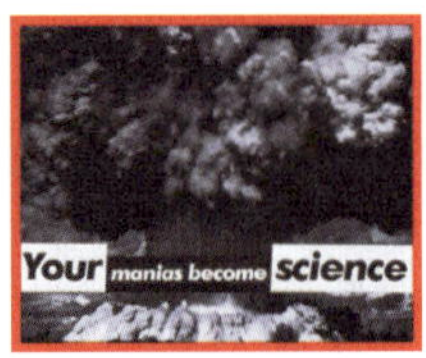

1981–1982

Her first foray into collage was a series of "pasteups." Her signature style would develop into bigger, digital collages with pithy aphorisms in bold font in black, red, and white bars.

1987 / 1989

Two of her most famous works, employing personal pronouns and direct address.

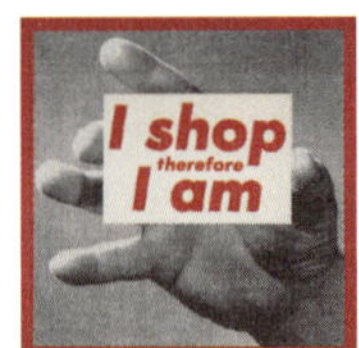

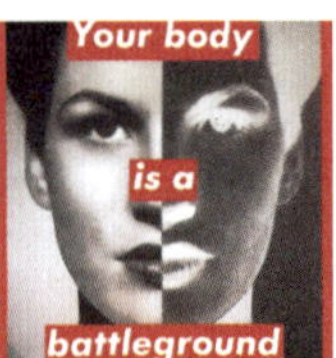

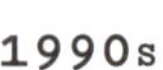

1990s

Her expansions into mass media featured the same style.

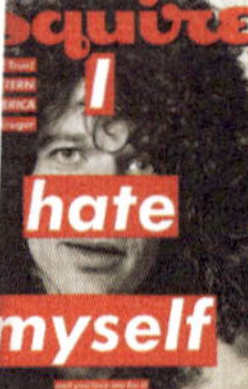

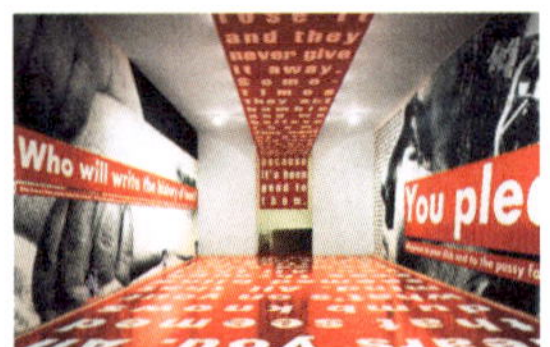

1991

Eventually the work became immersive . . .

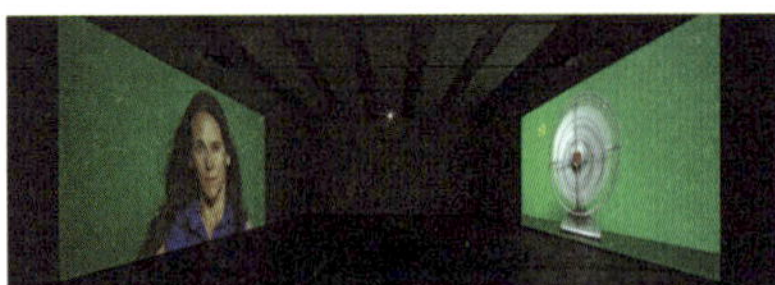

2010

. . . And incorporated sound and video.

1989 / 2019

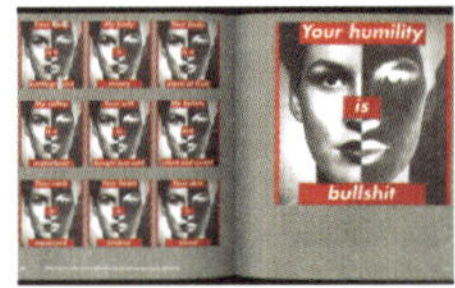

Why restrict the works to a single message? In an exhibition called *THINKING OF ~~YOU~~. I MEAN ~~ME~~. I MEAN YOU.*, what once was static became a morphing machine, allowing infinite variation.

2012

And was taken to the streets.

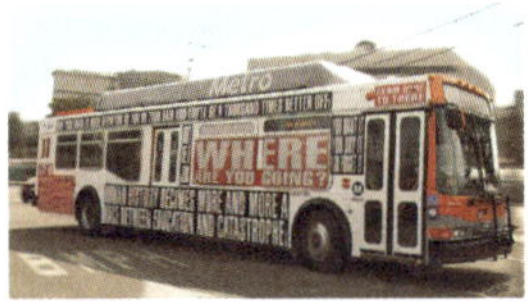

15

BARBARA KRUGER

Enough About Me / What About Me?

OCCUPATION: Visual Artist

WORK DISCUSSED: A Life's Work

BORN: 1945

AMONG THE WORKS I was most proud to have published during my career were two covers for *New York* magazine by Barbara Kruger. One was a picture of then New York governor Eliot Spitzer, with the word *brain* pointed at his crotch, which ran the week after his resignation over a prostitution scandal. The other was a picture of Donald Trump with the word *loser* plastered across it. That one came out a few days before he won the 2016 election.

It's not exactly surprising that Kruger is so good at cover making. A magazine cover employs the same image-and-text rhetorical economy that Kruger has made her life's work as an artist. Kruger got her start as a magazine graphic designer and pasteup artist in the late 1960s. She entered magazine work as a trade because she felt art was not available to someone of her social class (or gender), and then was able to adapt the skills she learned to a mode of expression that would come to have enormous influence. Her sense of the pivotal role of class has informed every bit of her art,[1] which is concerned with all the ways we are shaped by the expectations culture creates for us.

In time, she built a clear and powerful brand—a word she might hate for its crassness or embrace for its ubiquity as marketing lingo, I'm not sure which—but that in any event she calls "a signature style." This little timeline boils down how she got there—essentially, from pasteup (a now mostly dead, pre-digital practice of pasting words and images together to be photographed); to writing poetry (distilling words); combining photography and text in books, but keeping them separate; making artworks where the language is pithier; beginning to play with laying text on the photographs themselves; turning the text into an accusatory and self-implicating form of direct address (You/I); reducing the variables of typeface and color, creating what graphic designers call an "identity"; and eventually

1. What fuels their drive? You could ask that of any artist in this book (which I did, in different ways), but without drive, you're stuck at go. Add ideology (also true of David Simon) to the list of igniting factors (trauma, loneliness, joy, etc.). In Kruger's case, the art doesn't proceed without the outrage.

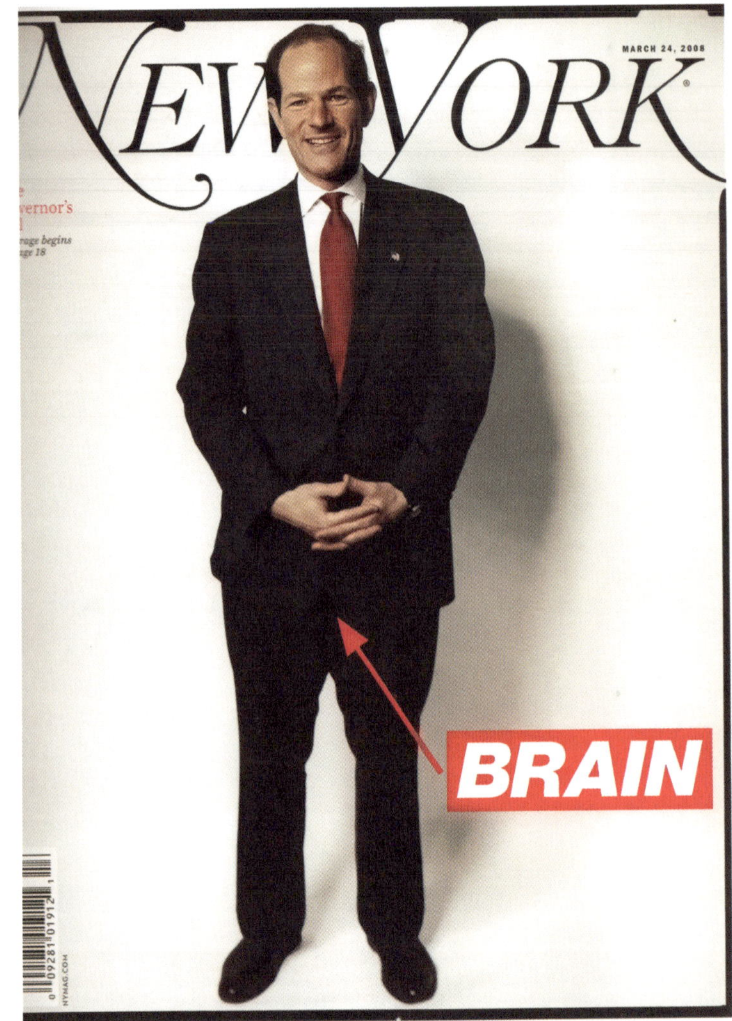

applying the picture and text sloganeering to a physical space, often surrounding the viewer. When you put it all together, it's remarkably linear.

I'd hoped we could find a particular moment in there somewhere when it all became clear, but Barbara Kruger is frustrating in a lot of ways. I wasn't allowed to "see" her,[2] only hear her voice (we spoke on the phone), and she refused to discuss the evolution of a single project. Ultimately I concluded that it didn't matter, because we could trace the evolution of that signature, which in a sense was a single work with multiple applications. Also, during the period of our communication, she was finishing a mammoth exhibition called *THINKING OF ~~YOU~~. I MEAN ~~ME~~. I MEAN YOU.* ("What's the title of your book?" she asked me. "Your title is really important."), which was sort of an anti-retrospective in that it included remakings of some of her iconic pieces, which I thought was relevant to this project. But mostly, I just liked her. She's combative and funny. I was in (perhaps predictable) awe of her dexterity with words and images. The perfect simplicity of that Spitzer cover made it maybe my favorite cover ever, anywhere. But the cover I wanted to talk about was Trump, which haunts me to this day. We eventually got to that.

Adam Moss: *Where are you?*
Barbara Kruger: The Springs [in the Hamptons]. I've had a little perch here, with rubber hoses for plumbing, for the past thirty years.
AM: *Thanks for talking to me. I want to be very respectful of the limits you've put on this conversation, so push back if we veer into uncomfortable territory.*
BK: Well, especially because this is being recorded. So I'm going to be especially retentive.
AM: *Were you interested in art as a child?*
BK: When I was growing up, I had absolutely no sense of what art was. Where I was, in Newark, you had a choice of taking a college course or a commercial course. And I took a commercial course, because that was laid out for me

2. I couldn't "see" Louise Glück, either, but in Kruger's case it was really extreme. She wouldn't give me rights to her images for this entry if I included *any* pictures of her, even stylized like the stamp-like portraits you see at the beginning of every other chapter. That's why hers is blank.

in terms of my class. When I thought of art, I thought maybe I could be an illustrator, because I was one of those kids who knew how to draw, as if that was a determinant of who was going to be an artist or not.

AM: *Did you get encouragement for your drawing skills?*

BK: Oh no, no. I just knew I had ability in that area. But my first attraction was to architecture. Because my parents never owned property. In fact, the little Springs place I'm in now is the first property anyone in my family ever owned.

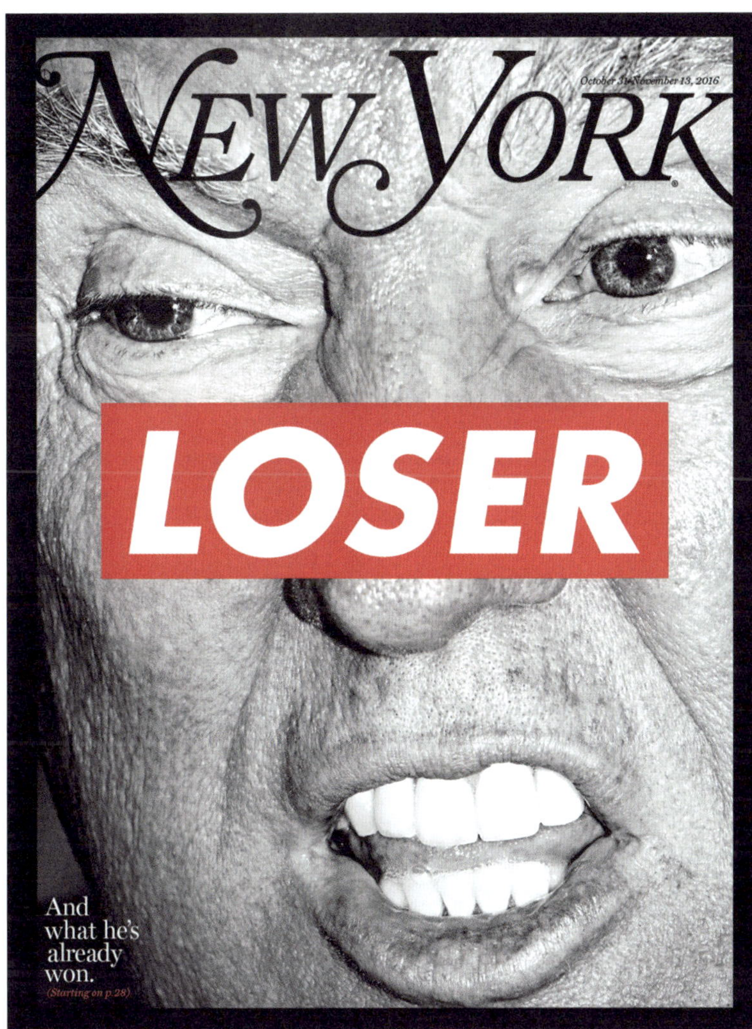

On weekends, we would look at model homes that we could never afford, in communities that would never have us. I just spent a lot of my teens drawing houses and plans for residential developments.

AM: *It was just kind of a private thing?*

BK: Oh yes. I didn't share it with anybody. I was just very engaged in the idea, though I didn't see it as such at that time, of the ways that the built environment constructs and contains us.

AM: *Was your family political?*

BK: Not really. But I did find a bunch of index cards for a speech I gave as valedictorian or salutatorian in high school. And I was shocked at how concerned it was with issues of class and race.

AM: *Were you a particularly verbal child?*

BK: Like many families, mine was more than problematic. But I think my developing language skills helped me through difficulties. And despite the problems, my parents never discredited my possibilities, which I know did happen to many of my peers who came from a much higher class level and were undermined in ways I wasn't.

Photos and Magic Markers Kruger went to Syracuse University and left after a year. ("I felt like a Martian there," she said. "It was mostly a class thing.") Then she went to Parsons and studied with Marvin Israel, a legendary magazine art director, most notably of *Harper's Bazaar*, and the photographer Diane Arbus. But she left there, too, still not feeling that making art was an available path for her.

She had to learn a trade. Israel steered her into graphic design and magazine layout, and she ended up at *Mademoiselle* magazine, where she did pasteup. She got the job by shopping a portfolio of imagined book covers.

AM: *As you started out in magazines, did you fantasize about making art for a living?*

BK: I didn't think about being a regular artist. There were almost no models for women, and I just hadn't been educated in art history or whatever. But during this time, the fluency I developed with pictures, through editorial media, really gave me a way of thinking about pictures and words that became the foundation of my work.

AM: *Were magazines fun for you?*

BK: Sure. I did do some illustrations of socks and shoes. It was cool. But I realized I didn't know what my future was. I just couldn't solve other people's problems in the way designers do. The hard part was figuring out what it means to call yourself an artist.[3]

AM: *But you were beginning to do your own art?*

BK: I did a lot of craft work. I did stitching. But somehow, to me, it was like work for women up the block. It was labor intensive and putting my brain to sleep. Meanwhile I started writing more, and that's where the fluency I developed in magazines came to be part of the recipe.

AM: *What were you writing?*

BK: Prose and poems. I did some readings, but that didn't last too long. I did some one-offs of what people leave in cars, like the back windows of cars and what were in them. And then I didn't have any money, so I was taking these visiting artists jobs, which were really visiting girl jobs, tangential jobs, and in all my travels I was taking photographs of architecture. It wasn't enough to just have these photos. I wanted to write the stories of those rooms. Eventually I did *Picture/Readings* [an art book], projecting narratives of people who were inside buildings I found compelling.

3. This "calling yourself" question, how important is that? People kept bringing it up. I guess it's pretty important, maybe, in the way that identity shapes work and makes you make sense to yourself. See Susan Meiselas, Gerald Lovell, and Tony Kushner, who all asked themselves the same question.

4. The "Pictures Generation" is the term applied to a school of artists, such as Richard Prince and Cindy Sherman, who were developing what Kruger called "a vernacular sort of signage."

AM: *Were there intimations in your mind that pictures with text was its own kind of art form?*

BK: Well, it was more organic than that. It was when I started putting them all together in one plane, and using direct address and pronouns . . . that clearly was a kind of invitation, a kind of activation.

AM: *Was anyone else doing that kind of work?*

BK: No, it wasn't really a thing. I remember talking to Marvin Israel and saying to him early on, "Why can't I be an artist with just photos and magic markers?" "Oh no, you can't do that." There was a history of so-called conceptual art, text art, but I would go to galleries early on and, man, I felt like a right-wing senator. I thought, *What the fuck. My dog could do that*. It was a conspiracy against my own intelligence. And this is where historical circumstance and social relations are so determinant in what we are. We were raised watching TV and movies, so there was this commonality of a vocabulary, which wasn't based on art historical paintings but was about popular culture and representation. I never considered myself a "Pictures Generation" artist,[4] but engagement with popular culture did allow myself and others to become visible.

AM: *Did you see an opportunity here? Was this something you talked about within your peer group?*

BK: Well, both really. Being an artist, most never make any money. We all feel disenfranchised and disempowered, and people forget the power of their own byline. And yet, they had the ability to start a conversation. That becomes a buzz, of fickleness and hotness. And you know how things happen. So, voilà.

AM: *And was there a moment when you felt, This is actually working for me?*

BK: It was when I started showing my large-scale photo works. For us, for my group, the showing was what was important. Showing did not mean selling. It wasn't about one work. Things are about a seriality. I remember when my name started entering the conversation, and my works began to sell, I made like $150 on each of those, because they sold like for

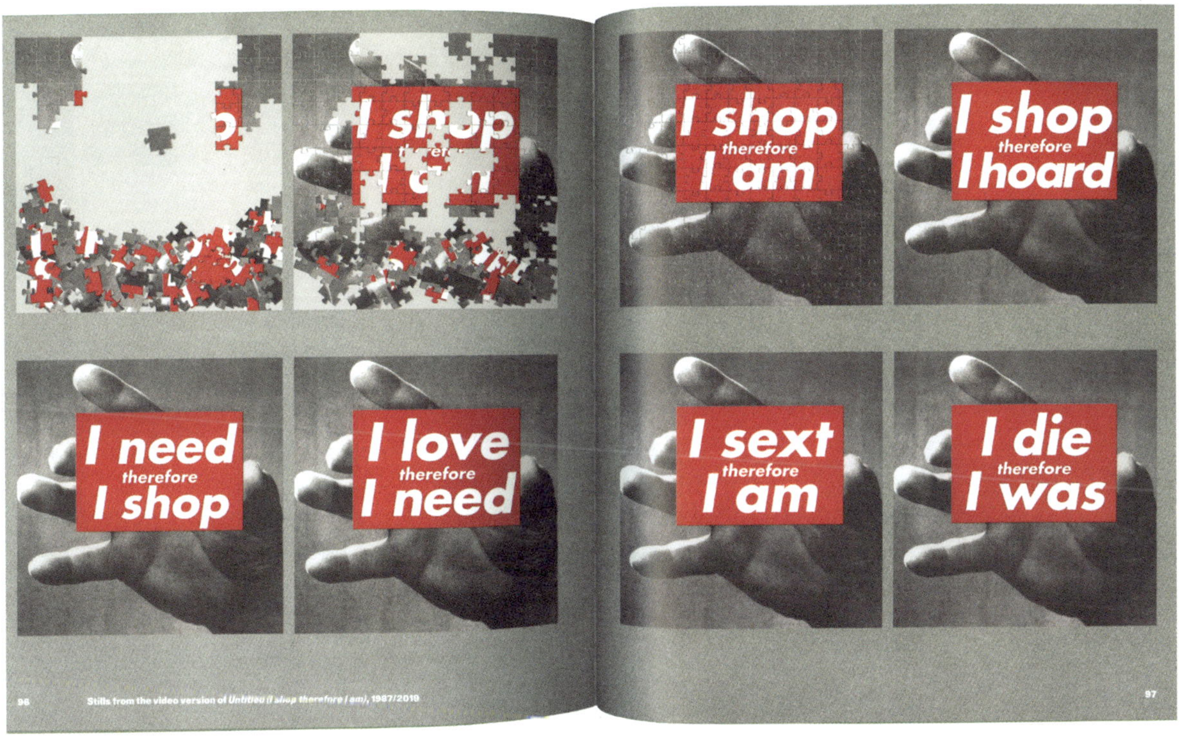

I shop therefore I am

I shop therefore I hoard

I need therefore I shop

I love therefore I need

I sext therefore I am

I die therefore I was

96 Stills from the video version of *Untitled (I shop therefore I am)*, 1987/2019 97

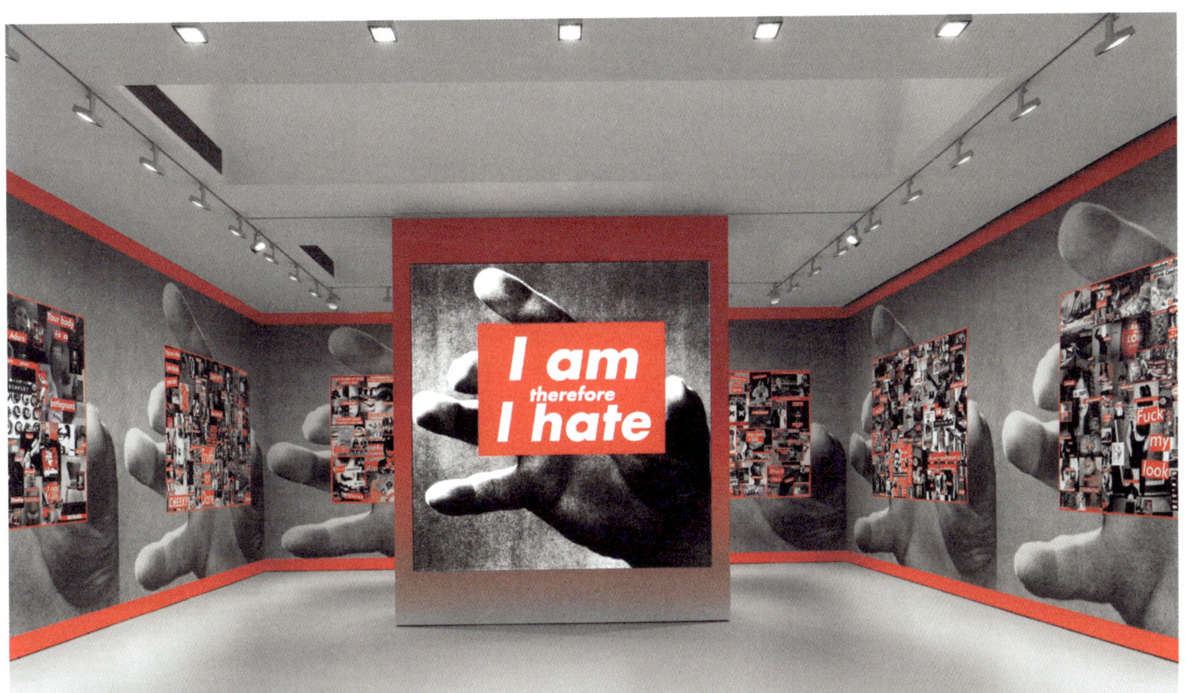

I Shop Therefore I Am, reinterpreted over and over, from her show *THINKING OF ~~YOU~~. I MEAN ~~ME~~. I MEAN YOU.* Kruger's work evolved to envelop environments.

$1,200, and then the frames and the prints were expensive, they were big. I remember carrying them on the E train. And then I realized I wanted to address the money, the newfound commodity status of the work.
AM: *You started to see yourself as a commodity.*
BK: Yeah. The work that said "Buy Me, I'll Change Your Life" or "You Are Getting What You Paid For." I discovered Walter Benjamin and Roland Barthes and started writing for small magazines and then for *Artforum*. I'd always dip into the Barthes because I loved the way he could approach big ideas in the most casual, secular way.[5]

You/Me We digressed into a long detour about media in the late seventies and my early days working at *The Village Voice*. I pressed her to return to her story.
BK: Ugh, I am so sick of the sound of my own voice, especially with the show coming out. You feel like a fraud. You know, what the fuck? You know, it's, like, enough. Enough about me / what about me? [She laughs.]
AM: *Do you remember the first time you used direct address? Was it* You Are Not Yourself*?*
BK: No, it was *Your Comfort Is My Silence*. I think that was the first of the works where pictures and words were in one plane.
AM: *So you sort of figured something out, and then created a whole bunch of works using this tool?*
BK: Yeah. And then they got larger and larger. The breakthrough for me were ones of scale.[6] And then at the beginning of 1991, bringing my engagement with architecture into it—I hate this word because it's become such a catchword, but they became more "immersive," there were walls and floors. I love working with space, and I trust my visual instincts to a degree, and I sort of know the materials I'm working with, I've developed a fluency in that, you know . . . ?

Hot We started talking about her friend, the critic Craig Owens, and she mentioned that what made him unusual was his self-doubt. I had remembered reading that she found doubt admirable.
BK: Well, doubtlessness can be very scary. Numerous belief structures have destroyed the world incrementally. In many ways we're living that right now.
AM: *How do you think that plays into your work?*
BK: In so many ways. No work, no painting, no novel, no movie is as brilliant and masterful or as failed and minor as it's thought to be. Things get pumped up, and that has to do with our value systems. In terms of the art world, and the speculative nature of markets—I tell my students, "If you become a hot, hot item, don't take it personally, because everything is so fickle. Somebody else will come along who will be younger and cuter and cheaper. And if you make it early, it's just so many years of performance anxiety."
AM: *The red and the black, and your typefaces, first Futura and then Helvetica condensed—were you creating a voice by limiting your tools? Is that fair to say?*
BK: I would say that I was developing a visual vocabulary.
AM: *The amazing thing about your vocabulary for me is how flexible your mind is in getting maximal power out of language. I mean, this is my profession—headline writing, for instance, is something few people know how to do. I'm interested in how you fixed on your tone. Your stuff is incredibly direct, accessible, and usually funny.*[7] *You've used the word* goof.
BK: I really appreciate your bringing up the goof. I mean, to me, Mel Brooks was the be-all and end-all, you know. I used to think Jerry Lewis was cute. People don't get how important the goof is in my work. I'm not talking about humor. Humor is far too genteel for me. I'm talking about comedy. It's such a powerful force that can be both liberating and horrendously shaming. By the Left and Right. And digitally—oh my

5. Roland Barthes is probably the second most-cited influence in this book (Melville being the first). Kruger certainly went further than Barthes in her own exploration of big ideas in the popular sphere: she reduced those ideas to slogans.

6. "Scale" seems to be the dividing line for many of these artists: bigger is better, or at least taken more seriously. (Personally, I don't see it.)

7. Kruger's voice is so well defined, and such an enormous part of what makes her work work. Getting the voice right, from which nearly all else follows—isn't that central to the evolution of every single project in this book?

God, where shame is such a hot commodity.

AM: *I know that you keep an archive of images. Do you also do that with phrasings?*

BK: Figures of speech that have been changed through culture, slang, which becomes very dated, I try to be careful about that. It's always a consideration, because I've done so many variations on my work. The images change with the text, and the words change with the images. I look back at works of mine that I think just suck. Don't ask me which ones.

AM: *Do you make a record of images and words as you're walking around?*

BK: Most of the images just come from googling, and earlier, Tumblr, Flickr. As far as some of the text, I have always been a café or diner writer. I would take a little notebook. I go to a diner in LA. I used to go to Caffè Dante on Macdougal Street. So much of my writing has happened in public places.

AM: *Why do you think public writing is so pleasurable for you?*

BK: There's something about the built environment, that culture that is constructing what you hear—the ambience, the conversations, the apparel, just everything.

AM: *Do you ever feel blocked?*

BK: I guess. But I'm not a painter that goes into a studio at ten in the morning and works until four. I'm not a writer who has to confront that page at the computer. I've done that. The way I work is very rangy. I can get these ideas when I'm sitting at a coffee shop or driving or in the bathtub, and I bring it to a place that sort of makes it work. And I think that's an advantage. I'm working all the time.

AM: *At this point, do you feel constrained by other people's expectations?*

BK: No, because there's never been a consensus about my work. I'm not everybody's cup of tea. Some people are needy—everyone has to love you. But everyone's just up for a fall, you know? You're not right. You're not good enough. You're in the wrong place at the wrong time. You just can't be everyone's idea of perfection.

AM: *I assume you're a voracious consumer of media—*

BK: I'd say yes.

AM: *Of memes? Which in some ways you anticipated? I mean—the juxtaposition of pictures and text for an effect—that's kind of what you do too.*

BK: I feel fine with it, I guess. Some of the things are so predictable. They're clever and some of them are funny. They embrace a kind of economy that is perfect for that space. I understand it so well that I don't really have to look at it. They're kind of verbal mirrors. They mirror the self—that crash of narcissism and voyeurism.

AM: *Do you watch TV?*

BK: Oh yes. *Ozark*. *BoJack Horseman*, please. I watch reality TV. Real Housewives of every locale, *Vanderpump*, any *Love & Hip Hop*. Reality shows are the most prevalent and brutal evidence of the sustaining, unrelenting power of stereotype and how people are so willing to act that stereotype out.

AM: *I wanted to talk to you about the Trump cover and Trump.*

BK: Well, when Jody Quon [photo director of *New York*] approached me, I thought right away, *What is the word he fears most?* And that's *loser*. There's nothing that comes close in Donald's universe.

AM: *You felt you understood him?*

BK: Look, I watched *The Apprentice* for years. I called him President Shecky. He was like Shecky Greene to me. People don't know what a tummler was. . . . He has a gift for that. People just don't understand his rhetorical powers.

AM: *So you didn't mean it as a predictor?*

BK: Oh no, I certainly didn't think, *This guy is gonna lose the election.*

AM: *You really didn't? Because I've spent a lot of time answering questions about that cover. And I say what you just did, about the power of that word for him and how it was meant to describe rather than predict. But I confess that, for me, it was in a way a prediction. An obviously catastrophic one. I love that cover, and am proud of it to this day. But I certainly expected him to lose.*

BK: Oh no. Do not underestimate white grievance.

16

DAVID MANDEL

What If Dr. Seuss Fucked Maya Angelou?

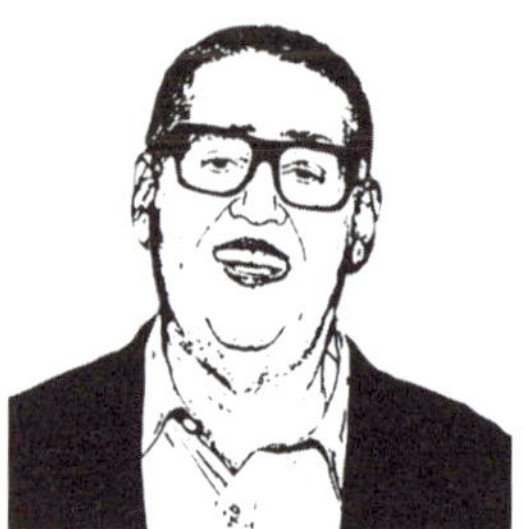

OCCUPATION: Comedy Writer / Showrunner

WORK DISCUSSED: *Veep*; Two Jokes

BORN: 1970

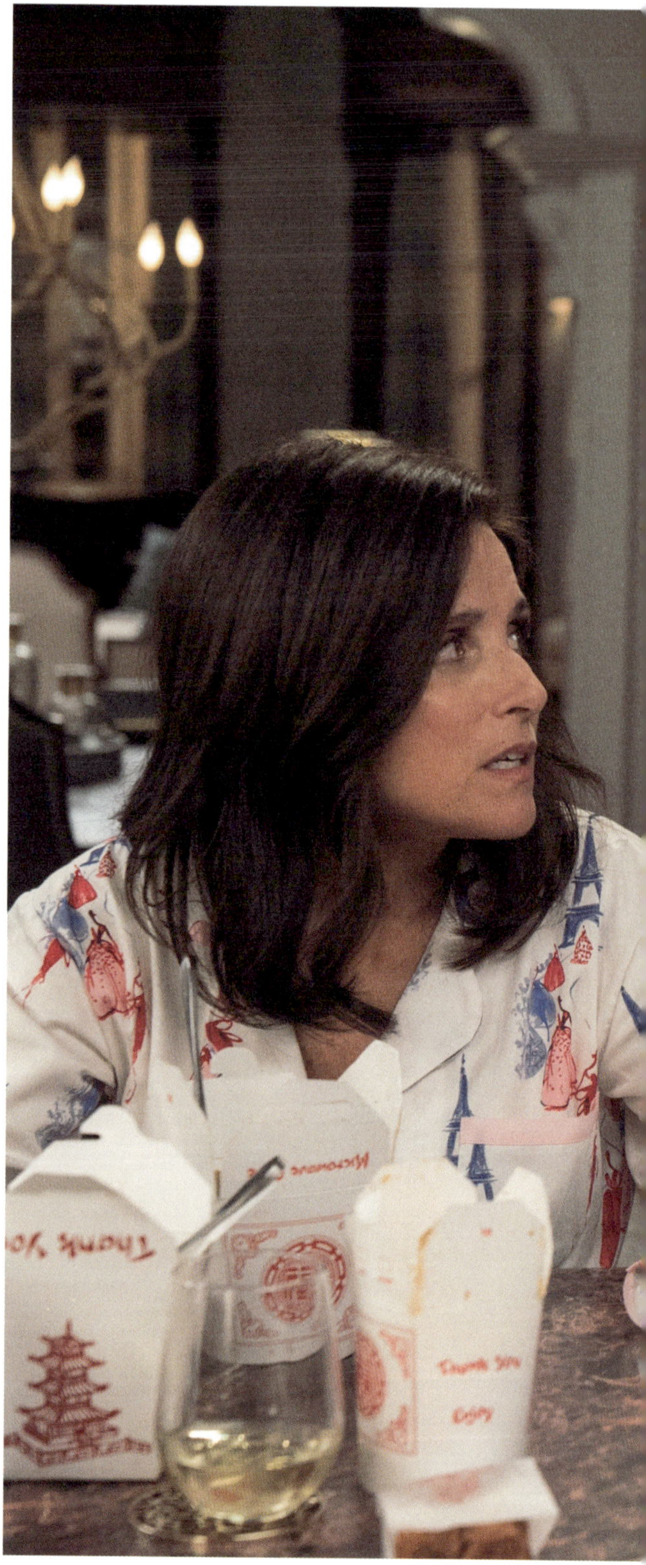

David Mandel and Julia Louis-Dreyfus on the set of *Veep*.

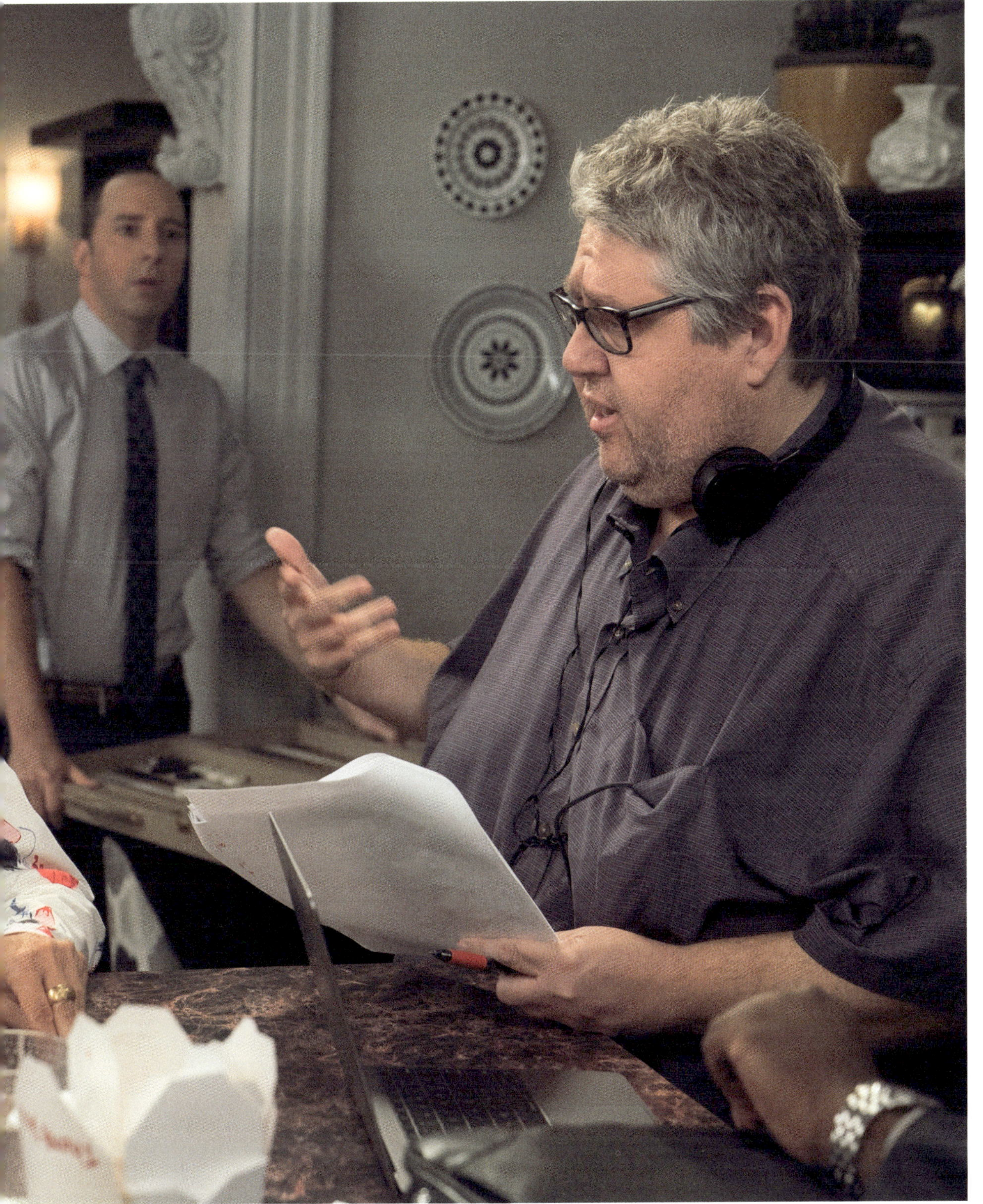

In the introduction, I mentioned a visit I once paid to the set of *Veep*. I was invited by Frank Rich, a good friend and a writer at *New York*, who was also an executive producer of the show. He thought it would be fun for me to come observe a shoot, and it was. *Veep* is an HBO comedy about a politician named Selina Meyer, played by Julia Louis-Dreyfus. She starts the show as an obscenely unscrupulous vice president and then goes on to various other political misadventures where she is pretty much foiled at every turn. The show was vicious and hilarious. It ran seven seasons, the last three overseen by David Mandel.

When I visited the set, I thought the fun would be just watching actors I admired acting; I didn't realize I would also see great comedy being written in front of me. Mandel is a big, boisterous guy with a big, warm laugh. The day I visited, I sat behind him watching him watch a monitor. A scene—short and inconsequential, basically featuring Jonah, a moronic congressman—was being shot on a set in an adjacent room. Mandel kept stopping the action to ratchet up a joke. (It was the offhand joke landing on a Jewish holiday that I referred to at the beginning of the book.) I now know that what I was watching was a familiar process where "alts"—options, some spontaneously generated, some written ahead of time—are offered to fine-tune a joke to its funniest calibration.

Mandel, who had followed a familiar comedy path to get to *Veep*—he watched a lot of *The Honeymooners* and *The Odd Couple* growing up, went to Harvard, became a *Harvard Lampoon* writer, graduated, and found himself writing for *Seinfeld* and *Curb Your Enthusiasm*—was hired after the show's originator, Armando Iannucci, decided to exit after season 4. Iannucci left the show at a narrative crossroads—or "a trap," in Mandel's words. Selina, who had briefly assumed the presidency after the president resigned, was running to be elected to the job, and the election ended in a tie. As part of Mandel's audition to run *Veep*, he had to pitch a solution. Mandel devised a short- and long-term scenario that would involve *Veep*'s version of hanging chads; Selina's loss to a younger woman, which would particularly vex her; and then shenanigans involving her post-presidency. The plotline won him the job. Mandel proved an excellent showrunner, who, in this account, first screwed up but then accurately diagnosed what exactly it was that made *Veep* successful, fixed what wasn't working, and figured out how to bring his own ways to a pattern already set by someone else.

Stories Before Jokes "I was taught to write sitcoms by Larry David—first on *Seinfeld*, then on *Curb*.[1] So first, my guiding philosophy: Is it really the funniest it can be? What can you do to get it there? No, that's not right. What comes first is story. If the story isn't working, you can papier-mâché over it with as many jokes as you want. But at the end of the day, it won't work. There are *Seinfeld* episodes I wrote where the stories never were quite right. They had some really funny jokes in them, but it didn't matter.

"In my first season of *Veep*, they made me hire three editors. I was like, Why three editors? When I got there, I realized Armando was just poring through huge amounts of improv footage, finding a show in the footage by going from edit room to edit room and working on multiple shows at once. I don't work like that. I love what he does. I can't *find* a show, do you know what I mean? His method results in some digressions that are wonderful and cloud-like in the way they float. And ours is a little more rat-tat-tat. But essentially, we come to a similar place.

"I go into a season with a rough idea and try to figure out very quickly where I want that season to end. I bring in guests, like the people who worked for Obama in Iowa, to help give us ideas. Pure story at this point, though if we think of something funny, we note it and bake it into the structure. And at some point we draw lines on whiteboards. Ten buckets, one for each episode. And we move things around. First, big-picture Selina things. And then, what's going on with her daughter, with Jonah. What if Jonah runs for something?

"Everybody in the writers' room gets to have opinions, but at the end of the day I'm holding the dry-erase pen. I show [the plan] to HBO and Julia [who was also an executive producer and basically the show's reigning monarch]. People get assigned scripts. Sometimes there's gang rewriting, but it's eventually going to go through my typewriter.

"That gets to a table draft, then we'll do a punch-up session where we go line to line trying to add more jokes, then that gets to the table read with actors. I'm listening for: Is it working? Is it long? Why are people confused? Why didn't this joke land?

"Then the script gets locked and we enter shooting mode. On the night before shooting a scene, Julia and I would talk through anything not working or lines that could be better. Or what seems too naked—like if Selina was almost saying what she wanted as opposed to acting on it. And it would go out to all the writers—we're looking for some options here."

Amping It Up That's how we get to the alts, but first Mandel wanted to mention an important lesson he had to learn as to how the show actually worked, something he didn't realize at first. After all the hoop jumping he did to get the job, the episode he wrote to start the season was inert. He panicked. *Veep* was a beloved series. "I knew we were going to be judged very quickly," he said. "I felt like I was being dropped right into a foxhole." He finally realized that plotting the right developments in the right sequence with funny jokes in between wasn't enough. *Veep*'s mojo lay in its pace and density.

"My first episode was kind of a disaster. Eventually I rewrote it, and sometimes I think that they loved that rewritten episode because the first one was so wrong. And the thing is, it honestly wasn't that different. It was very much people talking—Selina woke up and talked to Gary,[2] then she went out and gave a speech. There was, how do I put this? A lack of chaos. It was almost painfully logical. Not that that was what anybody identified it as. But what it took was almost taking the scenes and mushing them together because there wasn't enough happening. And then suddenly it was *Veep*."

When Mandel realized this, he pushed the throttle as far as it would go. "In any given scene, there were at least two or three things they're supposed to be discussing. That was a big difference—on *Seinfeld* and *Curb*, they're talking about one thing. Here, the show is pretty speedy. I amped it up to where it's fucking fast. I added more story. I started dipping into the characters' personal lives, which definitely thickens things up.

"And then in the edit room, basically anything that was unnecessary, be it words, breaths, pauses, whatever I could squeeze out of it, I did."

The Alts Mandel has a tight grip: the alts process I witnessed is a vivid expression of that. He spotted any weakness in the script and put out a call to the writers for new options, which were usually just adding new juice to a joke, a maneuver that inevitably involved tinkering with the specificity of the language.[3] The writing process was collegial but also competitive: "These are type A comedy writers. They're not trying to destroy each other, but they take pride. Somewhere in there is an egotistical one-upmanship."

Generally, the alts were sent to him the night before. "I write my own line or I take half of this and half of that. There's no formula. I will take all these alts, and I'm just circling anything.

"As we start shooting, I just start yelling the alts [to the actors] as I read or as I'm coming up with them myself, or someone whispers something in my ear. And I yell that out." They do one take after another. "I jam a Gary line in, jam a Richard line,[4] any place

1. Comedy writing in particular is like a daisy chain of influence.

2. Gary was a personal assistant or "body man"—a lapdog comically loyal to Selina in spite of all of her abuse.

3. As they're shooting, they rarely seem to throw out a joke and start over, they just keep reworking the joke they've got to make it better. Was that because at that point it was too difficult to start over, or because reducing what you permit yourself to fix brings the most successful (funniest) result? Maybe the second.

Ep. 607 - INT. COMMUNITY ROOM - KESHER ISRAEL GEORGETOWN SYNAGOGUE - DAY (DAY 1)

...

JONAH: So anyway, Adonee-ai, blessed be he, was like: "Moses, you must lead the Jews out of Egypt into a land of milk and honey." And Moses was like, "What, no pork?" That was a Jewish joke.

RABBI: And that land is called–

Scripted and shot

JONAH: I dunno, Israel?

ALTs Shot

JONAH: New York?

JONAH: Hanukkah (THIS AIRED)

ALTs not shot

JONAH: Egypt?

JONAH: Milkenzhonee? Is that it's Yiddish name?

JONAH: Palestine?

In the transcript the order of shooting seems to match. We tried "Israel" then "New York" then "Hanukkah" then "New York" again, then went back to "Hanukkah" for the last 4 takes.

I can wedge something in, I'm gonna. It's like a live rewrite, or live editing. We're on comedy adrenaline. And there's nothing more satisfying than that, except playing it to a room and hearing the laughter."

That excitement was very visible to me as I watched the crew's laughter build on the day I visited the set. Taking it in, it seemed as if he were subjecting the joke to a plebiscite: the biggest laugh from the crew wins. Turns out, it wasn't as democratic as it looked.

"The honest answer," he said, "and I don't want to sound like a giant asshole here, is I know when the laughter is coming. It's gratifying to hear, but I have no fucking doubt about how funny it is when I'm done. I'm definitely paying attention to how much people laugh on the set. But when I'm in the edit room, all that disappears. At some point I'm sitting alone with the editor. Not all comedy writers work this way, but I'm a laugher. I definitely want to laugh." Generally, he said, whatever he laughed hardest at got aired.

He couldn't recall the Jewish holiday joke I'd seen that day on the set. Ever obliging, he found another Jewish joke (Jewish jokes were not exactly rare on *Veep*) and wondered whether it might be the one (it wasn't, but we talked about it anyway). We settled on it and one other to examine. The jokes' alts were reconstructed by an associate, who sent them to Mandel. Here are the jokes, with the variations they considered, attached by arrow. You'll want to read the jokes and alts together along with Mandel's reasoning patter.

The Jewish Joke

David Mandel: "Sometimes there's a clear winner, but not here. The easiest way to explain this is, Jonah's an idiot. And these are quote, unquote 'Jewish jokes'—by definition we want them to be a little bad and a little antisemitic, but not too antisemitic. I'm not sure Jonah has hate in his heart, but he's definitely dumb and quasi-racist. So let's see. Israel wasn't doing much. The milk thing, I think that's supposed

ALTs Submitted:
PRESIDENT MEYER: Sounds like Dr. Seuss fucked Maya Angelou in the yuzz-ma-tuzz./in the humpf-humpf-a-dumpfher./in the flunnel/in the wumbus/in the diffendoofer.

Transcripts show:
After about 11 takes as scripted, you tried this
PRESIDENT MEYER: Sounds like Dr. Seuss sloozal-von-fucked Maya Angelou in the yuzz-ma-tuzz...
then
PRESIDENT MEYER: Sounds like Dr. Seuss fucked Maya Angelou in the yuzz-ma-tuzz, pulled out and sprayed her with snoozily-scuzz...
then the last two takes and what aired was this:
PRESIDENT MEYER: Sounds like Dr. Seuss fucked Maya Angelou in the yuzz-ma-tuzz and then filled her all up with snoozily-scuzz.

to be a Yiddish word kind of, but not, whatever. New York I guess works, it's right on the edge of Hymietown [a phrase Jesse Jackson had once used to refer to the city]. Which I thought I could get away with, because of its connection to politics. And during that season, Jonah's engaged to this Jew, who was like what would happen if Sheldon Adelson and Rebekah Mercer had a daughter. She wants him to convert, and he likes the idea of that, makes him feel 'chosen.' If the joke was anti-Jewish in a way, it would undercut his love of converting. And so Hanukkah felt stupid in a good way with Jonah, but not undercutting."

So that's how they arrived at the Jewish joke. We moved on to another joke he suggested, that he particularly liked.

4. Richard was a Selina aide. The salient point about him is that he was cheerful and comically oblivious to the cynical machinations of everyone else on the show.

5. "Great artists steal," in the words of Picasso, even to make an extremely dumb, very funny, ten-second joke.

6. The original dialogue on *Moonlighting* went like this: *David:* We're looking for a man with a mole on his nose. *Security Officer:* A mole on his nose? *Maddie:* A mole on his nose! *Security Officer:* What kind of clothes? *Maddie* [to David]: What kind of clothes . . . ? *David* [to Maddie]: What kind of clothes do you suppose? *Security Officer:* What kind of clothes do I suppose would be worn by a man with a mole on his nose? Who knows? *David:* Did I happen to mention, did I bother to disclose . . . ?

The Dr. Seuss Joke

DM: So Selina's running for president again. We're starting with this notion of a rally, with, you know that call-and-response thing that Obama used to work the crowd with. And Selina's trying to do that, and not getting any response. But her opponent has this natural affinity for the crowd. As we were writing the scene, we came up with this notion of fusing Dr. Seuss and Maya Angelou, which seemed very funny. Selina's the perfect person to hate both Dr. Seuss and Maya Angelou.

So now it gets complicated. I was a huge fan of the show *Moonlighting*. There's this great episode when they're trying to find a Chinese guy with a mole on his nose.[5] This is when *Moonlighting* was at its greatest, and the guy they're talking to just turns it back and forth into this Dr. Seuss thing[6]—and that left an indelible mark on my comedy psyche. [During the alts] I said I think there's an opportunity to stretch this line out into something more absurdly *Veep*-y. I ordered up what the joke

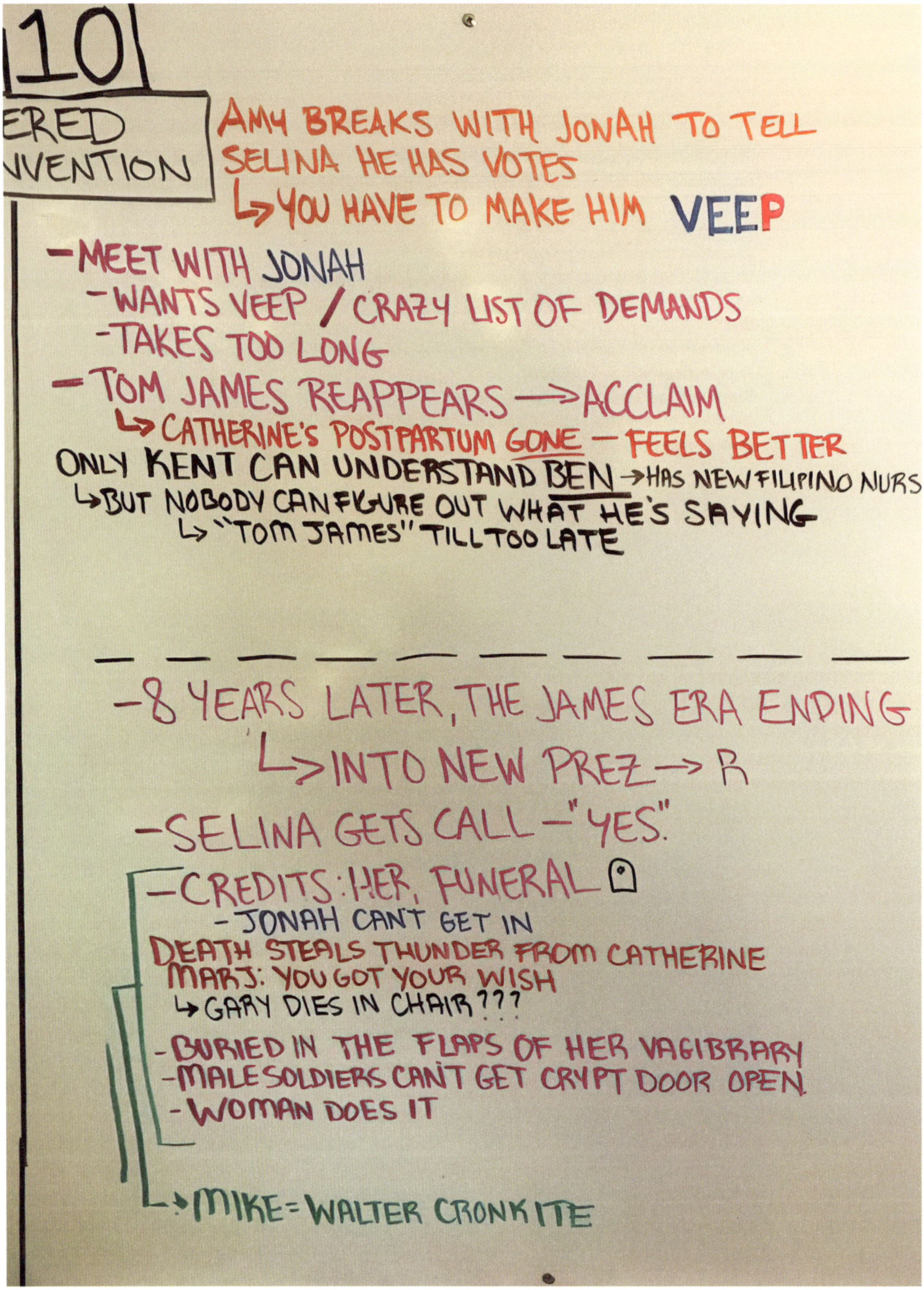

10

ERED
NVENTION

AMY BREAKS WITH JONAH TO TELL SELINA HE HAS VOTES
↳ YOU HAVE TO MAKE HIM VEEP

- MEET WITH JONAH
  - WANTS VEEP / CRAZY LIST OF DEMANDS
  - TAKES TOO LONG
- TOM JAMES REAPPEARS → ACCLAIM
  ↳ CATHERINE'S POSTPARTUM GONE — FEELS BETTER

ONLY KENT CAN UNDERSTAND BEN → HAS NEW FILIPINO NURS
↳ BUT NOBODY CAN FIGURE OUT WHAT HE'S SAYING
↳ "TOM JAMES" TILL TOO LATE

- 8 YEARS LATER, THE JAMES ERA ENDING
  ↳ INTO NEW PREZ → R
- SELINA GETS CALL — "YES."
- CREDITS: HER FUNERAL
  - JONAH CAN'T GET IN

DEATH STEALS THUNDER FROM CATHERINE
MARJ: YOU GOT YOUR WISH
↳ GARY DIES IN CHAIR???

- BURIED IN THE FLAPS OF HER VAGIBRARY
- MALE SOLDIERS CAN'T GET CRYPT DOOR OPEN.
- WOMAN DOES IT

↳ MIKE = WALTER CRONKITE

should be, which rarely happens. What if Dr. Seuss fucks Maya Angelou—how do we take this further? I can remember sitting there with the staff, trying to find the right one. And someone came up with "yuzz-ma-tuzz" and then Dan O'Keefe [a fellow writer] added "and filled her all up with snoozily-scuzz." And it was just exactly what I wanted.

How to End a Show Here is a whiteboard that shows the series plotline as it's being worked out. It was for the last season, but it's not what came to pass. Moving from the micro to the macro, I asked Mandel to discuss how he ended the series, because I was interested in how external events—Donald Trump on the one hand, and Julia Louis-Dreyfus's cancer on the other—influenced his thinking.[7]

David Mandel: This is basically what the end of the show looked like right before Julia was diagnosed with cancer.[8] We'd won an Emmy Award on Sunday night. And Monday morning I got the call she had cancer. So this—what you see on the whiteboard—is the original ending. Basically it was building to this notion Selina has, to make Jonah veep if she's going to be president again. She goes to meet Jonah, who is particularly assholey and has a crazy-long list of demands. The gist was that that takes too long, and Tom James [who had been Selina's original veep pick and was her sometimes lover] makes his move and is elected president. And then we jump eight years and Richard is elected president. And she gets the call from Richard. There was the thought that he was going to say, "Will you join me on the ticket?" And she just goes, "Yes," like she doesn't even let him finish. Or we just cut away, *Sopranos* style. Or the halfway cheat, where you just see the biggest fucking smile on her face. And then you jump ahead again to her funeral, the funeral of the only woman to be vice president twice.

That was where we were headed when we took a hiatus while Julia got treated. The biggest thing that happened during the interim is that Trump changed. As it became clear she was going to be okay, Trump was hitting the gas. He got crazier. He got more Trumpy, and he was pretty Trumpy to begin with. So I had this existential crisis. We were making fun of a model that doesn't exist anymore. The ongoing structure of *Veep* was, she tries to do something and it backfires. And it ruins her. So much of the show is based on the notion of either her being embarrassed, or saying the wrong thing or being seen the wrong way. All these concepts just instantly started to feel outdated. This was really bothering me. That led to the idea: in a world where Donald Trump gets to be president, why can't Selina be president? Why is Selina the only one paying the price? In a post-Trump world, what seems shameful no longer seems shameful.

We started talking about these larger questions like, What does it take to be president these days? What is she prepared to do? What is the worst thing she could do—that would make her earn the presidency, but that would just be horrifying? And ultimately, it was, you have to kill Fredo.[9] Like the moment when Coppola feared that people might like Michael Corleone too much. What do you do? You kill Fredo.

And really, what is the only thing she cares about? Gary. So we decided she's gonna kill Gary [not literally—she betrays him in a particularly awful way], basically bury him in the woods. And that just changed everything—obviously the finale, but we went back and looked at the whole season and darkened it, because all of a sudden we had to play in what was politics now. Sometimes things we were making up were happening by the time the episode aired. Like no matter how horrible and dark we wrote things, America seemed to be getting there as quickly as it could.

7. My own experience is that radically shifting gears can produce miracles if you're set up for them. On 9/11, at the *Times* magazine, we threw out the entire issue we had been laboriously planning and made a new one in seventy-two hours, a collage of fragmentary imprints of that freighted day, which was deeper and even more artful than many we'd taken months to make—probably the most meaningful (to me) of my whole career. That's because the talent at the magazine was so rich that with little input of my own, I could (mostly) point in another direction and watch what happened. That issue of the magazine, borne of crisis, which we called *Remains of the Day*, was just sitting in waiting. This is an endless footnote just to mention that talent hibernates.

8. When Julia Louis-Dreyfus was diagnosed with breast cancer in 2017, *Veep* went on a two-year hiatus.

9. Fredo was Michael's feeble brother in the *Godfather* movies. Michael offed him for being disloyal.

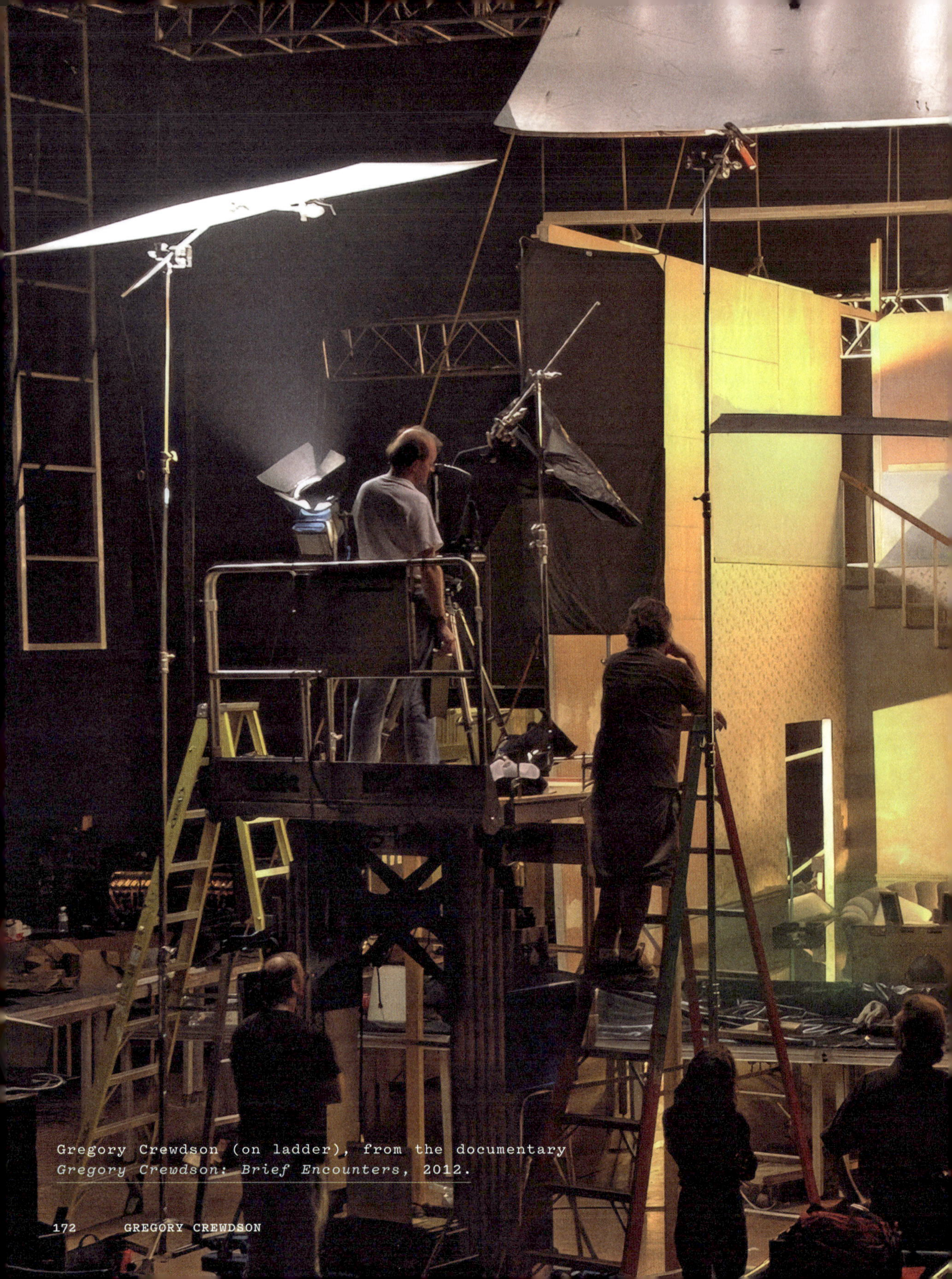

Gregory Crewdson (on ladder), from the documentary *Gregory Crewdson: Brief Encounters*, 2012.

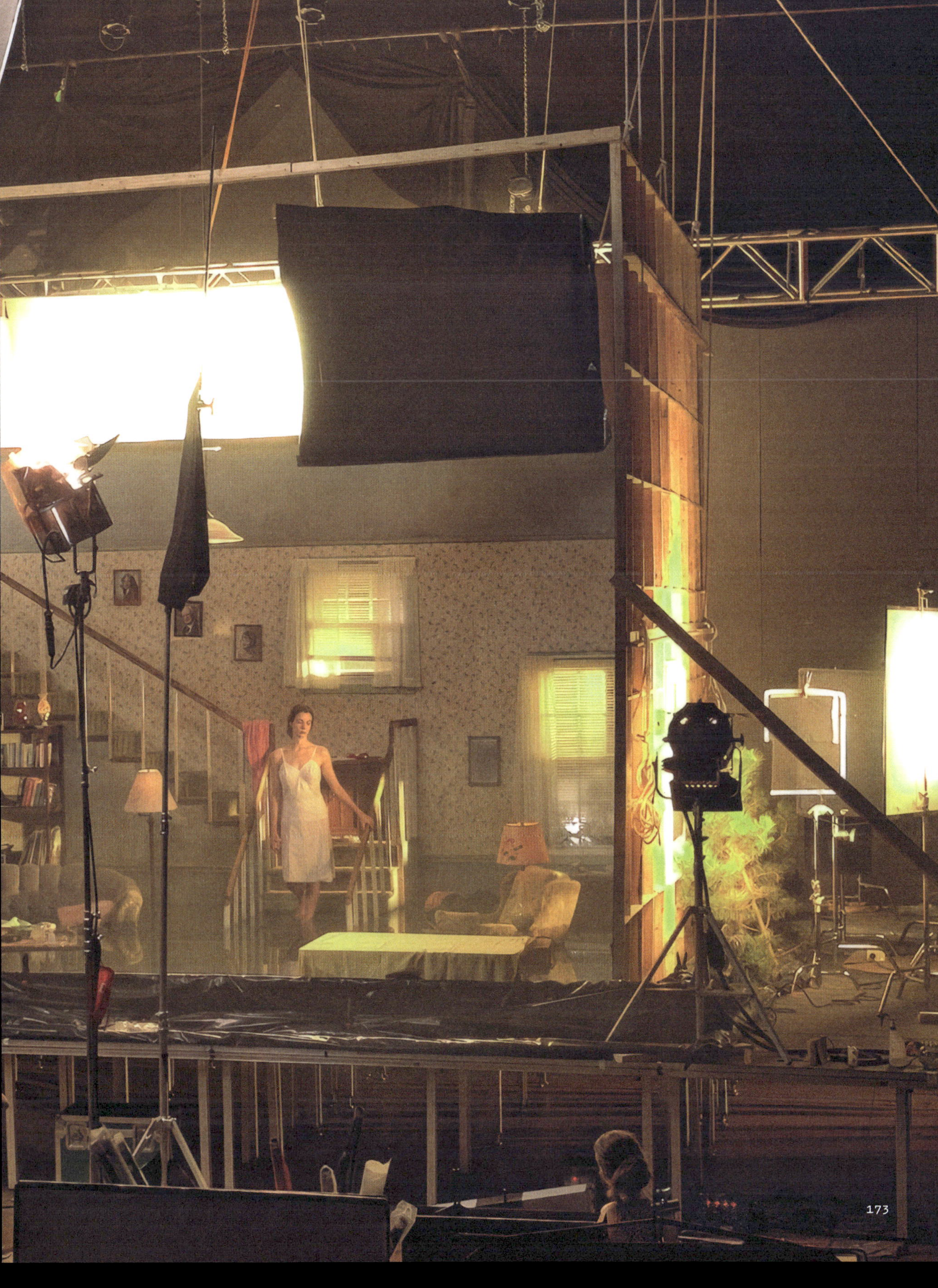

17

GREGORY CREWDSON

There's Only One Way It Could Possibly Be

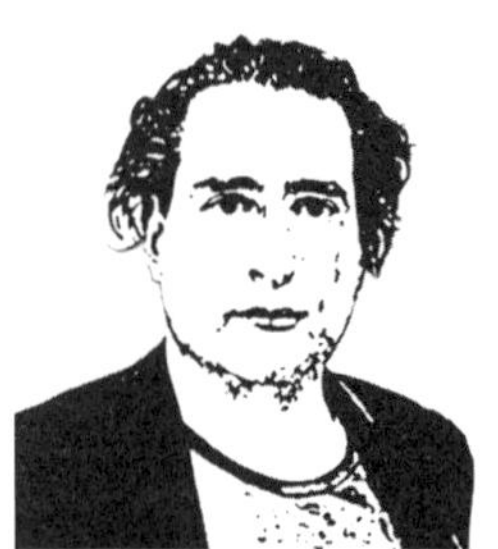

OCCUPATION: Photographer

WORK DISCUSSED: *Redemption Center* (2018–2019)

BORN: 1962

GREGORY CREWDSON IS a photographer who makes large-scale prints that resemble stills from a movie. Each image captures a moment, poised between a before and after that is entirely up to the viewer to devise. They are exquisitely lit staged dreamscapes: gigantic productions (and also gigantic prints), involving an indie-movie-size crew and many months—sometimes years—of pre- and postproduction. The pictures live in their own genre, somewhere between film and photography.

I have been drawn to them ever since Kathy Ryan, the photography director of *The New York Times Magazine*, first showed me the work when I was the editor and we were looking to begin a program of fine art portfolios in the magazine. She wanted Crewdson to inaugurate the series. He proposed a project that might involve actual movie stars—an exception for him (but also the reason why he was, for the first time, willing to have a publication show his work; we could help him procure the actors)—and be set in a Vermont farmhouse. It was expensive, but the resulting series, called *Dream House*, and ultimately featuring Julianne Moore, Philip Seymour Hoffman, and Tilda Swinton, was one of the more satisfying art projects we published during my tenure.

Crewdson's latest project at the time of our conversation, a series of photographs called *An Eclipse of Moths*, was set in a small industrial town, Pittsfield, Massachusetts, that is often the location of his shoots. His "star," in the case of the picture we discussed, was the man who runs the dump. But in a sense, it could have been a scene from any of his projects. You could edit his lifetime of images into a single motion picture—his imprint is that consistent.

"I always knew that I thought like a photographer, but that I love movies more." Crewdson was explaining how he came to invent this mutant art form I'd come to discuss. "I *love* movies, but this is how I know to do it—I think in still images. How do you tell a story in a still image? You tell it through form, light, atmosphere—they work as a kind of narrative code.

"My feeling is you're always just paying attention to that one central story that you feel like you're on earth to tell, and that that story is defined when you're coming of age as an artist. There's a very small window when you're open to influence,[1] and it's usually in your twenties. You think, *These are the things I love, these are the things I hate, these are my influences*. And then you spend your life working out those dramas."

In our conversation, he kept returning to this theme, as if he felt a little trapped in his sensibility. Is it really so fixed? Crewdson thought it was.

"I came of age in the mid-eighties. On the one hand, I was kind of inspired by the whole tradition of landscape photography like William Eggleston and [Joel] Sternfeld. And then I was going down to New York from graduate school and seeing modern photography like Cindy Sherman and Richard Prince and was very excited about their scale and artifice. And seeing *Blue Velvet*, and Eric Fischl paintings and reading Ray Carver short stories—and I kind of knew. And then you're stuck with those things."

The first tableau movie still–ish photo project (he doesn't have a name for them) that won him attention was a black-and-white series called *Hover*, which he made in the mid-nineties; the color-saturated *Twilight*, which he made several years later, made him art-world famous. He's done approximately nine of these projects, each generally more ambitious than the last. They've been shown in the Met, Whitney, and Brooklyn Museum. His work has been the subject of a film documentary. He is represented by the Gagosian Gallery and runs the graduate photography program at Yale. *An Eclipse of Moths* began its life just after he'd finished and shown another series called *Cathedral of the Pines*.

It was 2016. "I'm typically in one of three stages," he said, "preproduction, production, or postproduction. And the actual production of any body of work is unfortunately the shortest amount of time. When you finish a project, it goes out in the world; you kind of lose ownership in it. And there's a down element to it, a slight depression. At a certain point, it's time to get back to work. I'm a long-distance swimmer, and I feel sort of creative when I swim, where I just think openly about larger concepts or parameters. The last pictures were primarily intimate and in nature. So I knew for the next series I wanted to do something less intimate, more open—like emptied-out cityscapes with smaller figures. You try to make contrasting decisions to your last body of work. But of course, that only gets you so far because you can't really get away from yourself. You have one story that you continue to tell over and over. But . . . you do try."

The Hunt "Location scouting is just me driving alone, looking for *something*—I'm not exactly sure I know what it is," Crewdson said. "This can go on for months because there are no constraints on my time, in terms of budgets. Setting is very important to me. All the pictures in this series were made in Pittsfield, which is like forty-five minutes from my home."

As Crewdson explained it, he wanders around lost in a reverie until he reaches a particular location and sees a picture just appear before him. What struck me is he doesn't record the moment, the angle he is seeing, or even try to capture the location with his phone camera. The image gets locked; he sees it. "Something clicks," he said. "And I get a vague kind of image of what a picture might be." To some extent, he's made the photograph right then and there, in his mind. The rest—and there is a lot of rest—is just execution.

"I'm not that comfortable with cameras generally—I know there's a kind of contradiction there. And I'm dyslexic, but there's something about a still image that I completely get and understand. Once I see it in my head, it's ingrained. I have a photographic memory, I guess."[2]

1. Can influence leave that indelible mark only when you're young? That's not my experience, but I suppose I am way too impressionable—that's being a novice, I guess. Every new painter I like, I want to imitate immediately, and do. Of course, my own painting voice, such as it is, always subverts the imitations.

2. Memory! Several subjects mentioned having exceptional memories. Is memory relevant to creative expression? It must be helpful, at least.

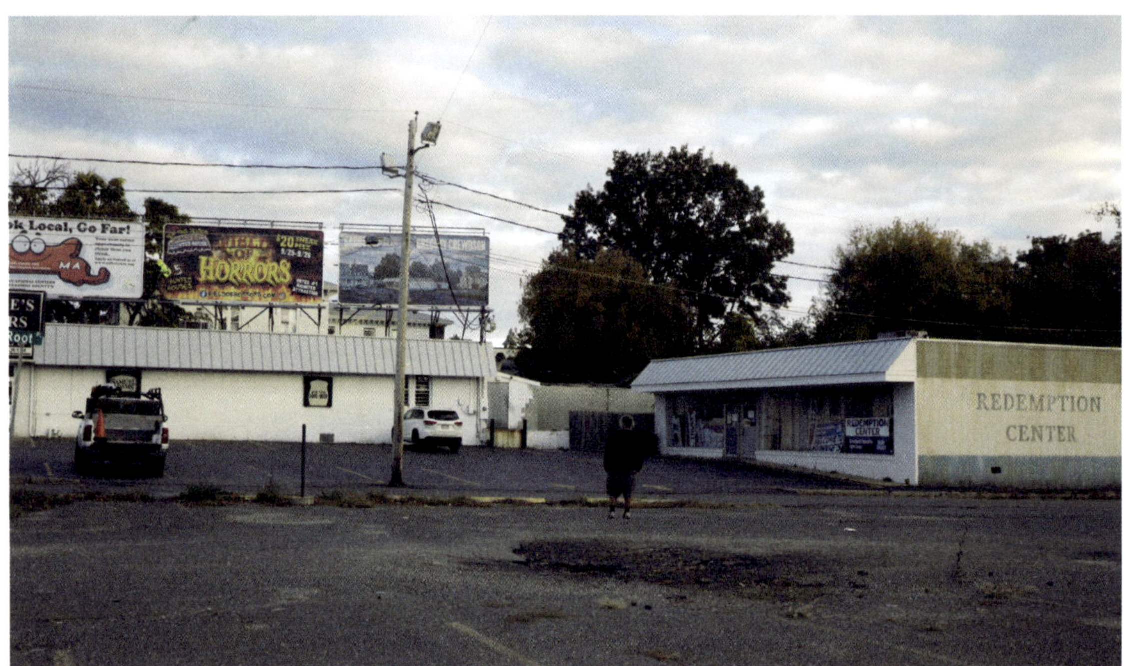

For the photograph titled *Redemption Center*, in *An Eclipse of Moths*, this is more or less the location he was looking at. (You can compare it to the finished picture on pages 180–181.)

"And then I bring in Juliane [a colleague, who is also his life partner]. I bring her to the location and I'll just literally sit there, describe where the frame begins, where it ends, what might be happening in the picture. And she'll take notes."

Crewdson does not tell her a story. He simply describes the picture he sees. "I'm interested in the moment. I almost don't want to know what's going to happen before or after. I work in motifs mostly. All artists do. All artists create iconography for themselves over a period of time. And that's kind of unconscious. I'm drawn to certain kinds of houses, cars, weather, light. So that's what I'm working with. And sometimes I'll come up with a scenario that has too much story in it, so I bring it back, simplify it, empty it out.

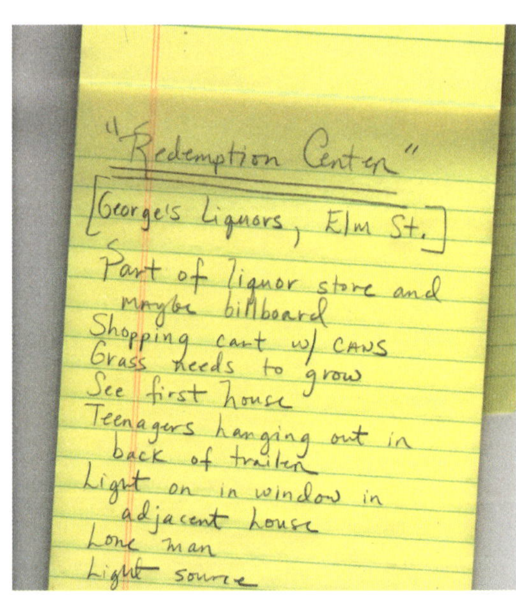

"Redemption Center"
[George's Liquors, Elm St.]
Part of liquor store and maybe billboard
Shopping cart w/ CANS
Grass needs to grow
See first house
Teenagers hanging out in back of trailer
Light on in window in adjacent house
Lone man
Light source

"Anyway, Juliane writes a kind of script—a textual description of the picture." The pictures that get made usually resemble these descriptions in nearly every way.

An Empty Lot That Haunts Him Many future viewers of *Redemption Center* will believe the picture is commenting on the opioid crisis because of its small-city despair, or that it is prescient in capturing a kind

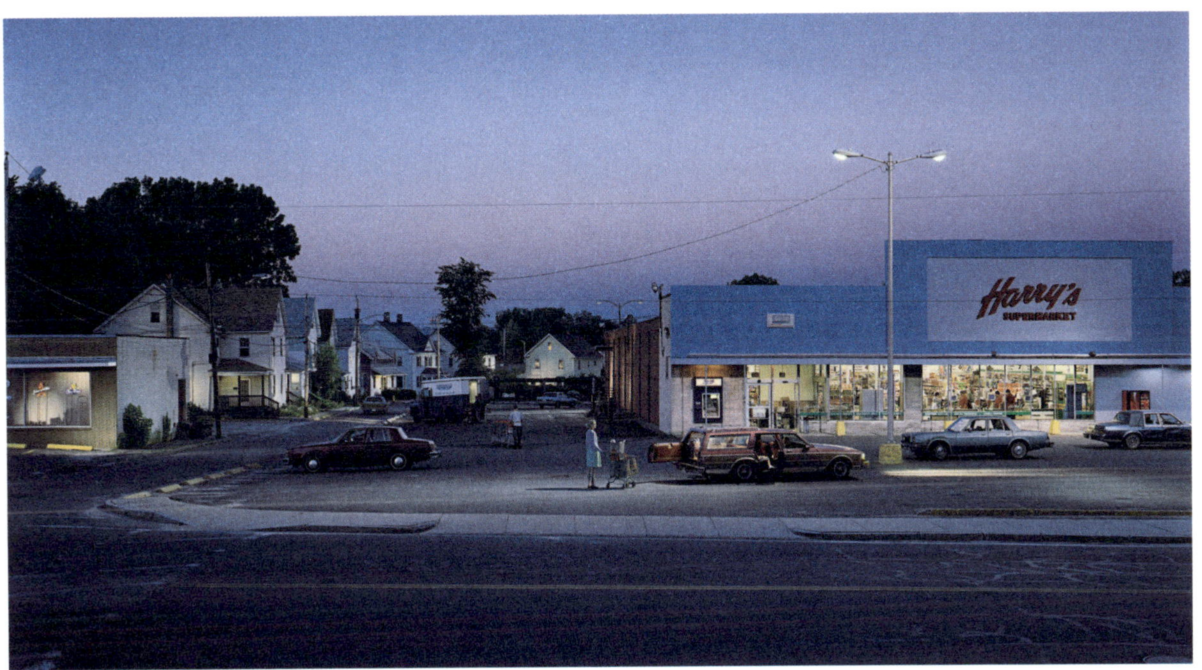

Gregory Crewdson, Untitled (2003-2008), from *Beneath the Roses*, digital pigment print, 57 × 88 in. © Gregory Crewdson.

of COVID feeling (at the time of our conversation, COVID was in full swing), but Crewdson had something else in mind.

"It was more about my feeling of brokenness at the time," he said, "searching for some kind of connection. And I just found myself thinking about the streetlamp as a kind of beacon—and that's how the series title, *An Eclipse of Moths*, came to be.

"I had made a picture many years ago in this location—for *Beneath the Roses* [another series]. There was a supermarket. I loved that supermarket: Harry's Supermarket. It was torn down. I liked the empty lot where the supermarket was, and I liked the redemption center that was there. My first thought was that the redemption center should play as a kind of metaphor. But the building was white, and I like everything to have a certain amount of muted color, so I knew I'd have to paint it."

A Silent Collaboration "Once I've settled on a location," Crewdson said, "I bring in my director of photography, who I've been working with for twenty-five years, Rick Sands. We talk generally about the project, but then [for each picture] we just sort of stand there at the location and—we don't talk about really anything, or we talk about anything but the picture. He tells me about his life, I tell him about mine, but meanwhile we're both just staring at the location. It's uncomfortable and a little excruciating, but he's trying to see what I see." Eventually, without speaking, Sands just knows what to do.[3]

Crewdson's crew grows to about forty-fifty people. "We're probably like a month out from production at this point. There are logistics—a budget, getting okays. And then because we've worked very closely with the city of Pittsfield, we ask them during this period not to pave any roads, not to mow lawns. . . ."[4]

The location had the bones of what he needed to work with, but he started to futz with it.

3. I love this moment. Mysticism enters the creative process in a whole new way—a Vulcan mind meld.

4. Pittsfield is a small city, but this is insane. The town would agree not to mow its lawns for a picture—even a big beautiful one? Crewdson laughed when I asked why the citizens don't revolt. "In Pittsfield I've become a known figure, for better or worse." In group projects, it helps to be persuasive.

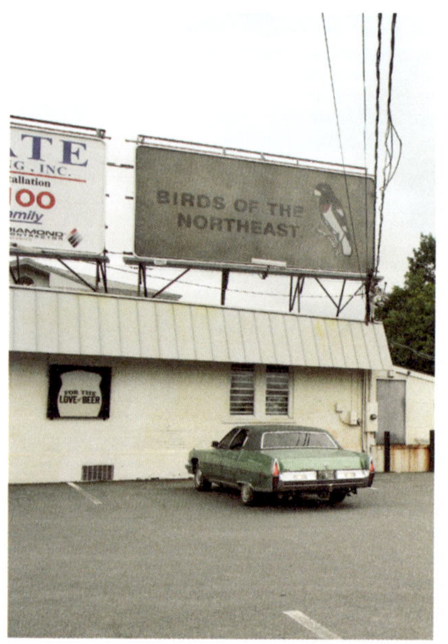

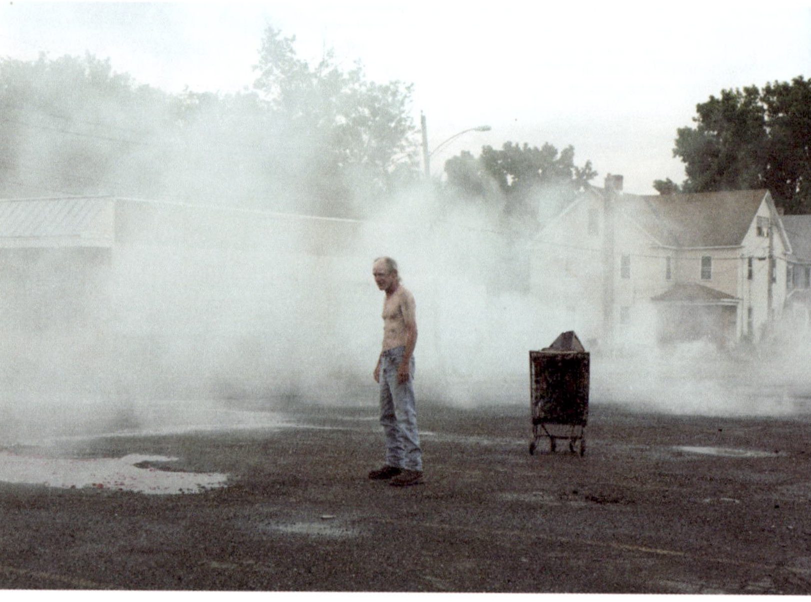

"I wanted my own billboard. So I worked with a graphic designer to design that billboard, BIRDS OF THE NORTHEAST. Birds have played in my pictures for years—nature, redemptive nature, the intersection where nature is growing provides almost a sense of possibility. . . .

"And I knew I wanted a central lamppost, and on the site there was just a pole, so we worked with the city to find an old lamppost."

The Dump Guy "I needed to find exactly the right person to be in the picture," Crewdson continued. "We try to use local people, people on the street. This guy happens to be the manager of my town dump. I always liked the way he looked, and then one day I just asked him: 'Do you wanna be in this picture?' And even two days before we were shooting, I hadn't figured out what I wanted him to be looking at. Then I noticed an indentation in the pavement that produces a puddle, and I thought, *Okay, let's put rose petals in there, that's it.*

"We wetted down the streets, rigged up two eighty-foot lifts with big lights, cast the two teenage boys hanging out near the recyclables in the back, used the fog machines to get a sense of the weather. . . .

"As we shoot, the camera never moves. We just make microscopic changes: How much of the face do we want to see? What's the attitude of the shoulders? And in my limited way, I direct the actors."

Making the Picture They shoot, he said, a hundred or so files for each picture, with different foci and different light, overexposure and underexposure, so that they can make adjustments in post-production. But he rarely wavers from the original picture in his head, and he didn't in this case. If this were me (and it really could never be) I'd cover myself in all sorts of ways so I still had the opportunity to change course. I'd keep all options open—what if that thing I saw in my head wasn't exactly right? That's just not the way Crewdson thinks. He's committed. But his doubt manifests itself in other ways.

"Every time we're on a shoot day, I wake up with an absolute pit in my stomach," he said. "I want to throw up, I'm just filled with anxiety. It's partially because there's a limit

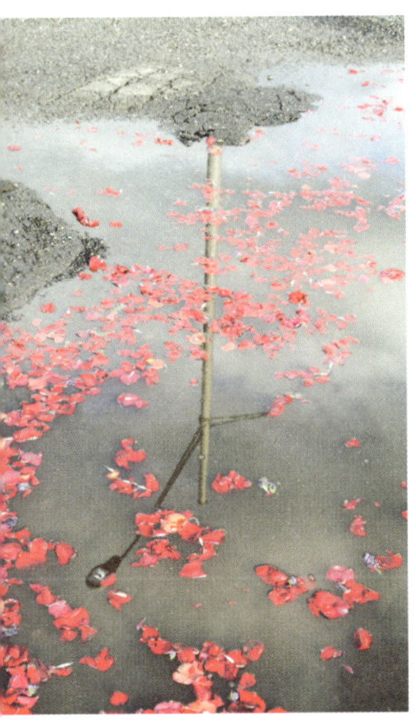

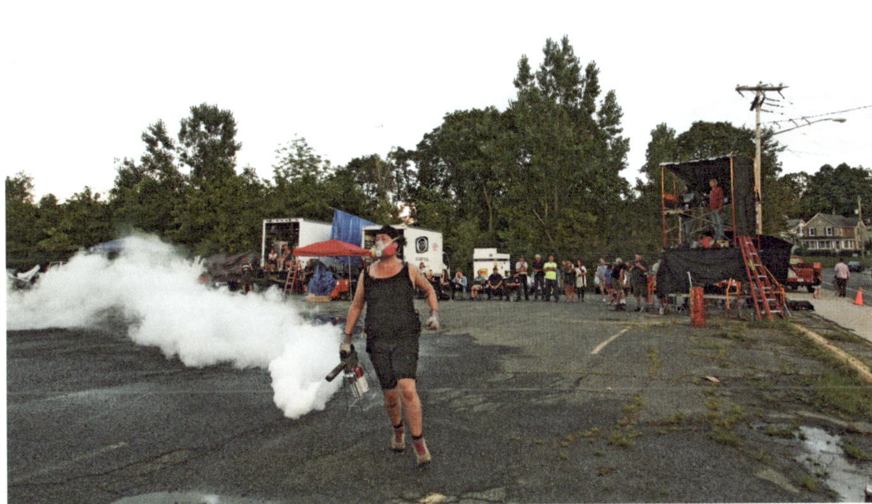

to what I can do at this point. I am constantly checking the weather, what the wind is going to be—I hate wind—and then the possible danger, with all the lights and stuff.

"But what happens is, as everyone's in their place, and the light is going down, you can physically see the picture coming to life. It's inexplicably peaceful at that moment. Everything makes sense. The beauty, the light, the stillness—it's my favorite part. This is it. It's right in front of me."

In this case, he was especially moved by the sky and the contours of the clouds, which of course he hadn't been able to control. He remembers being struck when the dump manager took off his shirt and revealed the patterns of uneven sun on his body; he couldn't believe his luck. In these situations, he feels a kind of artistic bliss, a "sweet spot" between what he can control and what he can't. But the feeling of serenity and satisfaction doesn't hold very long.

Once the picture is shot, he said, "I can't bear to look at it for at least a month." The distance between what is in his head and what he's captured in the frame widens. "Representation always disappoints," he said, laughing.

Then, after a while, his despondency lifted.

Okay After All "I look at it and say, *Okay, maybe it's not so bad.*[5] And then I start working again." He looked at all the files and took a bit from here and another from there, "to try to put it all together like a puzzle," he said. This is a long part of the process. Postproduction takes almost a year. Eventually the image gets made into a mammoth 50 × 88.9 inches print.

Finally the picture was done. And then he began the elaborate process of starting another one—the searching and the deciding and the casting (and hunt for funding, an entire other part of the process).

"It's funny, I'm awful at technique," Crewdson said. "I couldn't even develop a roll of film if you asked me to. Yet my pictures are super technical." He shook his head. "The most important thing is your story and finding a way to present that in physical form. There's only one way it could possibly be, and you've got to figure out how to do it."

5. A reoccurring sentiment: the work improves with distance as the artist forgets his intention and sees what's there instead.

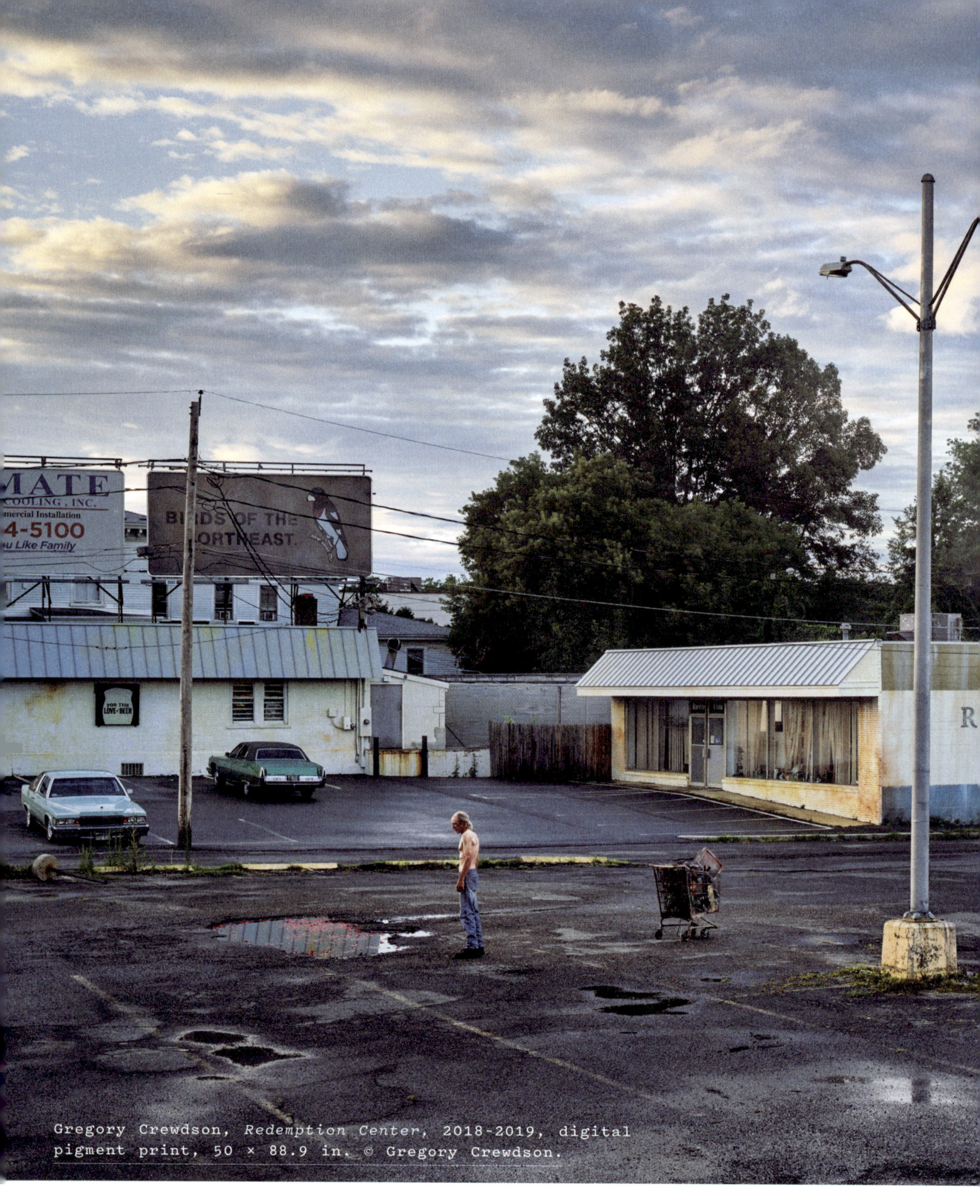

Gregory Crewdson, *Redemption Center*, 2018-2019, digital pigment print, 50 × 88.9 in. © Gregory Crewdson.

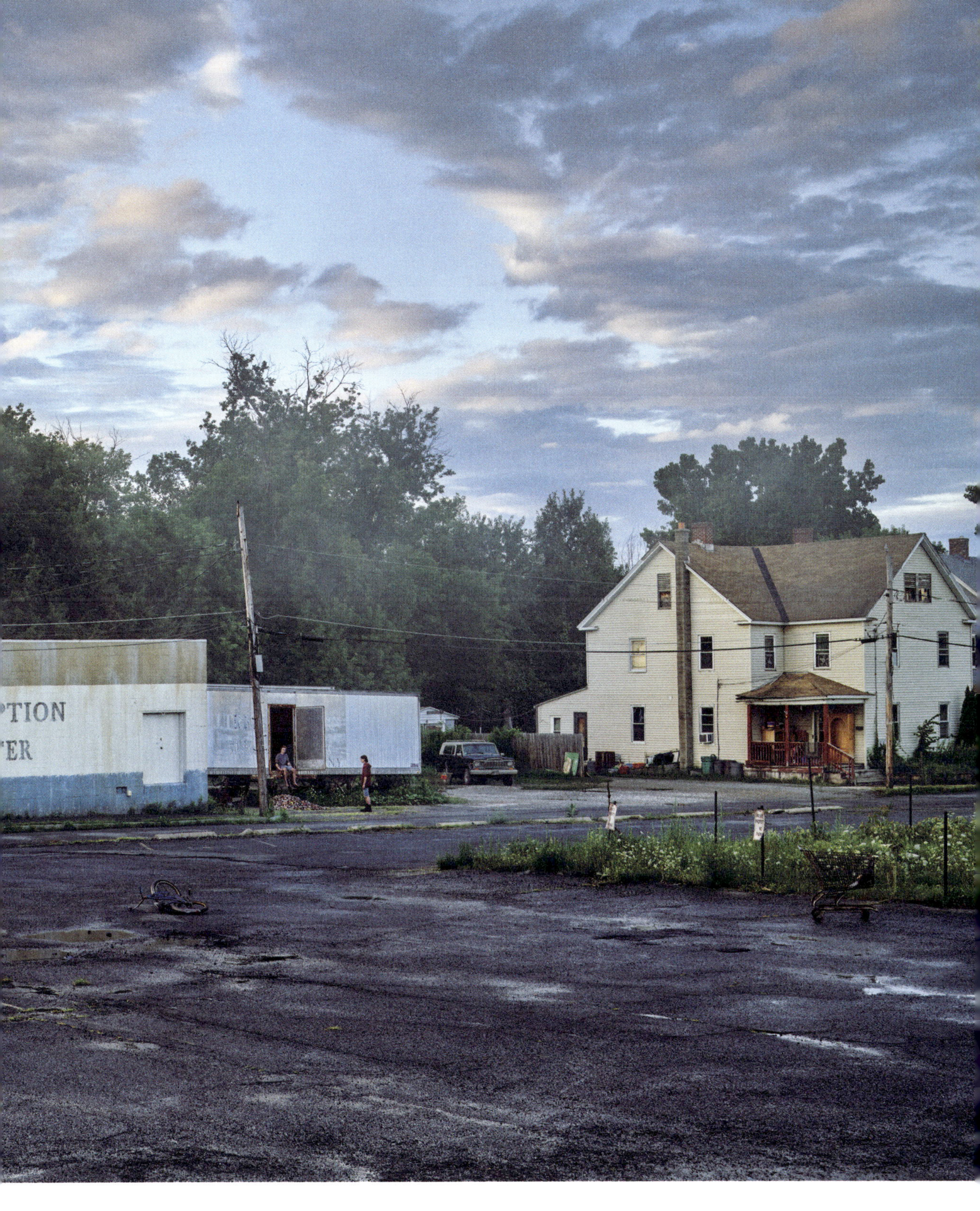
TION
ER

18

MARIE HOWE

The Unconscious Is Waiting to See If You Mean It

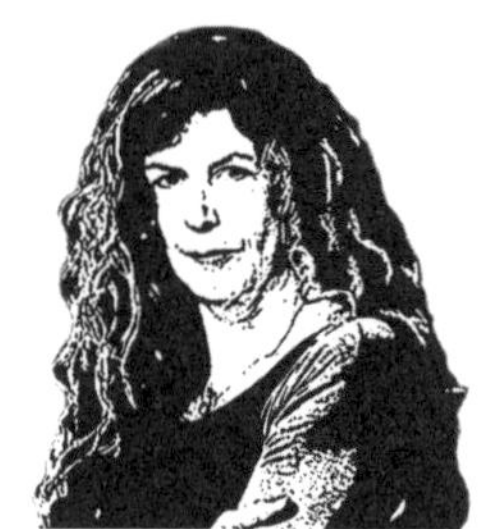

OCCUPATION: Poet

WORK DISCUSSED: "The Singularity" (2018)

BORN: 1950

"HOW DO YOU START A POEM?" I asked.

Marie hesitated. "I don't know," she said. "I've really been struggling writing. I haven't written anything I really liked in a long, long time."

Marie Howe is a gorgeous poet—her book *What the Living Do*, in particular, contains some of the most haunting, affecting poems I know. She had a reign as the New York State Poet, and is a poet other poets especially tend to worship. Shivering outside together under a heat lamp in one of those makeshift restaurant shacks that sprang up in the first fall of the pandemic, we were talking about "The Singularity,"[1] a poem she wrote in 2018 that became a viral sensation (by poetry standards) after she read it at the Universe in Verse conference that year, and then had another life later when it was made and distributed as an animated short. When I let her choose a poem to pick apart, she chose that one. The poem was written before COVID, but it was prescient in its grappling with the place of the human in a world not subject to its control.

"The great thing about this poem is that there was a deadline for it," Marie said.[2] Maria Popova, who runs the conference, had invited Marie to speak at the event, which concerns itself with the intersection of poetry and science. Because she was having trouble writing at the time, she remembered, "I was just going to read something from Walt Whitman, and Maria said to me, 'No, you write something,' and I decided I would try.

"It was forty-eight hours before the event. I wrote it by hand, in a notebook, on the living room couch. You carry these things around for years, and somehow it coalesces, and I know it's a cliché, but I'm writing to see what comes next. I wrote the poem out, then I might have written it again, and I probably typed it, changing it as I go. When I felt I had a beginning and an end, I walked into Inan's room"—Inan is Marie's daughter, then a teenager—"and I said, 'Can you listen to something,' and I read it to her, and she said, 'It's really good but the whole middle part is boring, and has to go.'

"And I said, okay, gone! And that changed everything."

Marie usually writes quickly. During this period, she said she'd been reading "all the books trying to understand the universe and time and space and that sort of thing. Stephen Hawking, Carlo Rovelli. Inan was taking physics and was very good at it, and we'd be talking at breakfast." Marie teaches an eco-poetry class to her students at Sarah Lawrence College. Many of her interests converge around trying to understand humans' place in the larger scheme of things. (Her poems often have religious themes. "When I started to write, I was always embarrassed by my theological interests," she said, but there is no denying they are central to her and have been since her very Catholic girlhood in Rochester.) This poem was, as she said, months and really a lifetime coming. But it was particularly sparked by the phrase Stephen Hawking uses to describe the big bang—"the singularity."

To begin our conversation, she had sent me its first draft, which you can see on the next page, along with the finished poem. Read the poem and the draft back and forth to follow along.

Line by Line The poem's first words, "Do you sometimes want to wake up to the Singularity / we once were," were there from the start. She paused for a moment in our little shack and considered the line. "'We once were,' those *w*'s—and then the *we* and the *you*. So it had its voice and its address—to you, to us. And that's really crucial to me—if I don't know who I'm talking to, then I don't know what I'm talking about."

At Inan's insistence, the next move had been to strip out the middle of the poem. "Mostly," Marie said, "I write a lot, and I take away things, say no. Subtraction is crucial. A poem is like crossing a stream, jumping from rock to rock." Or, put another way, "a poem has to have silence in it."

I handed her back the early draft she had given me, with my own editing notes to mark how it shifted. "Oh, all this is very interesting," she said. She read the first couple of stanzas out loud, verbalizing her editing process. "This goes, because it's too abstract," she said about a line she abandoned. "We already mentioned food, so this line is unnecessary. And I had to add 'home alone' to explain the pill drawer."

She was struck by how much she then wrote into the poem between drafts, which is unusual for her.[3] One phrase she added—"for every atom belonging to me as good belongs to you"—is Whitman's. "That Whitman quote is always in me." She turned to our fellow diners in the restaurant shack. "I've always wanted to make a video on my phone, just turn to her"—she gestured at our neighbor—"and her and him, to a hundred and fifty people, and have each of them say it. This line is the radical, remarkable truth. 'Every atom belonging to me as good belongs to you'—that quote *is* the singularity."

She saw that she added the words *Farsi* and *French* to the line about the ocean's language. "Oceans have a voice, but we can't hear it. But we were oceans. We have the memory." Intuitively, she felt listing languages helped get that across. *English*, *Farsi*, *French*—"Better to end with French, one syllable."

Then we got to the addition of "this awful loneliness." To me, the specific evocation of loneliness (along with the pills in the drawer) drove home the price humans have paid for colonizing "nature" (a phrase she has come to despise for its very suggestion that "nature is separate from us"). It was what made the poem so painful. She agreed it was "the absolute heart of the poem," but was focused on her use of the word *awful*. "Writing this line was the moment I realized this poem might work."

She was trying to get at the scale of the ecological horror. "I tell my students—'awesome' used to mean blinding, burnt, annihilating. We don't have a word for that anymore. Now we say that T-shirt is awesome." She mock shuddered. Awful, at least, has awe in it. To describe "how lonely we are in the world we made," it

1. The poem was originally called "Singularity." Marie eventually added the "The."

2. And here it is again—the invitation, the deadline. The taunt.

3. Not surprising, but the basic rhythm of add first, subtract later seems to be the way almost everybody works. Poets most of all.

DRAFT

THE SINGULARITY

Do you sometimes want to wake up to the singularity
We once were?

So compact nobody
Needed a bed, or food or money

Nobody hungry
Wandering in despair, in love,

Curled into a cot,
Hiding in the school bathroom

Pulling open the drawer
Where the pills are kept.

No more Nature. No
More Them and Us. No more testing

To determine if the elephant
Grieves her calf or if

The coral feels pain. Trashed
Oceans don't speak English

But we can wake up to what
We were before everything started.

When we were ocean
And sky was earth, and animal

Was energy and rock was liquid
And stars were space and space was not

At all – nothing.
Oh uncaused cause what made you move?

We have become unrecognizable
To ourselves: Anglerfish. Earth worms,

Barking dogs, Snowstorms,
Who remembers when we were

A singularity? When we were everything
With nothing around it.

(the last pea on your plate but also the plate the air, the table –)

Don't throw that plastic bottle into the ocean!

We are the fish! Remember?
Who wants to be a singularity again??

what we once was

No we, no was, no one.
Home at last. Home at last.

Home at last.

THE SINGULARITY

(after Stephen Hawking)

Do you sometimes wake up to the singularity
we once were

so compact nobody
needed a bed, or food or money

nobody hiding in the school bathroom
or home alone

pulling open the drawer
where the pills are kept.

For every atom belonging to me as good
belongs to you. Remember?

There was no *Nature.* No
them. No tests

to determine if the elephant
grieves her calf or if

the coral reef feels pain. Trashed
oceans don't speak English or Farsi or French;

would that we could wake up to what we were
when we *were* ocean, and before that

to when sky was earth, and animal was energy, and rock was
liquid, and stars were space, and space was not

at all—nothing,

before we came to believe humans were so important
before this awful loneliness.

Can molecules recall it?
What once was? Before anything happened?

No I, no we, no one, no was
no verb no noun

only a tiny tiny dot brimming with
is is is is is

All everything home.

would have to do.

She got to my favorite part of the poem, which she also added in the later draft—the stuttering *is is is* near the end. "The problem was, before the singularity, there wasn't a noun, but there was a dot"—poetry's power lies in its ability to convey such an enormous thought in just a few words. "There was no syntax, really, is what I'm trying to say. There was no subject/object." She mused on the words *subject* and *object*. "Those words would have been better," she said.

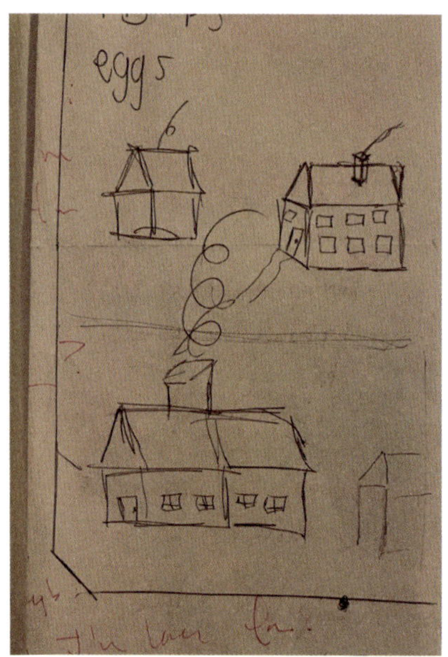

House doodle. Home at last? All everything home?

The last line originally read "home at last." She winced. "It's like a spiritual. You can't say 'home at last.'" She changed it to *All everything home.* But she wasn't entirely satisfied. "I mean, it's really a simple point. It borders on the sentimental."

Doubt The poem has won great acclaim, and she was happy with it but also, sitting here now in the damp cold, uneasy about her life as a poet. It was hard not to be moved by her doubt. I handed her another poem she had sent me, called "Hurry," which features Inan as a younger child, and asked if she wanted to talk about it.

"It's such a little poem. People love it, though," she said, sounding mystified.

"It's so simple," I said, in praise.

"Everything I do is so simple," she replied. "That's what I'm embarrassed about."[4]

She cast her eyes down. Still, as she read over "Hurry," she felt buoyed. "It's wild. It's encouraging because I'm really struggling, but here it is. When I slow down enough to feel—" She stopped herself. "The challenge of my whole life has been to slow down. I find it very difficult to be still—to endure it."

And at that moment during COVID, was pandemic life why she was having trouble

HURRY

We stop at the dry cleaners and the grocery store
and the gas station and the green market and
Hurry up honey, I say, hurry,
as she runs along two or three steps behind me
her blue jacket unzipped and her socks rolled down.

Where do I want her to hurry to? To her grave?
To mine? Where one day she might stand all grown?
Today, when all the errands are finally done, I say to her,
Honey I'm sorry I keep saying Hurry—
you walk ahead of me. You be the mother.

And, Hurry up, she says, over her shoulder, looking
back at me, laughing. Hurry up now darling, she says,
hurry, hurry, taking the house keys from my hands.

FOUND IN A JOURNAL

March 16 2018

Jackhammers early this morning. The sound of spring.
The light a gradually spring light.
Oh Lord. I am still stumbling. Lucie Luciie Lucie

Her body. Her hair. Her hair in that casket.
Her hands. Her breasts and her body her face.

A singularity is what was at the beginning. One thing and nothing else.

writing? "Even in lockdown, I'm so busy. I say I want more solitude, but I give it away. My daughter is old enough to be gone, but she's not, so I'm never really alone." Marie had been anxious, about the election, and more. "The world is so noisy," she said. "Who needs it, everybody's talking."

She had recently turned seventy, which may have been weighing on her more than she thought. Many friends she would show her work to are dead, she'd noticed lately.[5] "So it's like, who cares? You have to have someone waiting for you." And readers? "If I think about them, I can't write anything. When I write a poem, I have to pretend no one will see it."

I asked what emotion was most productive for her work—sadness? happiness? "Loneliness," she answered quickly.

Her best writing comes when, she said, she is "in my nightgown for days, not thinking about anyone else. It takes a couple of days just thrashing through the brambles to get to any type of clearing, and it's very painful. It's frustrating, you see all your limitations, but a lot of what is happening is the unconscious is just waiting to see if you mean it. I like it once I settle in, but the borders are tough." Once she passes into the other state, "that's the best feeling in the world—we're utterly ourselves and we're nobody."

Better A week later, I ran into Marie on the street—she lives down the block from me. She'd sent me some "inklings," as she calls them, that she'd found in her journals of poems and fragments. One mentioned money and food in a formulation she would use in "The Singularity"; one mentioned the singularity itself. She'd forgotten about both, which were written several weeks before she wrote the poem. We marveled about the subconscious. The poem, she remarked earlier, "uses me."

She was also excited to report she'd marked out a week to sit in her nightgown and work. As her friend and fan, I was relieved to see her anguish lift and sense of capability return, like she'd won a battle with her darker forces. At our tea, she had wistfully described what writing poetry was about for her. "It's self-forgetfulness," she said. "That is the suffering of being human—self-consciousness." When she can get beyond it, that, she said, "is the great liberation."

She was enthusiastic to get back to writing. "I don't know what I'm doing," she said. "But I never do. You only know later. A while later. And you go, *Oh my God, look at that.*"

4. *Simple*: such a strange word. Marie uses it here to belittle her work, and yet all the subjects in this book labor so hard to simplify their work, reduce it to its essence, elevate it. *Simple* is both the insult and the aspiration.

5. At the time of our conversation for the book, I chalked up this sentiment to pandemic weariness, but I've noticed in the time that has passed, she often brings up the death of readers she'd most relied on (her teacher the poet Stanley Kunitz especially). But it's true in so many contexts. Artists make art for a specific audience of their imagining. That audience is their collaborator.

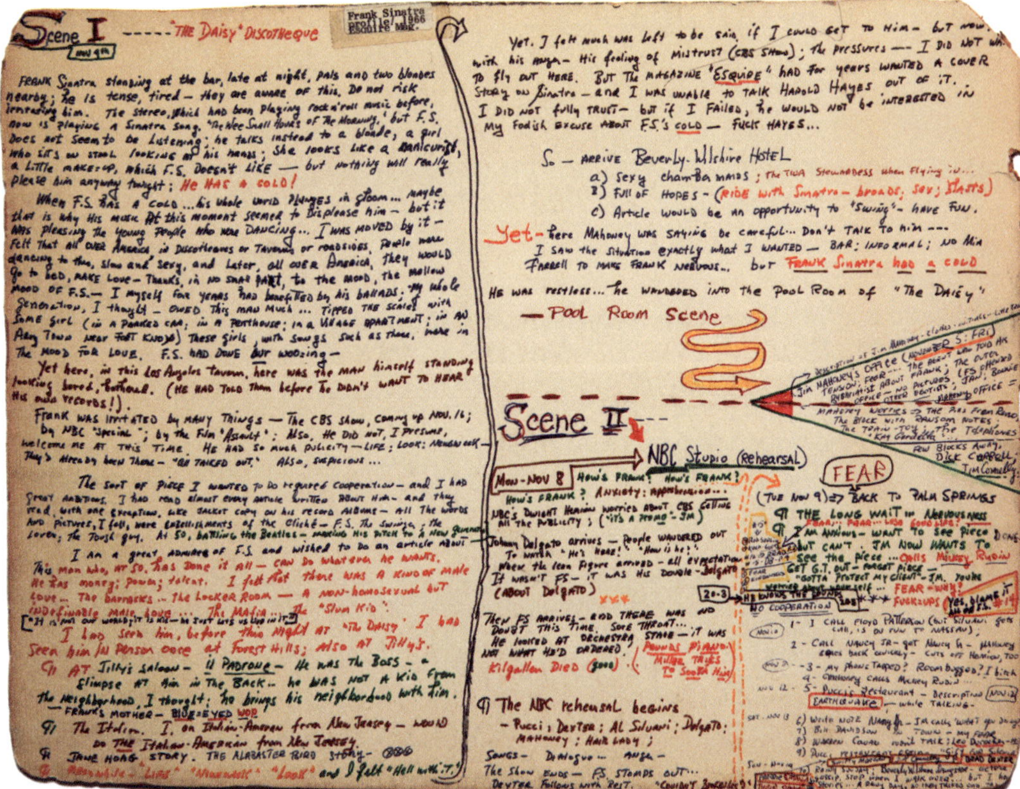

19

GAY TALESE

What the Hell Could You Ask Sinatra?

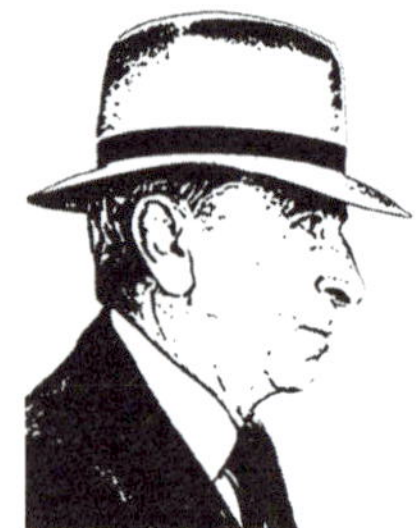

OCCUPATION: Writer

WORK DISCUSSED: "Frank Sinatra Has a Cold" (1966)

BORN: 1932

GAY TALESE WAS A little irritated that I'd come to talk to him about "Frank Sinatra Has a Cold," which he considers inferior to his other writing. But, among journalists especially, it is his most famous and influential work, and it is considered a pillar of the New Journalism, a label that came to describe nonfiction written with the conventions of literary fiction, except that it was not made up—at least, not most of the time.

Literary journalism was why I became a journalist. I devoured it as an adolescent, read Tom Wolfe, Joan Didion, Michael Herr—and Gay Talese. Only later did I understand that they (and others) constituted a movement, and that the movement had a name. Journalism was considered craft, not art, which rankled the more ambitious reporters of that time, who set out to prove that journalism in

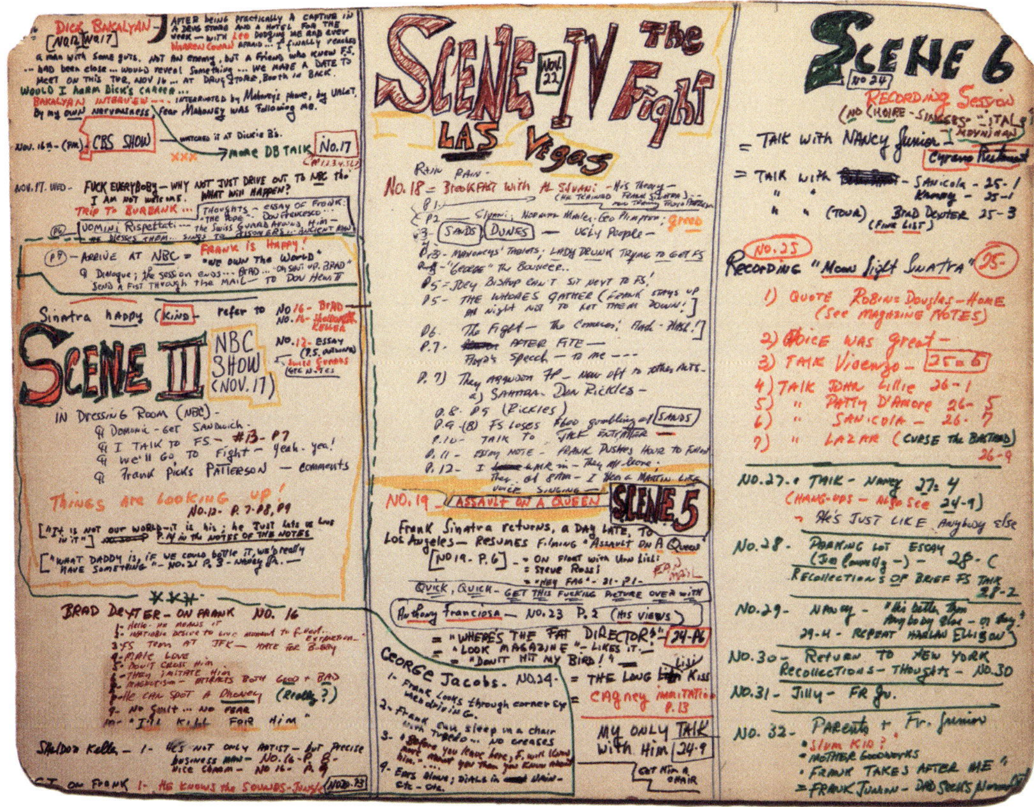

“Frank Sinatra Has a Cold,” meticulously and colorfully outlined.

the right hands could be literature. They structured their “pieces”—that’s what they called their articles—as short stories, built around scenes and action and dialogue. They wrote with an authorial confidence (godly omniscience or direct address) that traditional reporters generally found presumptuous—even vulgar. They did away with transparent sourcing, made no effort to appear objective, and replaced sobriety with swagger. Looking back, what most impresses is the arrogance they brought to the whole enterprise—which was the fuel for some extraordinary writing.

And of course their heyday, the 1960s and 1970s, was a time of great and fascinating turmoil, which was also central to their appeal. Fundamentally, the medium they were forging was to try to take fact and fuse it with imagination, but without compromising the fact, an exciting trick that few could pull off. (There were a lot of terrible imitators.) The genre has pretty much died down by now, whether because modern writers don’t have the talent or the moxie or the industry (these pieces were very difficult), or because readers don’t have the appetite. Or all of the above.

Talese was among the most restrained of the New Journalism set, and I always found the interplay of his literary ambition and the quiet of his prose to be especially effective. He is very much a gentleman. He met me at the door of his town house dressed in a suit, tie, and pocket square, a little anachronistic for this meeting, in his house in the midafternoon, but that’s his uniform even now. After some polite conversation, we went down to his writing studio, a basement he calls the bunker. He keeps every note—for the pieces

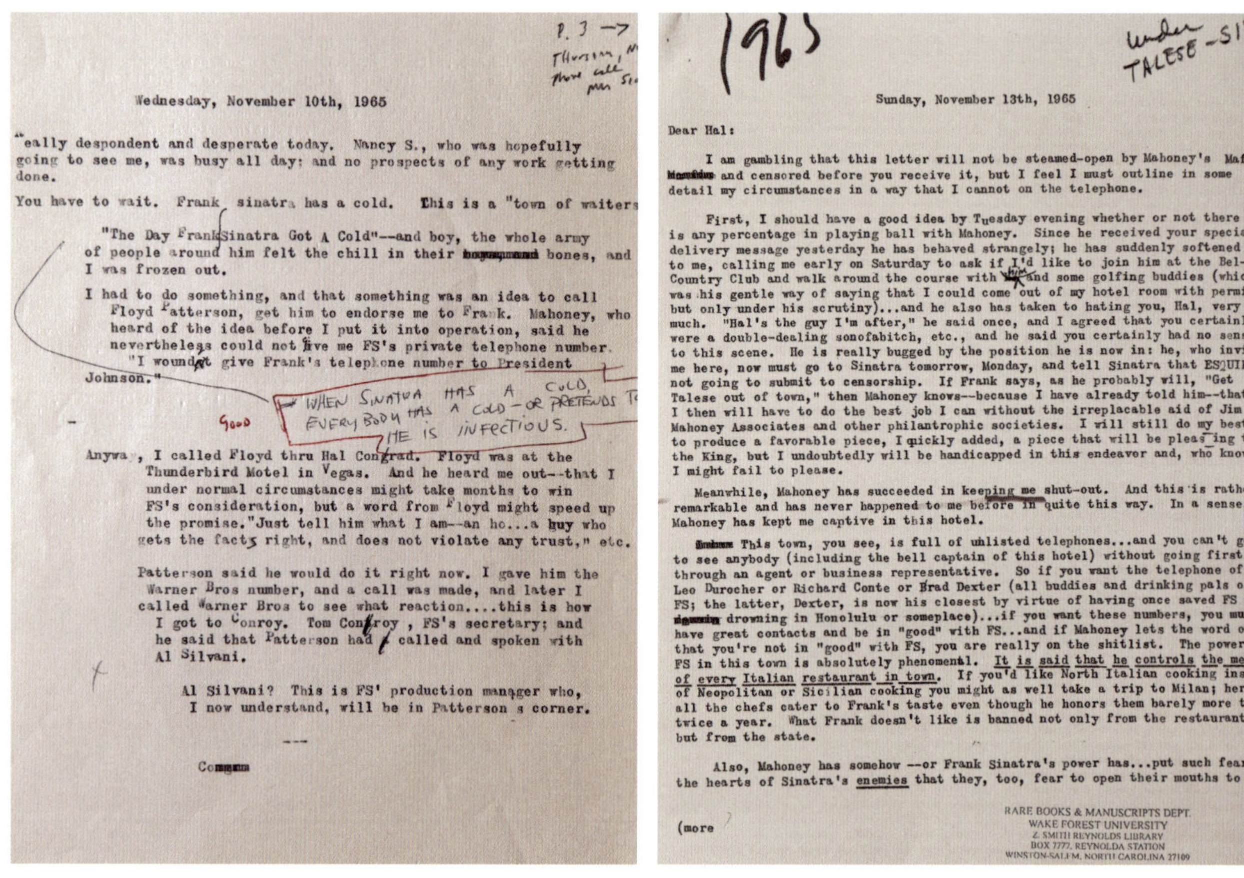

P. 3 →

Wednesday, November 10th, 1965

"eally despondent and desperate today. Nancy S., who was hopefully going to see me, was busy all day; and no prospects of any work getting done.

You have to wait. Frank sinatra has a cold. This is a "town of waiters

"The Day Frank Sinatra Got A Cold"--and boy, the whole army of people around him felt the chill in their bones, and I was frozen out.

I had to do something, and that something was an idea to call Floyd Patterson, get him to endorse me to Frank. Mahoney, who heard of the idea before I put it into operation, said he nevertheless could not give me FS's private telephone number. "I wouldn't give Frank's telephone number to President Johnson."

WHEN SINATRA HAS A COLD, EVERYBODY HAS A COLD—OR PRETENDS TO. HE IS INFECTIOUS.

GOOD

Anyway, I called Floyd thru Hal Conrad. Floyd was at the Thunderbird Motel in Vegas. And he heard me out--that I under normal circumstances might take months to win FS's consideration, but a word from Floyd might speed up the promise."Just tell him what I am--an ho...a guy who gets the facts right, and does not violate any trust," etc.

Patterson said he would do it right now. I gave him the Warner Bros number, and a call was made, and later I called Warner Bros to see what reaction....this is how I got to Conroy. Tom Conroy , FS's secretary; and he said that Patterson had called and spoken with Al Silvani.

Al Silvani? This is FS' production manager who, I now understand, will be in Patterson s corner.

Co

1965

under TALESE–SI

Sunday, November 13th, 1965

Dear Hal:

I am gambling that this letter will not be steamed-open by Mahoney's Mafi and censored before you receive it, but I feel I must outline in some detail my circumstances in a way that I cannot on the telephone.

First, I should have a good idea by Tuesday evening whether or not there is any percentage in playing ball with Mahoney. Since he received your special delivery message yesterday he has behaved strangely; he has suddenly softened to me, calling me early on Saturday to ask if I'd like to join him at the Bel-A Country Club and walk around the course with him and some golfing buddies (which was his gentle way of saying that I could come out of my hotel room with permis but only under his scrutiny)...and he also has taken to hating you, Hal, very much. "Hal's the guy I'm after," he said once, and I agreed that you certainly were a double-dealing sonofabitch, etc., and he said you certainly had no sensi to this scene. He is really bugged by the position he is now in: he, who invit me here, now must go to Sinatra tomorrow, Monday, and tell Sinatra that ESQUIRE not going to submit to censorship. If Frank says, as he probably will, "Get Talese out of town," then Mahoney knows--because I have already told him--that I then will have to do the best job I can without the irreplacable aid of Jim Mahoney Associates and other philantrophic societies. I will still do my best to produce a favorable piece, I quickly added, a piece that will be pleasing to the King, but I undoubtedly will be handicapped in this endeavor and, who knows I might fail to please.

Meanwhile, Mahoney has succeeded in keeping me shut-out. And this is rathe remarkable and has never happened to me before in quite this way. In a sense, Mahoney has kept me captive in this hotel.

This town, you see, is full of unlisted telephones...and you can't ge to see anybody (including the bell captain of this hotel) without going first through an agent or business representative. So if you want the telephone of, Leo Durocher or Richard Conte or Brad Dexter (all buddies and drinking pals of FS; the latter, Dexter, is now his closest by virtue of having once saved FS f drowning in Honolulu or someplace)...if you want these numbers, you mus have great contacts and be in "good" with FS...and if Mahoney lets the word ou that you're not in "good" with FS, you are really on the shitlist. The power FS in this town is absolutely phenomenal. It is said that he controls the men of every Italian restaurant in town. If you'd like North Italian cooking inst of Neopolitan or Sicilian cooking you might as well take a trip to Milan; here all the chefs cater to Frank's taste even though he honors them barely more th twice a year. What Frank doesn't like is banned not only from the restaurants but from the state.

Also, Mahoney has somehow --or Frank Sinatra's power has...put such fear the hearts of Sinatra's enemies that they, too, fear to open their mouths to

(more

Nightly notes, including (left) his arrival at his central conceit that when Sinatra has a cold, everybody does. On the right, a letter to Harold Hayes. Note the paranoia.

he did for *Esquire*, including those he considered his best, like one on Floyd Patterson called "The Loser"; for his classic book on *The New York Times*, *The Kingdom and the Power*; for his bestselling book on the Mafia, *Honor Thy Father*; for his study of the so-called sexual revolution, *Thy Neighbor's Wife*, which caused a scandal when it was published; and for the two books he was writing at the time of our meeting, when he was eighty-eight. And of course, "Frank Sinatra Has a Cold," a piece he never wanted to write but that follows him everywhere.[1]

Among the most famous attributes of "Frank Sinatra Has a Cold" is that it was, in journalistic terms, a "write around"—Sinatra wouldn't talk to him. But what makes the story endure is how Talese went about solving that problem, embracing the absence of its subject and building the story around the characters of Sinatra's posse. That's what Talese likes best about it too. The story is soaked in detail. The narrator is all-knowing. The piece has a fairly sophisticated structure—scenes wrapped within scenes (several of which he alludes to in his recollection). And all of it is plotted out in the colorful outline you can see on the opening pages of this chapter.

Throughout, Talese paints a world in which the protagonist is seen only through the reflection of the hangers-on who feed on him. But that wasn't Talese's intent. His editors wanted a profile of Frank Sinatra in which the reader actually gets to meet Frank Sinatra. That's what he flew out to Los Angeles to give them.

As he rifled through the notes in his boxes more than fifty years later, Talese found himself reliving the story. I am struck by a few things: How powerful a tool is simple observation—attention. How hard he worked to get at what might have been a simple entertainment story—believe me, people rarely work so hard to capture celebrities. Writing about the famous pays the rent, but most of its own practitioners view it, if they're being candid, as hack work (though, in the right hands, it's absolutely not).[2] And then, how Talese coerced the story out of his experience, writing about the same detail over and over again, as note, as summary, as outline, as draft, until he understood its meaning for him. Like for so many, his tenaciousness was pivotal.

GAY TALESE: I worked for the high school paper and I went to school in Alabama because I had a hard time getting into college. And then in Alabama, I met this Southern guy. And he said, "Since you like journalism so much, maybe you want to go to New York. You can talk to my cousin, who's the managing editor of *The New York Times*, Turner Catledge."[3] And that led to my getting a job as a copyboy there. I wrote a lot when I was a copyboy, mostly about obscure people, and I even got to write for the magazine—I was a pretty hot copyboy. I'm in the army for two years, and when I come back, I get assigned to the sports department, which was a good thing because they let me do what I want. And I guess I broke rules.[4] I wrote about a fighter once; I didn't even use his name. I wrote about a jockey. Why? Because Carson McCullers wrote a short story called "The Jockey." McCullers, Irwin Shaw, I read them, I reread them, I almost memorized them. I read the short story of Melville's, "Bartleby, the Scrivener," which of course you're aware of. And I wanted to write like Bartleby. I wanted to write about what Melville wrote about, which was nobodies. I wrote a lot about failures, because loser locker rooms are always more interesting. The *Times* let me because they were desperate to have sports writing that wasn't boring.

I wrote three books when I was still at the *Times*, and I started to write for *Esquire* on the side.

I quit *The New York Times* because I was sad. I couldn't get more than five thousand words. [Words are an extremely coveted currency for journalists.] Sinatra is, I don't know, fourteen thousand. I was making about $300 for the *Times*. And *Esquire* gave me the same salary, for only six pieces, that's all. Harold Hayes,[5] the editor, said, "You choose three and I'll choose three." So the first piece I did for Hayes was about Alden Whitman, the *Times* obituary writer. It was called "Mr. Bad News." I loved it, probably the best piece I did. Then Hayes says, "I want you to do Sinatra." I said, "No, Jesus. Everybody's done Sinatra." I argued about it, and he said, "Look, you have a cover guaranteed. It's all set. Sinatra's doing a big NBC special." And then I said, "And after, can I do Clifton Daniel [another *Times* figure, a managing editor]?" He agreed.

A Cold Is Not a Cold So, Sinatra was easy. I just had to fly there. And we used to have expense accounts, incredible. But when I got there, I called Jim Mahoney, his press agent, and he said, "Oh, gee, you're here." "Uh, yeah, I'm here,

1. Talese blames the attention he's received on Tom Wolfe. "He wrote a book called *The New Journalism*," Talese said. "No one ever heard of me until then. He coined it, and he made me the founder. Pissed a lot of people off. I didn't even know what he was talking about. But it brought me to the attention of the college crowd."

2. Some of the greatest magazine work has been written about celebrity. It's an irresistible—and even important subject, I think, even if it's usually just tossed off. Truman Capote on Marlon Brando. Lillian Ross. Wonderful. I published several stories by Lynn Hirschberg, at *Esquire* and *The New York Times Magazine*, that are, in my view, some of the best Hollywood portraits ever written. And "Frank Sinatra Has a Cold," of course.

3. Turner Catledge was the editor of *The New York Times*. It's a shame that connections of this sort matter so much in getting opportunities, but of course they do. I got my job as a copyboy—a *Times* lackey—the same way, although I didn't make anything like what Talese did of my own copyboy experience.

4. David Simon talks about this, too, viewing the breaking of the rules of journalism as almost a cathartic creative experience. Journalism has so many dusty conventions that it lends itself to convention flouting, but rule breaking as a first step toward art making is obviously true across fields.

5. Harold Hayes was the editor of *Esquire* from 1963 to 1973, during which he edited an amazing magazine, maybe the best run of a magazine ever. Hayes was the editor I most aspired to be, though in the one conversation I had with him, long after he left the field and I was just coming up, he depressed me with his bitterness about what magazine journalism had become. And those were still the pretty good days.

At 4:15 P.M., Jim Mahoney called from the NB
say, "Whom "It happened as I expected it would."
"Wha t?"
"Frank said no dice."
"You're kidding."
"No," Mahoney said. "He wouldn't go al
live up to the deal."
"There wasn't any deal--expect the one
"Well that's the way it is."
"You mean I won't be able to follow hi

No dice. Above and below, from Talese's nightly notes, recording dialogue, ruminations, etc.

when will I see Mr. Sinatra?" He said, "Well, Frank isn't feeling too well." "Oh." "He has a cold."

Well, I had thought it was all set. It was not all set. I thought, *I'll just go home; now I can get the fuck out of there.* But first I call Harold Hayes, and I say, "If you want me to come back, I'll come back. Or, I know you really want this piece, so I can try to do some research out here while I wait to talk to Sinatra." I knew people in Los Angeles. I knew a very important person, a guy named Jack Hanson, who owned a place called the Daisy—the Daisy discotheque.[6] He knew a lot of Sinatra people. He gave me some phone numbers. And then the phone rings one day and it's Mahoney. He says, "I understand you're talking to some friends of Frank. What are you doing?" I said, "How's Frank's cold?"

"I'll tell you what," he says. "You're not gonna see Frank." But he said I could go to a rehearsal and watch, if I kept my mouth shut. I knew the director of the special, named Dwight Hemion, whose daughter and my daughter went to the same school, but I didn't let Sinatra know that I knew Hemion. At the rehearsal Sinatra's voice cracked. His cold. And there was a guy who says, "Of all the people to get a cold, it has to be Sinatra, he couldn't have broken his leg?" I see Frank's double there. His driver, his bouncer. We were all watching Frank. All the studio heads, all the secretaries. And a trombone player from Nelson Riddle's band slipped a camera out of his pocket and snapped a photo of Frank standing there. Little stuff I knew I wouldn't use. And I wrote it up as a scene.

It's all about the scenes. 'Cause I always wanted to write scenes that seem like they're made up, but they're not made up.

The "Lede," as Lived A couple of days later, I go to see my friend Jack Hanson at the Daisy. It was dinner hour. And I see Sinatra over there at the bar! The lights were behind him, so you could see it was Sinatra. And the two blondes—you could certainly see that. He was with Leo Durocher, the baseball manager, and a guy named Brad Dexter, who was just hanging around. So I see him, and I wrote some notes. I write on these little shirt board things I keep in my pocket for this purpose.

It's always all about being there. No fucking telephone. Or tape recorder, worse. Because then you're surrendering the ear.

I look at Sinatra's shoes—unscraped, like they were never walked on—and he was smoking a cigarette. He lit the light, and the woman next to him was smoking too. After ten minutes,

I have been here three weeks. In that time I have seen Sinatra only at a distance, and rarely too; it is not easy to crack his inner circle. Today I called George Jacobs, but Stanley Parker answered the phone, and I could hear a football game on television in the background and voices, too, and imagined a room full of friends with drinks sitting around arguing, but not too offensively, about one thing or another--and Frank among tem, perhaps with his hair down--literally...

he went into the poolroom. And he was engaging in a heated conversation with Harlan—Harlan Ellison, a screenwriter.[7] And then finally Sinatra got up, left.

Then, when I go home to the hotel, I have my little Olivetti typewriter with me. Soft rap on the door. Chambermaid. Lovely French Algerian woman, blue eyes. And I'm writing about her and this fucking airline stewardess I met on the plane. So what I'm trying to say is, sure I'm on assignment to do Sinatra, but I'm also always writing about stuff that has nothing to do with Sinatra.

But Back to Sinatra I write, "Tonight I was at the Daisy, I saw Frank Sinatra, he was with two blondes."

And two guys—one was Leo Durocher. And here's this guy named Harlan Ellison, and Sinatra was bitch bitch bitching about Ellison's boots, his fucking Western cowboy boots. I wrote the whole scene up just as I saw it. The next day when I see Ellison, I say, "What were you thinking? Where did you get the boots? How much did they cost? Did you think Sinatra's gonna throw a bottle of bourbon at your face? That he was going to beat you up?" "No," he said, "I didn't give a shit." Sometimes journalism professors, critics, say, "How do you know what a person's thinking when you write these interior monologues?" Well, you ask the fucking person!

Every day on the road wherever I am, before I go to sleep, I read what I've written on the shirt boards and I type up my notes.[8] I'm thinking about Sinatra. He is a blend of power and fear. He surrounds himself with all these talents that are no match for his. Then there's all this stuff in the papers. About him angry and threatening to sue Walter Cronkite [who was preparing a report at the time that was rumored to be about his mob connections]. I write all that down.

Let's see. [Talese was flipping the pages in his folder.] I'm really despondent and desperate today.

I'm still no closer to seeing Sinatra. I'm waiting for the phone to ring, waiting for someone to liberate me from the helplessness and isolation and frustration and impotence. I can court people. I can con people. I can seduce.

Wednesday November 17th, 1965

So today, a day after the CBS-TV "special"--which incidentally I thought not very penetrating, a view confirmed by Gould in this morning's Times--I hope to get to Leo Durocher...also to get out to see the NBC "special" rehearsal, if I don't get tossed out.

I am to see Dick B tonight.

* * *

10 A.M. ...Thinking about Sinatra...He is a blend of the power and fear of men; he surrounds himself with those whose talent is no match for his, and this intimidates...he has this charm with women, making him the closest thing to a lover, ...He is a endlessly suspicious and fascinating study of American success. He gave up everthing for it--did what so few of us can do, those in the rut. Who live out our "winter dreams," thinking of that moment in the past, measuring everything against it; usually you ride with that which is familiar, the familiar wife and friends, the predictable reactions. He broke everything up and, like few men, realized that you can do this to a woman and still have her.

He is wildly , almost maniacal in his right to his privacy. But he is living vicariously for us. He has the wife, no longer married but she is there, she cares about him, he gets up at dinner parties and introduces her as "Nancy Senior" . . . Yet he is courting a girl, Mia, who is younger that his daughter Nancy, and one wonders how he justifies this, and what Nancy Jr., his love in the ballad, must think, Nancy with the smiling face.

He is such a liberal, but he is nothing of the sort in her relationship to a free press, but this , again, is the problem of not only him but the finks around him: to be with frank, you must sell out. You must. And if you do, the individual becomes subservient, eventually nothing but a faceless man, invisible man--Johnny DelGato's, who at one time had the dream of being an actor, and who took the part, and now is merely a stand in... one of many.

Dick He should have chosen to ignor that part in "Eternity." Just as Dick B did in his career. He turned down the "dialogue director," which would have put him in with Frank's clan again, but without balls.

ALL ACCOMPANIEST...Accompany him, and you play second-fiddle. They take the easy route, not learning from him the major lesson--do it yourself, make it yourself. Yet it is all so tempting to be in Frank's wild side--the helicopter, the jet, the wine and women, the villa in Rome, dipping a teenager, keeping a divorced wife, the love of children; having hoodlums and philanthropies; giving to charity and being so uncharitable.

More notes, more rehearsing of ideas and phrases.

6. Talese milks every contact. He is an expert at squeezing whatever he can out of his past experience—which seems valuable no matter one's medium.

7. Harlan Ellison was a novelist and screenwriter.

8. If you look through his box of notes, you can see he wrote the same scene over and over, changing just a few phrases each time, but the repetitive activity didn't just refine his language, it clarified for him what he was trying to say.

But if I don't get any response, I'm an inanimate object.

But I'm thinking . . . *Frank Sinatra's got a cold*. . . . And I'm thinking, *Oh boy, the whole story of people around him*. . . .

Nobodies This is written at night. Everything is written at night. Each page of my notes is dated, "1st day, 2nd day." I'm running up bills every day. I'm taking people to lunch and dinner. Minor actors, but they were available. Pucci, that's the bouncer, he used to be a professional football player. Pucci talked to me because his brother had a restaurant, and he wanted *Esquire*'s restaurant critic to write about it. I talked to the woman that carries Sinatra's toupee, the valet, people who worked in a band with Sinatra. Who the hell are these people? They're Bartleby people.

Oh, see. Then I go to the Ali-Patterson fight in Las Vegas.

Floyd Patterson is a friend of mine, I wrote thirty-eight pieces on Patterson. I call Patterson. I get tickets from Patterson. There at the fight sat Sinatra. Blue eyes. Kind of a religious experience. They just looked, staring.

On the twenty-second day, I finally talked to Nancy.[9]

I was supposed to talk to her before, but just as I was about to go over, the phone rang. It was a hard voice, Mahoney: "Didn't I tell you not to talk to Nancy?" Hayes had said to me that my phone might have been tapped, because how could Mahoney possibly know that I was calling Nancy Sinatra? But eventually I get to her.

Why did they talk to me? All these people wanted to be interviewed because they thought they were going to be a piece themselves. The most important connection I had was a guy named Jilly Rizzo, who is a pal of Sinatra, very close. Thuggish guy, but really important because he got me to Sinatra's mother. And the reason he would love me is because the last piece I wrote for *The New York Times* was on Jilly Rizzo's saloon in New York. He loved it. And when I was there, I saw Sinatra and I talked to some people outside the bar about Sinatra, wrote it on my shirt board thing and saved it—and later used it in this piece. As long as I was with Jilly, who was almost like Sinatra's consigliere, they had a sense that I wasn't doing anything funny or mean. And I wasn't. I only wanted to finish. I had to pay the rent. I had a daughter.

So, we're at thirty days at this point. My next step is to summarize it. While I'm summarizing, I'm sort of commenting on it. I'm sort of writing. And then I put it in some form. I'm thinking how the fuck to begin this. So now I'm thinking Daisy—here it is. This is what I wrote. That became my lede. And then here—here's a rough draft [see page 196]. It's not exactly how it ended up, but it's close [see page 197].

At the same time, I was pissed off because I was worried the piece was not working out. I had been unable to talk Hayes out of it.

But I don't trust Hayes. If the piece failed, he would not be interested in my foolish excuses about Frank Sinatra's cold. Well, fuck Hayes, but I didn't want to quit the story. Hayes scared me, and I didn't want to be there, but I didn't want to walk. So I told Hayes, "It's better without Sinatra. If Sinatra had talked to me, it would have killed it. What the hell could you ask Sinatra?"

I said to him, "I don't need Sinatra. There are a lot of minor characters in this story. Everyone is a minor character—and here's the story: When Frank Sinatra has a cold, everyone has a cold."

Later When I finished this piece, it wasn't like, *Oh, wow, boy, I wrote a piece of journalism people are going to be reading fifty years from now*. Not at all. I did get lots of letters, I saved every fucking letter.

I never heard from Sinatra. Years later, Sinatra's daughters said they thought it was pretty good. And now, the Sinatra family has bought it. For the movies. Got half a million dollars for that.

9. Sinatra's daughter and the singer of "These Boots Are Made for Walkin'," one of the great earworm songs of all time.

1965 The DAISY 273-3786 JACK HANSON owner

2

Thursday, ~~October~~ November 4th...

The Daisy ---this is a discotheque that may be spelled "The Daisy" and on this particular Thursday night, Frank Sinatra and Leo Durocher, plus a a couple of blondes, were at the bar, an and there were y0ung poeple--Les Brown8s shy son--and others—Dean Martin's Boy—.......they were in this place, and Sinatra bought the drinks and he was very kind to everyb9dy... and the record player, very loud, played Sinatra records ....and people danced... and I thought, "What must it belike to hear this song, these wonderf ul ballads " meant for lovers, and here is Sinatra, Mia Farrell*less...on this particulcar November evening with a couple of blondes that were nobody...he, Frank, who at this moment,--through his songs,--was getting everybody laid, --thru car radios, radios in lving rooms while Mum was asleep, in boats, in buses down from Bridgep9t,t, in floats, in yachts, in transititors...this Sinatra song, getting people laid...and hr listened to it, in this disquotueqeue,...and he was with this ~~kook~~ chick that you wouldn't turn around at...and it made you aware of the loneliness that Pat Mahoney spoke of when she said, in addition to the fact that he was a great guy, that they often put "put him into a car" and he, ~~[illegible]~~ bombed, went home alone....

===

Next to him, is this ~~fucmin~~ fuckin Dexter...who saved his life... and how this Dexter has a job.

===

Sihatra a arguing with these punk kids...didn't have a tie. "Don't play games with me" he shouted to one punk

See — Dec 4th notes ↓ more don't leak!

This punk, Harlan Ellison, Screenwriter "Oscar" — wouldn't get off the pool table —

See Dec 2 NOTES!

The lede, as observed in his notes on day 2...

3=

1st Draft

~~I had flown from New York to California the day before~~

tmmbhondesmmmdmmdmed

mmm sitting in the wee small hours of the morning in Beverly Hills private bar, next to two blonde girls who were unexceptional he uty, who looked in fact like manicurists; they were in their early thirties, and they sat on the stools, legs crossed, and one of them looked at ..held Sinatra's hand, to steady his gold lighter, and looked at his hands.

Sinatra's hands were nubby and raw, and his pinky finger protruded, stiff from a circulatory ailment, Behind the girls were Sinatra's men friends, very nervous; the only one who was ...more informal with him was Leo Durocher, but even Leo, who had once given Ty Cobb the hip, rounding second, and who was irreverent to the Babe Ruth, even Leo the lip ~~gave no~~ lip to Frank, particularly nights like this, when Frank could flare into ...a foul temper, a temper so quick that it takes an eye witness to describe it--sudden, volotile; --to make people wish they had not been there.

I had never seen this, but I, sitting in a table in the corner, wished I had not been there. I had been assigned to write a magazine profile on him, and while I had been enthusiastic earlier in the month, had lost much interest, ...the CBS thing, which was finished, would be a very revealing documentary, I feared, would leave nothing new for me to reveal, and I wantedto wait. But the magazine editor, after I had advanced my reasoning, mmmmmmm said that they had been trying for years to get a Sinatra coverstory; now, finally, he had agreed to not block it, mmmmmmh..agreed, through his publicity man, a 37-year old Jim Mahoney, had said that Frank had okayed it on sertain conditions--that he not be interviewed because he was "all talked out," having done the Life, Look, Newsweek earlier.

... as it appeared in his first draft...

Final Rush

Esquire
Jan. 10th '66

p. 1

Pub — April 1966

SINATRA

by Gay Talese

Frank Sinatra, holding a glass of bourbon in one hand and a cigarette in the other, stood in a dark corner of the bar between two attractive but fading blondes who sat waiting for him to say something. But he said nothing; he had been silent during much of the evening, except now in this private club in Beverly Hills he seemed even more distant, staring out through the smoke and semi-darkness into a large room beyond the bar where dozens of young couples sat huddled around small tables or twisted in the center of the floor to the clamorous clang of folk-rock music blaring from the stereo. The two blondes knew, as did Sinatra's four male friends who stood nearby, that it was a bad idea to force conversation upon him when he was in this mood of sullen silence, a mood that had hardly been uncommon during this first week of November, a month before his fiftieth birthday.

-more

... and in the final manuscript (which *Esquire* published pretty much exactly as is).

20

CHERYL POPE

A Kind of Derangement

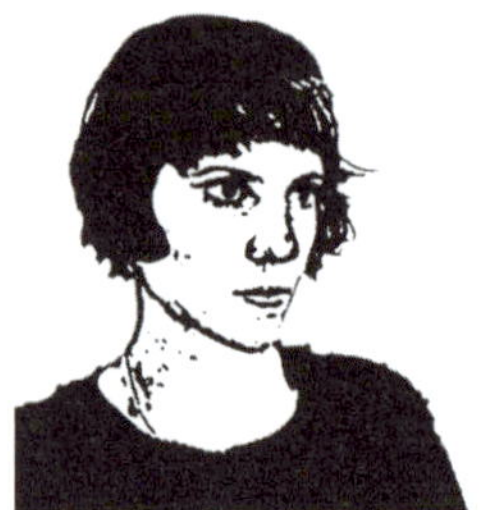

OCCUPATION: Visual Artist

WORK DISCUSSED: *Mother and Child on Blue Mat* (2021)

BORN: 1980

I WAS ON THE lookout for artists who keep records of minute iterations of their work, which few people actually do, and Mardee, the project manager of this book, sent me this unfinished image. Mardee is a big fan of Cheryl Pope, the artist of the emotionally fraught work the image was on the path to becoming, and knew that Cheryl had recorded the steps because she'd had a number of doubts along the way.

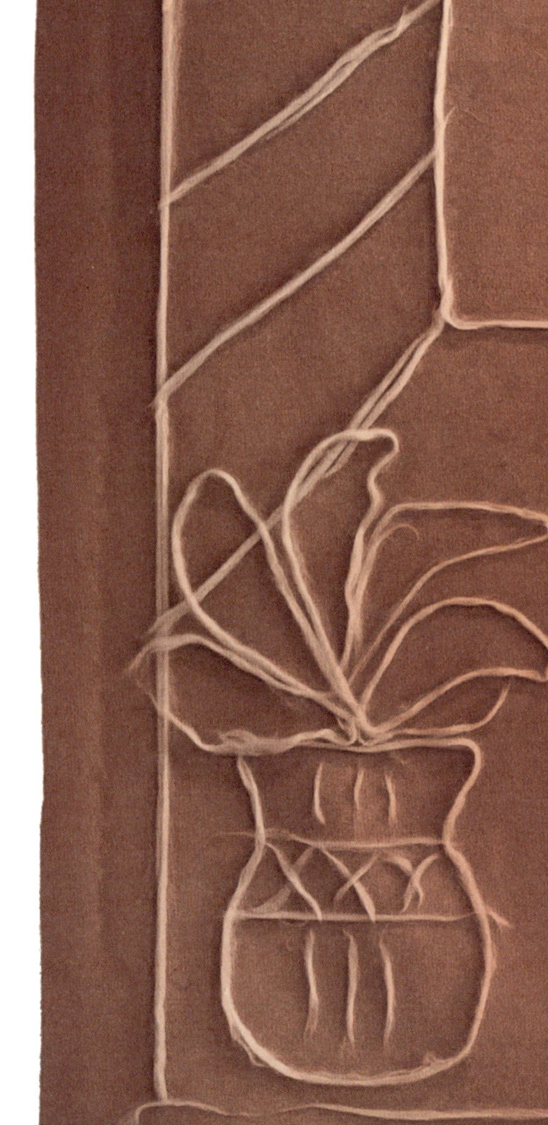

I didn't know Cheryl's art, and I didn't know the heartbreaking context of the image I was looking at, but I was drawn in by the beautiful emptiness of it—a consequence of it being essentially a study, but also, I later learned, because the work itself is about absence. And in fact, this simple gestural study of a mother and child in felt is actually my favorite version of the picture because it expresses that emptiness most poignantly.

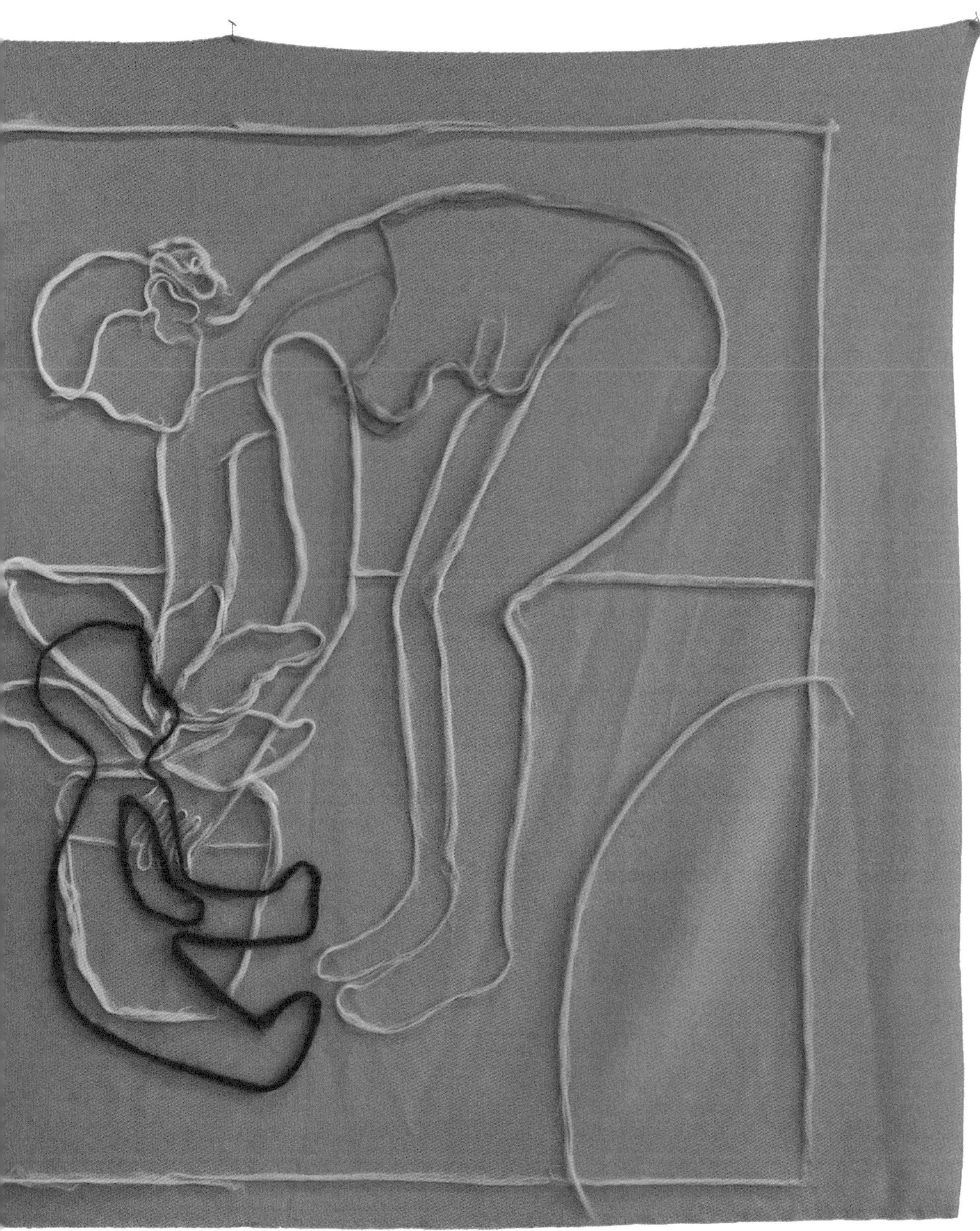

Cheryl is a Chicago-based artist who traverses mediums (textiles, installation, sculpture, painting, performance). This piece was a textile painting, an art form she taught herself. She is a disciple of the artist Nick Cave, who is best known for making *Soundsuits*, magical realist–style costumes that are equal parts performance, fashion, and sculpture. Cheryl ran Cave's studio and watched and sewed a lot.[1]

Cheryl made *Mother and Child on Blue Mat* after her third miscarriage, as her way of responding to the growing evidence that she would never give birth. This conclusion devastated her. Art can be compulsion, as the artist works something out through the making of it. That was certainly true here. Few pieces I've encountered are so powerfully motivated to slog through difficult feelings as this one. Making the work was, as she put it, her "way of painting through the motherhood" she would never have.

Cheryl started to make art as a child, receiving encouragement from an art teacher, and later found herself studying fashion at the School of the Art Institute of Chicago ("I would dream, I would see everyone in clothing I had never seen before. So when I woke up, I would try and draw that out. That's why I went into fashion"), where she met Cave. She works in different media, switches materials a lot, figures out how to make stuff by looking at YouTube or talking to knowledgeable salespeople at Home Depot. She is an avid boxer; she says that being in motion helps her to see things—it's one of her hacks. She doesn't particularly understand how she makes what she makes; she becomes obsessed and can't let go, like pretty much everybody else in these pages. "The way an image comes forward, I don't have a map for that. I have my mind just going, and then all of a sudden, I start to visualize it. Sometimes I think about myself as an employee of this," she said, pointing to her head. "Whoever up here comes up with the idea, I am just the laborer. It becomes a blur. I don't even remember much because I'm in such a neurotic obsessive state."

For this work, that state took hold right after she lost the last child. Her partner hadn't wanted the child in any case, and she was distraught. Eventually she and her partner split, which gave her the freedom to go forward with making the work. I asked her to narrate her way through it, decision by decision—including, as you'll see, regrets. She teared up as she walked me through the stages.

MOTHER AND CHILD ON BLUE MAT IN ELEVEN STAGES

"Okay, to start," Cheryl said, "this work happened out of survival. I had a miscarriage—my third—and lost my mind. It felt like a volcano erupting, like tectonic plates shifting." She started to "draw" the image on felt, which she intuited was the right medium, though she didn't know a thing about felt. "One of my students had used this felt-making technique five years earlier, and that stayed in my mind. I thought, *Oh, that's cool, I'm gonna remember that one.*" The technique required her to punch through the felt.

As for how she figured out how to work in this unfamiliar medium, she said, "I just did it. I was in a deranged state."

1. "I took this picture a few days after the third miscarriage," she said. "I'm in a really messed-up space here. One of my ways of coping, I realized later, was that I started amping up my plant life at home. Like: *Yes, I lost these babies, but I can grow things.* I was repotting everything." She took the pictures because she thought that the planting might "be telling me something." But meanwhile, she was making other images.

2. "This was the first one I did, maybe three days after the miscarriage. I'd had an image I'd been working on, of me sitting on the bath [when I was pregnant], and I took it out. And I see that she's sitting on

1. Most of the subjects of this book had mentors, incredibly important (and sometimes complicated) relationships. Would Stephen Sondheim have been Stephen Sondheim without Oscar Hammerstein?

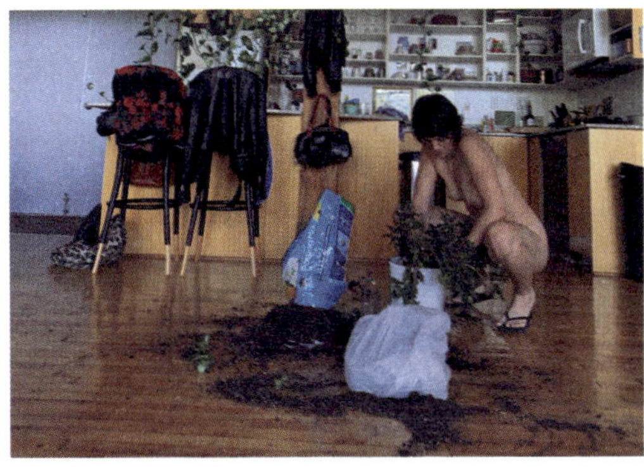

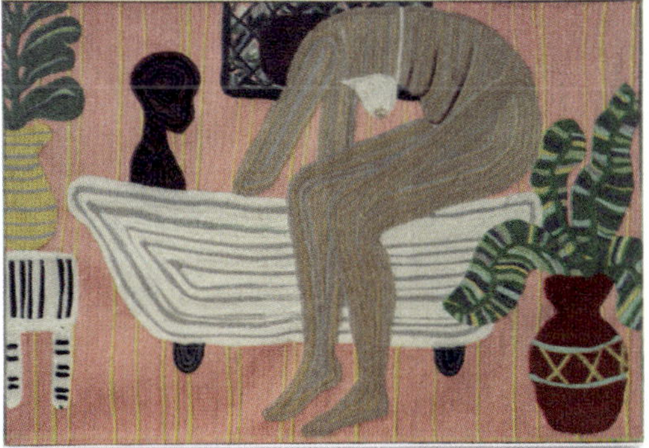

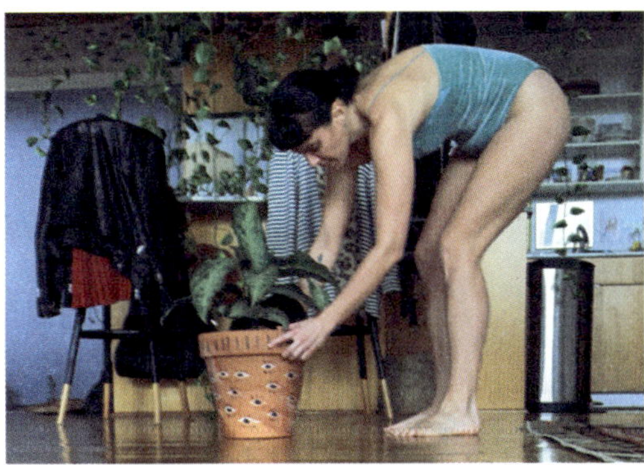

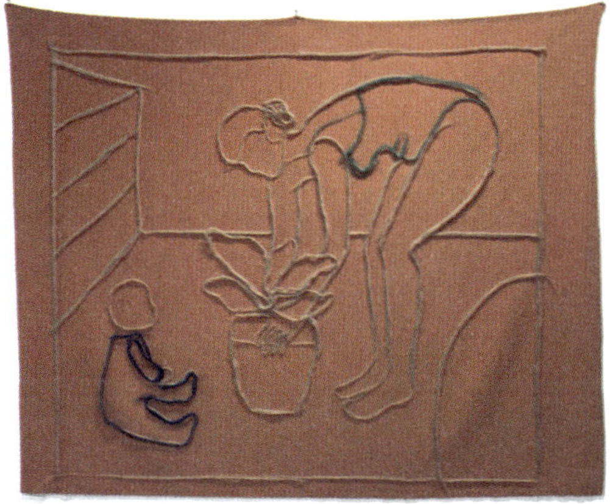

the bath because she's washing someone—everything was composed for a child to be there. My partner had been very against me drawing any of these images with the child until I had the child. But then once I'd had that third miscarriage, I thought, *You know, I've imagined this so many times, I wanted to give myself the gift of seeing what I had imagined*. My partner did not want the children. So I had been picturing myself as a single mom, seeing myself in these different moments—the bath, or another picture of me breastfeeding, which I did a year later. What I wanted to happen, what I imagined would happen, what didn't happen."

3. "When I went to begin what became *Mother and Child on a Blue Mat*, I couldn't find the plant picture in my phone, but I remembered it. So I re-created the scene and took several pictures of it. What I liked about this version was this shape, with her leaning down. I'm starting to make an oval."

4. As she began to work on the felt, she tentatively placed a child in the image, almost as an imagined witness to the mother and the plant. "When I looked at the photo, it was almost like I was talking to this baby that wasn't there. Where is the child—the child was absent, but was it present in the plant? Do I put the child [where the plant was]? I'm asking myself these questions. And when I started to do some research, I realized that [the impressionist painter] Mary Cassatt, who is the go-to for mothers and children—she also didn't have any children herself. So that was really critical. She gave me a freedom to say, 'I can do this.' Those miscarriages were my motherhood. People can hate me for it, but that's what it is. So I made this drawing. I love composition, composition makes any work work—the psychology, the feeling of a work for me, is in the composition. I was interested in this circle [the mother and plant] and this larger circle [including the child]. And I started to get this anxiety, like why is she picking up the plant? I want to pick up the baby—

"And I was going to leave it like that, but then I had a three-hour call with a friend who also had a miscarriage. While I'm talking to her, I'm looking at the image. And I got off the phone and I just—

5. "—moved the baby over: let me just draw him over here. But I didn't want to surrender the other drawing yet. This may be TMI, but I draw when I'm ovulating because I'm the most sensual. So my time window matters with these. And I record the image [of the two babies] because I think I really like this too. I like this echo, I like this as a misplace." She plays with the introduction of an illogic to the work by including a baby and its phantom. "I start going back and forth, and then I need to make a decision, and I say, *Okay, I'm going to make the switch*." So she'll move the baby instead of making a picture with the two babies in it.

"*Okay, I'm going to put him here and the plant there*. And they still make this nice circle. But I know I will use that image [of the two children] again someday[2]—I will return to it. And actually, now, I find I like that picture better than where I landed."

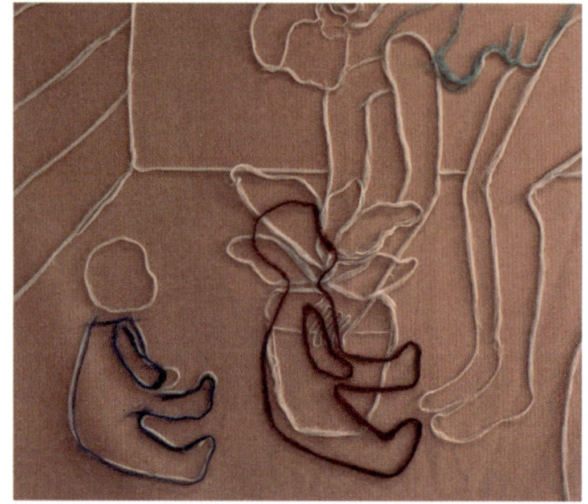

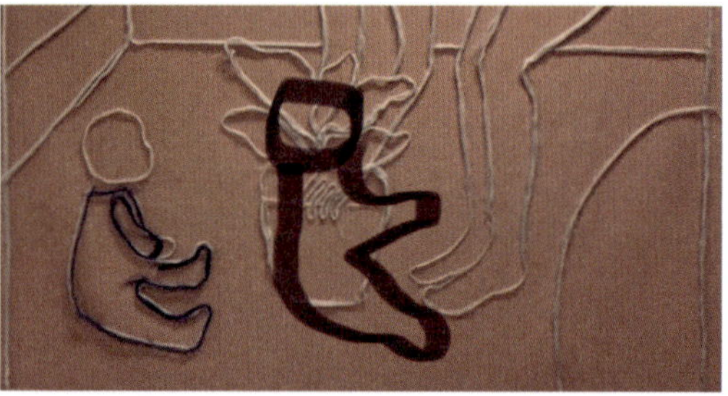

6. "Meanwhile, I'm just drawing these on my phone—I take a picture and draw on it with my finger—they're stages of apprehension. Studies."

7. She did a version with color swatches to see what would work: "I learned to do that during my fashion days."

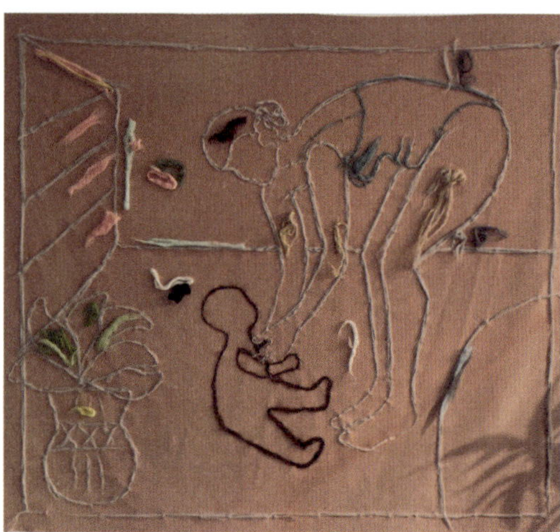

8. She begins to fill the picture in. "In the same way that with mothers, there's this ongoing relationship of the child disconnecting from the mother, I'm also thinking about connection and disconnection between the real and the imagined in my own situation with the child. This child did disconnect from me already.

"This [the miscarriages] happened three times. It's a cycle. That's why the composition is circular. I'm circling around this, I can't get out of it. . . . Color has to start to work with composition, it controls the way I move my eye. Someone asked Kerry James Marshall once, 'Why did you make that rug a pattern?' His answer was that otherwise it would be boring. Pattern keeps the eye irritated, active. So we stay engaged longer. I'm not following color theory, it's just intuition."

But Cheryl was also wrestling with

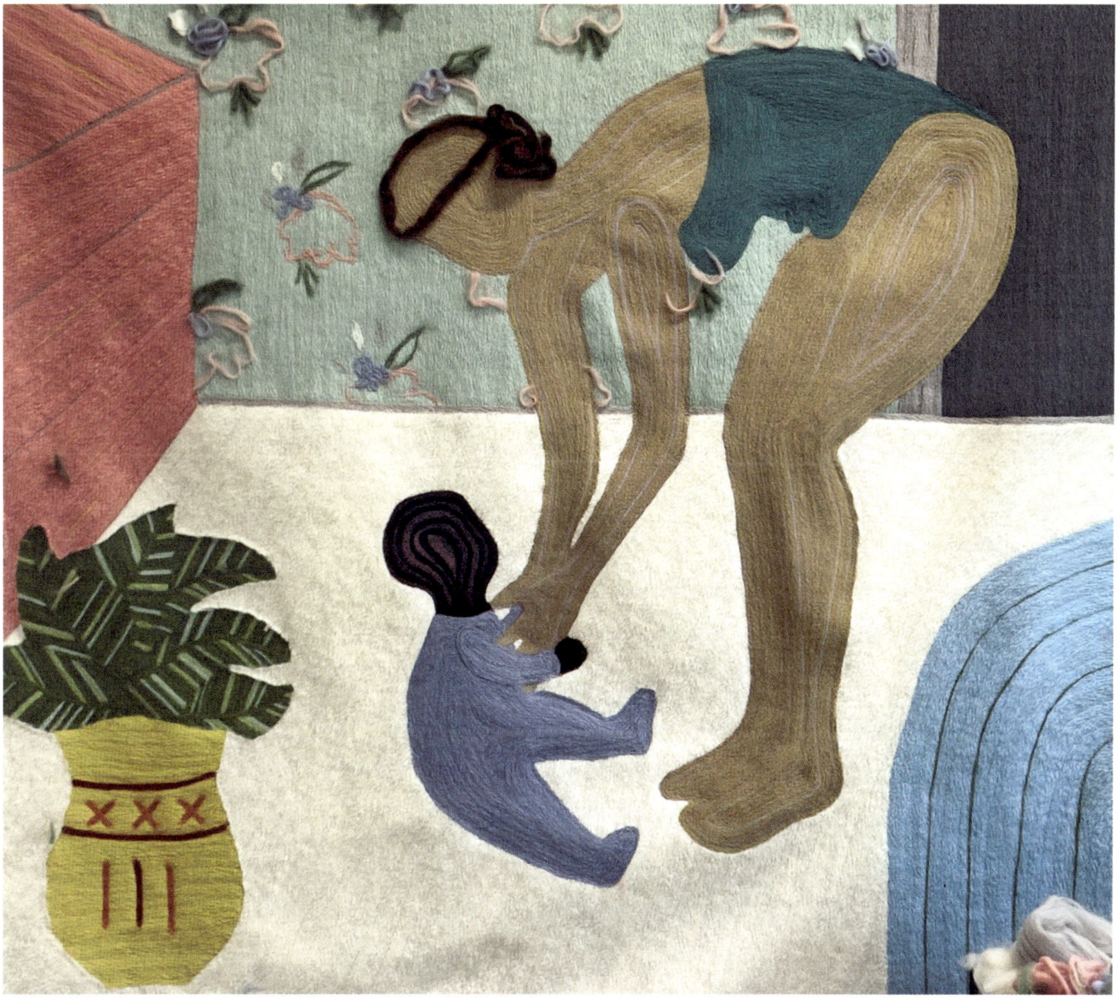

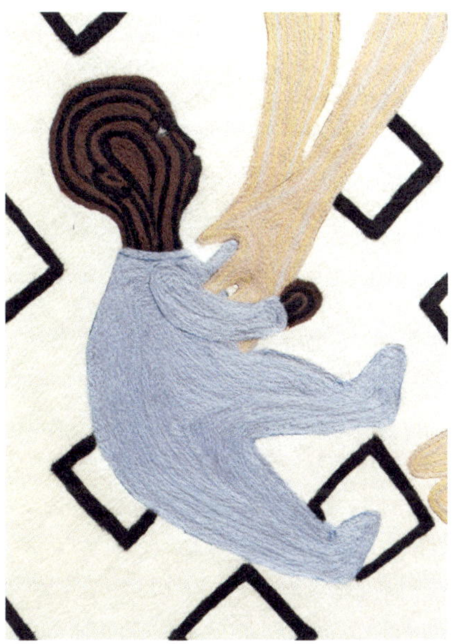

decisions. “Should I leave the floor white? Do I want to leave her hair like this?” And, especially: “How much do I keep telling and not telling in this image?”

Of particular worry was the skin color of the child. Her former partner, the baby’s father, is Black. She is white. “My anxiety is hyped up because I am worried about how people are going to read race in the picture.” She was making this picture in 2021, in an era when Black Lives Matter protests had heightened racial sensitivities, which unsettled her as she was making the image. She tried to put a softer brown rather than black to make him look mixed

2. Never waste a good idea.

race, but it doesn't work for the picture. "I'm well aware that a child is born lighter and can get darker," she said. But she is worried that because she's white, viewers will think she doesn't know this. "I have to tell everything in this one image," she said. "There's no room for nuance in this political climate. And that's suffocating."

9. Of all the decisions she had to make for this work, the hardest might be the decision to give faces to the mother and baby, or not—to make the picture specific or to generalize, to close it, in her words, or to open it.[3] "Finally," she said, after much deliberation, "I go all the way and give her [the mother] a face."

She noted that she put the face in because it frightened her to draw one on, and she knew if it scared her, she ought to try. She could always pull it back.

As she was talking to me, she used that phrase so many other artists use, that she was "listening" to the mother in her picture, waiting for it to tell her whether it wants a face or not. "Listening is at the ground of all of this. . . . In those moments of debate, I just tried to stay very quiet, listening for what she wants me to do."[4]

As for the baby, she said, "even at this moment, I'm stopping because I don't want to draw his face in. Because I can't imagine his face. And I've never drawn a baby's face. Am I scared? In my own mind I've never been able to imagine the face of the babies I've lost."

10. In the end, she gave the child a face. "So then I came into my studio and thought, *Just do it to see if you can do it*," she said. She kept the face.

11. Here is what the finished picture looks like.

But even after she was done, she had regrets about having included the baby's face. "Later when I looked at the piece, I went back to the gallery to take it down because it just tells everything. Everything is told here. But it was too late. Because then it became public."

"If you were to do the picture again, you'd do it without facial features on the child?" I asked her.

"One hundred percent," she said.

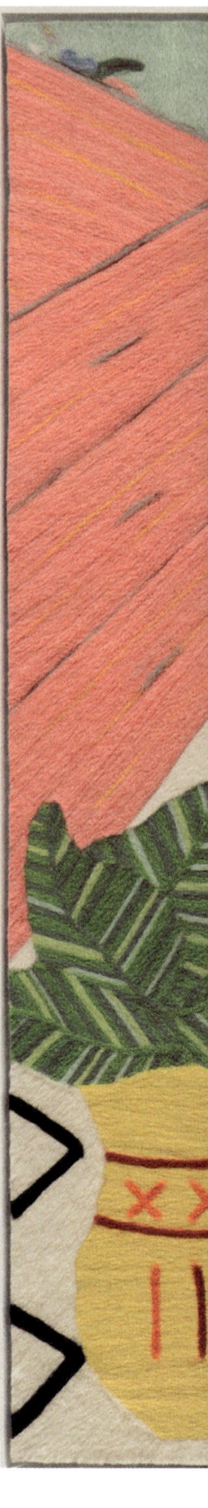

3. I found this particular quandary—what to make explicit and what to make the viewer/reader work for—ever present, across mediums. How to anticipate—and manipulate—what the audience will fill in has become a front-and-center question in my own painting.

4. "Listening." Again.

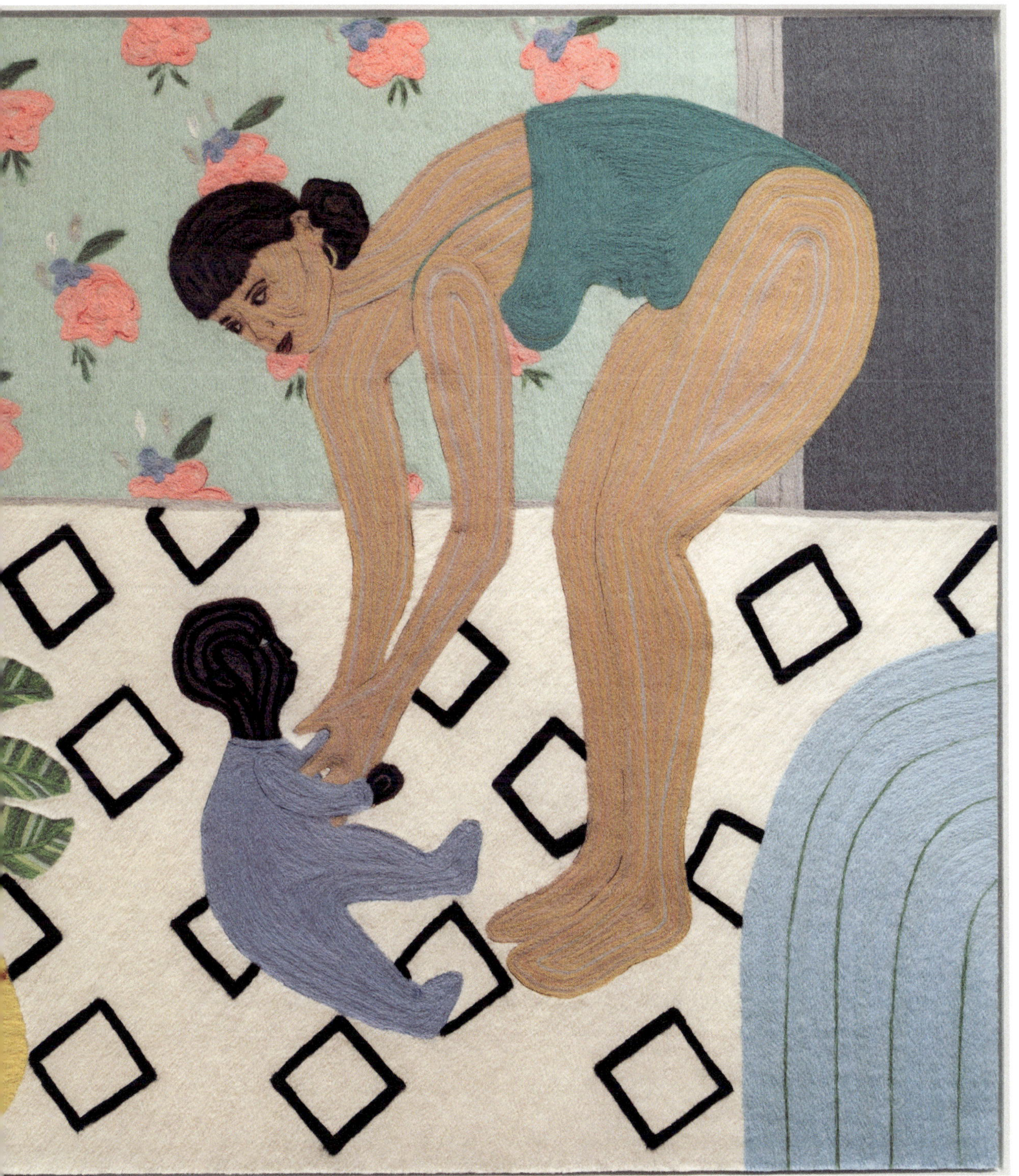

Cheryl Pope, *Mother and Child on Mat*, 2021, 50 × 61 in., wool roving needle punched into cashmere. Courtesy of the artist and Monique Meloche Gallery. Private collection of Halla Shami Sher.

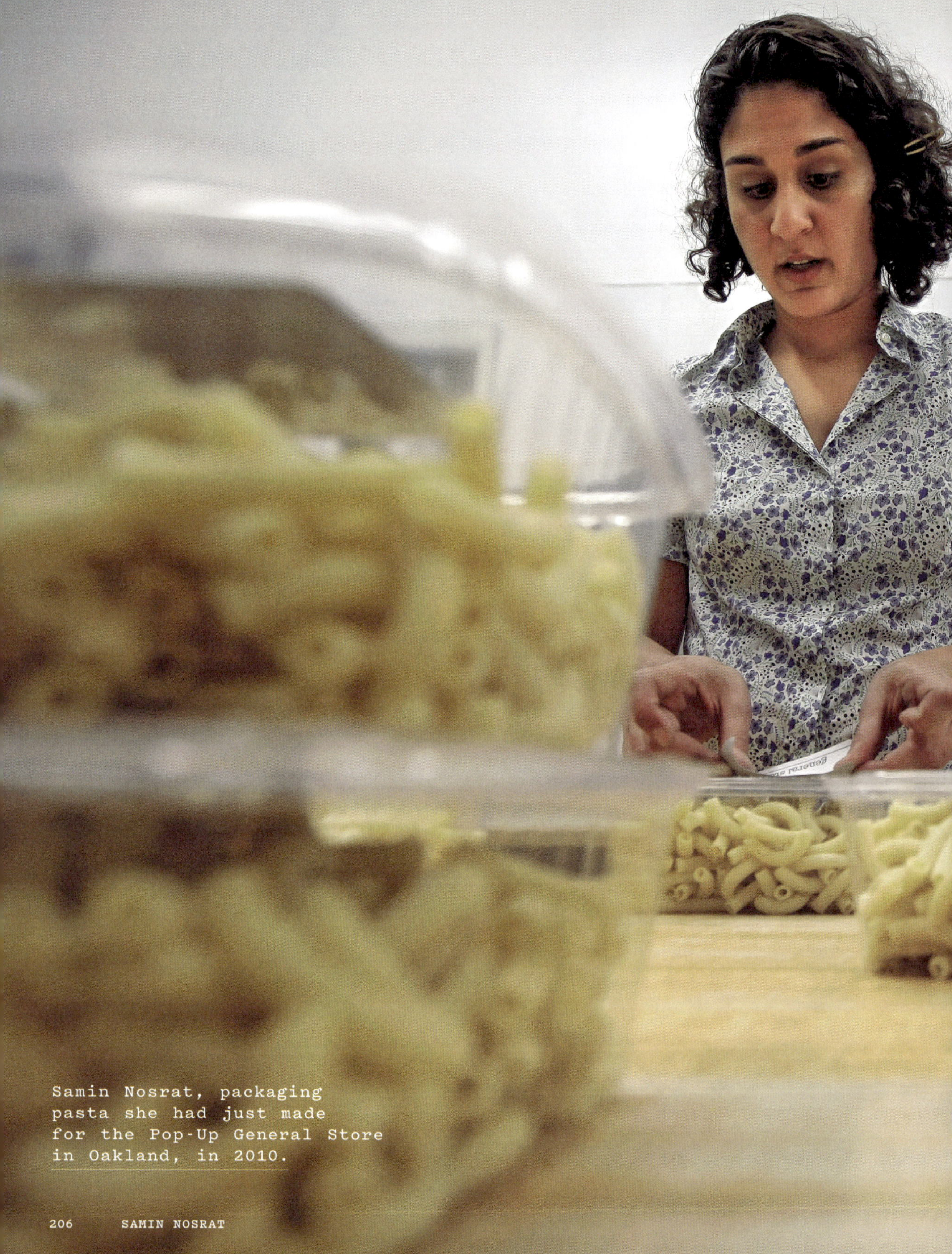

Samin Nosrat, packaging pasta she had just made for the Pop-Up General Store in Oakland, in 2010.

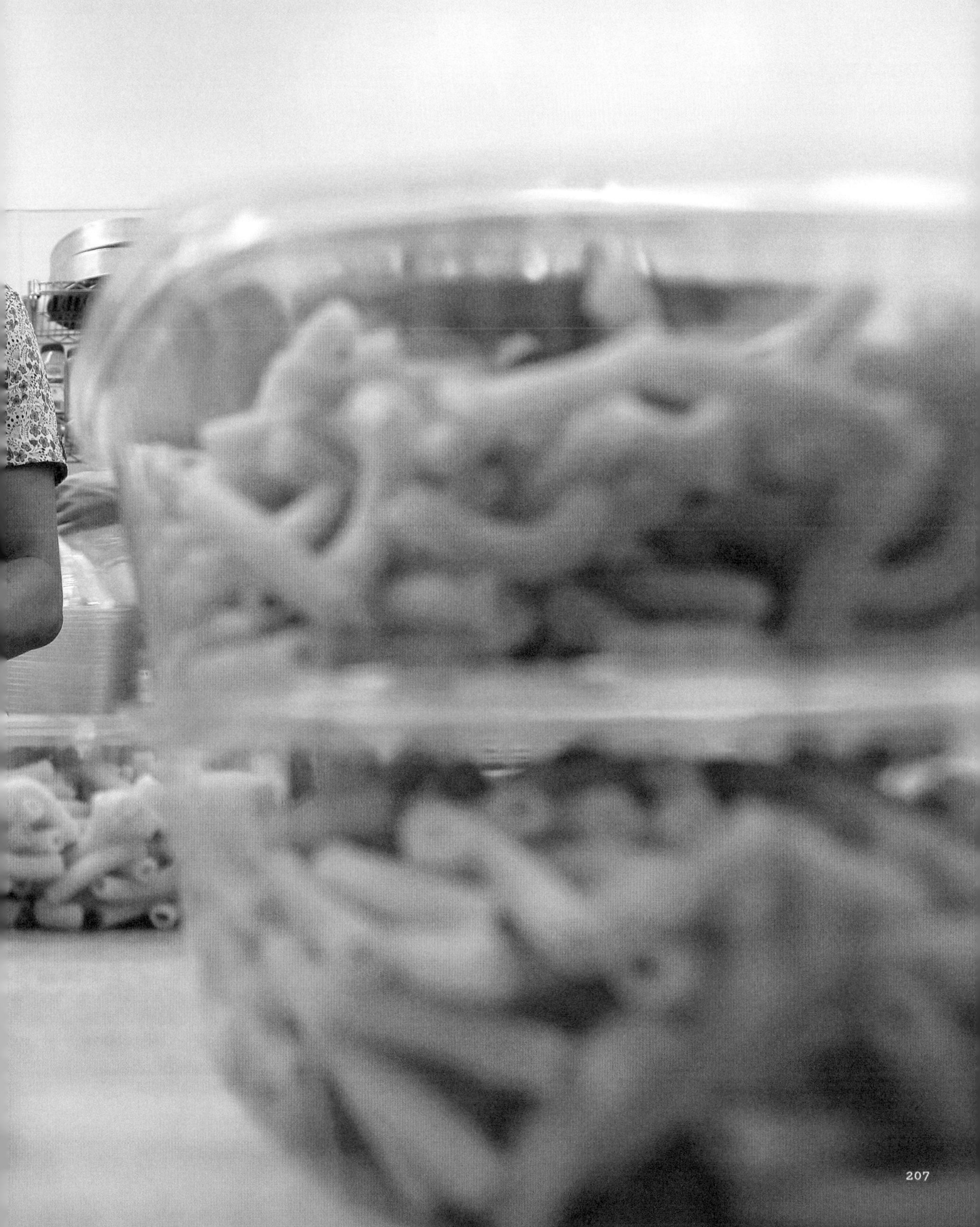

21

SAMIN NOSRAT

With Beginner's Eyes

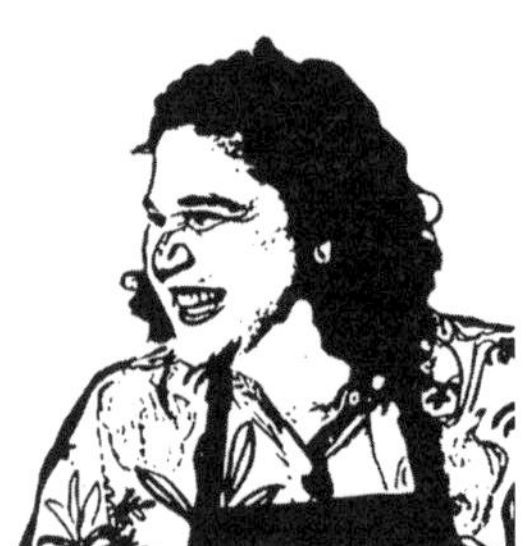

OCCUPATION: Cook/Writer

WORK DISCUSSED: *Salt, Fat, Acid, Heat* (2017)

BORN: 1979

SAMIN NOSRAT CHANGED cooking in my house and in the houses of many already accomplished cooks, thanks to the insightful and elegant formulation at the heart of her bestselling book and its Netflix series adaptation, that all cooking can be reduced to four elements: salt, fat, acid, and heat.

When I invited Samin to talk, I had been interested in the way cooking was like and unlike the other creative arts, and also in how an original concept itself can function as a kind of artwork. But during our conversation, she also dwelled on the process of writing—and then selling—a nonfiction book. Her path was illuminating, and so while not my chief subject, I went where she went, since getting your work out in the world absolutely informs the process.

There was a long lag time between when Samin agreed to talk and when I could speak with her. I learned later that she had been depressed. In the conversations for this book, I have tried to understand the mental states that go hand in hand with creating, so when we did reconnect, I asked if she'd be willing to talk about that. She very generously was, and since at this stage so much of her working life requires a public persona—the Netflix show, a podcast, and her performative presence on Instagram—the conversation went there as well.

As for the elements that led to her book *Salt, Fat, Acid, Heat*, there are many: the kitchen training, the doggedness, her intertwined ambitions as a writer and cook. But chiefly was the fact that she was able to envision something new at the exact moment before she would become too experienced to understand it had value. "I had to see it," she said, "with beginner's eyes."[1]

SAMIN NOSRAT: In August 2000 I started working as a busser at Chez Panisse and within a few weeks I was enchanted. I should back up. My family is from Iran, my mom cooked mostly Persian

1. I'm a big believer in "beginner's eyes." At *7 Days* we blundered into new story forms—personal, discursive, pre-bloggy—I might have dismissed with more experience, because I was either too jaded and thought it wouldn't work or too snobbish about the way someone is supposed to sound in a publication. Sometimes you can make the most original work when you just don't know any better.

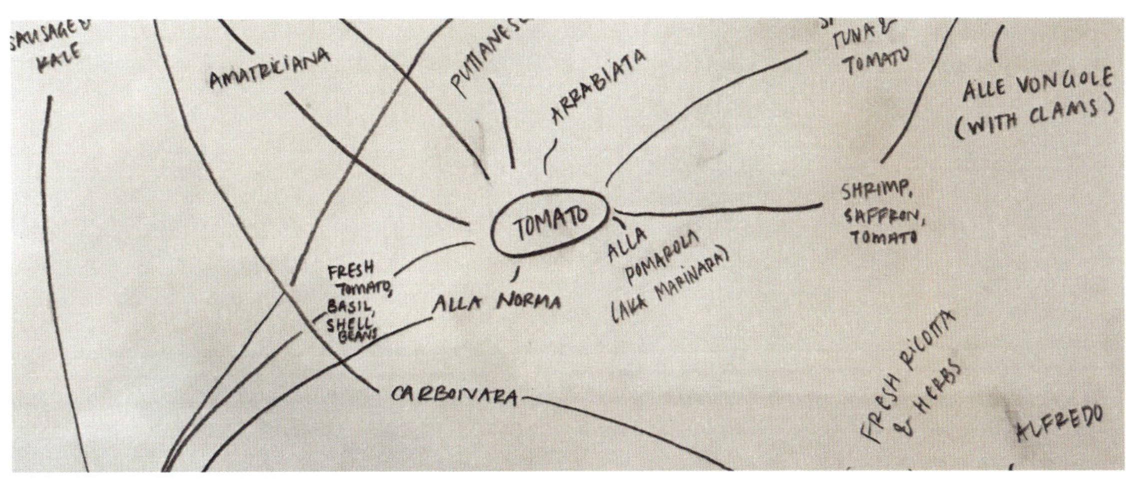

iguring out how much salt to use is not the easie
thing in the world, but it is the most crucial part of co
When I started working in the restaurant, I'd salt som
and bring it to my chef to taste, then be startled as
threw in handfuls and handfuls more to get it to
just right. How was it that these cooks could just po
~~in from~~ let the salt stream from the box for twent
seconds and still not have enough? Nothing was
too salty at Chez Panisse (unless I was making it)
too salty at chez panisse (unless I was making it) a few things about myself a

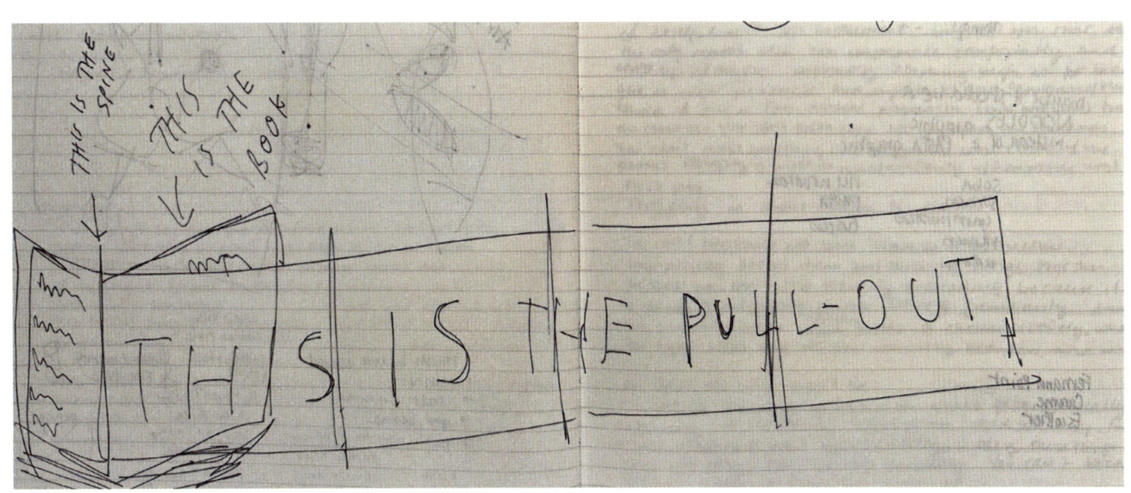

Making *Salt, Fat, Acid, Heat*: charting; writing; visualizing.

food for us. She was a kind of food hippie, using organic ingredients because they tasted closest to what she remembered in Iran. We lived in San Diego. We'd drive way across town looking for the perfect ingredient. So by the time I landed at Chez Panisse, when I was a senior at Berkeley, this sort of philosophy was not foreign to me. Okay, and also—I was a very overachieving immigrant, or child of immigrants. Being at Chez Panisse was the first time that I was in a little world where every single person was a bananas overachiever. I was looking around this restaurant that had been named the best restaurant in the country I don't know how many times. There were all these masterful cooks for me to learn from. And not just chefs, do you know what I mean? Like, cooks. I was a busser. I was a nobody. My first day was the twenty-seventh or twenty-eighth birthday of the restaurant, it was already older than I was. They're teaching me how to take out the trash. Turns out, there is a right way to take out the trash.

It was an incredible sensory education, in taste and smell. And an education in the way you set a table, how the linens should feel. Here you go, your first task is you're going to vacuum the dining room. And I remember feeling, *I can't believe they're letting me vacuum the floor.*

At the same time, I was a student who for my whole life only wanted to write. I wanted to study poetry, thought I would get an MFA or maybe a PhD. But every day I go to work, and it's magical. So I think, *Maybe I can do this*. It wasn't a coherent thing, just maybe I can try to cook.

I asked them if I could volunteer in the kitchen, and they let me do it one day a week, on top of my bussing. This is a rank well below an intern. I was the cooking intern's volunteer helper. And I was at the bottom of a very long list of people who wanted to work there for free. I was so in the way and helpless.

I was not particularly beloved by the chefs in the café. But one of the chefs in the restaurant, Chris Lee, took pity on me. I asked if I could ever earn an internship here. He said, "You don't know enough. Here's this stack of books. Pay attention. Go to the tastings. Watch how the cooks talk about tasting. And then come back to me in six months." He didn't think I would do it, but I did. Chris offered me up as a driver, going to farmers' markets and the Chez Panisse farm, getting to know the farmers, the produce.

And then I started cooking. Another chef there, who wasn't really interested in me, would assign the cooks to a dish. He would give, as far as I witnessed, very little instruction. But the cooks would get up and do it. I didn't understand. Nobody used recipes, nobody used cookbooks. One day it was Spanish food, one day Italian. I didn't know how people knew how to make every single thing in the whole wide world. And this is all in complete contrast to the thing you, Chris, have told me to do, which is cook directly out of these cookbooks. I had a headache probably for twelve months.

Patterns, Patterns, Patterns At the tastings, everybody's giving a sample of their dish. Every single time, the same few things happen, we're tasting the salad, we're tasting the soup. And it's, Oh this needs a little more salt. Doesn't this need a squeeze of lemon? Couldn't this use more Parmesan? Crunch? Olive oil? Over time I started to see patterns. *Huh, this is weird.* You know?

Eventually I got to the point where I was allowed near a stove. And once I get there, I started to see other patterns. *Oh wait, things are brought to a boil and turned down to a simmer. Oh wait, we put a braise in the oven at 475, then we turn it down to 325, the same thing.* I'm thinking, *Huh, interesting.* Then I go home and examine these recipes and I'm like, *Oh: pattern, pattern, pattern*. So one day, after a year and a half of this, I go to Chris—and I remember where I was standing in the kitchen, at the end of the big prep table, right by the

2. Michael Pollan is a best-selling writer on food and plants, among other things. He was one of my favorite writers at the *Times* magazine when I was editor.

3. Michael's class had a huge waiting list. To get in, Samin had to persuade him that he needed someone who'd worked in the food industry. She's very persistent.

sink—and I say, "I think I see a pattern." He says, "What?" I say, "Salt, fat, acid, heat. That's what everything we cook comes down to—salt, fat, acid, heat." And he said, "Yeah, everybody knows that."

I said, "Everybody does not know that! It's not in any of the books you gave me." He said, "No, but all good cooks know that." I said, "You know that because you've been doing this your whole life." He was like, "Whatever."

I said, "No, I'm gonna write a book about this. And it's going to be so easy. And short. And simple." I found a journal entry where I wrote, "I'm gonna write a book about this." I thought it's going to be twelve pages long, three pages for each thing. And I got a legal pad and started writing. And then pretty quickly I realized I actually have to learn how to cook to write this book. Everybody told me you don't know anything until you've been cooking for ten years.

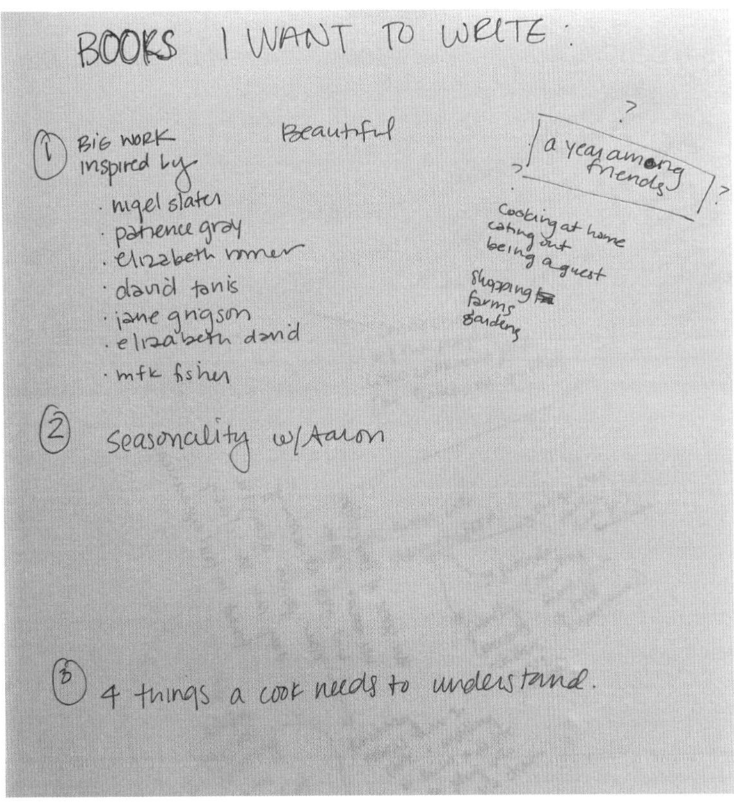

Books she wanted to write (early list). See number three.

But then because I had this framework into which I could file everything I learned, I filed it into all these folders. I went to Italy and helped a woman teach cooking classes, and so I could sort of test my thesis. From the minute you enter a kitchen, you might be the person who knows nothing. But then twenty minutes later, someone who knows even less than you comes along, and you have to show them how to peel an onion. So very quickly you have to develop a skill and a vocabulary for teaching people things.

I came back from Italy, and Chris had left Chez Panisse to open his own restaurant. So I went there to work for him, first as a line cook and then eventually like a sous-chef. And then I really was teaching young cooks. I was teaching them how to make a vinaigrette, what is buttermilk doing in roast chicken—and that's a balance of salt and fat and acid. I had to create a vocabulary to help me explain. I never let go of salt, fat, acid—it was always inside of me. But I have to say, I was not always happiest in a restaurant. I still wanted to be a writer.

At this point, I was pretty much running the restaurant kitchen. I looked at the restaurant reservations books every night, and I saw that Michael Pollan[2] was coming in for dinner. I was a huge fan of his, I'd read all his books. So I wrote a note to him after. I said, "Oh it was so nice to see you in the restaurant, I've been thinking of writing to you to see if I could audit your class." He was teaching a class at Berkeley called Following the Food Chain—food journalism.[3]

After the class, I applied for a Fulbright. I didn't get it. Michael said, "You don't need a

Fulbright, just start writing." I started writing for the [*San Francisco*] *Chronicle*. I didn't even know what a story was. I was saying, "I'm gonna write about beans." Actually, I still say I'm gonna write about beans.

A year or two after I took Michael's class, Michael was set to write a cooking book. And I know how he works. If he's going to write a book about cooking, he's going to need a cooking teacher. And I wrote him an email saying, "*I'm* your cooking teacher." We cooked every Sunday for a while. We would make food, and they [the Pollans] would invite all their friends. And I remember one day he wanted to do a pig roast, so we drove up to get the pig. On the trip, we were talking and I told him, "I've been putting this pressure on myself to come up with an idea of a book to write that would be groundbreaking." He said, "Write the book you already know." I said, "I guess the book should just be this philosophy that I have: salt, oil, acid, heat." He said, "No one's ever said that before. It's a gold mine."

I knew it was going to be hard because since the moment I first imagined this project, I had come to understand so much about cookbooks. I'd actually worked on two cookbooks that never happened—one with the woman in Italy I was working with, another with a friend who was writing a pickle book that just kind of imploded. The whole world of publishing made me feel so young and dumb.

Simple Is Hard But I thought a way to actually start would be to teach classes and write handouts for the classes. After all, I'd been teaching Michael. So I started teaching salt, fat, acid, heat classes. During this time I'm seeing the questions people have—"Oh, you need a diagram, here, let me draw you a diagram. Here's a list of emulsions. Here's a pictogram." All on butcher paper, these jankadoodle handouts. I also realized that as much as I wanted to instill the philosophy in them, they're still going to need a recipe. So that was a good thing for me to see too.

Then Michael wrote *Cooked*, and his agent—this was Binky Urban, a really powerful

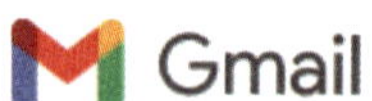

samin nosrat

you might be wondering...

samin nosrat
To:

Thu, Oct 13, 2011 at 10:20 PM

if I'm stalking you.

Well, the answer is yes!

I'm obsessed with your work. OB. SESSED.

And I have a secret dream (about to be not-so-secret):
that we can collaborate, and that you'll illustrate the cookbook (let's call it better-than-a-cookbook, actually) that I'm starting to work on.

I love your work. You are the Maira Kalman of my generation.

I am wacky. I write, I teach, I cook, and I am writing a book that will teach people how to cook.

You're probably thinking I'm a yahoo.

You're right.

agent—read the part of the draft which described me, and she said, "Oh wow, what a charismatic character. Does she have any book ideas?" And he said, "Well, yes actually, she has an idea." So I told her what I was thinking, and she said, "Yes, this is a good idea but it's too complicated, you have to simplify it." And I had no idea how to do that. I looked at the pages, the handouts—they were a mess. To make something simple is really hard.

This was the problem: salt and fat and acid are tangible materials. And heat is not. Salt comes in for the most part as a mineral. Fat and acid don't. How do I make any of this parallel? I tried many different ways. I brought it out to other agents in the meantime, who told me I wasn't qualified to write this book because I was not already a famous chef. There were agents who told me this book would never sell because all cookbooks need to have eight chapters; this book will never sell because it doesn't have photos. Strangely, it never occurred to me that anyone thought I wouldn't be qualified because I was a brown girl trying to write a general cookbook, but I'm sure that crossed some minds.

I was very confused. I am a sponge and obsessive, and I had paid a lot of attention to which cookbooks get published, which ones work and which don't, which ones I liked and didn't.[4] It took me about six months to distill and clarify my thinking until I could write a proposal. And in the meantime, I had been stalking the artist Wendy MacNaughton, who had been contributing to *Edible San Francisco*, because she's funny, she can convey stuff. I mean, here I am drawing these horrible butcher paper charts and at the time, Wendy was making all these Venn diagrams and they were so good. So I wrote her an insane email with a Venn diagram of all the people we knew in common.

I wrote, "You might be wondering if I'm stalking you. Well, the answer is yes. I'm obsessed with your work—obsessed, and I have a secret dream, about to be not so secret, that we can collaborate and that you'll illustrate the cookbook, let's call it better than a cookbook, that I'm starting to work on. I love your work, you are the Maira Kalman[5] of my generation." Blah, blah, blah. Wendy came aboard. We made like a forty-page, illustrated *Salt, Fat, Acid, Heat* proposal.[6]

I had to show publishers what I had in mind, because it was so radically different than anything that existed. I didn't want a recipe-filled cookbook. I wanted a book that teaches you to cook. I didn't want photos, I wanted illustrations—weird, funny things that were whimsical and silly.

And it worked. There was a fifteen-way auction and it went bananas. We sent it on a Thursday, and on Friday or Saturday the agent said, "You need to get on a plane and be in New York on Monday."[7] So I did. I went to meetings, and it was so exciting, nothing like this had ever happened to me in my whole life. I've never walked into a room before, ever, where everybody knew how to pronounce my name. All these old white people knew how to pronounce my name. And it didn't hit me until afterward that, like, *Oh my God, that means that they asked how to pronounce my name, so they could pronounce it correctly*. Never, in my whole life. And then I sold the book.

But you know, for the proposal, I hadn't solved the structure, I sort of just got to something good enough. I got through the high of, like, *Woo, oh wow, oh wow*. And then there was the inevitable low.

A Knife to the Heart I had to start writing. I wrote an almost entire first draft of the book, and it was not good. I wrote it like two and a half times. And I couldn't get there. There was one moment—I was supposed to have a phone call with the editor one morning. I was so desperate and sad—at my wit's end, I just didn't know what to do. The draft I had sent her, she had started on page one, her comments were perfectly nice. And they'd gotten increasingly

4. You have to really know the rules before you set out to break them.

5. Maira Kalman is an author and illustrator with a much-loved, exuberant style.

6. It's worth saying that the voice of this proposal anticipates the playful, pitch-perfect sound of the finished book itself. In Wendy MacNaughton, Samin had truly found a partner with whom it was possible to create in unison.

7. Samin ended up staying with Amanda "Binky" Urban's agency, but was represented by Kari Stuart.

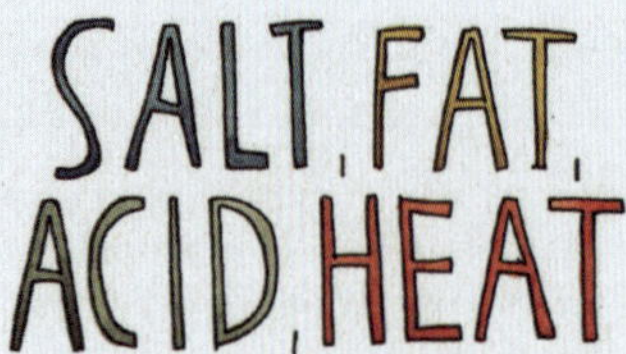

THE FOUR ELEMENTS of GOOD COOKING

by

SAMIN NOSRAT

illustrated by

WENDY MACNAUGHTON

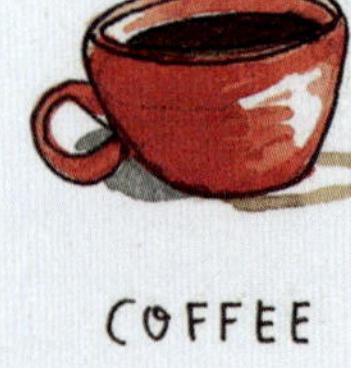

COFFEE

from ACID: CREATING THE PERFECT SANDWICH

Any good sandwich needs to have the elements of Salt, Fat, and Acid in balance. A good dose of texture and extra flavor (umami) never hurts, either! And it's always important to make sure there are enough moistening agents so that bread is never bordering another dry ingredient.

Let's deconstruct some classics to illustrate:

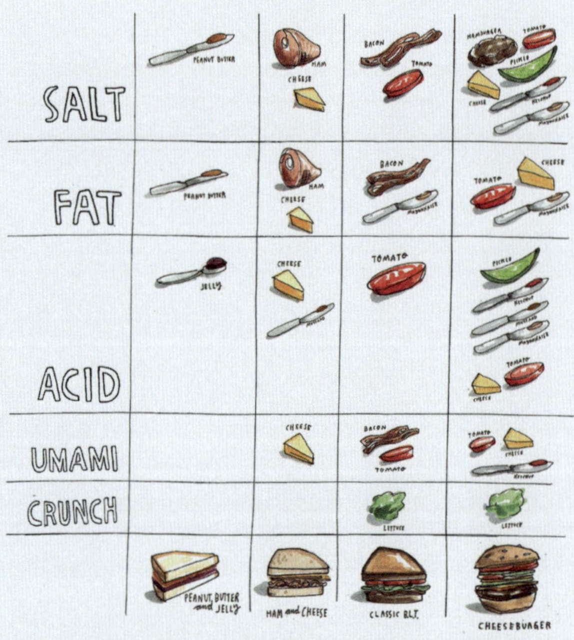

29

SALT·FAT·ACID·HEAT

SAMIN NOSRAT

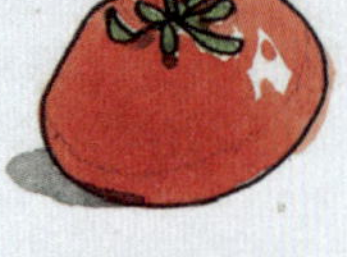

TOMATO

I want to write a book that teaches readers how to cook by defining and demystifying the four most basic, and most essential, elements of cooking. Salt, Fat, Acid and Heat are the variables that make our food delicious or bland, tender or tough, soggy or crisp, memorable or utterly forgettable. An understanding of the foundational science and techniques associated with each of these elements makes any cook a more sensitive decision-maker both in the kitchen and at the market.

Proposal: What Samin and Wendy MacNaughton proposed is, uncannily and unusually, the book they'd go on to make. The "Perfect Sandwich" chart didn't make it into the book, though many others they included did.

frustrated as she went on. By page sixty, her comment was like, "I don't know what you expect. I can't write this book for you."

It was like a knife to my heart. As the hardworking child of immigrants, I would never—you know what I mean? You think I'm not working hard enough? I'm trying! So this call was like a 911 call. I fell asleep the night before, and I was losing my mind. I woke up, we had a call at maybe 10:00 a.m., and it was Wednesday and the *Times* food section had just come out. Sam Sifton[8] had written this piece about burgers. What are you going to say about burgers? There's a new way to cook a burger? For whatever reason, I'm in bed reading the article. Trying to will myself to get out of bed and brush my teeth so I can talk to my editor. And something about it, maybe the way the article was formatted, something jumped out, something like blah, blah, blah . . . *flavor and science*. I brush my teeth, and I'm thinking, *Duh duh duh* flavor and science. *Flavor and science*. And then, *Oh my God, flavor and science!*

Dang *Science and flavor! That's what all these four elements have in common. The science of salt, the flavor of salt. The science of fat, the flavor of fat! Oh my God!* And forty-five minutes later I'm on the phone: "Dang, I found it!" Let's just say the editor was relieved.

And that was it. Of course, I had to master the science and I'm not even particularly good at chemistry, but at least I was curious. Eventually, when it was time for blurbs, I asked Harold McGee[9] for a blurb, and he wrote back and said to me in the nicest possible way, under no circumstances could I blurb this book because there are so many mistakes. Here is just a partial list. Twenty-four mistakes in it. I had a humongous panic. He said, "You need to have this book fact-checked in order for it not to be a joke." A fact-checker did catch a bunch of stuff.

By the time the book was about to come out, it was a really long journey. I remember going to therapy and I said, "I need help. Because I have let my opinion of myself and my happiness ride on what other people think of me, and if I do that with this, I am going to die." My therapist said, "You need to come up with your own definition of success and adhere to that. What would that look like?" I said, "It would look like giving everything I had to this book."

The day it came out, there were mistakes. They were super basic and it was embarrassing. I got something about osmosis wrong. But you know what? I'm still alive. I survived.

Showing Up I'm a person who gets depressed, and I am incredibly depressed right now. I spent a lot of last year depressed and didn't get much done. For the first time, I'm entering a phase where I am depressed and having to work. In the past, in my life, I've always just ignored my feelings, shut down, and worked. That's very much a cook's mentality—if you cut yourself or burn yourself, it doesn't matter, you have to get this plate of food made. But now I'm trying to pay a little more attention. Like, I don't know if it matters or not that I didn't produce pages last year. Maybe, maybe not.

I still have to show up in the world, and I still play by those rules—maybe one day I will say fuck 'em all. But right now, it's a box that I'm stuck in. My Instagram account is the metaphor for it. Sometimes I feel like I'm not going to play along anymore. And other times it's, I can't, I make money this way, I feel the financial pressure. Sometimes I feel I would have twice as many followers if I learned to play the game better. Other times, I don't know. I truly wish that I could just check out most of the time right now.

But you know, I'm back to work. It's fine, I'll get through it. I also feel a little bit of creative magic. The nice thing is I have a road map. I've done it once now, and I know the torture is part of it. So like, a little torture? I guess I'm doing it right.

8. Sam Sifton was then food editor at *The New York Times*, and later created their Cooking empire. Also, there are, actually, newish ways to cook a hamburger. (See the chapter on the svizzerina, page 354.)

9. Harold McGee writes on food science.

22

JOANNA QUINN & LES MILLS

Brain, Hand, Pencil, Paper

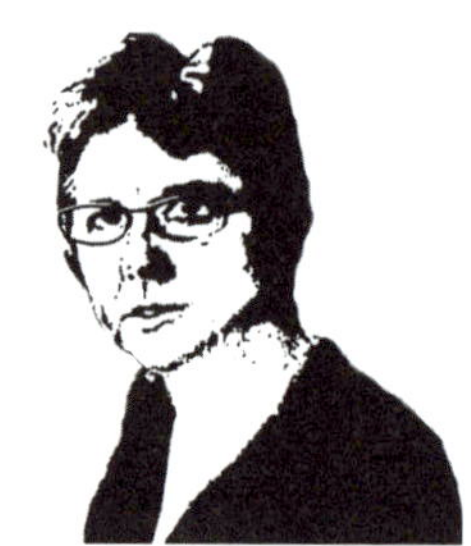

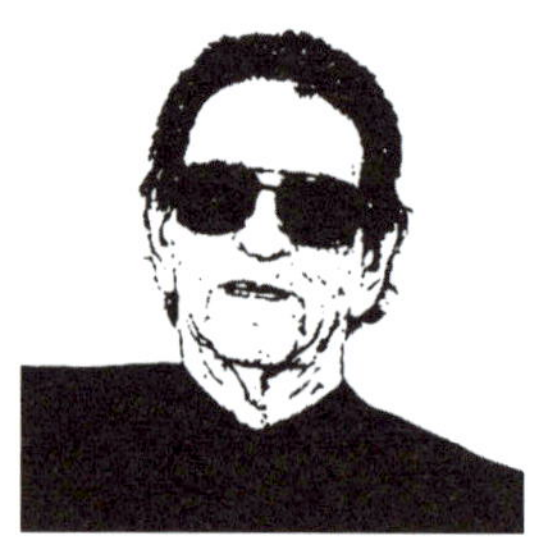

OCCUPATION: Animators

WORK DISCUSSED: Beryl (2006/2021)

BORN: 1962; 1942

Drawings by Quinn for the film *Body Beautiful*, working out the movement and proportions of her leading lady.

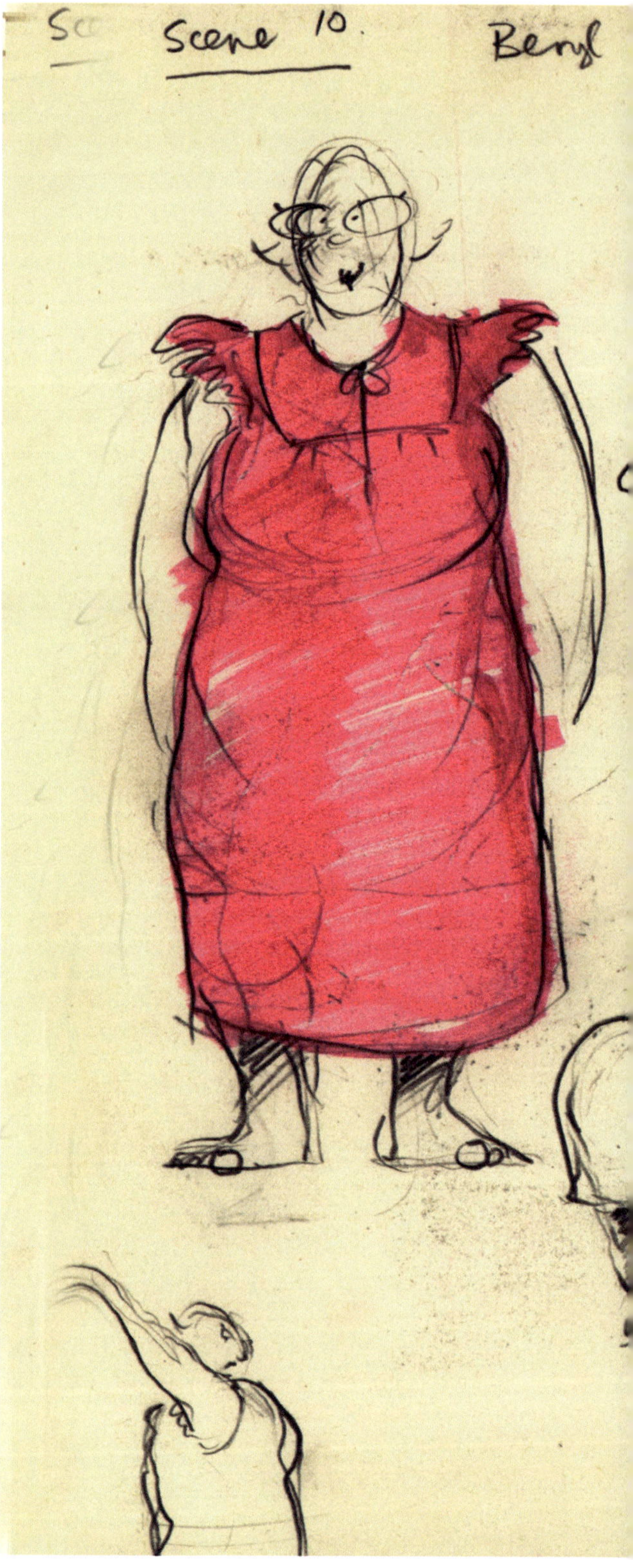

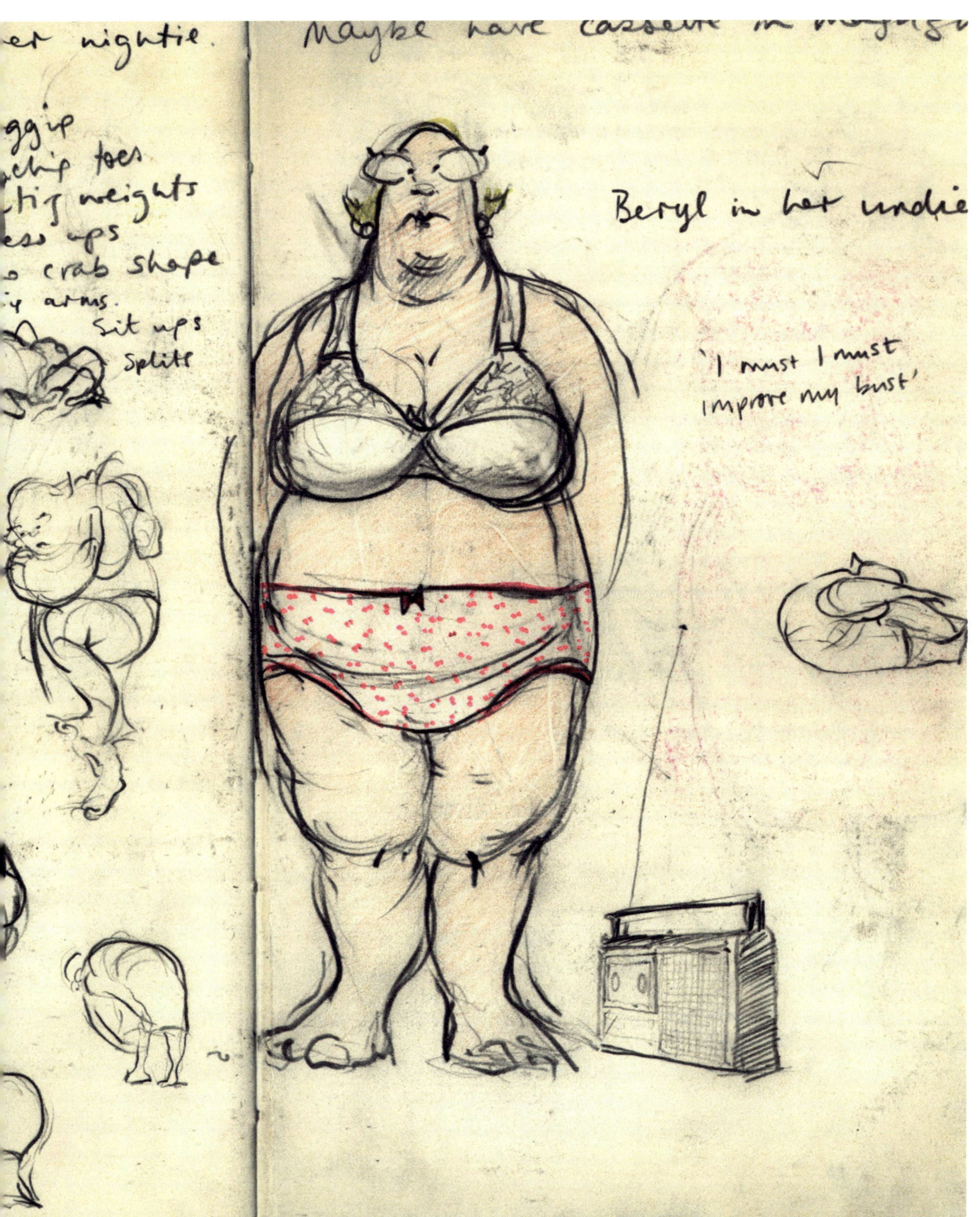

nightie.
Maybe have
weights
crab shape
Sit ups
Splits
Beryl in her
'I must I must
improve my bust'

DRAWING EXPRESSIVELY, with the right balance of precision and a free hand, takes practice, and a particular spirit—joy, usually. Joanna Quinn draws the people she sees at the bus stop from her window, draws in the middle of the night, has been drawing constantly since she was an only child in London. Compulsion or delight: Is there a difference? In any case, the person Quinn draws the most is one she made up decades ago: Beryl, the bodacious (brazen, curvy, prone to fuckups) protagonist of a series of celebrated animated short movies. Most of these movies she created with her husband, Les Mills, whom she met when he was her drawing teacher.[1]

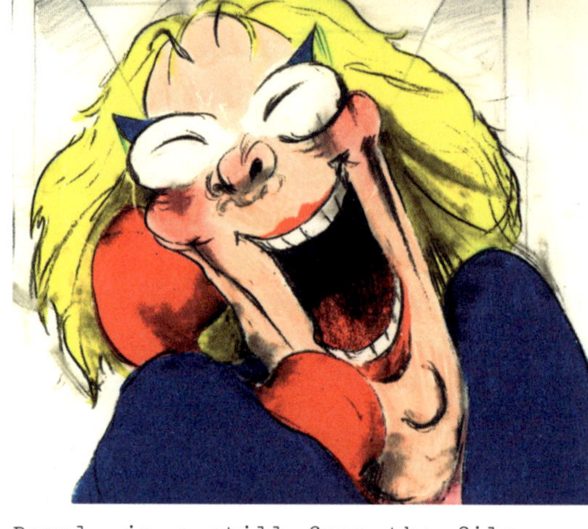

Beryl, in a still from the film *Girls Night Out*.

Quinn's bawdy heroine emerged, like so many creations in these pages, pretty much fully formed the first time out, though following years of rigorous training in life drawing. Quinn first imagined Beryl for a comic strip she drew as an undergraduate, and she reminds me a bit of characters I might have seen in the underground comics I devoured as a teenager, though she's a very British, contemporary version. For all Beryl's hilarious misadventures, she's a feminist heroine. I like the politics of Beryl (never explicit but strongly etched), and she makes me howl, but what I love most about her is her body. Quinn's bodies are big and fleshy usually, and very often unclothed. They're like a cross between the creations of the cartoonist R. Crumb and the painter Jenny Saville.

Beryl is a broad in the old sense, and maybe Quinn is too. Quinn doesn't seem to care about mainstream success or any of that. She—and Mills, who writes the movies, while she draws and directs—have devoted themselves to Beryl, even as she sometimes costs them money. (The movies are paid for by commissions mostly; she used to draw the Charmin bear for commercials, but found it soulless.)[2] They've made four Beryl movies, each more complex and outrageous than the last, but the short animated film is a category people are usually trying to break out of, since nobody sees them. Quinn and Mills don't care. They're mostly trying to please themselves. "There's only like four feature animated films I've ever liked," Mills said.[3]

Quinn goes to great lengths to protect the joy she gets from drawing. She draws with a pencil and paper, even though it would be far more efficient to draw directly onto a computer tablet and, she admits, nobody would ever tell the difference. When she feels her drawing is getting too stiff, she tricks herself to get back to her natural, freer style.

We talked mostly about *Dreams and Desires - Family Ties*, the third Beryl film and one she and Mills are particularly proud of, in which Beryl is given a video camera, which she uses to film her friend's wedding. Its point of view is very clever, with much of the material what Beryl "filmed," and it's loaded with winks—at one point she imagines herself shooting in the style of Leni Riefenstahl, for instance. Much hilarity follows—carnal, drug-addled, irreligious

1. Three of the subjects in this book at some point started collaborating with their older husbands or partners—Meiselas, Diller, and Quinn.

2. Quinn's Charmin bear is really a remarkably expressive, un-corporate creation, much loved by drawing enthusiasts and not at all lifeless as Quinn professes, though it obviously felt flat to her. Check it out online.

3. Quinn and Mills have never made a feature film, even though it's evident they could, and given the short movies, I imagine it'd be pretty wonderful. But they *choose* to work in this less popular and less lucrative form. Is this because they're less ambitious, or just the opposite—is making small films a necessary sacrifice to make the movies they want to make?

(Beryl gets stoned and sees Jesus pop off his cross—see page 16). As with every Beryl movie, it's all about Beryl's humiliation, but every frame of it is on her side. Quinn and Mills followed *Dreams and Desires* with a short called *Affairs of the Art*, which was nominated for an Academy Award.

Beryl from Nowhere

JOANNA QUINN: When people ask, "Where did Beryl come from?" for a long time I didn't know. I think when I was in college I got more political and realized I was always drawing men. I've always been a drawer, and as an only child, I spent a lot of time alone, drawing. I was drawing men all the time, yet my politics was feminist. Why was I avoiding drawing women? So I decided to make *Girls Night Out*, a comic strip about women, just about women. It needed a central character, and that was Beryl. It was Beryl's birthday, and her friends were taking her out and surprising her with a male stripper. I just drew her.

We did animation the first year in school. I did two little films. One was called *The Dancer*—I wanted to just try animating the figure. And then I did a film called *Superdog*, which was really awful, about a boy dog that tries to rescue a girl dog and she's all "bugger off" at the end. So I liked the observational stuff of the life drawing film and the comedy of the funny film. For *Girls Night Out*, I translated the comic strip into the film. I was just making my illustrations move. And

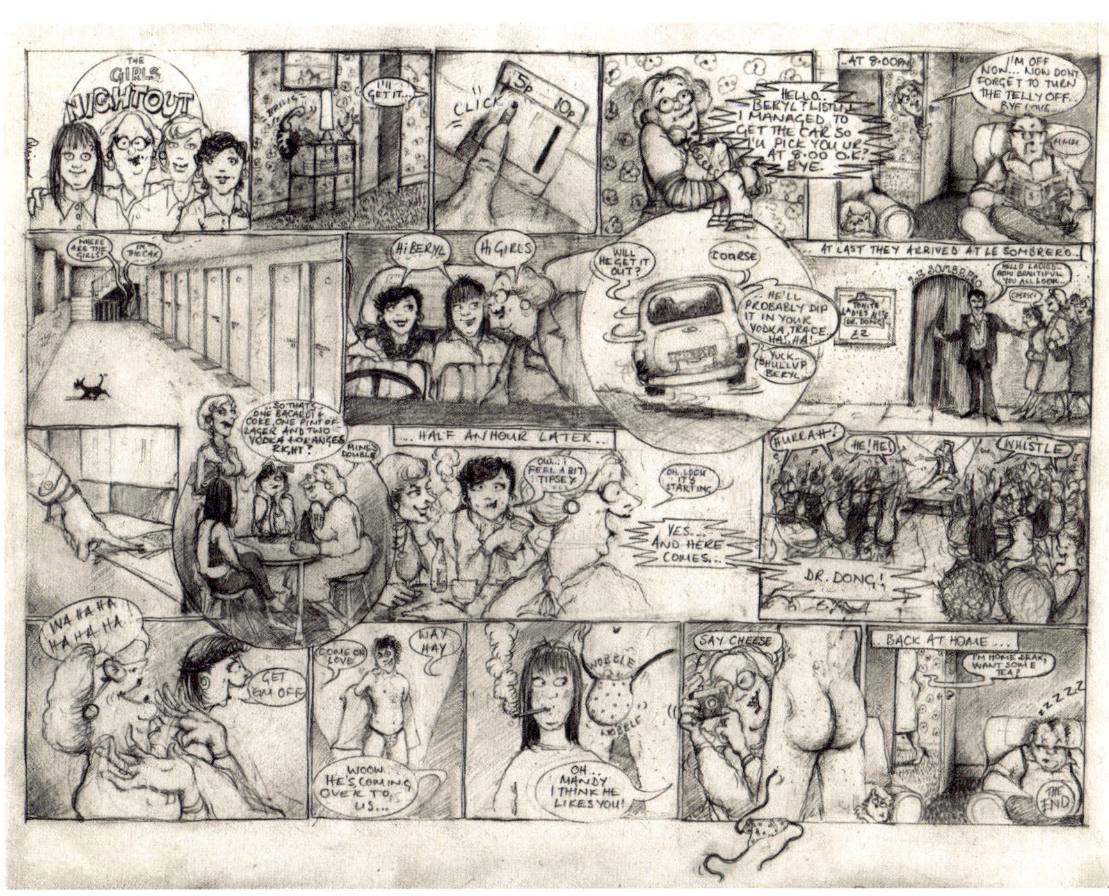

Beryl, as first created for an undergraduate comic strip.

I remember the feeling of, *Oh my God, this is magic*.

LES MILLS: I was her drawing teacher. And I realized, looking at her drawings, that they had huge dynamic potential, in terms of the way she drew and used movement, even in the still drawings. I would tell her not to rub out her mistakes: "You've got animation within drawings, you know."[4]

4. The principle of integrating mistakes into your work is a constant refrain here across genres.

Dreams and Desires - Family Ties (2006)

JQ: *Dreams and Desires* was really successful for us. It's won lots of awards. And the reason people like it is that it's a video diary, with the point of view of the camera throughout, which was really hard. People went, "Wow," because they'd never seen that before.

LM: Structurally it's a lot more disciplined than the other films. We used our own filmed video footage as references to explore camera angles and made references to seminal filmmakers like Eisenstein and Riefenstahl.

JQ: We had been stuck in the land of commercials for thirteen years. We made the film on the money we got from that. Making commercials is relentless. There's not much room for creativity, you're just making somebody else's idea come alive.

LM: As we were making the commercials, people were asking, "When are you going to make another Beryl film?" We were both feeling miserable that we weren't being creative, and we really needed to make a film. And we decided, "Okay, let's not tell the agency." I was able to delegate enough to other people and

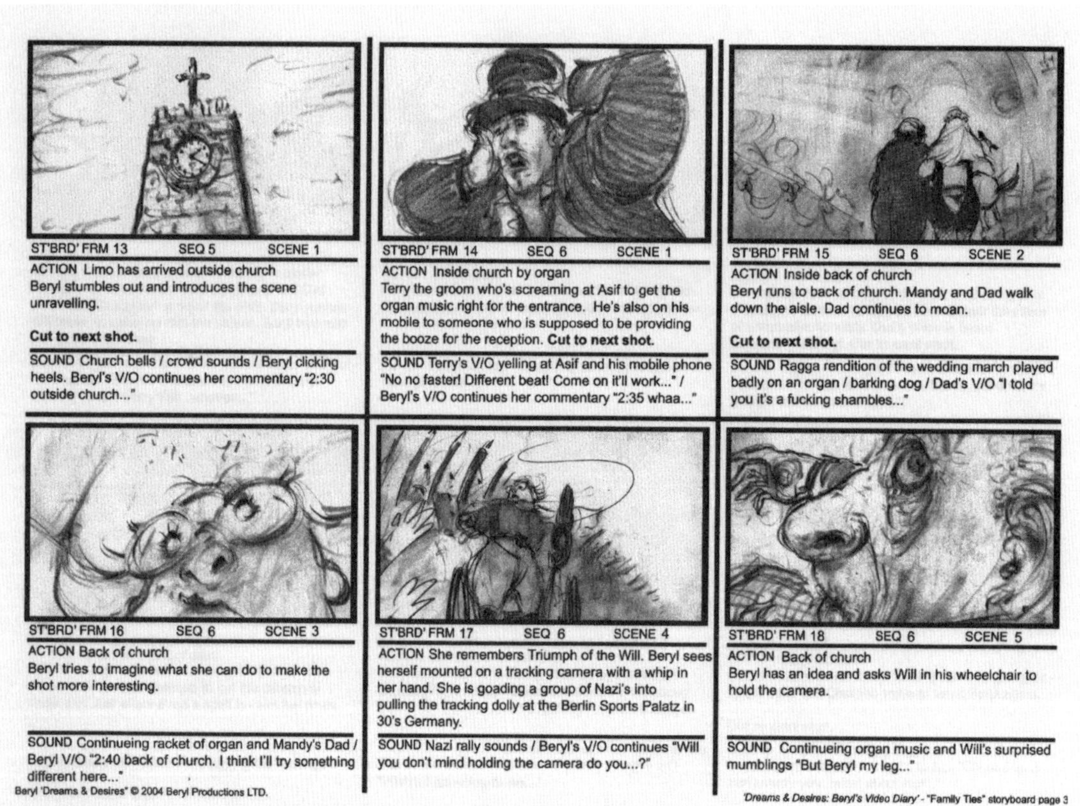

Storyboard for *Dreams and Desires - Family Ties*.

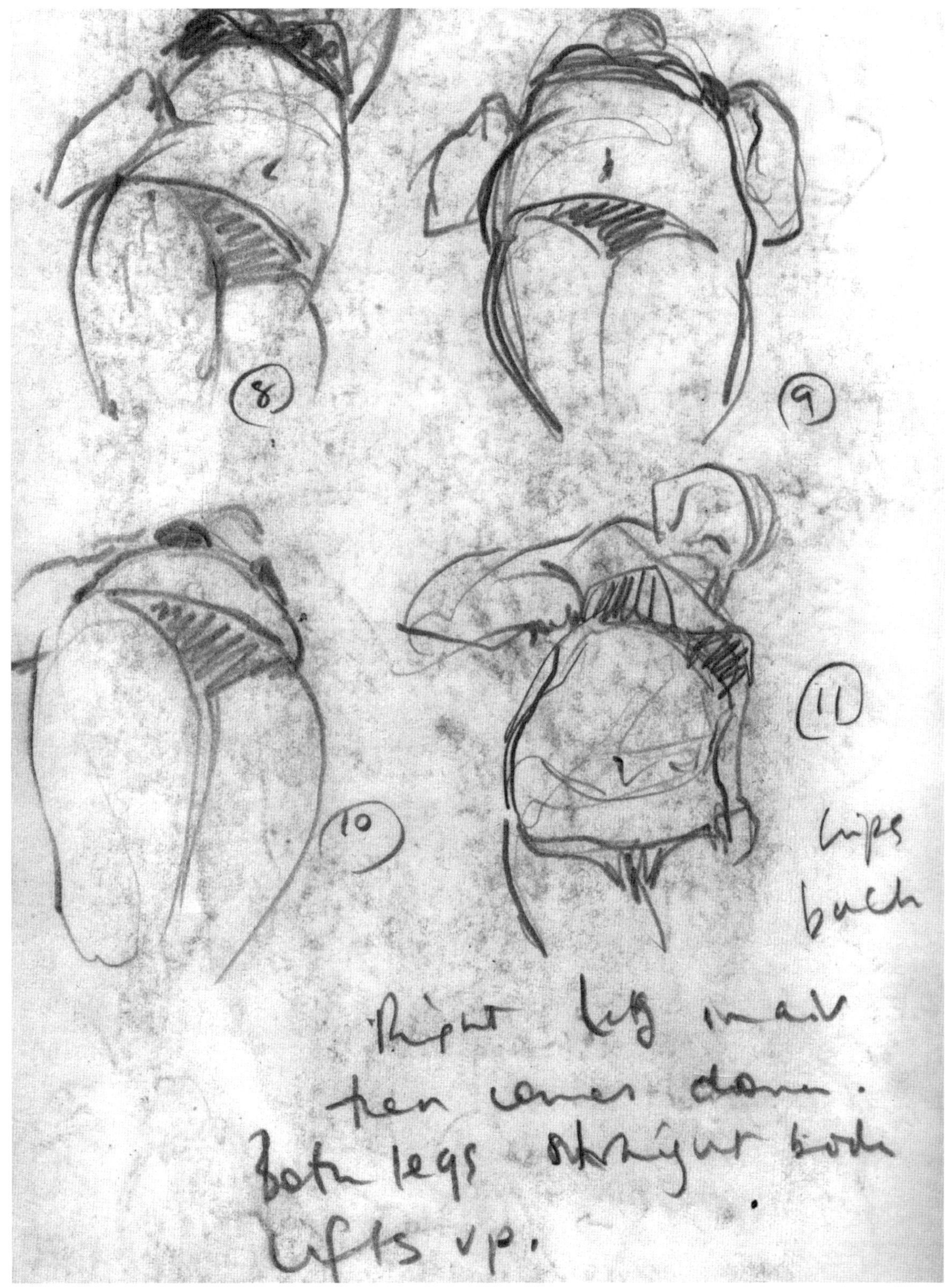

Mandy (another Quinn/Mills character), for *Dreams and Desires*.

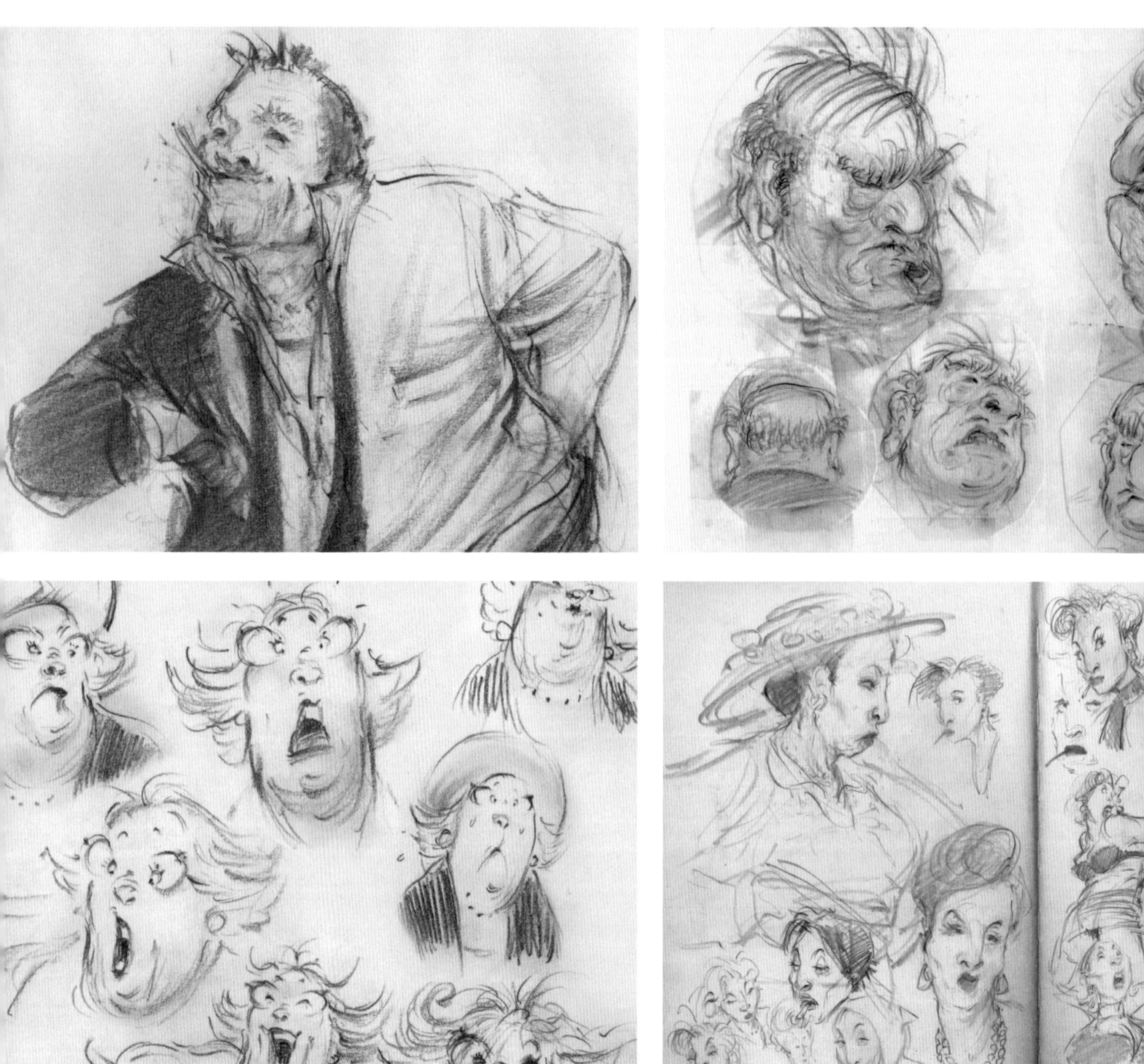

Character sketches for *Dreams and Desires*.

pretend I was in charge.

I had these cameras at the film school I was teaching at, which is where the idea we had for *Dreams and Desires*, of Beryl being given a video camera, and a friend asking her to video the wedding, came from. Beryl decided to go whole hog with the new camera, and explore it, read everything, and experiment at the wedding. And then it becomes sort of a disaster movie. My thing is, weddings are disaster movies.

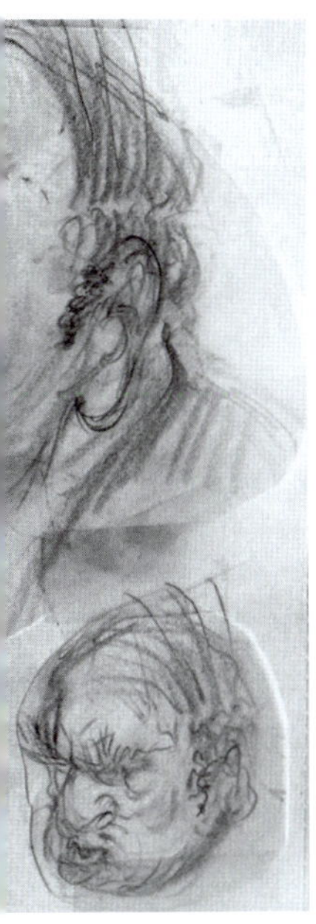

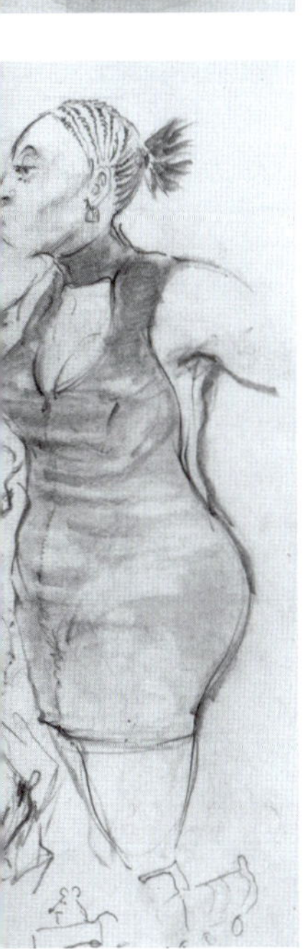

JQ: Les writes the script first. But not a script script. More like a short story.
LM: Then it's backwards and forwards, very much a team thing.
JQ: Before I storyboard, I take his script, and then start to do some ideas, draw. And then he goes, "Oh that's good," and tweaks his script. Generally, because I'm more interested in character, I make it more specific about the characters, bring more personality and humor in. Les is broader; I'm specific.

What we always try to do when we make a film is not use that many words and show what we need with the animation. But it never works. So we bombard everybody with language and bombard everybody with animation. We really start off not trying to do that. I think one of the reasons we work well together is 'cause I'm actually quite conservative, with a small *c*, and anxious about what people will think. Les'll go, "Eh, it'll be all right, just put it in."

I spend forever doing the storyboard. In the storyboard you're problem-solving—problems of continuity, where the camera is. Everything is set, so you don't have to worry about it later on. I blow up one of the frames, and I just animate it.

When we're done, we really aren't sure whether it was okay or just awful. When you're so focused on something, you can't tell. I think with *Dreams and Desires*, in the end we felt it was a bit relentless, there's no breathing space—you know, too in your face. Little did we know that we would go on to make a film that would make *Dreams and Desires* look really calm.

***Affairs of the Art* (2021)** *Affairs of the Art* was [so chaotic and long, for a short film] because it wasn't a commission, we used our own money to make it.[5] There was no deadline and nobody that we had to explain ourselves to. We knew the story; we had the storyboards. Looking back, we should have been more ruthless about it, said right at the beginning, this is going to be a ten-minute film, and chop stuff out. Because sixteen minutes—which is what it ended up being—it's sort of a halfway house. At film festivals, people see a film of sixteen minutes, they go, *Oh God*.

For *Affairs of the Art*, I worked for six months animating digitally, drawing on the Contiq—which is a giant tablet, you don't draw with a pencil. You just draw directly on to it with 2D software, everybody uses it now. But it made me realize I love drawing on paper, I just love the act, the simplicity of it. And my animation became really . . .
LM: Rigid.
JQ: Rigid. So I went back. I draw all the time. I've got piles of sketchbooks. And I do look out the window a lot. I love disappearing, being able to disappear in your work. The commercials nearly ruined me, because the style had to be flat and lifeless. So I had to break out of that. I broke my arm actually, last year. And so I started drawing with my other hand.[6] Les said, "Oh, your drawings are much better!" Sometimes I draw and not look at the page, but look at the person. The lines are all over the place, but you manage to catch something of the person. When I'm animating, my little thumbnails are the best thing. Brain, hand, pencil, paper, that's it. I realized, without it, how unhappy I was. It looked okay. . . .
LM: It didn't look okay—
JQ: Most people wouldn't be able to tell the difference. Actually drawing, it just makes me happy to draw. And it's more important to be a happy person.

5. It's so hard to impose discipline yourself. That's why external forces (commissions, audiences) keep being so important.

6. Similar to the move (hack) Kara Walker made in the first chapter.

23

WESLEY MORRIS

Writing in the Dark

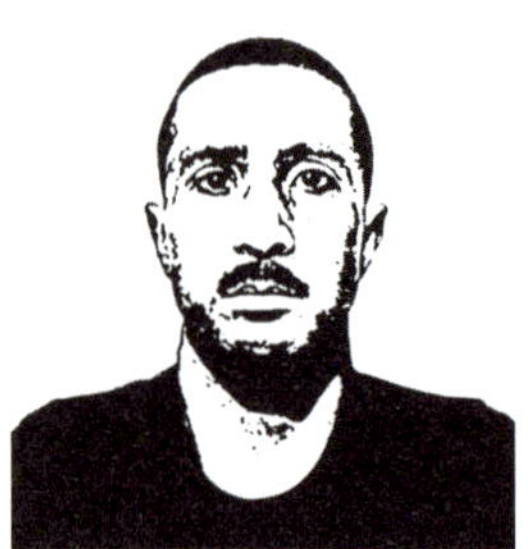

OCCUPATION: Critic

WORK DISCUSSED: The Notebooks

BORN: 1975

WESLEY MORRIS IS A critic at large at *The New York Times*, which basically means he is free to criticize, or riff on, almost anything: movies and television and music and also race and public spectacle and hairdos. He can write conventional criticism, but he's also remaking criticism as he goes. He co-hosts a wide-ranging pop culture podcast, once wrote a pretty unhinged blog, just for himself, on athletes' fashion choices, is writing a book of historical scholarship, and is constantly looking at new filters for his commentary. (One I liked especially was called "The Box," for "box office," which looked back at movies through the lens of their mass appeal in a given period, giving him an opportunity to offer an episodic history of popularity.) He is—thrillingly—all over the place.

I tried to hire Wesley at *New York* when he was working at a now defunct website called *Grantland*. Hiring critics was always one of the more interesting aspects of my editor job, because I found myself invested in finding ways to move criticism, which I read a lot back in the days when critics seemed to matter more (beginning for me when I was reading Dwight MacDonald and enthralled with Mary McCarthy), into a place where it might be culturally relevant again. I'm not sure I ever got there.[1] Still, I was enamored of critics who could really write, and who used the "review" as a vehicle to help readers think more expansively, less about the cultural object at hand than its context. Wesley always startled me with his range and delirious prose style. He's staking out a genre of his own. I wanted to know how he got there.

We met at his apartment in Brooklyn. It was strewn with books and paper piles and toppling DVDs (Wesley told me many of them were blaxploitation movies that couldn't be streamed that he was using for his research). He's a compact, muscly guy with a now famous mustache, which we'll get to in a moment. He made me some delicious biscuit strawberry shortcake. Before we talked criticism, we talked about the book he was writing or, at

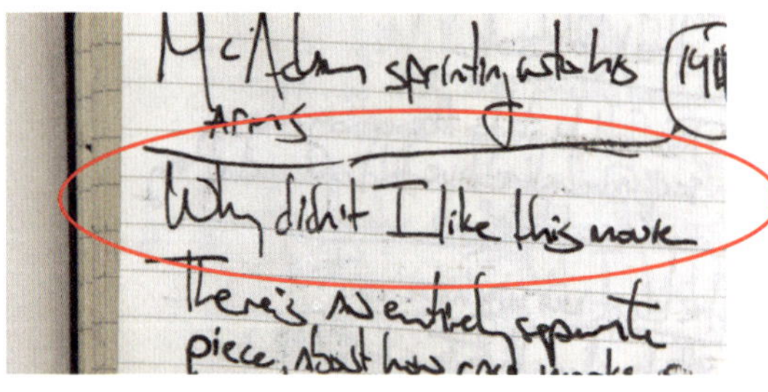

From his notebooks.

that moment, not writing. The book was, he said, "about the performance of Blackness—how much control do Black people have over their own image. How much control do I, as a Black person, have over mine?" The book was about the ways Black people play out scenarios that have been created for them by (white) cultural puppeteers, but he said he was wary of being the person "that's always telling you that this shit is rigged. That person usually gets drummed out of Blacktown for it." That's the way he talks; it's also the way he writes.

He was, more or less, willing to be drummed out. He'd made a career out of going his own way, though he was sometimes ambivalent about it. Figuring out where he fits in has been the overriding concern of Wesley's life in many contexts, as a Black man, a gay man, and a critic. Our conversation was about how he came to forge the original path as a writer that he has. That path is mostly one of acquiring influences, inhaling them, integrating and then discarding them, which, as it happens, is the recurring pattern with influence all over. He's a vivid example of absorbing and rejecting as a means to creating something new.

What Is a Critic? Wesley was drawn to criticism while at a boarding school in Philadelphia. "I didn't know what criticism was until a teacher told me that that was what I was doing," he said. He was in eighth grade. "We were supposed to watch a Hallmark movie called *April Morning*. So I read the book and watched the movie and just reviewed what the experience was like going from one thing to another. And [the teacher] said, 'This is not what I asked you to do. But, you know, what you just did is a job. People do it for a living. It's called movie criticism.' So I started reviewing movies for the school paper. Honestly, if the assignment had been to listen to some music and the teacher said, 'You know, there's a thing called rock criticism, you should do that for a living,' it might have been that."

He graduated from Yale in 1997, wrote movie criticism there, found his way to a job at the *San Francisco Examiner*, then the *San Francisco Chronicle*, and then eventually to *The Boston Globe* in 2002. All the while, he was reading what his fellow critics were doing and became both enamored of the critical wars raging around him and also whipsawed. Critical strategies were innovating and competing, and he found himself attracted and then repelled by almost all of them.

"Rock critics made claims," he said. "Like, this is the best or worst of the summer. Movie people didn't do that much. There was not a lot of flag planting. Well, Andrew Sarris"—who was promoting a polarizing "auteur" theory of moviemaking[2]—"was always planting flags. And Pauline Kael was trying to pull up the flags he'd planted. Then he'd do the same to her."

Kael's work was emotional, rooted in her gut as much as her head. Wesley responded to that. "I knew that I wanted to try to find a way to synthesize what I was reading, including Kael, who I spent a lot of time reading. I wanted to know how you wrote seven thousand words, or whatever, on *Shampoo*. I mean, it's a great movie. But I had never been given the space to, as a professional critic, even write one thousand words.

"And then there was the Hoberman era at *The Village Voice*, right?" Wesley said. J. Hoberman and his disciples were speaking in a more semiotic language, as music critics did—one that was thicker and more cerebral. "The way they thought about movies and the coded way that they would express things—you would have to interpret what they were saying. There was a lot of language turned in on itself. I found that very attractive."

But when Wesley started to write like that, his editor at the *San Francisco Chronicle* was not impressed. "She said, 'This isn't *Film Comment*.'" She was

1. One critic I hired who is absolutely advancing the possibilities of criticism is *New York* magazine's Pulitzer Prize–winning art critic Jerry Saltz. Jerry not only finds many forms for his criticism (he's invented an ingenious critical style on Instagram, for instance) but even his more conventionally located criticism is written in a loose, almost free-styleish prose style he builds from association—as much like a poet as a critic. He told me that when he sees an art show, he tries to keep linear thought at bay and lets words and their opposites float into his mind, which he then examines by playing psychoanalyst to himself. He also keeps a master-list of words he selects (from books or anywhere) almost arbitrarily, always searching for triggers for his writing. He has reams of legal pads full of them, an ongoing Saltzian glossary.

2. Auteur theory presumes that the director is the "author" of a movie—the only one who matters.

referring to the house organ of this sort of criticism, and it was a swipe at his trying to write in a voice that was more showy in its intelligence, often pretentious, and for a more specialized audience.

The *Chronicle* was a plainspoken paper, and it was grueling. "I can remember where I physically was sitting and the pressure I was under to finish things. Because at that point I was writing five reviews a week. I was a procrastinator, so I would be writing five reviews in thirty-six hours. And because I was in a second-tier market, everybody else in New York and LA would review a thing before I'd be able to see it." Meanwhile, criticism was changing again. Suddenly Anthony Lane, a dazzling stylist and very funny writer, had been hired into Pauline Kael's old gig at *The New Yorker*, alternating with the more erudite David Denby and setting up another feud of approaches to criticism. "The worst days were like when Anthony Lane had already written and delivered into the world a thing that I was sitting at my computer struggling to write.

"I was America's shittiest Anthony Lane adversary. I really wanted to figure out how he wrote such polished, informed pieces. The acuity, the humor, the concision. People dismissed him for being a jester. But then I became a Denby person, because he wasn't as flashy. There was something to argue with. I never felt Anthony Lane cared what we felt when we read it. I never wanted to write like Denby, but I respected his rigor. The thing about Hoberman was that he was really serious, looking at political valences. Everything was a politics to him." Also, unlike these other critics, Wesley wasn't really a movie nerd. "I was never obsessed. I never had a passion for this. I can go a week without watching a movie. I was more interested in being out in the world. If I was going to bring myself into the work, it was going to be to bring the life that I was living into the movies I was watching."

The Intimate Critic "I was having a lot of sex," he said, of the life he was living at the time. "I was meeting strangers, putting myself at risk to have a good time. I spent a lot of time by myself. And I'm a Black person doing that in a city where there weren't many Black people. It kind of made the act of writing about movies personal, even when I wasn't necessarily writing about myself. I was invested in the experience of intimacy between me and the thing."

Intimacy became his mark. That meant abandoning the authority of the all-knowing and embracing—reveling in—criticism's inherent subjectivity. Few critics really do that; it's difficult to give up the premise that you know better.

He moved to *The Boston Globe* and began to experiment. "I loved the freedom that I felt to be mad. And to love things. I tried to use profanity. I experimented with bringing myself into the stories, but not explicitly." His prose became less and less restrained.

Synthesizing Influences "I tried to figure out a way to do what Anthony Lane did, but sincerely." He was explaining how it started to come together. "To understand that there was a politics to everything, as Hoberman did. And try to still, with respect to Jim [Hoberman], have fun with it, and not let it ruin the experience of watching the thing. It was okay to like it. And you never got a sense with the boy critics that it was okay to enjoy any of this. The thrill was the intellect. I felt like I was on my own little island and never belonged anywhere.

"I figured out at that point who I was. I didn't have to respect anybody. I just had to follow my feelings.[3] And I was no longer reading other people to figure out how to do it. I can't stress to you enough how often I was reading Elvis Mitchell and A. O. Scott and Manohla Dargis [three *Times* critics, the last two of which are still his colleagues] before I could start to write what I was writing. At some point in Boston, I stopped caring. I distinctly remember thinking, *This is what I've been trying to do the whole time. This is what*

I've been trying to do." In 2012 he won his first Pulitzer Prize.

Lint But it's not as if the recognition sated him. He was still wandering creatively. He'd had a conversation with a friend after watching a Wimbledon match. "We were talking about how excellent Dulko's dress was and how bad Sharapova's was.[4] And she thought someone should write about what athletes are wearing. So I just started to." He began a personal blog he thought nobody would see, called *The Sportstorialist*, the first entry of which was on Andy Roddick and Roger Federer's tennis final in 2009. "I wrote about that because Roddick was so sweaty. And Federer was dry, couldn't have been drier." It turns out anything at all could be a prism for his writing. Later he wrote a piece playing off the lint in the hair of disgraced athlete Michael Vick in an interview with Bob Woodruff.[5] "They left that shit there the entire conversation. And I just thought that was the biggest fuck you ever."

Eventually he got a call from *Grantland*, which was sort of a sports site and sort of an anything-goes site. Bill Simmons, the sports columnist who was its editor, had liked Wesley's increasing turn to the odd. He told Wesley he could write whatever he wanted at whatever length, and he could also move *The Sportstorialist* into *Grantland*. Wesley was sold. That's where I first saw his work and tried to recruit him, but he wasn't going anywhere. He loved the job.

Eventually the *Times* called and said Wesley could have that same freedom as a critic at large but within an establishment institution. That invitation proved irresistible. He's been there since 2015.

His Self In 2020, he wrote a bizarre and beautiful essay called "My Mustache, My Self" that showed Wesley in all his plumage. It appears to be a personal essay about growing a COVID mustache that then reveals itself as a cultural exploration of the character Carlton from the television show *The Fresh Prince of Bel-Air* and that ultimately turns out to be a very sophisticated piece about Black identity and masculinity (and, in a way, it's a companion story to one he'd written also for the *Times* magazine, about the Black penis). The essay never flinches from an examination of self that is as perceptive and tough as that which he applies to fictional worlds as a critic. Here's one passage:

I knew before the summer's Black Lives Matter protests that my mustache made me look like a bougie race man: a professional, seemingly humorless middle-class Negro, a moderate, who believes that presentation is a crucial component of the "advancement" part of the N.A.A.C.P. mission, someone who doesn't mind a little respectability because he believes his people deserve respect. It's a look to ponder as the country finds itself churning once again over ceaseless questions of advancement and justice and the right to be left the hell alone.

I live a street over from a thoroughfare where the protests happened almost nightly in June and July. I could hear their approach from my living room. One evening, I stood at a corner, moved, as thousands of people passed: friends, colleagues, co-workers, some guy I went on a blind date with a million years ago, chanting, brandishing banners and buttons. Some protesters had their fists raised in a Black Power salute. So I raised mine. Not a gesture I would normally make. But there was something about seeing so many white people lifting their arms that goaded me into doing it, too. Mine kept lowering itself, so I had to jerk it to its fullest, most committed extension. I felt out of control, like Edward Norton throwing himself around his boss's office in Fight Club; *like the kleptomaniac that Tippi Hedren played in Alfred Hitchcock's* Marnie, *trying to palm a stack of cash but her arm. Just.*

3. I think this seeped into his prose style as well, as it increasingly relied more on feeling than logic to propel its way forward—less analytic than impressionistic.

4. Maria Sharapova and Gisela Dulko. You knew that.

5. Here's a sliver of it: Michael Vick conducted the entire interview with a piece of something in his hair. It was small and white. Yet, even on a tiny screen, it was as big as Billie Holiday's gardenia. Maybe it was chalk. Maybe it was lint. . . . One of the most endearingly polite things you can do for a friend or a stranger is let him know he has, say, parsley in his teeth. Not to do so can be innocent. Often it is. But, occasionally, allowing a person to spend a whole day with an upturned shirt collar can also constitute an act of malice. . . . Woodruff was inches away. He was talking as much to the speck as he was to Vick. In saying nothing, *Nightline* was saying everything: You might be on top of the world right now, but there's something in your hair—and we're leaving it there.

Won't. Pick. It. Up. At some point, I stopped straining. This wasn't the struggle I came for. Plus, a friend told me later that I had made my fist wrong.

The essay itself proceeds along in his usual manner, even while he was, in a sense, reviewing himself. "I usually start with the simplest thing, which is that I've observed something. I just want to say it and get out. But at some point I'm going to ask myself, *Why do I want to say this?* And the piece winds up trying to answer a question it doesn't have to." The essay was the crux of the entry that won him a second Pulitzer Prize in criticism, which no one had ever done before.

SCRIBBLING WHEN THE LIGHTS ARE OUT: RANDOM NOTEBOOK PAGES

One of the reasons I approached Wesley was that I have always been curious about what critics write in the dark. When I've gone to movies or shows with critics, I've found myself craning my neck to read the scratchy pile of words they record in their notebooks, usually earning a hairy eyeball in return. Their notebooks are private; they're diaries of joy or disgust—or, maybe, shopping lists? I wanted to know. And as it happened, Wesley saves them all. I asked if he'd share some pages, and then we'd decipher them together.

WESLEY MORRIS: I began using notebooks when I was thirteen. I'd seen other people do it—Siskel, Ebert. I thought, *Well, I guess you're supposed to have a notebook and sit in the dark and write down things that occurred to you.* So I would just take a notebook to a movie theater. Some movie I was going to review for the school paper, I brought a notebook, and I was very proud of it. But you know, one problem is things are so dark. And you're just constantly writing over yourself, you can't read any of it.

Once I figured out how to do this job, this would happen: watching a movie and you'd notice that everybody in the critics' screening would write things down at the same time. And you'd think, *Huh? Should I be writing something down?* And then sometimes I'd just write things down when nobody else was. See if I could trick the other critics.

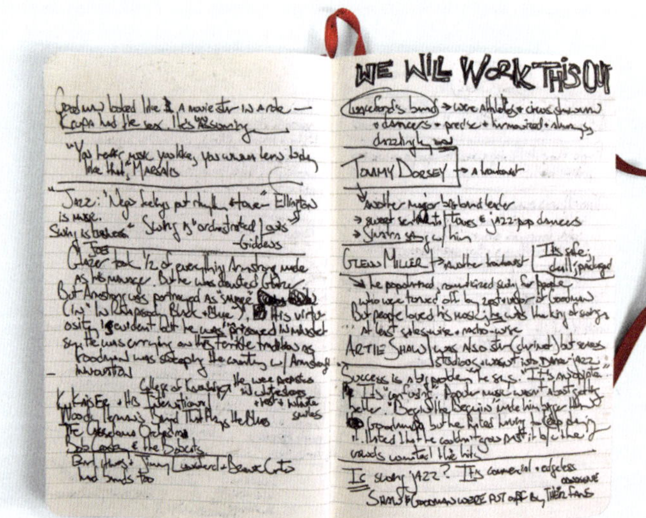

Ken Burn's *Jazz*

"We will work this out." Hmm. In my lowest, saddest moments, I think of music as the freest that white people and Black people can be to share ideas. Because it's not about spoken language, it's about some other language separate from history. But it's bound up in it. I did find this series thrilling; the amount of notes I took has to do with how well done the show was.

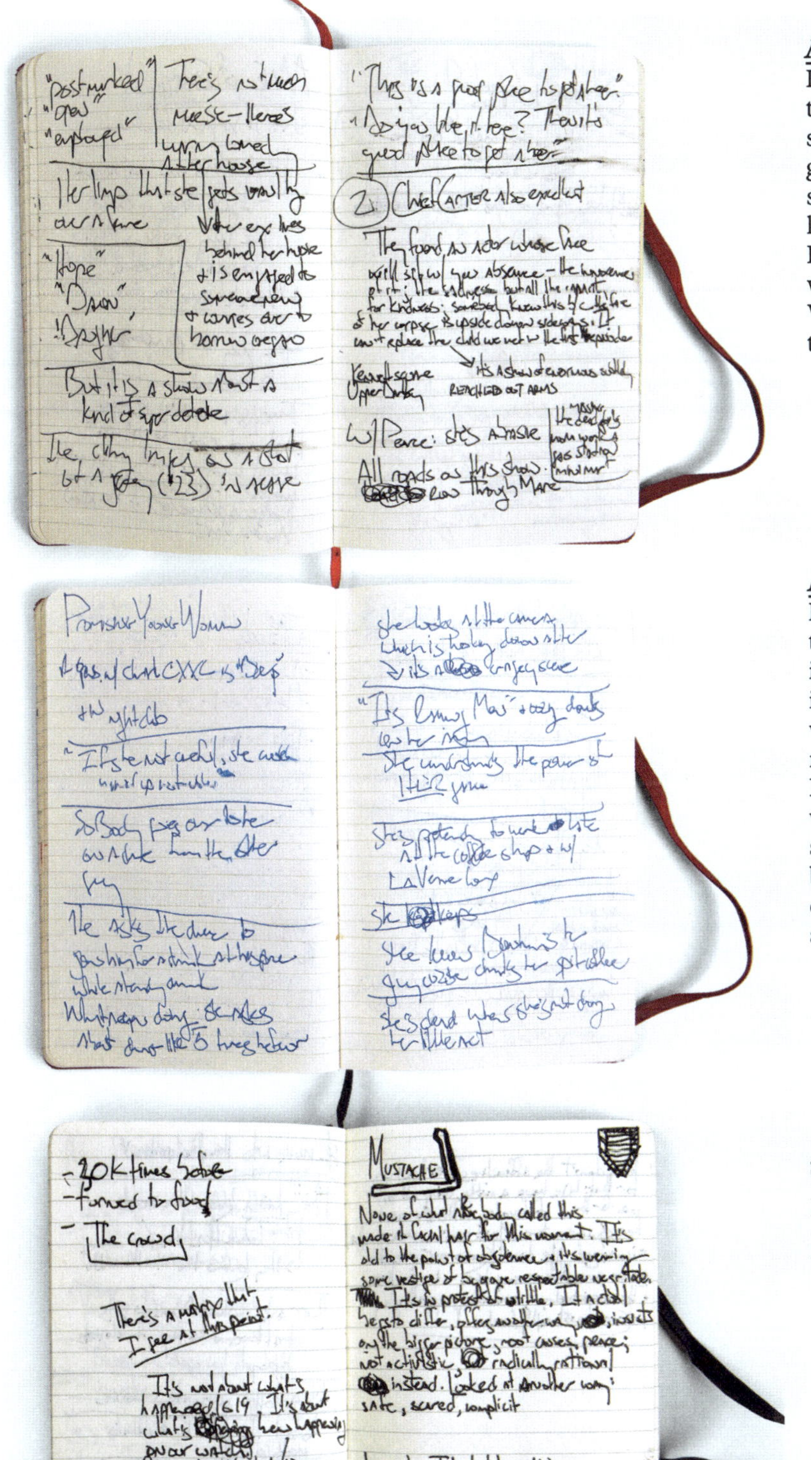

Mare of Easttown

I was writing about that girl that dies in the first episode—she was a genius. I thought that girl was going to be the whole show—and when she died, I kept thinking about her face. I don't know who that actress was, but I love casting decisions. Where do they find girls like these? That face.

Promising Young Woman

I watched this a couple of times. I thought even less of it the second time. The movie is afraid. It's such a symbol of where we are right now with respect to fun. Like it's bright. Like candy. But if you ate it, it would kill you. Right now, we seem to really want pleasure, but we also think we really don't deserve it. I'm working on a piece about it right now.

"My Mustachc, My Sclf"

This was for the mustache piece. I never used it. I must have forgotten I wrote that down. Which happens a lot.

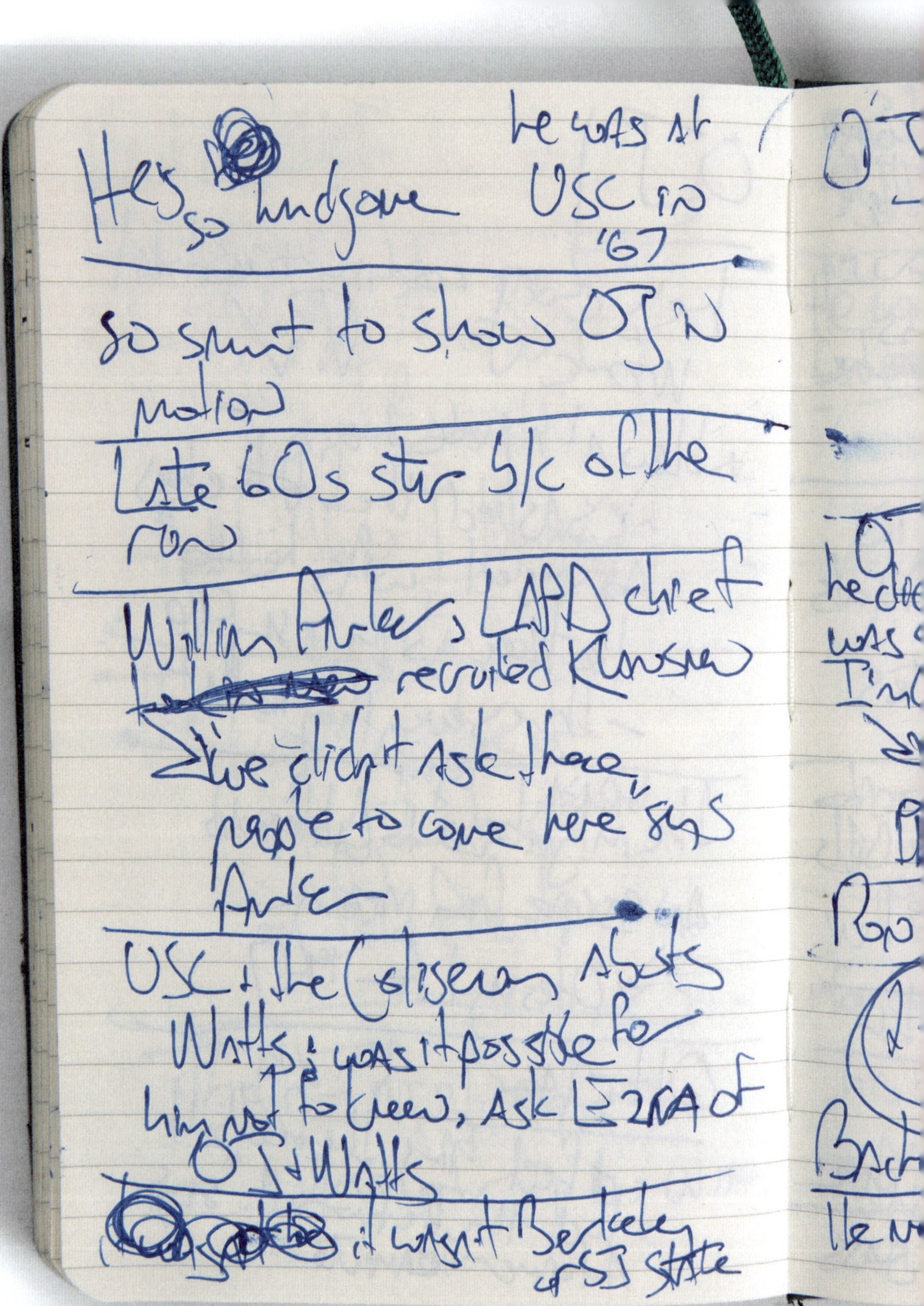

He's so handsome — he was at USC in '67

so smart to show OJ in motion

Late 60s star s/c of the run

William Parker, LAPD chief recruited Klansmen
"we didn't ask these people to come here" says Parker

USC + the Coliseum abuts Watts; was it possible for him not to know, Ask Ezra of OJ + Watts

it wasn't Berkeley or SJ State

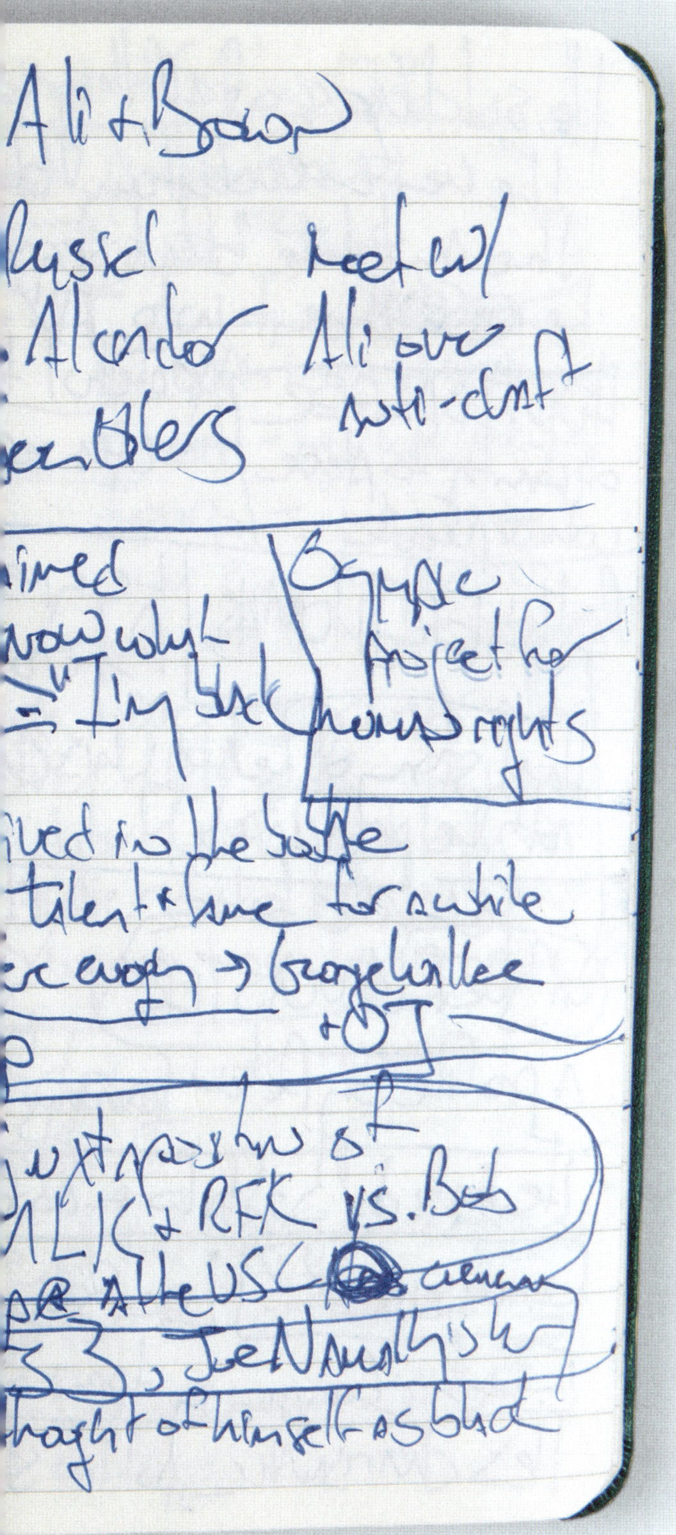

O.J.: Made in America

If you were a Martian and wanted to understand the United States of America, I would just say: watch this. There's something about the way it understands O. J. Simpson as a paradigmatic American. He was the rare Black person who was given the choice about how Black to be. People just accepted that. Even Black people were like, Okay, let's see how this goes. And what did he choose? He chose not to be Black. Every twenty-five years in the history of Black people someone makes this choice. For O. J., it was, *Fuck this. I want what the white guys have. This Black shit is trauma. Y'all Black people are the problem.* And what happens every time somebody leaves the plantation and runs off to the big house? Shit goes down. I mean, you can't do it. You cannot be successfully deracinated in this country.

The thrill of O. J. for white people was that he wanted to be like them, and they loved it. And then what happened? The very thing people have said was gonna happen forever. In all of history, Black men were always accused of killing white women—they can never prove it, but it's always, *blame the slave.* And now we finally get a Negro who really did just kill a white lady. And we can't fucking prove it! This is what Black people loved about that moment. Y'all can't catch him! This country is fucking ridiculous.

24

AMY SILLMAN

There, I've Killed It

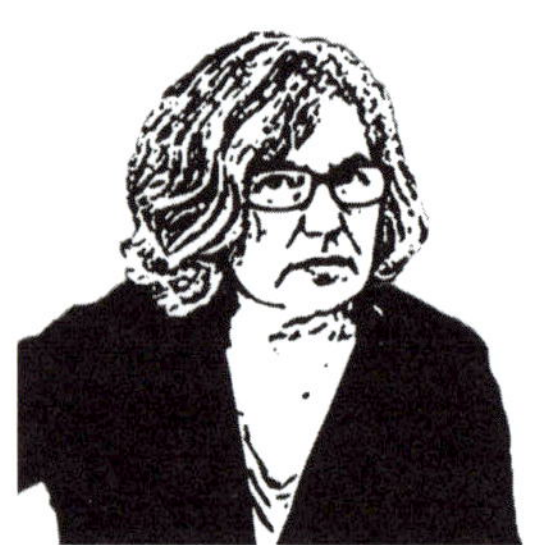

OCCUPATION: Visual Artist

WORK DISCUSSED: *Miss Gleason* (2014)

BORN: 1955

Adam Moss: *Do you ever think that one of the paintings you painted over was really the better painting?*

Amy Sillman: Oh, the best painting was the first one. I shouldn't have changed any of them.

AM: *So why do you change anything?*

AS: It's just neurotic. No good reason. It's entirely neurotic.

AMY SILLMAN IS AN abstract painter who does extraordinary things with color and shape, especially.[1] She's in the collections of MoMA and the Met and the Tate Modern. She also draws and animates and makes cool little zines. Her drawings are witty and crude. I thought of one series I love, of a figure barfing over and

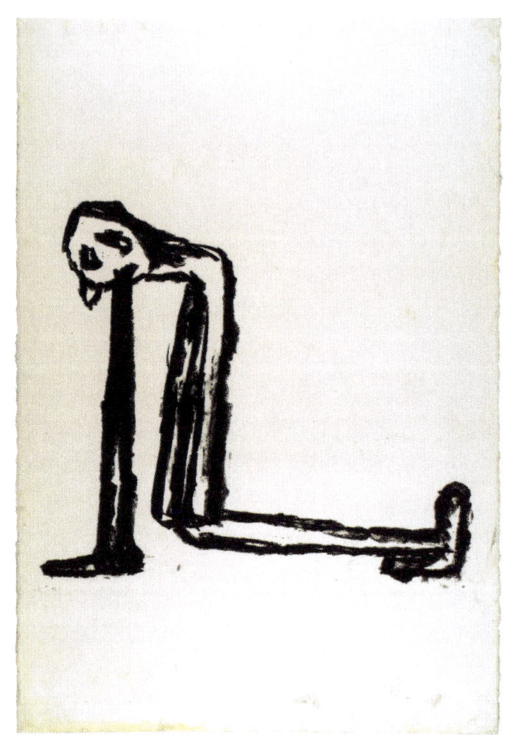

over again, as the perfect manifestation of the vomit stage (where artists spew their unmediated thoughts onto the page or the canvas) most creators talk about, though that's hardly what the drawings in the animation are about, since they are also political and pissed off. She's that too. She writes—in fact, she's one of the few artists I know who are truly verbal. She's funny and forthright, even while expressing very conceptual ideas. She compiled her writings in a fabulous little book called *Faux Pas*, which is also full of cartoonlike drawings and sharp chartlets. She is an intellectual and a comedian, direct and highfalutin at the same time, an abstractionist who, unlike most artists, actually wants to be understood.

And as it happened, Amy was also a dream subject for this project, because to reach the finish line of most of her paintings, she paints dozens of paintings, or even more, each usually pretty wonderful. Most are seen only by her, and only briefly, before she wipes them out. I talked to everyone in this book about self-sabotage (because I was looking for reassurance); it's a big theme, and it's the hell artists generally have to put themselves through on the way to the pay dirt of the work itself. But for Amy, it's actually what the work is all about: the struggle, the destruction. She is insistent that her painting—the final painting, the painting others see—is, in a sense, an arbitrary choice, like a game of musical chairs, where the music stops and that's the work. The obliteration isn't defeat. It's the point.

"I approach a painting with a brush," she said, "and it's got things working in it, but it's like I can't help myself. I'm thinking, *I'm gonna kill it, I'm gonna kill it—ah there, I've killed it.*"[2] If that sounds a little pathological (and it does to me), it's also riveting.

AMY SILLMAN: I learned to draw from a de Kooning–ish guy, to work with layers and erasure. Swipes and wipes. We learned all this doubt. And I don't know, I just started. I don't know what made me want to make paintings. Except for the indication that I got that you shouldn't be making them. Maybe I liked color, I don't know. As everybody knows, it was not okay to be doing painting in the late seventies. Then it was okay again, but I wasn't in any kind of cool crowd. And I remember making a lot of bad paintings.

The paintings were completely clueless. I had no content. I don't think I understood that I had no content, and I probably still don't. I mean, I don't think I have ideas per se. And I'd be willing at this point to say that might be true for a lot of people. You don't go into a painting with an idea. Green with yellow is not an idea. It's a kind of drive.

But I didn't know what I was doing for most of the time. I remember thinking the art world is crazy, like things are really happening in New York, but I'm nowhere near there. I have no gallery, no connections. I ended up living in Ahmedabad in the seventies, at an art colony there. I thought, *I'll just do whatever I want here, where no one will see it. I don't have to care. I grant myself this period where I can do whatever I want.*[3] I made drawings, layered drawings that I still like, that were dreamlike. And then they become paintings. In the nineties a really nice art historian came to visit me, and she said, "You should read *A Thousand Plateaus*, because your work has this endlessness."[4] She was picking up on this filmstrip quality that I think my work is about—something that keeps changing and moving. She basically gave me license to become a conceptualist. It was cool to find that out. Then I finally realized, over the last thirty years, that what I was interested in was the transformation of something into something else, and then to something else.

I start with, I don't know what, and then it looks terrible. And I ruin it. And then it looks maybe good. And then I ruin that. All the versions look completely different. First it needs clarity, then it needs a different color.

---

1. Amy's thoughts on shape can be found online, in a zine she made about a show (*The Shape of Shape*) she curated at MoMA. I really recommend her writing. The best of many great essays in *Faux Pas* is called "On Color." From it: "Making a painting is so hard, it makes you crazy. Before even the vicissitudes of color, you have to negotiate tone, silhouette, line, space, zone, area, layer, scale, speed and mass while interacting with a meta-surface of meaning . . . you have to go your own way, to cut away from your heroes and influences, and still be utterly conscious and literate about the discourse. You have to simultaneously diagnose, predict and ignore the past, present and future, all at once; you have to remember and forget at the same time."

2. I watch a lot of Instagram reels on art. Can't help it, they're addictive. One I keep laughing at shows a brush heading to the canvas as a voice repeats, "Don't do it, don't do it, don't do it!" with mounting—and to me, very familiar—urgency.

3. Another deal-with-self moment of bargaining.

4. All I can tell you about this book is that it "provides a toolbox for nomadic thought and has had a galvanizing influence on today's anti-capitalist movement." That summary is the clearest description I found anywhere.

You can see that it starts out perfectly good. Like I could have left it at that. And then I go, *That whole thing sucks*. And while it's happening, I'm in deep despair—

This one [we were talking at this point about one painting in particular], which could have easily ended there, crazily enough ends here.

—

Start "Is your first mark completely arbitrary?" I asked, because I'd heard that—that she has no intention at all when she begins a picture.

"Yes. A lot of time at the beginning I put the canvas on the floor, so I can't even control it. There's a wipe or spill or blob or stroke or something really simple."

Then she responds to that. And then responds to that response. All the while, she's digging, rummaging through the brain pan, as Virginia Woolf put it. Though she has her own analogies: "I've often told people that I feel like when I'm making paintings, I'm a radish grower. I'm feeling around, digging up these forms that I can hold in my hand. But I don't know what they're going to look like, or which one is going to be coming up." Also, elephants: "When you're painting, you're editing a blind elephant. It's an elephant under a sheet. You're editing something that you have no idea about. You're doing the same kind of brutal, scrupulous scalpel edit as you'd do to a text that was a mess. But when you're editing a text there's at least [something concrete] you can cut. Painting is an editing of a thing that has no framework, no idea.[5]

"The great challenge and reason and beauty of trying to be a painter is the impossibility of it, which is similar to the impossibility of a novelist or a poet, which is to manifest something or shape it from God-knows-what scraps and build a thing into a thing that has not been there before. You have no idea what it is. The journey is blind. You can take the sheet off the elephant and go, *Holy shit, that's it*."

Finish That's how we get to Amy's conviction that the end product—the physical painting—is no more relevant than the versions that came before it. "The picture is the vaguest analogy. The real thing is the dream. It's a condensation, a puff of smoke from inside you." The question of when to quit, when to freeze the puff into something material, then becomes a crucial question. I asked everyone, "How do you know when to stop?" because that's a question everyone always wants an answer to, but for her it really was a central query.

"An artwork has a philosophical condition, which is, I can control it. And you can say, 'Why didn't you stop?' And I can say, 'Because it wasn't satisfying yet.' I only paint for my own satisfaction, no matter what it looks like. You know, beauty isn't the goal."

"What is your relationship to the paintings you destroy?" I asked. As I watched her take a torch to some iterative versions I loved, I admit I felt a little sad. "Is it just like, *Okay, this is how I make a painting?* Or is there a sense of pain?"

"I think it's the other way around," she said. "It's not that I regret and mourn the gone paintings. It's that I make a painting to instantiate—manifest—regret. A lot of lost souls go over the cliff. But there's a really specific emotional purpose for myself, which is to enact a situation of rescue and regret."

The Making as a Thing Itself I ended up visiting Amy a couple of times after our first talk. She lives in an apartment in New York near Union Square Park with a terrace and a happy little dog that kept jumping up, wanting in on our conversation. (Her studio is in Bushwick, Brooklyn, where she heads most days from around eleven to seven.) I'd bike over to her place and we'd chat for a bit and then head to her computer. We'd get to work discussing the process pictures and narration she'd provided to explain the iterations of a painting she called *Miss Gleason*. It's a very large oil painting that took over six months to make. She picked it for our case because she liked it and realized she'd recorded all the

5. Though I felt that I might be imposing the word *editing* as a framework to understand many functions of artmaking, many subjects brought the word up themselves—in art, fashion, text obviously. It's a crucial stage; many felt it was the whole ball of wax.

6. Artists love their toys. Would-be artists too. More.

7. And she did. The show was called *Temporary Object* and opened in Naples, Italy, in April 2023.

steps on her phone. And because she's unusually introspective, she was able to recall her thinking as she made the picture (though what I've published in these pages is a very streamlined version—the progression of the entire painting in all its stages would have taken up the whole book). I figured it was as close as I was ever going to get to the interior creation monologue Sondheim had imagined, which I mentioned in the introduction.

But Amy wouldn't let me publish those pictures from her phone—like most artists, she's very particular about how her work is seen. Which put us at a standstill for a while, until she volunteered to make what she called digital drawings of the shifts the piece had gone through. As she started to work on them, she got very excited about the iterations as its own work, which was heady to watch. I liked the idea that our talks had spurred an art piece; I felt like a collaborator. She was really into the way the Photoshop renderings of the iPhone pictures looked. I was too; they were like art X-rays. At the printer, they told her they could print the images on all sorts of textures—canvas, aluminum. "Honey, we can do it all," they said, and she was thrilled.[6] So that's what she was going to do next—print the X-rays and exhibit them,[7] as well as turn them into an animation—looping process being what all her work is about.

The iterations you see starting on page 237 are mostly rendered in black and white, and show her reworking the forms over and over, with interruptions now and then to indicate how they looked in color (including these color versions was a concession to me; she didn't want to show any color versions at all, which frustrated me because color is so central to her work). You'll notice how drastically the painting changed as she went along; it's wild. It's a bit hard for you to see these versions in all their color and detail in these X-rays, but trust me when I say that there are at least five amazing pictures in here that she destroyed. But reading her narrative against the versions, you can get a clear sense of how Amy works—and works to subvert her work—as she goes along. Also, of how, for all the painting's abstraction, she was digging to find the figurative (arms, shoulders, nipples) or material objects (teapot, bottle) within. At one point, she was talking about her aches and pains, and found her shoulders and hips in the painting, the same body parts that had been worked over that day by a masseur. "It's literally a self-portrait," she marveled, but then, isn't everything?

As we talked, she suggested gallery shows she thought I should see, and gave me advice on my own painting, including one exercise she proposed after I told her I was struggling to make my work more abstract. (The gist: draw

STUMBLING INTO ART

I asked her, as I asked everybody, how she got started as an artist.

AS: It was a series of opting out of mistakes. So first it didn't work to go to college in Wisconsin, then it didn't work to work at a cannery, then it didn't work to study Japanese, then it didn't work to study illustration, then it didn't work to go to art school at the beginning because I felt I'd be too old. And then I became a painter. So I negated my way into the negative dialectic.

You know when you fall in love with someone that you feel isn't your type? Painting wasn't my type. But then I got more and more interested in it. The first thing that my drawing teacher said when I wanted to go be a painter was "You will be a waitress, not a painter."

But I was really good in my drawing class. So I said to him, "I would like to go to art school now." And he was, "No, you won't be able to." I was nineteen. I don't know if it was personal or structural. But he told me, "No, that's not going to work out."

a figure, or a couple—that's what she did—from sight multiple times over many hours; sleep; then the next day, draw the figures again from memory. And then keep distorting them as you move further away from your experience of the literal. It works.) She talked about other projects that were weighing on her that she'd promised to do: another show, a list of her favorite new books of the year, which flummoxed her because the main book she'd read that year was the Torah.

I began to like her a lot. There was something familiar about her, especially as she'd veer into conversations about the labyrinth of the psyche, where she placed all her explanations of where all this stuff came from. (Torah notwithstanding, she was firmly on the side of the great psychological theorists, and well schooled in them.) There was a lot of this talk in my house growing up as well, and she was direct and inquisitive, which I found comforting. She wanted to know what I was getting from the other subjects I talked to (all the subjects wanted to know that, actually), whether there were differences between men and women, poets and painters, gay and straight (there weren't, not meaningfully), that sort of thing.

We got to talking about aggression, which she brought up a lot in passing as relevant to process. "Or hate, is that what you mean?" she said when I asked about it. "I think hatred is part of art. A dialectic is of importance here, so the antithesis is basically the part where you negate, erase, efface, paint over, undermine, scrape, ruin. There's an urge in your painting, or my painting at least—looking for figures in it is like searching for your lover or parent or, you know, yourself. It's ego driven. And there's a part that's like a rageful id—you know, the part that says, *Absolutely not*. Then, at the end, it's like pulling something out of the wreckage, trying to care for it, heal it, or something." I asked whether it was the same when she writes. "All of it," she said, "is exactly the same in all kinds of art. *What the fuck is this, I can't work out this fucking paragraph*, and then you just move the sentence, and it's *Oh, look at that, great, exactly.*"

A couple of years ago, Amy came up with some ground rules for how to work. "Because I wipe over the painting so many times, I could just make one painting for the rest of my life, there's no reason to ever stop, you know? So I thought I needed to construct a score of moves that I could make. I figured out that I would allow myself an attempt at looking for a figure, a relatable figure. And then I had to try to do something radical with color. Then I would allow myself to wipe it out, add in destruction. And then there was one other move—making a kind of pattern or repetition of a pattern. I decided that I would give myself two passes of each. And that would give me eight layers. And there could be a ninth and tenth layer that were wild cards. And that was the point I had to solve the painting and get out." Which she didn't always do—"I'd ignore the whole thing, keep going"—but it gave her a structure.

Sometimes in our conversations, it sounded like she thought of making art as a game, as if she toggled between caring and not caring. "I think I work better when I'm like, fuck it, I can do whatever I want. Because it's all bullshit." I didn't believe she thought it was all bullshit—she cares, loads—but I knew what she meant.

It was all like that with Amy, though. Did she really not believe that the individual work mattered that much—where in her process she stopped? I had such a hard time accepting that, even as I understood the function that idea has for her. I admired her way of thinking and, sponge that I was, thought maybe it could be useful to try, but I knew I wasn't ready to surrender my attachment to the particular. It was still important to me to make one painting I felt was entirely successful. Would I ever? I suppose not, and that was one of her points. Still, didn't she ever make a painting just to make a painting?

She told me a story. Recently in Germany, she made a work for a show. The painting just emerged without any of this Sturm und Drang; it took her a week. "I loved it immediately and

I left it alone. And there was another in the same show that took me a year, took forever. They couldn't sell the one that was done in a week. And I happily took it back because I like the faster one better. But I got a greater sense of achievement from the really slow one. The one that I was desperately miserable making, but that I nailed. It's a very beautiful painting and somebody bought it and that's wonderful. No one wanted to buy the one that didn't have struggle in it."

"Were they right? Is it the better painting?" I asked. "Do you feel more satisfied by the one you struggled over?"

"Yes," she said, "but more love toward the easy one. I mean, I feel love toward each of them because they're all my relationships. But the easy one is such a pleasure. Like if you meet someone and have a great affair and at the end, no drama. That was great. Bye."

MISS GLEASON, IN THIRTY-NINE STAGES. AMY SILLMAN NARRATES.

(Note: all iterations are in color, of course, but only some color variations are represented here.)

1.

1. The painting is big, 84 inches wide by 91 inches tall. The first step was a thin wash of purple wiped on as a ground, like a sky.

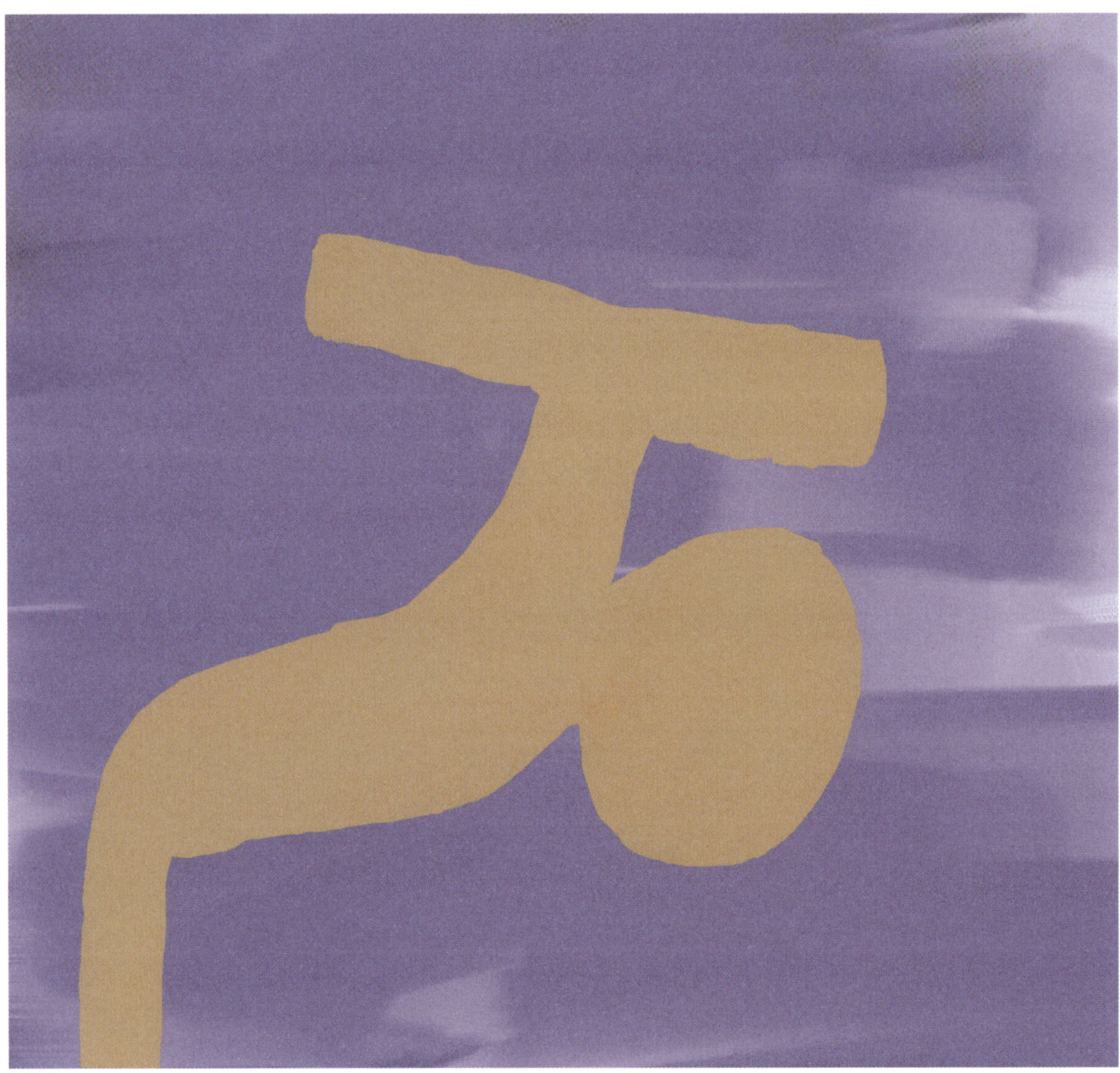

2.

2. Then, totally intuitively, I added one lone shape, some sort of saddle with a limb, or protrusion. Maybe I should stop? I probably should have but then I thought, *Nope, don't know what it is yet.*

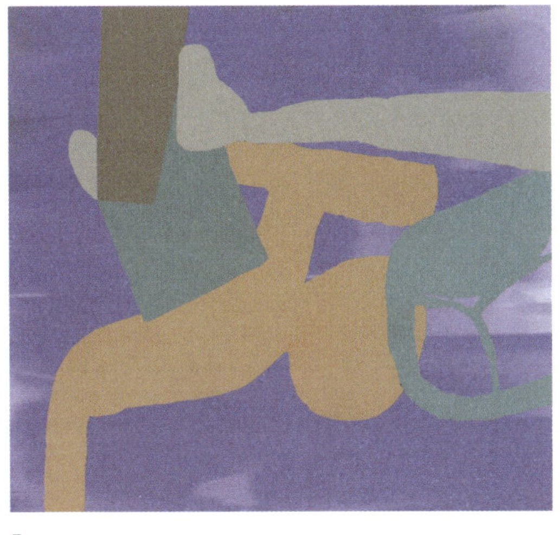

3.

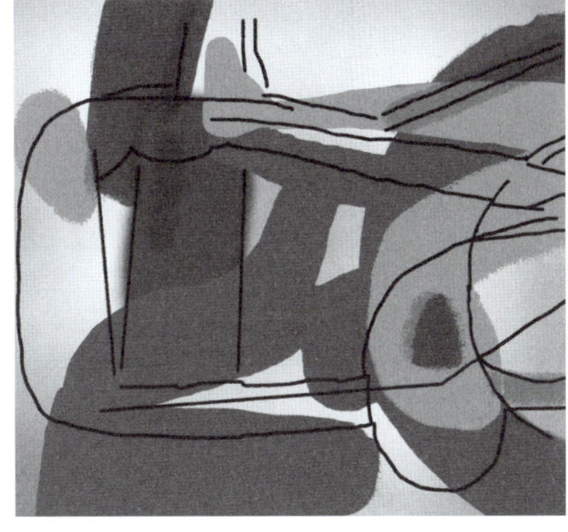

4.

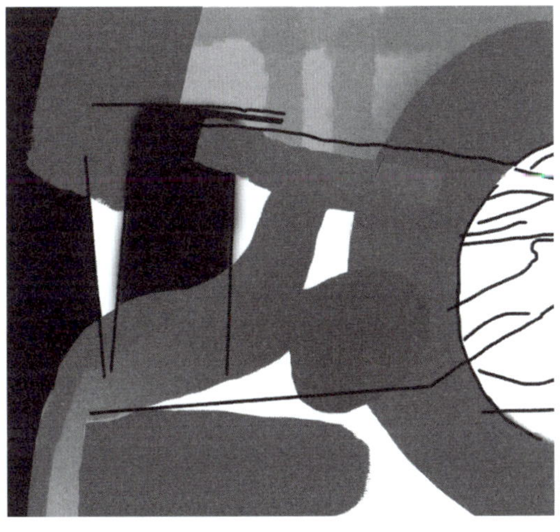

5.

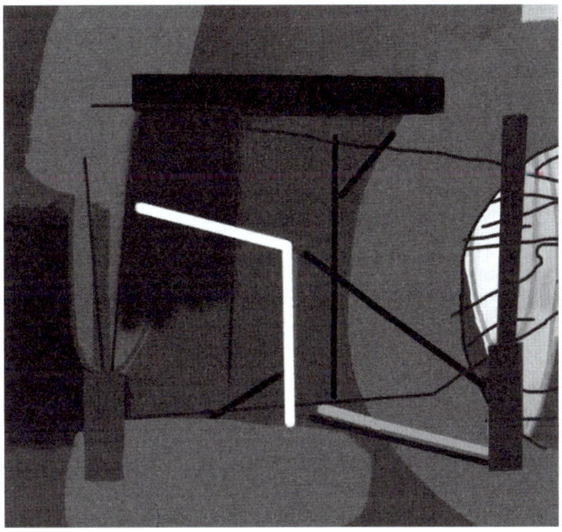

6.

3. Then came a pileup of beige, ochre, and blue-green shapes. I was trying to create a disequilibrium, an interruptive kind of jumble. I'm often aware of the instinct to paint a mark over the exact place where a brush mark begins.

4. Now there is a complicated bunch of shapes, but I need to clarify, so I add lines, which basically changes it from a shallow space with overlapping forms to a flattened linear diagram.

5. I continue trying to both clarify and complicate the whole thing, to heighten contradictions, and also to add color. So now we're off to the races, with space, line, and color all contradicting each other. I'm building up the painting's terms.

6. Many days go by where I'm flipping it upside down, and back again, adding lines and taking them out, and now I'm thinking, *Hmm, now what? It's just confusing.* I'm still negotiating between the diagrammatic and the spatial . . . and it's still kind of a mess.

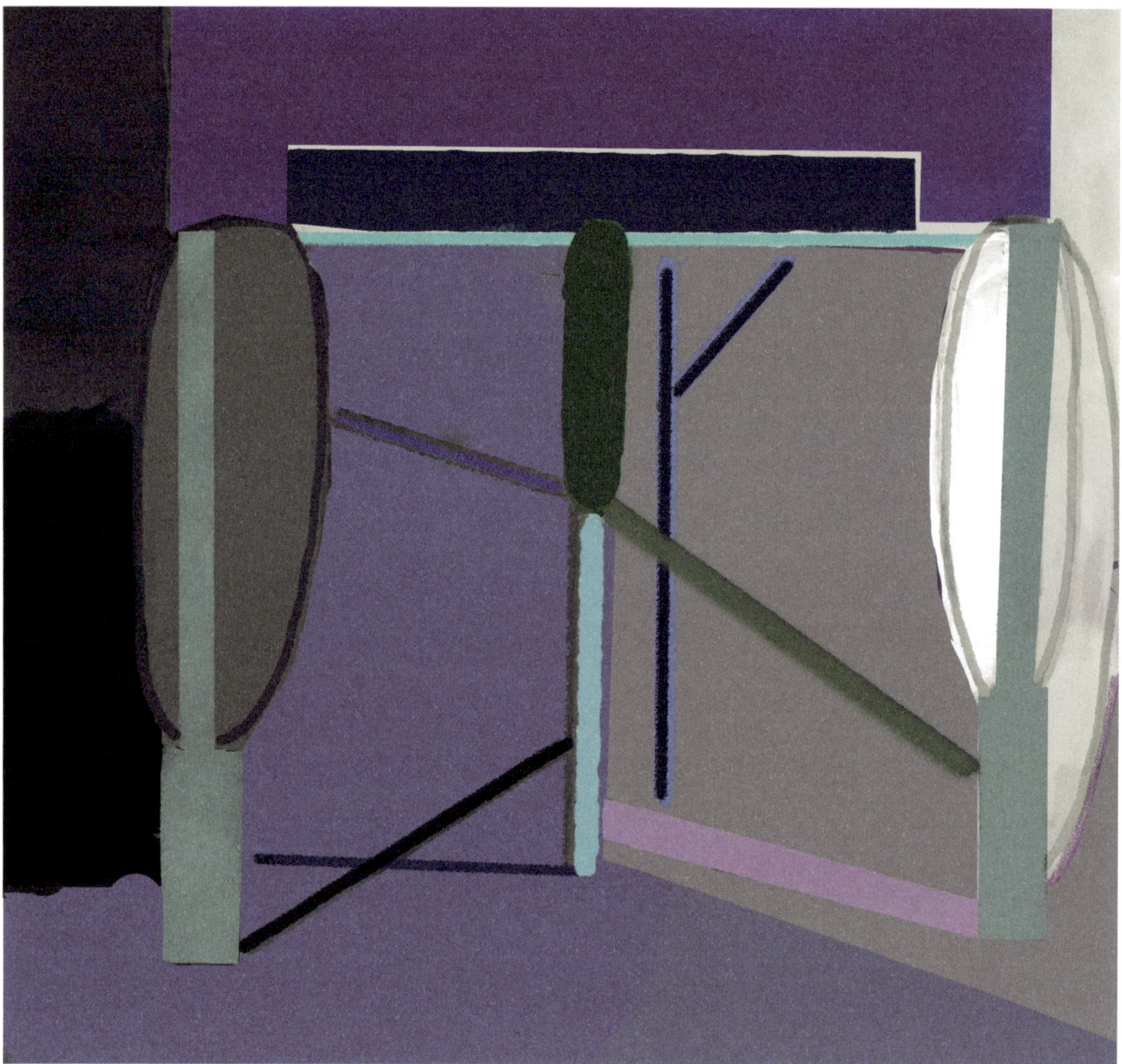

7.

7. I simplify the palette, there's a new gray-brown tonal ground with warmer, brighter colors up front. It has a kind of clockface in the center between two "trees." The painting feels emptier, and cleaner. The colors move around over the next few weeks.

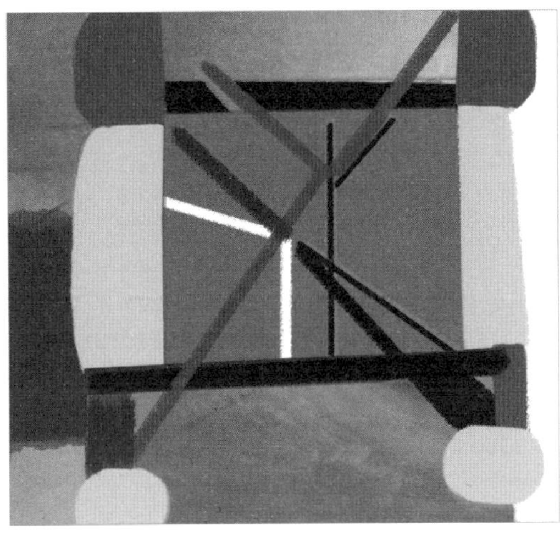

8.

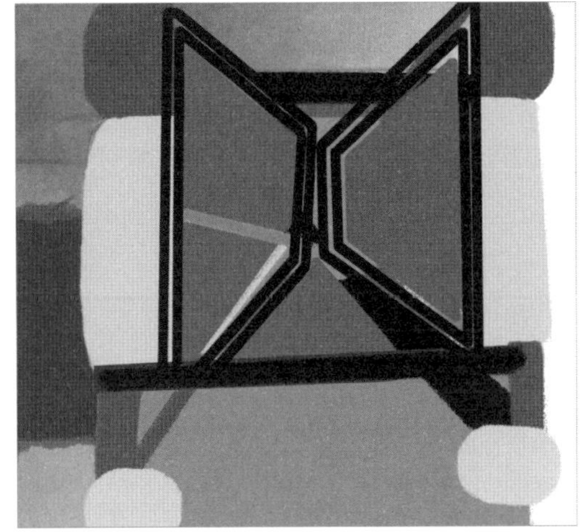

9.

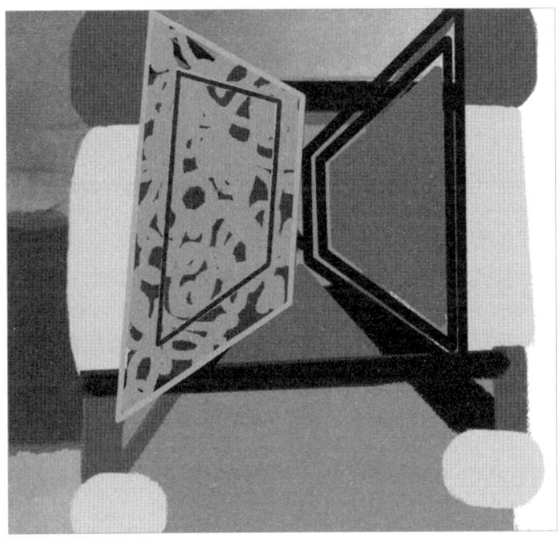

10.

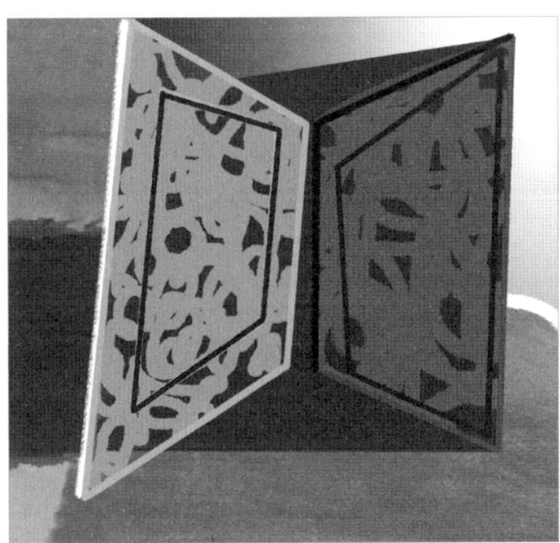

11.

8. At some point it turns into a valedictory kind of image, like a flag or Girl Scout medal, and I think, *I like it! Maybe I should stop!* I probably should have, but then I thought, *Nope. I don't know what it is yet.*

9. Then I get really angry at it. It's so flat, and I don't want it to be, so I'm trying to figure out how to make the space more dynamic, to squeeze it vertically or expand it horizontally. Some orthogonal lines are drawn on top, like window shutters, making the space perspectival.

10. But then I think, *No that's terrible—too heavy-handed,* so I add a kind of decorative treatment that flattens it again, kind of a bow or X-shaped thing.

11. It starts to look like an opened book. I tilt it back and forth to test which way has more weight, but it's still not working.

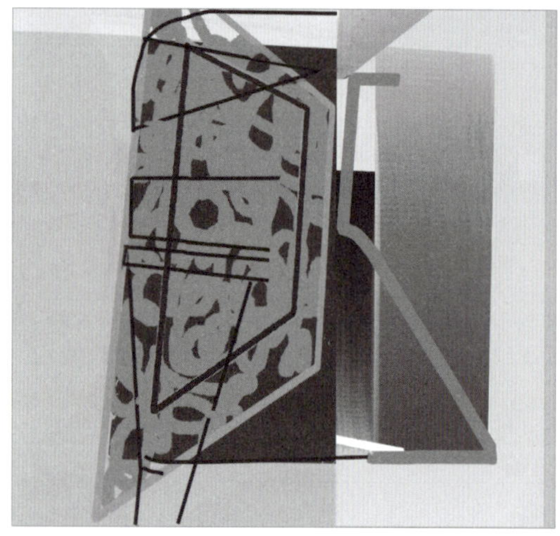

12.

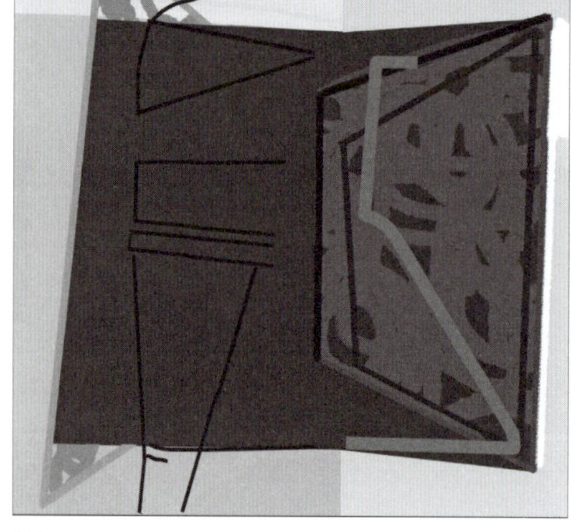

13.

14.

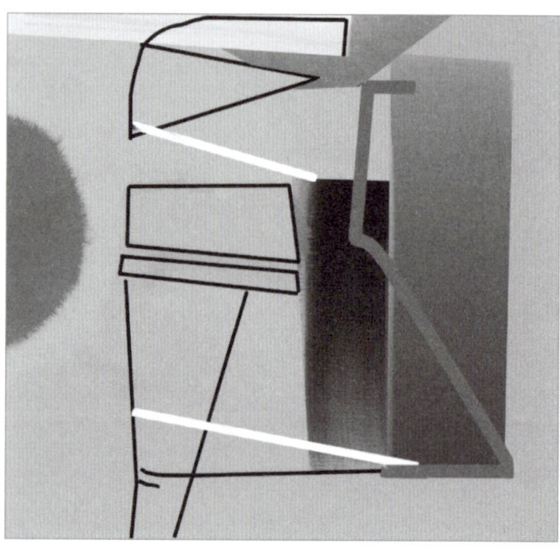

15.

12. I try painting the image in sideways to see if it works as an asymmetrical structure instead.

13. At this point I'm just fiddling with the painting's components, opacities, transparencies. I'm trying to work out the part-to-whole relations, and at the same time it's getting flatter and diagrammatic again.

14. At some point the parts aren't working, and I wipe a rather tormented purple field above it.

15. I somehow pull the flat linear forms forward from this murky ground again, and now it's got a stacked-up vertical on the left, like a diagram of a person. I'm also trying to balance the purple with a large green rectangle. It's like a Jenga game, finding a resolution between different parts and different colors.

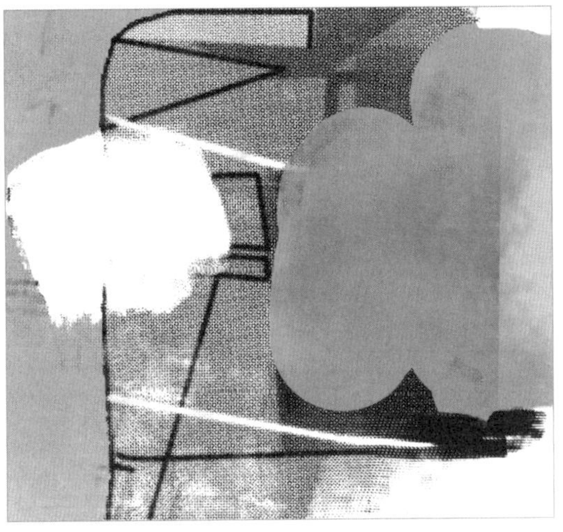

16.

17.

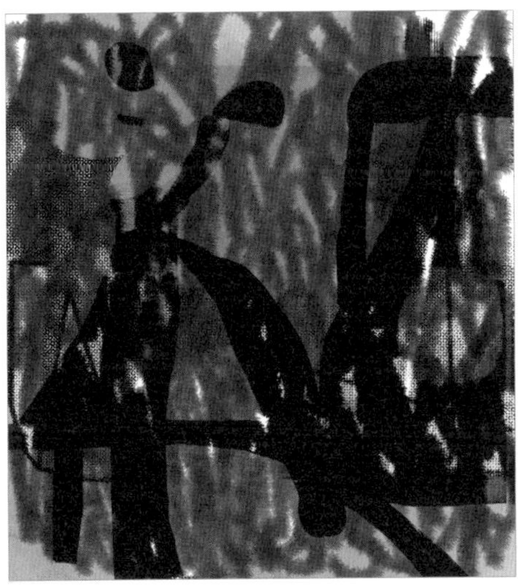

18.

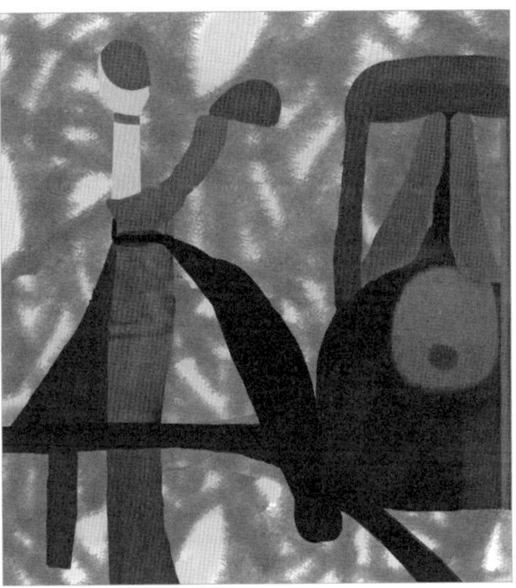

19.

16. Then I'm thinking, *Awful!* I wipe most of it out, put in some misty shapes and some patches to cover it. This painting has suffered a lot of wipeouts!

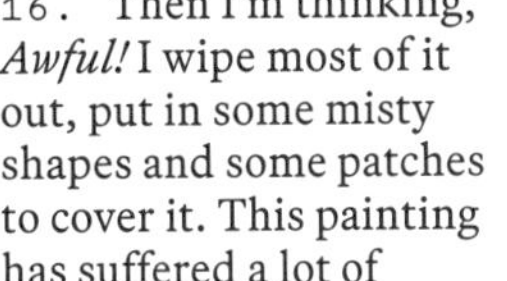

17. Then comes a total wipeout.

18. Then I turned it on its side vertically, and it got lost for a while. I don't have all the connecting images, but weeks go by with a series of desperate figure-ground maneuvers, figures that emerge and submerge continually into an allover fog.

19. Finally a pair of schematic figures stick, one on the left, a black silhouetted figure with a white head and neck, who was kind of waving or hailing the figure on the right, who was made like a kind of anthropomorphic object—a bottle with a kind of boob, with a nipple.

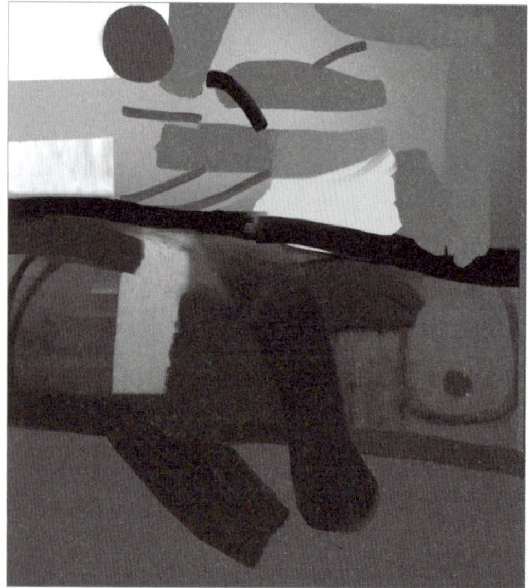

20.

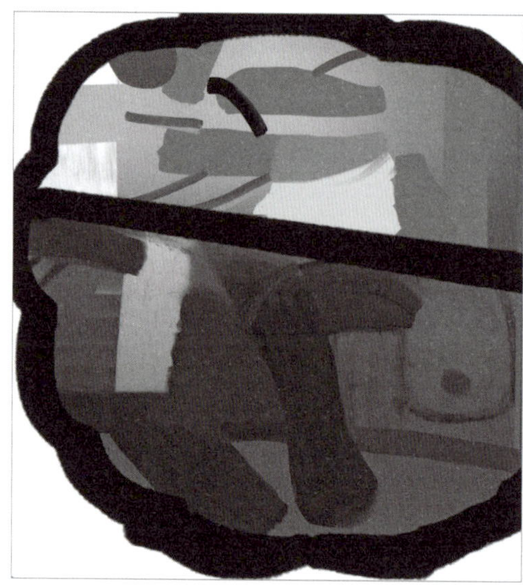

21.

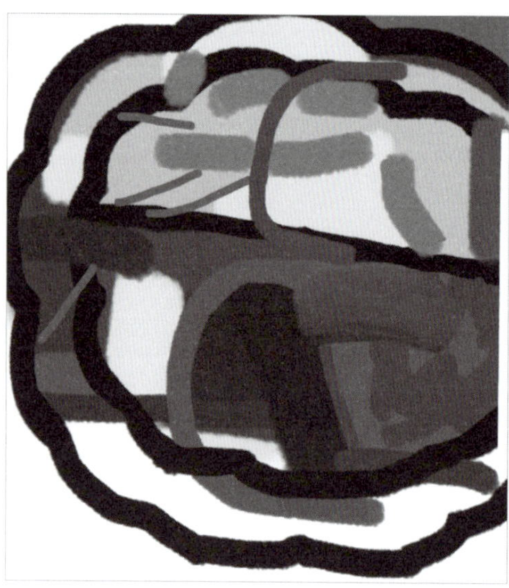

22.

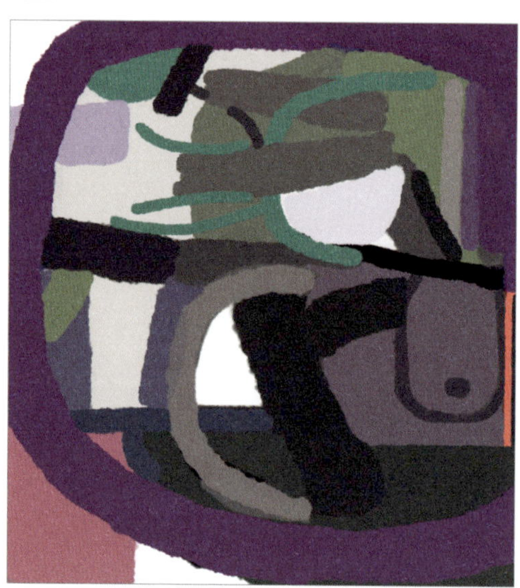

23.

20. The painting was flip-flopping between figures, and erasures. But I needed to steer it back to being a painting, not a diagram, so I dragged a big dirty fabric horizontally across it to energize the surface.

21. After mucking around between figure and structure for such a long time, I started worrying, *What should I do with the edges?* So I superimposed a diagram over the top, made of big arcs. At this point I was surprised in a good way, and probably should have left it, but instead I started fiddling around with the colors.

22. I was only adjusting colors and tones at this point, pulling ground tones out from underneath so the various blocks of color felt like light coming through a structure.

23. I turned it sideways again, and again considered leaving it. It was a nice painting at this point.

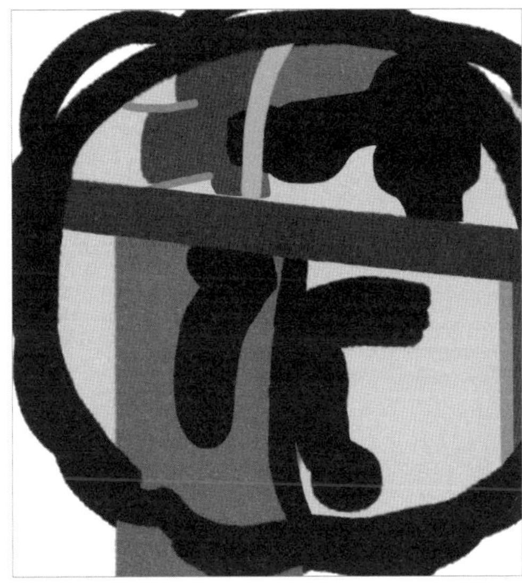

24.

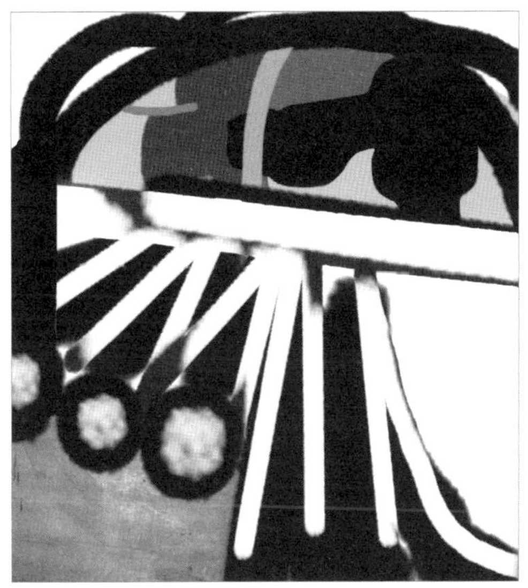

25.

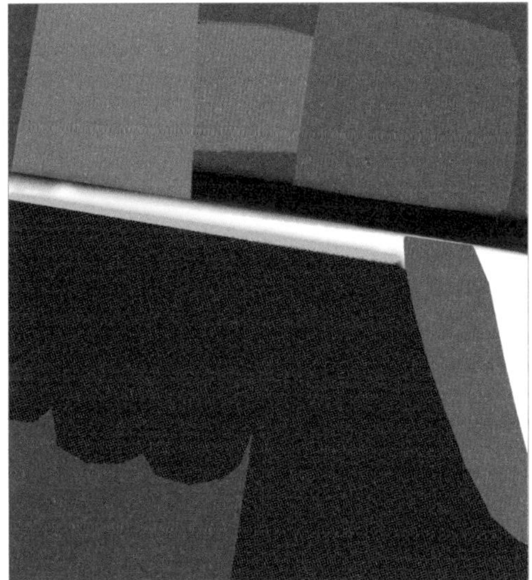

26.

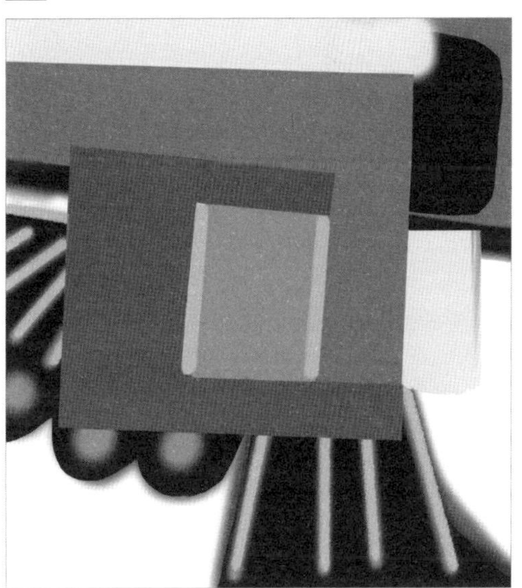

27.

24. But it kept evolving and went back to vertical. Now a border—versus interior structure—had been established, but I wanted to find the body again, something with some gravity. It went back and forth repeatedly until pendulous forms started to appear, like limp body parts or a droopy nose or spout.

25. Then things got complicated and went awry. The painting took a detour, and a pattern appeared at the bottom, like an awning or fringe hanging from a machine. The whole painting veered into confusing territory, and I realized I needed to make a big gesture, and deal with scale.

26. So I eliminated some narrative frippery and enlarged the geometry and colors into blocks.

27. The underlying narrative receded, and the color blocks took precedence.

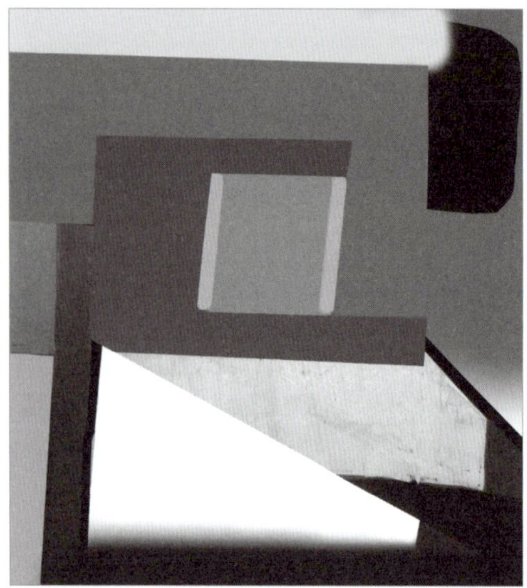

28.

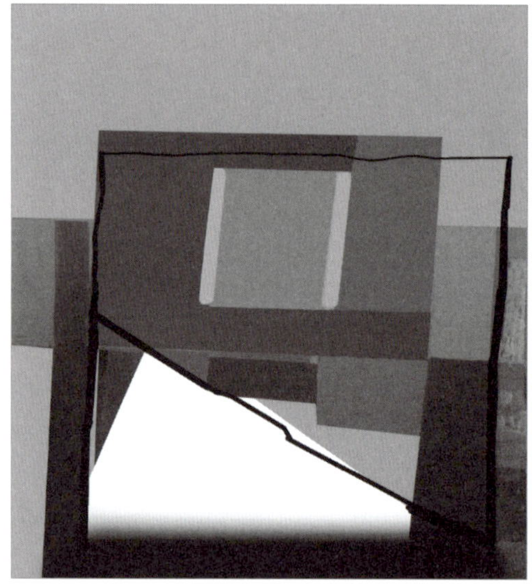

29.

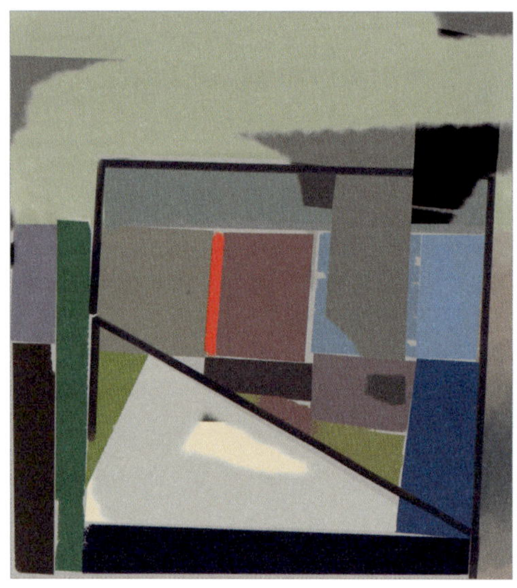

30.

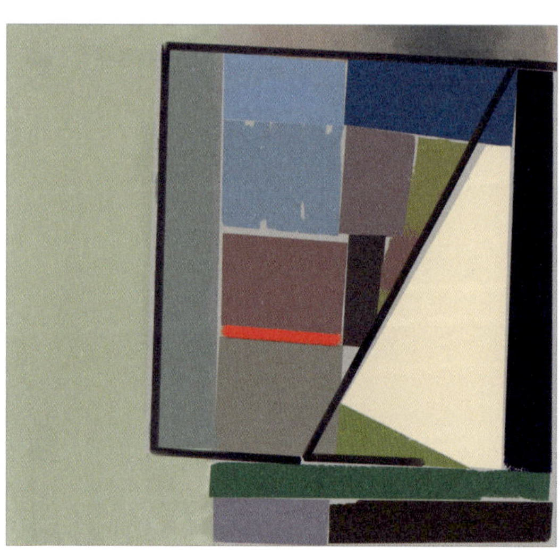

31.

28. Eventually a white triangle appeared and made the whole situation seem a bit unstable, like it was sitting on a seesaw or an unstable blade.

29. The white below made the upper part need more empty space, so I got rid of the top, and left it empty like a sky, and organized the shapes below into a kind of signpost or goalpost structure, something you could imagine passing under or through. The white triangle became its own form.

30. The grid kind of opened up. Air came into it.

31. I kept turning the painting from horizontal to vertical, and the white triangle became different things, from an empty plane of space to a sailboat going out of the picture to the right.

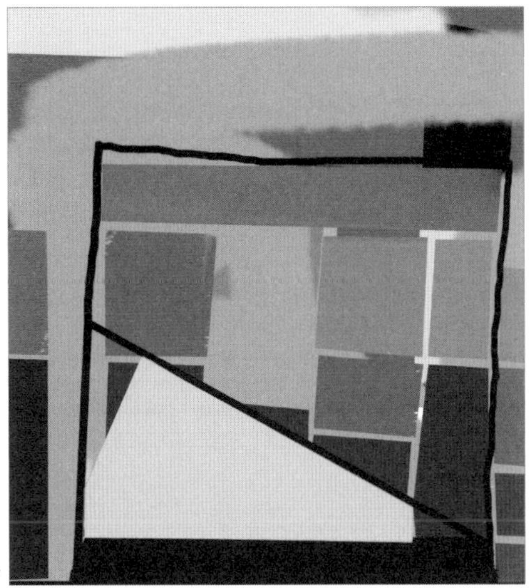

32.

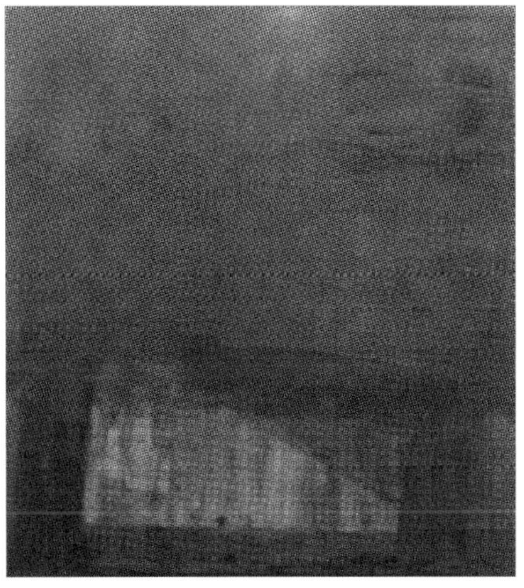

33.

34.

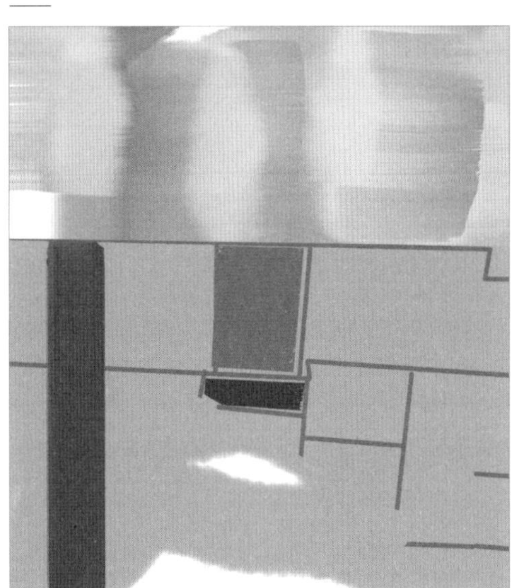

35.

32. I kept moving it around for a couple weeks, and started to get mad again, because I was getting tired of this endless indeterminacy—I flirted with wiping it out entirely again, but instead pulled a kind of fog around inside it.

33. I got mad again and covered the whole thing with a gray scrim that descended downward. Everything that had happened up till now was about to be wiped out, and I knew that I was getting to the point where it would soon be too late and I would lose whatever light was in the painting once and for all.

34. So I clarified the sky tone again, to rescue the light and regain some of the space. It was still a kind of shadowy mess, but there was a structure underneath again, below the cloud.

35. Then the weather kind of cleared up, the painting opened up again, and I found this tattered structure visible in it again, like a single post with a laundry line strung across it. I liked it.

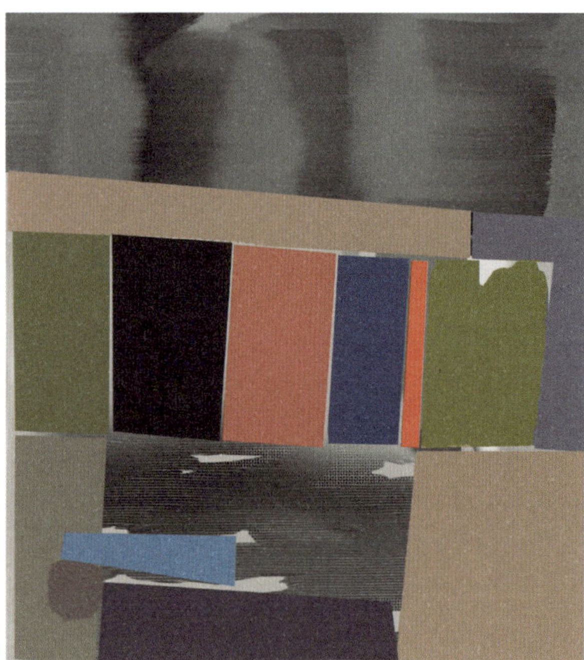

36.

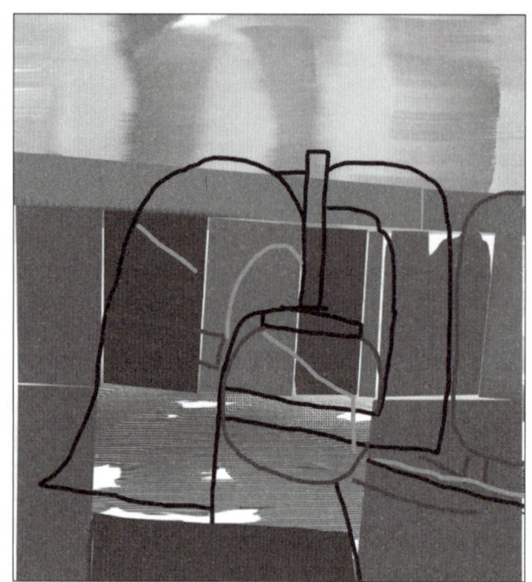

37.

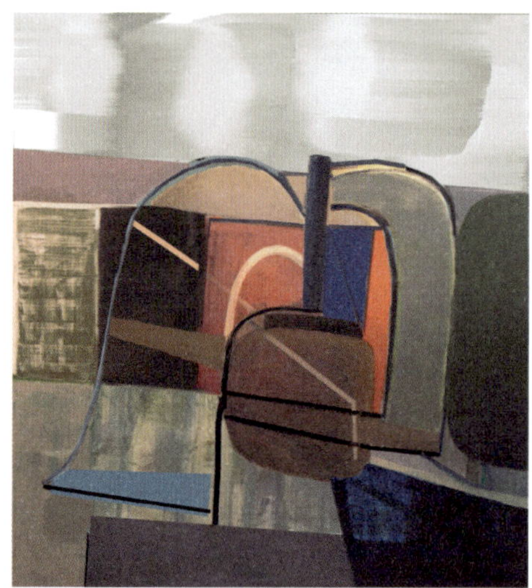

38.

36. I continued by adding a sequence of colors, like flags, that moved across the space in a horizontal line, each marked by difference to whatever was next to it: a cool, then a warm, then a dull scuffed color, etc., all hanging like sheets on a line.

37. I was thinking, *I've got to be done soon.* So I made the color blocks become a ground by imposing a drawing of a single figure-ish form on top, an object, a body like an apple or a teakettle, a torso with a kind of tilt, leaning over and down to the lower right side of the painting.

38. I clarified the teakettle body as the central figure, which comes up from the lower right and has a structure, like a sculpture on a pedestal, with some logic and some weight. On the right, it leans up against a dark green oval; on its left side it's more open, like a bell shape hanging in space. I liked it, and that was it.

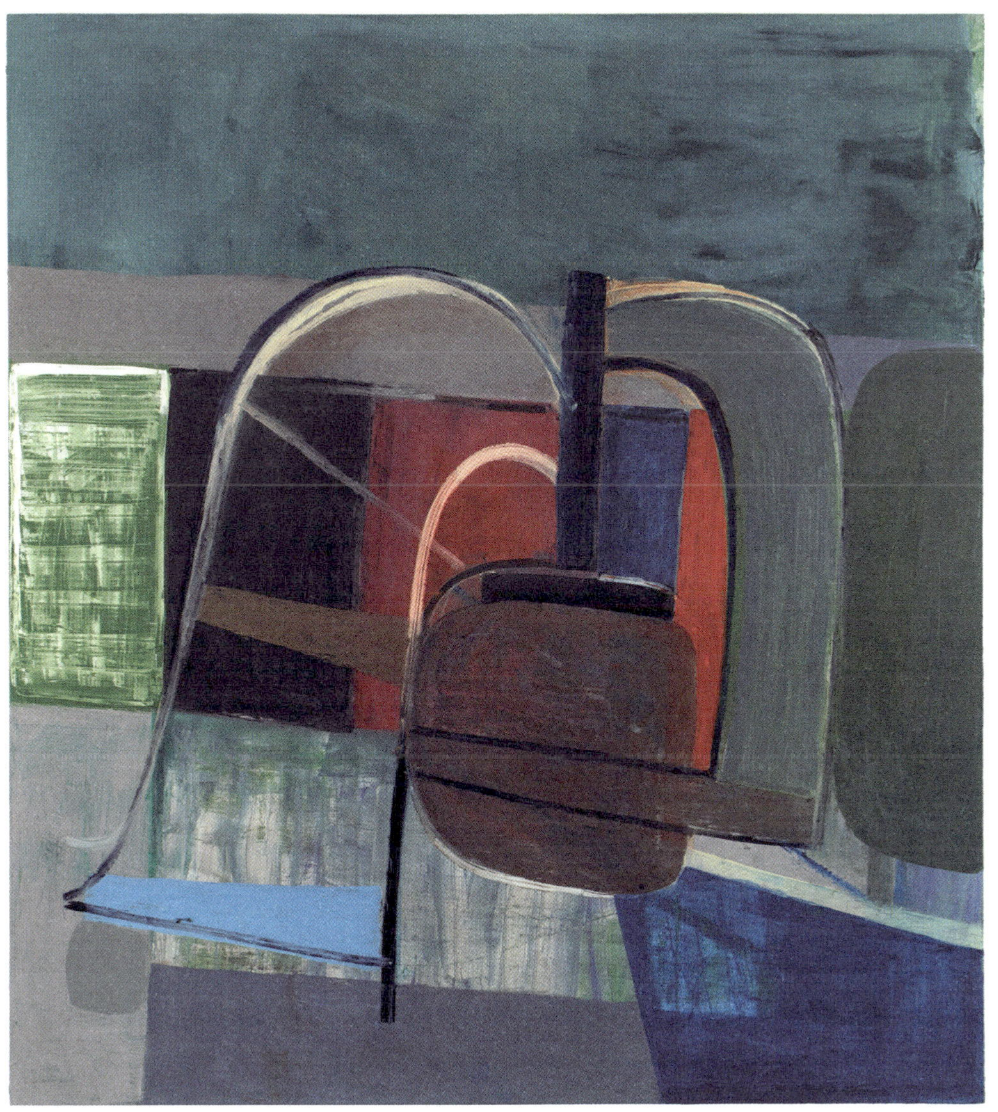

39. Amy Sillman, *Miss Gleason*, 2014. Oil on canvas, 91 × 84 in. Collection of Museum of Contemporary Art, Los Angeles. Courtesy of the artist.

39. I gave it a name, *Miss Gleason* (a private joke about a girl's name). I think the painting is a portrait of a girl. I figured out a space for the girl, and it was done.

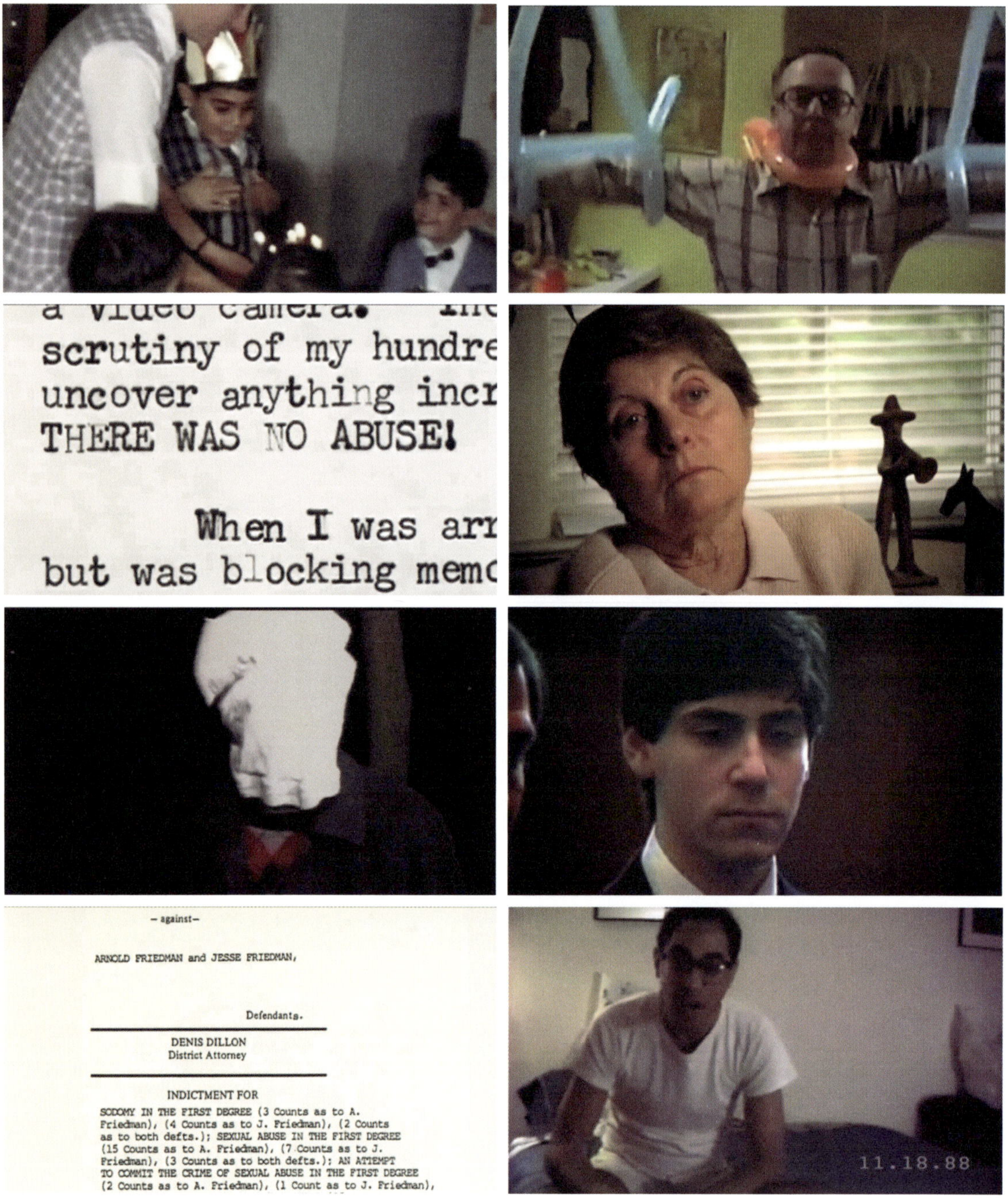

a video camera. The
scrutiny of my hundre
uncover anything incr
THERE WAS NO ABUSE!

When I was arr
but was blocking memo

—against—

ARNOLD FRIEDMAN and JESSE FRIEDMAN,

Defendants.

DENIS DILLON
District Attorney

INDICTMENT FOR

SODOMY IN THE FIRST DEGREE (3 Counts as to A. Friedman), (4 Counts as to J. Friedman), (2 Counts as to both defts.); SEXUAL ABUSE IN THE FIRST DEGREE (15 Counts as to A. Friedman), (7 Counts as to J. Friedman), (3 Counts as to both defts.); AN ATTEMPT TO COMMIT THE CRIME OF SEXUAL ABUSE IN THE FIRST DEGREE (2 Counts as to A. Friedman), (1 Count as to J. Friedman),

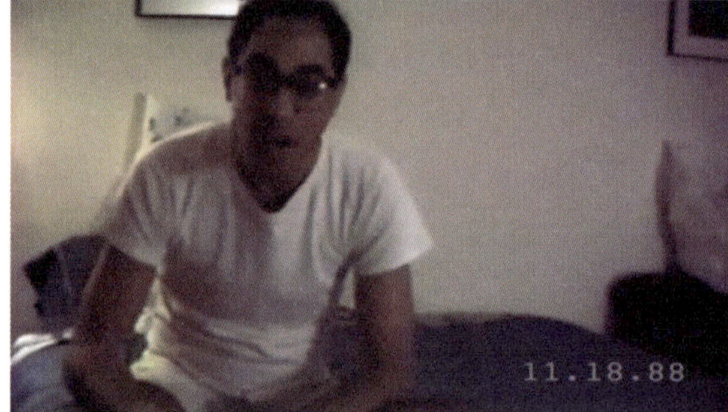

Scenes from *Capturing the Friedmans*. On right, top to bottom, the family: Arnold, Elaine, Jesse, David: "If you're the fucking cops, go fuck yourselves."

25

ANDREW JARECKI

Conjurer Extraordinaire

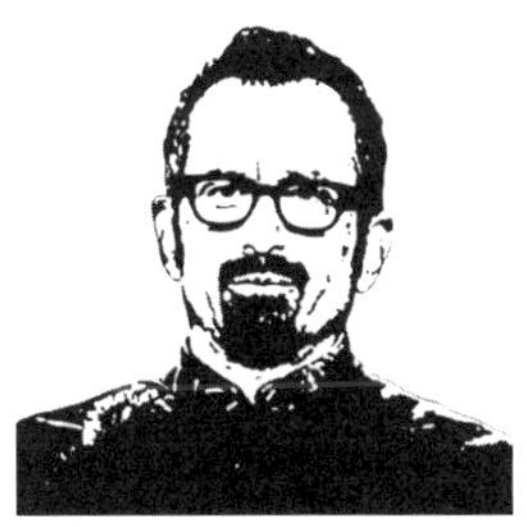

OCCUPATION: Documentary Filmmaker

WORK DISCUSSED: *Capturing the Friedmans* (2003)

BORN: 1963

ACCIDENTS FIGURE HEAVILY in the history of art. Still, it's a little difficult to believe that the brutal documentary classic *Capturing the Friedmans*, which I'd come to Andrew Jarecki to talk about, began its life as a movie about party clowns. Also that this complex, prismatic film was made by a novice, one whose central résumé item was that he was a tech entrepreneur millionaire. Sometimes fate really works like that. And when it does, considerations of the role luck plays in creation inevitably surface. But luck is usually earned, as it was in this case. And then the more interesting part is what follows it.

Andrew Jarecki is the son of a psychiatrist who wound up hugely successful in the gold business. His mother was a cultural critic. Jarecki was torn between business and art. He went to Princeton, toyed with going to drama school, and ended up in the family gold business, while also making a short film that was shown at Sundance ("If there's one thing that's the most 'me' thing," he said, "it's probably bridging these worlds"). Then, after observing how the process of figuring out movie showtimes and buying tickets was begging for disruption, he invented Moviefone, which allowed customers to use the phone and eventually the computer to purchase tickets. His timing was excellent: Moviefone was developed just before internet ubiquity but succeeded in time for Jarecki to sell it to AOL and make his own fortune.[1]

That's when he began a movie about clowns who entertain children at birthday parties, a project he'd mostly devised to teach himself how to make a full-length film. And this is what happened: a little while into the filming of the movie, Jarecki stumbled on a secret concerning one of those clowns, an entertainer called Silly Billy, whose real name was David Friedman. David's father, a math teacher named Arnold Friedman, had been arrested for allegedly raping

1. Jarecki said that what made him successful in business was that he didn't want to be seen as "another idiot son of a rich guy," so he prepared more, worked harder, etc. When he self-financed this movie, he was driven by the same fear of being branded a rich dilettante. "I knew how ridiculous it would look if I funded my own film and it was bad. I had to be swinging with two bats all the time."

young boys who attended the computer class he gave in his basement. David's brother Jesse was also arrested, accused of aiding in the alleged rapes. Jarecki abandoned the clown movie and made a child abuse movie instead.

Capturing the Friedmans revisits the alleged rapes, pitting one account against another. It documents the devastating impact the case had on David's family, as the Friedman children rally around their father and turn against their mother. It explores the forces unleashed in the town where they lived—Great Neck, Long Island—as the villagers became a modern lynch mob.

Because Arnold and Jesse were both convicted, and Jarecki didn't trust the verdict, the movie, in effect, retries the case, but *Capturing the Friedmans* is not really a true-crime documentary. It is a psychological swampland, and a marvelously complicated film. Truth is elusive, accounts are contradicted. "People are disturbed by ambiguity," Jarecki told me, and he built his movie around that discomfort. Its themes, which include our need to confess, tell secrets, and be seen, feel prescient for a movie made, as this was, at the beginning of the twenty-first century, before the Kardashians and social media. The film artfully weaves in some extraordinary footage from the Friedmans' home movies, turning its focus from the crime narrative to family trauma. It unspools with patience, one story layered on the next. It's the first documentary where I ever noticed a filmmaker successfully developing themes, principally around familial obliteration, I'd appreciated in other art forms. (Arthur Miller might have told this story.) But it was not the movie Andrew Jarecki thought he was making.

"I started out in one place," Jarecki said, "and everything changed."

ANDREW JARECKI: In 1999, when I sold the business, I immediately started thinking about making a film. I'd made one short, and I wanted something bite-size that would get my feet wet. Something really simple. I met a weird guy in a New York restaurant who was doing balloon twisting for kids, and he explained to me that there was a little culture of children's birthday party entertainers who were all friends.[2] Silly Billy was the number-one guy, and he was friends with Princess Priscilla and Professor Potter and Wacky Wendy, the paper plate lady. I thought, *These are people who live among children and haven't totally*

The Children's Entertainer Project

The Children's Entertainer Project is the working title of a documentary film whose mission is to explore the hidden artistry in the world of people who entertain children. While there are tens of thousands of Children's Entertainers in this country, from traditional balloon sculptors, magicians, and clowns, to one-of-a-kind artists and variety performers, this is a segment of the artistic community that has traditionally been overlooked by the media. As a result, the best performers across the country often are known only in their own geographic areas, and only through word-of-mouth and local press.

We are currently researching and shooting our subject, which began production in mid-2000. The finished film will be submitted to domestic and international film festivals that welcome documentary submissions, and other documentary outlets such as PBS and HBO.

The original pitch for the clown movie, before it became *Capturing the Friedmans*.

grown up yet, this could be a really interesting, weird story. I bet if I work on this, something will happen.

After a few months, I had still not reached out to Silly Billy. I was waiting, because if you're wealthy and you want your daughter to have a nice birthday party, he's who your assistant's assistant's going to call. And he's going to come over and do a show that'll be great for adults, because he's full of sarcasm and kind of a dark character to begin with, but maybe the kids are going to start crying, which is what happens at a lot of his shows. I thought, *I'll call him last*. When I reached him, he said, "Well, it's not much of a film if I'm not in it, now is it?" I'm thinking, *This is so great*. He's selling me hard on being New York's king clown, so I start filming him. There was a great editor I had met—Nancy Baker's her name—I started showing her the footage. And she said, "I kept asking myself, *What makes this clown so angry?*"

It was just such a clarification of what I'd been feeling. I thought, *All right, maybe this guy is going to be my film, I don't know*. So I kept going—meeting with him and meeting with other people. And he started dropping all these little weird hints. He would say, "You know I really don't want to talk about my father. He was a good father, I don't want to talk about it." And then he would say the most hateful things about his mother—"My mother is an idiot, my mother is sexually immature."

I remember thinking, *I've got to find out what's going on with Silly Billy's mom*. I had asked him a number of times if I could talk to his mother, and he always rebuffed me: "Absolutely not," he said, "she's going to say crazy things." Which obviously piqued my interest. As it happened, [Silly Billy] had been on *Candid Camera* as a kid, which was a real big deal, it was maybe the most popular show in America. And so I had gotten a copy of it, but in it he was running around playing with Christmas presents and it was boring. I'd put it to the side.

Silly Billy—David Friedman was his real name—calls me one day. He says, "You keep bugging me about talking to my mother. I never saw that episode of *Candid Camera* I was on. If you could use your filmmaker magic to get me a copy of that episode, I'll let you talk to my mother." I didn't tell him I had it already.

So I called Elaine, David's mother. I said, "You know David has arranged for me to come see you." She said, "Yes, I know." I said, "I just want to make sure you're comfortable." She said, "Well, to tell you the truth I'm not." And she went on, "I had a bad experience with a filming. People said it was going to go one way, but it went another. And it was very upsetting." I said, "Look, I don't think it's going to be the same. What was that, a motion picture?" And she said, "No, that was a television show. It was something called *Geraldo*."[3] I thought, *Oh, that's interesting*.

I get to her house. She says, "You follow me." In the back of the house, there's a tiny office with a little sofa and a desk. She says, "Put your camera there. Andrew, you sit there. I'll be back in a little while."

And on the writing table is a blotter. Facing me is a letter, a handwritten letter from her, ostensibly to some newspaper—a letter to the editor. But it had clearly never been sent. It said, "A deeply religious person, I was brought up in the Jewish faith to believe that truth and justice were the most important things. Truth and justice were never part of this case."

She comes back in, and we talk as if she hasn't led me to this document. The interview is largely in the film. We talk again the next morning. She says, "I don't really want to talk about his father because, you know, we were divorced." And when I say to her, "I hear from David and from your other sons, they've got these negative things to say about you, but they're glowing about your ex-husband," she says, "You know, it's classic that children side with the abusive parent. But we're not going to be talking about the Friedman case."

2. When Jarecki himself was twelve, he set up a little business as a magician and would work kids' parties. That propelled his interest in the clown film, but also tells you a lot about who he was at an early age. His business card read "Conjurer extraordinaire."

3. *Geraldo* was a tabloid program hosted by Geraldo Rivera, suggesting that there was something tawdry at play to motivate Rivera's interest.

That was all. She'd clearly been admonished by David—a filmmaker's coming, ixnay on anything other than I was a wonderful child. But she was dying to talk about her life.

So I call my assistant from the car, say, "Look up the Friedman case, 1980s, in LexisNexis."[4] She does, says, "You've got to pull over. I'm going to read you something."

—

A Secret Life The assistant read Jarecki a cover story from the Long Island newspaper *Newsday* called "The Secret Life of Arnold Friedman." It was the "most salacious, shocking thing," Jarecki recalled; the story reported that "hundreds of kids were raped in the house"—in the basement—by David's father, Arnold.

Jarecki was stunned. "I wondered how to go back to David to talk about this. At one point earlier he had said to me, after I probed a little bit about some of what he was saying, 'Oh you're a smart guy, you could figure it out.' So when I went back to him, I told him I figured it out. And he said, '*Uh-oh.*'"

Ultimately, Jarecki persuaded David to participate. Jarecki had read enough about mass hysteria in child abuse cases that he didn't necessarily believe the charge, and convinced David it was in his interest to tell him the story rather than risk exposure from a less sympathetic storyteller. This was both true and somewhat disingenuous.

"And little by little, he started to—I don't want to say warm to it—but he said, 'I know that subconsciously I want to tell this story. But I'm telling you, my conscious mind knows that this is not good for the clown business.' Still, David said he might cooperate, if it would help his brother Jesse get out of prison. And then he said this: 'I should tell you if you're thinking about this being your film, that I got a video camera shortly before the cops came to my house. So starting when the police came to my house that night and everything changed, I recorded the family falling apart. And I have twenty-three hours of video from that period.' I just thought, well that's going to change everything. That brings a whole new dimension to things. And I realized it was going to take a number of years to do right."

So, luck. Preposterous luck. The discovery of the story first, and very significantly, the footage later, made it clear to Jarecki that there was an extraordinary movie to be made, even if he did not have the experience to make it.[5] Jarecki did not lack confidence, or wiles. Little by little, eventually, he won the cooperation of nearly everyone he might need for his story—Elaine, Jesse, the detectives (for whom this was the biggest prosecution of their careers), some of the children who had made the accusations, pretty much every principal except one of the Friedman brothers. Ultimately, everybody talked, each for his own reason: "Everybody had a secret. Everybody wanted to tell me the secret, but didn't want me to tell the secret to anybody else.

"And so," said Jarecki, "the picture started to evolve."

Layers Jarecki set to work as both investigator and artist, not traits that usually coexist in the same person, but that might have something to do with being brought up in the vortex of business and art, logic and intuition. He proved a relentless, effective interrogator.[6] And then, armed with the epically clashing stories he was collecting, the telling of the story, by his account, seemed obvious. He and his editor Richard Hankin played the opposing versions against one another, over and over, which became the spine of the film. "When I first met with Fran Galasso, the detective, I asked her the most memorable thing about the case. And she said, 'I guess it was the fact there were foot-high stacks of child pornography in plain view.'" It wasn't until months later, when the records department sent Jarecki the stack of Instamatic photographs the police

4. Database of documents, articles, info of many kinds.

5. Jarecki had been working on the movie for a year at this point, shot hundreds of hours of film. But he was very happy to throw all that away. (He did make a little version of it, that appears as a DVD extra with *Capturing the Friedmans*.) It reminded me of the principle of "sunk cost" in creative work—that you just have to be ruthless with what you've already done in order to make something better.

6. I asked Jarecki what his business and film success had in common. He said, "I don't know if it's always a strength, but I just feel like I get myself into a mode where I don't hear the word *no*. It's elemental to my personality. In another life I would probably have been a stalker."

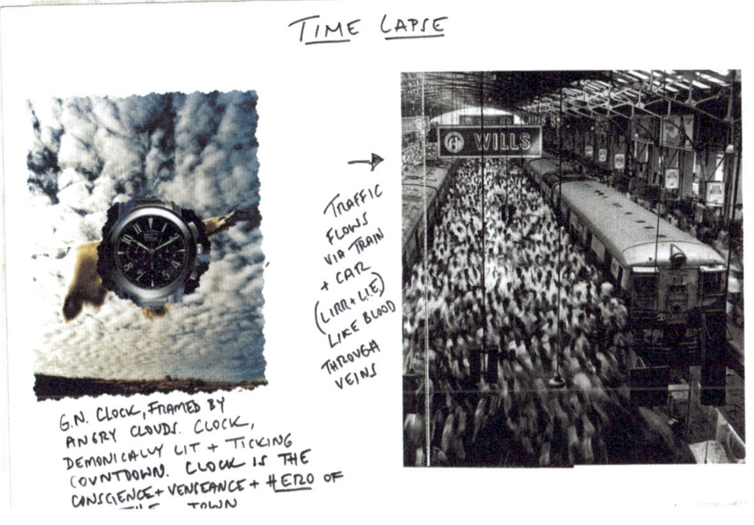

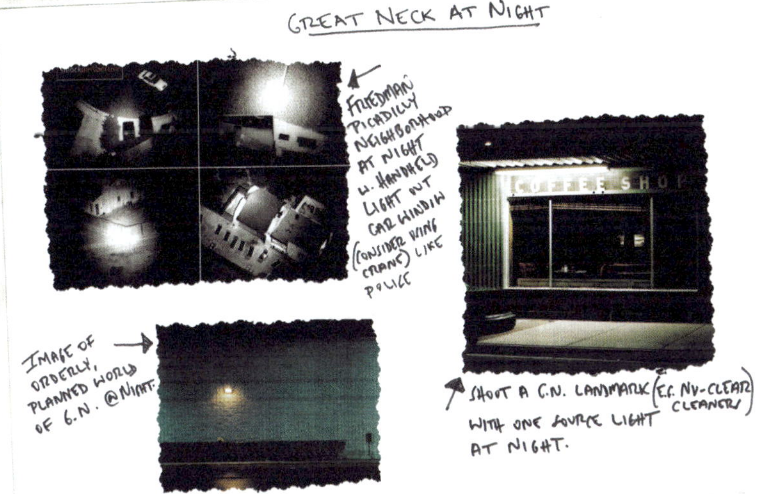

From Jarecki's collage board of metaphors...

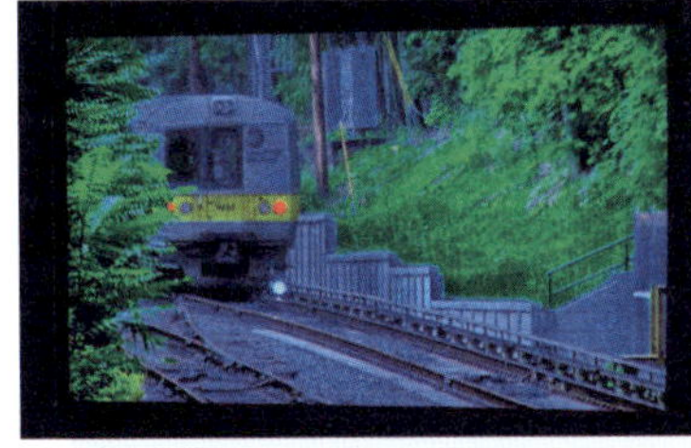

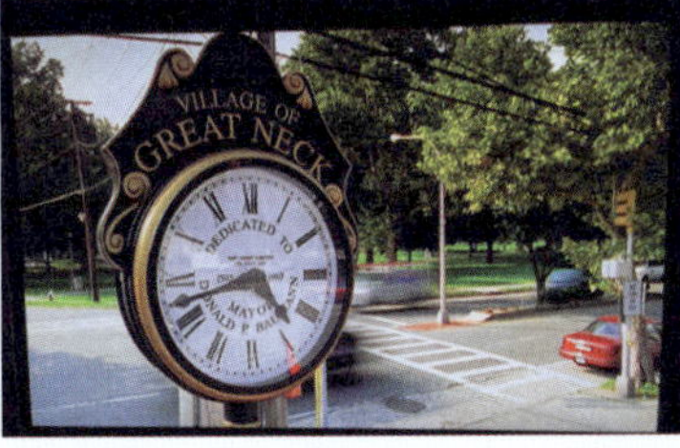

...and a couple of the images they became on film.

Andrew Jarecki didn't know much about how to make a movie like this, but he'd taken on a producing partner, a childhood friend, Marc Smerling, who was also a cinematographer. Smerling told him to go to a bookstore: "Find photography books, and as you flip through them, look for what speaks to you. And then just start tearing pages out or taking pictures of stuff and start collaging." That's what these are: mood boards, and excerpts from a memo to his visual staff to help him explain what he was seeing.

"Sometimes it sounds silly to talk through the metaphor," reads the memo, "but I had a strong feeling as I was driving through Great Neck, of it as a biological organism, with blood coursing through it, and community T cells coming in to eradicate the Friedmans, who were like an unfriendly virus. The trains were like arteries, bringing in nourishment to support the organism."

As he was ripping through the books, he saw a clock, and fixed on the threatening passage of time: "Jesse Friedman's life was in the process of being destroyed," said Jarecki, "and the community was saying we've got to eliminate him, right now. Every day Jesse would wake up and suddenly there was a second indictment and a third and accusations of hundreds of rapes. I wanted the viewer to feel anxiety. The Great Neck clock became very important."

took when they went to the Friedman house, that he saw there were "no foot-high stacks of anything, anywhere around the house." Then, he said, once you put those two things against each other, her account and the photographs, "it kind of tells you how you're going to tell the story."

But Jarecki was after more than building a case. He'd tripped on a narrative of almost unfathomable literary potential. He recognized its depths, even as he didn't know what to do with it. "It's a process," Jarecki said, of following a formula and then breaking the rule two seconds after you start.

I asked him whether he methodically plotted out how he was going to tell the story, because the telling was not at all straightforward. He did, but also thought the way his mind organized material might subvert the movie. "I remember writing an outline and then sitting with Richard and thinking, *Are you being a businessman about this? Are you cataloging things and trying to systematize something? Is this process going to get you what you want? Or is the process going to suck the life out of watching the film?* Writing it all down makes me feel less anxious," he said, but then the footage suggested its own path.

Jarecki was alert for metaphor, which turned out to be everywhere he and his editor looked. (A good editor, he said, is somebody who feels the material in an exaggerated way. When he's cutting something, he knows what emotional impact it's going to have.) "You go into the edit room, and you start talking about something like, what about the footage of the little girl in the ballerina costume?"—there's this seemingly irrelevant bit of a home movie, of a young girl (Arnold's sister when she was little) twirling on a roof—"what's up with that piece of footage, what does it mean? Well, I don't know. On the one hand, it's simple and beautiful, from a time before all these terrible things happened to the Friedmans. On the other hand, it's a grown man up on a roof with a little girl, and he's making her dance and filming it. It's innocent and guilty at the same time—voyeuristic; it makes you uncomfortable. So you kind of blow up your outline, and you start to wonder, Who's going to be talking under this footage, what kind of music is going to be under it?

"You look at sequence, courtroom testimony, moments—and then you just have this abstract figurative process of saying, *What feels right here? What's going to carry the emotional storyline while I'm here scrambling to make sure I make all my points?*"

To some extent, as often happens, once he was in motion, the elements seemed to fall into place on their own—he just needed to get out of the way. At one point, he was filming the main accuser sitting in a suggestive pose, the boy's hands drifting downward as if he were masturbating as he relayed his story of the assault, a piece of disturbing—and very effective—footage in the film.

"He is obviously a very troubled kid. And I almost fucked that scene up by asking him too many times to sit up. Because I'm thinking, all I want to do is make a good movie and I want it to look like a professional job. Eventually I'm thinking, *What am I doing? I'm supposed to be capturing reality here.* I didn't realize until later how much digging around in his pants he was doing because I was mostly looking at his face."

Jarecki rejected voiceovers and visual reenactments, which might have made telling the story easier. "I think you can do something more abstract and it gives room for the audience to bring their imagination to it." But the film is complicated, and he was looking for ways to pace it. He used plenty of footage of a playground in Great Neck. The ticking clock is an important theme (the case is hurried through the courts), and he found a clock in the town that helped him underline the point nonverbally (see page 255). And he hired a composer (two, actually; the first he fired because his score didn't work) to create underscoring orchestration that

7. One interesting note about the composer, Andrea Morricone. He created the fundamentals of the score right after a conversation with Jarecki, on a rooftop, without a piano or any other instrument. Composed it right out of his head. How does anybody do that?

heightens the film's operatic scope.[7]

Ultimately, what Jarecki was learning as investigator complicated his role as filmmaker. Because while he came to believe that the abuse in the basement never happened, he also concluded that Arnold was in fact a pedophile and had abused others. And took his innocent son Jesse down with him. Jarecki never says this outright in the film because nothing is said outright—many viewers would later report that they didn't know what to believe. But this point of view, with his growing belief that Jesse was the true victim of the story, undergirds the film.

Telling a Story Of all of Jarecki's decisions, the most important is the one declared in the very first beat. The film opens with home movie footage of Jesse introducing his father to the movie's audience (the home movie and now this one) with obvious adoration. Arnold beams, childlike. There's a brief snippet of Elaine, saying, "Let's face it, he liked pictures." Double meanings abound, as they tend to when you're looking for them. There's another quick slice of a home movie skit, with a little sign: WARNING THIS SHOW MAY BE HAZARDOUS FOR YOUR HEALTH. One portentous beat after another, all culled from the treasure of found footage. Soon he cuts to David squirming, saying there are some things about his father he doesn't want to discuss—a vestige of the clown film—which he then undercuts and punctuates with an excruciating snippet of a video diary David made after the arrest. In it, David tells whoever has found this footage to stop watching, this is private—adding, "If you're the fucking cops, go fuck yourselves." It's awful.

Jarecki arranged these five harrowing minutes to set out the film's themes and metathemes, and to tell the viewer that Jesse is the emotional center of the movie—pay the most attention to him. "We probably tried fifty other things," said Jarecki. "But the reason that opening worked is those are the stakes: What separates tragedy from melodrama is that there has to be something lost when a person is taken down. Arnold Friedman may be the tragic hero. But Jesse is the stakes. As for David, who cares about David? He's a very sad character, and he creates the momentum of the story. But at the end of the day, I'm not going to cry over anything having to do with David. It can't be a story about Arnold. It wasn't a good idea for Arnold to be the Pied Piper of Great Neck. And surely not a good idea to bring Jesse in as an assistant. Because once they knew Jesse was potentially an exculpatory witness, he had to become part of the problem, he had to be even more vicious than his father. Little by little, the viewer starts to feel a little outraged that they were taken in. And yet they're confounded, because at the core of it, Arnold is not necessarily a great person. I always say in the editing room, both things can be true. Arnold can be a wonderful teacher, even a good father, but he can also be a pedophile who destroyed his son's life."

The opening takes the entire byzantine saga and creates a hierarchy of sympathy, with Jarecki asserting Jesse's place as the film's principal character. We won't really meet Jesse again until the last third of the movie, after the case in all of its wobbliness has been relitigated on film. But in the end, the movie is not so much an indictment as it is a story about a very tragic, very fucked-up family, made up of people Jarecki got to know intimately.

At one point Seth, the brother who didn't participate, told Jarecki that he was destroying his family. Troubled, Jarecki went to see Robert Coles, a child psychiatrist and kind of ethics guru, for counsel. Coles gave him his benediction, told him he was doing the right thing. By the time Jarecki finished the film, he came to accept that his project had been mostly for the good, even as he was still beset by some ambivalence. "I felt all of it. I felt I had done right by them. In any case, I felt I had captured reality."

The film won the Grand Jury Prize at Sundance, was nominated for an Academy Award, and was (especially by documentary standards) a box office hit. Most critics praised the

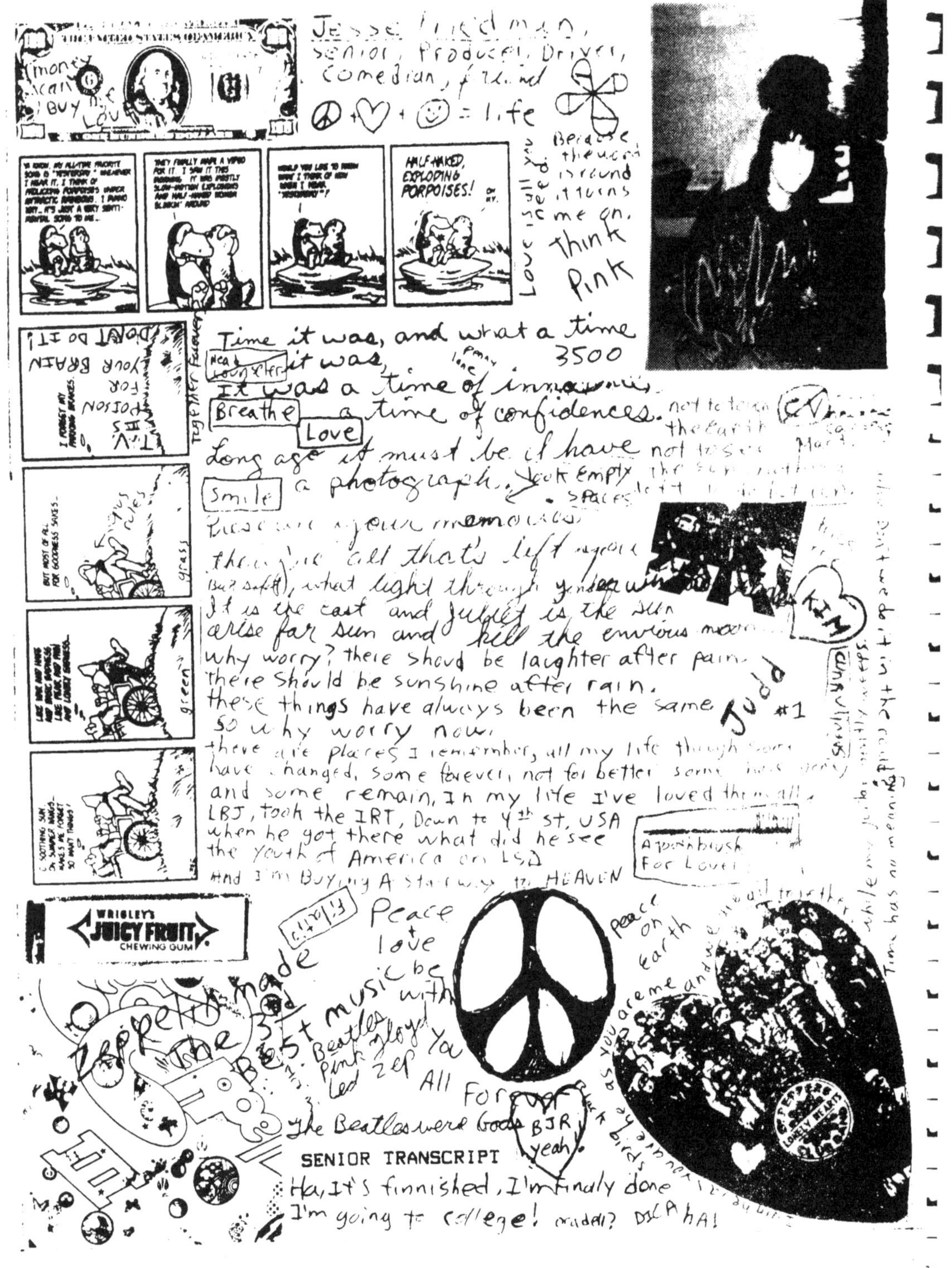

Jesse Friedman's yearbook page. Jarecki's belief in Jesse's innocence and, in a sense, though he never says so, his determination to save him, was the driver of this movie. Jarecki says that seeing this page was the ignition.

movie, although Jarecki later got some grief over elisions of testimony. Also, when it came out that Jarecki helped pay for Jesse's appeal, some felt that the movie's calibrated ambiguity was a con. Documentaries will always be vulnerable to criticism that the filmmaker distorted facts in the service of art, but still, I've watched the movie over and over, and it never ceases to astonish me.

Another Accident? Several years later, Jarecki engaged in another project requiring the subject to invest him with a trust that seems beyond comprehension. That was *The Jinx*, the HBO series investigating the role of real estate scion Robert Durst in the murder of two people, and the disappearance of a third. Durst was a pathological figure who agreed to talk after seeing a fictional movie Jarecki had made about Durst's life, called *All Good Things*, which Durst thought was fair. I won't go into details about that movie or the series, which could make its own chapter, but I'll offer here Jarecki's account of how he obtained Durst's confession in *The Jinx*, which would ultimately lead to Durst's arrest. Durst later died in prison (as did Arnold, by the way). The confession, which they discovered at the eleventh hour, came about this way:

"We were very far down the path of finishing the series. There's a terrific editor who I've worked with, and she's very thorough. We were cleaning up the audio so that we could finalize the footage, and she went to the scene that we had in the Regency Hotel conference room [where they were interrogating Durst with evidence that appeared to nail him]. Bob [Durst] was in the bathroom, and there were two microphones on the same track. My microphone and his. And there was a boom mic in the room, so there were a few microphones going on at the same time. In order for [the editor] to make it as crisp as possible, she's getting rid of all the extra junk. So you just remove the room noise, or whatever it is, and when she muted the two tracks, mine and the room track, she hears the door close in the bathroom. Before, all the tracks were mushed together. But when she has muted the other tracks, she hears him close the door and say to himself, 'There it is, you're caught.' And when she heard that, she just freaked out.

"Bob's in the bathroom for like seven or eight minutes, and they find another drive and there's all this noise on it. There's loud peeing sounds, there's toilet flushing, and you know, he says a dozen kind of amazing things. Shifting his perspective all the time, sometimes he's talking like Bob, sometimes like me, he's just kind of free-associating in there."

The series is very good and might have been successful without this audio, but with it, it was a sensation.

So again, luck? Once maybe, but this was ridiculous. You can't ignore the fact that Jarecki's work seems strewn with crazy, fortuitous accidents.

Still, Jarecki was built for this. His investigative logic and his supple emotional instincts lead him places. I asked Jarecki why people seem to tell him things. "I've always had a slightly overdeveloped sense of empathy," he said. "And I think Bob felt that, because it isn't fake. There are moments when I'm obviously arranging, manipulating—but my friendship with Bob was real. I guess you can fake empathy. But if you can see the good in people—Bob might have killed three people, but he always had a reason. There's an internal logic to Bob.

"And I have a good nose for when somebody has a story or when somebody is not sharing something. I have a bit of a spider sense for that. In the Friedman case, based on everything David was saying, I could feel in my bones that Elaine must be dying to talk about her life because he was treating her unfairly. I felt she felt unlistened to. People want to be seen. Wanting for their moment on earth to be recorded in some way. They want to know that they've made their mark."

This seems as good a place as any to say that luck is important in all feats of creation. But it's more like the predicate than the sentence.

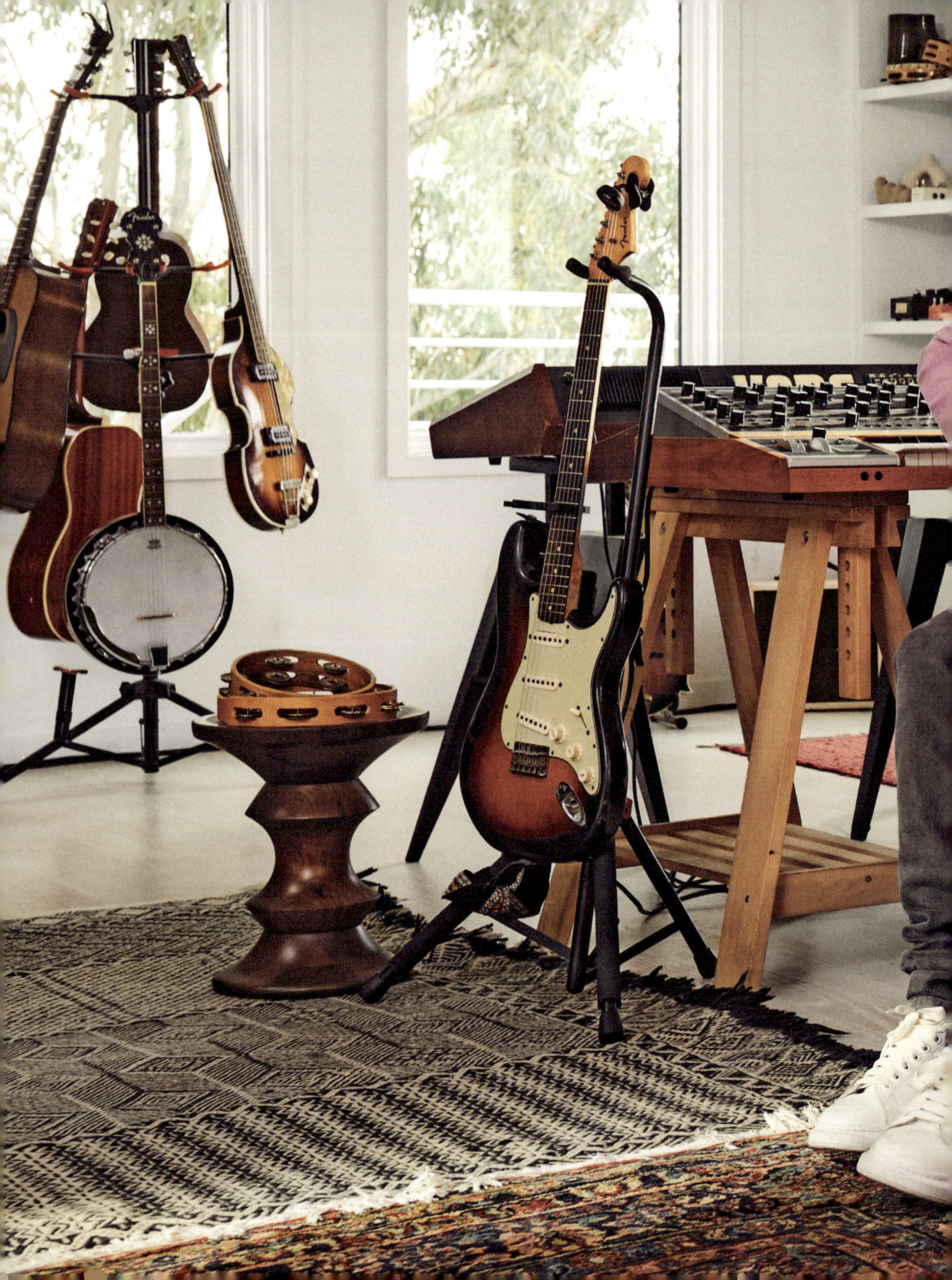

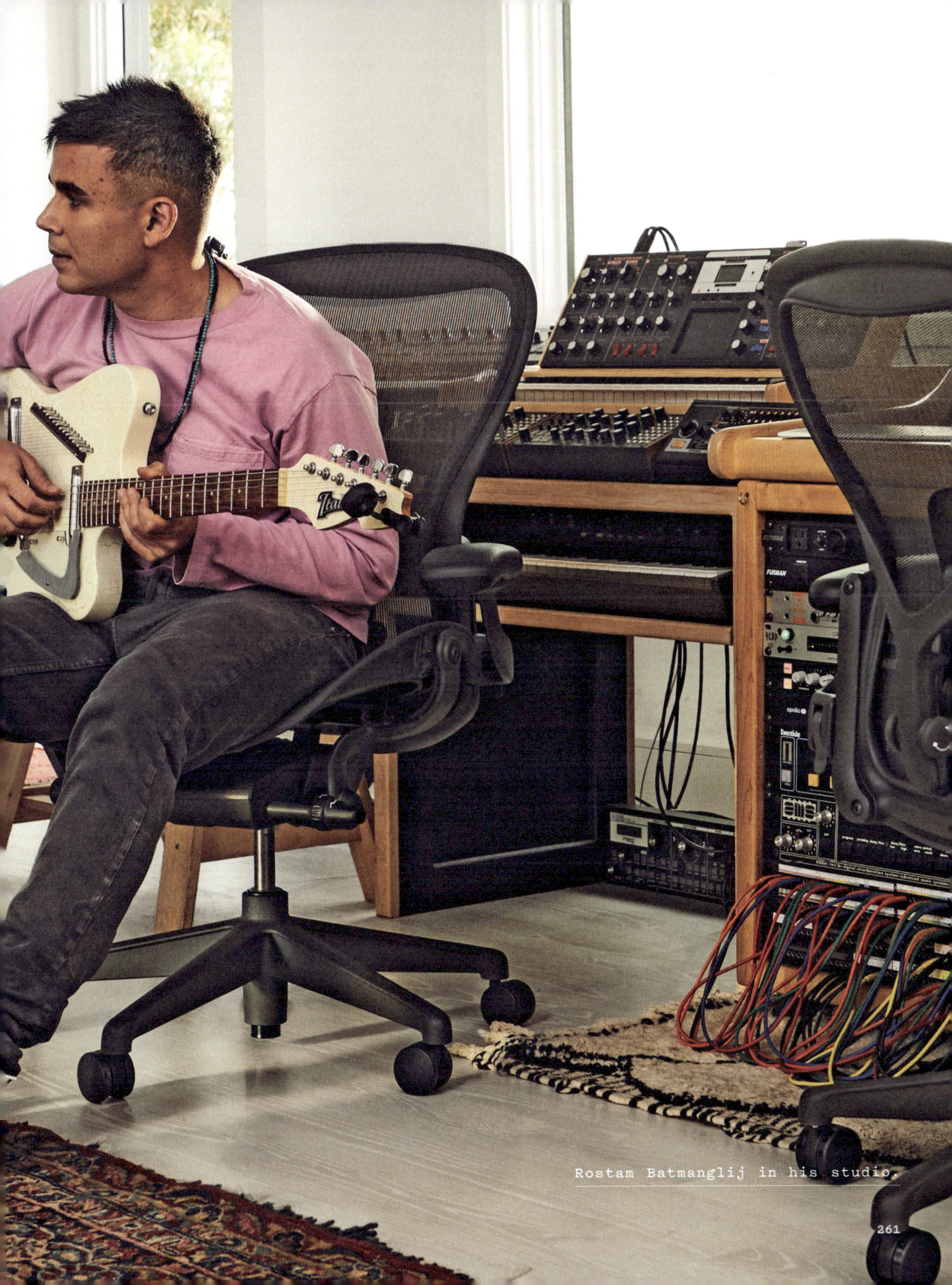

Rostam Batmanglij in his studio.

26
ROSTAM
The Song on His Phone

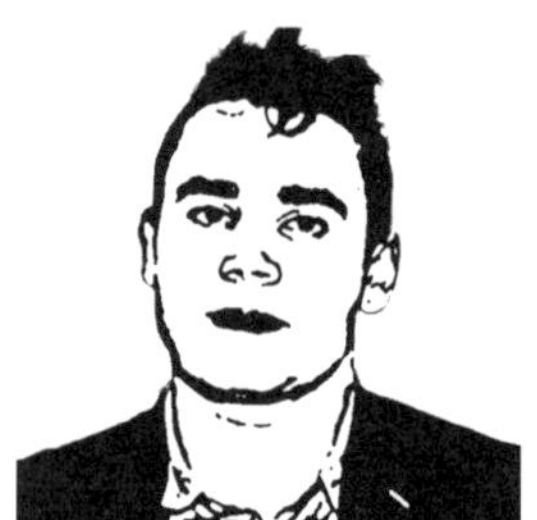

OCCUPATION: Singer-Songwriter
WORK DISCUSSED: "In a River" (2018)
BORN: 1983

ROSTAM BATMANGLIJ IS AN indie musician who was a founder of the band Vampire Weekend before he struck out on his own as a performer and producer. He has a very particular sound (and voice) that I love, and I listen to his music a lot. As a child he had a pretty intense musical education—piano, flute, guitar, and music theory.[1] "I started writing songs as a very young kid—I would write melodies, write them out on sheet music. When I was around thirteen or fourteen, I included lyrics as well. They weren't very good, but it was a pursuit." At Columbia University, he met Ezra Koenig, and soon the two (with two other musicians) joined to create Vampire Weekend, a huge (and very influential) band of the new century. Rostam also produced the records and functioned as what one reviewer called "the sonic consigliere," merging the many musical influences at play. In 2016, he broke off to try his hand at making his own music as, simply, Rostam. We sat down to talk about a beautiful song of his, "In a River."[2]

ROSTAM: I had been working as a producer with the singer-songwriter named Maggie Rogers on a song called "Fallingwater." I kept hearing a mandolin as a missing piece in the song that would make it something new, so I got a mandolin and I tried it. And Maggie immediately said no—too country, too much twang. She was probably right. But I had a mandolin all of a sudden. I had barely played a mandolin. But if you know the chord shapes for a guitar, they're the same chord shapes on the mandolin, just upside down. It isn't hard.

It was June, maybe of 2016. I was sitting in my living room with this new mandolin and just started playing. As I was trying to get familiar with it, a chord sequence started coming into my fingers and I sort of kept playing with it—just three chord shapes.

I made a recording on my phone—just me singing and playing the mandolin at the same time. From that first recording, a few of the lyrics are already there. Some are gibberish. Some are English words not in the right place.

This was one of those cases where the melody, the lyrics, and the chords arrive somewhat simultaneously. There are some songwriters who refuse to write a song unless it comes to them that way, but I'm a little more agnostic—I'll do anything that ends up at something I'm happy with.

I can't really explain where the song came from. That is one aspect of songwriting that I feel I've trained myself to turn off, because as soon as you start analyzing it, you are tampering with something powerful: your subconscious. But let's see. I was in Los Angeles, it was June, I was getting ready to go to Massachusetts to be on a beach. There are no rivers to swim in in Provincetown.[3] And yet it came to me as it came to me. The concept came from my experiences there. It's important to place yourself inside a concept when you're writing a song. Because that's when you can let your mind do all the work. And then it's important not to be too loyal to the concept at the expense of what might happen.

For a while I let it rest. Inevitably, these things live on your phone and you can listen to them at any time. Sometimes late at night, you'll just go through the various bits before you go to sleep and you listen to these little recordings that you make. Sometimes, it's a piano part. In this case it was something resembling a song. And then you decide what you want to work on—what gets promoted to the big leagues.

The voice memo serves as a music scrapbook, but I also use the Notes app, which becomes a scrapbook for lyrics. I started playing with the words, changing, shifting back and forth. Sometimes it's about trying to write more lyrics without an intention for them to fit in anywhere. I just kept going back, and getting happier and happier. So I was working on the lyrics; I was touring a bit. In January, when I got back to LA, I was feeling a little pressure because I was staring down the barrel about two weeks from going on tour again, so I started recording "In a River."

When I write a song, it's always connected to recording. Moving between recording and songwriting, the two inform each other, and you get inspired to write more. When I say *recorded*—well, the original recording on my iPhone just of me singing and playing—that's the first incarnation. But then the process of recording something properly is to record each thing in isolation—the mandolin and then the vocals. This early recording was slow—way slower than what it became. I remember not being sure that the song needed a bridge, but then getting to a point where I could hear the first verse, the second verse, and the two choruses and saying, *Oh, obviously yes.* So then I wrote a bridge. I had the melody; I had the chorus. I had the lyrics. And then I felt the songwriting was done.

This song is unique because it was probably performed fifty times before its final recording.[4] On tour, I played "In a River" with my touring band at every single concert. I remember telling the musician who was playing the mandolin during the show that we had to get the tempo exactly right. On nights where he played it too fast, it was missing something. Speed is a huge question mark with a song. Faster, it has energy but sometimes loses intimacy. If it's slower, sometimes the groove is improved and it can become more sexy or more powerful.

Following the bridge of the song, there's a part where I sort of yelp, like, "Woo!" And as soon as I would do that, people would clap. The more we played the song, the more I found that if I raised my hands above my head and clapped, then they would too. After the tour, I booked a few days at a recording studio.

What I wanted was to have this sort of live feeling enter the song—so much music is made nowadays with no fluctuation of tempo. There was a sound, too, the sound of five hundred people clapping at the same time.

1. Another instance of rigorous training at an early age. Almost all of the subjects of this book started young.

2. This is the only song of his he owns outright. He uses it to fund philanthropic projects. It appears on no album ("It's my 'Hey Jude,'" he says), but several versions of it appear on Spotify.

3. He is often my neighbor there, which is how I got to know him. Sometimes you can hear his music wafting through the trees.

4. Moses Sumney also brought his unfinished song on the road at first, and playing it in front of audiences helped him figure out what the song ought to be, as it did here.

DRAFT

Even in the background
With the lights on the field
Somewhere to my right or left
Is a body I can feel

We are swimming
With no clothes on
In a river
in the dark

We are holding
One another
We are holding
We are holding on

So forgive me if I'm too bored
And forgive what I should say
I ain't got no time to get old
But I got nothing to play

We are swimming
In a river
With no clothes on
in the dark

And I'm holding
Yeah I'm holding on
To you,
Yeah I got you by the arm

We are swimming
In the river
Naked
In the sun

And I'm holding
I am holding
I am holding
Holding on

RIFFINGS ON HIS PHONE

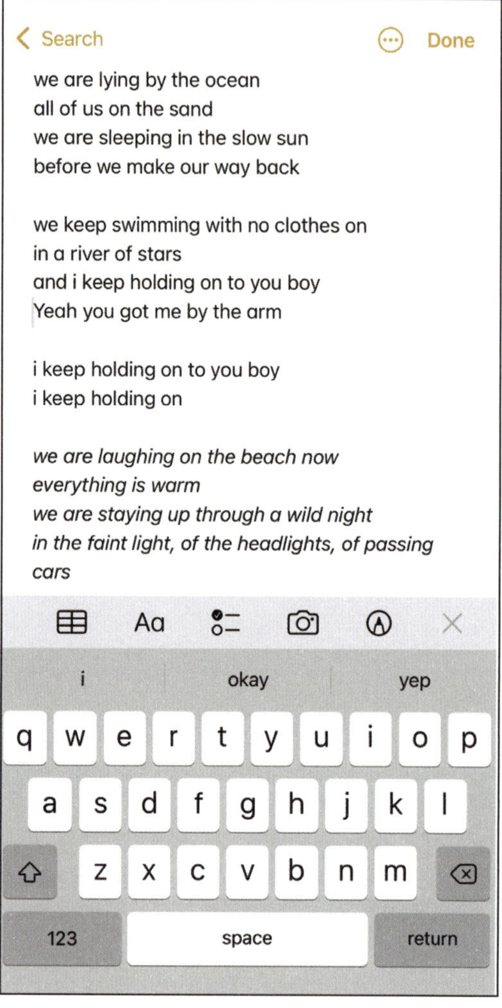

We recorded the YouTube video of one of the concerts and put it inside Pro Tools. The claps arrive with the snare drum, and there's two fiddle solos that happen at the same time, so that's kind of where the energy comes from.

And the ending? Well, a thing about this song that's kind of unique is that it ends with a chorus that's low-key and mostly has different lyrics. I guess you could call it a coda. It's like a slow end. I don't really remember why I did that. It might have been that I had extra lyrics. I was trying to overwrite so that I could take my favorite lyrics and put them in the song. I think I might have written them to try and see if I could beat the chorus that I had.

Coda So Rostam tucked them in the end, and that's the song you can hear on Spotify. It's a song I listen to a lot. But maybe I've been wrong about what the song means. The key

IN A RIVER

Slide into the cool mud
Underneath the pines
Somewhere to your right or left
Is my body you can find

We are swimming with no clothes on
In a river in the dark
And I am holding on to you, boy
In the faint light of the stars

So you wade out across the marsh
Water up to your waist
Carry our stuff above your head
Till the dune comes to a crest

We are swimming with no clothes on
In a river in the dark
And I am holding on to you, boy
In the faint light of the stars

But sometimes I feel it
In a dream I know I've been there
We were sleeping by the ocean
We were laughing on the warm sand
We stay up all night
And we wake up in the sunlight
We got dreams we keep together
We got time to spend, oh, hell yeah

We are swimming with no clothes on
In a river in the dark
And I am holding on to you, boy
In the faint light of the stars

We are lying
On the beach now
Everything is warm
We are staying up
Through a wild night
In the faint light
Of the headlights
Of passing cars

lyric is "swimming in a river with no clothes on." When I offhandedly referred to what seemed obvious to me—that it was about skinny-dipping with some boy (which is also how most music critics described the song)—Rostam smiled.

"Well, that's what you say it's about," he said.[5] "I feel a little nervous to say what I was drawn to about that lyric [because] it evoked some thoughts about—well, specifically the metaphor of the womb, maybe at a place where you're sort of swimming with no clothes. I think that was in the back of my head. And then this other concept of, like, death, ascension, traveling through space. Which is not what I was thinking about directly, but maybe that's what drew me to the lyric as being good."

He dug through his phone and found an early note where he is playing the lyrics. He read the lyrics and narrated:

"'*We are lying by the ocean. All of us on the sand. We are sleeping in the slow sun before we make our way back.*' So definitely more literal. '*We keep swimming with no clothes on, in a river of stars, and I keep holding on to you, boy, yeah, you got me by the arm.*' Terrible. '*I keep holding on to you boy, I keep holding on.*' So this is, yeah—this is embarrassing, I'm cringing at my own work. But, you know, you have to do the bad stuff to get to the good."

And then Rostam scrounged a bit and found the original voice memo—the one from that first night on his phone. "Don't judge me," he said. "It was called 'In a River with No Clothes On,' which is a terrible name. But here goes. Hmm."

We listened, both staring intently at his phone as if it were a discovered relic. You can hear him on the mandolin, singing and talking his way through fragments of song. Barely a minute into the recording, he sings that line around which the whole song is built: "*We are swimming with no clothes on, in a river in the dark.*" I remarked to him that the surprising thing (I am always surprised by this) is how much he had in that first moment.

"Yes, and there was also that lyric, '*Somewhere to your right or left is your body you can find.*' No. '*My body you can find.*' Right. I liked that immediately."

5. See Marc Jacobs for a similar exchange over the creator's meaning for a work versus how it is received.

27

IRA GLASS

Laugh Here

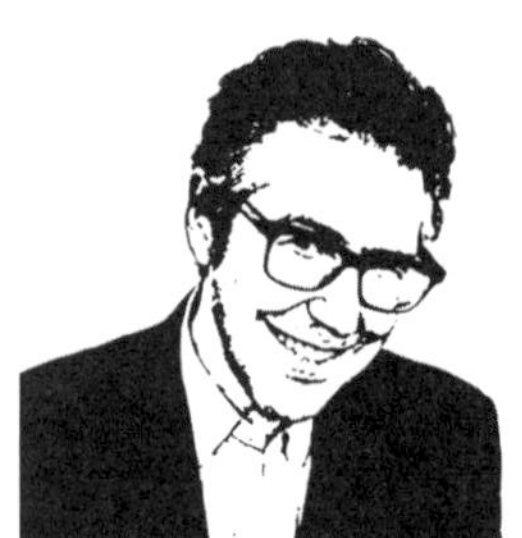

OCCUPATION: Radio Host

WORK DISCUSSED: *This American Life* (1995)

BORN: 1959

IRA GLASS'S AFFABILITY, along with his ferocious discipline and creative ambition (also that voice), make for an unusual cocktail, and is what turned *This American Life* into such a successful joining of journalism and art. Glass is a pioneer I've long admired. After years working his way up in public radio, he acted on an idea for a new kind of radio program, which became *This American Life.* And with it, he invented that casually nasal sound and intimate, unspooling style that has together become—and this is especially evident in the age of podcasts—the ubiquitous voice of oral narrative. In a sense, he created an art form. As someone who spent my career in a related field, I thought I might learn a lot by talking to him. Also, he's an anxious Jew. We had that in common as well.

For the most part, these chapters are built around specific case studies, and Ira and I tried to parse a couple of different episodes, but honestly, it was too complicated to make that work in these pages (a problem he would understand).[1] So I ditched the episodes and focused instead on how *This American Life*—and that sound—came to be. The way Ira discusses creative work has a Yankee quality I could relate to, so I wanted to start there.

Adam Moss: *I was hoping we could discuss the relationship of anxiety to drive, because I think it's an important note for the book, and people often, at least implicitly, bring it up. And you're candid and articulate enough to—*

Ira Glass: Nice flattery! As a fellow interviewer, I'm respecting the flattery. All right. I need a harsh deadline to get anything done. Without it I can really float. And I'm anxious about it being good. Like, all the time. My experience of most stories is that they're trying to be mediocre.[2] I mean, occasionally a person is such a good talker, and the story is inherently interesting, and the stakes are so good, and they're funny, and it has so much feeling, all you have to do is get out of the way. That doesn't happen often. Generally, because we're building around tape, there's enough to make work if you try really hard. And in every draft, it's just going back and forth between being sparkly and matte. And matte is usually a long part of the process. There are stories where much of the time I'm wondering, *Are we gonna have to kill them?* And only at the eleventh hour do they get to be good enough. It's only through an act of will that things are not mediocre.

Every episode feels like it's down to the wire. The thing just goes out on Friday night on the public radio satellite, and then it has to exist. I'm anxious about it getting done, and I'm anxious about it being good. I'm anxious in general. At least it's anxiety about something in a world I can control. If anything, I've really organized so much of my life to do away with personal relationships, and to spend more time inside the battle against inefficient storytelling. For better or worse, as a number of my girlfriends and my ex-wife pointed out, a lot of my energy has gone into that. I don't even think of it as anxiety. There came a point in making last week's show, where to get the thing done, basically I was getting up at six in the morning and just working until I went to sleep at night.[3] It wasn't a great way to live. But it was certainly a simple way to live.

AM: *There's a quote I read of yours that I think pretty perfectly encapsulates the creative predicament. It starts "Well, nobody tells people who are beginners . . ."*

IG: Oh, that. It's something I said off the cuff years ago. Should I even refer to the fact that it exists as a quote?

AM: *Sure. But we're not talking for radio. [Ira laughs.] I could always edit that part out.*

IG: Oh, right. Well, basically it's a quote where I express what my experience was in my twenties, which is, if you want to do creative work of any kind, there's a period where your ambition is greater than what you're actually able to make. Like in my case my ability definitely was lower than my dreams for myself. But I was smart enough. I could tell the difference between good and bad. I think that people don't talk about this. There's a time when you have a dream and you have enough taste to know what's lacking, but your abilities don't get you there. And I think people just die on the rocks of that, that point when they write songs and their songs aren't that great, and they're rational about that, not deluded, and they stop. I was really stuck there for a very long time.

AM: *So they have the ambition, but not the skills, and most people just don't wait it out. I think that's very true.*

IG: There was a point where every year *This American Life* would do a poetry show. One year a producer pitched an idea, and I said, "Oh my God, I did that story when I was a baby reporter. Why don't you go back and listen to it and see if we can pull the tape out or something." And she went back and listened to my story, which was only from a decade before. And she said, "Wow. There's no sign from the tape that you have any talent for radio. There's no good writing. The story doesn't make any sense. You seem to have no aptitude for radio at all."

AM: *It couldn't have been that bad.*

IG: The drama of my twenties was wondering if I was ever going to get there. I would have these simple stories I was trying to make on my own, and I would take weeks. I was just a bad writer and so insecure as a picker of tape.

AM: *So how did you emerge from that?*

IG: Really, you just have to work your way out of it. That's the only way. You have to be rigorous, you have to be a soldier, you have to fight. It's only by making a volume of work that you'll be forced to confront what it is that you don't know how to do, and learn

---

1. So that you understand some of the variables that go into making a radio story, the main case study we were going to talk about was a very interesting one-hour episode about the SATs, which Ira planned to report and narrate but ultimately felt he didn't have enough authority to do. He passed the job over to the writer Paul Tough, who'd written a book on the subject and whose reporting formed the basis of the story. One problem solved. Then changes in the news forced the story to be radically reoriented three times. Then they couldn't get the narrative to work. Then it was saved by the discovery of some old tape. The show made me cry, but it would take about twenty pages to explain here.

2. I think you could sub in pretty much anything for *stories* in this sentence.

3. For what it's worth, I really related to this sentiment. It was how I felt about my magazine work before I didn't. "You must have had this experience as a magazine editor," said Ira. "Sometimes you're putting out an episode or a show or an issue of magazine, and it's not that good. Everything's very professional. It's just not that interesting. It takes just as much work to make a thing that's mediocre as it does to make the good version. And it's really soul draining." "I felt like that," I said, "when the difference between good and great was very visible to me, and it would drive me crazy. But then suddenly it wasn't. I felt, *I'm not burning anymore*. And as soon as I started to feel that, I knew it could get contagious. I just had to remove myself from the environment." "Wow," he said. It was clear that it was not at all what he felt, though we'd been at it nearly the same amount of time. He was very much still slugging.

to do it. Oh, and the other thing is, you need to show your work to other people and have them tell you what they don't like. There was a period when I would pay this guy fifty bucks to tell me what I was doing wrong.

How *This American Life* Works

AM: *Let's break down how you make a show.*
IG: Well, our regular pitch process is that we have a story meeting every week.
AM: *Sounds familiar. Are they competitive? I always wanted our pitch meetings to be a little scary. I thought it would bring out better ideas. I still think so, but I got a lot of shit for that.*[4]
IG: If anything, there's an overweening attempt at niceness. Very often, a few of us have to be the ones to bring down the ax. And then there are stories where everybody's on one side of it and I'm on the other. Often I'll give in.
AM: *And the stories themselves?*
IG: The thing radio can do peculiarly well is make you attached to a person. The medium is built for it. So first and foremost is the tape. You're always just building around tape.
AM: *I used to think "voice" was that for magazines.*[5] *If the story was confidently, charismatically told—that is, if the reader wanted to be in the writer's company—you could fake your way through the rest. But for you the crucial element is the tape?*

4. I'm not making any excuses (and I still feel fear can motivate—not a fashionable thought these days), but it was from my elders at *Esquire* that I learned meetings should make you cry, because that's what happened at their meetings. One's chain of mentors can be very decisive.

MUSIC MIX NOTES: IRA'S EDITS

Ira's editing notes (in black type) in response to the mix notes for the sound in the SAT story, called "The Campus Tour Has Been Cancelled." Ira's endearing manner—his radio voice, and the voice with which he talked to me (identical)—comes through clearly in how he talks to his staff.

ACT 1 PART 1 - Daniela (SN Mix, DC Notes handing off to IG)

Commented [1]: @ira@thislife.org I just did a test -- confirmed that we can remove the buzz with no ill effects on Paul's voice. I also sent him an email about troubleshooting his setup before retrax. _Assigned to Ira Glass_

0:09 Ira, I started music early -- I think we'll get away with it because there's going to be that two-way with no music before it? If not here, you could also start music at 0:26 under "There was a group" but I think you'd still want to dump it under her second piece of tape. Which is maybe a little short?

:08 I like music here! I think Pluck Up works great till you get to the quote. Then it and the philips are sort of serious and monotonous under the quote in a way that doesn't seem to know she's being funny and this is a funny quote. To me, there's something sort of neutral and flattening about Pluck Up that's not working for us here. **THURSDAY NOTES:** Hi stowe! Cold light of day! I think there probably isn't a section of pluck up that's gonna work with the later part of her quote. I think find something else to support the lightness and fun of the quote. And then ... note that when you get the second quote, it's not quite a record-scratch moment but it's a big change, hitting failure with the SAT.
SN: Two alts in. I can do a fade out on Summer Equinox if you prefer -- I couldn't resist the show-off clean ending.
Holy damn. Summer Equinox is great. Expositional where it needs to be. Light and funny where it needs to be. Cold stop at the perfect point. Yes yes yes.

~~:18~~—Cut .12 s]econds pause before "getting amazing grades" I know that's a very specific number!

~~:32~~—Cut .2 sec before "for most of high school"

~~:34~~—Listening in the studio, she doesn't sound as loud as Paul when she enters. I know on the meters it's close.

~~1:27~~—Ira, I pulled her under the trax here because I couldn't figure out an elegant way to end her quote. You could cut the "Um" and end on the exhale but it feels a little abrupt. Or we could sub in a different "Not" from somewhere else? Or maybe this works. Please advise.
I like what you did! Let's keep that.

~~2:03~~—I worry about his performance without music. Can you start under "when it came time for the SAT"? I pasted the start of the song where it could go. That nice music break 12 seconds into the song lands at a nice place. Let's do secret pocketbook. McGinley - I say with respect - is exactly the kind of repetitive boring melody I abhor. And in any case, a little too dissonant I think for this spot. Lose the music around 3:15ish, where she starts comparing her performance to theirs. SN: Pocketbook fixed.

Commented [2]: These are fighting words.
Commented [3]: I said them with respect!
Commented [4]: You can use that trash when you're working with Nadia and Sean and Dana.
Commented [5]: I say with respect
Commented [6]: hahaha

4:07 Courtin. Love it. Perfect. Perfect placement too. Great post. Yes.

5:29 both these are great. Hard to choose. I think the lower one but wanna hear one more time

Admissions officer story SN mix IG notes

~~:14~~—Love the Lemon. How do you beat the energy and forward momentum of that? Pulling it out a little earlier than you did.

IG: Without decent tape at the beginning, it's hard to make something good. Often we're really excited about something but the tape is like, ehhh.

AM: *And does that mean the story's doomed?*

IG: Not always doomed, just hard. The simplest way to think about it came from Julie Snyder, who went on to do *Serial* with us. She sometimes thinks, like, *What are the moments of a piece that I'm looking forward to?* There have to be a bunch of moments like that.

It's just a lot of stage-managing: How much is this person going to be a character, how much are we going to develop this argument, do we want to go funny here or serious here? And radio is so sensitive. I don't know if it's like this in print. Pacing is so hard. How long do you linger on a point—one more sentence, or half sentence?

At first it's a written draft, a script. A lot of the things you're figuring out are the mechanics of the drama. Like for you to invest emotionally, you have to have someone you care about. But honestly, so much of a radio story is about when do you slow down, where do you have a beat for feeling, and where do you have a beat for information. In a way, it's very traditional drama.

5. And isn't it true that *This American Life* is all about voice—not the stories, maybe, but the show itself, which is built around a (particularly lovable) animating persona? This voice-first idea reappears everywhere from paintings (Gerald Lovell) to novels (Sheila Heti) to books about cooking (Samin Nosrat). Voice doesn't have to be lovable, but it does have to be strong and distinctive. I knew this in my magazine life, but inasmuch as it creeps in, I also run away from it in my painting life. A voice requires commitment, which in painting terrifies me.

~~2:44~~—Hard to choose between these two. McGinley gives more gravitas. But the momentum of Kimborough helps this very academic story. Held it in a tad longer than you.

~~6:06~~—Slawin great. The other's a little bouncy for kids not going to college in this spot. SN: I'm glad you picked this one. Not sure I've ever actually used this track.

~~9:10~~—hard choice. Courtin - for forward motion.

~~9:25~~—Let's cut this: Quinlan said they're very aware of the correlation between a student's SAT test scores and what kind of background they come from … and they factor that into how they looked at the scores …

~~10:01~~—Cut this: But this year the Ivy Leagues pushed their announcement date back a week to April 6th because they were so flooded with applications once they went test optional

~~10:55~~—We need a section break here. My suggested solution: let's return to the Lemon music that started the story. I threw it in there. Theoretically it could start under the end of the last Quinlan quote by it's more of a section break if it just starts in the clear. Check my levels and the general approach and all?
SN: I like it. I gave it a little more space before the needle drop.

~~12:11~~—There's a recut voicetrack with new wording on an "edited retakes" line I made, just above the narration line. Can you incorporate this recut in the piece?

> One thing that became a LOT more important to Admissions people I talked to ... now that they didn't have SATs: seeing the rigor of a student's curriculum, like how many advanced placement courses kids took, that kind of thing… and what they got ~~on them~~ in those classes.
>
> Understandable of course … but it obviously gave a boost to students from high schools with more resources … that offered lots of advanced ~~AP~~ classes.

~~12:18~~—Both great. Let's do Un Moraliste. It gives an air of "what will happen" to the next section in a nice way.

~~14:27~~—Sure! Let's do the Leyton Brown! The left channel was insanely quiet compared to the right so I boosted. SN: Dumb thing about that song! Thanks for catching.

Top MT mix IG notes

~~:46~~—In the studio she doesn't sound as loud as me when she enters. Also on the meters she's a tad lower. Can you boost?

~~:52~~—both musics are great, in different ways. And they both develop nicely. Ulrich is better and more appealing until you get to that melody at 1:22 then it's sort of distracting. Let's do the blue dot. I faded out a little later than you did.

~~2:12~~—These are nice but Ulrich is a too minor key and low-key for this triumphant moment. Courtin is good but the post is just too lounge-ironic kitchy. Too unfeeling and just … kitsch. Can you find something else? Play to the happy excitement of it. And start a little later. Right after she says "we're going test optional" around 2:19. I know that's very on the nose!!

And then stories go through many, many drafts. I'm working in a medium that rewards editing and reediting and reediting. Changes, nips, tucks, all the way to the moment it goes on the air.

AM: *How do you build a show?*

IG: It can take different forms. Usually there'll be one story we've been working on for a long time, and then everything else will come together really fast—not the best way to work. The shows have themes, but you might notice a story is not really on theme. And my feeling is it doesn't really matter. Like it's nice when it's tight, but it's also fine if it's just three good stories. The other thing I could say about the structure is the structure of the show is best story to worst.

AM: *Huh. You couldn't really tell that from listening. So it's the same theory as newspaper?*

IG: What do you mean?

AM: *Well, the assumption for years at newspapers was that people would skim, they're not reading for pleasure, just information. Now that's obviously changed, but that was the theory of the pyramid news structure—all the important stuff up front. The magazine idea was the opposite—lure people in so they're forced to read to the last paragraph to figure it out.*

IG: That's like our thing, where I feel we're constantly baiting people forward—both through narrative structure, but then literally saying what we're going to explain. Reading Roland Barthes in college, his theories of narrative, totally informed how I decided to make radio stories. He talks simply about how having plot creates a question that people want answered. People want to know what's going to happen next so you can hold their attention. That's why *This American Life* starts the way it does.

AM: *How important is delivery?*

IG: Super important. Each of us records our voice tracks, everybody's now trained to direct; they say, "Go slower, pause here, you're overselling, you're not selling enough." For people who've never been on the radio, sometimes for a twelve-minute piece, we'll spend two and a half hours in the studio with them. People will read like they're reading a report in front of a class, when you really want to talk like you talk. You just want to be talking.

Differently

AM: *Did you know how to do that right out of the gate?*

IG: Figuring out how to perform on the radio took me a decade before I did *This American Life*. I did a local show with two friends for five years, just to train myself to sound different from other NPR reporters. Like in my early scripts, I would write "laugh here," reminding myself, *Oh this line is funny*. David Sedaris once saw one of my scripts; he's like, "You write *laugh* in the script?"

AM: *Ha. So we're getting to how you came to create* This American Life. *You wanted to sound different because you had a different idea of how radio should sound?*

IG: Before *This American Life* there was a kind of story that I liked when I heard it on the radio. I was making some stories like it in my job as a producer for *All Things Considered* and *Morning Edition*.

There was feeling, with a plot and characters; you just get pulled in. I thought somebody could make a whole show of these. And you wouldn't narrate it like an NPR host, there wouldn't be any effort to be the official voice of officialdom.

AM: *Did you have a specific idea of the voice you were working toward, or was it just intuitive?*

IG: It was completely conscious. And I really struggled over it. In a certain way I still do. I still like to perform my lines, make it sound like I'm really talking. But it's my least favorite part of the week.

AM: *I think of you as having invented a certain kind of intimacy on the radio. Am I giving you too much credit?*

IG: No, I agree with that. [*laughs*] I invented it in this form. Honestly, there were good performers on the radio—Susan Stamberg, one of the original hosts of *All Things Considered*, is a much better performer than I am. But

I guess I invented this particular sound. It was an attempt to sound like the person I really am, but talk my way to bits of tape in a structured story. It doesn't seem like much of an innovation now, but at the time it was really new, like new to the point where we had to talk program directors into picking up the show. Because they felt, "Well, is there going to be a real host?"

And the use of music was different. Once you start adding scoring, like a film, the thing starts to have the feeling of film. It's partly the way we do music, it's partly my tone. It took me a long time to get to a point where I thought that it worked.

AM: *Did you have it figured out before you pitched* This American Life*?*

IG: When I started the show, I had the sound. If you listen to the first episode, it's there. It's not clear what we're going to do is narrative. There was basically a piece of performance art on it. It was more of a grab bag, but then we were good at narrative, so we just felt like, "Let's head towards that."

AM: *Why do you think you were the one to figure this form out?*

IG: I can work for a really long time and I don't mind. [*laughs*][6] Really, it was just that it took so many hours to make this material and I had nothing else interesting to do in my life. And I started working at NPR when I was nineteen. By the time *This American Life* went on the air, I was an experienced radio producer and had worked with the best people for years, just as a statement of fact. I knew how to do radio inside and out. And there weren't people with that much experience doing something that wasn't traditional. I was lucky in that the very first person at NPR who gave me a real job was this guy named Keith Talbot, whose job was to invent new ways to do documentaries. And so from the very beginning, the questions were like, How do you make a show, structure a show, think of a format that nobody has ever made? Every show we would remake the format, with different kinds of narration. For a show about people who live on the ocean, the narration was two guys sitting on a pier. And one of them had an imaginary friend. And he would tell stories about the imaginary friend. I know that sounds terrible, but it was great.

What I'm doing in a way is so square. But Keith put me in the frame of, you can really move anything around and create a new aesthetic. I experimented for years. I did little stories with that kind of feeling to them, and then I thought to build it out to a full show. And honestly, it seemed to me like such an obvious idea. I thought, *If I don't get this on air fast, somebody else is going to.*

AM: *Is what you're doing square because that's what you like? Or your ability? Or because it's who you are? Would you rather it be weirder?*

IG: It's square because I've consciously made a product, where we're saying to you in the first minute, we're going to give you something really interesting and appealing. I'm going to take you by the hand, and I'm going to tell you why this is interesting. That's a square choice, a middlebrow choice, that's an aesthetic choice that, for a bunch of reasons, like the aesthetics of the stuff I loved as a kid, feels comfortable to me. My cousin Philip Glass, I mean, this is not his thing.[7] This is what he came to destroy. Just immerse, and let people figure it out. He's proud of me, but his reaction to what I do is "That seems boring. Just really old-fashioned." There are producers on the staff who very much want to push the show in a different direction. One producer is just like, narrative schmarrative. And that's fine, if you can make it interesting.

AM: *Are you more inclined to experiment now than you were at the beginning of the show? Do you find yourself loosening up or tightening as you go along?*

IG: When you're on the air for twenty-five years, you really are just looking for anything that'll seem fun to do. Anything that's shiny, you run towards.

6. A tolerance for tedium has to be one of the least celebrated and most important traits of a successful artist.

7. There are few less-narrative-oriented artists than the composer Philip Glass—who is in fact Ira's cousin.

28

SIMPHIWE NDZUBE

I Am a Portal

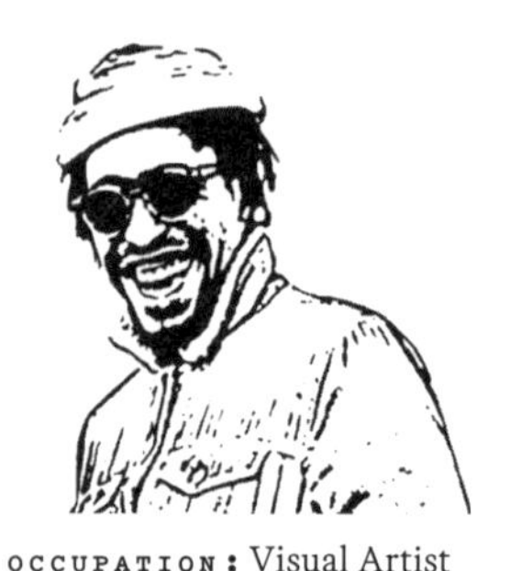

OCCUPATION: Visual Artist

WORK DISCUSSED: *Hunter* (2021)

BORN: 1990

THE PHRASE *WORLD-BUILDING* is frequently used to describe what artists do, but seldom is it as apt as it is for the work of Simphiwe Ndzube, who populates what amounts to a Marvel-size, richly imagined universe across his entire body of work. The world even has a name, the Mine Moon. Simphiwe is a South African artist living in Los Angeles, but I went to visit him in a gallery in Soho, where he was having a show. He is curious, wide open; it was impossible not to fall for him immediately. On the walls were pictures built from textiles and paint and collaged with photographs of his own body parts (eyes, tongue, ears). In the center of the space were life-size sculptures, all depicting scenes from the folkloric epic of his own imagining that he's been populating for years, with mysterious beasts and villagers in colorful clothing on top of them. Like several of the other artists in this book, he called himself a portal through which the world was built, though in his case with the active help of his ancestors. But it wasn't entirely as mystical as that.

Art from Dung Not very long ago, he was a boy in Eastern Cape, in South Africa. Simphiwe was a postapartheid child of a single mother, raised in his early years by his grandmother. "What I remember from that first week in school is I drew a candle, a lit candle, and my teacher was amazed by it. And then from that point on, she would use me to draw diagrams. Pretty terrible diagrams, but . . ." He began to see himself as someone who could draw, also as someone who could draw better than his classmates. He was imaginative and competitive;[1] that was his nature. The kids of his village made wire cars. His overriding thought was, *How do I make one that's better than the others are going to make?* And then he continued: "We played house, like dollhouse. We'd use dung to make furniture."

He learned pantsula, an expressive, acrobatic South African dance style, and when he was old enough, he competed. Dance consumed him, but he was meanwhile painting pictures of the villagers—"hustling portraits," as he put it, for whatever cash he could get.[2] When he was eighteen, his mother died, leaving him parentless. Painting helped him grieve.

The first painting that was meaningful to him, he recalled, "was me and my sister as children, I have a little belly and skinny legs. We are standing outside. In the background are all these graves; it's a really dark painting. Two kids trying to figure out where else to go. The moment was like, *Oh shit, we don't have a father. Now our mother's gone.* It became clear that I had nothing else important that I needed to be doing other than to create.[3] And to avoid dealing with a lot of what was happening."

He found his way to art school, where he rebelled against its preoccupation with modern European and American art—he wanted something rooted in South Africa's difficult history. One school break he began to experiment and was surprised by what seemed to emerge: work that was mythic but definitely contemporary; indirectly political, with themes of subjugation. "It looked primitive, and playful," Simphiwe recalled. "Then I made a series of these things in chalk pastels and acrylic, on brown paper. And I posted one of them, and there was interest from a gallery. I got the confidence to go ahead and be weird. The weirder I got, the more approval I got."[4]

Recognizing that he was onto something, he steeped himself in magical realism, started reading Gabriel García Márquez, Isabel Allende, and Haruki Murakami. He found himself "entertaining an idea of a possibility of a fantastical space." He moved to the US. "And being in LA, I realized I could just give it a name. So I called it the Mine Moon."

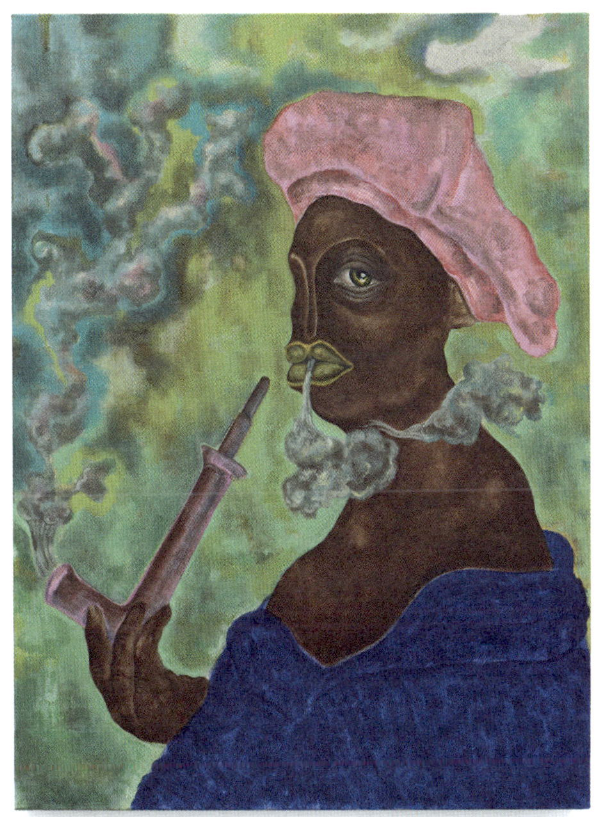

At the gallery, he pointed to one picture of a mother smoking a pipe. It helped him understand that the work in the gallery was a product of her hallucinations. But also, of course, his.

Hallucinations "All of it," Simphiwe said, "is based on my parents' experiences, and what happened around them. I was born in 1990, in the transition from apartheid. My world was completely optimistic, but then everybody else who's older than me is angry. They say, 'You guys don't understand.'

"I think about ways dreams function," he continued. If you look at his work, you

1. Is a competitive spirit helpful to an artist? I guess it's helpful to fuel any drive—that is, in the right proportion.

2. Selling work at an early age was also critical to Maria de Los Angeles's trajectory.

3. In a tender exchange, Simphiwe showed me some drawings he'd made to communicate with his sister when she was in a hospital. He drew, she drew, they passed drawings back and forth. Drawing was its own language.

4. In the interest of pattern tracking, maybe it's worth noting the importance of validation—what one gets approval for, especially: when and from whom. Approval for one thing and not another does seem to nudge you here and not there.

know you are eventually going to be talking about dreams. "You never have intentions to dream certain things, but then . . . What is it called when you direct your dreams?" "Lucid dreaming," his studio assistant suggested, and he nodded. "You can go into dreams with intentions to have control, and there are exercises to get to that point." We talked about Salvador Dalí's famous experiments trying to capture his dreams immediately after jolting himself awake with a falling spoon,[5] which Simphiwe found amusing but intriguing. "The way dreams function is the way I can allow myself to work. I make meaning out of it only when the painting's finished. It's almost like a waking-up moment. If I open myself up to be a vessel, there are stories of my lineage, genetic memory, that my parts remember that have nothing to do with me. I look at it," he said, "as a way in which magic happens."

Simphiwe's got a vigorous mystical bent, but he doesn't suggest things *just* happen, which I'm glad about because of my impatience with magical talk (my problem, not his). I wanted to know the concrete steps he takes to build the artifacts of this world. His method is rigorous. "I very often begin out of nothing, pages from books or magazines, images I've stored. I will start off with a composition I like. That gives me the map, then I'm trying to make marks, erasing, fixing, changing. With acrylic, it dries fast. It's methodical. I know if I follow the steps, I will most likely arrive at a painting that looks like Simphiwe."

He flips back and forth between painting and sculpture. For either, he might start with clothes, actual fabrics from Goodwill, or pictures he's cut out. "Hang the clothes, draw it, see how it feels first." In a sense he's building a dollhouse, like he did as a child. "Then there's the face; the face needs to be complete. And then I pin the hands in different directions. When I'm ready, I do the washes. Then I draw whatever the landscape is. And then I block it in. The painting is done. I just need to make it convincing."

He has plenty of starting points—his palette usually proceeds from ultramarine blue, he has to fix the movement of the body before he knows what to do—but otherwise, he just plays. How does he know it is done? "If I were to do anything else with it, then I'd really fuck it up."

We returned to the idea of himself as a portal. I asked if there were ways he opens that door.

He paused. "I mean, weed is definitely one of them."

I'd been hoping someone would bring up weed—it's not so far away from Salvador Dalí's spoon—a tool to unleash the imagination. In any case, he wanted to talk about it because these days, weed was very much on his mind. "Weed just relaxes me. It makes me think, *Okay, there are things not making sense, but you know, keep them coming*. There's been some dependence with weed, I must say. I try sometimes to see what happens when I don't smoke weed for a couple of days. And it's a little bit harder, but I can work longer. With weed, it peaks and drops right away. I'm trying not to rely on any substance to create."[6]

He gets to the studio, looks at images, frequently naps in the afternoons. Then, when his assistants leave and he is alone, he starts making his mythological world, working into the night. I was curious about the world's contours—its rules or constraints; that is, what defines it—but my question was too pragmatic. He just shook his head.[7]

"I make so much from impulse, pure impulse," Simphiwe said. "Very often I don't understand it myself."

He recently finished a sculpture called *Hunter*. I asked him to narrate its evolution.

5. For this method, Dalí would hold a spoon while starting to doze. The spoon would drop, waking him up, and he'd jump to work, squeezing that optimal moment between the conscious and the unconscious for all it was worth.

6. But drug use does actually loosen you up for creative purposes, right? Not necessarily. Some studies show that cannabis actually makes you *less* capable of "divergent thinking" (the analogue for creativity); LSD makes you plenty divergent but hampers your organizing functions enough that you're useless to make anything. Regardless, many artists love their drugs—opium and hashish are thought to have highly influenced Picasso's Rose period, for instance. A school of thought places inebriants at the start of recorded creation, positing that cave paintings were made during druggy rituals.

7. Among the aspects of his work that most puzzled me was the fact that he'd created the Mine Moon without a particularly structured sense of how it worked. I'd talked to many artists about worlds they'd made (in TV, novels, movies, art); so much effort was taken to establish the rules within which they operated. With Simphiwe, it was all feel.

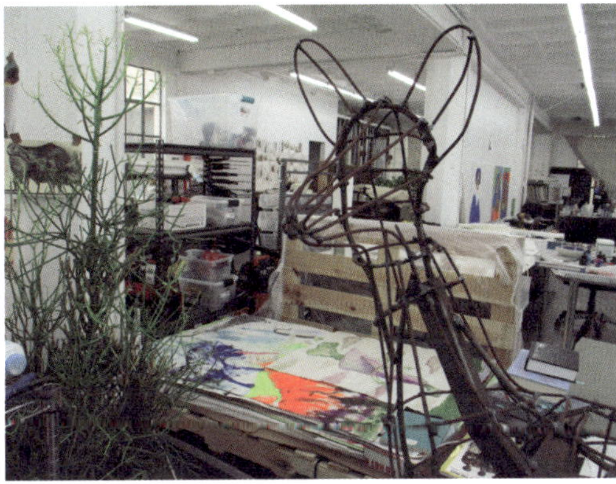

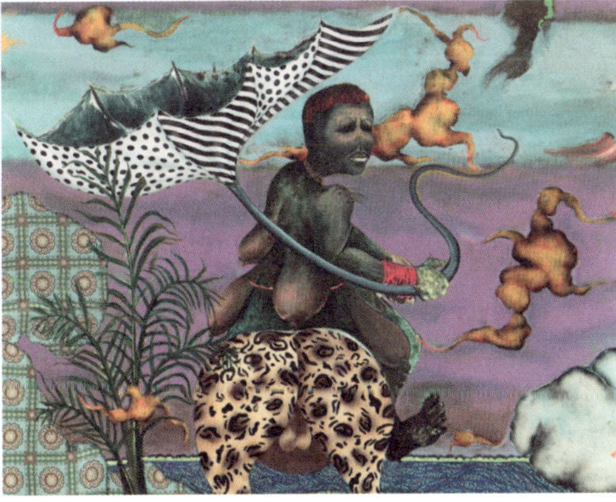

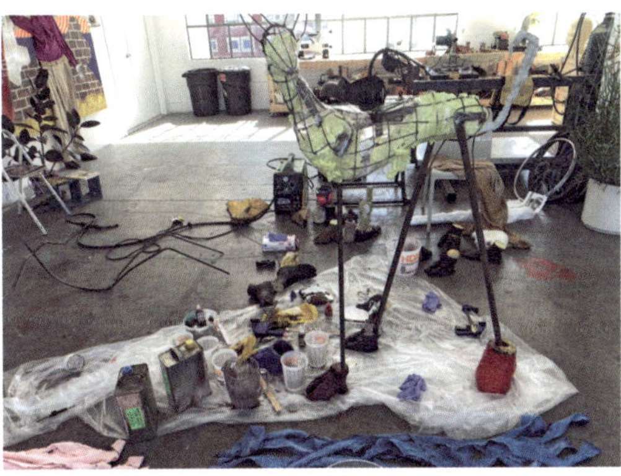

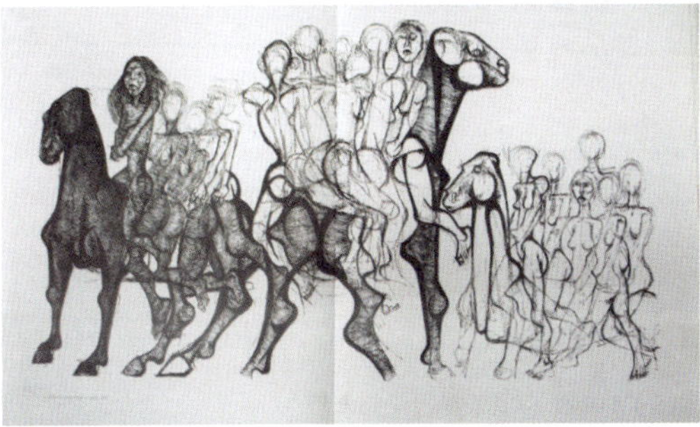

1. **Simphiwe started with a dog.** I'd made this sculpture of a dog—a metallic skeleton—that had been sitting in the studio for almost a year. It was sitting there for the longest time, chilling. I just didn't like it, couldn't see where it was going to go.

About a year later I began making a series of paintings, of figures riding totem spirit animals. And as I was looking at the paintings, I looked over at the dog, and just immediately thought, *Maybe that's not a dog*. I realized what bothered me was its four legs.

2. **So he amputated his dog's legs.** I cut off two of its legs. Then I welded one back on. Now it had three legs, and it really became so much more interesting as a form. And all of a sudden I knew exactly what to do.

3. **Because he'd been looking at some Dumile Feni drawings . . .** Feni's like the African Picasso. He's got all these bronze sculptures; I'm obsessed with them. And I started to look at his studies of figures and horses and how he could elongate and stretch them. I'm thinking, *How can I look at the old masters and channel them? Maybe I could bring them alive again, insert them into my own work.*

4. **And back at a sculpture he'd already made.** I'd done this other sculpture in 2018 of a figure riding a beast. A beast of burden. So I was also thinking, *How could I bring back that piece?* I had been thinking through this idea, about an elder that has to carry—through labor, back-breaking labor—the next generation. It was autobiographical to me, but I was also looking for ways to make it timeless, mythological—broad enough that it's not limited in meaning. In that first sculpture, the figure has an arm [or leg] that is a shovel. I realized I wanted to revisit this series. I imagined them one day coming together, having sort of a procession into Noah's ark. I thought of them as

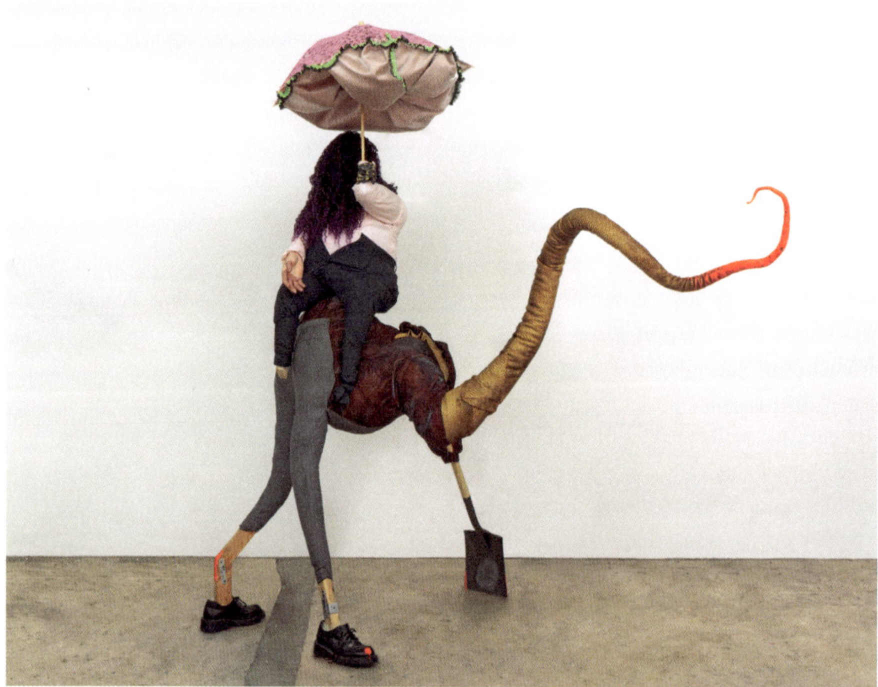

two generations, the youthful figure on top sitting on the shoulders of giants.

5. **He drew a sketch of what a new sculpture might look like.** I wanted the figure to look like it was made of ultramarine stone. I was thinking of a super-blue naked figure with a slight lumpy belly and a flag, carried by this three-legged creature.

6. **But the reclining figure didn't work.** That was the idea. But when I started welding, I was met with very practical complications—the neck's going to be weird to read because the head of the cat and the head of the figure were too close. I wasn't sure if I would want then to elongate the figure, have an even longer torso and neck. But that became more difficult to build with my hands. Also I wanted to use [a cast of] my own feet, and visually it did not make sense, because the feet were too big. So I gave up. I thought, *Maybe not now.*

But there were those paintings I'd made, some of which I had in the studio. I looked at them and thought, *The painting has the figure sitting up, why not try to make the sitting upright one from the painting?*

7. **With the posture solved, he started to build the sculpture.** I wrapped it up—and it looked like a mummified sort of ancient-looking . . . cat? It's like a sphinx cat but also an African wild dog, with the ears.

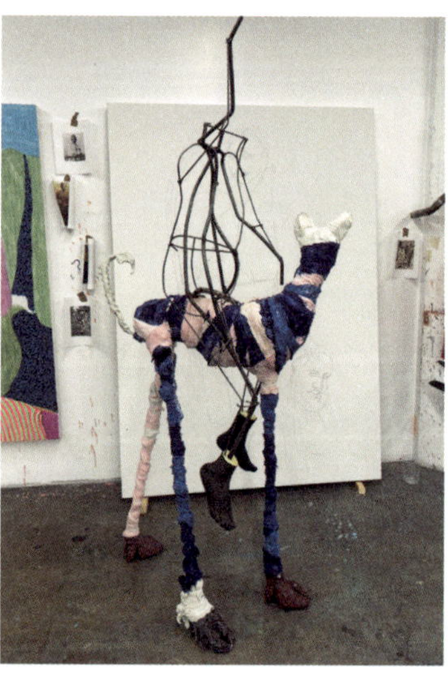

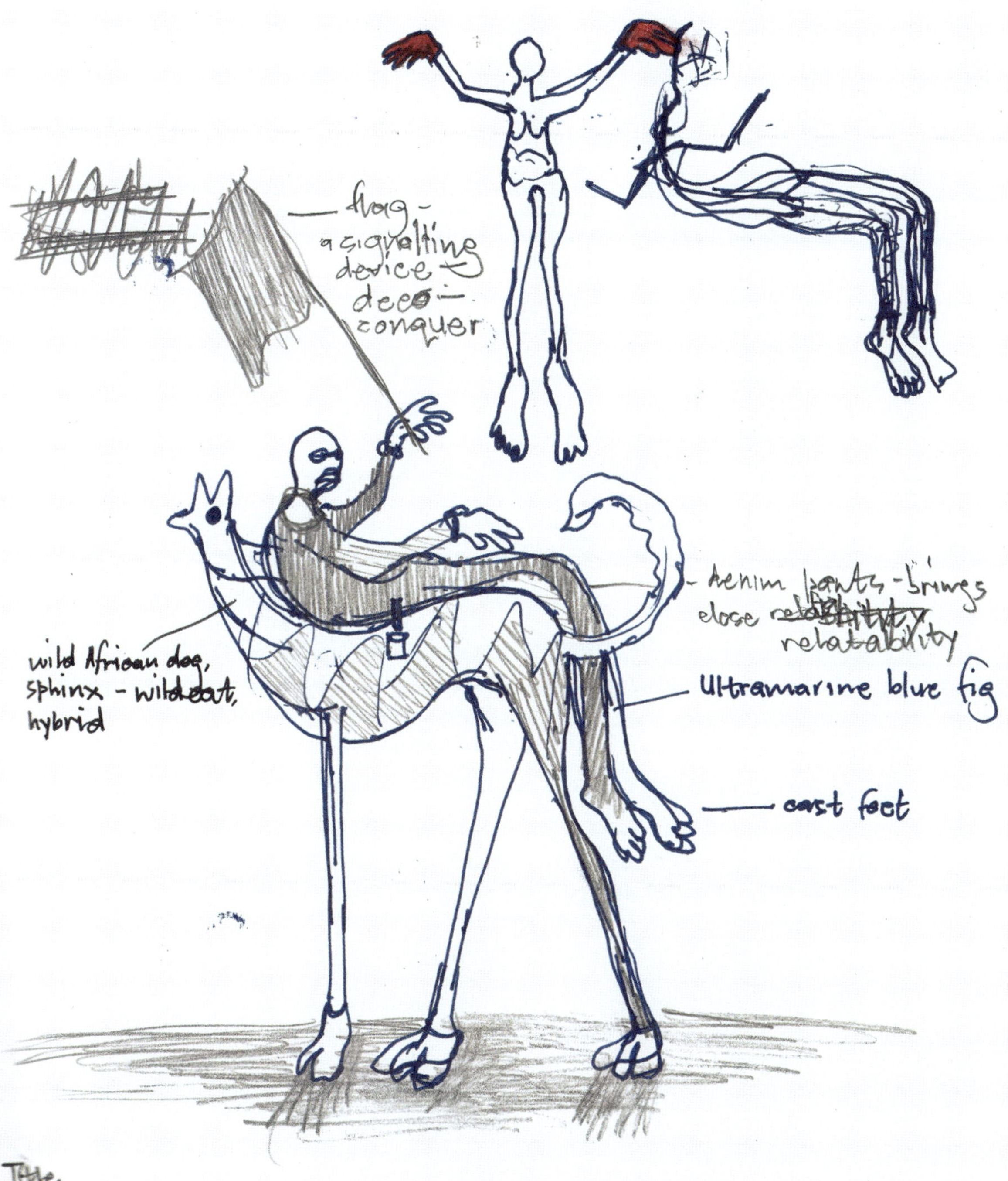
sculpture for Sadie Coles
flag -
a signalling device
deco -
conquer
denim pants - brings close relatability
wild African dog, sphinx - wildcat, hybrid
Ultramarine blue fig
cast feet
Title

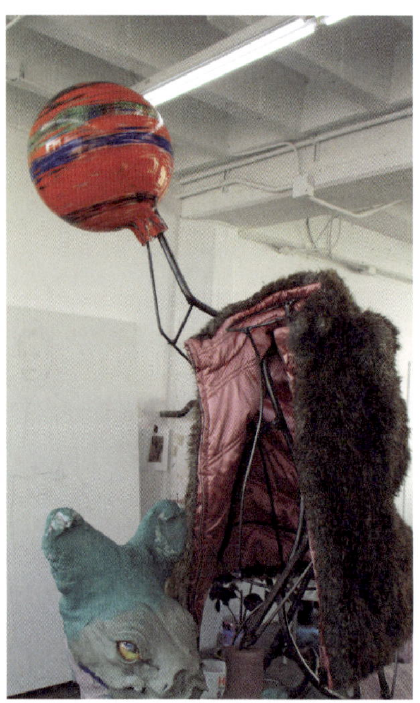

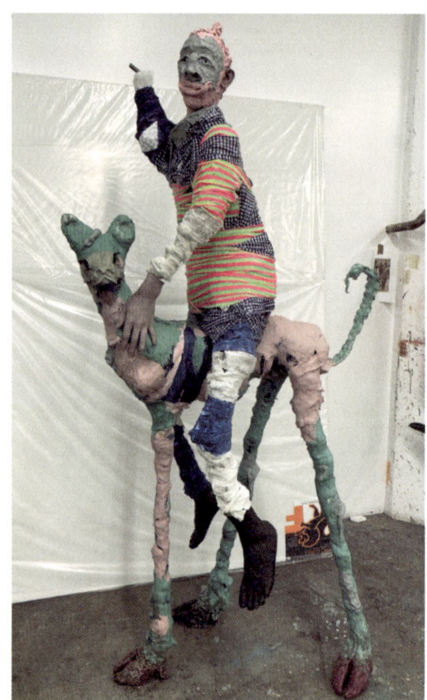

8. The head was presenting problems, so he experimented, using balloons to show him the way. I was trying different heads, weighing possibilities. I'd try things, and then I see, *Oh, it's not working.*

9. But then he got it. He moved forward, layered fabric on the sculpted figure, and switched up his materials to make it sturdier. I'm trying to create blocks of texture. It's the first time I'm using glass eyes. And I'm building it a new way—with epoxy molding paste rendered on top of a fabric stiffened with cold glue over chicken-wire mesh. I've had issues with sculptures breaking in transition. The question is, How do I make it more physically resilient, but also mythologically more open?

10. The face wasn't going the way he'd planned, but he was okay with that. The face is very hard because with sculpture it comes out however it wants to come out. I brought in dentures so it would feel abstract and real at the same time. Playful elements, but also sort of repulsive.

11. And then there was that flag he'd imagined. Did he really need it? What would the flag mean? It's an interesting statement, but is it really important as a symbol?

12. The night before it was set to go out to the gallery, he was still not satisfied. He was agitated, indecisive. Literally the night before, I was still entertaining the flag, I was putting the metallic ball there to see what it might look like. I'm still wondering, *What could the flag be?* I went back and forth, not knowing.

And then the hands, I was obsessed with the hands! At one point I had the hands wide open. I had some latex gloves I bought in South Africa I was also thinking I might bring into the work.

13. He made a last-minute decision to abandon the flag. And with no time to spare, he arrived at a hand gesture that was finally exactly right. I had a thick amount of clay, and when it was wet, it created this super-lumpy shit-looking hand. It looked muddy; it was falling off. It was the final touch. Nice, interesting, and funny—at least I think it's funny. I didn't want to force anything. In the end the easiest things to happen become the ones that feel effortlessly right.

14. The sculpture was done. I shipped it out. It had been a month since the drawing. I think the sculpture is a masterpiece, an absolute masterpiece. But it took its time.

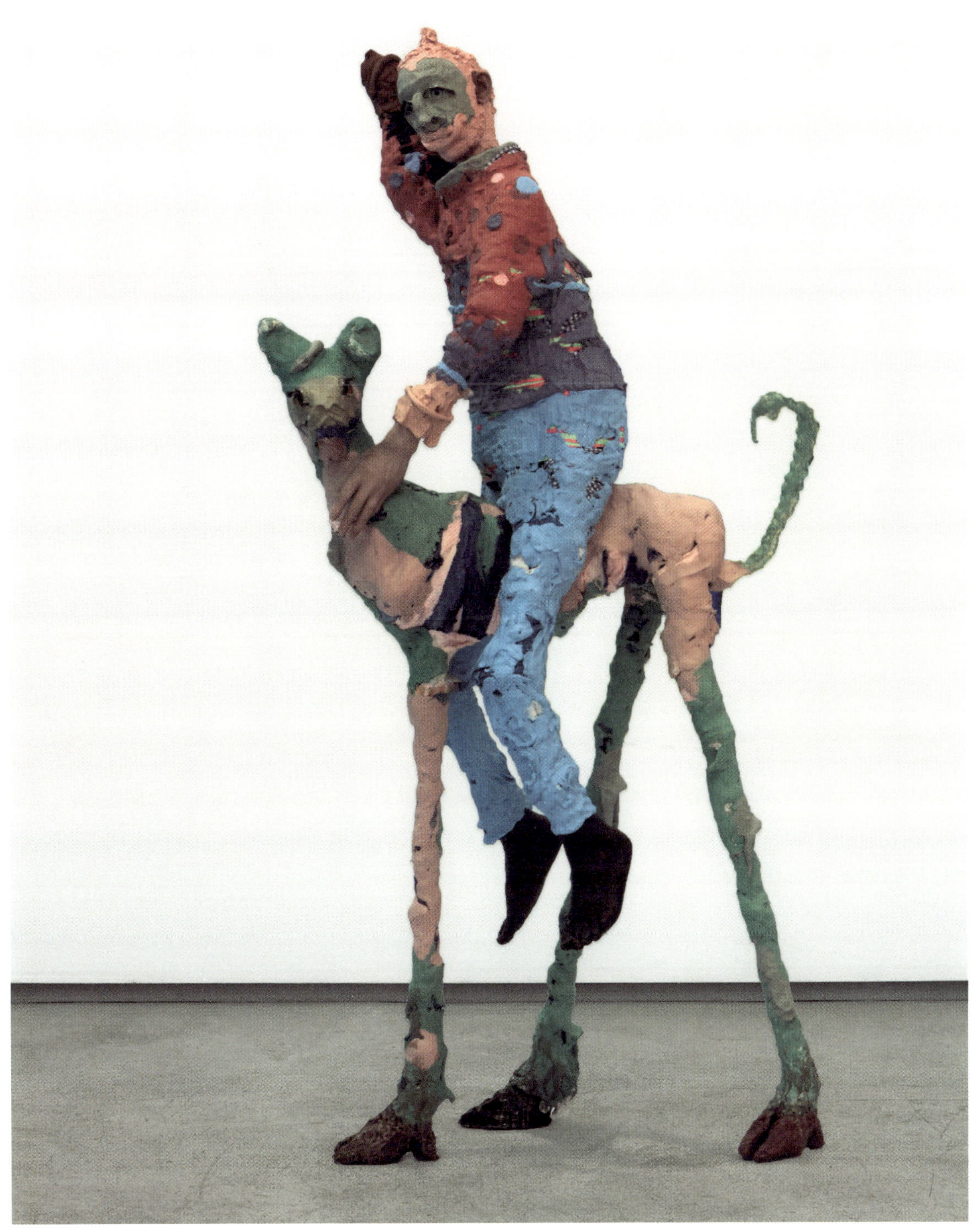

Simphiwe Ndzube, *Hunter*, 2021. Metal, fabric, resin epoxy, chicken wire, glass eyes, false eyelashes, silicone; 80 × 39.75 × 24.25 in. © Simphiwe Ndzube, courtesy Sadie Coles HQ, London.

29

DEAN BAQUET & TOM BODKIN

A "Rothko" on A1

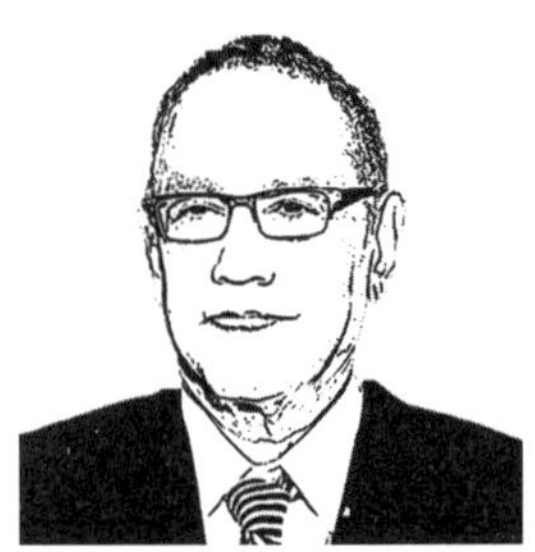

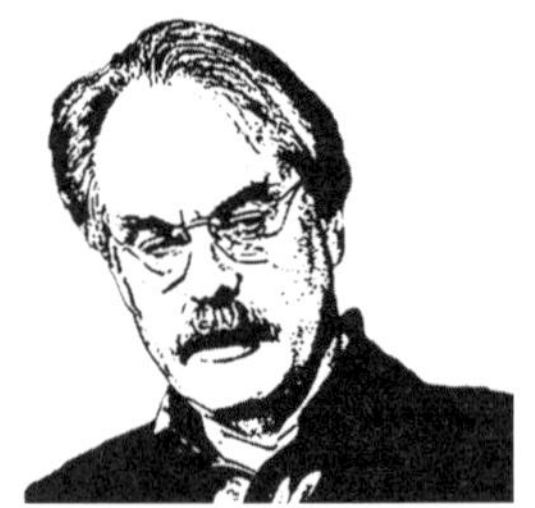

OCCUPATION: Editor, Designer

WORK DISCUSSED: *New York Times* front page (May 24, 2020)

BORN: 1956; 1953

WHEN I GRADUATED from college, I went to work as a copyboy at *The New York Times*. Less than a year later, I left because I felt like such an oddball there. In those days, people didn't quit the *Times*. But the paper was a forbidding place, with customs meant to discourage deviant behavior, and when I was twenty-one, I guess I wanted to be deviant. What used to be called the Establishment—and the *Times* was nothing if not that—fascinated me, but also held little professional allure. I was still an adolescent, and the *Times* was full of grown-ups.

I left, went to *Rolling Stone*, then *Esquire*, and then started a small, unconventional magazine called *7 Days*.[1] When that folded, I was invited back to the *Times* by Joe Lelyveld,[2] then the managing editor, an imposing journalist with a subversive spirit who generally saw the value of making trouble even inside an institution he revered. Joe had admired *7 Days* and felt that maybe the *Times* could use some of its spirit, though I was never exactly sure what that meant. I was barely thirty.

Basically, I was supposed to go around and ask questions that might help the hidebound think differently. Most of the staffers wanted no part of me, but I found some colleagues who wanted to bend the place a bit and used me as a safe vehicle with which to give that a try. We did some interesting projects, most of which never came to pass. In spite of efforts like Joe's, The *Times* wasn't really ready to experiment much, and while that was frustrating to me personally, I came to feel that generally it was for the best. The *Times* was a traditional institution that struggled with change. It could tolerate incremental movement, but anything more threatened to undermine all that was right with it.

Eventually, I found my way to the *Times* magazine, which I overhauled along with my boss Jack Rosenthal, in ways that were perceived to be

1. As mentioned, *7 Days* was a scrappy New York weekly staffed mostly by kids (me included). The magazine was not the most sophisticated publication, but it had a strong pulse and, somehow, an original voice.

2. Joe Lelyveld, who went on to lead the paper, was the closest thing to a mentor that I ever had. He taught me everything I know about serious journalism. At the same time, he was hoping my un-*Times*ness would rub off on the paper. It was a fairly hopeless project until I got to the magazine. But all told, the *Times*'s imprint on me was much greater than my imprint on the *Times*.

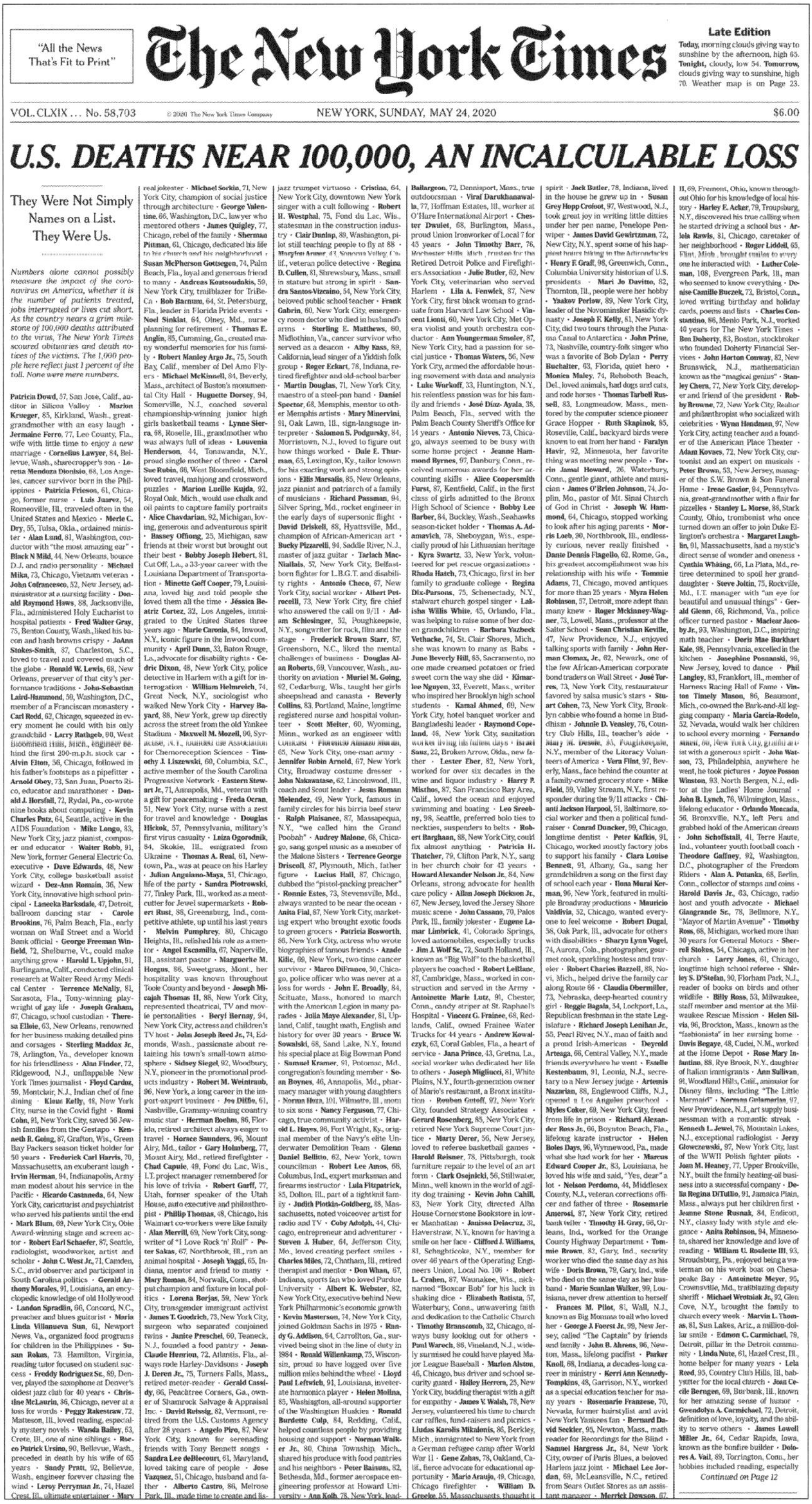

"All the News That's Fit to Print"

The New York Times

Late Edition

Today, morning clouds giving way to sunshine by the afternoon, high 65. **Tonight,** cloudy, low 54. **Tomorrow,** clouds giving way to sunshine, high 70. Weather map is on Page 23.

VOL. CLXIX ... No. 58,703 © 2020 The New York Times Company NEW YORK, SUNDAY, MAY 24, 2020 $6.00

U.S. DEATHS NEAR 100,000, AN INCALCULABLE LOSS

They Were Not Simply Names on a List. They Were Us.

Numbers alone cannot possibly measure the impact of the coronavirus on America, whether it is the number of patients treated, jobs interrupted or lives cut short. As the country nears a grim milestone of 100,000 deaths attributed to the virus, The New York Times scoured obituaries and death notices of the victims. The 1,000 people here reflect just 1 percent of the toll. None were mere numbers.

Patricia Dowd, 57, San Jose, Calif., auditor in Silicon Valley · **Marion Krueger**, 85, Kirkland, Wash., great-grandmother with an easy laugh · **Jermaine Ferro**, 77, Lee County, Fla., wife with little time to enjoy a new marriage · **Cornelius Lawyer**, 84, Bellevue, Wash., sharecropper's son · **Loretta Mendoza Dionisio**, 68, Los Angeles, cancer survivor born in the Philippines · **Patricia Frieson**, 61, Chicago, former nurse · **Luis Juarez**, 54, Romeoville, Ill., traveled often in the United States and Mexico · **Merle C. Dry**, 55, Tulsa, Okla., ordained minister · **Alan Lund**, 81, Washington, conductor with "the most amazing ear" · **Black N Mild**, 44, New Orleans, bounce D.J. and radio personality · **Michael Mika**, 73, Chicago, Vietnam veteran · **John Cofrancesco**, 52, New Jersey, administrator at a nursing facility · **Donald Raymond Haws**, 88, Jacksonville, Fla., administered Holy Eucharist to hospital patients · **Fred Walter Gray**, 75, Benton County, Wash., liked his bacon and hash browns crispy · **JoAnn Stokes-Smith**, 87, Charleston, S.C., loved to travel and covered much of the globe · **Ronald W. Lewis**, 68, New Orleans, preserver of that city's performance traditions · **John-Sebastian Laird-Hammond**, 59, Washington, D.C., member of a Franciscan monastery · **Carl Redd**, 62, Chicago, squeezed in every moment he could with his only grandchild · **Larry Rathgeb**, 90, West Bloomfield Hills, Mich., engineer behind the first 200-m.p.h. stock car · **Alvin Elton**, 56, Chicago, followed in his father's footsteps as a pipefitter · **Arnold Obey**, 73, San Juan, Puerto Rico, educator and marathoner · **Donald J. Horsfall**, 72, Rydal, Pa., co-wrote nine books about computing · **Kevin Charles Patz**, 64, Seattle, active in the AIDS Foundation · **Mike Longo**, 83, New York City, jazz pianist, composer and educator · **Walter Robb**, 91, New York, former General Electric Co. executive · **Dave Edwards**, 48, New York City, college basketball assist wizard · **Dez-Ann Romain**, 36, New York City, innovative high school principal · **Laneeka Barksdale**, 47, Detroit, ballroom dancing star · **Carole Brookins**, 76, Palm Beach, Fla., early woman on Wall Street and a World Bank official · **George Freeman Winfield**, 72, Shelburne, Vt., could make anything grow · **Harold L. Upjohn**, 81, Burlingame, Calif., conducted clinical research at Walter Reed Army Medical Center · **Terrence McNally**, 81, Sarasota, Fla., Tony-winning playwright of gay life · **Joseph Graham**, 67, Chicago, school custodian · **Theresa Elloie**, 63, New Orleans, renowned for her business making detailed pins and corsages · **Sterling Maddox Jr.**, 78, Arlington, Va., developer known for his friendliness · **Alan Finder**, 72, Ridgewood, N.J., unflappable New York Times journalist · **Floyd Cardoz**, 59, Montclair, N.J., Indian chef of fine dining · **Kious Kelly**, 48, New York City, nurse in the Covid fight · **Romi Cohn**, 91, New York City, saved 56 Jewish families from the Gestapo · **Kenneth R. Going**, 87, Grafton, Wis., Green Bay Packers season ticket holder for 50 years · **Frederick Carl Harris**, 70, Massachusetts, an exuberant laugh · **Irvin Herman**, 94, Indianapolis, Army man modest about his service in the Pacific · **Ricardo Castaneda**, 64, New York City, caricaturist and psychiatrist who served his patients until the end · **Mark Blum**, 69, New York City, Obie Award-winning stage and screen actor · **Robert Earl Schaefer**, 87, Seattle, radiologist, woodworker, artist and scholar · **John C. West Jr.**, 71, Camden, S.C., avid observer and participant in South Carolina politics · **Gerald Anthony Morales**, 91, Louisiana, an encyclopedic knowledge of old Hollywood · **Landon Spradlin**, 66, Concord, N.C., preacher and blues guitarist · **Maria Linda Villanueva Sun**, 61, Newport News, Va., organized food programs for children in the Philippines · **Susan Rokus**, 73, Hamilton, Virginia, reading tutor focused on student success · **Freddy Rodriguez Sr.**, 89, Denver, played the saxophone at Denver's oldest jazz club for 40 years · **Christine McLaurin**, 86, Chicago, never at a loss for words · **Peggy Rakestraw**, 72, Matteson, Ill., loved reading, especially mystery novels · **Wanda Bailey**, 63, Crete, Ill., one of nine siblings · **Rocco Patrick Ursino**, 90, Bellevue, Wash., preceded in death by his wife of 65 years · **Sandy Pratt**, 92, Bellevue, Wash., engineer forever chasing the wind · **Leroy Perryman Jr.**, 74, Hazel Crest, Ill., ultimate entertainer · **Mary**

real jokester · **Michael Sorkin**, 71, New York City, champion of social justice through architecture · **George Valentine**, 66, Washington, D.C., lawyer who mentored others · **James Quigley**, 77, Chicago, rebel of the family · **Sherman Pittman**, 61, Chicago, dedicated his life to his church and his neighborhood · **Susan McPherson Gottsegen**, 74, Palm Beach, Fla., loyal and generous friend to many · **Andreas Koutsoudakis**, 59, New York City, trailblazer for TriBeCa · **Bob Barnum**, 64, St. Petersburg, Fla., leader in Florida Pride events · **Noel Sinkiat**, 64, Olney, Md., nurse planning for retirement · **Thomas E. Anglin**, 85, Cumming, Ga., created many wonderful memories for his family · **Robert Manley Argo Jr.**, 75, South Bay, Calif., member of Del Amo Flyers · **Michael McKinnell**, 84, Beverly, Mass., architect of Boston's monumental City Hall · **Huguette Dorsey**, 94, Somerville, N.J., coached several championship-winning junior high girls basketball teams · **Lynne Sierra**, 68, Roselle, Ill., grandmother who was always full of ideas · **Louvenia Henderson**, 44, Tonawanda, N.Y., proud single mother of three · **Carol Sue Rubin**, 69, West Bloomfield, Mich., loved travel, mahjong and crossword puzzles · **Marion Lucille Kujda**, 92, Royal Oak, Mich., would use chalk and oil paints to capture family portraits · **Alice Chavdarian**, 92, Michigan, loving, generous and adventurous spirit · **Bassey Offiong**, 25, Michigan, saw friends at their worst but brought out their best · **Bobby Joseph Hebert**, 81, Cut Off, La., a 33-year career with the Louisiana Department of Transportation · **Minette Goff Cooper**, 79, Louisiana, loved big and told people she loved them all the time · **Jéssica Beatriz Cortez**, 32, Los Angeles, immigrated to the United States three years ago · **Marie Caronia**, 84, Inwood, N.Y., iconic figure in the Inwood community · **April Dunn**, 33, Baton Rouge, La., advocate for disability rights · **Cedric Dixon**, 48, New York City, police detective in Harlem with a gift for interrogation · **William Helmreich**, 74, Great Neck, N.Y., sociologist who walked New York City · **Harvey Bayard**, 88, New York, grew up directly across the street from the old Yankee Stadium · **Maxwell M. Mozell**, 90, Syracuse, N.Y., founded the Association for Chemoreception Sciences · **Timothy J. Liszewski**, 60, Columbia, S.C., active member of the South Carolina Progressive Network · **Eastern Stewart Jr.**, 71, Annapolis, Md., veteran with a gift for peacemaking · **Freda Ocran**, 51, New York City, nurse with a zest for travel and knowledge · **Douglas Hickok**, 57, Pennsylvania, military's first virus casualty · **Loiza Ogorodnik**, 84, Skokie, Ill., emigrated from Ukraine · **Thomas A. Real**, 61, Newtown, Pa., was at peace on his Harley · **Julian Anguiano-Maya**, 51, Chicago, life of the party · **Sandra Piotrowski**, 77, Tinley Park, Ill., worked as a meat-cutter for Jewel supermarkets · **Robert Rust**, 88, Greensburg, Ind., competitive athlete, up until his last years · **Melvin Pumphrey**, 80, Chicago Heights, Ill., relished his role as a mentor · **Angel Escamilla**, 67, Naperville, Ill., assistant pastor · **Marguerite M. Horgus**, 86, Sweetgrass, Mont., her hospitality was known throughout Toole County and beyond · **Joseph Micajah Thomas II**, 88, New York City, represented theatrical, TV and movie personalities · **Beryl Bernay**, 94, New York City, actress and children's TV host · **John Joseph Reed Jr.**, 74, Edmonds, Wash., passionate about restoring his town's small-town atmosphere · **Sidney Siegel**, 92, Woodbury, N.Y., pioneer in the promotional products industry · **Robert M. Weintraub**, 96, New York, a long career in the import-export business · **Joe Diffie**, 61, Nashville, Grammy-winning country music star · **Herman Boehm**, 86, Florida, retired architect always eager to travel · **Horace Saunders**, 96, Mount Airy, Md., tailor · **Gary Holmberg**, 77, Mount Airy, Md., retired firefighter · **Chad Capule**, 49, Fond du Lac, Wis., Walmart co-workers were like family · **Alan Merrill**, 69, New York City, songwriter of "I Love Rock 'n' Roll" · **Peter Sakas**, 67, Northbrook, Ill., ran an animal hospital · **Joseph Yaggi**, 65, Indiana, mentor and friend to many · **Mary Roman**, 84, Norwalk, Conn., shot-put champion and fixture in local politics · **Lorena Borjas**, 59, New York City, transgender immigrant activist · **James T. Goodrich**, 73, New York City, surgeon who separated conjoined twins · **Janice Preschel**, 60, Teaneck, N.J., founded a food pantry · **Jean-Claude Henrion**, 72, Atlantis, Fla., always rode Harley-Davidsons · **Joseph J. Deren Jr.**, 75, Turners Falls, Mass., retired meter-reader · **Gerald Cassidy**, 66, Peachtree Corners, Ga., owner of Shamrock Salvage & Appraisal Inc. · **David Reissig**, 82, Vermont, retired from the U.S. Customs Agency after 28 years · **Angelo Piro**, 87, New York City, known for serenading friends with Tony Bennett songs · **Sandra Lee deBlecourt**, 61, Maryland, loved taking care of people · **Jose Vazquez**, 51, Chicago, husband and father · **Alberto Castro**, 86, Melrose Park, Ill., made time to create and lis-

jazz trumpet virtuoso · **Cristina**, 64, New York City, downtown New York singer with a cult following · **Robert H. Westphal**, 75, Fond du Lac, Wis., statesman in the construction industry · **Clair Dunlap**, 89, Washington, pilot still teaching people to fly at 88 · **Marylou Armer**, 43, Sonoma Valley, Calif., veteran police detective · **Regina D. Cullen**, 81, Shrewsbury, Mass., small in stature but strong in spirit · **Sandra Santos-Vizcaino**, 54, New York City, beloved public school teacher · **Frank Gabrin**, 60, New York City, emergency room doctor who died in his husband's arms · **Sterling E. Matthews**, 60, Midlothian, Va., cancer survivor who served as a deacon · **Alby Kass**, 89, California, lead singer of a Yiddish folk group · **Roger Eckart**, 78, Indiana, retired firefighter and old-school barber · **Martin Douglas**, 71, New York City, maestro of a steel-pan band · **Daniel Spector**, 68, Memphis, mentor to other Memphis artists · **Mary Minervini**, 91, Oak Lawn, Ill., sign-language interpreter · **Salomon S. Podgursky**, 84, Morristown, N.J., loved to figure out how things worked · **Dale E. Thurman**, 65, Lexington, Ky., tailor known for his exacting work and strong opinions · **Ellis Marsalis**, 85, New Orleans, jazz pianist and patriarch of a family of musicians · **Richard Passman**, 94, Silver Spring, Md., rocket engineer in the early days of supersonic flight · **David Driskell**, 88, Hyattsville, Md., champion of African-American art · **Bucky Pizzarelli**, 94, Saddle River, N.J., master of jazz guitar · **Tarlach MacNiallais**, 57, New York City, Belfast-born fighter for L.G.B.T. and disability rights · **Antonio Checo**, 67, New York City, social worker · **Albert Petrocelli**, 73, New York City, fire chief who answered the call on 9/11 · **Adam Schlesinger**, 52, Poughkeepsie, N.Y., songwriter for rock, film and the stage · **Frederick Brown Starr**, 87, Greensboro, N.C., liked the mental challenges of business · **Douglas Alan Roberts**, 69, Vancouver, Wash., authority on aviation · **Muriel M. Going**, 92, Cedarburg, Wis., taught her girls sheepshead and canasta · **Beverly Collins**, 83, Portland, Maine, longtime registered nurse and hospital volunteer · **Scott Melter**, 60, Wyoming, Minn., worked as an engineer with Comcast · **Florencio Almazo Morán**, 65, New York City, one-man army · **Jennifer Robin Arnold**, 67, New York City, Broadway costume dresser · **John Nakawatase**, 62, Lincolnwood, Ill., coach and Scout leader · **Jesus Roman Melendez**, 49, New York, famous in family circles for his birria beef stew · **Ralph Plaisance**, 87, Massapequa, N.Y., "we called him the Grand Poobah" · **Audrey Malone**, 86, Chicago, sang gospel music as a member of the Malone Sisters · **Terrence George Driscoll**, 87, Plymouth, Mich., father figure · **Lucius Hall**, 87, Chicago, dubbed the "pistol-packing preacher" · **Ronnie Estes**, 73, Stevensville, Md., always wanted to be near the ocean · **Anita Fial**, 87, New York City, marketing expert who brought exotic foods to green grocers · **Patricia Bosworth**, 86, New York City, actress who wrote biographies of famous friends · **Azade Kilic**, 60, New York, two-time cancer survivor · **Marco DiFranco**, 50, Chicago, police officer who was never at a loss for words · **John E. Broadly**, 84, Scituate, Mass., honored to march with the American Legion in many parades · **Julia Maye Alexander**, 81, Upland, Calif., taught math, English and history for over 30 years · **Bruce W. Sowalski**, 68, Sand Lake, N.Y., found his special place at Big Bowman Pond · **Samuel Kramer**, 91, Potomac, Md., congregation's founding member · **Sean Boynes**, 46, Annapolis, Md., pharmacy manager with young daughters · **Norma Roza**, 101, Wilmette, Ill., mom to six sons · **Nancy Ferguson**, 77, Chicago, true community activist · **Harold L. Hayes**, 96, Fort Wright, Ky., original member of the Navy's elite Underwater Demolition Team · **Glenn Daniel Bellitto**, 62, New York, town councilman · **Robert Lee Amos**, 68, Columbus, Ind., expert marksman and firearms instructor · **Lula Fitzpatrick**, 85, Dolton, Ill., part of a tightknit family · **Judith Plotkin-Goldberg**, 88, Massachusetts, noted voiceover artist for radio and TV · **Coby Adolph**, 44, Chicago, entrepreneur and adventurer · **Steven J. Huber**, 64, Jefferson City, Mo., loved creating perfect smiles · **Charles Miles**, 72, Chatham, Ill., retired therapist and mentor · **Don Whan**, 67, Indiana, sports fan who loved Purdue University · **Albert K. Webster**, 82, New York City, executive behind New York Philharmonic's economic growth · **Kevin Masterson**, 74, New York City, joined Goldman Sachs in 1975 · **Randy G. Addison**, 64, Carrollton, Ga., survived being shot in the line of duty in 1984 · **Ronald Willenkamp**, 75, Wisconsin, proud to have logged over five million miles behind the wheel · **Lloyd Paul Leftwich**, 91, Louisiana, inveterate harmonica player · **Helen Molina**, 85, Washington, all-around supporter of the Washington Huskies · **Ronald Burdette Culp**, 84, Redding, Calif., helped countless people by providing housing and support · **Norman Walker Jr.**, 80, China Township, Mich., shared his produce with food pantries and his neighbors · **Peter Bainum**, 82, Bethesda, Md., former aerospace engineering professor at Howard University · **Ann Kolb**, 78, New York, lead-

Baillargeon, 72, Dennisport, Mass., true outdoorsman · **Viraf Darukhanawala**, 77, Hoffman Estates, Ill., worker at O'Hare International Airport · **Chester Dwulet**, 68, Burlington, Mass., proud Union Ironworker of Local 7 for 45 years · **John Timothy Barr**, 76, Rochester Hills, Mich., trustee for the Retired Detroit Police and Firefighters Association · **Julie Butler**, 62, New York City, veterinarian who served Harlem · **Lila A. Fenwick**, 87, New York City, first black woman to graduate from Harvard Law School · **Vincent Lionti**, 60, New York City, Met Opera violist and youth orchestra conductor · **Ann Youngerman Smoler**, 87, New York City, had a passion for social justice · **Thomas Waters**, 56, New York City, armed the affordable housing movement with data and analysis · **Luke Workoff**, 33, Huntington, N.Y., his relentless passion was for his family and friends · **José Díaz-Ayala**, 38, Palm Beach, Fla., served with the Palm Beach County Sheriff's Office for 14 years · **Antonio Nieves**, 73, Chicago, always seemed to be busy with some home project · **Jeanne Hammond Byrnes**, 97, Danbury, Conn., received numerous awards for her accounting skills · **Alice Coopersmith Furst**, 87, Kentfield, Calif., in the first class of girls admitted to the Bronx High School of Science · **Joseph W. Barber**, 84, Buckley, Wash., Seahawks season-ticket holder · **Thomas A. Adamavich**, 78, Sheboygan, Wis., especially proud of his Lithuanian heritage · **Kyra Swartz**, 33, New York, volunteered for pet rescue organizations · **Rhoda Hatch**, 73, Chicago, first in her family to graduate college · **Regina Dix-Parsons**, 75, Schenectady, N.Y., stalwart church gospel singer · **Lakisha Willis White**, 45, Orlando, Fla., was helping to raise some of her dozen grandchildren · **Barbara Yazbeck Vethacke**, 74, St. Clair Shores, Mich., she was known to many as Babs · **June Beverly Hill**, 85, Sacramento, no one made creamed potatoes or fried sweet corn the way she did · **Kimarlee Nguyen**, 33, Everett, Mass., writer who inspired her Brooklyn high school students · **Kamal Ahmed**, 69, New York City, hotel banquet worker and Bangladeshi leader · **Raymond Copeland**, 46, New York City, sanitation worker living his fullest days · **Israel Sauz**, 22, Broken Arrow, Okla., new father · **Lester Eber**, 82, New York, worked for over six decades in the wine and liquor industry · **Harry P. Misthos**, 87, San Francisco Bay Area, Calif., loved the ocean and enjoyed swimming and boating · **Leo Sreebny**, 98, Seattle, preferred bolo ties to neckties, suspenders to belts · **Robert Borghaan**, 88, New York City, could fix almost anything · **Patricia H. Thatcher**, 79, Clifton Park, N.Y., sang in her church choir for 42 years · **Howard Alexander Nelson Jr.**, 84, New Orleans, strong advocate for health care policy · **Allan Joseph Dickson Jr.**, 67, New Jersey, loved the Jersey Shore music scene · **John Cassano**, 70, Palos Park, Ill., family jokester · **Eugene Lamar Limbrick**, 41, Colorado Springs, loved automobiles, especially trucks · **Jim J. Wolf Sr.**, 72, South Holland, Ill., known as "Big Wolf" to the basketball players he coached · **Robert LeBlanc**, 87, Cambridge, Mass., worked in construction and served in the Army · **Antoinette Marie Lutz**, 91, Chester, Conn., candy striper at St. Raphael's Hospital · **Vincent G. Frainee**, 68, Redlands, Calif., owned Frainee Water Trucks for 44 years · **Andrew Kowalczyk**, 63, Coral Gables, Fla., a heart of service · **Jana Prince**, 43, Gretna, La., social worker who dedicated her life to others · **Joseph Migliucci**, 81, White Plains, N.Y., fourth-generation owner of Mario's restaurant, a Bronx institution · **Reuben Goteff**, 92, New York City, founded Strategy Associates · **Gerard Rosenberg**, 85, New York City, retired New York Supreme Court justice · **Marty Derer**, 56, New Jersey, loved to referee basketball games · **Harold Reisner**, 78, Pittsburgh, took furniture repair to the level of an art form · **Clark Osojnicki**, 56, Stillwater, Minn., well known in the world of agility dog training · **Kevin John Cahill**, 83, New York City, directed Alba House Cornerstone Bookstore in lower Manhattan · **Janissa Delacruz**, 31, Haverstraw, N.Y., known for having a smile on her face · **Clifford J. Williams**, 81, Schaghticoke, N.Y., member for over 46 years of the Operating Engineers Union, Local No. 106 · **Robert L. Crahen**, 87, Waunakee, Wis., nicknamed "Boxcar Bob" for his luck in shaking dice · **Elizabeth Batista**, 57, Waterbury, Conn., unwavering faith and dedication to the Catholic Church · **Timothy Branscomb**, 32, Chicago, always busy looking out for others · **Paul Warech**, 86, Vineland, N.J., widely surmised he could have played Major League Baseball · **Marlon Alston**, 46, Chicago, bus driver and school security guard · **Hailey Herrera**, 25, New York City, budding therapist with a gift for empathy · **James V. Walsh**, 78, New Jersey, volunteered his time to church car raffles, fund-raisers and picnics · **Liudas Karolis Mikalonis**, 86, Berkley, Mich., immigrated to New York from a German refugee camp after World War II · **Gene Zahas**, 78, Oakland, Calif., fierce advocate for educational opportunity · **Mario Araujo**, 49, Chicago, Chicago firefighter · **William D. Greeke**, 55, Massachusetts, thought it

spirit · **Jack Butler**, 78, Indiana, lived in the house he grew up in · **Susan Grey Hopp Crofoot**, 97, Westwood, N.J., took great joy in writing little ditties under her pen name, Penelope Penwiper · **James David Gewirtzman**, 72, New City, N.Y., spent some of his happiest hours hiking in the Adirondacks · **Henry F. Graff**, 98, Greenwich, Conn., Columbia University historian of U.S. presidents · **Mari Jo Davitto**, 82, Thornton, Ill., people were her hobby · **Yaakov Perlow**, 89, New York City, leader of the Novominsker Hasidic dynasty · **Joseph F. Kelly**, 81, New York City, did two tours through the Panama Canal to Antarctica · **John Prine**, 73, Nashville, country-folk singer who was a favorite of Bob Dylan · **Perry Buchalter**, 63, Florida, quiet hero · **Monica Maley**, 74, Rehoboth Beach, Del., loved animals, had dogs and cats, and rode horses · **Thomas Tarbell Russell**, 83, Longmeadow, Mass., mentored by the computer science pioneer Grace Hopper · **Ruth Skapinok**, 85, Roseville, Calif., backyard birds were known to eat from her hand · **Faralyn Havir**, 92, Minnesota, her favorite thing was meeting new people · **Torrin Jamal Howard**, 26, Waterbury, Conn., gentle giant, athlete and musician · **James O'Brien Johnson**, 74, Joplin, Mo., pastor of Mt. Sinai Church of God in Christ · **Joseph W. Hammond**, 64, Chicago, stopped working to look after his aging parents · **Morris Loeb**, 90, Northbrook, Ill., endlessly curious, never really finished · **Dante Dennis Flagello**, 62, Rome, Ga., his greatest accomplishment was his relationship with his wife · **Tommie Adams**, 71, Chicago, moved antiques for more than 25 years · **Myra Helen Robinson**, 57, Detroit, more adept than many knew · **Roger Mckinney-Wagner**, 73, Lowell, Mass., professor at the Salter School · **Sean Christian Keville**, 47, New Providence, N.J., enjoyed talking sports with family · **John Herman Clomax, Jr.**, 62, Newark, one of the few African-American corporate bond traders on Wall Street · **José Torres**, 73, New York City, restaurateur favored by salsa music's stars · **Stuart Cohen**, 73, New York City, Brooklyn cabbie who found a home in Buddhism · **Johnnie D. Veasley**, 76, Country Club Hills, Ill., teacher's aide · **Mary M. Desole**, 93, Poughkeepsie, N.Y., member of the Literacy Volunteers of America · **Vera Flint**, 97, Beverly, Mass., face behind the counter at a family-owned grocery store · **Mike Field**, 59, Valley Stream, N.Y., first responder during the 9/11 attacks · **Chianti Jackson Harpool**, 51, Baltimore, social worker and then a political fundraiser · **Conrad Duncker**, 99, Chicago, longtime dentist · **Peter Kafkis**, 91, Chicago, worked mostly factory jobs to support his family · **Clara Louise Bennett**, 91, Albany, Ga., sang her grandchildren a song on the first day of school each year · **Ilona Murai Kerman**, 96, New York, featured in multiple Broadway productions · **Mauricio Valdivia**, 52, Chicago, wanted everyone to feel welcome · **Robert Dugal**, 58, Oak Park, Ill., advocate for others with disabilities · **Sharyn Lynn Vogel**, 74, Aurora, Colo., photographer, gourmet cook, sparkling hostess and traveler · **Robert Charles Bazzell**, 88, Novi, Mich., helped drive the family car along Route 66 · **Claudia Obermiller**, 73, Nebraska, deep-hearted country girl · **Reggie Bagala**, 54, Lockport, La., Republican freshman in the state Legislature · **Richard Joseph Lenihan Jr.**, 55, Pearl River, N.Y., man of faith and a proud Irish-American · **Deyrold Arteaga**, 66, Central Valley, N.Y., made friends everywhere he went · **Estelle Kestenbaum**, 91, Leonia, N.J., secretary to a New Jersey judge · **Artemis Nazarian**, 88, Englewood Cliffs, N.J., opened a Los Angeles preschool · **Myles Coker**, 69, New York City, freed from life in prison · **Richard Alexander Ross Jr.**, 66, Boynton Beach, Fla., lifelong karate instructor · **Helen Boles Days**, 96, Wynnewood, Pa., made what she had work for her · **Marcus Edward Cooper Jr.**, 83, Louisiana, he loved his wife and said, "Yes, dear" a lot · **Nelson Perdomo**, 44, Middlesex County, N.J., veteran corrections officer and father of three · **Rosemarie Amerosi**, 87, New York City, retired bank teller · **Timothy H. Gray**, 66, Orleans, Ind., worked for the Orange County Highway Department · **Tommie Brown**, 82, Gary, Ind., security worker who died the same day as his wife · **Doris Brown**, 79, Gary, Ind., wife who died on the same day as her husband · **Marie Scanlan Walker**, 99, Louisiana, never drew attention to herself · **Frances M. Pilot**, 81, Wall, N.J., known as Big Momma to all who loved her · **George J. Foerst Jr.**, 99, New Jersey, called "The Captain" by friends and family · **John B. Ahrens**, 96, Newton, Mass., lifelong pacifist · **Parker Knoll**, 68, Indiana, a decades-long career in ministry · **Kerri Ann Kennedy-Tompkins**, 48, Garrison, N.Y., worked as a special education teacher for many years · **Rosemarie Franzese**, 70, Nevada, former hairstylist and avid New York Yankees fan · **Bernard David Seckler**, 95, Newton, Mass., math reader for Recordings for the Blind · **Samuel Hargress Jr.**, 84, New York City, owner of Paris Blues, a beloved Harlem jazz joint · **Michael Lee Jordan**, 69, McLeansville, N.C., retired from Sears Outlet Stores as an assistant manager · **Merrick Dowson**, 67,

II, 69, Fremont, Ohio, known throughout Ohio for his knowledge of local history · **Harley E. Acker**, 79, Troupsburg, N.Y., discovered his true calling when he started driving a school bus · **Arlola Rawls**, 81, Chicago, caretaker of her neighborhood · **Roger Liddell**, 65, Flint, Mich., brought smiles to everyone he interacted with · **Luther Coleman**, 108, Evergreen Park, Ill., man who seemed to know everything · **Denise Camille Buczek**, 72, Bristol, Conn., loved writing birthday and holiday cards, poems and lists · **Charles Constantino**, 86, Menlo Park, N.J., worked 40 years for The New York Times · **Ben Doherty**, 83, Boston, stockbroker who founded Doherty Financial Services · **John Horton Conway**, 82, New Brunswick, N.J., mathematician known as the "magical genius" · **Stanley Chera**, 77, New York City, developer and friend of the president · **Robby Browne**, 72, New York City, Realtor and philanthropist who socialized with celebrities · **Wynn Handman**, 97, New York City, acting teacher and a founder of the American Place Theater · **Adam Kovacs**, 72, New York City, cartoonist and an expert on musicals · **Peter Brown**, 53, New Jersey, manager of the S.W. Brown & Son Funeral Home · **Irene Gasior**, 94, Pennsylvania, great-grandmother with a flair for pizzelles · **Stanley L. Morse**, 88, Stark County, Ohio, trombonist who once turned down an offer to join Duke Ellington's orchestra · **Margaret Laughlin**, 91, Massachusetts, had a mystic's direct sense of wonder and oneness · **Cynthia Whiting**, 66, La Plata, Md., retiree determined to spoil her granddaughter · **Steve Joltin**, 75, Rockville, Md., I.T. manager with "an eye for beautiful and unusual things" · **Gerald Glenn**, 66, Richmond, Va., police officer turned pastor · **Maclear Jacoby Jr.**, 93, Washington, D.C., inspiring math teacher · **Doris Mae Burkhart Kale**, 98, Pennsylvania, excelled in the kitchen · **Josephine Posnanski**, 98, New Jersey, loved to dance · **Phil Langley**, 83, Frankfort, Ill., member of Harness Racing Hall of Fame · **Vinton Timely Mason**, 86, Beaumont, Mich., co-owned the Bark-and-All logging company · **Maria Garcia-Rodelo**, 52, Nevada, would walk her children to school every morning · **Fernando Miteli**, 60, New York City, graffiti artist with a generous spirit · **John Watson**, 73, Philadelphia, anywhere he went, he took pictures · **Joyce Posson Winston**, 93, North Bergen, N.J., editor at the Ladies' Home Journal · **John B. Lynch**, 76, Wilmington, Mass., lifelong educator · **Orlando Moncada**, 56, Bronxville, N.Y., left Peru and grabbed hold of the American dream · **John Schoffstall**, 41, Terre Haute, Ind., volunteer youth football coach · **Theodore Gaffney**, 92, Washington, D.C., photographer of the Freedom Riders · **Alan A. Potanka**, 68, Berlin, Conn., collector of stamps and coins · **Harold Davis Jr.**, 63, Chicago, radio host and youth advocate · **Michael Giangrande Sr.**, 78, Bellmore, N.Y., "Mayor of Martin Avenue" · **Timothy Ross**, 68, Michigan, worked more than 30 years for General Motors · **Sherrell Stokes**, 54, Chicago, active in her church · **Larry Jones**, 61, Chicago, longtime high school referee · **Shirley S. D'Stefan**, 90, Florham Park, N.J., reader of books on birds and other wildlife · **Billy Ross**, 53, Milwaukee, staff member and mentor at the Milwaukee Rescue Mission · **Helen Silvia**, 96, Brockton, Mass., known as the "fashionista" in her nursing home · **Davis Begaye**, 48, Cudei, N.M., worked at the Home Depot · **Rose Mary Infantino**, 88, Rye Brook, N.Y., daughter of Italian immigrants · **Ann Sullivan**, 91, Woodland Hills, Calif., animator for Disney films, including "The Little Mermaid" · **Norman Gulamerian**, 92, New Providence, N.J., art supply businessman with a romantic streak · **Kenneth L. Jewel**, 78, Mountain Lakes, N.J., exceptional radiologist · **Jerzy Glowczewski**, 97, New York City, last of the WWII Polish fighter pilots · **Joan M. Heaney**, 77, Upper Brookville, N.Y., built the family heating-oil business into a successful company · **Delia Regina DiTullio**, 91, Jamaica Plain, Mass., always put her children first · **Jeanne Stone Rusnak**, 84, Endicott, N.Y., classy lady with style and elegance · **Anita Robinson**, 94, Minnesota, shared her knowledge and love of reading · **William U. Roulette III**, 93, Stroudsburg, Pa., enjoyed being a waterman on his work boat on Chesapeake Bay · **Antoinette Meyer**, 95, Crownsville, Md., trailblazing deputy sheriff · **Michael Wrotniak Jr.**, 92, Glen Cove, N.Y., brought the family to church every week · **Marvin L. Thomas**, 81, Sun Lakes, Ariz., a million-dollar smile · **Edmon C. Carmichael**, 79, Detroit, pillar in the Detroit community · **Linda Nute**, 61, Hazel Crest, Ill., home helper for many years · **Lela Reed**, 95, Country Club Hills, Ill., babysitter for the local church · **Joan Cecile Berngen**, 69, Burbank, Ill., known for her amazing sense of humor · **Gwendolyn A. Carmichael**, 72, Detroit, definition of love, loyalty, and the ability to serve others · **James Lowell Miller Jr.**, 64, Cedar Rapids, Iowa, known as the bonfire builder · **Dolores A. Vail**, 89, Torrington, Conn., her hobbies included reading, especially

Continued on Page 12

May 24, 2020. The front page becomes a memorial.

radical within the institution (principally, conceiving it as a publication with properties associated with a freestanding magazine, rather than a newspaper supplement) but that to me seemed modest. When I became the magazine's editor, I became more aggressive in testing the *New York Times*'s boundaries, which made me both allies and enemies at the paper. In retrospect, I realize that I felt freer to experiment than my colleagues because the validation I sought was from outside the paper—I wanted to impress my old magazine crowd more than the newsroom. I've come to see that where you direct your need for approval has a lot to do with the kind of work that you do.[3]

Eventually I was promoted into management (though I was reluctant to leave my hands-on job at the magazine), and in my new role I attended the Page One meetings. The front page of the *Times* was in many ways the paper incarnate, the repository of all its values. What the *Times* said on its front page set the agenda for government, other media, its readers' very sense of what was right (and mostly wrong) with the world. Its influence was almost incalculable. And so it was kind of a sacred page, very carefully programmed, with rituals of placement and language mostly only intuited by its readers but very much understood within the institution. Journalists at the paper marked their career progress by how often they appeared on the page. Editors cowered in the Page One meetings because they were generally meant to; fear was a leadership tool that created conformity.[4] In the conversation that follows, I speak with two of the editors in those meetings, Dean Baquet, who was the national editor when I was at the *Times* and would go on to become the top editor, which he was at the time we talked; and Tom Bodkin, who was (and is still, though with less of a day-to-day role) the paper's chief designer.

I wanted to talk to them because on May 24, 2020, I awoke to a startling sight. I unfurled the newspaper I still read on paper every morning. The front page was not like the front page the paper had been publishing since 1851, but something else entirely: a public monument memorializing the first one hundred thousand COVID deaths, hundreds of names in tiny type (like Maya Lin's Vietnam memorial, in a sense) under one headline. In effect, it was a single image, a wail of grief.

Categorically, it was a work of art rather than information, and while you can argue about whether it succeeded or not (I thought so, but some others I know were less sure), you couldn't help but see it as an astonishing and wrenching departure from tradition in an institution particularly attached to it.

As I asked my old colleagues to talk about how the page came to be, I also hoped to get some insight in how creativity can work within an institutional setting—the *Times* being historically a pretty straightjacketed example—and how executive decisions, a simple yes or no, can also function as artistic acts.

A lot has changed since I was there in the nineties and early aughts. Number-one change dwarfing all others: the internet, which has dissolved the paper's physical form to an enormous extent, making it, as media jargon has it, digital first. For that reason, the paper's front page is a kind of relic, which no doubt liberates its makers from the page's heritage, though A1 (as it is called) is still important. In so many respects, the context in which journalism (and authority, which is almost indistinguishable from the *Times*'s self-concept) operates has changed substantially, which made the wrecking ball to the page possible. But still, though conditions matter, so do the makers themselves.

From 2014 until he stepped down after our conversation in 2022, Dean was the paper's editor—to my mind, as good (aggressive, highly creative within the paper's traditions, sensitive but not knee-jerk to shifting currents) as any the paper has ever known, a transformational

3. Another way that validation works. Where you seek it matters as much as where you get it.

4. And it worked! For my first several years sitting in at Page One meetings, I may have opened my mouth twice. I was terrified.

5. Howell Raines, the executive editor of *The New York Times* from 2001 to 2003, when I was at the paper, had a turbulent tenure, and resigned in the wake of the Jayson Blair scandal and a staff revolt over his management style. But he had a big, and lasting, effect on the paper.

figure, especially given all the change he'd had to navigate. He says the fact that he was not a *Times* lifer (he left his post as national editor to edit the *Los Angeles Times* before returning to *The New York Times*) gave him permission to toy with *Times* conventions. As for Tom, he's a perfectly calibrated design chief for the *Times*, a traditionalist at heart who is talented, smart, and unusually strategic, a mix that always made him an extraordinarily effective innovator within the paper. The three of us spoke twice on Zoom, Tom from his country house, Dean from Los Angeles, where he'd been editing the paper remotely, which also seemed inconceivable to me.

Adam Moss: *I was looking at every front page in 2020. It's an incredible run of history. There's the Trump impeachment trial, then the first premonition of COVID, and the mounting awareness of its impact, month after month. There's the election, of course, and then just six days after the year is over, the January 6 insurrection. So I suspect they'll be teaching this in high schools. But it's covering this first year of COVID that I want to talk about—in one narrow sense, which is the way it changed the front page of the physical newspaper. I'm fixed on the day, observing the one hundred thousandth COVID death, that you devoted the entire page to a wall to wall tiny-type roster of COVID lives lost. That was just such a departure from the* New York Times *that I worked at, which was not really that long ago. I wanted to discuss how you got there, and how you see the front page, in this period of its fading influence, at least as compared to the paper's digital reach. So let's discuss what you think you were departing from.*
Tom Bodkin: You know, it's funny. I don't think we were departing all that much. Even though it looks like we are. My focus as the designer is all about augmenting the content, making it clearer, and giving people an emotional connection to it. But it's all based on the very solid, basic values that the *Times* has always had. Were you at the paper when we went to color?
AM: *Yep.*
Dean Baquet: Me too.
TB: Well, my biggest challenge was to convince people, because there was a huge amount of resistance, both internally and externally, to color—that it would dilute our values, be like *USA Today*. . . .
DB: By the way, I was one of the idiotic resisters.
TB: You were not alone! The great majority of *New York Times* employees were against it, the great majority of the public.
AM: *What's the mission of the page to you both? Like, for example, it's obvious that the front page has always been about creating a hierarchy of importance according to the* Times*—to say* this *is more important than* that.
TB: Definitely, but it's also about presenting a physical representation of the *Times*'s values. The size of the headlines, the drama you try to create or not. It needs to be substantive, but we want it to be entertaining too. It represents us.
DB: But I think we've shed some restrictions in order to realize the vision you've described. If you go back in time to when I was national editor, if the vice president was mentioned in the top of the story, the vice president's picture had to be on the front page. A photograph couldn't work its way onto the page based on its news value. So the values are even more pure now because we're more honest about the hierarchy. And then the internet has changed the way I, at least, think about what stories go on the front page.
TB: What I do today, I couldn't really do pre-Dean. [Dean laughs it off.] I'm serious. Changes in media have helped us open up a bit. But editors tend to be very literal thinkers. That's just the way they're trained. They're not meant to be imaginative.
AM: *That's pretty much how I remember it.*
TB: Once you get to visual representations, if you're rigidly literal, you're not going to get across what you want to get across, and on the front page we were locked. I gotta say, you know, what's his name? [*laughs*] [Former executive editor] Howell [Raines][5] . . . did a

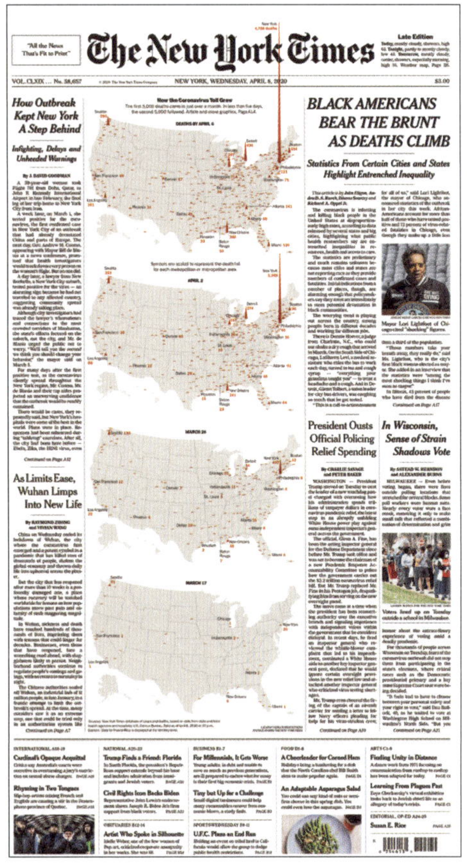

"All the News That's Fit to Print"

The New York Times

VOL. CLXIX . . . No. 58,657 — NEW YORK, WEDNESDAY, APRIL 8, 2020 — $3.00

How Outbreak Kept New York A Step Behind

Infighting, Delays and Unheeded Warnings

BLACK AMERICANS BEAR THE BRUNT AS DEATHS CLIMB

Statistics From Certain Cities and States Highlight Entrenched Inequality

President Ousts Official Policing Relief Spending

In Wisconsin, Sense of Strain Shadows Vote

As Limits Ease, Wuhan Limps Into New Life

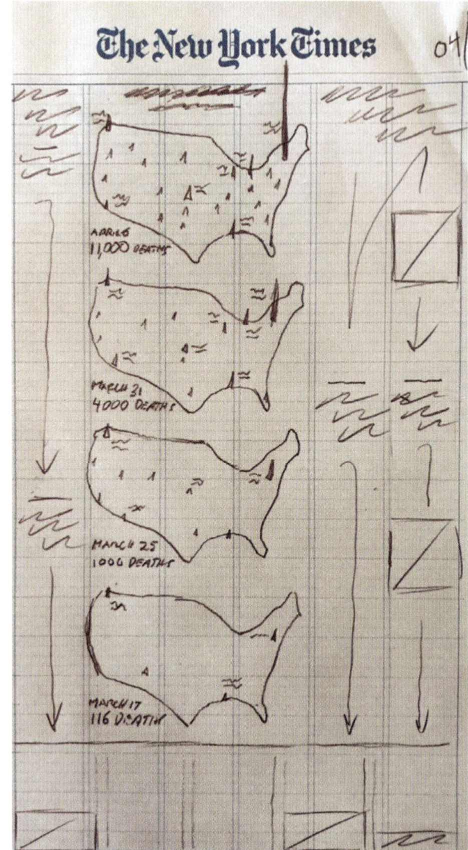

Steps on the way to May 24. A graphic takes over most of the page and pierces the logo (with a page one drawing by Tom. Such front-page sketches are made by designers after the editors' discussions).

little bit of the freeing up.

DB: Howell?

TB: I hate to admit it. But he did, partly just because he was really interested in photography.

AM: *Well, Howell was really trying to make sure every front page was dramatic. He would talk about it in those terms. He thought like a magazine editor—or a television producer.*

TB: That's right. And one of the things that got in his way, is he wanted *every* page to be dramatic. Sort of to an almost equal level. So it's hard to modulate things. I mean, we're not going to do what we did with one hundred thousand deaths without its magnitude. It's a great example.

AM: *Dean, your tenure coincides with some first-person stuff on the page.*

DB: More than that, we lead the paper with analysis pieces now. You have to be able to tell the difference between habit and true traditions. Newspapers used to put first-person material on the front page one hundred years ago all the time. The traditional *New York Times* lead of the paper, that's a silly tradition, to my way of thinking.

AM: *If it's not a banner head [a large headline running the width of the paper], I think people don't even know what the paper is saying is the most important story.*

6. A nut graph is the paragraph where the writer makes the case for the story's significance.

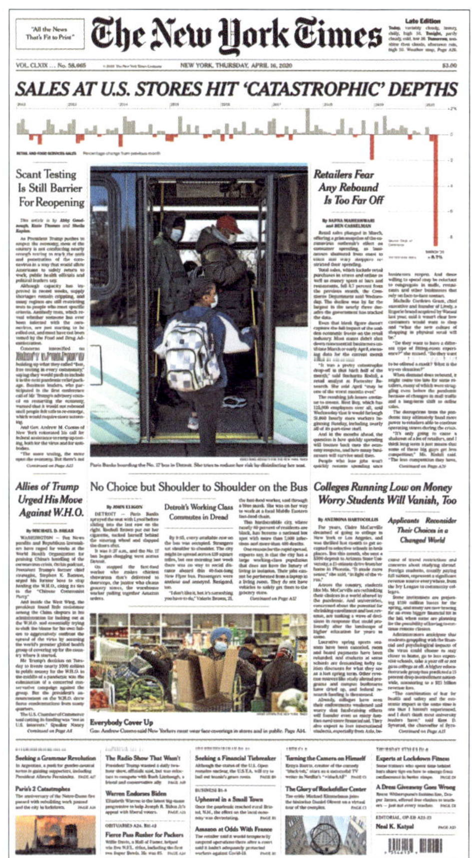

"All the News That's Fit to Print"

The New York Times

Late Edition

VOL. CLXIX ... No. 58,665 — NEW YORK, THURSDAY, APRIL 16, 2020 — $3.00

SALES AT U.S. STORES HIT 'CATASTROPHIC' DEPTHS

Scant Testing Is Still Barrier For Reopening

Retailers Fear Any Rebound Is Too Far Off

Allies of Trump Urged His Move Against W.H.O.

No Choice but Shoulder to Shoulder on the Bus

Detroit's Working Class Commutes in Dread

Colleges Running Low on Money Worry Students Will Vanish, Too

Applicants Reconsider Their Choices in a Changed World

Everybody Cover Up

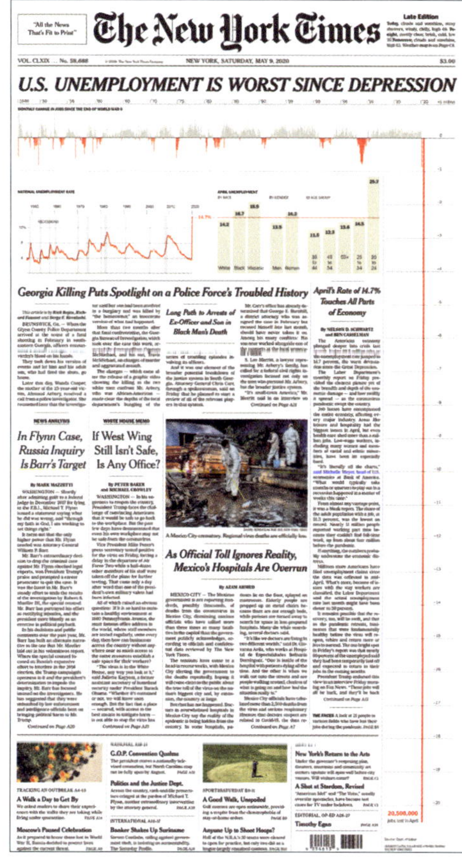

"All the News That's Fit to Print"

The New York Times

Late Edition

VOL. CLXIX ... No. 58,688 — NEW YORK, SATURDAY, MAY 9, 2020 — $3.00

U.S. UNEMPLOYMENT IS WORST SINCE DEPRESSION

Georgia Killing Puts Spotlight on a Police Force's Troubled History

Long Path to Arrests of Ex-Officer and Son in Black Man's Death

April's Rate of 14.7% Touches All Parts of Economy

In Flynn Case, Russia Inquiry Is Barr's Target

If West Wing Still Isn't Safe, Is Any Office?

As Official Toll Ignores Reality, Mexico's Hospitals Are Overrun

A six-column graphic where a sub-headline might go. Then, a graphic takes over the crucial right column, where the lead story goes.

DB: I always thought if you wanted to do a graphic of how *The New York Times* has changed, and I can say this now, rest his soul, you could monitor the reduction of front-page stories by Robert Pear [who covered Congress and policy]. Because frankly, most of those stories were not that important. But the paper had to be dressed a certain way, in lead-of-the-paper clothing. It had to have a certain kind of lead, a certain kind of nut graph.[6] I think that newspapers, not just *The New York Times*, inflated stories that were not that important in order to meet this standard. And it was sort of ridiculous, right? If you look at traditional *Times* leads in the paper fifteen years ago, you'll see modest changes in Medicare policy that were not that important. But they looked like lead-of-the-paper stories.

TB: I have a philosophy about design that I sort of refer to as progressive engagement. When people look at something complicated like *The New York Times*, they first have an overall impression. What is the tone of the day? What is the feeling? And then they start focusing in.

DB: That's very much an artist's or painter's construct, right? People get a feeling, then look at detail?

AM: *Who are you editing the front page for at this point?*

DB: Well, internally we've changed. The big front-page meeting doesn't exist anymore. There is a meeting; we talk through the front. But you have to acknowledge that even though there is still such a thing as the most important story of the day, if it happened early, you've got to find a way to tell people something different. I mean, even if you—the reader I mean—are not on your phone constantly, you have a general sense of the news through osmosis and conversation.

Also, what is news has changed a little bit too. The budget, the things that used to dominate the front page, are not as important as changes in the way people live their lives. I'm driven very much by the belief that *The New York Times* has to have as high a percentage as possible of things nobody else has. You know, Joe Lelyveld, who I love. I hope Joe doesn't read your book. [I laugh.] There were two quotes in my mind from Joe about the front page. One, in retrospect was silly, as much as I love him. I broke a story with Jeff Gerth years ago, as a reporter, about the Clintons, and I don't even remember what it was, but Joe wanted the presentation to be restrained, which I respected. But his quote was, "I want people to think we're sort of reluctant to bring them this news." As much as I love him, that's ridiculous. But I also remember one other thing that he said that was powerful. Someone, maybe Arthur Sulzberger Sr., someone from the family, died, and Joe said something like, "What I like about this front page is that it looks like the paper's in mourning." And I thought it showed such respect for the role of the front page.

AM: *But both comments reflect the extent that one of the functions of the front page is to create an affect. The first was tentativeness, the second grief.*

TB: One of the things that print, at the scale of a newspaper, can do that is very difficult digitally is work like a canvas—express very broad emotion, but also offer detail. The internet is very much a sequential experience. You're scrolling.

7. We spoke for the first time on May 13, 2021. It was the day the CDC relaxed its COVID mask mandate.

8. In 2000, Dean left the *Times* to become managing editor of the *LA Times*. He returned in 2007.

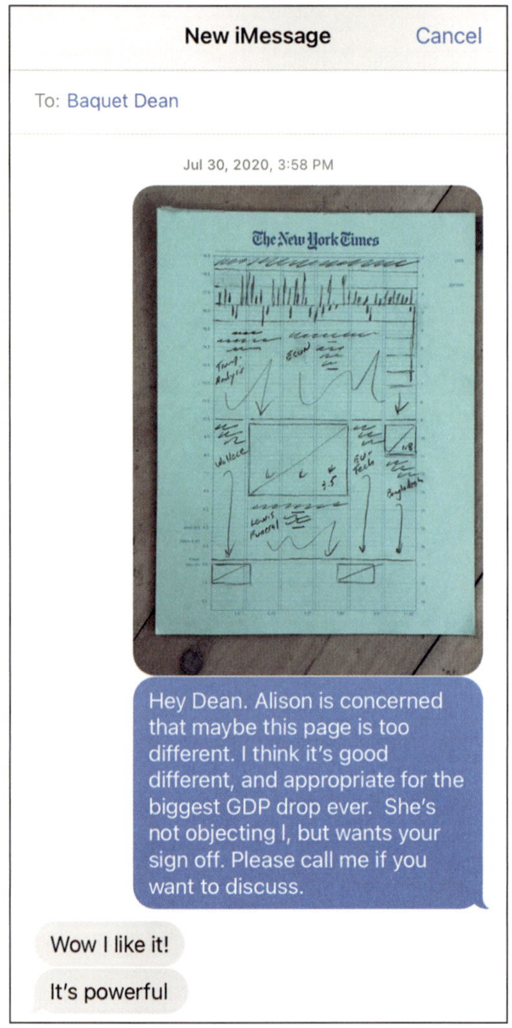

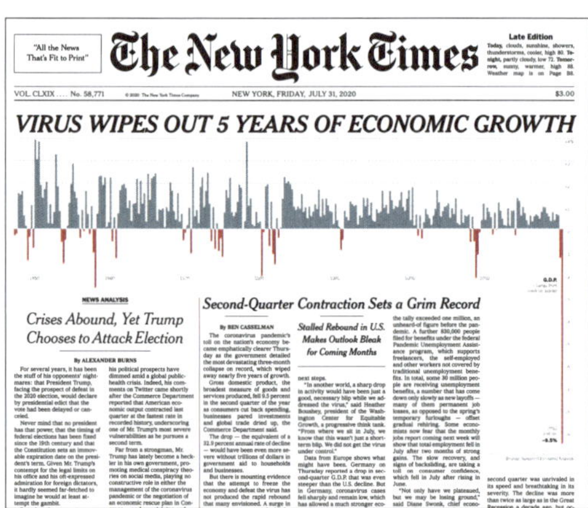
"All the News That's Fit to Print"

The New York Times

Late Edition

VOL. CLXIX .... No. 58,771 — NEW YORK, FRIDAY, JULY 31, 2020 — $3.00

VIRUS WIPES OUT 5 YEARS OF ECONOMIC GROWTH

NEWS ANALYSIS

Crises Abound, Yet Trump Chooses to Attack Election

By ALEXANDER BURNS

Second-Quarter Contraction Sets a Grim Record

By BEN CASSELMAN

Stalled Rebound in U.S. Makes Outlook Bleak for Coming Months

Text exchange between Tom and Dean over a July 31 page one design that broke convention again.

AM: *Is there an extent to which the declining print readership actually liberates you? I think the answer is going to be no, but I'm just asking.*
DB: It's funny. I was going to say yes. I don't feel pressured to get some stories on the front page. They'll get good play somewhere else.
AM: *The print edition has different readers than your digital edition.*
TB: Yes, the print reader has made a very deliberate choice. So for them you want a slower, maybe deeper experience.
AM: *Do you make the page for historical purposes at all?*
DB: You know, today we had a conversation. I argued that we needed a banner about today's news, about the lifting of the mask restrictions.[7] The science desk tried to convince me that we shouldn't use it as a banner, that we didn't learn a whole lot more about the science. And my view is that when people go back and look at the front pages of *The New York Times*, you've got to have a banner headline on the day they were told they didn't have to wear masks if they're vaccinated. That is a fucking big deal. There are moments.
TB: The moment thing is super important. Often I have to argue for a bigger head than my colleagues want to use. But Dean understands. And I think part of it is because he does appreciate art.
DB: It's also because I left the paper.[8]
TB: Yes, that helps.

SPEAKING IN A DIFFERENT LANGUAGE

I wanted to ask Dean about another huge shift in the front page, the use of more subjective language that came with covering the Trump administration.
AM: *Can we talk about the other stories of 2020? Specifically, I want to ask you about the escalation in the language you used to describe Trump, especially in front-page headlines.*
DB: The first discussion was over the word *lie*. I mean, all politicians lie, right? But he was clearly playing in another league. In the back of my mind, I was looking for a moment to use it. And the one time we did it, it was so clear. It was when Trump backed off from his statement that Barack Obama was not born in the US. And he went further than that—he said, "I have hired people, they're looking at it, and they're finding very interesting things." So when he finally said he didn't hire anybody, he conceded that was a complete lie, and we used the word *lie*. But I still wanted to make it that I had to sign off every time we used that word. Because I was wary of slipping, [of making it difficult to] extricate from it.
AM: *I was wondering if you were.*
DB: I mean, some of the loosening up of language should continue. We should never have done all of the crazy backflips newspapers went through to keep from using the word *racist*. In retrospect, that was ridiculous. But I think the way we've made it easier to extricate is that we didn't use the word *lie* too often. I was a jerk about it sometimes. But there was another powerful front page when we decided to really call him out for subverting the election.
AM: *One that really struck me—it was a six-column banner on a piece of news analysis by David Sanger. The headline said "Trump Escalates Push to Erode Trust in Vote." And the deck read "baseless attacks threaten a process in place since 1788." And yet, that day's news wasn't all that different than what he had done the day before. So you were making an overall characterization.*
DB: That's the one I was thinking of. I just wanted to do it. It was a drumbeat. We probably could have written that headline three, four days before. But we needed a vehicle to call it in a more dramatic way.
AM: *Do you feel you go over the line sometimes?*
DB: I'm not shy about it. We go overboard sometimes. On the headline on the story about the George Floyd anniversary, we used the phrase "call to action." I thought that was too much [that the *Times* was implictly making a call to action as well].

AM: *All right, let's talk about the COVID pages. The way I see it, you had three front pages before the May 24 issue, where you were dipping your toes in a major disruption of storytelling techniques through graphics on the page. On March 27 you have a job losses graphic extending downward from a horizontal graph, taking over the right-hand column.*

On April 16 you use a graphic as the second line of a banner headline—it's about stores.

And then May 9 was very dramatic, with unemployment figures plummeting down the right column.

TB: There was one other.

AM: *Where you pierced the logo . . .*

TB: And the peak went through the logo. I liked that one a lot.

AM: *So, all of these were departures before you got to the one hundred thousand day. I wouldn't call them baby steps, because in other times they would be considered gigantic. But in the end, they pale next to the one hundred thousand page. Was there a debate among all those literal editors?*

TB: Yes. There were real concerns, but people were willing to let go of some of them. These numbers are almost a metaphor, and a lot of things artists do are metaphorical. I mean, this is not normal. And I feel almost an obligation to do something different. I want them to look at this page and say, "Shit, the *Times* must think this is really huge."

AM: *Was there a sense of momentum, one of these changes emboldening the other?*

TB: The first was the hardest, in terms of convincing my colleagues that it was going to be okay. But once we did it, the reaction was positive, right? After the first, I felt, *Okay, we should look for other moments*. And the next moment was when retail sales fell to nothing.

AM: *Did you feel that you were in any danger of hooking the reader into an expectation that you're now going to be speaking in this more dramatic language?*

TB: No, because variation is important. And you don't hit one hundred thousand deaths every day.

AM: *Okay, so the one hundred thousand deaths.*

TB: I think what probably happened was Marc Lacey, [then the national editor], said something like the day was coming in a month or so, and we've got to be doing something special for it. And Simone Landon [a graphics editor] had the idea to gather all these obituaries; and then an algorithm was written to pull them all from different sources.

AM: *So it was imagined as a project for inside the paper.*

TB: I wasn't even aware it was going on. My initial thought was hundreds of tiny little pictures. Because what I do, this is my designer's head, is I try to reduce things.[9] And what I'm thinking is we want to express two things: the magnitude, and the humanity. It's one hundred thousand people dying. So, you know, what does that look like? Tiny faces filling the whole page.

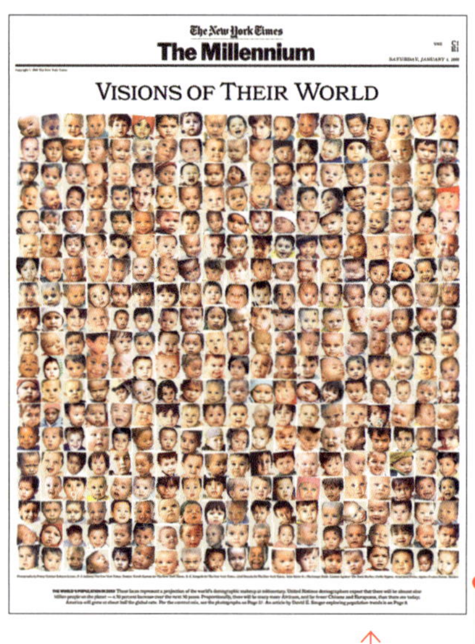
The New York Times
The Millennium
VISIONS OF THEIR WORLD

A grid of faces of the sort Tom first imagined had been employed for a special section in 2000.

I started talking to the picture desk about it. And they were, "Man, that's gonna be hard to get a hundred thousand, you know?"

So maybe two or three weeks before, Marc Lacey calls and he says he's seen all these special pages now, and I think, you know, a lot of names would have the same impact. I thought the important part was the putting nothing else on the page. And I knew that would actually be very hard to get anybody to agree to, except Dean.

AM: *You brought this to Dean?*

DB: You sent me a text, or an email.

TB: I'm pretty sure that's exactly what I did. To work at *The New York Times* effectively, you have to be very good at strategy. I didn't have the patience to convince every literal editor. I knew that the editors would say, "Well, don't we need a few refers[10] at the bottom of the page?" I decided I'm not going to discuss this with anybody, I'm just going to fucking do it. And then I'm going to show it to Dean. Because I knew Dean would get it immediately.

AM: *Okay.*

TB: And at this point I'd been convinced that a typographic solution was actually better.

AM: *In some ways it deviates less than the pictures.*

TB: Correct! We fooled around with a lot of ways of doing it, different columns and stuff. And I thought, even though six columns isn't maybe the best way to present this content, I want six columns and column rules—minimal other changes to the page.

AM: *Let's switch points of view. Dean, what do you remember?*

DB: Tom emailed me a mock-up of the page. And I don't remember having any hesitation at all.

AM: *Really?*

DB: Maybe I've romanticized it a bit. But . . .

[Dean's phone rings.] Okay, let me call her back.

TB: [Tom looks at his phone.] Yes, she's calling me now because she wants to make a headline change on the page. . . .

[They return to our conversation.]

DB: So my recollection is no hesitation.

TB: I knew you would get it.

DB: It did not feel like it wasn't *The New York Times*. I got a couple of calls from editors who said, "You sure?"

TB: I didn't realize that. Really?

DB: I won't tell you who. Anyway, like twenty minutes later, just because whenever I deviate, when I deviate that much, I sent a copy of it to A. G. Sulzberger. Just because the publisher should not be surprised. And my recollection was, he had a one-word response: "Wow."[11]

TB: It didn't really matter what day we did it, because we were approaching one hundred thousand. So we decided to do it on a Sunday. Partly because of the circulation on Sundays. If you're gonna do it . . .

—

Dean hops off to deal with the front-page problem that the editor had been calling about. Ultimately Dean does not get the banner head he wanted. In spite of his belief in the magnitude of the CDC decision, the foreign desk editors convinced him that a Middle East development was significant enough to interrupt the banner. That development would prove to be not very significant. So, by the way, would the CDC rulings on masks. COVID surged again, masks came back on, the day was not so important after all. Front pages are not prophecies, though sometimes they pretend to be.

We talked again a few weeks later.

—

AM: *Back to the one-hundred-thousand-COVID-deaths front page—what was the reaction mostly?*

DB: It was almost all overwhelmingly positive. The only negative comments we got were from the school that thinks COVID is overstated. They started to look at each case to find whether there were a couple of people . . .

AM: *Who hadn't died of COVID?*

DB: And they actually found one or two. Between editions, we changed a couple of them. But really the reaction was good. They got what Tom was trying to do. You know, I'm a big Rothko fan.

Because Rothko was trying to do the impossible. He was trying to paint emotions. I actually thought that page was trying to portray a feeling. Nobody was going to read it name by name. It was like a Rothko. And the longer you look at a Rothko, the sadder you get.

9. In this way, a designer works like any artist—reducing. Editing is explicitly about distilling, but all art is a form of condensation.

10. A "refer" (pronounced "reefer") describes a bit of copy that directs you to other copy. The bottom of the front page is taken up with refers.

11. I never worked for A. G., but I did for his father, Arthur. Once I made such a terrible mistake (approving an image in the magazine that employed S-M imagery) that the paper had to run an editor's note distancing itself from my decision, which is a serious slap. Arthur pulled me over and said, "Not a smart move, but I hope you ignore the note and just continue what you're doing." Most of the rank and file were less interested in change than the leaders were; he actually valued rule-breaking. So, if you just barged ahead and pretended you didn't know you shouldn't—at least in my experience—you were rewarded for it.

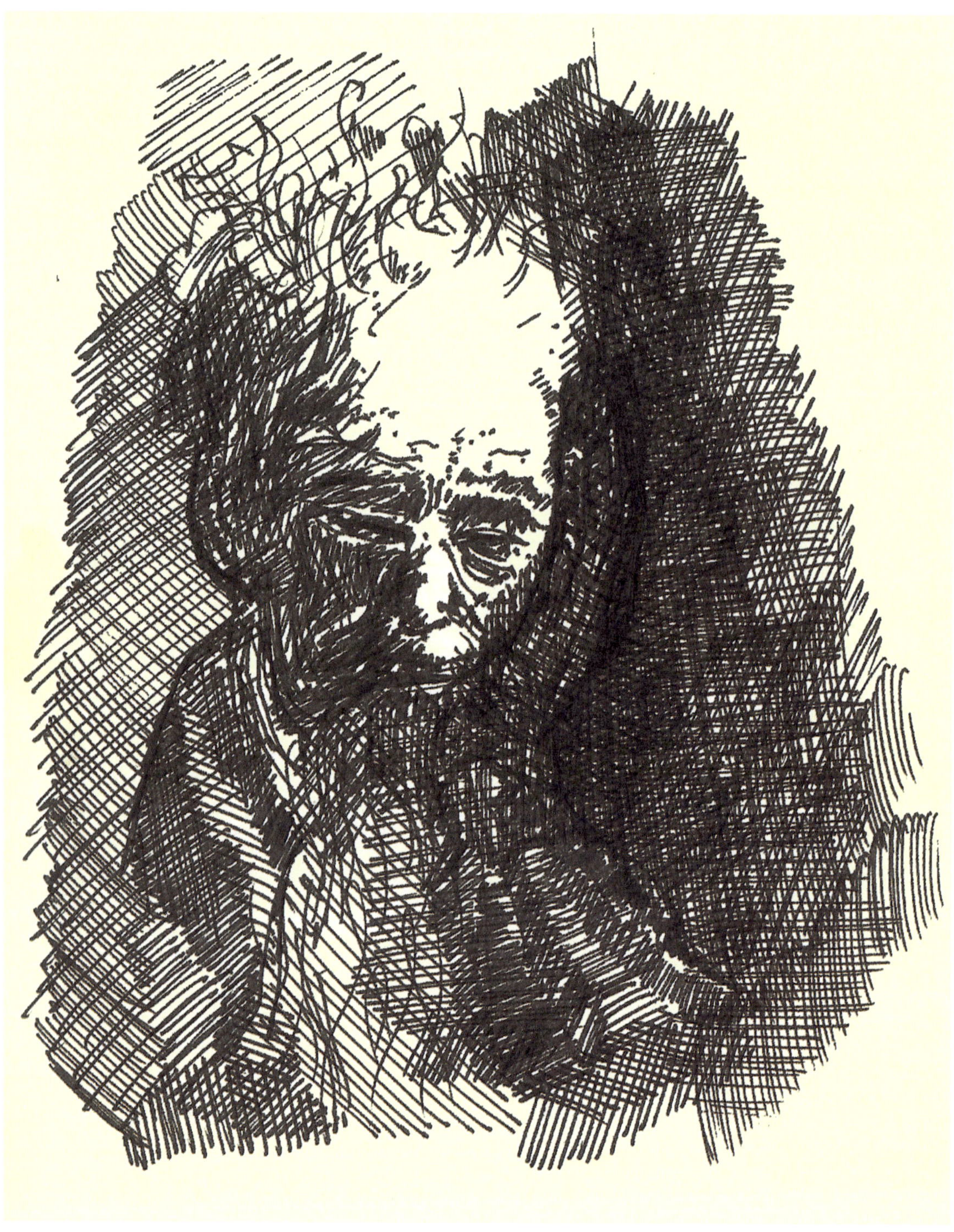

A page from Max Porter's notebooks. "I think I ripped this off from a Rembrandt etching," he said. "Rembrandt's etchings seem to me almost the pinnacle of human creation in some way–the meeting of science and art. It's as good as we've ever been."

30

MAX PORTER

Itchy Little Breakthroughs

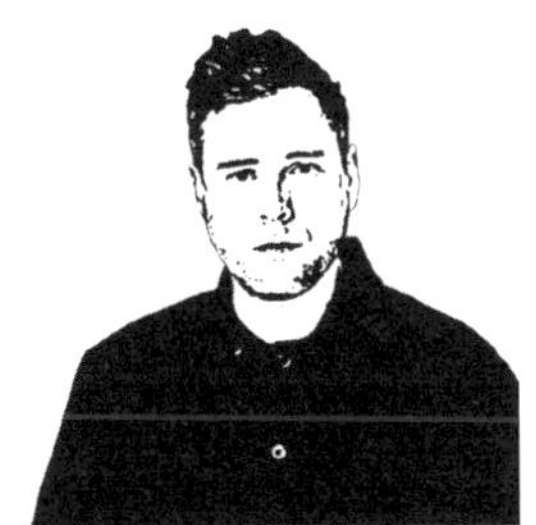

OCCUPATION: Writer

WORK DISCUSSED: *Tobias Llewelyn Raggs 1891 (:Unconscious Throughout)*

BORN: 1981

AFTER I LEARNED that Max Porter works out his books by drawing in notebooks, I—as a fan of both drawing and notebooks—felt a special urgency to talk to him for this book. Max, who used to be an editor,[1] writes books that defy classification: a little prose, a little poetry, a lot of imagination. His first book, *Grief Is the Thing with Feathers*, features a big bossy crow who visits a father and his sons, grieving for the loss of their wife and mother. It was something of a sensation—winner of the Young Writer of the Year Prize, the international Dylan Thomas Prize, short-listed for the Goldsmiths Prize for experimental writing, translated into twenty-seven languages, adapted into a play with Cillian Murphy. His second book, *Lanny*, is about the eponymous character, a "5-year-old dreamer, whose infectious sweetness is matched only by his verbal precocity and otherworldly connection to nature"—that's from a *New York Times* review whose headline described the book as "Rich, Twisted, Gloriously Cacophonous." It was short-listed for the Booker Prize.

I sought Max out for lots of reasons—I liked his books a lot, and creative ambition was what he was all about—but I really wanted to see the notebooks. "My notebook is the microbial fungus of ideas and images I draw on when I'm writing," he said when we first spoke. He was just as excited to talk about notebooks as I was (it's a rarefied interest, I know). Notebook-making runs in his family. "I have one of my grandfather's sketchbooks I keep as a holy relic."[2] Max is always drawing, drawing as he's thinking and talking, letting his thoughts, both deep and ordinary, pass through his arm to the page as images and word bursts. "Not a day will go by when I haven't drawn, even if it's a shopping list, where I've turned the word *tomato* into a drawing of a tomato," he told me. "I also vandalize books. The books I've

1. Naturally, because of my own experience, I wanted to know whether his editor head interferes with his writing. His response: "I have voices in my head saying, *That's not original, that's repetitive, that's a cliché, that's familiar formulation, that's*... So I have this sort of rigor that is also pain, while I'm writing, and I occasionally can break through that and just write. And then I have to sit down with it and think, quite brutally and dispassionately with myself, *Is that of any artistic or intellectual merit?* And that's my life." It's impressive that he can break through that voice in his head. I'm still working on that.

2. His grandfather was an art historian, classically schooled, very intent on disciplined learning. "He would sit us outside a church and say, 'Draw the church.'" That's how Max learned to draw.

loved most in the world are full of drawings." His notebooks make a compelling case for sketching as a form of editing, helping clarify the noise of thought. It's as if he needs his arm to make sense of the thicket of his brain.

Max came to his experimentalism—a too-blunt description of his style, but a reasonable shorthand, I think—out of a process of creative elimination. He was an art polymath. "My writing grew out of a discomfort I had between art and music and writing," he said. "When I made music, I felt I should be writing, and when I wrote, I felt I should be painting, feeling I wasn't good enough at any of them. I'm limited by my lack of skill. And one of the reasons I fell into writing *Grief Is the Thing with Feathers* was because in the fragmentary form, half poem, half essay, I started to feel good *enough*. It was more like a collage. I have to have the imagistic material in order to be interested in the project."

He is invested in trying to discover ways to tell stories that elide the straightaway. "The idea that readers are thick and you know they need help," he said, "I think it's bullshit. The last thing you want when you open a book is someone explaining." But at the same time, he continued, "I don't want experimentalism for experimentalism's sake. Because that excludes the reader. Being on soggy ground is only worthwhile if you land on firm ground." Like many modernists, but maybe more so, he is particularly interested in exposing the artifice of storytelling. "How do I tell the reader that it's true and also imagined? This is my fundamental difficulty as a writer and the reason I keep trying. My hope is that you're rigorously attentive to editorial and critical discipline while you're writing, but you're also free and inventive and happy, having accidents. You want to try and create a blend. And I don't think you can fake that blend, which is one of the reasons notebooks are so useful, because you're in training to achieve it all the time."

Tobias Llewelyn Raggs He sent me pages from the journal where he's been working through a project he's been playing with for the last couple of years. I asked him to annotate it. You can see how he needed the notebooks to help him make it out: it's a complicated set of interlocking boxes. For these purposes, what you need to know is that the project plays off the Victorian tale of Sweeney Todd, which was the source of the Stephen Sondheim musical.

3. The movement in most of these chapters is the mind barfs out the complicated thing, then the artist's conscious self simplifies it until it is intelligible/fabulous. Max's way is to take the complicated thing and first *further* complicate it. Then he uses the drawings to strip it down.

4. The notebooks are just one step in his process. Then comes the pain. Here's a little description I really liked of the agony of writing the novel he'd just sold: "I had bloodshot eyes, I was shaking and bit my fingernails all down. I wrote a beginning. I wrote forty thousand extra words, sat with it for a week, had nightmares, shuffled it, went for long walks, talked to people about it. Went basically completely mad, and then took those forty thousand words out and was left with the twenty thousand I'd started with, which I then polished. Like, an insane fortnight of dithering and back-and-forth. But in it I felt bubbling along this acceptance that that is my creative process, and it's good. And it's hard. And it's generative; other things will flow out of it."

THE EXCEPTION THAT PROVES THE RULE

"I've just sold a novel this week," he said (exclaimed, really, not something I think many people actually do). It was *Shy*, which would be published in 2023. "I was thinking when I went for a walk up a hill this morning, *I must tell Adam this, that I sold my new book this week to a publisher here*. It's the only book I've ever written that *isn't* from a notebook. It's come straight out of one single drawer, and the only research I did, the only preparatory work, was this one single doodle."

He was speaking from Bath, England. We were on Zoom. He drew a picture, held it to the screen. "It's a boy . . . in a pond . . . wearing a backpack, in nighttime. That's it. The book is about an unhappy boy in the nineties who doesn't want to live, set over one night. I wrote it fast. And now I'm a believer in those things people talk about—flow states?[5] I've spoken so positively about the notebooks I wonder if I'm too reliant on them. This was the only time I think in my entire life where I've literally run from the table downstairs in my flat, to the upstairs to get started, you know?"

Sweeney Todd is a barber who goes off on a murderous tear; his corpses are made into meat pies. Toby is an innocent boy who comes to work at the pie shop. In Max's version, Toby/Tobias is kept in the basement by the Todd character, whose name is Barton. But that's just the setup.

"It's a revisionist Victorian novel," Max explained, "one in which the protagonist might have a sense of what is coming—industrialization, exploitation, war. He can see what's coming. And he doesn't like it."

To complicate matters (Max is very intent on complicating matters),[3] the story goes back and forth in time and is set in a theatrical black box, in darkness. "I wanted to stage it in a melodramatic setting," Max said. "What if I locked this guy in the dark, and have him riff on his own identity, his story, the future. What if he's an actor? Could he play all the parts? Could he audition people for the parts that he has in mind? Could it all be a kind of confession for the tortured Western male ego? And I started building this novel in the pages of this notebook."

So you can see a little of the dense forest of Max's mind.[4] You can't compare the notebook pages with the finished novel, because there isn't one, but the notebooks do provide a pretty good snapshot of a creative brain moving very fast, while serving as an instrument of grounding and refinement. "I'm trying to avoid it being a gimmick, but I'm trying to harness the magic of said gimmick or said trickery. And view it with real feeling and not make it corny as shit. The notebook pages are me working out how to do something as preposterous as having the play script meet joke meet therapy session meet melodrama."

5. Mihaly Csikszentmihalyi coined this concept to describe that zone of complete productive absorption that has always reminded me of a hallucinatory drug trip—or playing a pinball game with a very high score. I've experienced it now and then. It's bliss.

THE "TOBIAS LLEWELYN RAGGS 1891" NOTEBOOKS

Here are some pages of his drawings, along with his notes, which he's using to help himself understand a book that, as we spoke, was only just coming into focus for him. He deciphers:

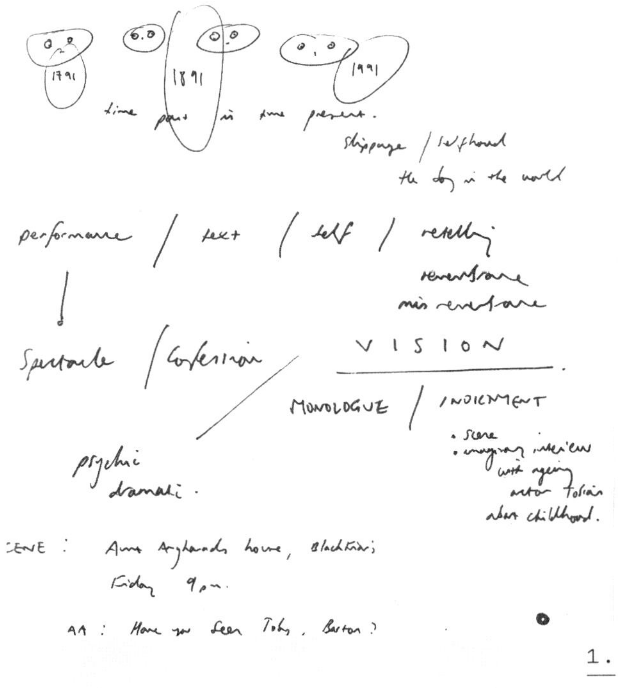

1. The idea is that Tobias would be a character who would move through the time zones 1791, 1891, 1991. It would be a novelistic device, without any of the smoke and mirrors of a novel pretending it isn't doing that.

2.

2 . Oh, that waiter figure? That's Barton. He's the impresario, the Sweeney Todd guy, the guy who's locked Toby in the basement. And this is Toby saying in a sort of postmodern way, "If we're going to have this character, let's flesh him out a bit." So these are notes around the character—physical notes toward a person building a character. And of course, that's me trying to figure out the character too. I'm using this notebook to try to make physical what's in my head.

3 . This is me thinking of how one would physically stage this. This atrium is the literal cellar he is in. The eye above the head is his thoughts. And the eye above him is the omniscient narrator in my eye. At this stage I'm wildly disconnected from any practical sense of how would I do this and just trying to be ambitious. I do six or seven of these pages in a burst. And then I think, *Ah, fuck, what am I up to here*, and put it back on the shelf. Go pick up the kids or something. At a certain point—this is quite crucial—I bring this notebook up to my bed, so that when I wake up in the night with itchy little breakthroughs, I can go straight into this notebook, and then bring it down here tomorrow.

4 . I'm having fun here. I've gotten rid of the anxiety over how it's structured, so I'm just having fun, padding it all out. Whenever I (or Tobias) woke up drenched in sweat or tears, terrified from the vision, I thought his aunt would sit on the edge of the bed and say, "Tell me." The person he trusts most in the world

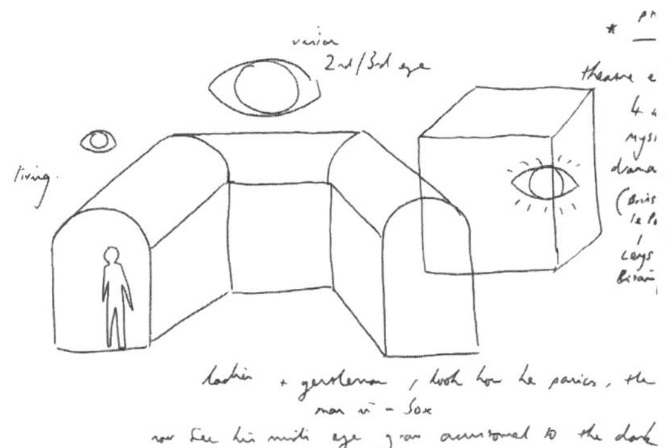

3.

etc.

"TELL ME"

4.

becomes us, the reader. I think the breakthrough I'm getting at here is how would I create a sense of intimacy out of this really preposterously kitsch theatrical setup?

5 . I'm trying to work out his prose style. Is it one block of thought with stage directions, asides, with everything leveled? How would he speak? I'm thinking, *Are the stage directions in brackets?* And my little revelation when I had it, which admittedly isn't very exciting on the page, is that in between his dashes and the bracket sits his selfhood. The little dashes are Tobias, and the brackets are the author's voice.

5.

Tobias
Llewelyn
Raggs

1891

1 : THE LIGHT
2 : THE DARK

(:UNCONSCIOUS THROUGHOUT)

6.

6 . Llewelyn is my father's middle name, and I think ultimately one has to accept in a kind of psychotherapeutic way that I'm always writing about my dad. My dad syndrome leaks into every book. And I thought *Tobias Llewelyn Raggs (:Unconscious Throughout)* might be a good title.

At the time of our talk, Max still wasn't sure what he was going to do with *Tobias Llewelyn Raggs*. But his many notebooks are full of other unrealized projects and life ephemera. "When you read your notebooks, you remeet ideas. You reintroduce them to who you are now." Some random pages:

7 . I wrote a novel about a pagan saint called *Uncumber*. Uncumber is an actual [folk] saint. Begged God to save her from an unhappy marriage, and he gave her a beard. And I've translated it into the twenty-first century. The novel is a love triangle between her and her assassin and her hagiographer. And this was the drawing I did when I realized I wanted to do it, when I was committed to the idea. This was years of thinking condensed into one happy idea. I'm still playing around with it. My wife thought it was too weird. There was some truth to that, but also I was beginning to think it would make a fantastic play. So I was speaking to a producer last year who loved the idea. It's being commissioned as we speak.

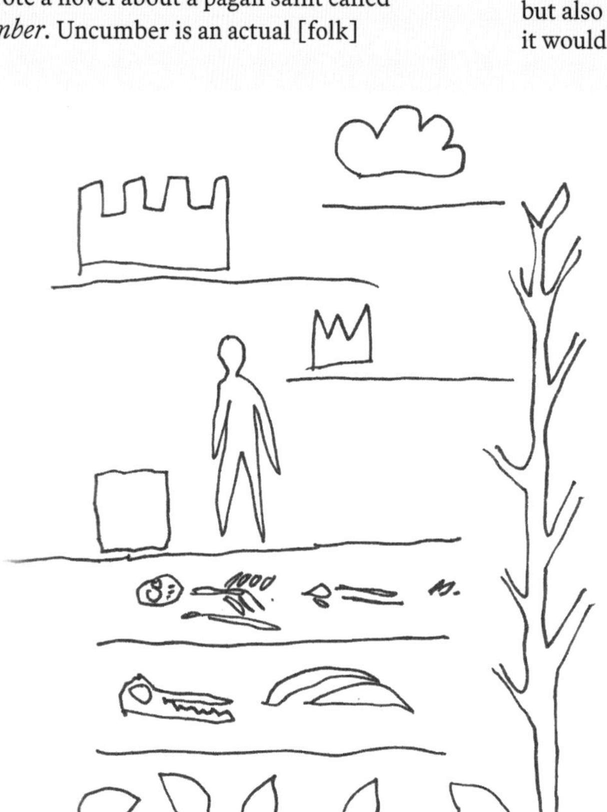

7.

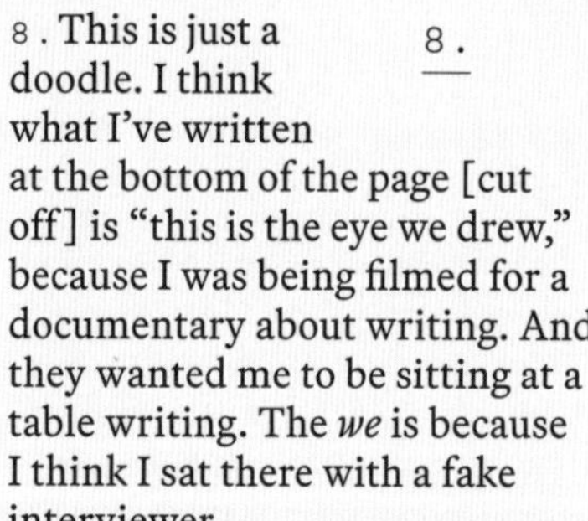

8.

8 . This is just a doodle. I think what I've written at the bottom of the page [cut off] is "this is the eye we drew," because I was being filmed for a documentary about writing. And they wanted me to be sitting at a table writing. The *we* is because I think I sat there with a fake interviewer.

9 . This one makes me sad. It's a very stylized reproduction I have of my father on a beach. I've done it from memory. And just annotating it, thinking about my children. He is showing the photographer that he is strong. I've written "showing me his strength"—I guess I'm thinking about inheritance. This is about as close to keeping a diary as I get.

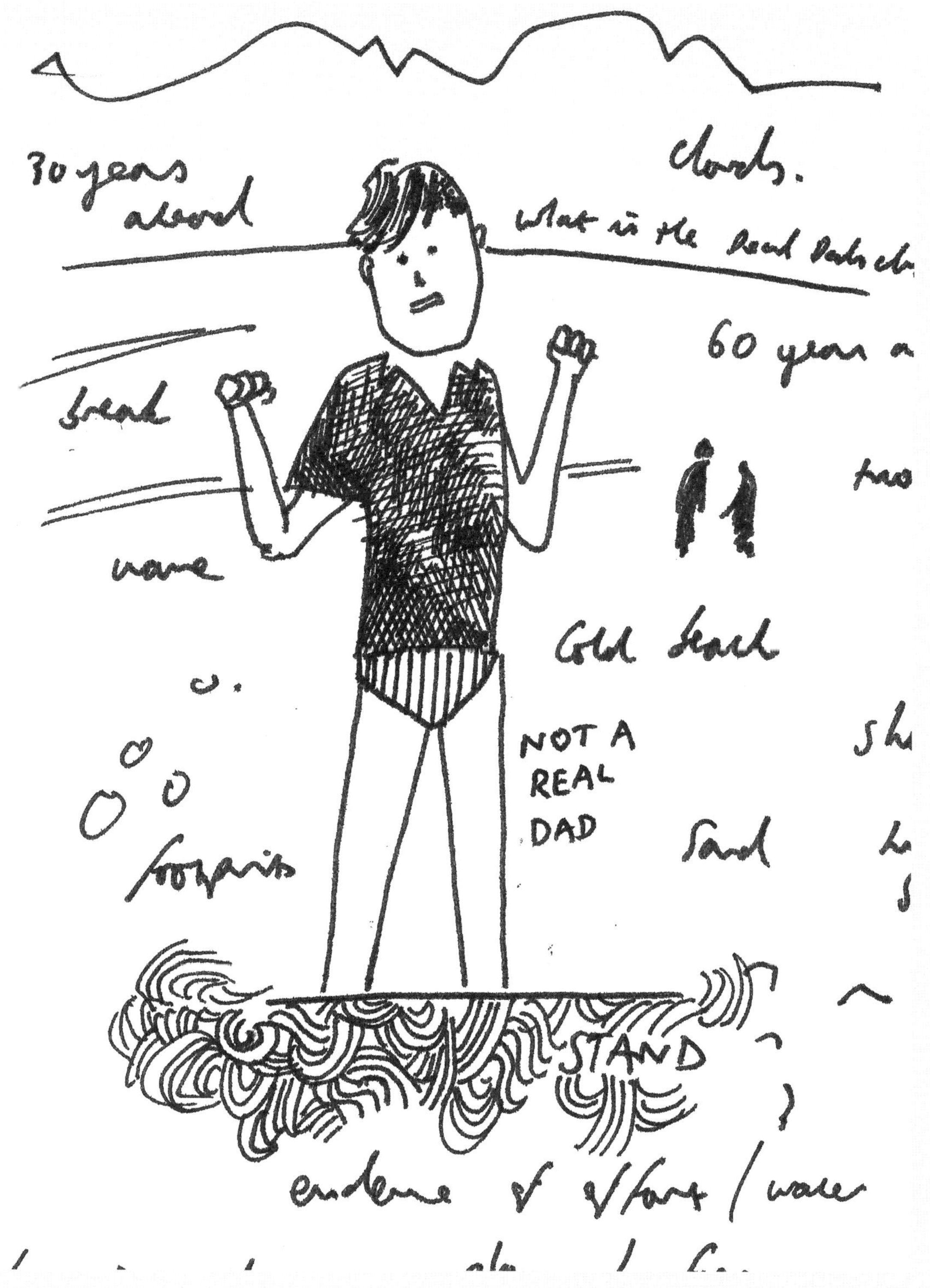
30 years abroad
clouds.
break
wave
Cold beach
NOT A
REAL
DAD
footprints
Sand
STAND
9.

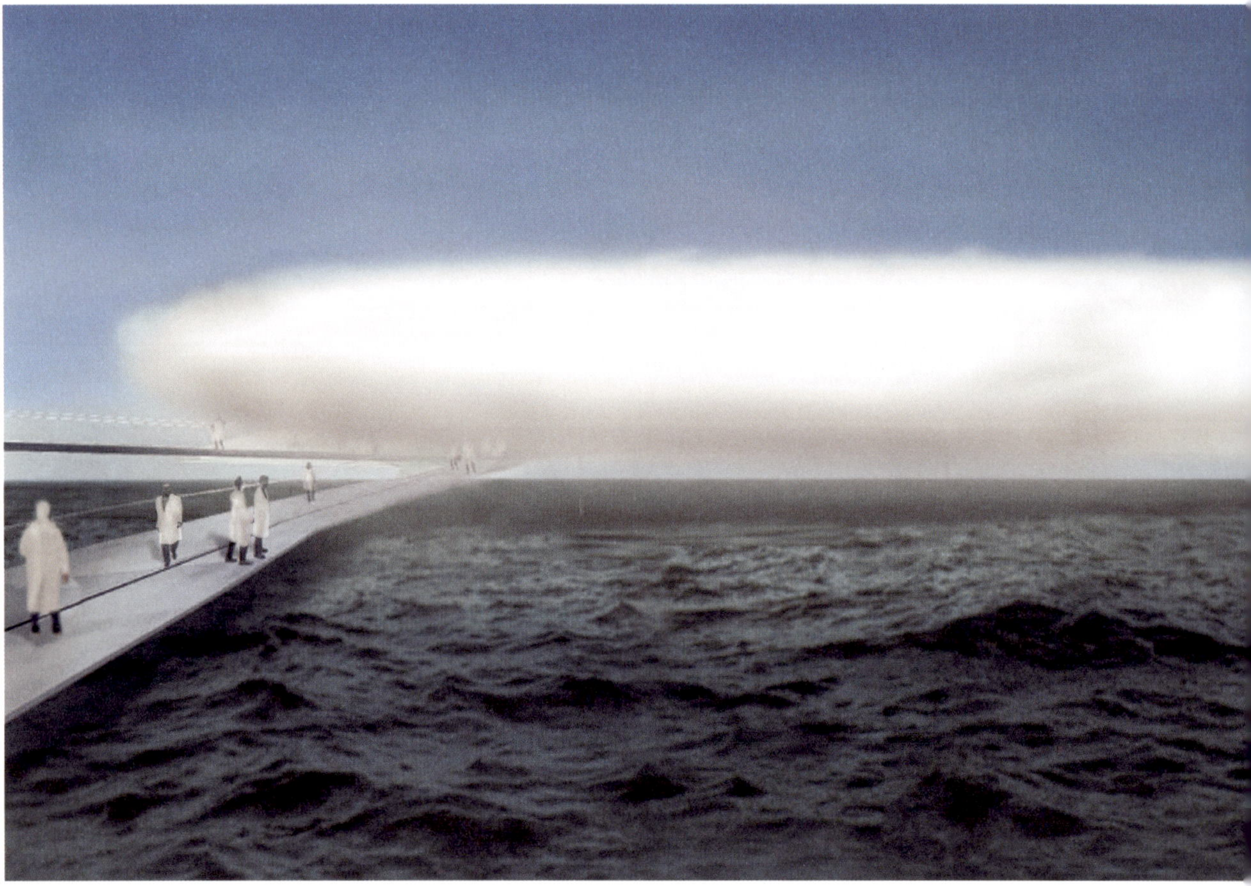

31

ELIZABETH DILLER

Theory and Fog

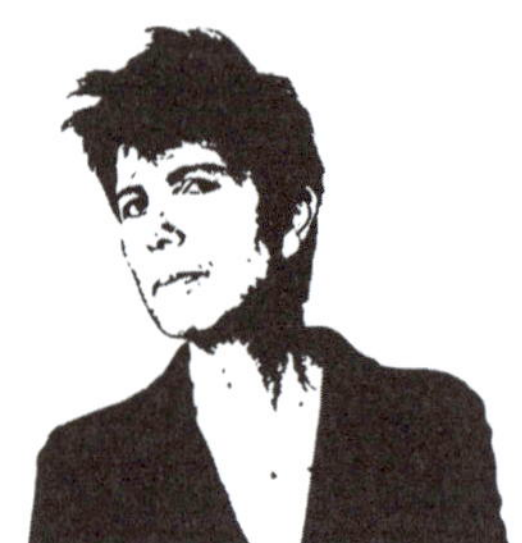

OCCUPATION: Architect

WORK DISCUSSED: The Blur Building (2002)

BORN: 1954

WHEN I FIRST SET OUT to talk to Elizabeth Diller, I thought we'd discuss one of the projects she and her colleagues at Diller Scofidio + Renfro have taken on that have altered New York City. Maybe we'd talk about the High Line, the park built around abandoned train tracks, which reimagined an urban idyll. Or the renovations at Lincoln Center and MoMA that intelligently reshaped two pivotal New York cultural institutions. Or even the Shed, a shape-shifting, *Transformers*-like performing arts venue in the otherwise execrable Hudson Yards. So much of modern, cultural New York has been touched and made better by Liz Diller's hand. Trophy buildings are always fun to gawk at, but they don't generally improve

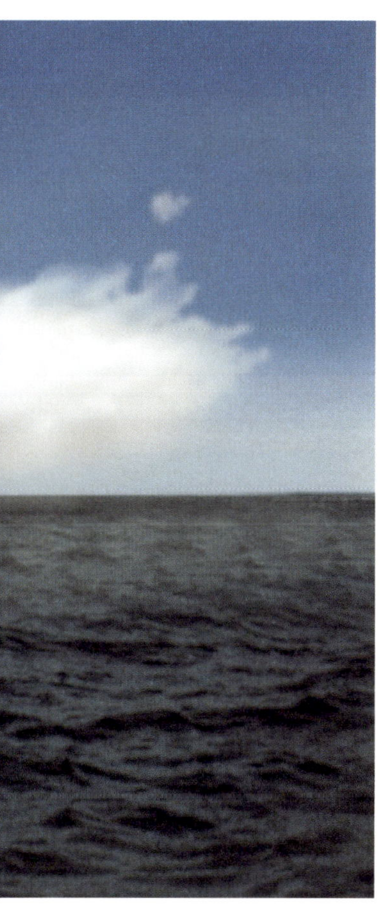

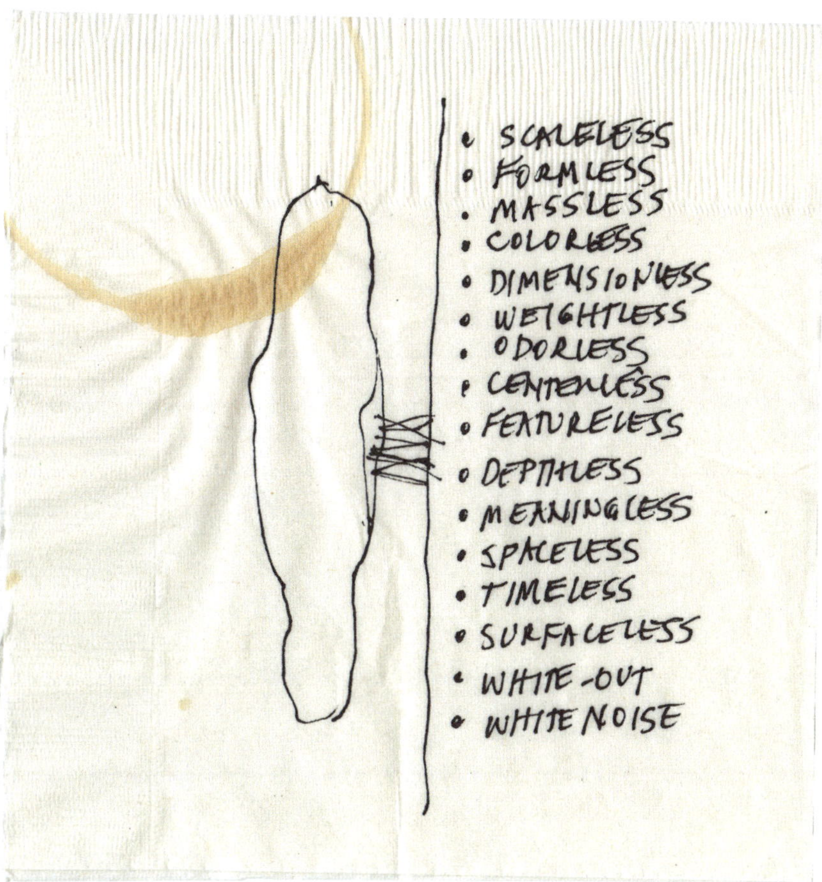

The Blur Building imagined as rendering and as napkin drawing (complete with coffee stain).

people's living experience. For the most part, the restrained and typically introverted work Diller and her team do has a positive, practical effect. It's more about brains than drama.

But as I started poking around Diller's past work, I came upon something dramatic in the extreme—dramatic to the point of uselessness—and I couldn't let go of it, even though I hadn't experienced it myself and never would. That project, certainly no secret to anyone who follows her and her work, is the Blur Building. The Blur Building was made entirely of water. It sat, temporarily, on a lake (Lake Neuchâtel, in Switzerland), as part of an expo in 2002. The "building" was a wildly inventive spectacle, a work, more or less, of art for art's sake. It was a building whose material was as much theory as fog.

Elizabeth Diller is cool and cerebral, but also slyly playful. She began the firm with her husband, Ric Scofidio, her professor before they married. Diller, whose parents emigrated from Poland when she was five, is a multidisciplinary artist as much as a straight-ahead architect. The firm's early work included many art installations (including 2,500 traffic cones in Columbus Circle, a spectacle I would like to have seen). The project Diller seems to describe with the most enthusiasm[1] was the Mile-Long

1. I found myself listening for what the subjects spoke about with the most excitement. For Diller, it wasn't anything about this project particularly, it was when she talked about conceptual art, which was perhaps the road not taken for her. At one point she also mentioned she wanted to direct a movie.

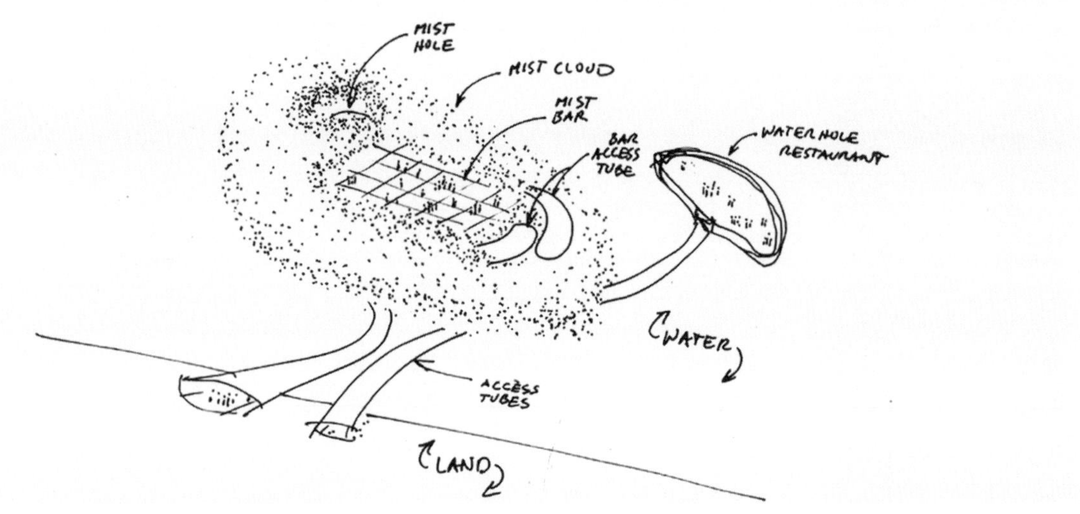

Blur Building, sketch.

Opera she staged with a thousand singers at the High Line.

The Blur Building was one third art installation, one third performance piece, and one third building. It was the product of a vision, simple and immediate, that she (and her husband) could see but nobody else could, and that she herself tried to complicate before it was reduced to its pure misty essence—a project, like much great art, insane and obvious at the same time.

ELIZABETH DILLER: Some of our projects are commissions and some are just out of our own research. They come, you know, from nothing, so there's no brief, right? The first imaginings are likely to be sketches. I used to keep sketchbooks, not in a very orderly way, just whatever was around. And then I started to doodle, on anything, a napkin or menu or whatever. I think the act of actually drawing something, sketching, imprints something in my brain. And it's important to record because my memory is really bad. I have lots of ideas. They evaporate like dreams unless I write them down, or sketch.

Something nags at me, and I don't really know how to get there when I believe in that nagging thing. And then there are also the old agendas that keep coming up. Like the complexities of vision, issues of voyeurism, exhibitionism, control, surveillance that somehow come into every project. It's like a parallel agenda.

Blur Originally, there was a competition for the Expo 2002 in Switzerland.[2] My studio was asked by a couple of collaborators if we wanted to do it. Our work was known to some of these Swiss folks, just because we're interested in large-scale projects. I think the High Line was maybe in the works. There was no particular brief—it was solely to make a proposal for a large-scale installation. We were shown the location and asked for an idea.

Our team was largely focused on landscape. And we came up with some ideas around the landscape, cutting through the landscape, making a sort of typography covered by flowers. I was pushing the team to build on the lake, because though the lake was the backdrop, maybe it could also be the experience, even the building material. Everyone thought it would be too big a risk to take, we would lose the competition. I said, "Let's take a chance." So

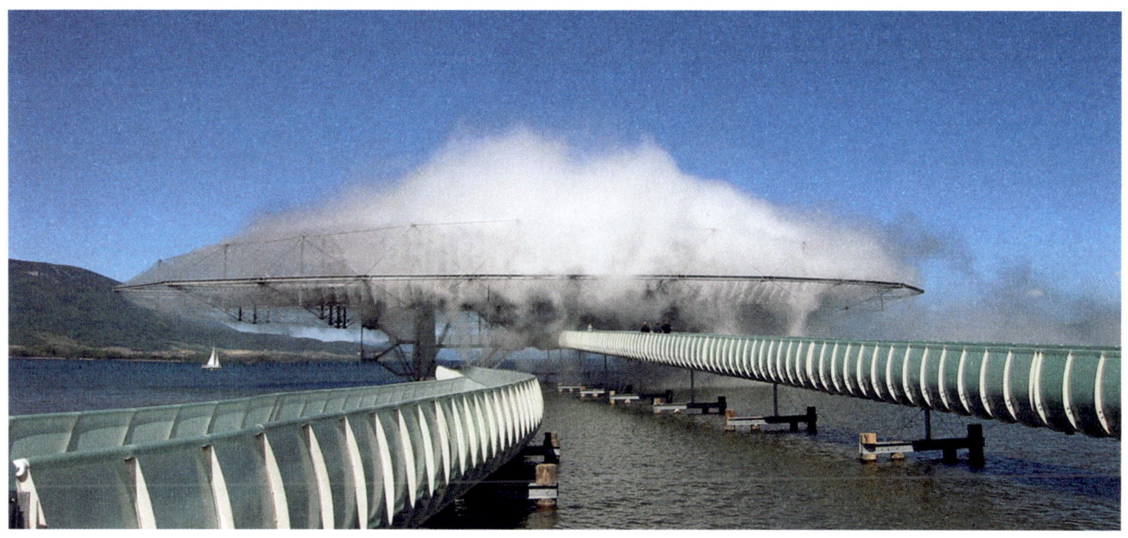

Blur Building, real thing.

we sort of split apart and did different things.

We were thinking of the problem of vision, and this was the first years of the 2000s, so we were also preoccupied with technologies. Our early inspiration was about the water—can we atomize water? As a critique on our ocular-centric culture.[3] Can we block off vision, can we problematize it in a kind of beautiful way? And then we got a vision of the cloud bank. Just like that. It was partly surreal, you know? It sort of popped into our heads. You know you can't explain every thing, right? There's this critical analytical mind that's kind of reading the place. And that's rational. But then there's also a kind of itch you keep wanting to scratch. You know, like Ric and I might be in the middle of dinner and find ourselves drawing on a napkin, and all of a sudden, you think of something. It rarely comes when you're focusing. It's indirect; one thing starts the sparks that connects the other synapses. I wish I knew how it works because I would want to trigger that more often.

Can This Be Done? So we had this fog bank with no other reason to be but problematizing vision. And it just made total sense to us. That was followed by, Can it be done? The artist Fujiko Nakaya had done a project in a 1970 expo of a building that was totally obscured by fog. So she was the expert. We went to her and said, "We want to make fog. We don't want it to be a building, there's no interior, just fog." And she said, "Well, you can't really do it. Because the fog isn't going to stay in one place." And then we said, "What if we made a thinking structure, which, when the wind blows [it registers the shift and] it makes more fog?" She introduced us to some guys who manufacture nozzles, for agriculture.

Oh, I forgot the part where we won the competition!

We just wanted to make a cloud on the lake. An ozone inspiration. So, for the purposes of the expo, we showed a cloud. But once we won for God knows whatever reason, we said, "Oh fuck, how do we actually make this?"

The process became fuller and more

2. Commissions/competitions help, as I've noted before—but especially open-ended ones, giving one the structure of an invitation but a wide expanse within which to roam.

3. The podcast *99% Invisible* featured an influential study done in the late fifties on creative personality, one notable segment of which was a study of quite-famous architects. The researchers concluded that their subjects had arresting personalities, were nonconformist, preferred ambiguity over order, were able to make unexpected connections, were courageous, and self-centered, but not, typically or necessarily, that intelligent. If Liz Diller had been among the subject pool, she would have blown that last finding out of the water. She is conceptual first, aesthetic later.

interesting as we developed the structure, a tensegrity structure [a three-dimensional base, which plays tension and compression pressures against each other for stability], very lightweight with four points that touch the lake bottom.

We got a structural engineer involved, and at some point we decided that we wanted to add another layer of sound. We asked Christian Marclay[4] if he would collaborate. He made a beautiful soundscape out of drips.

The Braincoat That Wasn't And then we also began to envision the "braincoat," a raincoat that could be worn in the structure, that would sense out other people, because you couldn't really see who you were passing by, but you might be able to respond to them in some way. The idea was that you could fill out this questionnaire, and we worked with the writer Douglas Cooper.[5] We would make a compatibility index, sort of like matchmaking. When you come close to someone, there's a little display on their chest—pink was affinity, green was the opposite.

We were working with IDEO;[6] we designed through it to a certain degree. But we didn't end up making the coat, because we had a sponsor for it and we lost the sponsorship. I was very upset that we lost it. But people encouraged me, saying, "It's really good, just what it is, without the raincoat." The raincoat was a hard loss.

Then we thought about projecting on the fog, and you can see some of these were bad ideas. Because you can't actually project on fog. And we wanted to put in a restaurant that would be a dry space with a hole, and then the two parallel glass walls would have special fish.

Then there was the lake. One of the things we didn't anticipate was the water quality. We started to test the water. And, well, we were just panicked, totally panicked. Because if [polluted water] is in your lungs, you know, it's Legionnaires' disease. We could kill off an entire population! We went to work on the filtration system.

What Makes a Bad Idea A bad idea is something that's extraneous to the whole thing.[7] The self-editing process is as creative as putting the ideas on the table, you know? So we decided that this was not about video or restaurants.

4. Christian Marclay's artistic work is often about sound, but he is probably best known as the maker of the twenty-four-hour film *The Clock*.

5. Douglas Cooper is a novelist and short story writer.

6. IDEO is a large and influential design firm.

7. Simplify! Again. The Marie Kondo principle as applied to art.

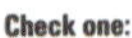

Check one:

Sinner or Saint

Beauty or Beast

Puccini or Prince

Most or Least

Saunter or Mince

Fight or Faint

One love or Two

Old World or New

Back Door, Front Door, Do Not Enter

Left or Right or Center

Separate, Overlap

Satin or Burlap

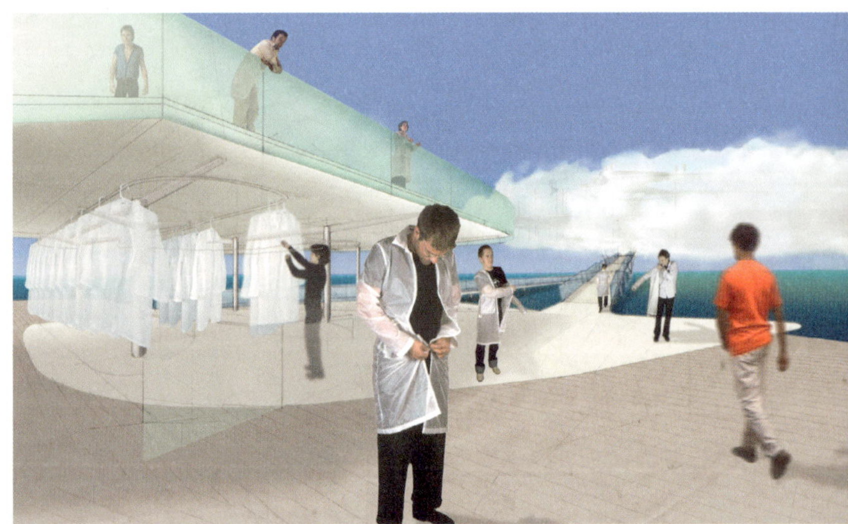

Abandoned: The Braincoat. The matchmaking questionnaire.

Shortly before we spoke, a project in London—the Centre for Music, a concert hall for which the firm had done a very ambitious design—was scotched.
ELIZABETH DILLER: So, you know, architecture. So much of our work is based on competitions or direct commissions, and these projects are never secure. Funds need to be raised. Approvals are needed—from the city, the general public. Take the High Line. It was a competition before it was a real thing. There were five different visions, and ours was selected. You may not win; chances are you won't. But you have to enter with the belief that you're going to get it. Otherwise it's hard to muster up the energy. You have to sort of fall in love with someone with the potential of being rejected.
For the music center, we won the project—unexpectedly, by the way. But Brexit made it very difficult for the orchestra, and COVID made it nearly impossible. And that was that. Disappointment is structured into architecture, and we are used to it. But every time it happens, it's crushing.

This was an exposition with nothing to see and nothing to do, except contemplate our dependence on vision. In any project, there are more ideas than there's really space for. One idea is stronger without the other. The problem with a lot of people who do creative work is a tendency to oversaturate projects with too much. And it turned out that some of the ideas were totally unnecessary. What was most interesting was just getting lost in the fog. The surreal image of the cloud was what made us win. In the end, all of these other elements might have been a distraction from what was really powerful.

The Experience of Blur You'd enter the building on a ramp. Someone would just come into focus and then pass. You didn't exactly know where the stair was. You couldn't see. A gust of wind would come in, and the cloud would move. And then it would fill back up, very quickly. Architects typically build things where you can predict, more or less, how people will behave. In this, we knew so little. And then there is this thing people call the ion effect. I didn't really take it seriously. But then we did the piece, and I felt it myself. When a certain kind of light would hit the water, it created a kind of ethereal, beautiful feeling. It made you kind of overwhelmingly happy, like a drug, you know?

We got really bad press for the project, though that didn't stop people from coming. [Over a million people visited.] The response was, "Why would you put money into this problem of fog?" Fog was a bad thing. Afterwards it became a national symbol. We realized in reading about it that it came to symbolize Swiss doubt. Switzerland was always sort of this in-between thing. That hadn't been in our mind at all. Some people even had a religious reading of it, that it had to do with the Ascension.

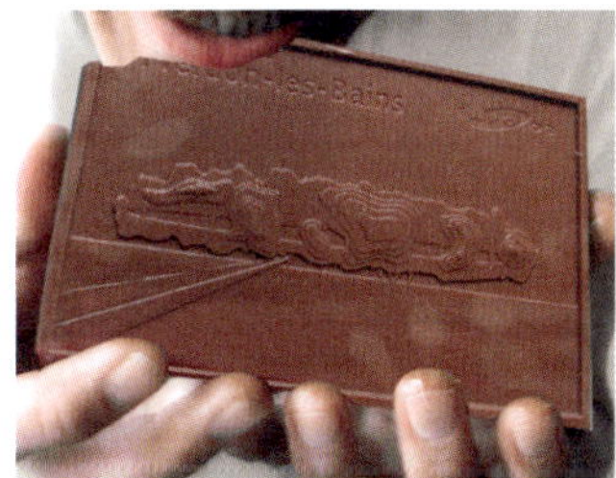

Blur Building chocolate bar.

—

PS After we talked about Blur, Diller and I discussed public space in New York, a subject I think a lot about. Most of it wasn't relevant to the Blur project, but I'll just leave you with this, as an indication of how Diller's mind works while thinking out loud:

"I've always thought that all ground floors should just be open, and you should be able to walk through every building, to the other side through the block—it should just all be public. These spaces could be porous and leaky. Not private taps, you know?"

I loved that idea.

32

IAN ADELMAN, CALVIN SEIBERT

Here Today, Gone Today

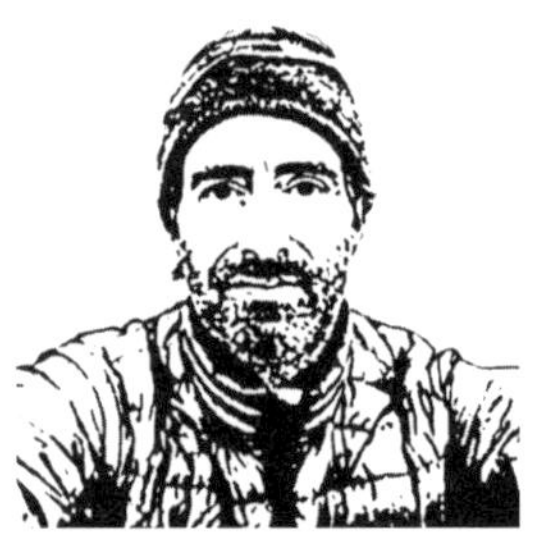

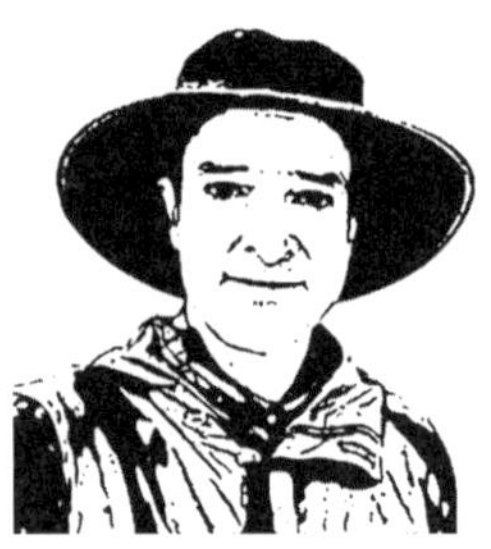

PURSUIT: Sandcastles

WORK DISCUSSED: Todos Santos Castle (2002)

BORN: 1971; 1958

ONE DAY AT LUNCH, Ian Adelman took out his phone and showed me a picture of a sandcastle he'd built. It looked like an architectural model: precise, ambitious, spectacular. Ian and I had worked together for years. He'd designed the sweep of *New York*'s digital publications, each its own nation with its own visual language. In his digital design work he was a world-builder, like pretty much everyone else in this book. Also, at the intersection of journalism and the internet, in a medium that leaned more toward utility than art, he was, in my view, one of the first true artists.

But that's not why I wanted to talk to him. Once I saw his sandcastle, I thought it would be interesting to talk about art as a hobby—not a term he liked, because it trivialized the effort, but still, as something you do because you love doing it. Ian was, in his own way, an Elizabeth Diller of the sand.

During the pandemic, Ian was building sandcastles feverishly. He'd moved to Water Mill, a beach town in eastern Long Island. Mornings he'd get up early and set about creating a new structure, one that would more or less disappear by day's end. That seemed interesting to me, too, creating something meant to perish. So I went to his house one day, and we talked about sandcastles.

An Arty Kid Ian's mother was a painter. He grew up largely without a television, exercised his imagination building forts from materials he found in the woods. "I made models, scale models, this whole diorama thing. Even before I thought about it as a term, urban planning, I was interested in shapes, roads, how everything interacts." He used fabric paints to make rock T-shirts—his friends asked him to draw on their jeans. He designed the lettering for his yearbook.

He was just an arty kid, restless at the beach, so when his father, who was a scientist, made drip castles in the sand, Ian would join him. Later, Ian went to the Rhode Island School of Design, became a graphic designer, and eventually came to join us at *New York*. The only

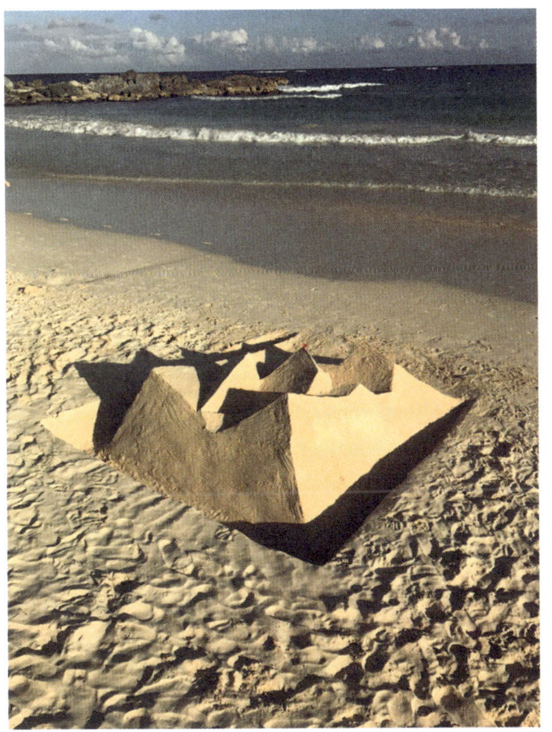

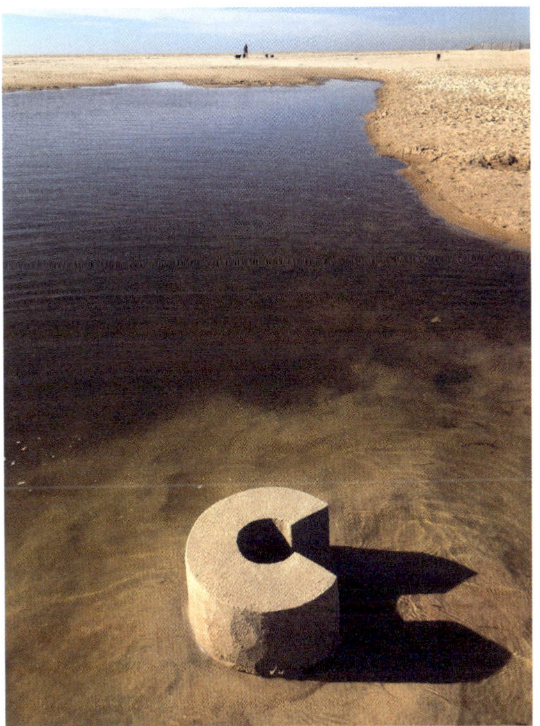

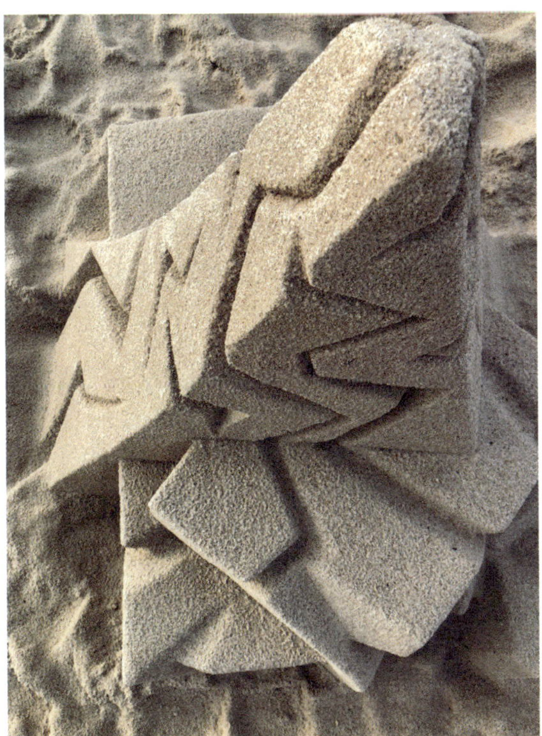

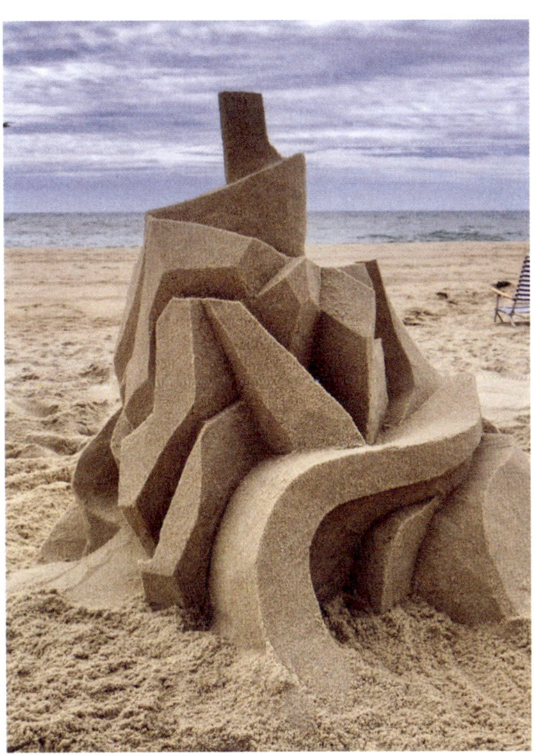

Selections from Ian's oeuvre. Top left, Tulum. The rest, Water Mill.

castle building he did at that time was as a way to relieve his boredom while everyone else was lying around in the sun.

A Trip to Tulum One visit to Tulum, a beach town in Mexico, changed all that. "When I first went to Tulum, it was the first time I experienced sand that I could basically sculpt," Ian said. "The sand was so fine, it was like making a snowball. And clean—no pebbles or small rocks or driftwood. Because the Tulum sand sticks together so well, I could make different things, like a whole bunch of spheres joined together. The sand was like clay. I improvised. I wanted to create something that in the sun would look like a dazzle camouflage, all angles, ideas like that."

When he returned home from Tulum, he got more obsessive—building castles in Water Mill and Brighton Beach, Coney Island (he became a student of sand, the way a surfer might of waves, looking for where the sand was most promising—and settling for where it was, at least, available). He'd spend the better part of the day alone, making increasingly ambitious angular structures.[1]

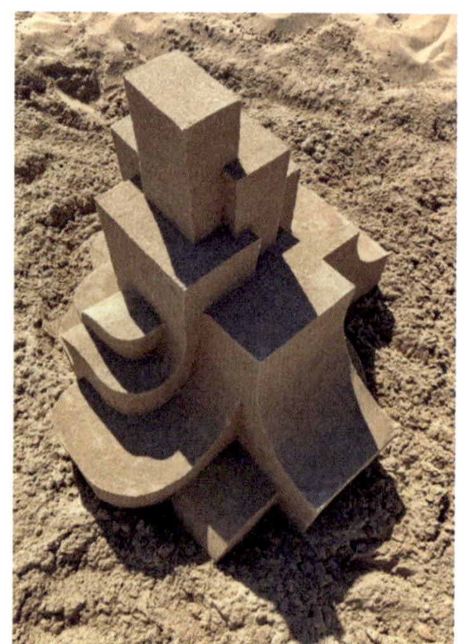

Another, on Brighton Beach.

Building "As I was doing it more, I really wished I had something to form things more effectively. So I went to the hardware store and bought some masonry. I had never carried water to make sand wet, I would just kind of dig down to the wet sand. But once you introduce your own water and combine that with the hand tools, it opens up another world. I often have the desire to outshine the thing I did the day before. Over time, that's harder to accomplish. But with tools,[2] I could approach it with a particular intention."

Sometimes Ian gets an idea and sketches it so he internalizes it, but he rarely brings the drawings to the beach. He goes in the early morning, when it is empty. He avoids the sun, which is a castle killer because it dries out the sand. He's fond of arcs, intersections, planes, swoops, topographic maps, letter forms. "I've made things that feel like they belong in some sci-fi world. It's that intersection of the kind of rectilinear architecture that is part of the popular imagination of the future, as rendered by the people in the past. You see *Dune*? There was a lot in it that made me think about things I've made."

The Tao of It Ian describes his psyche as he's building as one of almost perfect focus, no wandering grocery lists or stray anxieties, just a locked-in state with the sand. "I decide something is done when I run out of time.[3] Part of the appeal of working sand is that it's temporal. Because it's temporal, stakes are lower. Sometimes people ask if I've thought about working in stone. I'd be frozen, I'm not ready to do it.

"Glass is really the closest thing. In its liquid state, you can manipulate it with your hands, there's a full spectrum of stability, and it's incredibly tactile. That doesn't mean I'd feel comfortable with it. It requires years of training. Sand is freeing. You don't have to worry about wasting material, and you get instant feedback on all the decisions you make. I'm pretty disappointed if I'm not happy with it, but in the end it's just sand. If I spend a long time building something up and a big part of it falls off, it's frustrating, but you can still find a way to make it into something. And sometimes the castle's actually intact the next day. I can just dump water on it, pack it down, and put more on top of it, turn it into a bigger thing. Then, once it's bigger than you, it takes on a whole other dynamic. Definitely more dramatic. I get excited thinking about it. Just that feeling."

The word *feeling* comes up a lot as he's talking. Not emotional feeling—actual body sensation. All of Ian's obsessions are physical in significant part: he is an intense cyclist and cycle builder, also a DJ. "As things get bigger, the physicality takes on a whole other thing.[4] I like to ride my bike in traffic because I love the feeling of always calculating, but also the way you use your body responsively. I think of working with sand the same way."

Performance Sandcastles are made in public: "People are always part of the equation." Generally he is left alone, but people sometimes try to engage him. "I was at Brighton Beach, and a man came over who'd emigrated from the Soviet Union, and he saw something in the forms that made him think about constructivism. We just talked for an hour about Russia and the Soviet Union. And I liked that because it *is* a performance."

And then there are kids. "Kids are typically awed when you're building—until you leave, then they want to kill it." Ian recalled one instance when a young boy started to build his own castle near the one he was building. "He came over and said, 'Look, I'm an artist too.' "

Instagram Ian records all his castles and posts them. "I'm making two things now, the castle and the picture. The picture is its own piece. In many ways it's an opportunity to get validation. And when you start posting stuff, then it's almost like you're expected to deliver."

For a long time, as far as Ian knew, he was the only one pursuing sandcastle building with this sort of zeal. "And then there's one I made with balls of sand. Someone commented that it's almost like Calvin Seibert level. I was like, *Who's Calvin Seibert?*"

That's when he learned he had a doppelgänger, who was also making dramatic architectural structures in the sand. They weren't exactly like his, but they were close. Calvin Seibert, who is a sculptor who'd moved recently to Denver, is an Instagram superstar. "I love a lot of the stuff he makes," Ian said. "It's without question super impressive. All the time people send me images of his work and say, 'Look at this guy, he's copying you.' I'm like, 'No, he got there first.'"

I thought it might be interesting if I hooked up the two of them for a conversation.

A Conversation with Calvin Seibert

Adam Moss: *Calvin, how did you start making castles?*

Calvin Seibert: I grew up in Vail, my father started Vail, and so I was surrounded by construction. I played in the sand piles of construction sites, and my mother, in order to keep me out of the sites, had a full load of sand dumped in our yard. A truckload. And then I started to make things out of concrete, using my mother's KitchenAid mixer to mix concrete.[5] We made roads and dams and little ponds.

I always thought I was going to be an architect. But looking back now, I understand I was really a sculptor. I went to New York and went to SVA [School of Visual Arts], would make castles at Jones Beach, the Rockaways. My sculpture was always architectural—the sandcastles have always been architectural, kind of modernist, hard edged.

Ian Adelman: Precision is a pattern for you.

CS: But I've been trying to let that go. My whole life is about letting go. Because my early sandcastles were very severe, symmetrical, precise in their evenness. And that's just a trap.

AM: *You make sculptures now with other materials?*

CS: I've been making stuff out of cardboard. In New York, I'd visit the galleries on recycling

1. It's worth noting that what Ian does for a living requires him to work in a company, with a team, which isn't always the most satisfying way to make art—maybe especially for Ian, who has strong convictions and can get gummed up when he thinks a process has gone awry. Building castles is a project free of consensus building—just Ian alone in the sand with his hands.

2. His tools include: shovel for moving large amounts of sand; two buckets (either five-gallon contractor style or smaller collapsible) for carrying water; sometimes a larger tub (rigid or collapsible) for mixing sand and water; masonry pointing trowels, various sizes (roughly triangular, with a pointed tip); margin trowels, one inch and two inches wide; dull five-inch kitchen knife.

3. Reasons people decide a work is done: It feels done. Completely arbitrary. There's a deadline. They're sick of it. They're bored. They're afraid they're going to screw it up. And here: the sun is going down.

4. The physical sensation of making art? I've now heard it a few times, mostly for visual artists.

5. Dumping dirt in the yard? Allowing him to mix concrete in a kitchen appliance? Calvin's mother was an exemplary enabler.

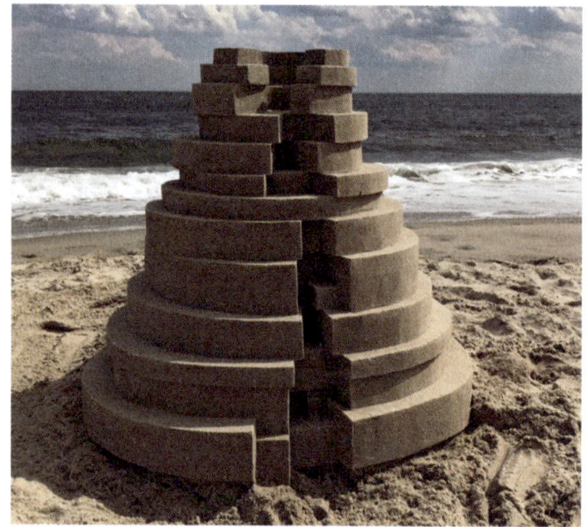

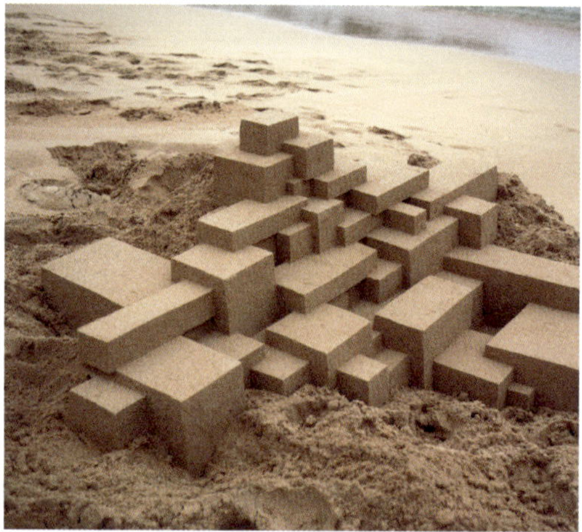

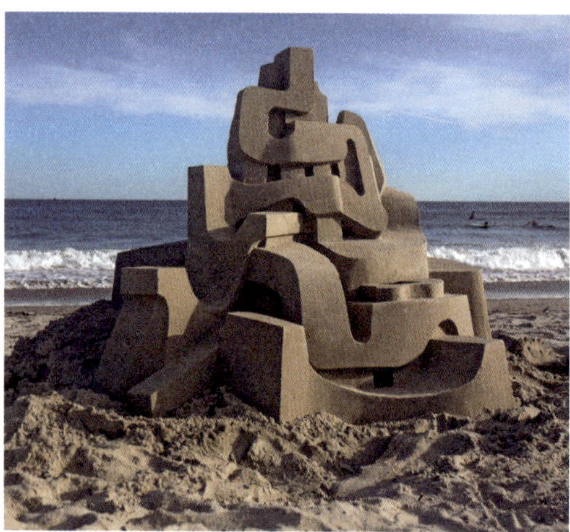

Three by Calvin Seibert.

days and get this really clean cardboard out of the garbage. But at the same time, I was going to the beach to make sculptures out of sand.

AM: *Were you attracted to the perishability of it?*

CS: Didn't care. Still don't. I do drawings that go into boxes, and I never look at them again. I just like doing it. I've never had much ambition in terms of getting my work seen, though obviously I often I take pictures.[6] And I'm ambitious about the work itself.

IA: For me a very specific thing happens. And I don't want to suggest that it's necessarily the same for you. But I have ADD, right, and I take medicine for it, but one characteristic they say of people who have ADD, they have this ability to hyperfocus. The only distractions are the formal ones within the thing you're making. There's something about these intense, isolated moments of focus that are deeply satisfying.

CS: It always goes the same way for me. I'm very optimistic at the beginning. And by noon or when it's really hot, I just want to go home. But I get through that, and by four I'm much happier. It gets better; that's a constant. And I think a lot of artwork is like that; the next morning you wake up and realize it's not so bad.[7]

AM: *Of course, with sandcastles, there's rarely a next day.*

CS: Sometimes you can get a really nice picture the next day, of the half-destroyed castle.

IA: Do you come to the beach with a plan?

CS: I usually arrive at the beach with no notion. Well, one notion—I say, yesterday you made curves, today you're going to do triangles. I need to keep expanding the variety within the parameters of what I've set. I have these tried-and-true solutions. I try to fight them. But you can't knock a castle down and start all over because you run out of time.

IA: How do you know if something's working?

CS: It's working if I'm surprised by it.

They discuss tools. Calvin recommends plexiglass sheets, which allow him to make

6. If you make art and no one sees it, are you an artist? A question I think about sometimes, because I am so loath to let people see my work.

7. As I've said, a pretty universal experience. Bad at night, not so bad the next morning. Even I have experienced it.

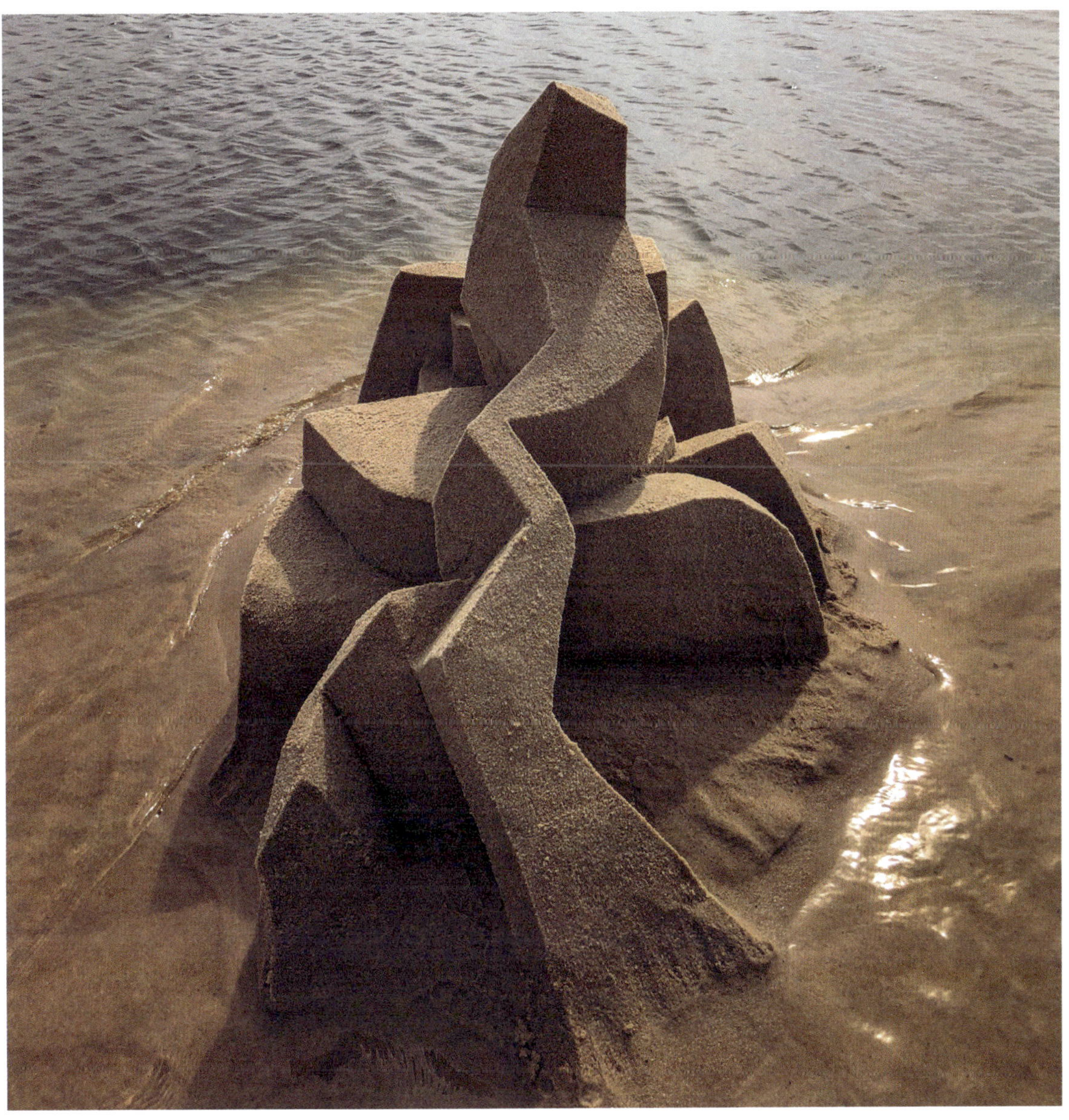

By Ian. Water Mill.

smoother edges on the structures. They compare styles, with Ian saying he would find it impossible to be quite as precise as Calvin, who says, "I spend almost half the time just making it look clean. If I didn't care about making it clean, I'd make something twice as big." Ian nods and then says, "I just don't have the patience."

They talk for a while.

IA: I feel like I could talk about this stuff all day. One last question. How do you feel about the passersby?

CS: Just a little would be nice. I like some human interaction, but not too much.

IA: In my experience, the most frequently asked question is, "What is it?"

CS: Yeah, I don't know what they're expecting. I say, "It's a sandcastle."

A CASTLE IN TODOS SANTOS, IN EIGHT STAGES

Ian Adelman: It was New Year's Day, we were flying out the next day. I knew the sand was great.

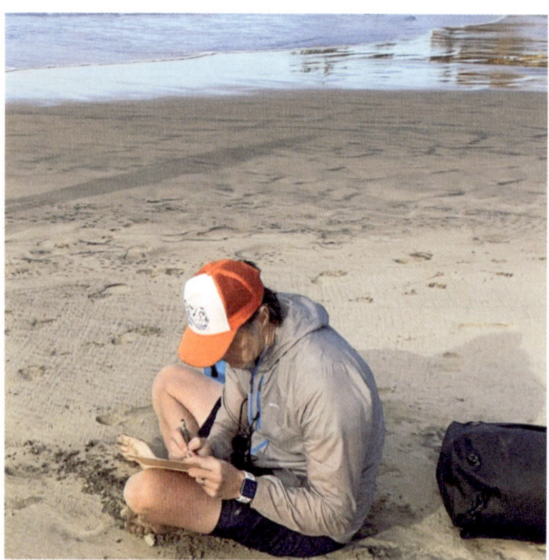

1. I wanted the forms to intersect. I often like asymmetrical, sloping things, and I like making solids that intersect. So I knew I wanted to do that.

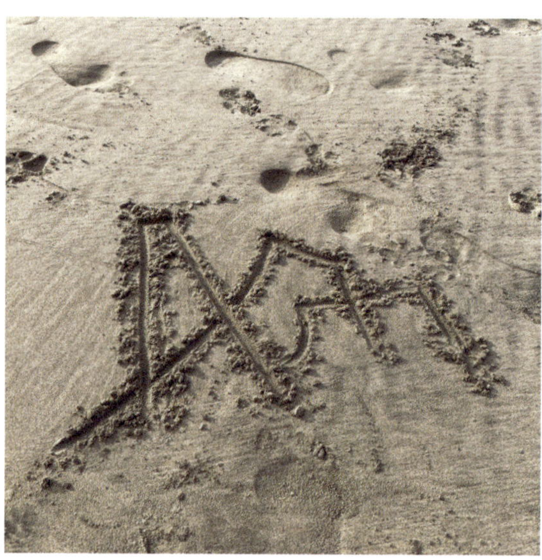

2. I began at seven thirty in the morning. I drew in the sand so I could remind myself what I was trying to do.

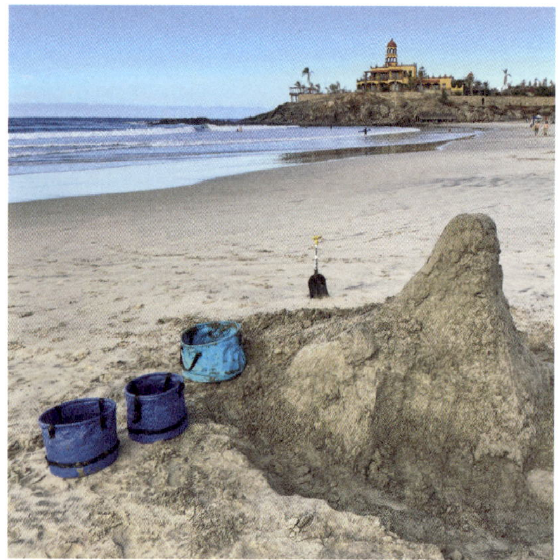

3. My plan was to go there and start building maybe a half hour after high tide, so there would be tide line.

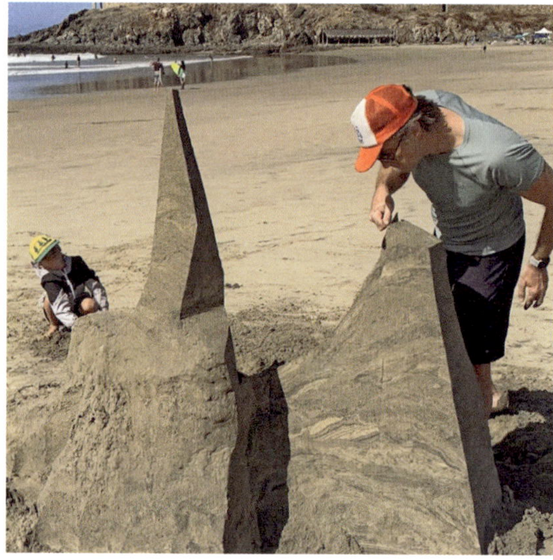

4. The water would be close to me while I was building. Also the sand had been underwater, and it's incredible sand, so I could just start digging and piling.

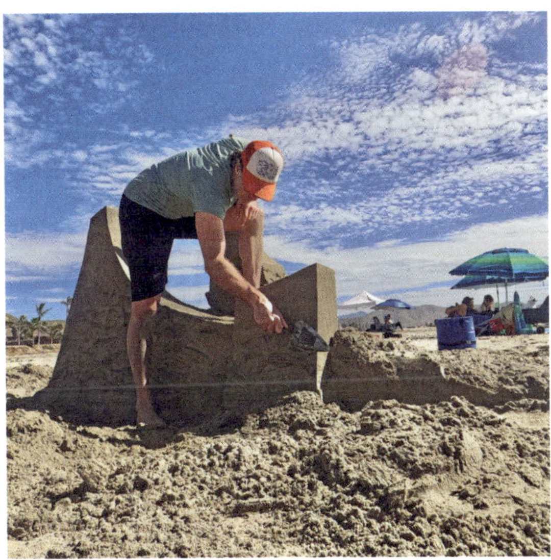

5. I'm thinking, *Am I going to be happy with how this feels? What am I going to do with this right now? Am I going to embellish it?* This is literally all I'm thinking about.

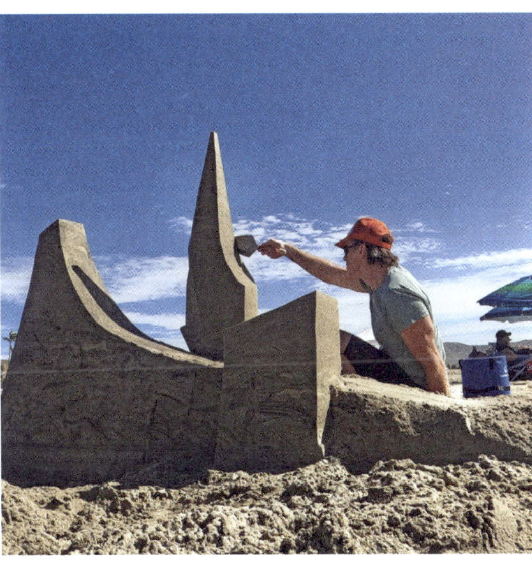

6. There's always a first cut. And immediately I start going away from my plan. In my sketch there was a symmetrical tower. But as soon as I did that, I wanted something different.

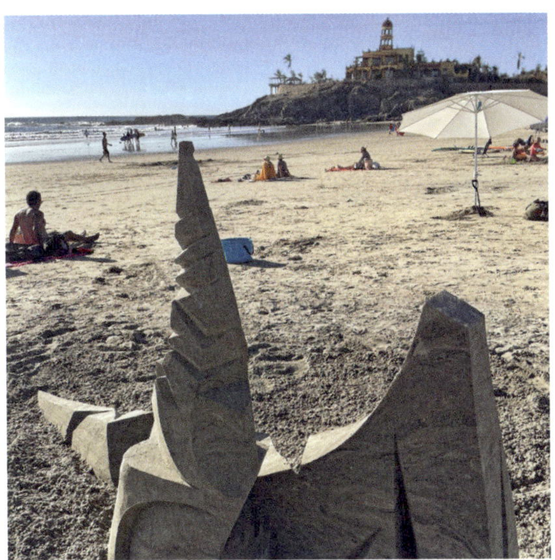

7. At some point I took a big slice out if it. I lost the crispness, so I turned it into a curve. The striations are super satisfying. Especially as it gets smoother. It really does look like stone.

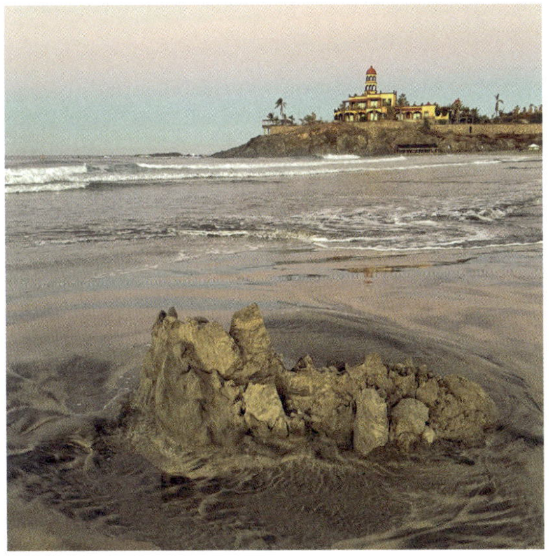

8. I completed the structure eight hours later. And I actually ended up not being super happy with it—it ended up even more elongated than I imagined. And then it was gone.

33

TYLER HOBBS

The Computer Has a Hand Too

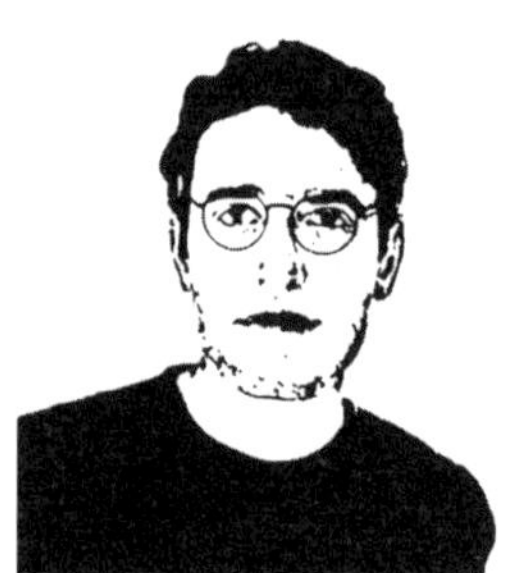

OCCUPATION: Visual Artist

WORK DISCUSSED: *Fidenza* (2021)

BORN: 1987

NFTS WERE BOOMING, and though I was both cynical and ignorant about them, I had a sense they might have a place here. So I turned to Tyler Hobbs. He is an Austin-based artist famous for a series called *Fidenza*, several works from which were selling as NFTs for up to $3 million on the secondary market. But I wasn't just following the money. I was interested in the way a machine could be a collaborator. I knew that Tyler thought about that a lot, because he's a lucid writer who explains, with great care, what he is doing and why he is doing it in essays on his website. Tyler had made *Fidenza* to be sold on a platform called Art Blocks. His art was a code, from which he would generate 999 works, whose specific characteristics he couldn't control. The important artistic work was in building a masterpiece of an algorithm that could then generate a high percentage of sublime creations.

Though this work is, in one sense, made by a computer, there was an artist at the helm. Francis Bacon said that all interesting work was accident, though you have to create the conditions for the right accident.[1] And it turned out that that was exactly what Tyler did—which, when I thought about it, disarmed my skepticism about the genre.

As it happened, NFTs weren't the genre anyway. They were merely a method by which the work got distributed and then bought. Tyler is a generative artist,[2] though he didn't know that there was a name for it when he started making work by programming it. Decisions, and his reactions to his decisions, were explicitly Tyler's tools in making art with an algorithm, just as they are for any artist working in any medium.

TYLER HOBBS: I grew up drawing and painting all the time. I made comic books, took after-school painting lessons copying Van Gogh, Monet, Renoir. I was pretty good, but I had competing

1. Bacon is hardly the only artist to talk about the value—really, the indispensability—of accident in making work, but his comments on the subject, which run throughout a book of his conversations with David Sylvester, called *Interviews with Francis Bacon,* made a deep impression on me. I highly recommend the book.

2. Generative art refers to art made through an autonomous system, often a computer.

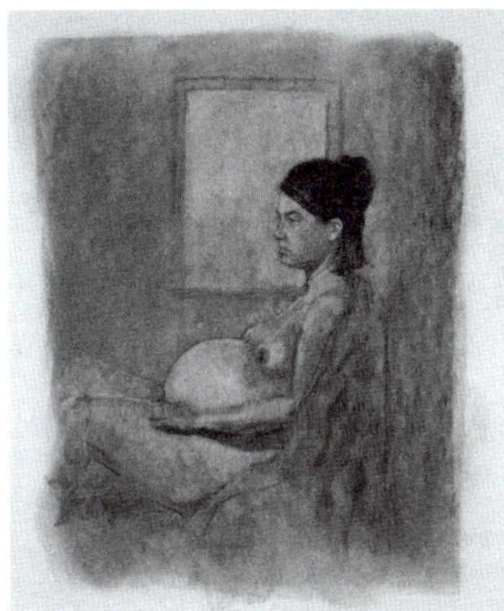
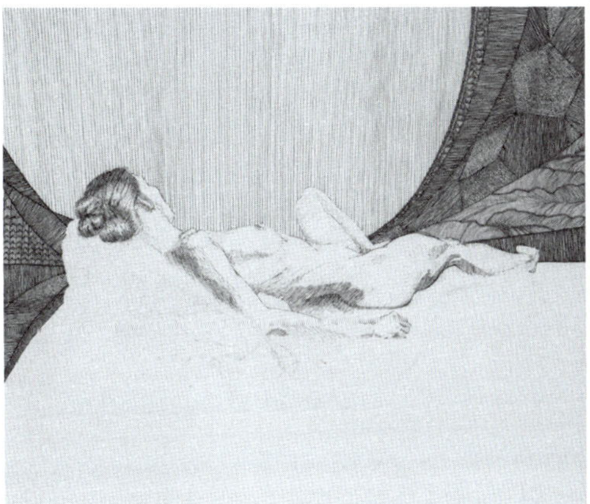
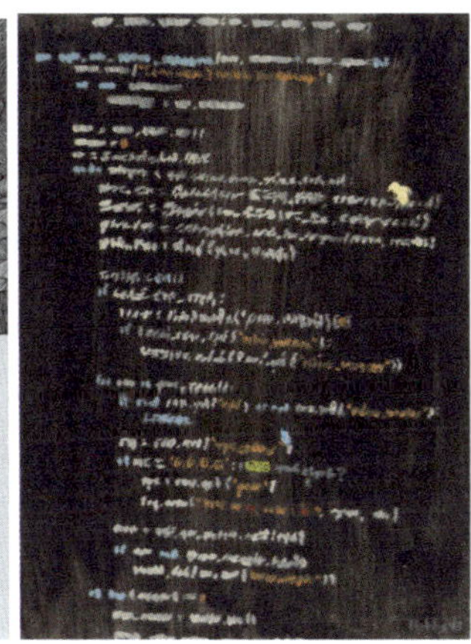

interests—skateboarding, music [a punk band, jazz drumming], computer programming. In my early twenties I decided visual art was it. So I redoubled my efforts in learning the basics—composition, color palette—and got really into figure drawing especially.

Everything to me was figurative until I started working generatively, because it's much easier to start with something that's known, right? I didn't have the imagination that I needed to create original compositions from whole cloth.

The important thing is, I was trying to follow the traditional route, paying my dues, eating my vegetables. And at a certain point, I realized I had squeezed as much juice as I could out of that, and I needed to make something original. I was twenty-seven.

I was working as a programmer at a local tech start-up in Austin. I had heard the advice for artists, that you need to bring into your work what you're passionate about. I looked at my own life and realized programming was that for me. It just clicked. It's how I think about problems. I knew it had to be part of my artwork. But it wasn't clear to me how.

Here's an example where I attempted to introduce mathematically based elements into my figurative work. It was transitional, from 2013.

But I didn't yet know anything about generative art. So I did strange experiments. I made paintings that were like coding environments. I did programmatic manipulations of photographs. I went on many long walks. I wondered if there were aesthetics that were particular to the coding environment. Could I observe coding through the lens of painting and extract something interesting? By aesthetics, I was thinking of maybe the stereotypical hacker scene in a movie, where text moves across a black background. Not quite that, but arrangements of shapes and colors, abstract design elements.

So my first attempt at merging these two was to literally paint these patterns. It did not turn out very well. But it wasn't the worst thing ever. It's just kind of boring.

The next one I did was around programmatic manipulation of a photograph or digital image. And having a photograph as a starting point was comforting. They weren't bad, and they were enough to entice me to continue. But they weren't it, exactly.

And then I tried one other direction, which was to paint a painting using mathematical components, like sine waves, you know, and quadratic curves. I don't have that one to show you, I think I must have painted over it. And actually, it was reasonably interesting.

But while I was painting, I had a thought: *Why don't I write a program that creates the painting? Why am I doing this painting by hand? Why am I trying to measure out a sine wave on a canvas instead of writing a program that creates the work itself?*

The Art Is the Program I made my first work with that in mind. And it was immediately interesting to me. It was more interesting than any of the paintings I had been making, and I didn't think I had ever seen anything like it before. I created the painting out of mathematical primitives; it uses a lot of curves. And I used randomness in the program, to shift detail around.

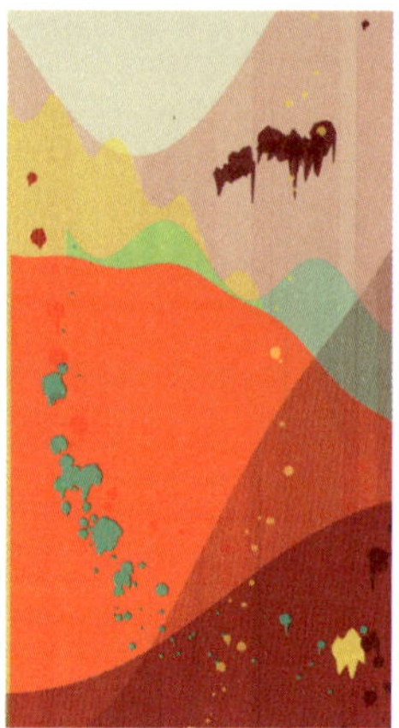

I did not have a final composition in my head, and part of what made it successful for me was that I had not been able to visualize the abstract composition ahead of time, which I had been able to do for figurative work.[3] But this was nice because it was iterative and discovery oriented. I would just try things, see what happened. Sine waves were the first thing I worked with because I found them aesthetically pleasing and they happened to be very easy to code.

I started making several works per week, for a few years in a row—I had like five hundred generative works in the span of these few years. I honed programming skills, refined types of calculations about creating artwork, and consumed lots of work about artists, trying to educate myself visually. I started to get much more interested in abstract artwork, needing to learn more about what's already out there. I got very heavily into the New York school of abstract expressionists, Rothko especially.[4] Digital art tends to be cold and rigid. It's just not that compelling to me. I had come from painting; I wanted to see how the vibrance and texture and chaos of paint on canvas could translate to the digital world.

But it was a big mental shift. When you're creating a painting, you're thinking of every aspect of a particular image, constructing it and fine-tuning it. For generative work, you're finding ways to abstract and extract it. You're

WHAT IS AN NFT?

TYLER HOBBS: Okay, let me define the terms here. An NFT is just an online record of a sale, and it's particularly important for digital artwork because it helps someone get recognized as the legitimate collector of the artwork. The Art Blocks model is, they take the code and they write it to the block chain, so collectors can come in and say, "I want to purchase an NFT that's generated from that program." I don't know what's going to come out, neither does Art Blocks or the collector. And there's an output size—so for *Fidenza,* I said there were going to be 999 NFTs created from that program, no more. So this is the first time I had no ability to curate what's coming out of the program. Usually I can cherry-pick the images I like to sell as individual works, but not here. So it really raised the bar for what I needed to do in terms of a consistent high-level output from the program. And I have to introduce a lot of variety as well. Particularly with *Fidenza*, I introduced so much variety there were many surprising outputs, even to me.

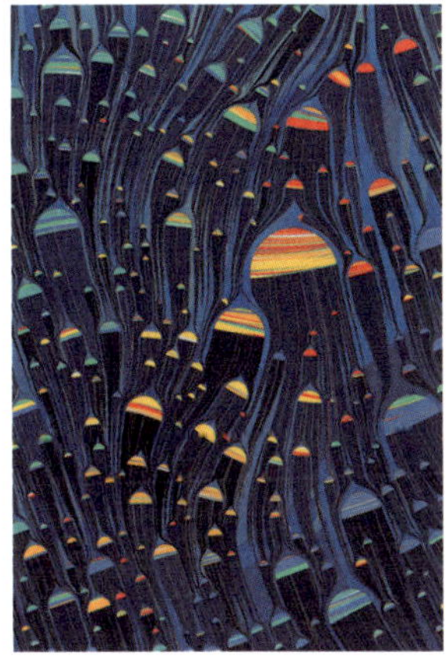

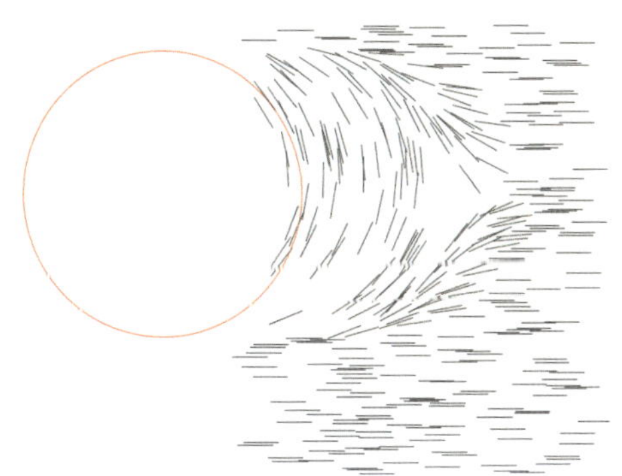

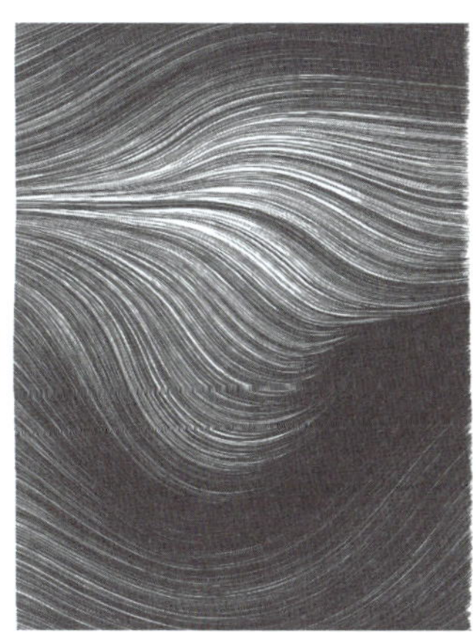

turning it into a system: *What is it about this style of image that I enjoy? Is it the balance of the shapes? Or the distribution of color? How can I generalize those?*[5] Because it's code, it has to be incredibly explicit. The computer never gives you anything for free. I had to rely on my ability to iterate to get to a good final point, which has been so much more successful for me than trying to dream a masterwork and then bring it to reality. And sometimes the computer randomly suggests something new to me. I heavily rely on those moments for inspiration.

The weakest position for an artist is to have a blank canvas. Many, many times I have just said, *Okay, I'm literally just going to draw horizontal lines on the canvas so it's not blank anymore.* As I'm developing the work, I have every image and version of the code. Oftentimes there was a point in the middle where I could have gone one direction or another. It's very fruitful for me to go back and say, *Now I'm going to explore the other route and see where that leads me.* So it's not a blank canvas. It makes me much more productive, and I can move fast.[6]

I started selling the work directly on my website, and getting commission offers. I went full time as an artist in about 2017.

I thought this really worked. It's called *Ectogenesis*. Sometimes works have a way of creating themselves, and the best you can do is analyze it after the fact and say what happened there that made this so good. For me, a big part of what made this successful was the color distribution, and the importance of creating pockets of vibrancy surrounded by larger areas of desaturation.

Flow Fields Before I actually made *Fidenza*, I should explain how I got there. I was interested in this idea of curves flowing, distorting the grid so curves swerve in interesting ways. This image is the very first thing I ever put down in a program. The circle represents the distortion to the grid. It was helping me visualize whether the code was working in the way I intended.

Two days later I made this, the first actual work using a flow field, which is a way to generate curves that don't tend to overlap. Programming tends to be rigid and squared off; creating an organic curve is a pretty difficult

3. In a sense, not being able to imagine the work liberates you from the maddening distance Michael Cunningham identified, between the thing in your head and the thing you are able to produce.

4. Even when subcontracting aspects of his abstraction to the machine, he approached the field the way any abstractionist might, by reading, analyzing, trying to make sense of why it worked when it did. Also, as I'm tracing recurrences in these notes, I should register that Rothko wins the prize for visual artist most cited.

5. I could never make this kind of art (besides the fact that I wouldn't want to, I am also a digital incompetent) but thinking about how generative art forces you to analyze or break down where it's going awry or succeeding (also what you're liking in it) really helped me in my own painting.

6. Art making involves an immense amount of tedium. This is the unfortunate truth. Programming substitutes its own tedium for tedium on the canvas. But then, *whoosh*.

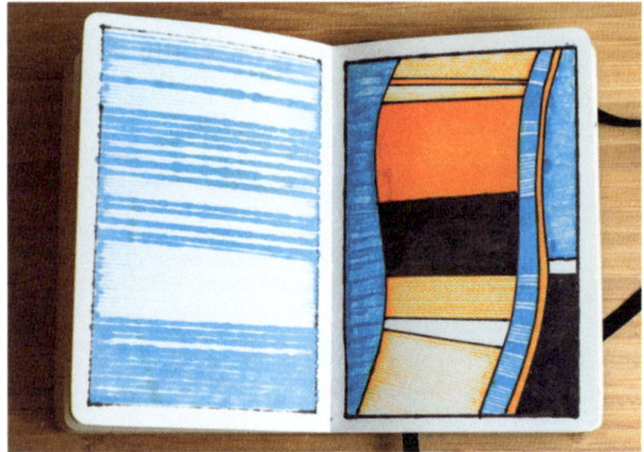

Occasionally he draws: "For some work I start with a compositional idea, which is hand drawn. But it is an outlier for my process."

task. Before this, I didn't have the means to achieve that programmatically, and I don't think many other people did either.

And then this is two days later. It shows how I was able to take the flow fields to create more complex constructions and add color to it. That delivered the early hints of what was to come later with *Fidenza*.

And I had really started to pay attention to the spacing. This one reminded me of corals and sea anemones. It had an organic quality to it while being very simple. The shapes are not overworked, not pretentious, and I loved that.

I started to introduce more variety and more variations of scale, more dynamic compositions. The positions of the segments, the thickness, these are all randomized. But they're randomized within a window. Which gives me a sense of control, but still gives the computer room to surprise me with something unexpected. In this I was liking the rhythmic quality particularly.

So now I started to move into color. There are a million ways colors can go wrong that just become obnoxious or overbearing. The way it works is I define a color palette by hand. I hand select the color and assign a probability to each color—so, a 70 percent chance of a shape being white, 20 percent chance of it being blue, and so on. Lots of surprises occur, some good, some really bad.

These are just sketches, not finished works. I'm just playing. For some of them, maybe there's a distance of an hour between them. I can move fast.

This gets closer to a finished work. It was for an interior mural that a company had commissioned. It was the same session as the preceding images—in 2020.

And, finally, *Fidenza* I started to hear about NFTs in '21. Started hearing about Art Blocks, which is a particular platform that serves generative art through the block chain. I felt it would be a natural fit for my work. I submitted an application to Art Blocks in 2021, said, "Hey I'm Tyler, Art Blocks sounds awesome, I have this program I think will really work well." I showed them these sorts of outputs and said this is the kind of thing I would like

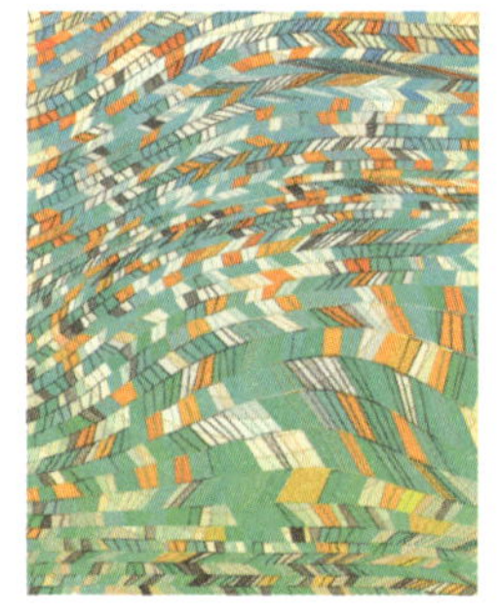

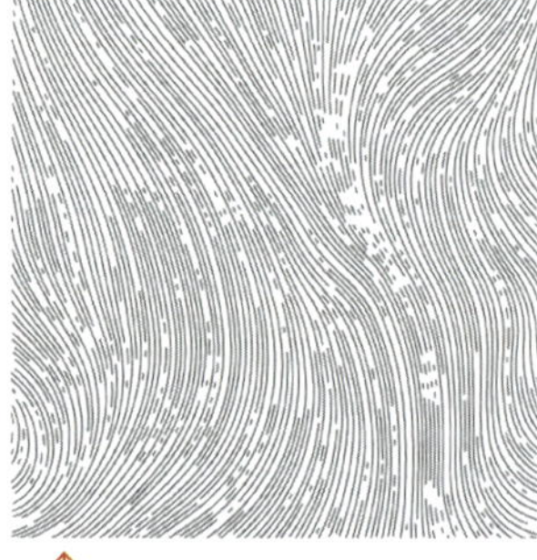

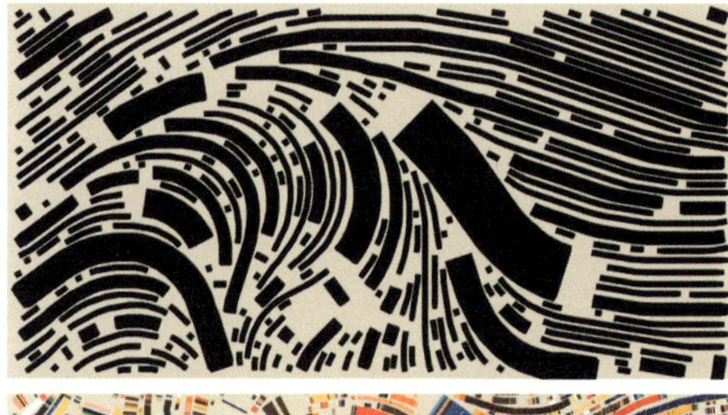

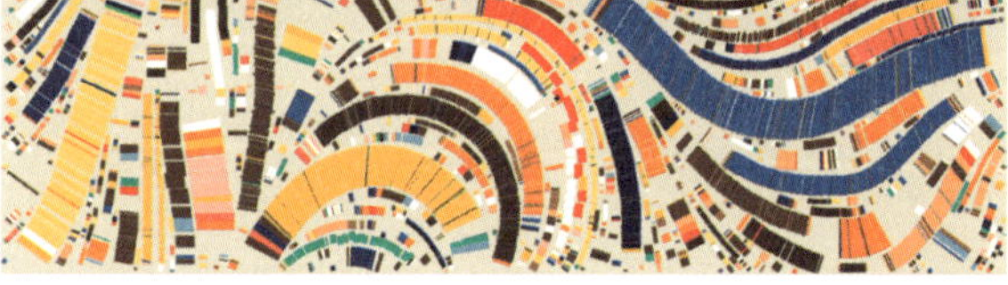

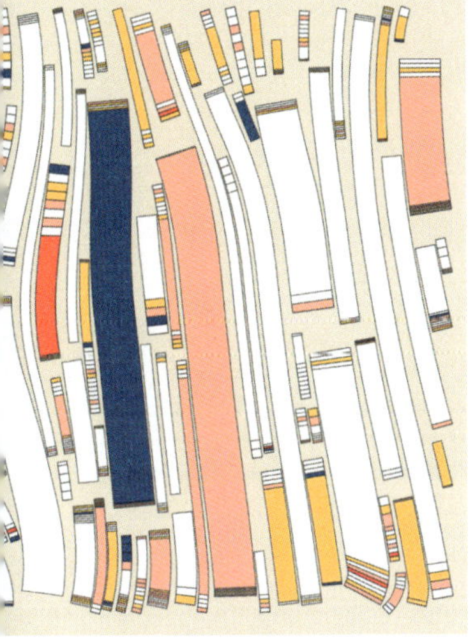

Fidenza #982.

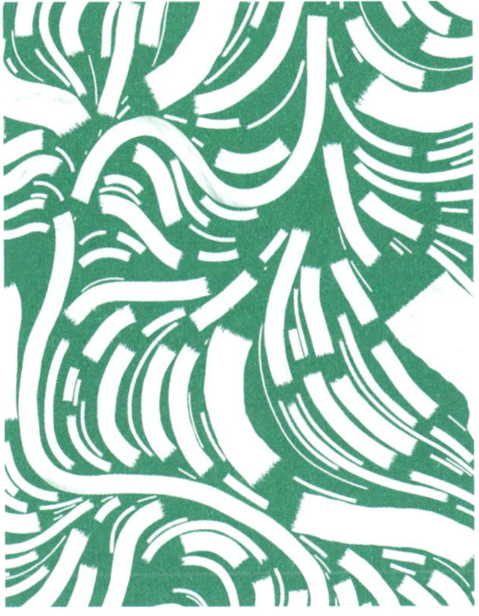

Fidenza #410.

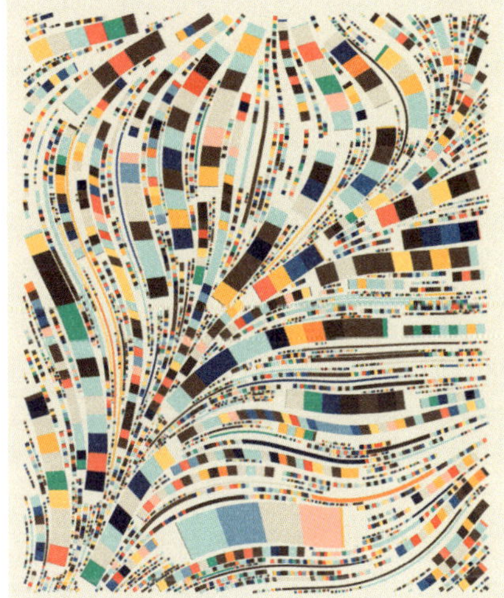

Fidenza #313. (This is the one that sold for over $3 million.)

to release, and they were incredibly excited about it.

So after Art Blocks accepted my application, I had three or four months to get to the finished *Fidenza* output. And I went to work experimenting with variations. Instead of thin curves, I used thick, curved rectangles. I designed them with fourteen unique sets of colors. I shifted scale. I made "small" shapes very rare, jumbo (nice, chunky shapes) the most common, and jumbo extra large rare again. I played with different textures ranging from a painterly look to a more graphic appearance. I allowed for outlines. And I added a "collision check, no overlap" feature, and they created two different modes where these checks are not as strict, including one that removes checking altogether.

And that was it. I was making hundreds, thousands of outputs, so I had a very good feeling for the kinds of things the algorithm would do, while surprising me.

I wanted it to be 99 percent acceptably good, the top 25 percent to be quite good, and the last 5 percent, when things combine in an unpredictable but beautiful way, magical. So when I felt comfortable that that's what the program might produce, I just released it. On June 11, *Fidenza* became available for sale.

Here's what emerged I'm more confident now. I have a better feel for what it takes to create a high-quality work. Whereas before I might have put in one, five, maybe ten hours on one project, now I can spend up to two hundred hours.

As for *Fidenza*, the primary sales from the algorithm were soon eclipsed in the secondary market. On the secondary market, you can see a particular image and buy that. (I can't tell you which ones I like best—my collectors would kill me. But there's no best single one.) And for me, the nice part is there's a 5 percent royalty that goes to the artist on secondary sales, which in my case was massive—*Fidenza* came along at an interesting time, because NFTs exploded immediately after I put it out,[7] and *Fidenza* did particularly well. The works started selling for one hundred times what I had originally sold them for. And so I was lucky that I was allowed to reap some of the rewards.

7. By the time I was finishing this book, the value of NFTs had substantially declined. But Tyler still really believed in them; he thought they would always rise and fall. During this period, AI became hot. Could AI be my collaborator in the writing of this book? I experimented with ChatGPT. I did find it helpful, even, in a sense, creative when I pushed it explicitly for looser, less linear responses, and some were pretty interestingly disarranged. But alas, I did have to write the book myself.

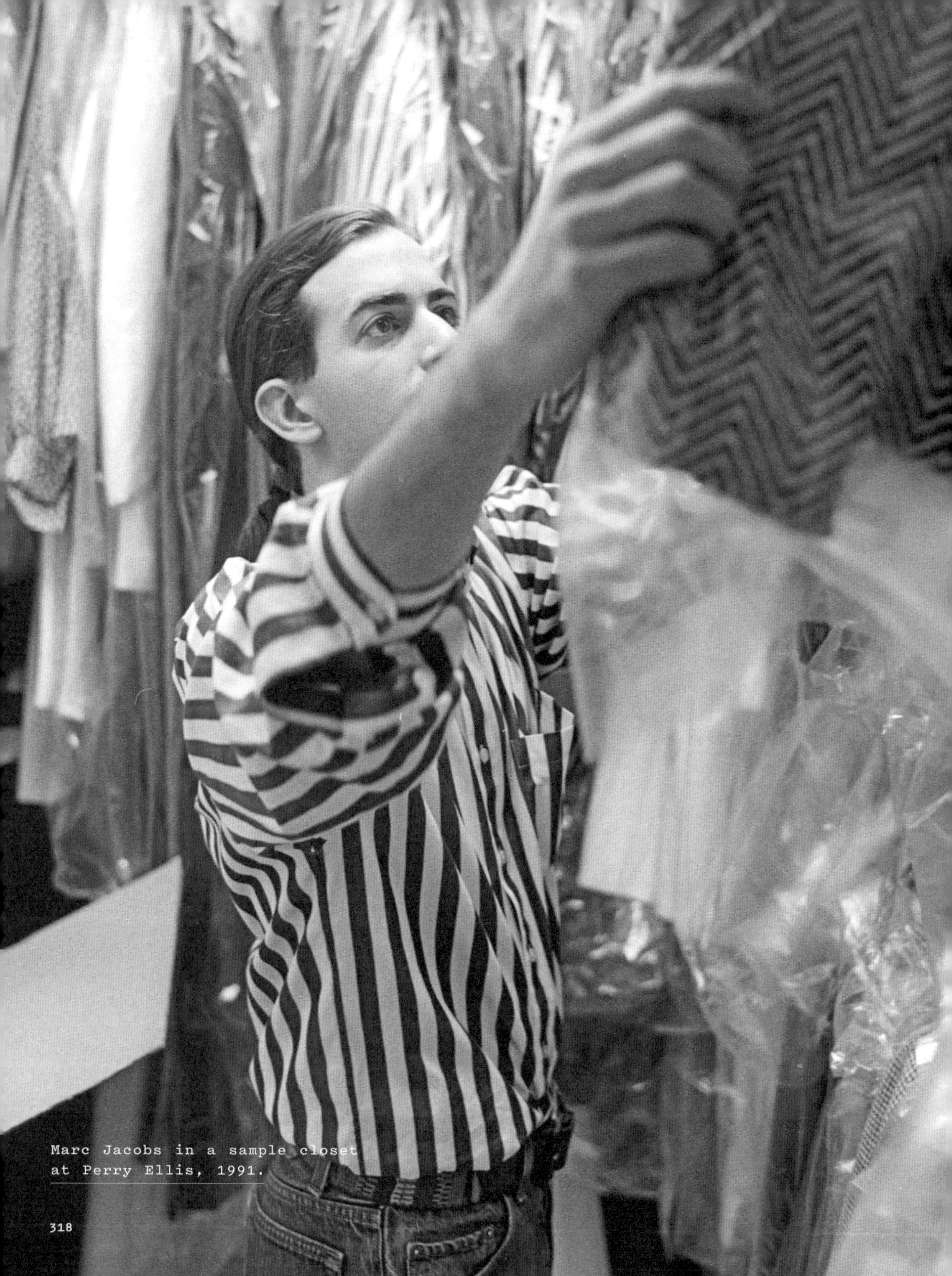

Marc Jacobs in a sample closet at Perry Ellis, 1991.

34
MARC JACOBS
It Is *Always* Harder

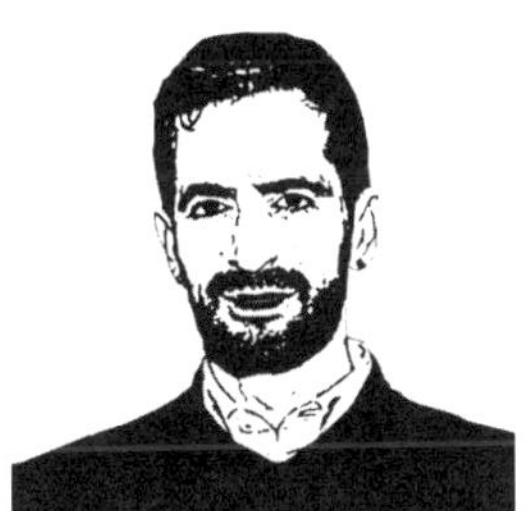

OCCUPATION: Fashion Designer

WORK DISCUSSED: Striped Jersey Dress (2021)

BORN: 1963

IN MY OLD editing jobs, I would go to fashion shows during "fashion week" in New York. Many of the fashion houses were advertisers, and it was important to show your face. It sounds like fun, but it wasn't—not for me. The kissy social swirl was amusing, but I couldn't help thinking it was alot of posturing for what was, in the end, usually ten minutes of show to dress up commerce like art. And the clothes didn't interest me much, although that was mostly because I didn't understand them. When I sat next to the critics and editors who knew fashion, and they would explain what I was seeing, I became more impressed. But even they had disdain for much of what was on the runway. Most of the houses would trot the same look out, season after season. And all "week" (in reality it was closer to two weeks) the fashion cognoscenti would wait for the one show that never failed to thrill them, whether it fully succeeded or not. The last night belonged to Marc Jacobs, for he was considered the true artist of American fashion.

And actually, to my surprise, I saw why. Over and over, Jacobs would reinvent himself. In a world numbed by branding and the necessity of repetition, he never did the same thing twice. His clothes were alert to changing times, but not in a way that felt reflexive. They were intelligent, witty—conceptual and yet also mostly beautiful. He was not just making a statement. And his shows themselves were theatrical spectacles, so that was a kick too. I couldn't wait to talk about them with my knowledgeable colleagues.

Jacobs's career was an alpine range —vertiginous ascents and descents. A precocious talent, he went to the High School of Art and Design in New York and then to Parsons and shot to fame quickly, the youngest designer to win the Council of Fashion Designers of America award for "new fashion talent." He designed for Perry Ellis, was notoriously fired for designing a (very ahead of its time) "grunge" line; had his own popular eponymous label; triumphed at Louis Vuitton before eventually leaving, presumably

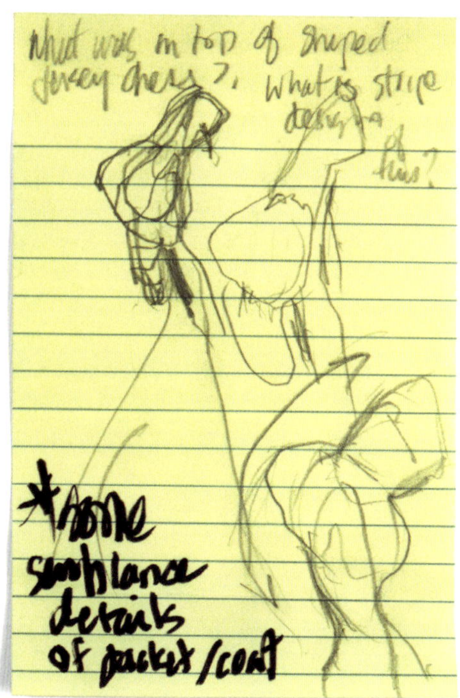

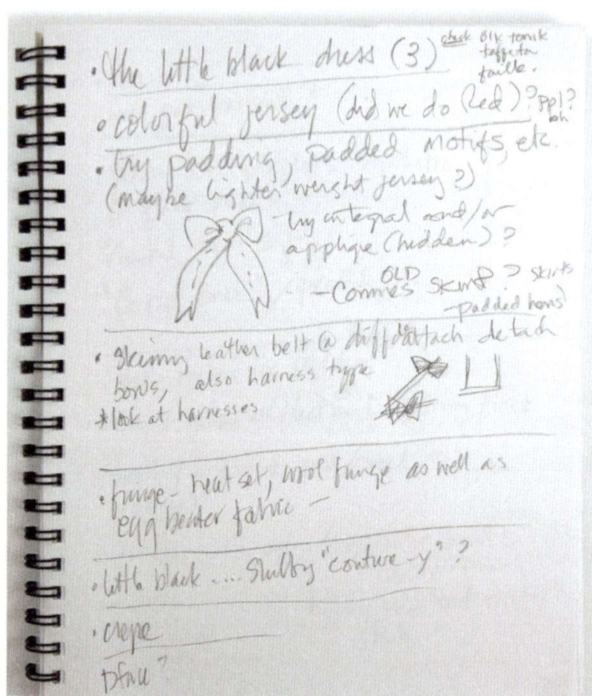

Sketching, describing.

not of his own choosing; and saw his empire shrink. Throughout, he has lived a very public life—his drug use and sex life and cosmetic surgery have always been all there for the world to see. He never hid any of it, and was candid and human, even while living a life made for a tawdry miniseries. He frightened me personally a bit (in that nerd to queen bee kind of way), but I also thought he was marvelous.

What does it mean to be an artist in a fiercely commercial—and often vicious—context? Marc Jacobs is just raw enough, and just calloused enough, to maneuver through it. This took years of practice, but it must also be a function of a very unusual character, because his MO was there from the beginning. He descends a rabbit hole, takes what's useful, descends another. He allows ideas in, but is rigorous about dismissing false leads. He is vulnerable and tough, open and shut. He preserves his instincts, which usually serve him.

I went to visit him in his Soho office smack in the middle of COVID to talk about the first collection he did after lockdown, which had received rapturous reviews. He wanted to talk about one dress, the first he made after the quarantine hiatus and the last he finished before the show. The building was nearly empty, I was let into his office, and he descended a stairway—very Hollywood. Then he took me through the making of this elegant striped dress, one decision after another.

MARC JACOBS: Generally, when it's time to do a new collection, we get together and start talking. It's very similar from season to season. We talk about fabrics, about colors; everything comes up. And I'm not a very linear thinker. So I'm lucky to have Joseph, who is the director of the studio.[1] He's able to decipher things from my conversation. Things start to stick. Some drop out, reappear later, or go away.

I do sketches to try and transmit an idea or thought—midnight, three in the morning. And

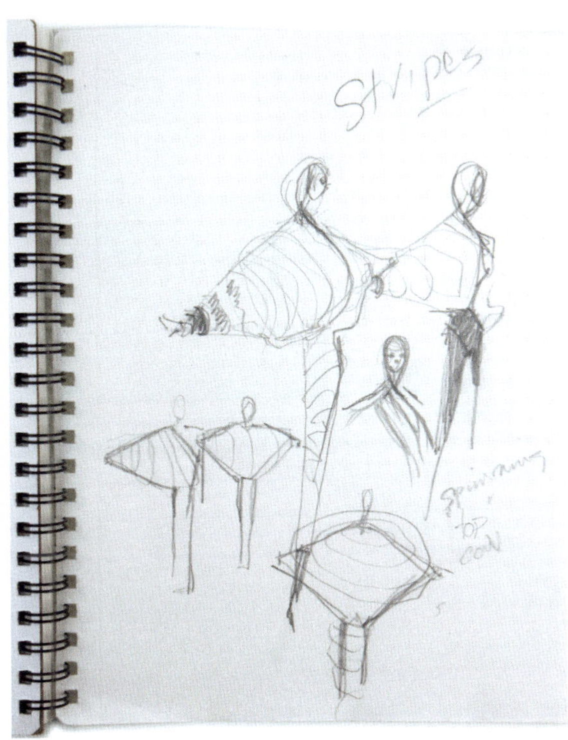

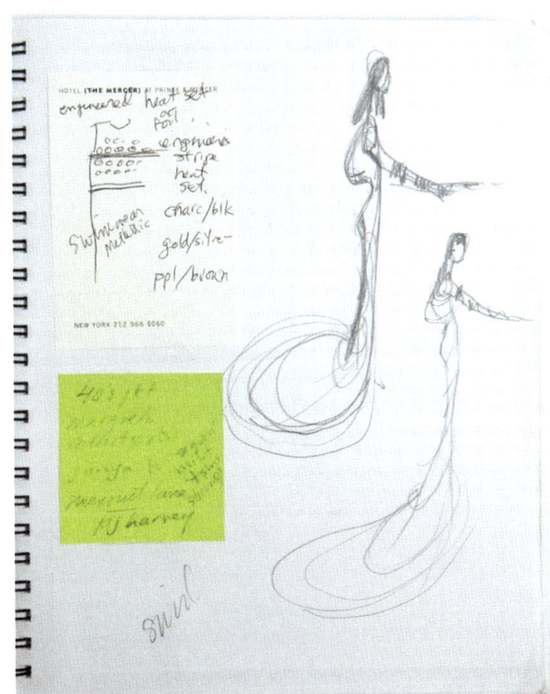

then I come in with a pocketful of them. But it's only a starting point. And it's a little silly that I have to say that out loud, but I feel like I do, every time, say, "This is only a sketch."

Time becomes the greatest editor. The only way to get things done is to finish.

The Dilemma This Time We had stopped during COVID. We just couldn't figure out any way to create something during lockdown, and I felt it was a really smart decision to not do anything. So we checked in with each other. And we thought, we're not going to even attempt to do something until we're all together.

I like to work towards the goal of a live show,[2] whether it's for one hundred people or four hundred, in the Armory or the library or in our store. What motivates me is the idea of making clothes for a performance, a theatrical performance. So we took a break, we all had a lot of time to think, and then we were able to be reunited.

The windows were all open, we were masked, it was weird. We rely on Italian mills to make fabric; how were we going to do that? They can't come here. There were new obstacles. So we started to think, we have to be really mindful of fabrics, maybe we should use the fabrics we have left over. And then we decided we were going to do the show with Bergdorf's exclusively—the clothes would only be available in one place. I felt that by doing something rare, a small amount at that price level—no wastage, no overages of fabric—that actually felt responsible.

This Dress, the Thread This dress was the first piece we talked about and the first piece we started. We were still working on it like up to a week before the show.

Here's how it began. I thought:

1. Joseph Carter is the creative director of women's ready-to-wear.

2. Among his other attributes, Marc Jacobs has always been a showman. His runways have featured a giant sun orb lighting the proceedings, a marching band, headphones for the audience to hear the soundtrack, models walking out from the interior onto the streets, Lady Gaga. For years, the audience had to wait hours for the show to start, but the shows were usually worth it.

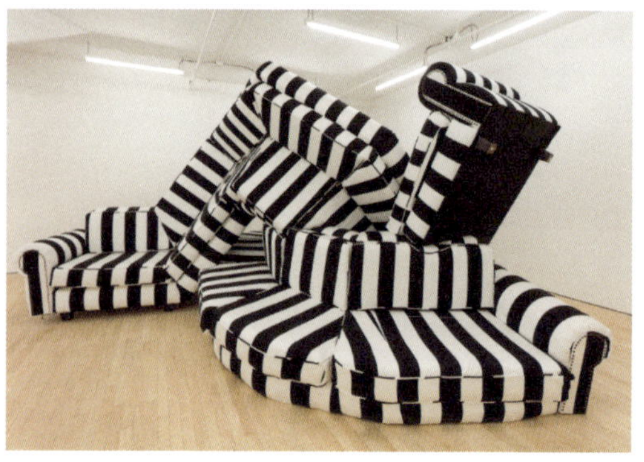

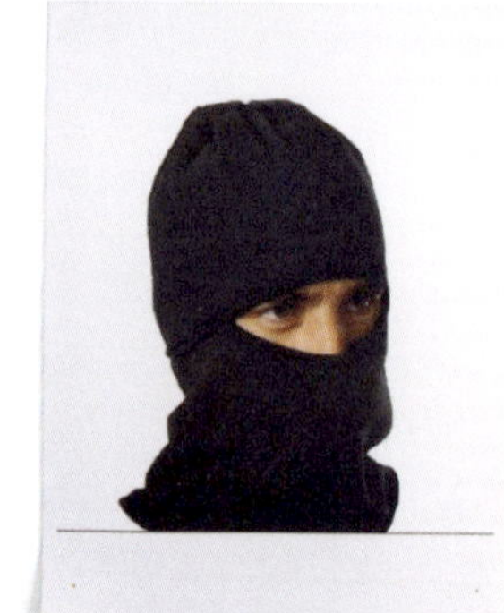

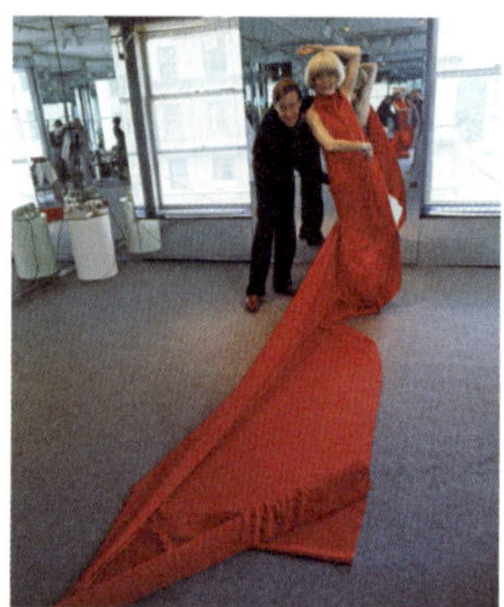

References.

What have people been wearing during lockdown? Sweatpants and T-shirts. I didn't want to show sweatpants and T-shirts necessarily, but maybe we should do some kind of T-shirt that could be long—that could be a T-shirt dress. And I always say this, so it wasn't new, but to my mind there was some new importance to it. I was like, we should start with jersey because it's comfortable. It feels good. It's not restrictive. We started looking at images of dance and fashion where there was a lot of movement.

We created a collage board and said, "Well, what kind of jersey would that T-shirt be in? What color? Solid or patterned?" And I said it should be a striped shirt. But then: Printed or knitted? And I said it should be stripes, with two colors we piece together. And then everyone started playing. We bought jersey in Midtown, we had leftover jersey from the previous season, we played.

I thought about this couch by Borna Sammak that I remember loving.

And then, I don't know, I like the idea of stripes being kind of irregular and maybe creating some optical pattern. I like the idea of it feeling like it's twisting or moving, turning around the body.

We started playing with squares that were different-size stripes, and we cut holes in them and we had a model come. We made a hypnotic sort of spiral. We just layered squares and rectangles.

And then: Maybe it should have a hood?

So it became kind of a hoodie over a T-shirt dress. The conversations went back and forth. Maybe the circular thing is a square. Maybe this, maybe that. It got distilled into this shape, like a turtleneck T-shirt dress.

And then, maybe the hood belonged to something worn over the dress. Maybe a puffer? The thing just kept getting layered and layered, but they were all just scraps. I mean, it wasn't a real dress, or a real coat or anything. It was just panels and panels.

But still, the jersey felt too . . . kind of limp. And once I saw the roundness and the body of the down piece, I thought we should try trapunto, which is when you put padding between the two layers of jersey and there's a lot of stitching. So even though it was a jersey, it had kind of a squishiness to it. Then the fabric became padded, quilted. It just evolved like that.

We were entertaining the idea that if we weren't able to do a show, these things had to make great photographs, right? I thought, whatever we did, it would be shown in the store. So the most important thing to me was to see the figure from the side. I thought, *Well, if this were a photograph, I think the hem of the dress should make a beautiful shape on the floor.* So we made it very long.

And the points of the square that we had originally cut became bigger, longer, with wider stripes on the bottom. We put our house model Christina on a white seamless and we placed the points so it had this amazing shape. Like

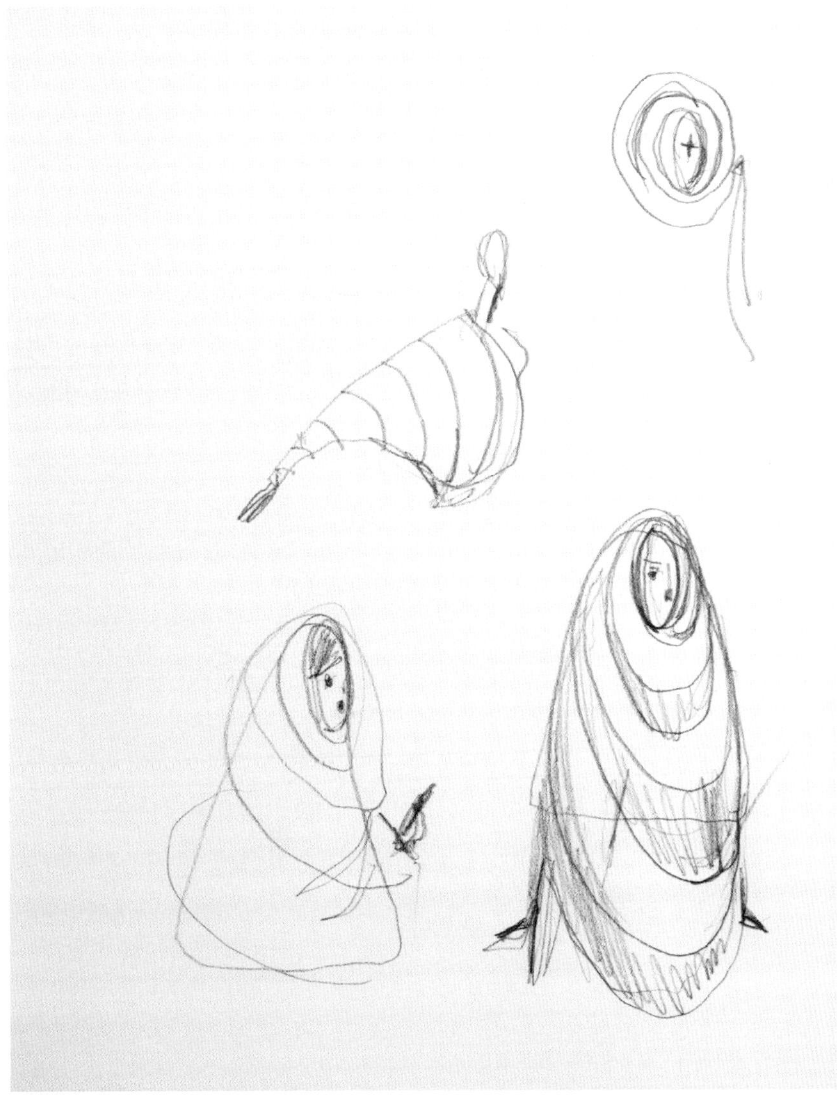

Imagining the hood. (I love this drawing-ET in Marc Jacobs.)

an op art thing.

I started thinking, *Each look we do, we'll find an environment where it's camouflaged. The striped dress on the striped floor, the dress disappears, or morphs into the floor. Just think of these as images.*

In my head, I have lots of insecurities and doubts. I was excited, but I wasn't sure we had it. So like I said, it ended up being stitched and padded, but in the interim, we also tried strips of jersey to make up the black-and-white stripes. So each one of the black stripes was made up of twelve little strips of black fabric and then the white stripe was six little stripes of white fabric. We tried using sweatshirt fabric because it had more body than the jersey we ended up using. We tried it with all the seams on the outside—maybe that would give the stripe more texture. We tried cutting the jersey in different directions to see if it changed the way the dress fell. We tried different ways of working the fabric, and different stitch samples.

It was the first piece we started working on, and we were still . . . I mean, I don't want to say perfecting, because it wasn't perfect in the end. But it was pretty good.[3]

—

As we were looking at the dress, I asked whether they were meant to be prison stripes, thinking he may have been thinking that way because of the lockdown. It was the wrong thing to say.

—

MJ: I *hardly* think it's prison stripes. Okay, I don't know why I insisted on a stripe, it's funny. But I always think a striped T-shirt is like the dumbest thing. When I was a little kid, all my T-shirts were striped. It's classic. *The Cat in the Hat.*

But what you said about the prison stripes—I've stopped correcting people. People would come backstage after a show and say, "Oh, I love that it was so *Mary Poppins.*" It wasn't *Mary Poppins.* But that's fine. That's what you saw. As long as people see something, you're fine.

So prison, or thirties Berlin, or *Cat in the Hat,* or rave. It's like, great.

—

Critics of the collection (who tended to see lockdown) were drawn to the progression of the show, which led to a release from the cloistered nature of the clothing.

—

MJ: That was a conscious thing. I had started to collect images of the way people covered their face. I had doctored a turtleneck and pulled it over my nose. We created a mask, a hidden identity. A hat and hood and a turtleneck, and all you saw was eyes. As we worked through it, we thought, "How covered should everyone be?" And then, "What if we then repeated the show, uncovered—strip them of all the layers." Kind of like concealed identity and then release: *Okay, you can see my face now.* I was a little afraid that when we stripped down each of the humans in the show, their outfits wouldn't look *enough*. You can't do something like that unless both versions look great.

But when we started doing the fittings, we thought, Okay, this looks amazing without all the head coverings. And we got excited because we knew that this idea was gonna work.

—

And it did. The show was generally seen as a triumph.

—

MJ: But if we'd had no deadline, we'd still be working on that striped dress. [He laughed.] I know I would want to stitch it differently.

3. Where was the customer/audience/viewer in all of this? No doubt, Jacobs was attendant to what might sell, but I believe his sense of customer desires seems to be mostly internalized—he designs principally by instinct, which often works out, not always, and which is why his career has had so many ups and downs. In any case, what appears in stores are usually commercial adaptations (for him and all designers) that are quite different from what he shows on the runway. In my own case, I always edited for myself, and when I felt that I wasn't the magazine's audience anymore, that was another reason I quit.

CONVERSATIONS WITH HIS SHRINK

MARC JACOBS: There's always a reason I feel more unsure than ever. This season it was like, "Oh my God, we haven't done anything for a year; it has to be incredible." And I remember saying that the last show we did, with all the dancers—Karole Armitage did the choreography—if this is the last show I ever do, I'd die a happy man.

Which is a wonderful feeling—until you have to do another show. I had to get past that and say, well, this is going to be something else. I'm not sure it'll have the same emotional pull. But you know, my shrink helped me. He said, "Just go to work and do it. You know you say this every time, there's always some reason why it's worse than ever." I don't know if it's me who feels this way or if it's reality, but there are always more obstacles than there were the time before. And I always feel it needs to be better than the one before.

My psychiatrist said to me, "You know, you have evidence that proves that this is your process—and something good comes of it, right? So will it be the best thing you've ever done? Don't know. But you will do something good. Because it's just the way it goes."

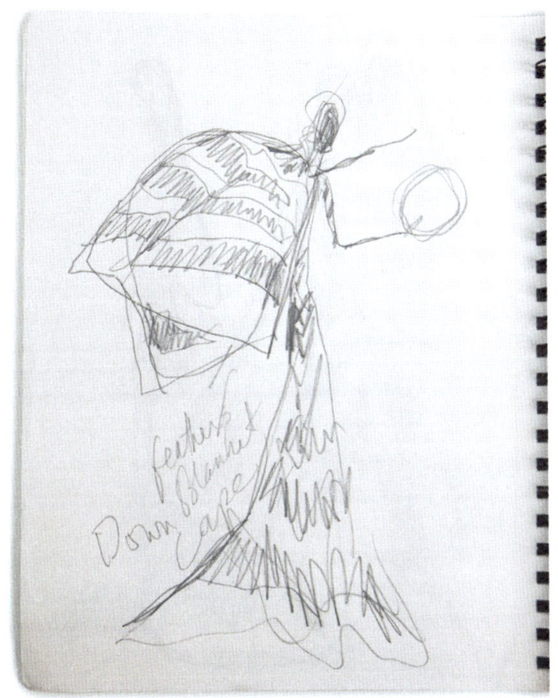

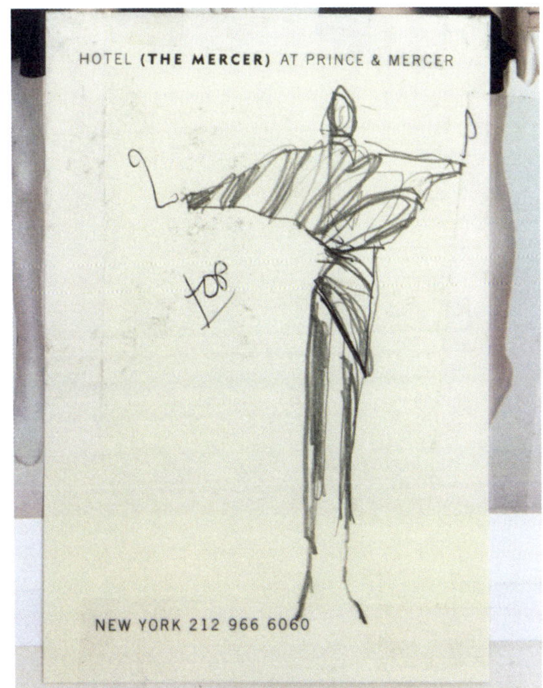

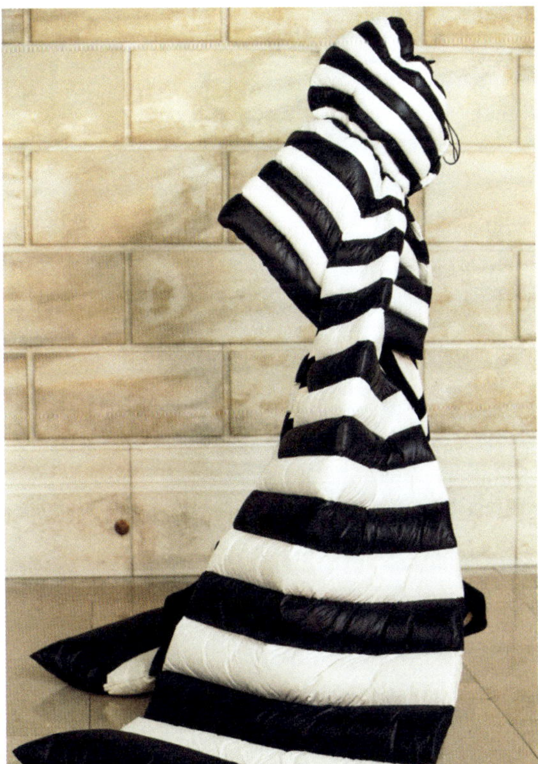
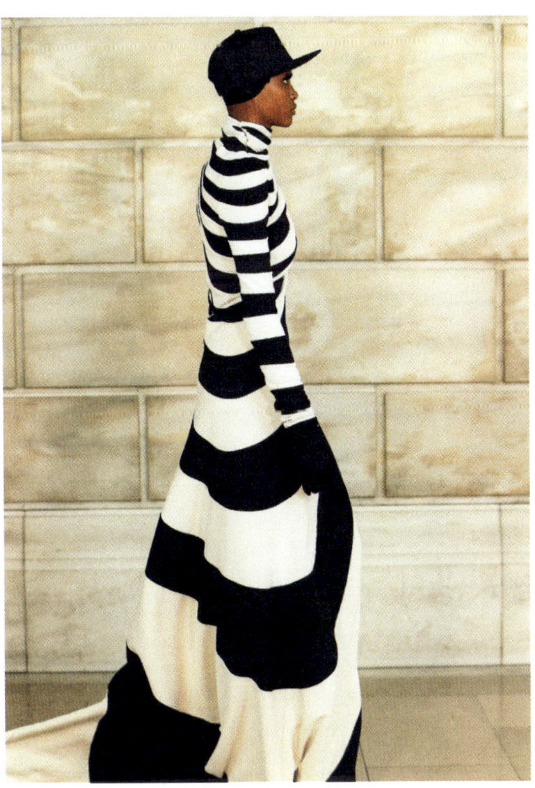

Top row: Jacobs's sketches of the striped dress. Bottom row: Two versions of the dress itself, hooded and not.

35
GRADY WEST
Alter Ego

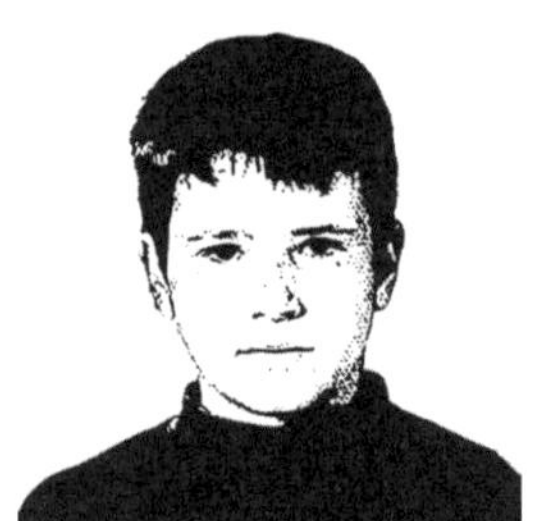

OCCUPATION: Performance Artist
WORK DISCUSSED: Dina Martina
BORN: 1963

THIS CHAPTER MIGHT sit in the you've-got-to-be-there zone, but I'll give it a go. Dina Martina is a character created by a man named Grady West, who plays Dina in a one-person, one-hour show of meandering monologue and excruciating song styling. It's technically a drag show, but not in the way you might expect. The show often tours in the places likely to understand Dina (Seattle, New York, et al.) and in in-residence summers in Provincetown, where Dina is the reigning act, halfway between arthouse and madhouse. Grady calls her (or him, for he is talking about himself) a clown, which is true as far as it goes, but a clown more like Buster Keaton than Bozo, Dada on two hairy legs.

The Stranger, a paper in Seattle, described West's creation like this: "The primary fact that one must understand about Dina Martina—beyond her stature as a superstar entertainer without peer—is that she is in possession of not one shred of discernible talent or grace. Her voice sounds like a cat having an epileptic fit on a chalkboard, her body moves like two pigs fighting their way out of a sleeping bag, and her face looks like the collision of a Maybelline truck with a Shoney's buffet." Dina Martina is a cult figure, revered within ironist circles. "Performance art never looked so good," said Whoopi Goldberg; John Waters described her as going "way beyond drag into some new kind of twisted art."

The central conceit is that Dina is 100 percent blind to her absurdity. She speaks in an invented dialect, exchanging hard and soft *g*'s (*jift* for *gift*), twisting idioms, performing a lounge act. She sings painfully, appears in crudely constructed videos, and tells stories of her life—about growing up in Las Vegas, and her daughter Phoebe, who is played by a puppet, and her best friend Doreen, heir to the Kotex fortune. It's definitely hit and miss, but you don't mind the misses because the bizarro universe Grady has created has no cracks. While feeling spontaneous, it is a wildly, deceptively disciplined act.

I had originally decided not to bring

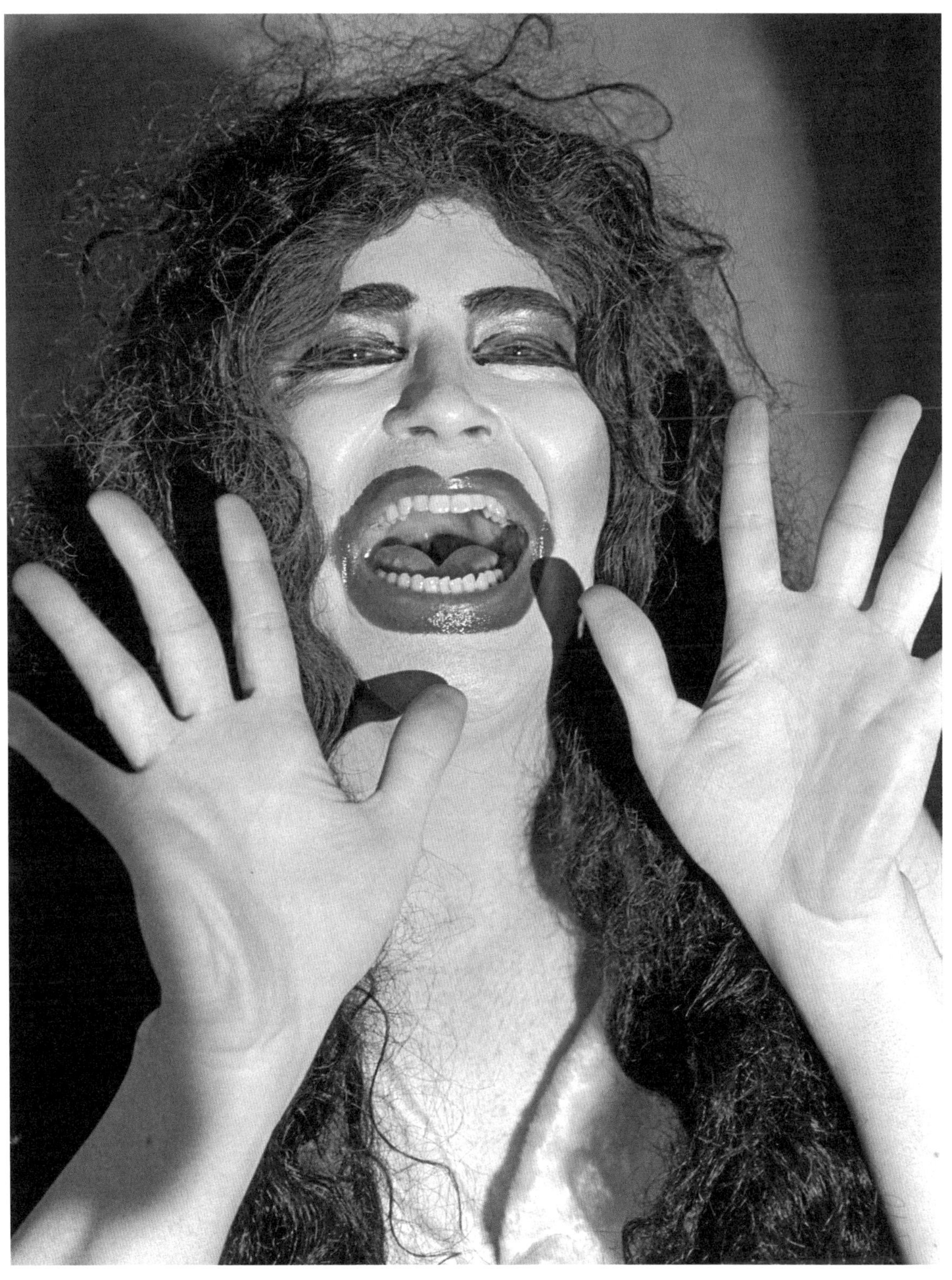

Dina Martina, a glam shot.

performers into this book, but I had wondered what it was like to invent an alter ego as your life's work, and then, for much of the time, live it. Grady rarely breaks character or talks about Dina (he requested that his "stamp" picture on the preceding spread be of him as a young boy; I obliged), so I was surprised when he agreed to talk to me about her, but I think he was himself interested in thinking about how Dina came into the world. And what surprised me (though I should now be realizing that this happens a lot) is how full-blown she was in her first imaginings. She was conceived in a moment when ironic burlesque was flourishing, in many respects as a reaction to AIDS. (Timing, it seems clear from these conversations, matters a lot.) I found myself particularly interested in how the show moved from blurted improv in its first days to a constructed, ingenious performance. Also, in what is happening in Grady's mind as he performs her. Playing Dina is like a very functional dissociation.

We spoke in Provincetown and later in New York, when it was nearly time for his summer show, which he had written none of.

GRADY WEST: Well, let's see. Both my parents were married and divorced five times each. And my mom was an alcoholic. It was a happy childhood. My mom would usually hang out with her two best friends, Rose and Pat. When they got together, they would drink and do weird voices and you know, crack each other up. So I would do my damnedest to get them to laugh. It usually worked; they were lubricated.

The first thing I wanted to be was a fireman, because of the cool trucks and the outfits. But then I fancied becoming an actor. The school play was an "original" musical, which meant that the choir teacher took every Broadway hit from the last forty years and glued them together. I, no surprise to anyone, can't sing, and yet I had one of the meatiest parts. But it was awful. I was awful.

They videotaped it and showed it to us the next day in class. Everyone but me was going, "There I am! There you are, Mary. There you are, Ted." And I'm just sitting there alone, seeing me suck and just shrinking, smaller and smaller. My dream of becoming an actor died at that moment. I thought, *What am I gonna do now? I'm not going to be an actor.*[1]

Waiting for the Punch Line I was a class clown, a goofball. But, I mean, there was a lot of darkness there too. I guess what I found funny was always like this: non sequitur, very bizarre. I remember one time doing a skit with my sister—there was a commercial for a detergent or something called Swans Down. And for some reason I tied it into a burglary, where someone's going to say "Hands up" but instead they say "Hands down." It made sense to me, but my sister just turned to me and went, "What?" I said, "Just say it!" So she did. And my dad and our grandparents, who were the audience, just sat there, waiting for the punch line. And I said, "There it is!"[2]

I graduated high school, worked at a restaurant. A guy I knew a little who'd worked there before asked some of us if we wanted to perform at this thing he was putting together. He had been commissioned to put on a show on Saturday afternoons—no cover, no door person, just word of mouth. He wanted to bridge the gap between the Seattle Art Museum and the Lusty Lady, an erotic dance place next door, so he was looking for "a tawdry lounge act peep show." I thought, *I'll do a bad lounge act. And hopefully it'll be funny.* Really low stakes. It was in the afternoon. What can it hurt?

Dina! I just thought of myself as a woman, sort of a wallflower. I didn't sit up all night dreaming it up. I mean, malapropism and wordplay is something I've always loved, so that went into the character without me really thinking about it. Dina's first hair was a ten-dollar Halloween closeout Morticia Addams wig I found at Hallmark. Bad makeup, no powder. I poured it into my hand, put it all over, and it was bloppy and shiny, and then I wiped it away and smeared lipstick around my mouth.

And then I went on.[3]

When I came offstage the first time, all the other performers were saying, "Oh my God, that was really funny, that was amazing, that was great." And I said, "What did I say my name was?" 'Cause I think I knew I wanted it to be Dina, so I guess I just rhymed it. A friend said, "I think you said Dina Martina or something like that." So that's how she got her name.

She was more demure when she first arrived. But there was that weird self-confidence. And most pervasive, the complete lack of self-awareness. Lack of objectivity about her ill-fitting clothes and her rat's nest hair. But it was all very spontaneous. From that first day, Dina had a faux continental accent. It developed over the years, but pretty early on I realized that certain words are fun if I do a soft *G* as opposed to a hard.

Since the early eighties I'd collected elevator music, Muzak-y stuff. So when I went onstage that's what I sang to. One of the first songs I sang was from the Golden Gate Strings performing *The Monkees Song Book*. I sang the Monkees theme. I said, you know, something like, "I'm Dina Martina, and people say I monkey around."[4]

The peep show lasted four nights over the course of a month. I threw my cheap wig away but six or so months later, I got a call to say they were doing a one-night cabaret. So I got another one and then, over time, I was invited to perform Dina at more cabarets around Seattle. At one, maybe two years after the peep show, someone asked me to go on, and then I find out they were doing a drag cabaret. Everybody but me is in traditional drag, doing lip sync, looking absolutely flawless. And they said, "Oh—what's she doing there?" I said, "Hi. I'm in the show too." And the more I got into Dina, I could just feel their assholes tightening. They thought I was making fun of drag. Some Southern queens pinpointed it immediately. They said, "Oh, you're a booger queen." Because that's what they call deliberately messy drag.[5]

I performed at another cabaret, where the only thing I remember was I had a really good pickle display—I'm a connoisseur, and this was the best pickle display ever. I thought, I'll do my interpretive dance to "Music Box Dancer" with a tutu on the pickle, and I'll dance with it. I now see how necessary it is to know what the audience wants to see. That night it was all women wanting to see women comedians. When I went onstage it was *noth-ing.* Tumbleweeds and crickets. I learned a lesson. I threw away a third of what I planned to do. I forgot about the pickle, who was offstage. But I didn't care that I'd bombed. I loved doing it so much. And bombing makes you a better performer.

I kept taking what gigs I could get. And it just grew. The first full-length Dina show was in '93. I was freaking out, people were pouring in, there were lines outside, and I was there with my index cards, and I was like, "I don't know what I'm doing!" And Dan Savage [who would go on to become a popular sex columnist and podcaster] was running tech. He said, "Calm down." I said, "No, let's make it free. That way they can't really complain, can they?" And Dan said, "No, we're still going to charge." He said to me, "*Figure it out!*" He told everybody, "Nobody talk to Grady for the next fifteen minutes." And in those fifteen minutes, I figured it out.

Development Eventually I thought [the show needed more construction]. I thought I should squeegee some of the dead air out of it. Her personality meshed really good with dead air, but I also realized I needed to pick up the pace a bit. You know, when you play venues where people are so drunk, you have to start

1. "Was there a sense that Dina was a response to how devastated you were in high school watching yourself act?" I asked him. "Were you at all determined to create art out of the worst possible version of yourself?" "That's giving me too much credit," he answered. "I'm not an ambitious person." But really, it has to be true a little. Or maybe I've just spent too much time on a shrink's couch.

2. Where does a sense of humor come from? Science is clueless. But in Grady's case, it's truly a mystery, because his humor is so specific. How does someone start to think like that? Similar to the questions I keep asking about where one's signature/imprint as a singer or painter comes from.

3. During the AIDS epidemic, in gay circles especially, a deeply ironic style of cabaret took root—*Hedwig and the Angry Inch* came out of that cultural moment, and Dina Martina did too. It's hard to separate Dina from that context.

4. For the unaware, the Monkees were (originally) a sitcom boy band. Their theme song went "Hey, hey, we're the Monkees. And people say we monkey around. But we're too busy singing to put anybody down." Immortal.

5. Like others here, Grady stumbled into a tradition, then inverted it in his own way.

barreling through, not give them any room.

And then also, I started filling in Dina's [backstory]. For the first Christmas show I did, I came up with a daughter I called Pho-ebbie. I'd been out thrifting, and I found this rag doll that was this big. I thought, *This is weird. Funny. Borderline creepy. Maybe Dina could adopt this kid.* And I put her in, suspended from a string on a pulley. So that's how it went.

Going Pro Still, it took me probably until the early 2000s before I actually got it through my head that maybe I could do this for a living. It was still a sideline until I started performing in Provincetown in 2005. And then I was able to start touring. I basically got enough exposure that I was able to book in New York, and eventually London and LA. There were several points when I'd just freak out, thinking, *Oh my God, this is the time everybody is going to realize I have no talent.* But the remedy is remembering, *Grady, they're not coming to judge you. They're just coming to have a good time.*

Over time I started scripting it. And I am basically not an eleventh-hour producer, more like a twelfth-hour producer. I go to my computer and think, *Oh God, tickets have been sold. It opens tomorrow. And I haven't written it yet.* I go through my hundreds of pages of ideas, and I just glue things together from that. But the format of the show doesn't have to have a story arc or redemption at the end, or conflict.[6] So I just do whatever feels good. I don't analyze. Opening night is my dress rehearsal. To the point where I have bought outfits and never tried them on, and during a video segment I'm changing my outfit and realize, *Oh shit, I can't fit into this.* One time the dress was so much smaller than I expected that I unzipped it, put my arms through the sleeves and just had it in front of me when I went onstage.

Over the course of a run, I add little bits here and there. But I don't improvise much. They give me fifty-five minutes, not a minute longer. But sometimes, I don't know. Earlier this year because the show was outside for COVID, there was this huge V formation of birds. And I was doing the monologue and thinking, *Should I say something?* I just stopped and said, "Oh, look at the birds." It got a big laugh. So that's kind of what you live for.

Two Places at Once

Adam Moss: *When you're onstage, you're talking and thinking at the same time?*

Grady West: Yes. It's a weird thing because you really have to not let yourself run away with the conversation in your head, because you'll lose your place in the monologue.

AM: *You never get exhausted by Dina?*

GW: Oh God, no.

AM: *Does Dina bleed into your Grady life?*

GW: After all these years of malapropisms, they're always in the back of my mind. Sometimes I'll start to say something, and I'll think, *Wait, is that the actual way to pronounce it?*

AM: *My favorite bit from this year's show was when you came out and sang, to the tune of the Weather Girls song "It's Raining Men," "It's raining* them.*" Did that come to you in a second, or was it sort of a developing idea?*

GW: No, it came to me two and a half years ago, and I just sat on it and thought I could never do it. I was afraid people would think I was anti-trans or anti-nonbinary. And it's not that. Then I was like, what the hell. You can do it in a way that people won't have room to think you're being a dick about it.

I was going to end the show with it last year and have this talk about how these people are rare, beautiful creatures like a unicorn. And then have a big unicorn floaty thing in the pool. I'd jump on it at the end of the song and say, "Thank you, good night." And then have a really long awkward pause, with me swimming, paddling with my hands to the other side of the pool. Which is funny in theory, but I thought it might actually be stupid and go on too long.

AM: *Stupid is good.*

GW: Stupid can be good. But it's not always good.

6. Whether accidentally or not, Grady created a structure that fit his MO. The character is a mess, so the show is allowed to be a mess—no linear anything, no narrative, no theme. Still, it makes its own peculiar sense.

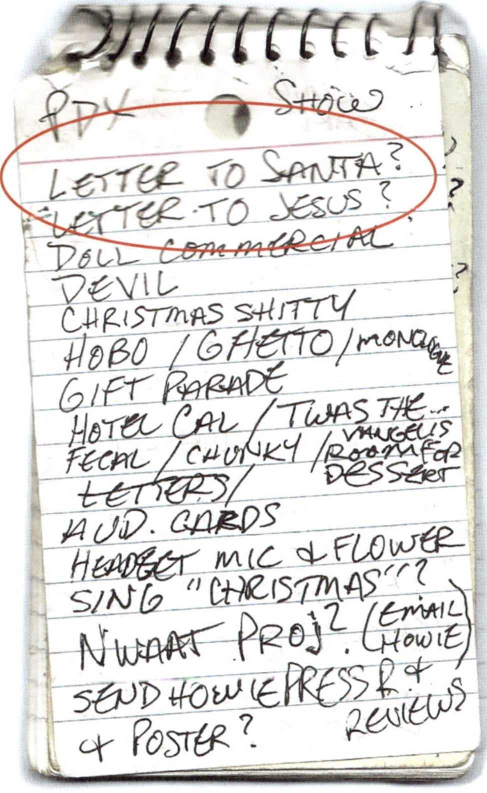

1.

Germs of jokes. Or not.

2.

Dina Martina is as close to a direct-from-the-brain expression of the way her creator just looks at things as any "work." But there are steps in between. As Grady is wandering around, he jots stray thoughts in his notebook. Some make it into his act, some don't. They aren't exactly jokes, but they offer a pretty clear biopsy of Grady's broken worldview. He tried to make sense of a few.

1. Santa/Jesus These ended up in a Christmas show, as a video segment. The video opens with Dina writing Santa, "Dear Santa, how are you, blah, blah, blah, what's going on?" The letter to Jesus opens with "Dear Jesus, how are you. I'm fine. Do you have Santa Claus's address? I sent him a letter, but it keeps coming back. He must have moved off of Thirty-Fourth Street."

2A. Choking Hazard Dina would occasionally talk about the Bible and just say it was a choking hazard. And that it makes a wonderful coaster. I know none of these jokes make any sense. I just think of things, you know there's got to be a joke in there somewhere.

2B. Big, Juicy Flies Oh, that's one I never used but I love the idea. You know, like those big bumblebees, only flies. And Dina and Doreen pick them up, and say they're like raisins with wings, I don't know. A lot of my ideas aren't worth developing. I guess it was a hot summer day when I wrote that. And you'd see a fly, and think, *Where the hell did that come from?* It should be in *The Guinness Book of World Records* or something. There's a lot of liquid in there.

36

WILL SHORTZ

The Brain Is a Slide Carousel

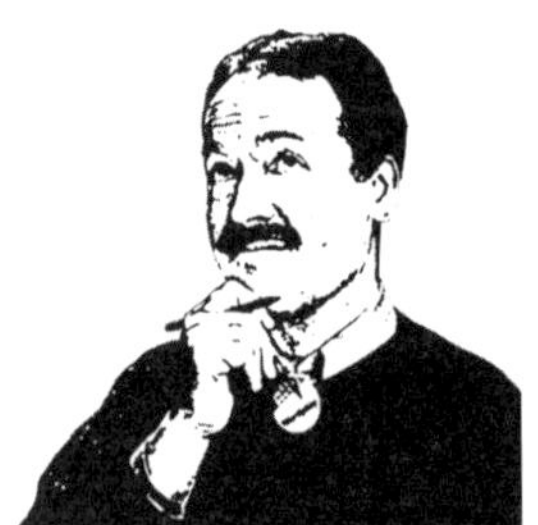

OCCUPATION: Puzzler

WORK DISCUSSED: "Driving Around" (2018)

BORN: 1952

ARE LOGIC AND CREATIVITY opposite? Not at all: even the most unrestrained surrealist or experimental novelist is working within a grid of their own logic. There were moments in my conversations for this book that I began to believe that setting up that grid and solving problems within it was the primary act of creative process, and I've never entirely let go of that. In any case, that was my own logic for wanting to talk to Will Shortz, the crossword editor of *The New York Times* (that, and thinking that an edit of a crossword puzzle would be fun to pore over, which it was).

I briefly supervised Will (though just barely; we did have a funny encounter at the time, however, which we discuss below). When he began at the *Times* in 1993, where he came from *Games* magazine and NPR, he was flying solo. These days the games department at the *Times* is enormous—its puzzles are hugely popular and multiplying. For instance, in the last couple of years, Will helped introduce[1] the highly addictive Spelling Bee (an anagram-like game, which I play on the subway). In 2022 the *Times* bought *Wordle*, which brought infinitely more puzzlers into the fold. And Shortz spools out new puzzles all the time.

We talked about the puzzling mind (to which I kept seeking parallels with the art mind).[2] Will has been obsessed since childhood. He began making puzzles when he was eight, and he sold his first one at fourteen. When he went to college, he created a major he called enigmatology. "Enigmatology is actually the study of riddles," he said. "I broadened it to mean the study of all puzzles. I created one course on crossword construction. Every few weeks I'd go into my professor's office with a new crossword I'd made and sit next to him as he solved and critiqued it. I found professors in the math department to help me make math puzzles. For logic puzzles, I found someone in philosophy. And I took a course in the psychology of puzzles—what's going through our brains as we're solving puzzles, and why we as humans feel compelled to solve puzzles when we're faced with problems in everyday life."

The attributes Will thinks make for a good puzzle solver do overlap somewhat with those that appear to mark a successful artistic mind, especially having rigor and play in balance. Puzzle solving is about finding linking associations—that's true of art making as well and, in a broader sense, all kinds of thinking.

"To solve puzzles, you need a level of language," he said. "But also a flexibility of mind. A sense of playfulness. And you need to like being challenged. Somebody once told me he never does crosswords, because he's afraid of failing and feeling stupid, which is a silly way to feel. I mean, it's just you and the puzzle. But there is a skill of the top solvers that just blows me away. They can look at the first four down clues and get all the answers before they go over the grid and fill them in. My mind won't do that. I can't fathom a brain that can hold all those things in mind at once.[3]

"I started out doing the Jumble puzzles in newspapers. I could typically do it in five to eight seconds. I just go boom, boom, boom. And I'm very good at anagrams, which requires you to break words into individual letters. Years ago I was in France watching TV in a hotel room. There was a game that involved French anagrams. I'm not at all fluent in French, but I got a nine-letter anagram on the show before the contestants did. My mind is flexible, which makes me a good crossword editor, but you know I'm also crazy about table tennis. For table tennis you need constant focus.

"I'm a pretty good solver. I'm not the world's best. I think among average people, among my friends, I would be a genius. But at World Puzzle Championships, at an event of literal geniuses, I am not a genius.

"Here's a crazy thing. You hear about this phenomenon all the time. People are solving a crossword, they get stuck, come back fifteen minutes later, and immediately get an answer they couldn't think of before. What do you think has happened? I had a professor who compared the brain to an old-fashioned slide carousel. The slide drops down, and you move to the next one. The second time the puzzle comes around, the carousel is in a different position, and the brain connects somehow."[4]

Over time, puzzles have gotten more sophisticated and also more popular. "It's hard to compare it with the crossword craze of 1924 and '25, or the Rubik's craze of 1981"—this is where Will's mind just goes—"Or even the sudoku craze of 2005 and '06. But generally, puzzles are more popular now, and the reason I think is that more people use their brains as a living. There's less manual labor, more computer programming. And when you're done with your regular work, you can't turn your brain off. It wants to keep going.

"I like to devise new puzzles. For Spelling Bee, there was something similar that appeared in British newspapers. Theirs had a letter in the middle as well, with four to nine letters around. My important change was that the middle letter can be repeated. I said, you can repeat any letter, which makes it more interesting. I called it Spelling Bee, which I think is a really good name—the central letters have the shape of a hexagon, which gives you a sense of a beehive. And that improves the puzzle visually, and the visuals of a puzzle are very important. And we've said you can now use four-letter words instead of starting at five, which makes it easier. Without four letter words, we were going to run out of combinations after so many years. Now I think the puzzle will go on forever.

"My hope is to devise a crossword in which clues can have two different answers. That's never been done before. And the reason is that, you know, I think one of the reasons people do crosswords is to bring order out of life. We're faced with many problems and we do the best we can. What's great about crosswords and other human-made puzzles is that there is a perfect answer. Finding perfection is something we don't experience much in life. Two

1. Will worked with Frank Longo, who is the Spelling Bee editor.

2. See Stephen Sondheim and John Derian.

3. This description of the toggle between play and rigor is such a good description of the opposing traits you need to make art. Needless to say, I can't fathom it either.

4. I don't want to push this games/art thing too hard, but isn't this exactly the same for painting, writing, etc? It is for me. Walk away; that's when you figure it out.

Merry Go Round
Sam Trabucco
168 18th Ave.
San Francisco, CA 94121
sammyt628@gmail.com

JUL 1 2018

accepted 5/7/18

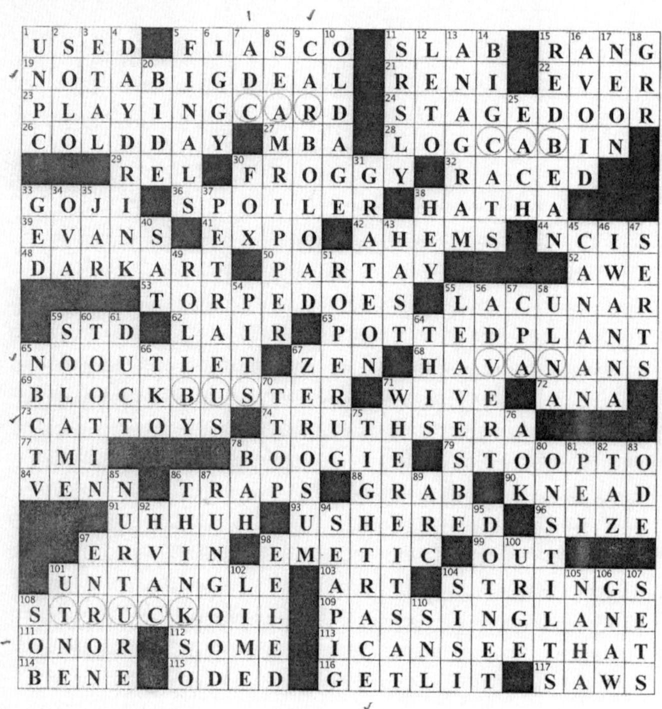

Workarounds
On the Road
Driving You Crazy
Going Crazy
Slow Drivers
→ Driving Around

The completed grid.

perfect answers violates this basic reason, and that's what makes it elegant."[5]

Creating a Puzzle Of all the puzzles at *The New York Times*, the crossword is still the nucleus, the classic. So I asked him to share the making of one. These days he gets around two hundred submissions a week from regular constructors and new ones, and picks seven. The puzzle Will chose to discuss here was a Sunday puzzle (midrange difficulty) from a regular constructor named Sam Trabucco, which was originally submitted as "Merry Go Round" but which Will retitled "Driving Around." You can see the completed puzzle above. "Every theme

5. Finally the analogy completely falls apart. There is no "perfect" solution to art.

Sam Trabucco

ACROSS

Clue	Answer
1 Played for a fool	USED
5 ~~Hot~~ Total mess	FIASCO
11 Big piece of cake	SLAB
15 Buzzed	RANG
19 ~~"That's alright!"~~ "Don't worry about it!"	NOTABIGDEAL
21 ~~"Crucifixion of St. Peter" painter~~ Guido —, painter of the "Crucifixion of St. Peter"	RENI
22 ~~"Will I — learn?"~~ "Do I —!"	EVER
23 Feigning ~~incapacity ["Someone's asleep at the wheel!"]~~ lifelessness	PLAYINGCARD
24 Play out?	STAGEDOOR
26 ~~A school may declare one over frostbite concerns~~ Metaphorical time in hell	COLDDAY
27 Future exec, ~~they hope~~ maybe	MBA
28 Accessed ~~as Twitter ["This guy's gonna make them miss their flight!"]~~ with one's password	LOGCABIN
29 Seminary study: Abbr.	REL
30 ~~Certain amphibian, in kid-speak~~ One who "went a courtin'" in an old kids' song	FROGGY
32 Hurried along	RACED
33 ~~Trendy berry~~ Asian berry marketed as a "superfood"	GOJI
36 ~~Something many "Game of Thrones" fans seek to avoid~~ "Darth Vader is Luke's father," e.g.	SPOILER
38 Yoga variety	HATHA
39 Lily Potter's maiden name in the "Harry Potter" books	EVANS
41 ~~New product~~ fair	EXPO
42 Attention-getters	AHEMS
44 ~~2003 "JAG" spinoff~~ Longtime CBS police procedural	NCIS
48 ~~Evil practice~~ Voodoo, e.g.	DARKART
50 ~~Dated slang for a bash~~ Quite a bash, in slang	PARTAY
52 ~~It's inspired by the incredible~~ Partner of shock	AWE
53 Wrecks, as one's chances	TORPEDOES

The clues as submitted, with Will's edits. The solution is in the column on the right.

answer contains the name of a vehicle," he said, explaining the puzzle's ground rules. "It's an elegant concept. It's not made by a computer. A human thought of this idea; a human could execute it. When I'm choosing a puzzle, I'm looking for a fresh idea for a theme. Then if I like the theme, I look at the fill. What makes a good fill in a crossword is basically names and phrases that people know. You can have the occasional obscurity, but mostly you want the grid to be filled with lively, colorful, familiar vocabulary. Then, if the constructor can write good clues, that's a bonus. But if I need to, I can rewrite the clues myself."

On average Will rewrites half the clues. That was the case with this one. You can see all his changes on the left and the pages that follow, with his explanations below.

WILL SHORTZ: 5 across was "Hot Mess" [for "fiasco"]. I think he threw that in to sound current. But a fiasco has nothing to do with a hot mess. "Total mess" is what it is. I like precision of language.

19 across: "That's alright!" [for "Notabigdeal"]. Well, I wouldn't do that because that's a nonstandard spelling of *all right*. So I changed it to "Don't worry about it."

Okay, the next one, "*Crucifixion of St. Peter* painter," was perfectly fine, but I like to give context to answers. If you don't know this artist [Reni], and you get it from the crossings, then you ended up, "Well, I don't know." But by giving the first name it gives context, you've learned something.

Let's jump to . . . 26, "a school may declare one over frostbite concerns." The answer's "cold day," so that seems stretching it to me.

The actual way people use it is "it'll be a cold day in hell when blah blah." So that was a way to clue it [metaphorical time in hell] that reflects the way people really use the word. For 29, the clue was "Sem Study." I don't know that most people know what S-E-M is an abbreviation for, so I wrote it out, "Seminary Study, abbreviated."

Mmm, let's see, 33, "Trendy Berry"—answer's "Goji." The *Times* crossword has a shelf life of five to ten years, so I don't use trendy because five years from now it's not trendy.

For 36, "spoiler," "Something many *Game of Thrones* fans seek to avoid." I instead wrote "Darth Vader is Luke's father." I don't know—that just made me smile.

41, "New product fair" was too specific for "Expo." An expo is just a fair. And also, I wanted to make it harder—for "Fair," you might first think just average, or light-complexioned.

For 59 [not pictured], the answer is "STD"—it can be clued as "sexually transmitted disease" or "abbreviation for standard." I will always go with "standard" because STDs are such an unpleasant subject. And I'm not a prude—I had "brown-nosed" in a crossword once.

104 was just a matter of being more challenged. For "Strings," he had "Puppet masters pull them"—that seemed too easy for a Sunday puzzle, so I changed it to "Big part of an orchestra."

Here's one clue that I like a lot. It was 80 down. His clue was "Walking Up?" but that didn't make grammatical sense. And I thought "like some clowns and beachside houses" was fun. When you read that clue, you think, *What could clowns and beachside houses have in*

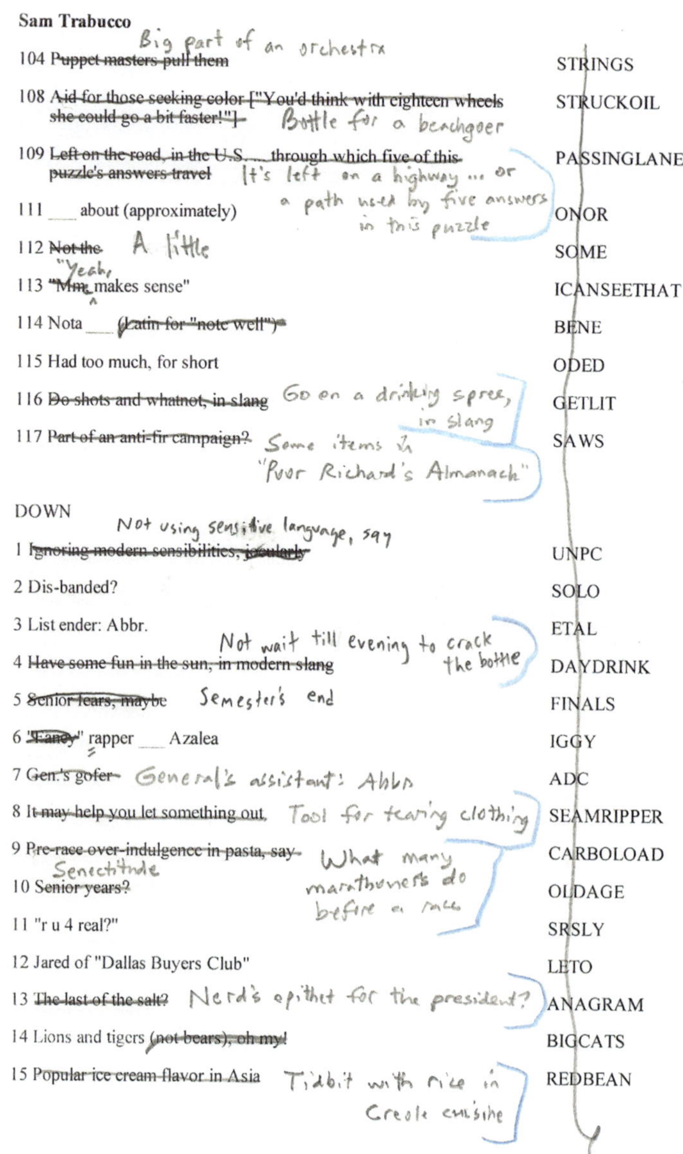

Sam Trabucco

104 ~~Puppet masters pull them~~ Big part of an orchestra — STRINGS

108 ~~Aid for those seeking color ["You'd think with eighteen wheels she could go a bit faster!"]~~ Bottle for a beachgoer — STRUCKOIL

109 ~~Left on the road, in the U.S.... through which five of this puzzle's answers travel~~ It's left on a highway ... or a path used by five answers in this puzzle — PASSINGLANE

111 ___ about (approximately) — ONOR

112 ~~Not the~~ A little — SOME

113 ~~"Mm,~~ "Yeah, makes sense" — ICANSEETHAT

114 Nota ___ ~~(Latin for "note well")~~ — BENE

115 Had too much, for short — ODED

116 ~~Do shots and whatnot, in slang~~ Go on a drinking spree, in slang — GETLIT

117 ~~Part of an anti-fir campaign?~~ Some items in "Poor Richard's Almanack" — SAWS

DOWN

1 ~~Ignoring modern sensibilities, jocularly~~ Not using sensitive language, say — UNPC

2 Dis-banded? — SOLO

3 List ender: Abbr. — ETAL

4 ~~Have some fun in the sun, in modern slang~~ Not wait till evening to crack the bottle — DAYDRINK

5 ~~Senior fears, maybe~~ Semester's end — FINALS

6 ~~"Fancy"~~ rapper ___ Azalea — IGGY

7 ~~Gen.'s gofer~~ General's assistant: Abbr. — ADC

8 ~~It may help you let something out~~ Tool for tearing clothing — SEAMRIPPER

9 ~~Pre-race over-indulgence in pasta, say~~ What many marathoners do before a race — CARBOLOAD

10 ~~Senior years?~~ Senectitude — OLDAGE

11 "r u 4 real?" — SRSLY

12 Jared of "Dallas Buyers Club" — LETO

13 ~~The last of the salt?~~ Nerd's epithet for the president? — ANAGRAM

14 Lions and tigers ~~(not bears), oh my!~~ — BIGCATS

15 ~~Popular ice cream flavor in Asia~~ Tidbit with rice in Creole cuisine — REDBEAN

Sam Trabucco

Clue	Answer
16 Sidestep	AVOID
17 It's under Helium in the Periodic Table	NEON
18 ~~Angry~~ dog's warning	GRR
20 Endure	BIDE
25 Per	EACH
30 ~~Network with notably partisan reporting~~ ___ News	FOX
31 ~~Bother~~ Annoy, in a way	GRATEON
33 ~~Alternative to HS, for some~~ High school equivalency, for short	GED
34 ~~Egg donor's donation~~ Donations to some clinics	OVA
35 ~~That's my jam (container)!~~ Pantry item	JAR
37 ~~Onetime~~ David ___, CIA director ~~David~~ under Obama	PETRAEUS
38 ~~"Sup!"~~ "Watch it!"	HEY
40 Took a breather	SAT
43 ~~Biblical verb form~~ Possess, as thou might	HAST
45 ~~Palestine, once~~ Old Testament land	CANAAN
46 "Pick me! Pick me!"	IWANNA
47 Some ~~renowned~~ Spanish ~~paintings~~ murals	SERTS
49 Elapse, as years	ROLLBY
51 Braided floor covering	ROPERUG
54 ~~(The) worst~~ Where coal miners work	PITS
55 Doesn't bother	LEAVESBE
56 Telly pitch	ADVERT
57 1040 reviewer, for short	CPA
58 Humerus connection	ULNA
59 "How ~~boring!~~ uncool!"	SOLAME
60 "Yer darn ___!"	TOOTIN
61 It may bring a tear to one's eye	DUCT
64 "___ Is Us" (65-Down drama)	THIS

common? The answer was "On stilts." Would you get it? When you do, it's a little aha.

—

Where the Mind Goes For 30 down, for "Fox," he struck out "Network with notably partisan reporting" and replaced it with ___ News.

I stopped him there. Does he make a conscious effort to steer clear of controversy—like politics? "Clues shouldn't take sides," he said, "they should be factual. And it probably is factual that they are a partisan network. . . ."

"But you're just being extra cautious?"

"Yeah, I guess. A comment that I read every once in a while is from right-wing solvers, who say that 'the only reason I subscribe to your rag is for the crossword.' You know, it's a broad audience."

I was struck by how loaded all these choices were, which reminded me of the awkward encounter I alluded to earlier, back when I was supposed to be Will's minder at the *Times*. The puzzle's name was "Homonames," and some eagle-eyed *Times* readers interpreted that to suggest it was all about gay sex—and possibly of the rougher variety. I was asked to investigate.

"Oh yes, I remember," Will said. "Instead of Carrie Fisher the actress, it was C-A-R-R-Y F-I-S-S-U-R-E. Rex Reed was W-R-E-C-K-S R-E-A-D, and he was notably gay. And Jim Nabors was also in there, as G-Y-M."

Will professed to be horrified at the time, and said that none of those references were intended.

"It's a stretch," he said to me, perhaps extending the allusion, but it was a reminder of how powerful the subconscious is, for solver and constructor alike.

37

SHEILA HETI

A Map of Her Mînd

OCCUPATION: Writer

WORK DISCUSSED: *How Should a Person Be?* (2010)

BORN: 1976

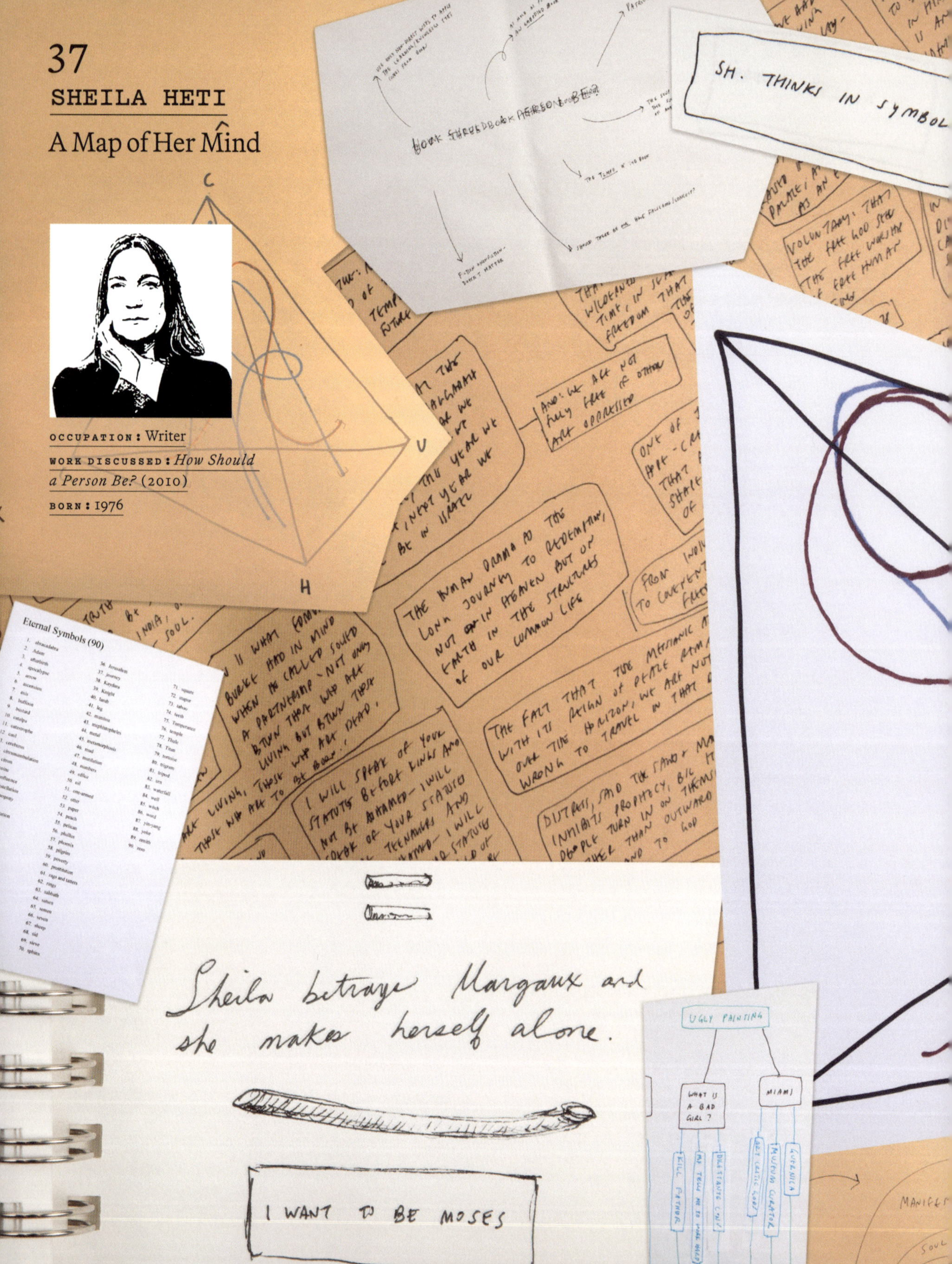

BOOK THREE

states
near-death
in a relationship
middle of the night
March
wanting
privilege
death

archetypes
the quiet woman
the father
children
psychiatrist
the muse
God
the newly single
the contingent girl/boyfriend
the male artist
the female artist
king of Morocco

elements of nature
the single brain
the void
animals
sexual attraction
the soul
wealth
beauty
lack of preservation
family
persona
holes/gaps
structures
spirit of the time

symbolic objects
the pot
the head/brain
the fur coat
feet
hair
tape recorder
a book
computer
work of art
bed
movies
cell phone
gifts
painting
food
water

symbolic places
the home
movie theatre
subway
party
the city
"The surface"
taxi cab
basement apartment
New York
the gallery
the art fair
the web
the bar
the restaurant
old folks home
the street
dinner party
the airplane
airport

scarcity

abundance

MX
GOD
SH

I CERTAINLY THINK THAT'S WHAT GOOD ART DOES; IT LETS THE WHOLE WORLD UNDERSTAND THE WHOLE WORLD THROUGH IT — IT'S NOTHING IN ITSELF; JUST A FRUIT. THAT'S MY AMBITION; TO MAKE SOMETHING SO FULL, THAT EMBODIES EVERY MEANING, DUALITY, SHOULD AND SIMPLE AS MILK.

ALL THE TIME MY IDEAL OF TEACHING HAS BEEN TO DELVE ON BEHALF OF THE IDEA THAT PEOPLE ARE RESPONSIBLE FOR THEIR OWN ACTIVITIES, THAT THEY ARE REALLY, IN A SENSE, THE AUTHORS, THAT ULTIMATELY THEY ARE WHAT THEY HAVE TO CONSIDER. THEN FOR THEM TO BEGIN ASSIGNING THEIR OWN TASKS AND MAKE THEIR OWN CHOICES AND DECISIONS IN THEIR DUALITIES TO THEIR NEEDS AND NOT IN LIGHT OF SOME ABSTRACT

THE EARLY LINE PAINTINGS WERE STILL PAINTINGS IN A TRADITIONAL SENSE. THEY HAD ALL THE ACCOUTREMENTS, ALL THE ASPIRATIONS OF A PAINTING. THE LATE LINE PAINTINGS, WHICH BY THE WAY WERE ESSENTIALLY THE SAME MEANS — STRAIGHT LINES ON A SINGLE COLOURED GROUND — WERE TO BE MY FIRST SUCCESSFUL ATTEMPT NOT TO PAINT A PAINTING. IN 1981, I STILL DIDN'T KNOW HOW TO DO THAT. I'M NOT EVEN SURE WHAT I WAS SETTING OUT TO DO. I WAS JUST FOLLOWING A LINE OF ENQUIRY, AND AT THAT POINT, I HAD TO JUMP.

WITH ME, ART IS ALWAYS ABOUT A SCULPTURE FOR PEOPLE TO USE. I DON'T WANT TO TELL PEOPLE HOW TO USE IT. BUT I THINK THERE MUST BE SOMETHING IN ART THAT GETS YOU TO THE POINT OF THERE BEING A DIFFERENT REALITY, OF HAVING ANOTHER KIND OF EXPERIENCE.

ALLOW THE ESSENCE OF THE BOOK TO REVEAL ITSELF TO YOU WHEN YOU'RE DONE.

"THE BOOK OF COCAINE"

ESSENCE

FATE

THE UNIVERSE OF THE BOOK

BASE ELEMENTS

THE HUMAN
HUMAN QUALITIES
HUMAN TYPES
DYNAMIC ACTIONS

METAPHOR
SYMBOLIC PLACES
SYMBOLIC OBJECTS
SYMBOLIC GESTURES

CONTEXT
STATES OF TIME
OF NATURE
REALMS OF THE GODS

MANIFESTATION · CONTINGENT DECKS

SOUL
MOVEMENT TO AND AWAY FROM SOUL
MOVEMENT AWAY FROM SOUL
DEVELOPMENT OF SOUL

CULTURE
LIGHTS OFF + ON
LIGHTS ON
LIGHTS OFF

ESSENCE · DECKS U, H, G

FATE
UNIVERSAL SYMBOLS
HUMAN STATES
ACTIONS OF THE GODS

SHEILA HETI HAS written many different kinds of books, novels like *Ticknor*, *Pure Colour*, and *Motherhood*, as well as nonfiction book projects of various types, some a little more conventional than others but all pretty bold in toying with form. I reached out to her after *The New York Times* published an excerpt of a new project she'd been working on: she'd broken down years of journal entries, and recombined sentences alphabetically (*A* sentences, then *B* sentences, then *C*) from her journals so that they created a kind of narrative progression. She has an unusual mind; I wanted to tap it.

One of Sheila's most original books is also one of her best known, *How Should a Person Be?* That's the novel whose evolution we traced. *How Should a Person Be?* is about a character, named Sheila, trying to forge a moral path after a divorce and while at a point in her life when she fears, as she put it, that she has no soul. She has failed to deliver on a play commission and is worried that she is a failure. She has a heated, self-destructive, and sexually graphic affair. Her friends have a competition to make the ugliest painting; the ugly painting becomes a metaphoric motif. Much of the book is in the form of transcribed conversations with her best friend Margaux. Real-life Sheila has a best friend named Margaux. Real-life Sheila taped her conversations with Margaux. Real-life Sheila divorced and failed to write a play. Real-life Sheila had such an affair. Real-life Sheila's friends had an ugly painting competition. *How Should a Person Be?* is a work of fiction, absolutely, but also, in Sheila's account, one she had to live (enact, in her real life) in order to write it.

How Should a Person Be? is now considered one of the pivotal works of "autofiction," a blend of fiction and autobiography. *How Should a Person Be?* was met with polarizing reactions—"Reviewers," wrote one, in the *London Review of Books*, "describe wanting to throw the book across the room or stock up on copies to give to friends, sometimes both"—but has since become something of a classic to many (especially young women), who are drawn in by Sheila's candor, her winning voice, and the book's thrilling bludgeoning of the conventional novel.

One of its tougher readers was the critic James Wood, who called it "messy" and "narcissistic." So I was surprised to hear Sheila, who came over one day to tell me the book's story, say that Wood was on her mind as she was writing the novel because she felt he might admire her attempt to rewrite a novel's rules. "I read a review by James Wood," she said, "about Flaubert, *Madame Bovary*. He wrote, 'This is how Flaubert revolutionized the novel.' There was one paragraph where Wood said Flaubert privileged 'seeing.' I thought, *I'm going to do the opposite of all that.* Because I hated *Madame Bovary.* I hated the conventional realist novel. And that was a huge driver when I set out to write *How Should a Person Be?* I thought, *Instead of seeing, I'm going to privilege [speaking] details, in the recording of conversations.* The thing about a novel like *Madame Bovary* is that the narrative voice always retains a cool composure. And I thought, *Okay, my narrative voice is going to lose its composure.*

"I thought I was writing my book for James Wood. I thought he would like my book," Sheila said. Not that she seemed to care much when he didn't. She has strong convictions about novel writing. She finds most fiction boring. "Because I think there's a texture missing. Because [much of what a novel used to do] is not necessary. You have TV." She likes novels of voice not unlike her own, though she has plenty of reservations about her own work as well.

Sheila lives in Toronto, and projects what you might consider a Canadian unflappability. She is kind and quirky, but not at all as eccentric seeming as I'd thought she might be from her work. And yet there was clearly a little bit of the lunatic in there somewhere. When I had described this book's project to her, explaining that I was hoping to find physical entrails of her process, she said she might have what I needed, and brought over an enormous trove of notebooks, notecards, and huge sheets of paper containing what she called maps. You can see some of them collaged on the preceding spread, looking a little like the crazy quilt of clues Carrie Mathison plastered on her wall in *Homeland*.[1] To understand and write her book, Sheila had devised a cosmology, which she kept elaborating in charts, or lists, and that worked as her compass. In a way, the maps provided a clear view of the obsession that lurks within everyone, maybe artists especially. They were also beautiful and elegant, works of art in themselves, even though they were never meant to be seen by anyone. "Writing *How Should a Person Be?* was the hardest I've ever worked in my whole life," she reflected. "It wasn't like I was writing a novel about myself. I had no template."

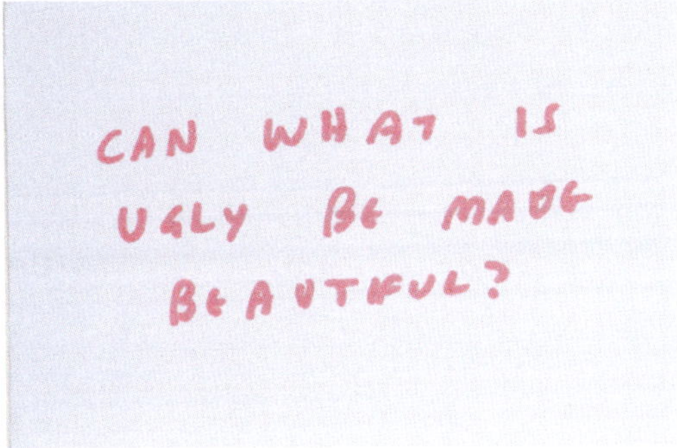

Note to self. A theme of the painting competition, and of the book.

So that's what we talked about, how she found her way—with the help of her maps.

SHEILA HETI: It was 2005. I was separating from my husband. I had just published my novel *Ticknor*, in the voice of the historical figure George Ticknor, and I found that process . . . unjoyous. I ended up writing about twenty pages a year. Painstaking. And all alone. And I thought, *I can never write in that way again.*

I moved to Montreal, got an apartment of my own. And I started to read the Bible. I don't know why.

I was emailing with a lot of people, really long emails, that's what people wrote back then. I was now separated, somebody else was getting divorced—all sorts of dramatic things were happening. I started to number the emails like the Bible: the Book of Margaux, like that. Numbering the passages.

I had also been reading this famous article about Linux called "The Cathedral and the Bazaar," which advocated for open sourcing in software. I thought, *Maybe I can open source a novel. Maybe that'll get the bugs out faster. Maybe I should model my process on Linux.* So the process itself would involve showing friends multiple drafts, not believing my brain was the best brain to write the book.

When I moved back to Toronto, my husband and I broke up. I started spending more time with my friend Margaux Williamson, who's a painter. We talked and talked, nonstop. I was thinking, *Maybe my studio can be out in the world rather than in my room*—the opposite of what it was for my previous book, which was so unbearable.

So that is what I'd been thinking about, but I had no subject. I always have this conviction that it doesn't matter what you write about, the subject will come. And then, because I had just gotten divorced, and I was wandering and lost and totally discombobulated, and wasn't sure I was a moral person, that became the subject of the book.

It was so gradual. Oh, and I was really into the reality show *The Hills*.[2] So another of my thoughts was, *How can I make a book like* The Hills*?* What that meant is that I'd have to orchestrate things to happen.

I was taping the conversations I was having with my friends. We would go to brunch, and one brunch someone asked, "Who can make the ugliest painting?" And I said, "We have to really do that, so I can tape the conversations and make it part of my book."

Margaux and I talked a lot about Paris Hilton. At one point I had considered writing an article about her. You remember when

1. On the TV series *Homeland*, Mathison was a CIA agent who, in fits of mania, covers her wall with clues, which in their brilliant combination provide her with a map to help her pursue a terrorist case. I kept seeing Carrie's code wall when I looked at the pile of charts Sheila brought over.

2. *The Hills* was one of the more popular, influential, and insipid reality shows of the early 2000s. Like all of its kind, the "reality" is manipulated.

Britney Spears cut her hair off, Lindsay Lohan, all these girls were getting in trouble—they were seen as ruining America. Margaux found them fascinating. She said, "Paris Hilton is like Andy Warhol." I did write the article, though it was never published. The article was a kind of transcribed dialogue in which Margaux defends Paris Hilton. Which I thought for a while might be the center of the project. Maybe it became two or three sentences of the book.

So I had the Bible. Paris Hilton. Me and Margaux. The ugly painting competition. I was trying to put these elements together.

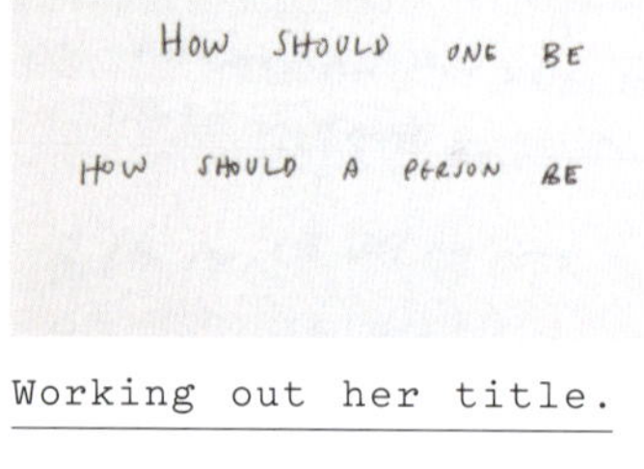

Working out her title.

Two thousand six was the big year, the year of discovery. And I'm not sure what order it all happened in. But I wrote what became the prologue. Just in a spontaneous push—it was about 90 percent of how it ended up in the book. "How should a person be" was the first sentence of the prologue.

In 2006 I was at Yaddo [a retreat for artists and writers] and already had this phrase, "How should a person be"—but I wasn't sure it was gonna be the title. On my wall I'd written: "How should a person be," question mark. Margaux came to visit me there, and she said that should be the title of the book.

I thought, *I'm going to become this Paris Hilton slash Sheila.* In order to write the book. It wasn't like putting on a costume. You suppress parts of your life and exaggerate others. It was fun, you know? I think that's why Andy Warhol was so interesting to me. Because that's how I understood what Warhol was doing.

Oh, one more thing. Before I had the title or had written the prologue, I had started a book with my friend Misha Glouberman called *The Moral Development of Misha*. I wrote like seventy pages of it. About him as a character, walking through the world solving people's problems. A Jesus figure. I never did anything with it, really. I gave it to him. He liked it. Later, I wrote a book with him called *The Chairs Are Where the People Go.* For a long time, *The Chairs Are Where the People Go* and *How Should a Person Be?* were the same book.

Margaux and I went to Scope, at the Miami art fair, and she read the prologue on the plane. It was kind of in the voice of me as a character on *The Hills*. That voice just came out.[3] And she loved those pages, loved the voice. She said, "This is the best thing you've ever written."

I sent it to Mark Greif,[4] and he said, "This is great. Now you need to write another three hundred pages of it." So I thought, *Okay, I have the voice.*

The reason the character's name is Sheila in the book is because when I was transcribing our conversations, I just kept writing Sheila, Margaux, Sheila, Margaux. And Margaux liked it. I tried to change the name, but it just seemed so fake because I had been looking at these transcripts. Margaux said, "If you change the names, it looks like we're hiding something. But if you leave the names, it's just so weird." She thought what I was doing was really weird. I didn't think it was weird.

I was in the book, I was living the book, but I started to think, *I need a narrative.* I wanted people to get to the end of the book, and I understood that to get somebody to the end, you need some kind of arc. In 2008 or so I started moving away from Margaux a bit, and that was a bit of drama in our friendship. I got the idea, oh, I have to betray Margaux in the book. Because I want to be a good person, and I'm always somebody that runs away from relationships. That might work for drama, as a plot, in the book.

My idea of plot was that I needed to create a forest of symbols for myself, that would be the world that Sheila and Margaux were walking. So I wrote down five hundred, six

3. The voice, in a sense, preceded the book and made it possible to write. That's usually how it works.

4. Mark Greif is a cultural critic, author of the book *Against Everything*, and one of the founders of the journal *n+1*.

5. Sheila writing down scenes as she experienced them is a little like Sofia Coppola's translating her own broken toe into her character's broken toe. But maybe the analogy stops there.

Airplane
1 message

Margaux Williamson
To: SHEILA HETI

Almost out of Vancouver.
Here is Martin Heath's number: I told him you would be calling shortly once you've figured out the date with the university
They keep taking us off and putting us back on the plane - here in Vancouver.
It was so nice to see you yesterday. What a goddamned treat.
I woke up this morning feeling terrific still about my teenager hamlet short and excited for you with your book.
I found this in a two week old new york times magazine article today about Carl Jung's unpublished unseen "red book" (about his journey to find his soul) that they will be putting out next month:
(this is him talking to one of his patients about her writing her own book)

"I should advise you to put it all down as beautifully as you can - in some beautifully bound book," Jung instructed. "It will seem as if you were making the visions banal - but then you need to do that - then you are freed from the power of them.. Then when these things are in some precious book you can go to tehe book & turn over the pages & for you it will be your church - your cathedral - the silent places of your spirit where you will find renewal. If anyone tells you that it is morbid or neurotic and you listen to them - then you will lose your soul - for in that book is your soul."

I suspect your book will be more comprehensible.
It is a miracle to find a live channel of life and where your plug fits it's hole. and then it becomes part of it.
I am feeling optimistic about everything today. I don't need to distract myself from anything. All of my thoughts are a pleasure today.

They have told me no more communications!
We are going to take off.
LOVE YOU.
What a world you help make.

hundred scenes that were real moments.[5] And then I turned them each into a single word, like *pigeon*. The plot of the book is lights go on, lights go off. She starts to develop her soul, then the lights go on. And the last three scenes the lights go off.

Okay, this is the part that's really hard to explain. But I'll do my best.

—

The Cosmology Sheila does try to explain, with the help of the mountain of materials she has brought. It's clear this was not a rudimentary exercise; it's something she worked out over a very long period of time, repetitively. There are piles of notes, drawings, cards. It takes the form of a card system, with echoes of tarot. I don't understand it. You won't understand it. Sheila herself doesn't fully understand it. But what's key is that it helped her write the book: "Sheila betrays Margaux and she makes herself alone," Sheila told me. "I understood that. But I couldn't see the whole thing. I was really desperately trying to see the beginning, middle, and end, writing the book and trying to understand the book at the same time."

Having despaired over trying to make sense of it for me, Sheila wrote me a few weeks later. She'd found an email in which she described the system to Lorin Stein, her editor at Farrar, Straus and Giroux, after he had rejected the book (a point in the book's evolution that we'll get to), hoping to change his mind. You might want to refer to that collage on pages 338–339, but don't work too hard to decipher it. The fact of the system rather than the particulars is what matters. Here is an excerpt of Sheila's email to Stein:

IMAGINATION IS COMBINATION.

I created four decks of cards. Each deck represented a different aspect of the universe or life. I broke all the elements of life into four, and those four were: human qualities / actions of the gods / universal symbols (tree, mother, etc) / contingent symbols (paris hilton, a street in Toronto—things pinned to a particular time and place, not comprehensible across cultures and time).

There were 30 different actions of the gods, 60 different human qualities, 90 universal symbols and 180 contingent ones.

Also, there was a grid, a four-pointed triangle (that is, a 3-D triangle) and each point represented one of either actions of the gods, human qualities, universal symbols, contingent ones.

Anyway, I decided the book would have several main sections, and would proceed in this order:

1) movement away and toward soul
2) movement away from soul
3) lights go on and off
4) movement toward soul
5) lights go on
6) lights go off

Parts 1, 2 and 4 represent the individual; parts 3, 5 and 6 represent the culture.

Each section was given a number, representing how long it would last in the course of the book.

The way I came up with those numbers (essentially, to be brief) was I came up with (and wrote down in short paragraphs) about 600 ideas for scenes; a scene might be something that happened to me in the past three years, or an important idea that had occurred to me in the past four years, something in the news, whatever.

There were, of course, very many scenes that didn't fall into any of those six categories, and those scenes were discarded.

From the scenes that were left, I wrote down key words which reflected the main ideas of each scene (the airport, secrecy, pacing, responding to a request, the critic). These words were then put into the four categories that I mentioned earlier—the decks (contingent symbols, actions of the gods, human qualities).

The universal symbols I took randomly (using a numbering method) from the Penguin Dictionary of Symbols.

So then I had four decks of cards, each with a different number and colour, the colour representing which of the four decks (universal, gods, etc) and the number referring to that deck's list of key words.

When I came to write certain parts of the book, I could randomly draw one card from each of the four decks, having before me a universal symbol, a contingent symbol, a human quality and an action of the gods—as well as a place on the squiggly line within the triangle, so I would know the relative weight of each of those four elements to each other, and then I would begin to write—and what I would write would try to make sense of how those four elements interacted with each other.

What might a scene be that (for example) necessitated (determined by the random drawing of four cards):

fucking (an action of the gods, naturally!)
being-for-others (human quality)
ascension (universal symbol)
andy warhol (contingent symbol)

This was the method by which I wrote many passages of the book.

This email did not change Lorin Stein's mind. But Sheila was undeterred.

—

SH: I kept creating new systems because I didn't know how to write the book. What's the plot? What *is* a plot? And then, practically: How much dialogue should be in the book? What portion should be transcribed conversation? What's the tempo of the book?

There was a point in the book in which I had come up with ten new commandments. I remember one: Be honest and transparent and give away nothing. Then I thought, *I can't actually put those in the book, because I'm not Moses. I want to be Moses, but I'm not Moses. This is gonna be what Margaux and I learned, and I'll put that in the book.* I started sprinkling sand throughout the book. I had to indicate that we're wandering in the desert.

I realized the book needed the body; it was too cerebral. That's when I put the sex in. After the end of my marriage, I'd had this affair with a guy. It was sort of mind-blowing. So I wrote all the Israel [his name in the book; the scenes are explicit and somewhat self-abasing] passages. And I gave them to the guy to read. I didn't think it was for the book, it was just spontaneous writing, I thought maybe it would be for its own book, "Chastity." And when I did put it in the book, I thought, *No one's going to notice anything except this sex stuff.*

I didn't know where I was going. I didn't know how to finish the book. I had so many different endings for the book. One night I woke up and said, *I'm going to write a scene about squash.* It just kind of came to me. And I wondered, *Why am I*

6. "At one point I wondered, 'Did I just use Margaux to write this book?'" Sheila said to me, after I'd asked about their relationship now. She said she continues to be very good friends with Margaux, though their relationship has changed over the years. About her role in the book, "Margaux felt mixed," Sheila said. "Because she's an accomplished artist in her own right. And it's a big part of her public identity, and I don't think that's necessarily always what somebody wants. But she loves the book."

writing this scene? But then it ended up, of course, being the end of the book.

At some point, I sent it to Margaux[6] and she told me, "It's not done." And that was really devastating because I didn't really know how to get it done. I was glad to be accountable to her because part of why I was writing the book was I was trying to become a more moral person. She'd read one hundred drafts. And I had failed with the play. I wasn't going to fail with this.

She said, "If you betrayed me, I would not forgive you so easily."

So I cut stuff, wrote new stuff. Tried to think more deeply about it. I kept trying, rearranging, trying to find the heart—the feelings.

Then I felt exhausted, like I can't go further. I didn't know what else to do with it. Everybody I showed it to gave me permission to publish it, even those who didn't really like it. "Israel" (I had changed his name, but everybody knew who he was) was very angry about it.

Lorin had said, "Who cares about you and Margaux? Maybe you should put it in the drawer." And that threw me off course for a few months. I felt hopeless. Is anyone going to get this? But I came back to it because I just had to write it.

> "I can't offer on it, although you know that I do love her writing. The project, really a conceptual novel, seems to pull Sheila in a direction that I don't think is her strongest, and I could not reconcile the "docu-drama" style of the later sections of the book with the more appealing sections where her voice, and her direct address, are more in play. I adore her writing, but this project attempts to do something that, in the written word, is very hard to pull off, and just as hard to sell."
>
> "I sat down with the Heti this weekend and plunged in, but I'm sorry to say it just isn't for me. I sympathize with the main character, and I was interested in the friendship with Margaux—what she said about friendships between women seemed very true and familiar to me, and great to read. Ultimately though I couldn't get excited about it, in the way that you would want an editor to be. It may be a case of something being *too* close, too familiar. It's terrible, the kind of gut instinct thing that can kick in when a voice or consciousness feels too close to one's own. In any case, a regretful decline on this one."
>
> "I'm terrifically sorry to have had this for such a long time without getting back to you. I'm also very, very sorry to say that this is the kind of book I've had absolutely no luck in acquiring since I've been here, and I don't anticipate having much luck acquiring going forward. If I'm speaking confidentially, I would say that what I expect to have success with here is fiction that is much more middle-of-the-road conventional. In terms of some of the more graphic sexual content, and the experiments she is doing with form, I know that too many people in house would see those things as turn-offs."
>
> "Though Heti's voice is distinctive and appealing, I'm afraid I feel like this book would be too small for us. I really like her characters, and her prose is witty and accessible—I just wish that the story felt more cohesive. As it stands, the elliptical scenes end up making it difficult to find a narrative to follow, and in the end I worry that the experimental approach would make this a tough sell."
>
> "Sorry it took me so long to get back to you on Sheila Heti's novel. What a strange duck of a book! It's awkward at times, but honestly so, and more often that not quite lovely and elegant, even when it describes the kind of floundering embarrassment so many of us have felt in our twenties and early thirties. Unfortunately, I had some trouble finding my place in the story. Am I to take things like the extended silences on the bus with Marguax at face value (in which case I have trouble believing them) or as impressionistic gestures to represent spaces between them? (And if I have to ask, am I really understanding her work?) And how do I sell a book about failing to write a play? I guess I just didn't have the enthusiasm I'd need to launch the book in the US so I feel I should pass."

Excerpts from some rejection notes Sheila received.

Finally, I felt I'm never going to be able to finish this book because it's my life; if my life keeps changing, the book keeps changing. I remember being really troubled about that. But finally I did finish, and publish it.

—

How Should a Person Be? was rejected by many publishers before House of Anansi in Canada put the book out in 2010 (see some of the rejection notes above, which Sheila saved). It was two years before an American publisher, Henry Holt, finally released it.

—

SH: I think I did the best I could writing it, and I feel good having written it. I think I knew it was something special because of what Margaux and I had lived together. It was the best period of my life. It was a time of artistic struggle, but I remember it as a time of joy.

I was just trying to make rules for myself to live by going forward. And I feel like I live by them. The main rule is just value people. I felt like that spirit probably is in the book. But as a reader—I don't know if I would like to read *How Should a Person Be?* I don't know, yes or no. Like maybe the book did fail. I just don't know if it failed or not.

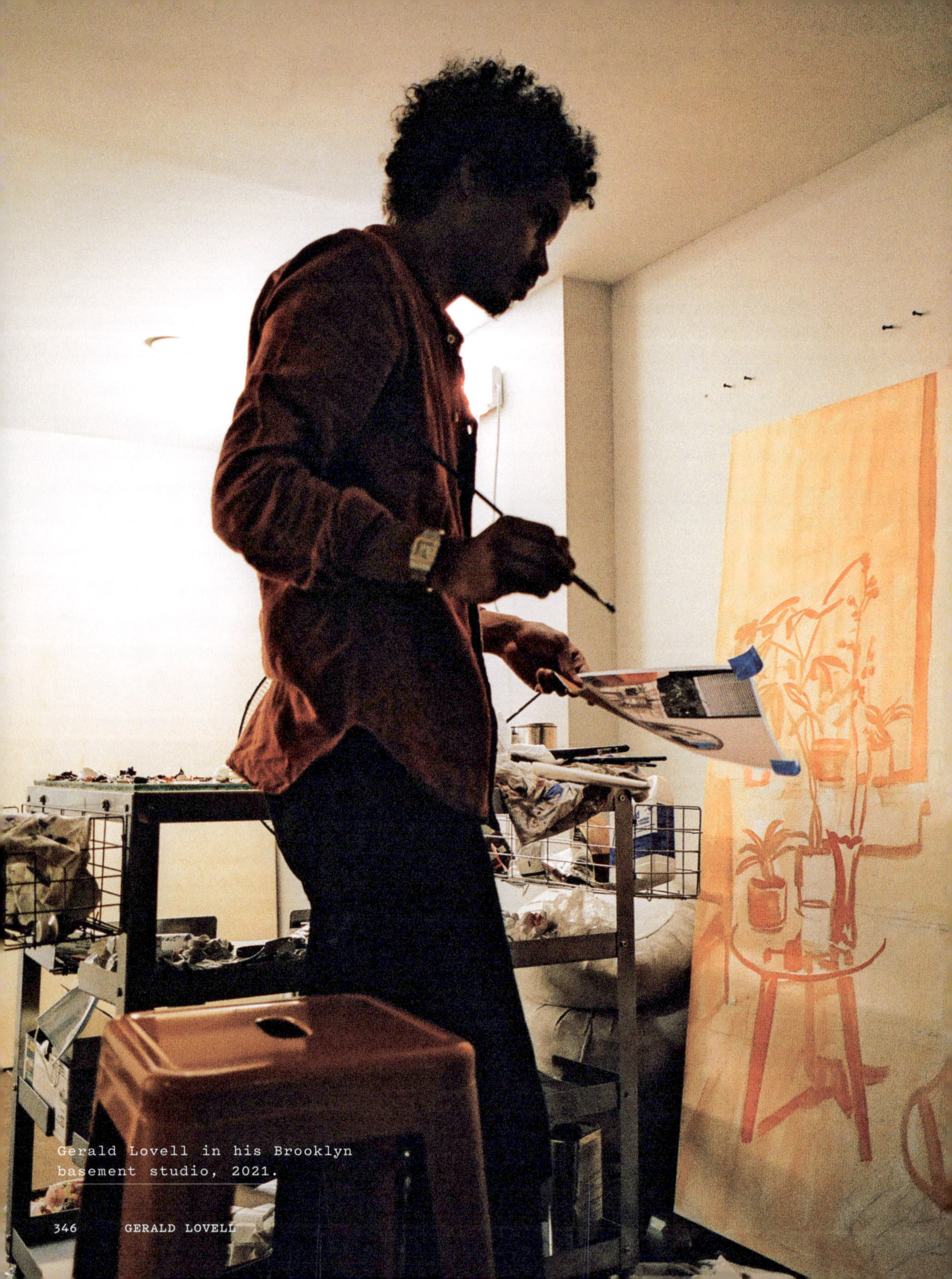

Gerald Lovell in his Brooklyn basement studio, 2021.

38

GERALD LOVELL

I Am Begrudgingly on the Wall

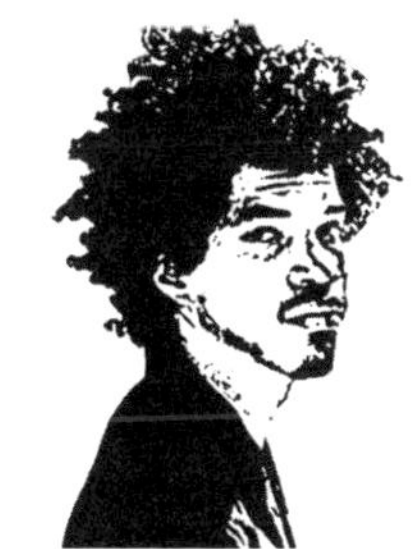

OCCUPATION: Visual Artist

WORK DISCUSSED: *Chameleon* (2021)

BORN: 1992

GERALD LOVELL IS an artist I found on Instagram. Most of the artists in this book are seasoned veterans; I was looking to talk to someone at the front end of an art career. I was immediately taken by Gerald's work, which depicted scenes of contemporary young Black life (his)—pictures of friends painted in impasto tile-like globs. I kept scrolling and found my way to an art infatuation. His paintings had Lucian Freud's texture and Alice Neel's charisma, which is precisely how I'd love to paint myself. He's hot right now, young (just turning twenty-nine when I visited), and self-taught—a graphic design school dropout. The mythology around him is that he learned to paint by watching YouTube videos, which intrigued me. It turns out to be true, but only a little bit; mostly he learned by figuring it out for himself. He hadn't been painting all that much longer than me.

He'd recently moved to New York from Atlanta, and I went to visit him in his new apartment in Bed-Stuy, Brooklyn. Gerald is sweet and slender, boyish. I feared from reading about him that I wouldn't get a whole lot because he's usually shy and doesn't say much, but I was wrong. I'd happened on him at a moment when his life was shifting dramatically, and as much as it scared him, he was also interested in the change and wanted to talk about it. "It felt like I was jumping into the ocean," he said, about coming to New York and giving being a big-time artist a try. We were standing by the door of the apartment his gallery had found for him, before going downstairs to his studio. The ocean was fun so far, but full of sharks. "The art world is a big mystery. It can get competitive—very toxic really fast," he said.[1] He looked away. "And I'm not really competitive at all."

I didn't know him, but anyone could see that his identity was shifting. Not long ago, he had been doing whatever work he could pick up and feeling lost. And now? "It takes a lot to say,

1. Why does the "art world," whatever it means to those who fear its judgment, have such a hold on artists, no matter how experienced they are? It feels medieval. Every field has its gatekeepers—its guild—but for art especially, its perceived power is mythic and heavily influences how artists work and what they make. Art-world approval has huge financial stakes; it also builds and (mostly) breaks spirits.

'I'm an artist,'" he said.[2] "Because there are so many expectations that come with it. And as soon as you say it out loud, the next questions are along the lines of well, 'How *successful* an artist are you? Where are you showing?'" The art world tends to suck the blood of young artists if they succumb to caring about their place in it. Gerald was trying not to care, but also it was clear he did. Who wouldn't?

We went downstairs, where he pointed to the wax on his table. He'd been playing with building even more texture into his paintings ("I want to make it look more grotesque"), which excited me as someone now invested in his work, but I was also interested for myself. I grilled him on his method, both to record here and to steal ideas. Several paintings were on the wall in various stages of incompleteness. A couple were self-portraits. His success so far had come from looking at and documenting the lives of others, conjuring a vivid social world of friends growing up together, almost like the cast of an ensemble series you might see on Netflix.[3] But now he'd started to turn his work on himself, not coincidentally at a moment when he was breaking away. "I'm really drawn to self-portraits right now," he said. "I feel like I've given my friends to these walls, and it's done a lot for me, just putting them in places where they're admired, but now I want to address some problems I've had for a long time, and just figure that out." He was talking personally, not about art particularly.

One of the half-finished paintings was of him shirtless, with a pair of scissors in his hand. I told him I liked it. He said he was having to move quickly on that one, because it was slated to be sold at Art Basel in Miami. That's the picture you see represented here.

We'll get back to that picture.

2. That naming thing again.

3. And, as it happens, Gerald's paintings were featured in a Netflix movie called *Really Love*.

4. Jurell Cayetano is an Atlanta artist whose paintings bear some similarity (in content if not in style) to Gerald's—expressive portraits of his friend group. Their work has sometimes been shown together.

5. This book is not about skills, but they're obviously an essential part of any process, and these days you really can get guidance everywhere. The internet ushered in a golden age of free skills training online, which is fantastic if sometimes confusing. I spend hours sometimes watching instructional videos, and it doesn't—usually—feel like a waste of time. I even took an IRL class with a guy I found on Instagram; I just liked the way he taught in thirty-second reels, and he was good at three hours too.

But meanwhile, he works on many pieces at once and is both exhilarated by his ability to make something out of nothing and at war with the grind. The demand for his paintings was growing, and he wanted—he needed—to feed it. He wakes up at six on a good day and is basically working day and night. We toured the room and found ourselves at another portrait of himself. He showed me how he'd been spending a lot of time going over the repetitive detail of the background. When he's exhausted, he moves from the fun stuff to the tedium, which he can do with less conscious effort. But this painting was taking him a while. "When I first set out, I was like, *Oh my God, this is going to be really great*. But I know for sure it's not going to be finished to my satisfaction before Art Basel, so now it has to sit for a while." This was in some ways a good thing. He was happy to be living with the painting awhile longer. But that meant he had to turn most of his attention to the scissor picture. "Everyone's like, 'Produce, produce, produce.'"

Lost As a child, Gerald was skilled at drawing, lackluster at school. He was directed to the Art Institute of Atlanta-Decatur by a teacher, but once there thought he needed to be focused on something he could make money from. He landed on graphic design, which he dismissed pretty quickly because he wasn't interested in dealing with the capricious clients that come with the job. He transferred to a traditional school before dropping out. And then he moved to Atlanta, he was working all the time, and he was at sea.

"Eventually I crashed at my friend's apartment. I was sleeping on the floor in the living room. And we used to get drunk all the time, and one night I was like, 'I don't know what the hell I'm going to do.' And my friend Jurell,[4] who is an amazing artist himself, said, 'Well, you could try your hand at fine art. You have technical skill. If you worked out a particular style you could call your own, yeah, you could, you know . . ." I didn't know if he was serious. And in the following days, I went

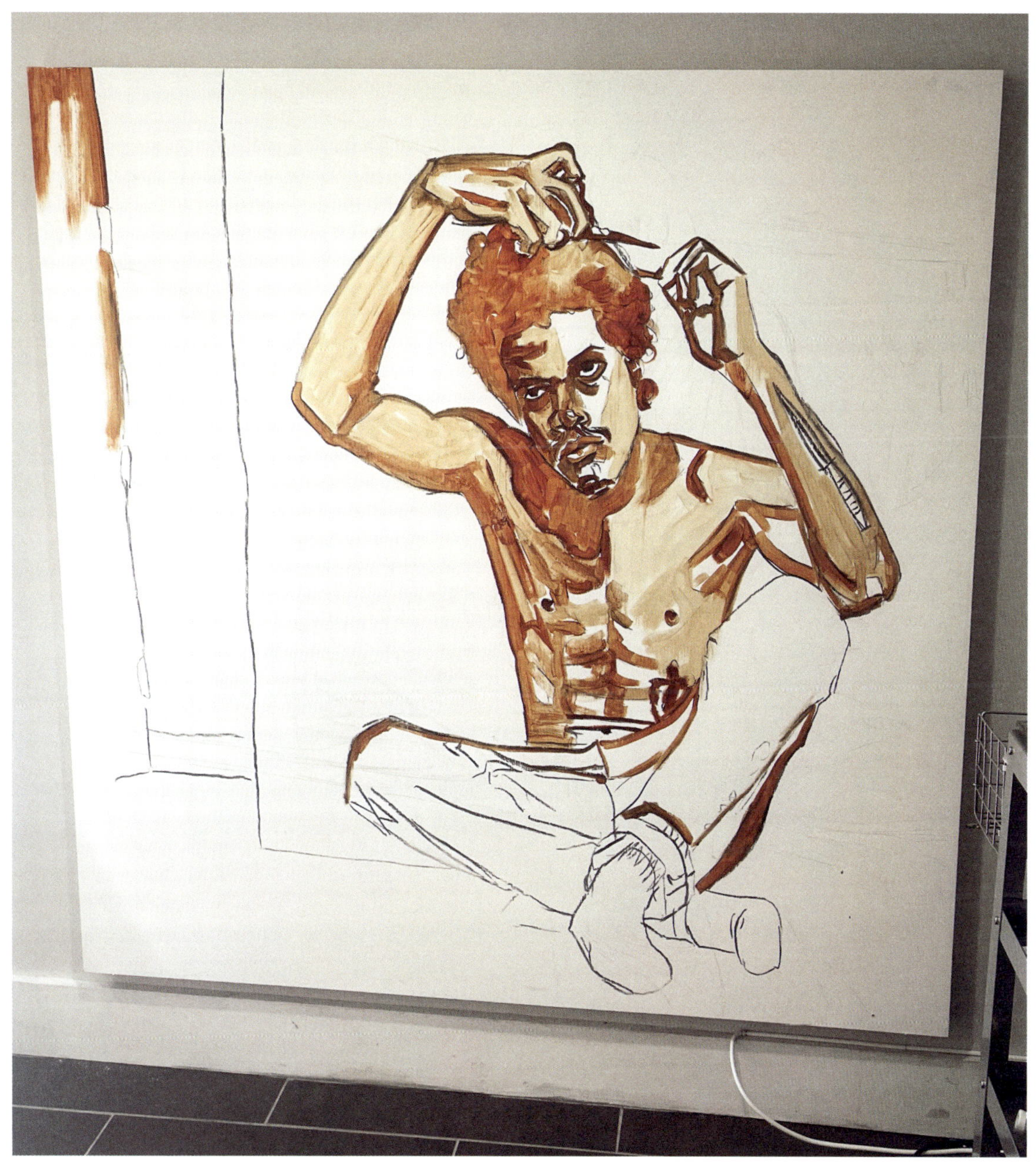

exploring. Doing the YouTube thing. I looked up painting techniques. YouTube is a university; you can find out how to do anything.[5] I just learned different ways—like different tricks with impasto itself."

Impasto is a way of painting with thick strokes of paint. Lovell became entranced with loading paint on his brush, and was a quick YouTube study. He began to paint in a corner of the living room where he slept, and the essential feel of his paintings just materialized. He started painting portraits built from these tiles of paint, and they looked amazing. He was developing a style, just as Jurell had

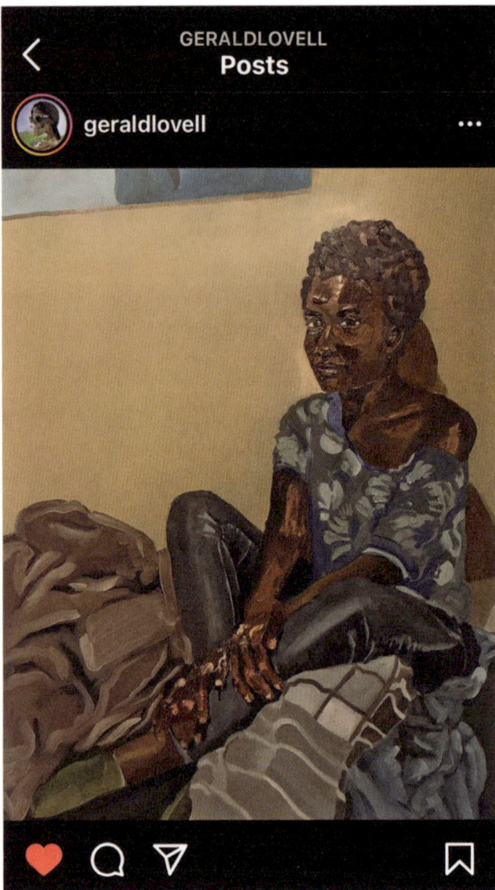

suggested, but by Gerald's account, it wasn't deliberate at all. He wasn't even mimicking anyone, as artists tend to do when they start. Then he found himself staring at a Van Gogh painting. He had always liked Van Gogh, and now saw things in Van Gogh's work he hadn't seen before, because he was looking for it. "Van Gogh didn't do layers. He went from thick paint onto the surface," he said. "And I was, *Oh that's just like me!*"

Really fast, he began to make a series of portraits, drawn from photographs and built with impasto—just as he does now. He wasn't sure where this now-apparent signature style came from. "I was like, *Whoa, this is crazy.*" He made a self-portrait in burnt sienna and ultramarine blue, two colors in combination he would come to rely on for his skin tone. "I showed it to my friend, and he was like, 'Yeah, keep doing that. You don't need help from anyone anymore.'"

Taking Pictures Gerald found his subject matter in casual photos he would take of his friends, from which he would then paint, exaggerating a bit. Eventually he would try to control these photographs more because they became so central to his work, but in a way he was documenting his set the way many people do on social media feeds. "But I made the executive decision I wanted everyone to be looking at me." (That stare back is a key characteristic of his work.) He hit a stride, "made like four of them," and posted these paintings on Instagram. He started to get inquiries from galleries.

When he arrived with paintings in hand, the galleries were unimpressed. The pictures were small; they didn't make much of an impression. He wasn't deterred. "There's a level of ego that's present in order to make something you've made and be like, 'No, this is good,'" he said. "Because if you don't do that, no one else will believe in you. You can't let your insecurities surface."[6]

He started to paint ferociously. "I would do a lot of overnights, like I had to get something done. And I was just never good with jobs." He was working at restaurants and in retail. "I'm definitely the employee that will just no-show and never show up again. I've done that at least five times. My heart wasn't there." His heart was in his canvases. He experimented a bit, mostly with what parts of the painting should be flat and what should be built up with paint. In time, he would figure out how to separate the pictures, painting his backgrounds flat and keeping his figures in impasto. (Part of the reason was economic—impasto takes a lot of paint, and he had to be sparing with it.)

Then he took a trip to LA, saw a bunch of Kerry James Marshall paintings, among others—painters he came to admire—and came back with a conviction. "The work needs to get bigger. It needs to get bigger, it needs to get better."[7] When he increased their size, that helped; the paintings became more ambitious. He made a painting he called *The Woman with the Eyes*, which was the first time he said he felt elated. "That was the first one that's like this size. It wasn't just face, shoulders. And I thought, *Well, every painting going forward has to give me the same feeling this painting has given me.*"

Himself He quit his jobs, secured gallery representation. His work started to sell seriously; he took going big to an extreme, painting a five-story mural called *Grace* that brought him more attention. He moved to New York. And now we were staring at the self-portrait I was drawn to when I first entered the room. The one with the scissors.

It was a daring picture for him—"It's the first time, like, I don't have a shirt on. I've never rendered [a naked torso]—that's like half the body." Like many artists, he has some interest in painting nude figures, but he's self-conscious—about his own figure, but he's also too shy to ask anyone to sit nude for him: "I don't know if I can find someone ever to pose naked." Finding a model to strip, which he could do very easily, doesn't interest him. His pictures are too personal for that. They are about his relationships, including with himself.[8]

What he noticed he was mostly taken with in this picture was his stare, which, right now, was looking back at him. He was liking the brooding eyes and their window into his dissatisfaction. Gerald was very open; he hadn't seemed to harden yet. And he recognized that his discomfort was good material for his art. "I'm starting to settle into accepting that I'm not a child anymore," he said to me. "I'm like an adult. Like, really an adult. Even though I feel like an adult in a child's body sometimes. And that's where all these self-portraits are coming from."

Central to the image was the scissors. "So I cut my own hair," he said. "Before this year, I've had dreads. I didn't have any spiritual connection to it, it was just easy to groom, and I liked the way it looked. But I came to realize there are things culturally that I was trying to avoid by having dreads. My grandfather was from Puerto Rico. There's a lot of racism in being both Black and Puerto Rican. There are Puerto Ricans who will be, you know, 'I'm not Black.' And I've never really felt truly connected [to my Puerto Rican side] because I didn't know Spanish. And then moving here, and seeing so much [Puerto Rican] pride, neighborhoods where the flags are everywhere, I don't know, I felt like my dreads were hiding a part of myself. I've had Black experience, I identify as Black. But also, you know, I'm living alone, there's a lot of self-reflection going on."

He posed the photograph with the scissors with the intention of making a painting of it, and did it in one take. He got the uneasy look he wanted. "I was not happy, and I knew I was not happy." He gestured over to the eyes in the painting: "Once I reached his eyes, I was like,

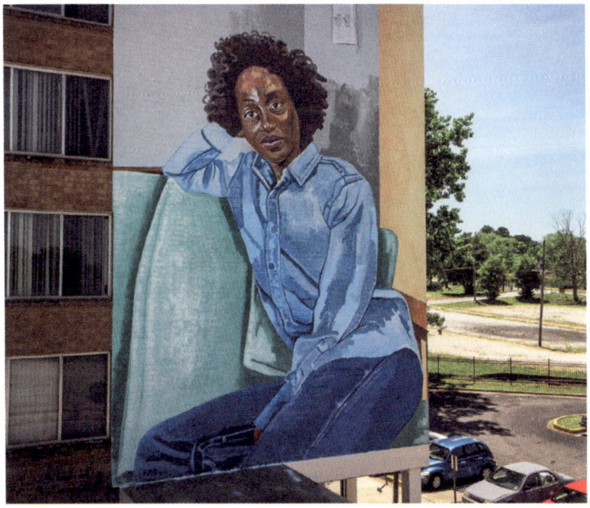

6. In so many respects, art making is about confidence. You need to project it in your work because otherwise your audience gets anxious, and truly, also, you need to have it inside somewhere because otherwise it's impossible to create anything. For all Gerald's introverted personal manner, he was an art extrovert.

7. Scale, I suppose, signals confidence.

8. Gerald paints portraits, which involves likeness—a challenge for many artists, even experienced ones. But Gerald paints only people he knows, himself included. Likeness is a funny thing. David Hockney: "If you draw someone you don't know you struggle for a likeness. You think maybe it should look like them and you don't know what people look like really. Whereas friends you learn slowly they have many faces. When I draw people I know well, I don't bother about the likeness. It is always there somehow." I find that myself. If you really know the subject, something in your brain does all the work. Even if your picture doesn't look like them, it looks like them.

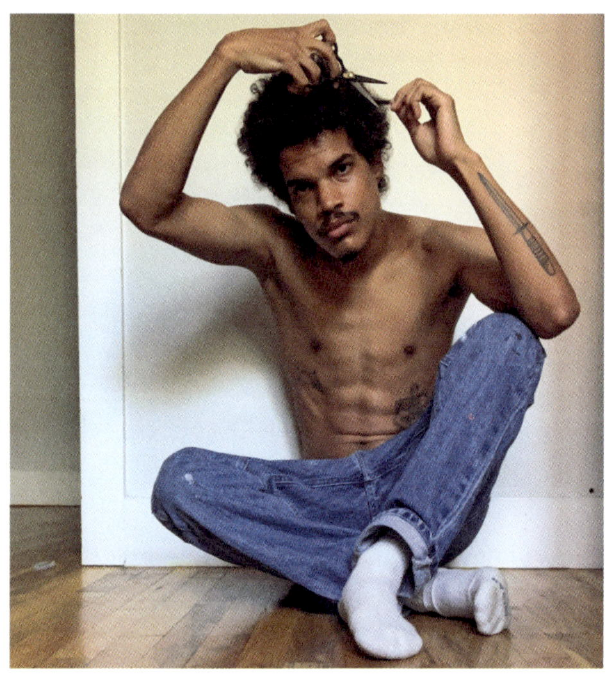

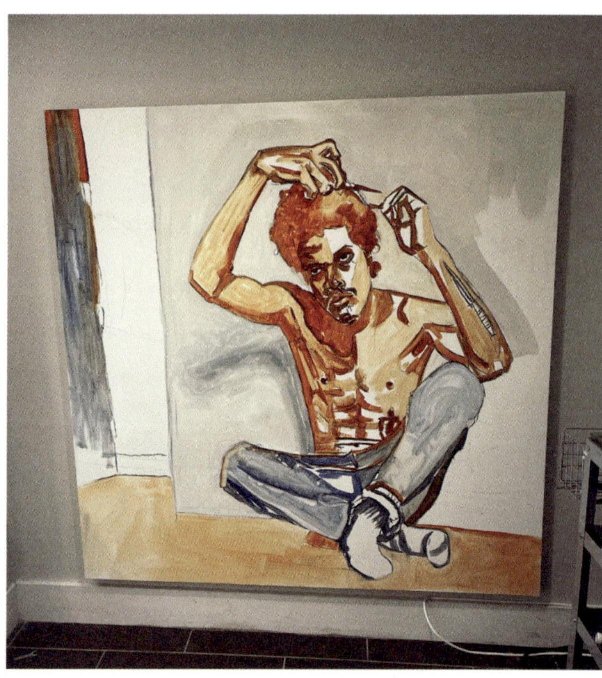

The source photograph, on to finish.

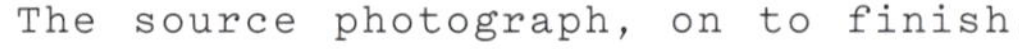

Oh no, this is going to be great. I look tired and like all the things we are.

"I think the painting itself isn't hard," he said. I found myself getting envious again, thinking about how little he's daunted by the more ordinary challenges of art making, like just getting the paint to do what you want it to do. The technical work comes easily to him, even as he's vexed by the more personal aspects of its presentation. "People talk about mastery and stuff, they love to throw that word around. But if the work still makes you uncomfortable, unsure of yourself—do masters still get unsure?"[9]

He was a little embarrassed by this painting, "because there's no way to present a huge painting of yourself without it coming off like a vanity thing." We talked about its vanity, and I reassured him the painting seemed honest, not grandiose. It was hard to resist giving him a little hug.

Stages After he was done, we spoke again, and I asked him what he was working through as he continued with the picture. The last figure is the final work.

"Getting a composition to work in a square was really tough," he said, "but I liked how the legs and the arms made a circle of C's in a nonsymmetrical way; I thought that was pretty cool. Technically, the hardest thing was the hair. I didn't put highlights on it the way I usually do—the shininess came from the medium. But the hair is nothing but green and red on top of each other. And then the tattoos—I painted over the tattoo, then I went back with a brush and carved it out of the paint while it was still wet."

When you look at the painting's stages, you see that the thing he was most drawn to about it—the eyes—were in place from the very start, the product of a few simple marks. There's nothing particularly bravura about them, but he's right, the whole power of the picture is in the eyes. Everything we had talked about during my studio visit was in the painting. "I

9. From the evidence of all the conversations I had for this book, yes.

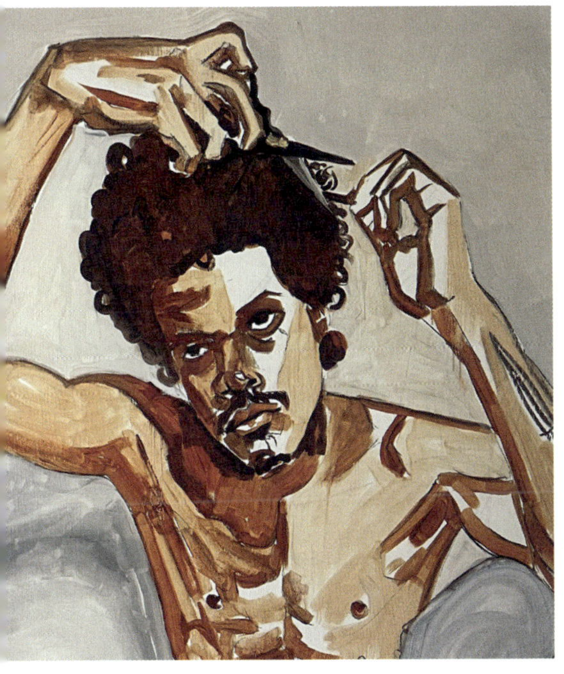

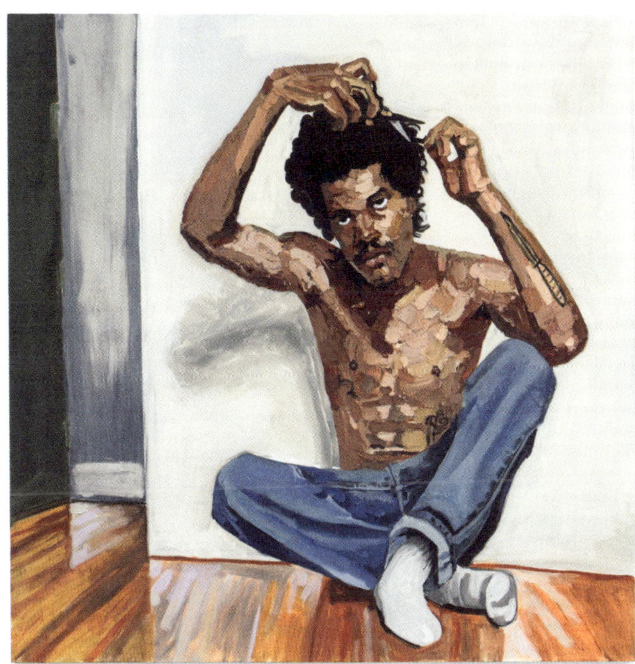

Chameleon, 2021, oil on panel, 60 × 60 in. Courtesy of Gerald Lovell and P·P·O·W, New York.

really love this painting," he said. "I feel like I'm begrudgingly on the wall. Honestly, there was a lot of stuff I was working with then—like my place in the art world, and feeling like that world is an unhealthy atmosphere for an artist." He appeared to be feeling sturdier now, but he loved the snarl in his expression. "It feels like a moment in time where I was just documenting my own personal angst."

"I ended up calling the painting *Chameleon,*" he said. "I was painting a version of myself that I wanted people to see. Automatically, people just assume I'm nice. I wanted to look mean."

In December the self-portrait was sold at Art Basel.

One More That should be the end of this story, except among the other pictures offered for sale, there was this one, of me.

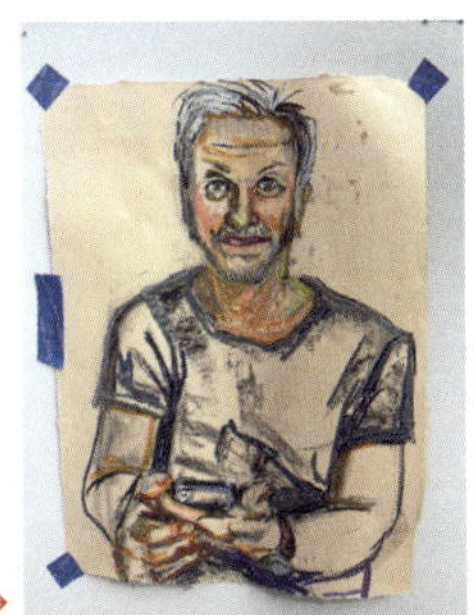

Here's how it happened. At times, when we talked, I found Gerald staring at me in a way I couldn't place. As we were finishing, it become clear I was fodder. Gerald asked to take my picture, I said sure, and then he snapped me with his phone.

Several months later, he texted me this drawing. It was not the most flattering version of me, or at least not the way I want to look, but it caught an affect of mine I recognized. I was impressed, pleased, and hoped he might even give it to me. A week later, I learned that he planned to sell it. I was shocked. That sensitive boy was actually a snake! But soon any uneasiness I felt turned to excitement. Gerald is, after all, an artist—a gifted, perceptive, and hungry one. An artist is a thief. So is a journalist. Like for all the subjects of this book, I had come here to steal something from him for my purposes, so it was only right that he stole something back. And I was interested in what he saw in me. I grew to like the idea that this image might someday live on a stranger's walls.

39

JODY WILLIAMS & RITA SODI

Stay Simple

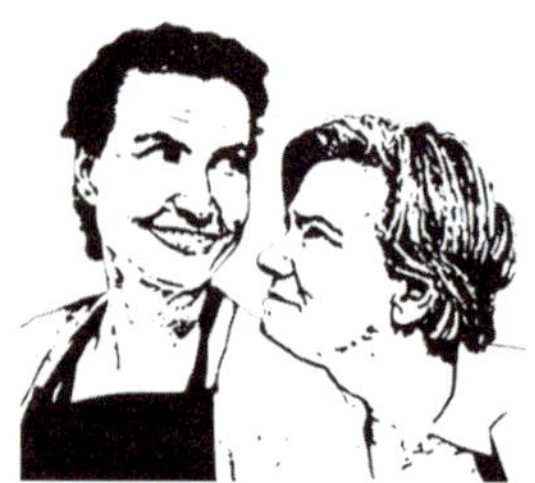

OCCUPATION: Chefs/Restaurateurs

WORK DISCUSSED: Svizzerina (2014)

BORN: 1963; 1961

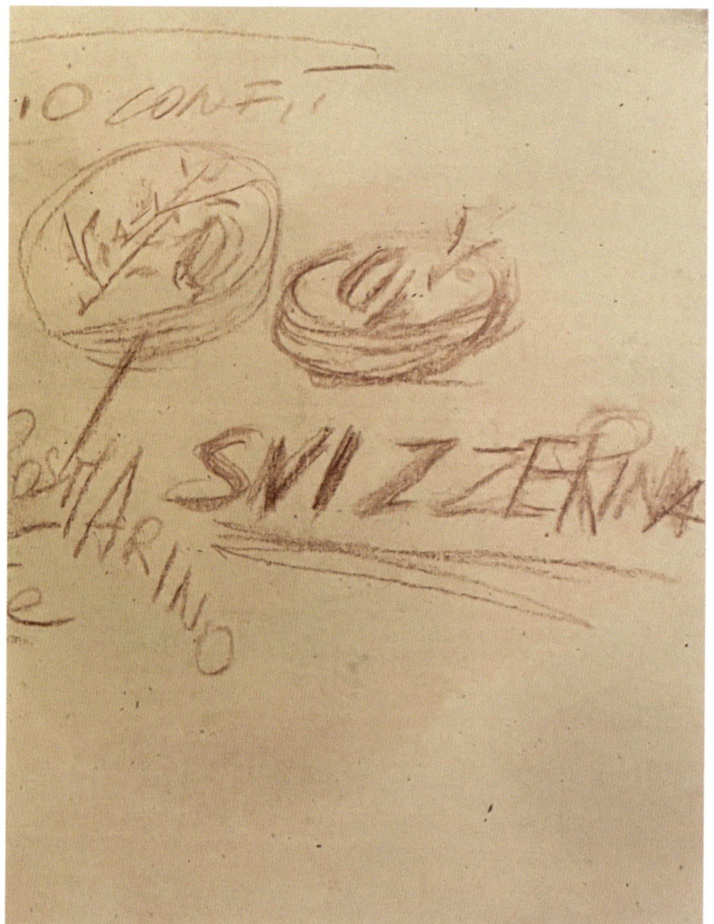

Svizzerina imagined.

WHEN I'M HUNGRY and tired, I want a hamburger. And when I'm particularly cranky and want to indulge myself, what I crave is a svizzerina. The svizzerina is a crunchy disc of chopped strip steak that is almost vermilion inside, with a little rosemary and confit of garlic on top (so emphatically not a hamburger, per its makers). It's really delicious. And it is, to me, a work of art.

Is it a work of art like a painting or a poem? I suppose not, but I include it here because (a) I was curious about how Rita Sodi and Jody Williams had arrived at the svizzerina's perfect simplicity; (b) as with the entry on Samin Nosrat (page 208), I wanted to know how the process of creating food compared

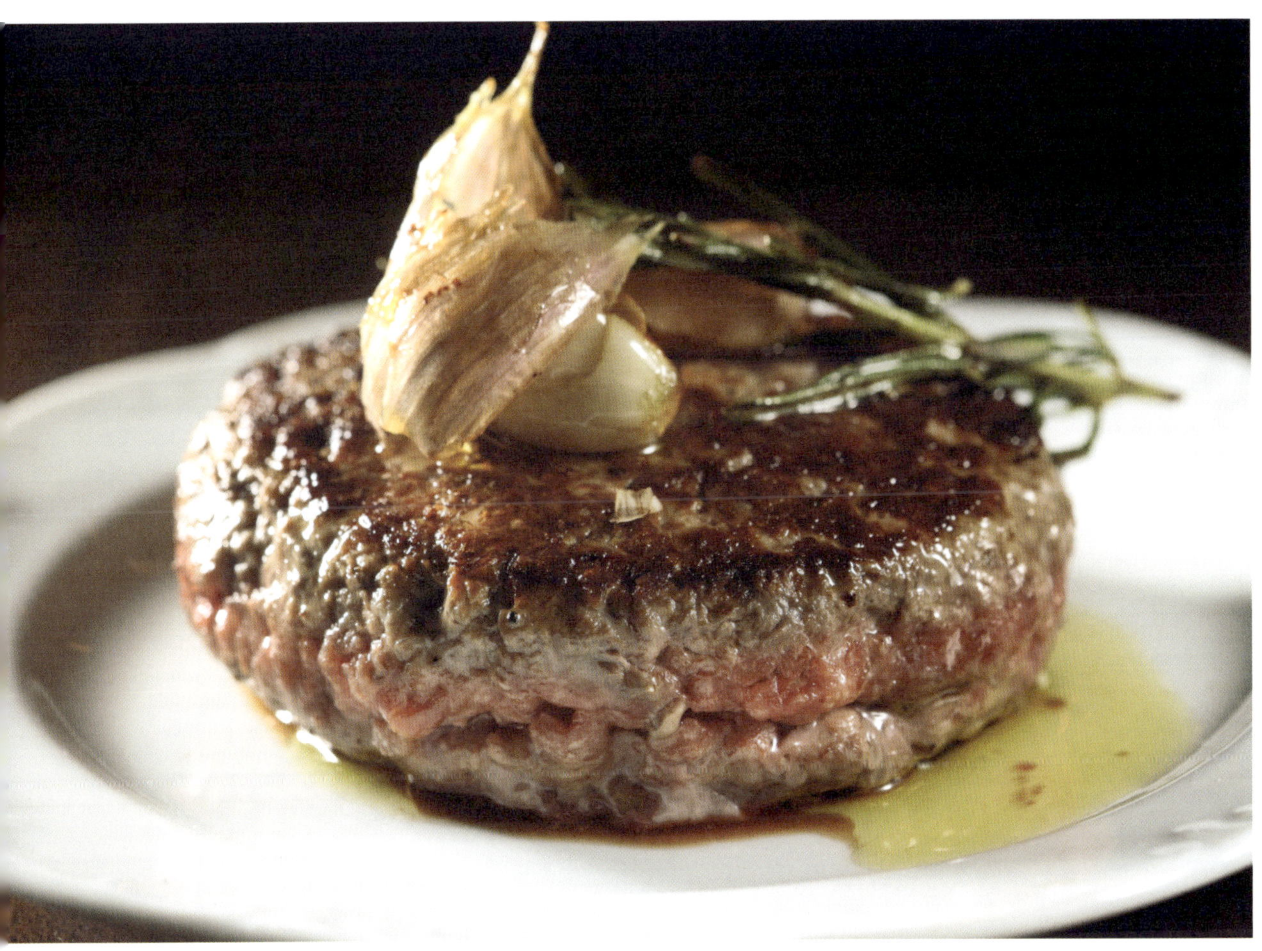

Svizzerina realized.

with the other activities in this book; and (c) I wanted an excuse to keep ordering it. The svizzerina is served at a kind-of trattoria named Via Carota, which *The New Yorker* called "New York's most perfect restaurant," and which also serves a simple/complicated version of a green salad that Samin declared, in *The New York Times*, the "best green salad in the world." Via Carota is just one of four delectable neighborhood restaurants (and one bar) the couple own within a four-block, very bougie radius near my home. During the period I was talking to them, they had just taken the lease for a fifth.

Jody and Rita each has her own restaurant—they are a stone's throw from one another. Jody's is French, called Buvette; Rita's is Italian, called I Sodi. Jody saw Rita at I Sodi gnawing on a lamb bone and says maybe that was the moment she fell in love. They started dating soon after. They make an odd couple, geometrically and in temperament. Rita is angular, taller, more reserved. Jody is softer, closer to the ground, more garrulous. Jody had restaurant training; Rita started her restaurant pretty impulsively, knowing little about the business of food, though she was a serious cook. Rita is a measurer, Jody more of an improviser. "We start with a different opinion on everything," Rita said, when I asked how they make decisions together. "But the more we work, the more we agree."

A Restaurant Together It's often said that restaurants are imbued with love—they mostly don't make a lot of sense economically (though that's not true for this couple, who do very well), so passion has to play some part. In Jody and Rita's case, that takes several forms. Rita said her interest always starts with memory: "The flavor I'm missing, the smell that I'm missing. I start with this. The biggest part is nostalgia." Jody said, "I think I bring to the table a little gluttony—the desire to eat and have it all." Then there is the passion for creating expressive environments in which food and setting take on the quality of an emotion; a need to use the restaurants to make their own relationship work; and a more primal need to be loved back by their audience or, in this case, customers, along with the battle not to let this need screw them up, which I recognized from my conversations with conventional artists. Here's Jody's account of the beginning of Via Carota:

"I was doing Buvette, Rita was doing I Sodi, and we were dating. And we were so busy and crazy at planning, I said as a joke, 'If we really want to see each other, we should open a restaurant together.'

"And then we looked down the street and we saw, what was it? This restaurant [which had been the site of many failed restaurants before], and you know, it's sad when a restaurant sort of languishes, then decays. And darkens. So we said, 'Let's do something there. An ode to Via Carota'—we were referring to Rita's place on Via Carota [in Tuscany] that we had spent some time in together. Then it was, 'Okay, call 'em up.' There's always this moment when I look at Rita and she says, 'Let's do it.' She does not hesitate. And then it's like hell or high water, we're gonna see it through.

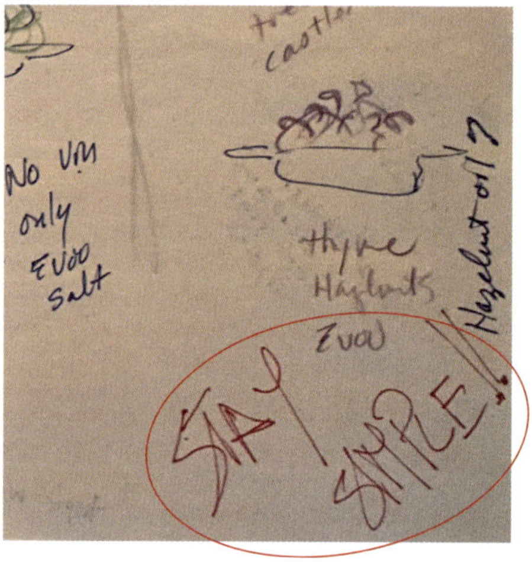

"It's not perfect sometimes, we learn along the way. We do slow openings; it takes us six months to improve and be confident.[1] And we never really feel confident. We feel like we need to apologize. I'm gonna take your money and you're gonna put this, right now, in your mouth? Sometimes it's just painful.

"I mean, will people come? Can we get maybe sixty for lunch and one hundred for dinner? We're totally panicked."

Simple Their idea for Via Carota was unconventional: a restaurant built around side dishes, with food ambition but without food formality. They just wanted what they wanted (and what they understood diners wanted), a restaurant with no airs, where people could eat however they liked. "We were envisioning a menu that sort of is deconstructed, so you can really have the freedom to eat all the sides. We never really want to eat all the meat and fish on the menus—we just keep eating all the beans."

I was there the very first night. I walked by, saw that it was open, and took a seat at the bar. A few months later, I couldn't get in; the place was mobbed. It's been that way for a decade. It's probably my favorite restaurant in the world.

The first time we talked, Jody hauled out a bunch of old papers she'd saved, some of which are represented here. (Rita, incredulous: "I don't know why we never threw those out.")

On one page is the directive "Stay simple." I asked Jody what that means. "You might feel compelled to do something to be liked. Will you love me? I want to be loved, you know, I can overdo it. Yeah, so stay simple. It's good when

1. Their restaurants take forever to open. And sometimes, as with the restaurant we were sitting in during our conversations (called the Commerce Inn), they can take another while to catch on. But, like all the subjects of this book, in spite of their professed lack of confidence, Jody and Rita have faith it will work—otherwise they'd just give up. I realize this chapter is about a sublime piece of chopped meat, but for all its amorphousness, faith keeps returning as a core principle. Simplicity too.

2. This is also, I suppose, a recipe. For what it's worth, the word *recipe* came up a couple of times (Machine Dazzle; Barbara Kruger) to describe an artistic formula, or signature.

you can no longer take away.”

That dictum especially informed the creation of the svizzerina, their own little *Mona Lisa*. Here is its evolution, which does in fact follow a familiar artistic pattern. It took them about a day to devise:

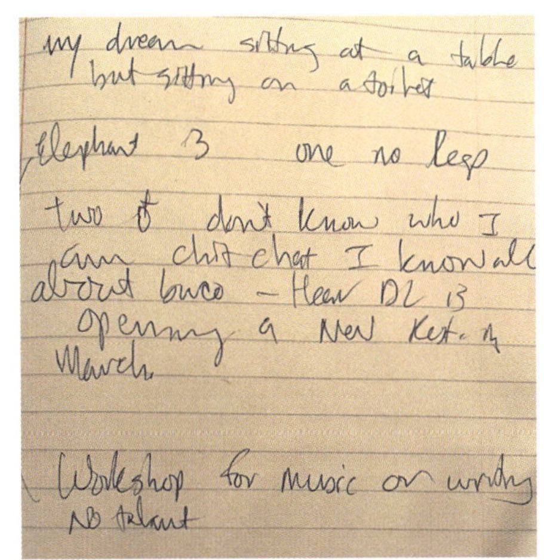
my dream sitting at a table
but sitting on a toilet
Elephant 3 one no leg
two of don't know who I
am chit chat I know all
about ... – Hear DZ 13
opening a New Rest. in
March
Workshop for music or writing
no talent

Dream from Jody Williams's journal: sitting at a restaurant table, which is a toilet. The brain is a blender.

1. Pose a problem.
Jody: “At first we were thinking, would we want a hamburger? And we’re like, ‘No. We can’t do that.’ Because that’s all anybody focuses on. I mean, we love hamburgers. But it just didn’t fit on the table. A hamburger is a sandwich, a hand food, right? It would disrupt the sharing, for one thing.” Nevertheless, it seemed they’d really need a hamburger-like thing.

2. Dig deep; or start with what you know.
Jody: “And then we realized we had, inside Rita, the stories of the svizzerina. The svizzerina is what they grew up eating in Italy. It was like for iron, if you’re run down. And there’s a French seared steak, raw. It’s a bistro thing. Like cooked steak tartare.”

3. Allow yourself not to know what you’re doing.
Rita: “We tried everything.” **Jody:** “We didn’t have a lot of confidence.”

4. Consider your materials.
Jody: “You could do rib eye, but you get better texture with the New York strip.”

5. Begin.
Jody: “And then you can take the fat cap off. You chop the fat, you chop the meat.”

6. Complicate.
Rita: “The fat has a different consistency than the meat. When you chop it together, it’s a bit of a mess. If you divide the consistency, it’s easier to chop, and more precise.” **Jody:** “So we chop the meat, and then we’re missing the fat and folding it back in. And it’s becoming brighter with the fat—if there’s not enough, like a forty-sixty ratio, you put more fat into it. Fat is where the flavor and joy is. You don’t season it. You put the steak back together.”

7. Make it yours.
Jody: “You’re gonna do it on a flattop. It’s gonna be hot, so you can really sear. It’s very rare. You want the meat to sear and crunch. You’re looking for two extremes. You need your seasoning on the outside—salt and coarse pepper—’cause you’re not seasoning inside. Because then it’s like making meat loaf. You want it very rare inside, so the fat sort of becomes opaque inside.” Sometimes people ask for it to be less pink. Usually, they say no. **Jody:** “You eat it like this or not at all.”

8. Experiment.
Jody: “We’re not gonna do hamburger, but let’s put a piece of bread under it, do you want to do that? Let’s do it with focaccia—no, that’s gross.” So no bread. “I added fried onions on top. Boop, boop, boop, boom. Like an onion sautéed, caramelized onions on top.” No onions. “Potatoes. We tried a couple different potatoes. We’re not going to dumb it down by fearing that someone’s going to want french fries.” No potatoes. “Sometimes we don’t know what we want; we change our mind in the middle of everything. And then all of a sudden we just did the garlic confit and some rosemary fried in olive oil over it. And we thought . . .” **Rita:** “That’s perfect.” **Jody:** “When you can no longer take away, the dish is done.”[2]

40

TAYLOR MAC & MACHINE DAZZLE

Don't Hold Back

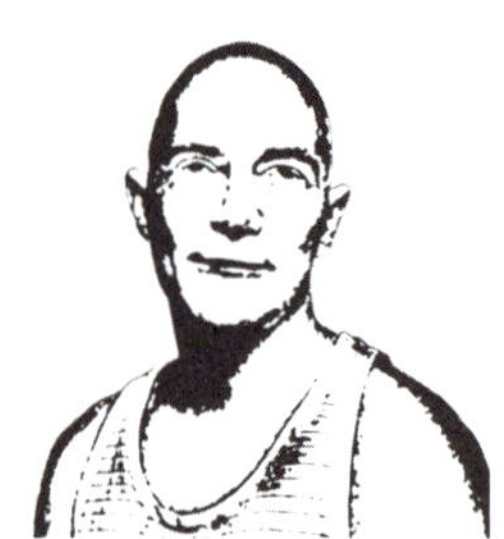

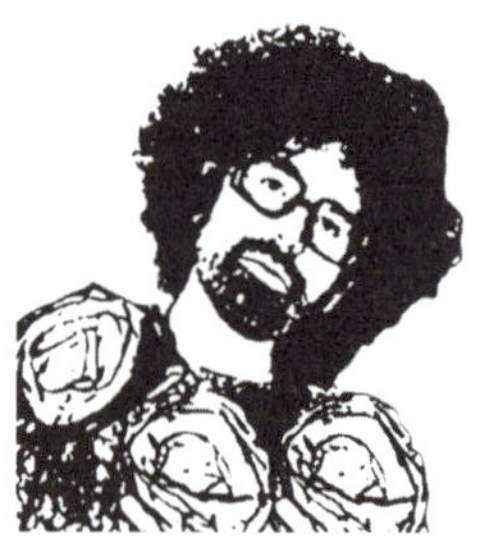

OCCUPATION: Theater Artist / Costumer

WORK DISCUSSED: *A 24-Decade History of Popular Music* (2016)

BORN: 1973; 1972

Collaborators: For the *24-Decade* show, Machine Dazzle dresses Taylor Mac.

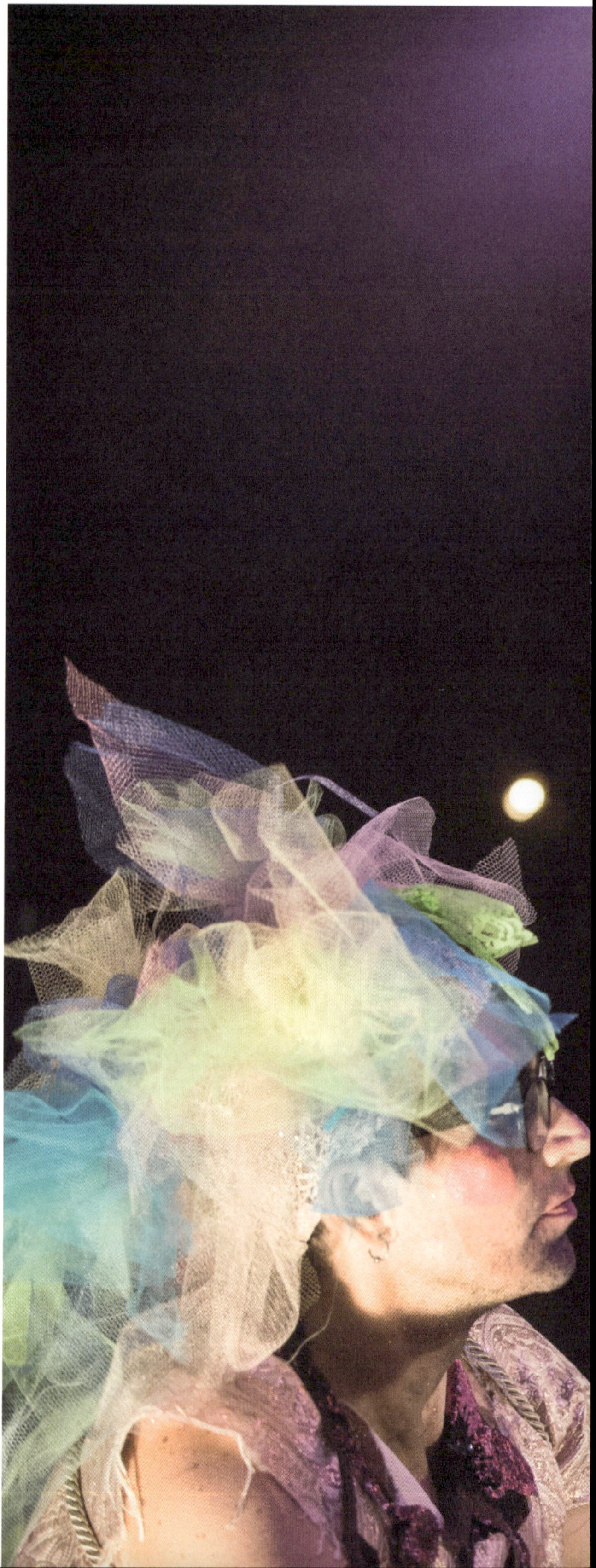

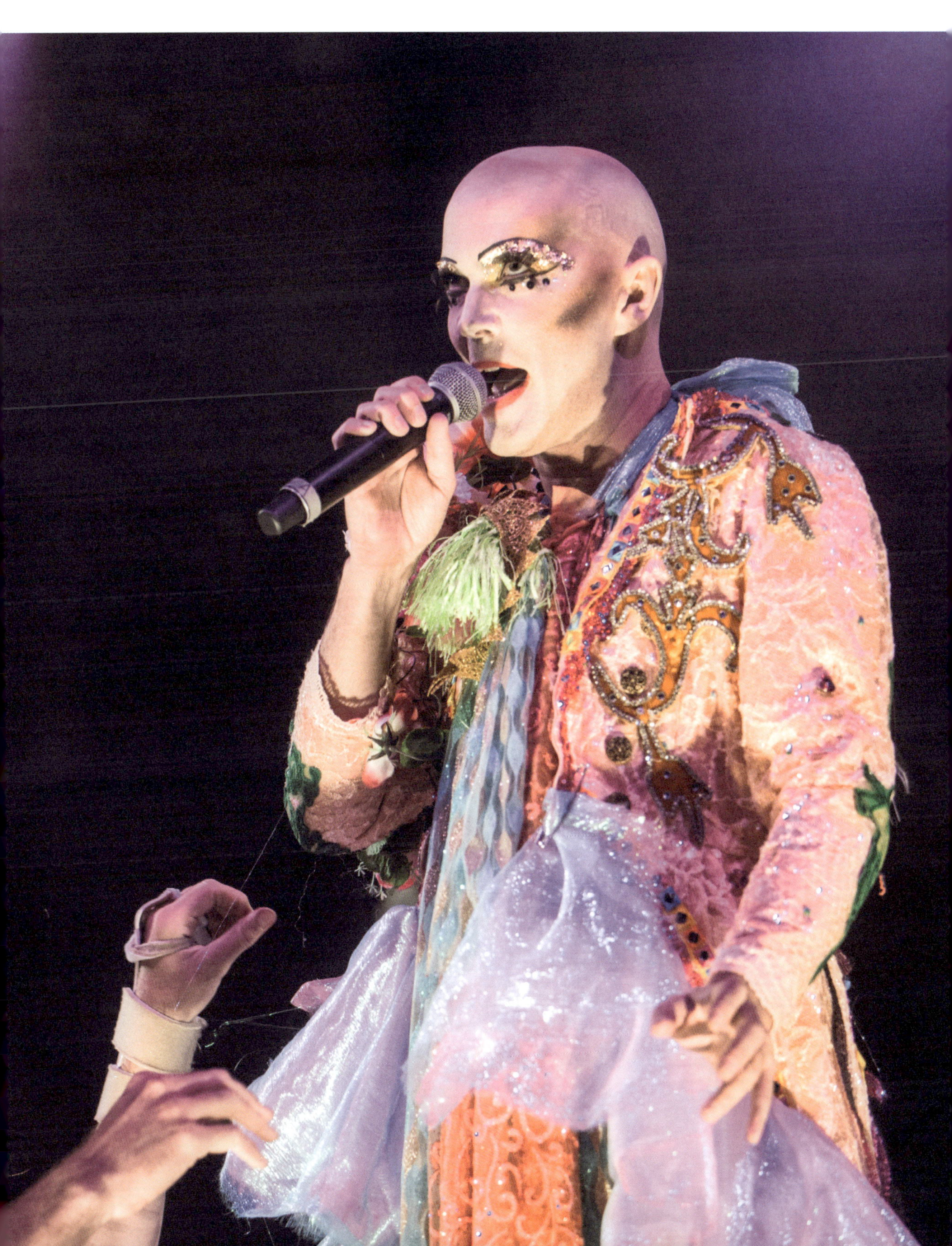

OVER TWENTY-FOUR HOURS, from noon to noon, the weekend of October 8, 2016, I was an ecstatic captive of the performer / theater artist Taylor Mac in a theater in Brooklyn. I know the date because the performance I saw, *A 24-Decade History of Popular Music*, occurred only once, and never will again, in its full twenty-four-hour duration. Some of my friends were going. I hesitated because, well, it was twenty-four hours. I was afraid of feeling like a prisoner, and I really hate immersion theater experiences, but I went anyway, persuaded it was a once-in-a-lifetime kind of thing. Wesley Morris (see page 224) called it "one of the great experiences of my life."[1] And it was for me too.

We often see creators as godlike because we are asking them to take control of our experience (reading their book or listening to their music), but I've never seen such a vivid demonstration of that God principle in action as I did that weekend. It was probably the single most ambitious piece of theater I've ever encountered, in a life of going to a lot of theater. Over twenty-four hours, Taylor (whom I knew a bit) took the audience through the entirety of American history, one decade at a time, from 1776 to 2016, offering an inverted, or "queer," mirror as a lens. Each hour was another decade. Each told the story of that decade from the point of view of a marginalized (Black, Jewish, gay, etc.) community. Each used popular songs of the decade—spirituals, folk, pop songs, TV theme songs—to tell its story.

We moved through the American Revolution and Reconstruction, Prohibition, and civil rights. One decade might be set in a Jewish tenement, another on Mars, for each decade was also its own little happening,[2] with Taylor inviting audience members to join in on the telling. So, somewhere in the third or fourth hour, Taylor pitted Walt Whitman against Stephen Foster in a fighting match and asked the audience to pelt the loser with Ping-Pong balls. Later, Taylor restaged the Oklahoma land rush by coaxing the audience to grab whatever territory near their seats they could get their greedy hands on and not let go; turned the theater into a queer alternative version of a high school prom in which we were all commanded to dance with a same-sex stranger; fed us soup on an approximation of a Depression breadline; woke up whoever was sleeping at the nineteen-or-so-hour mark with a kids' marching band they'd invited to enter and blast our eardrums, thrillingly. All the while, Taylor bossed us around, crooning and belting and exhorting, and we surrendered. It was very culty. We might have done anything for Taylor, our leader.

There were 650 of us. Taylor was above us on a stage. The orchestra was behind. (There was a loft to nap in if we were fading.) Throughout the twenty-four hours, Taylor lured us to fall in love with the entire entourage: the musicians; the helpers, whom they called the Dandy Minions; each and every one of the collaborators. Then, one by one, each member of the troupe was banished from the stage, so that by the time we reached the end, Taylor was up there alone.

One of those particularly beloved collaborators was Taylor's costumer, friend, and, for this show, dresser: a man named Machine Dazzle. Taylor had come up mainly as a downtown performance artist before getting more mainstream recognition (winning a MacArthur "Genius Grant" and writing a Broadway play; the twenty-four-hour show was a Pulitzer finalist). Machine had started out making costumes for a troupe of dancers that mostly did nightlife gigs. They found each other and started to play together on a piece of Taylor's called *The Lily's Revenge*.

They would go on to work together on other

1. Wesley Morris on Taylor Mac: "Mr. Mac gave me one of the great experiences of my life. I've slept on it, and I'm sure. It wasn't simply the physical feat. Although, come on: 246 songs spanning 240 years for 24 straight hours, including small breaks for him to eat, hydrate and use the loo, and starting in 1776 with a great-big band and ending with Mr. Mac, alone in 2016, doing original songs on piano and ukulele."

2. *Happenings,* defined by the *Oxford English Dictionary* as "a partly improvised or spontaneous piece of theatrical or other artistic performance, typically involving audience participation," fascinated (and frightened) me as a child of the sixties, when they were popular. They've fallen out of favor, but the term pretty well defines what this was.

3. This book is not really about collaboration. But what's more striking—the silence and secrecy of theirs, or the conjoined twin-y sensibility that makes it work?

4. They still perform the show sometimes, though just a clump of decades at a time. There's an HBO documentary on the twenty-four-hour event.

Taylor performances (these theater experiences don't fall into an obvious genre). But *A 24-Decade History* would be each other's masterpiece. For this show, Machine dressed Taylor in costumes he'd constructed for each decade, which were each Machine's own rendition of the period—a telling of American history that existed on a plane parallel to Taylor's. They weren't so much costumes as wearable dioramas, dresses and headdresses made of objects that might have been invented during the period, or were just the product of Machine's (mostly hilarious) riffs on the decade's meanings. So the dozens of dresses were made of frankfurters and eyeballs and cassette tapes full of coded references you might grasp or not before Machine yanked them off Taylor and replaced them, for the next decade, with an even more flamboyant sculpture for Taylor to wear. That's what they were, too, sculptures. They were their own spectacle—in a sense, their own show. Years later they got a couple of floors of their own at a show celebrating Machine's work at the Museum of Arts and Design, called *Queer Maximalism*.

That's an apt description of both their work. Unlike other, more meticulous artists, they're not at all bothered by—in fact they relish—the mess of being all in. Each is very devoted to their own invented, twisted fire hose of a vision, which happily intertwine together.

I really admired the way they fed off each other's talents, and wanted to talk to them together. They agreed, and we sat in my kitchen trying to piece the evening together and discuss how they got there. Their collaboration is very unusual. I was surprised at the extent they worked separately—in fact, each had little idea what the other was doing. That's a product of knowing each other so well and being years in sensibility sync, but it's just not how most artistic partners work. Taylor held secrets from Machine; in turn, Machine wouldn't tell Taylor what he had made until he showed up with it.[3]

We decided to focus on something they called the blind reveal, which was the happening they created to end the decade when Braille was invented. For an hour, a ways into the show, the audience was blindfolded and asked to flirt with each other, playing musical chairs in the dark and ending up on a stranger's lap. For this conversation, Taylor and Machine wanted to talk about what the audience would see as the blindfolds came off. Taylor's costume was, after all—as Machine put it—both costume and set. The moment was, they both thought, a spectacular opportunity (after removing our blindfolds, they had one shot to startle us), and the two spent the better part of years, as they workshopped the show in shorter increments (in effect training for this one-night-only performance), trying to get it right.[4] The costume evolved, and eventually involved Taylor in a harness—flying in the air, in a resplendent cloud of balloons.

MAXIMALISM'S BEGINNINGS

"I had a very supportive mother in terms of being an artistic human being, and a negative mother in terms of being queer," said Taylor. "So it was mixed messaging. But I can't say it was a good childhood, I'm sorry. And I think this is where Machine and I are a little similar. We stored up all the things that we imagined and wanted to do. And then we got to the age where we could do them, and then we wanted to do them all. Don't want to hold back anymore."

"When it was time for art class," said Machine, "I would do the assignment one hundred times; everyone else wouldn't even do it once." That zeal eventually developed into an aesthetic. "I have a million ideas. I want all the ideas in there. And I'm going to kill myself to do it."

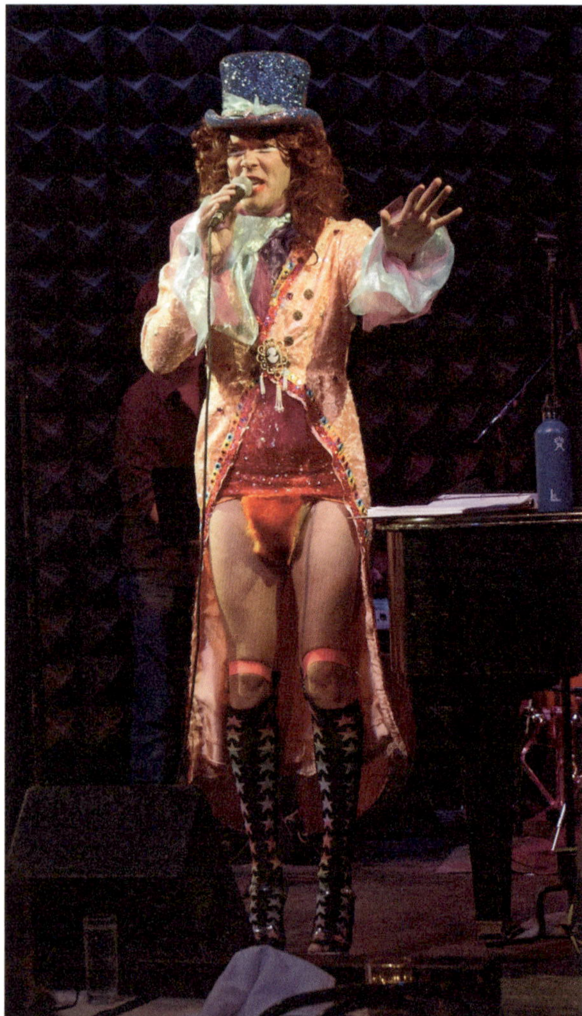

The blind reveal: first try (Joe's Pub, Manhattan).

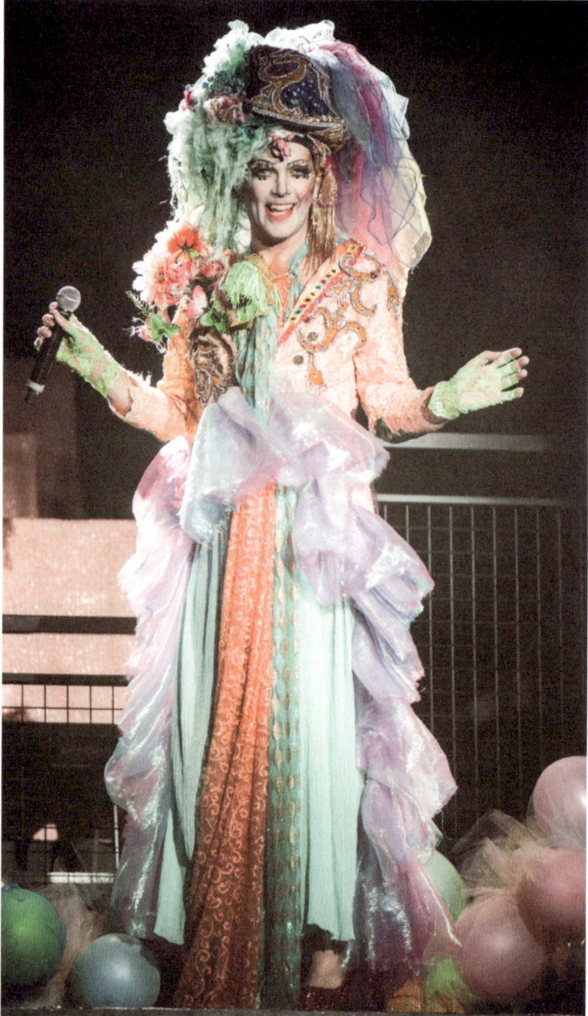

Another (St. Ann's Warehouse, Brooklyn).

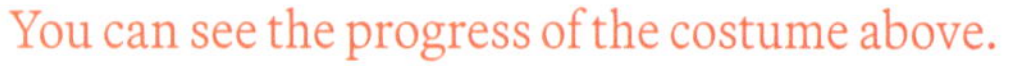

You can see the progress of the costume above.

Taylor Gets an Idea

Taylor Mac: We were working on this other play, *The Lily's Revenge*. *Lily* was a five-hour play with thirty-six people in it, and at some point I realized that the play was subconsciously reenacting an AIDS Walk that I went to in San Francisco when I was fourteen. I'd never met an out homosexual before, and suddenly there were thousands all at the same time. I found myself chasing that feeling, of wanting to stage that experience, without really knowing I was doing that. And I thought, *Why don't I do that consciously for my next big project?* I started to think about that, looking for a form for it. I don't remember exactly when I thought of popular music, but I was thinking that the content is communities being torn apart and then building themselves as a result of being torn apart. And the thing about a popular song is that it's not reaching for the hem of God, it's reaching for community. You remember the song because we repeat the chords a million

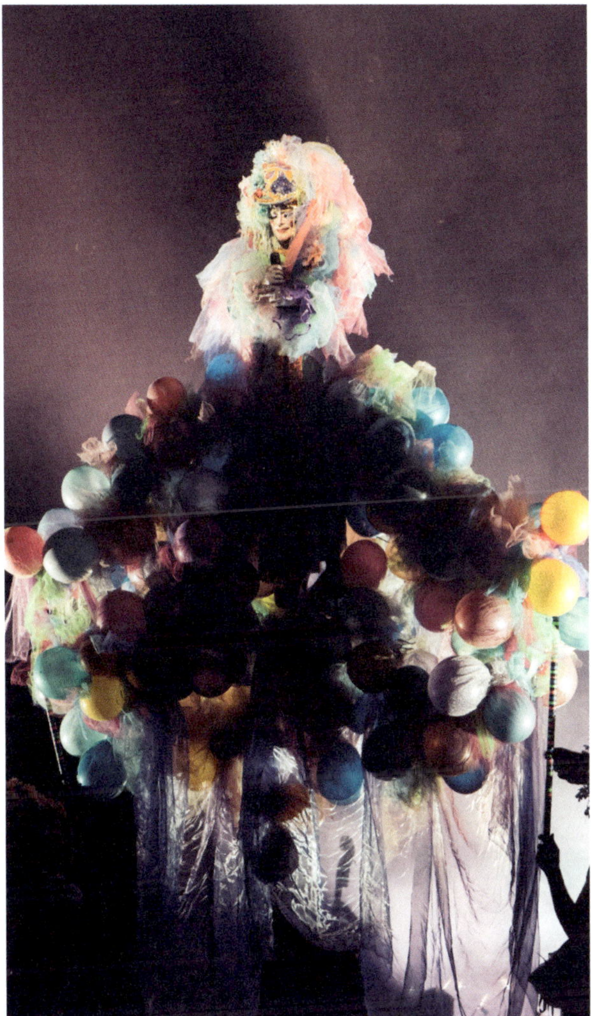

And again, in the air (Berlin): the Dandy in the Cloud.

times. The queer part is that what connects queer people isn't our sexuality, it's that we're outsiders. So I thought, *Can queer people be a metaphor?* And then: *I'M gonna be the metaphor*. One queer body will be the metaphor for America, while grappling with the history through popular songs. That was kind of the idea.

Adam Moss: *And the twenty-four hours of it, that it would take on the full sweep of American history through twenty-four decades, was that there from the beginning?*

TM: What became a kind of happy accident—I wish I'd thought of it before—was that I just realized one day that I was literally joining 240 years. And so that was . . . twenty-four hours. One for every decade. So the math just started working out.

Yes, and then Machine came on. Though in my mind Machine was always on board—

A Secret Project

AM: *Machine, do you remember when Taylor explained the idea to you?*

Machine Dazzle: It didn't happen right away. [He turns to Taylor.] You didn't spill. I remember you were in Europe. And you were like, "Machine, I need an 1890s-inspired outfit." I didn't know what it was for at first. You had something in your mind. As far as I knew, it was for a photo shoot. I never saw you, we never had a fitting. But you kept that costume, the one that had patches of candy. And then months, or even a year later, you asked me to do a 1970s thing. You were like, "Now I'm doing the '70s. And while you're at it, let's do the 1930s too." I thought, *Well, okay, this is interesting*.

AM: *You never asked Taylor what the costume was for?*

MD: No. And then you [*to Taylor*] called a meeting and came to my workplace; I was a jewelry designer. And you said, "What I want to do is a twenty-four-decade show." You spilled that we were going to do twenty-four decades in twenty-four costumes. But I still—I had no idea it was going to turn into a marathon! I thought what's great is I had the luxury of time to just figure out ideas and start little piles of sketches.

AM: *And was the basic aesthetic in place from the very first costumes you made?*

MD: No, the early ones were a lot more experimental. They would fall apart. They were very garbage-y.

TM: One of them was even on paper. And it only lasted the night I wore it.

MD: I started working on the opening look [the American Revolution]. The wig is made

from macaroni. And then I added a witchy vest thing that actually says thirteen, with stars on them—because you know, thirteen, great number. And then an old pair of gloves, and then better gloves.
TM: And meanwhile the shoes are perpetually evolving, being repurposed.
AM: *Taylor, at what point did you start to see it as a marathon?*
TM: Well, the concept was that I was going to workshop all these decades at Joe's Pub, where I would break even paying all the musicians, like maybe if I was lucky I'd make a hundred bucks. And then eventually we'd put it all together, and it would be real ragtag, you know? But beautiful. Along the way these producers—Pomegranate Arts, they did *Einstein on the Beach*—saw it, and they came aboard, and then it was like, this vision [to do the entire sweep at some point] can actually happen. We'd done maybe ten workshops, maybe half the decades. But once they came on board, we started doing these decades again. And part of my concept at that point was we would make it *with* the audience. So it would become a ritual. You would want to come back to see how the decade evolved. We would workshop it for many, many years. It was like a Ponzi scheme: we could be booked for the next five years with one show.

Anyway, we couldn't really rehearse. We'd just make sure all the song charts were correct. But no one would ever hear what I was going to say onstage.
AM: *Had you written it out?*
TM: Yes, but no one had heard it.
AM: *Did each decade's script change a lot over time or just on the margins?*
TM: Often a lot. Whole new concepts.
AM: *But you didn't tell Machine you'd be doing all the decades together in one show?*
TM: I think I didn't tell everyone because even though people are pretty game with the big projects, I always get a little flak for having ambitious ideas. . . .
AM: *Do you? I mean, that's who you are—*
TM: Well, it's like, why do we have to work so hard?
MD: Except me. I would never. . . .

Bigger

TM: Machine's always the one who says, "Oh wait, bigger, yes, let's go!" Also, I don't like to say fully what the concept is right away because it may change. I kept that to myself for a few years. It got to the point where I was asking myself, *Do I have to get butch, do I have to get aggressive about having a vision and defending my vision?* It's not fun to have to do that with your collaborators who you love.
AM: *How much time would you give yourself to work out the particulars of each decade?*
TM: Months before. I work very "content dictates form." So I would say, *What's the decade about? Okay, let me go hunt for songs from that decade.*
AM: *And you would decide what the decade was about, as opposed to it being a conversation among all of your collaborators?*
TM: Yes. I put an offering on the table. I want to have the thing people are responding to. But I don't ever dictate to Machine what to make. Because Machine never tells me what to make.
AM: *You don't give Machine any parameters at all? I mean, obviously you told him you wanted to do it in drag. . . .*
TM: I don't think I even said that.
MD: There was only one thing you ever asked for specifically in twenty-four decades. You said you wanted something to represent a man and a woman, and I showed up with the most basic thing, but it really works: a lock and key. A heart-shaped lock and a big floppy key.
TM: I might have said something like, "It's all a metaphor for robber barons." Also, I need a costume that I can take off and put on an audience member. Functional things. But that's all. I just know what he does. When we started working with each other, we were drawn to each other, to our aesthetic.
AM: *So a couple more questions before we get to the blind reveal. I'm curious because I found it so affecting: the banishment of the troupe onstage, one by one, decade by decade, when did that come into your thinking?*

TM: That was also early on—like, within the first week of realizing I wanted to do this, because it all had come from the AIDS epidemic. I wanted the show to get harder as it goes along. And so it was important that you feel a loss. I wanted the audience to be surprised, but feel it. Okay, we're losing the tuba player. The audience cheers, but they don't really connect to what is happening until the twentieth century, when they start losing people they've gotten to know. They start to gasp.

AM: *As you were workshopping the show, what would shift? The music, your language, the theme?*

TM: All of it. We would try different songs, different concepts. "This song isn't doing anything, can we make it minor? Can we slow it down?" I mean, generally, how do you rehearse something like this? How do you rehearse blindfolding an entire audience? We would have to experiment during the performances.

AM: *Can you take me through a song change?*

TM: Okay, here's one. So this was the decade of the fifties into the sixties. We were doing that Pete Seeger song "Turn! Turn! Turn!" We'd rehearsed it in the music studio, but when we got to the concert, it was like, blah, horrible.

AM: *Because it was treacly?*

TM: Honestly, it was because none of the musicians liked it. So the thought was, maybe we should do this *Peter Gunn* song [the theme song to a popular 1950s TV show] instead. I said, "Can we play this?" And then everyone loved it. It became a staple. It's one of the only ones we really mash up. . . .

AM: *So you mashed it up with "Turn! Turn! Turn!"*

TM: Yes, it just gave us excitement from the get-go.

The Blind Reveal

AM: *Let's move on to the blind reveal. What was it?*

TM: Well, you know, four hours in the theater is a long time for most people. I've gotten them up in the first decade to stand for a song, and then it happens again in the second decade, the women stand up and go, "Ooooh," and then in the third decade, people stand up and play beer pong, spitting at each other. But when the fourth hour is over, I thought, *They've been staring at the lights the whole time, we just need to do something radically different*. So I was researching the decade and it was roughly when Braille was invented, and I thought, *That's perfect*. That was in France, and in America, the War of 1812 was over, people were committing to the idea of America in a way they hadn't yet. So they had to figure out how to see anew, feel anew, listen anew. And it just felt right. We need a bit of a palate cleanser, after all. And if I put it in too late in the show, we might put people to sleep. So I just thought now is a good time to blindfold them, and then we can make them do musical chairs.

AM: *At a certain point, you're going to tell them to take off their blindfold, and there's something you wanted them to see. And I assume this is the thing you kept rethinking.*

MD: It started along these lines. At one of the earlier shows at Joe's Pub, I showed up with a dandy outfit to represent the decade because it was like the height of the dandy—all these highly effeminate . . .

TM: Cis men. There is even a song about the dandy in that decade.

MD: But I didn't know about that. I did my research about the decade. I didn't know there were songs. I'd never been to a rehearsal. I just showed up an hour before Taylor goes onstage. He hadn't even tried on the costume.

TM: Eventually, Machine's concept was that it would be the most amazing outfit in the show.

MD: Because by that point, they were blindfolded. And when the blindfolds were removed, I kept wanting to make it bigger and bigger. And when we had the capabilities to fly you through the air, somehow it got even bigger. First Taylor was revealed somewhere on the other side of the room.

TM: Up in the loft, yeah.

MD: But when we started going to theaters where you could fly in a harness . . .

TM: The audience freaked out.
MD: I could do something huge! And that's why I covered you in balloons.
AM: *But at first, in the pictures you sent me, the look was fairly demure.*
MD: That was at the beginning, when we were doing little bits of the show at Joe's Pub. With the wig? And the top hat?
TM: It wasn't particularly fabulous at all.
MD: Well, no . . .
TM: This is what I found out about Machine. Often he will show up with something jaw-dropping right off, nine times out of ten. But then the one time, he'll show up and it'll be "Okay, this is the beginning of an idea. . . ."
MD: That was before I found my recipe. I kept building on it. The top hat that exists now is still the top hat. I turned a dress into a jacket. It's just so embellished you don't see it anymore. And one day I'm blowing up balloons and covering them in tulle. . . .
TM: This is a man who loves working, so the goal isn't to get it done. The goal is to work.
AM: *Talk about the recipe.*

Machine's Recipe

MD: I didn't figure out the recipe until we had workshopped about half the shows out. All of a sudden I realized, *Wait, this outfit is solid black, the Jewish decade was black, the thirties were black*. And then I just knew I had to do more. I rarely take away.[5] I add things. I love all the pageantry. But I was really only starting to get all this at Joe's Pub. I realized that when Taylor walks on the stage, he's not only the costume, he's the set, he's the props. I've got to give the audience something to look at.

So then it was, "I know you look absolutely silly. But the audience is going to love it. Trust me." Sometimes when I'd watch Taylor, I'd think, *Maybe that costume's a little too easy. I think he could handle more*.

And then of course I kept experimenting. I looked at what they're wearing at the time. That's where I started. That's what most historical designers would do—the silhouettes of the time. It's a piece of the pie, but not the whole pie. And somewhere it clicked. What was *new* at the time? And then: What was invented? How can I turn the inventions into a costume? The second decade was when the steam engine was invented. And so I put steam stacks into Taylor's costume. At first they were tulle. But then I got the balls to do dry ice and boiling water.
TM: He would put boiling water on me backstage.
MD: Well, not on him, exactly. But, you know, emotions become sculpture.
AM: *I assume you imagine that the audience is subliminally getting it, even if they're not seeing it precisely.*
MD: Most people would never get all the references. I want people to figure it out, or go, *Aha*. Anyway, [for the reveal] at first it's a dress turned backwards and cut open like a dandy jacket with tails. I wanted it really colorful. And there was this weird codpiece that was really mal-fitting. It was like fur. And then I just wanted it to be pretty. And then, once the audience was blindfolded, it changed.
TM: I'm basically in my little panties and shoes. Or barefoot. And then Machine would come out with one part of the outfit and put it on me while I'm singing. I'm singing with a microphone and he's got to put things over my head.
AM: *Which the audience isn't seeing.*
TM: We want them to be concentrating. So while they're blindfolded, we're asking them to pass a flower on, tease the person next to you with your flower—while I'm taking off my shoes, creeping around.
MD: So what happens is we get you dressed, you end up somewhere in the theater, or you're in the harness and you're flying. And then they take off the blindfold. And it's big. And it's pretty. It's the kind of thing you want to look at and adore, like a flower.
TM: Like, this is what I've been wearing the whole hour, and now you see it.

5. Most of the other chapters are consumed with subtraction. This is the opposite.

6. This outfit was the centerpiece of Machine's museum show, though his other costumes may have been more interesting to look at close up, since they were like outsider-art folk sculptures, layered with objects that appeared as if they had been scavenged from a landfill—maybe they were. The dandy outfit was mostly balloons, meant to look gorgeous at a distance, which it did.

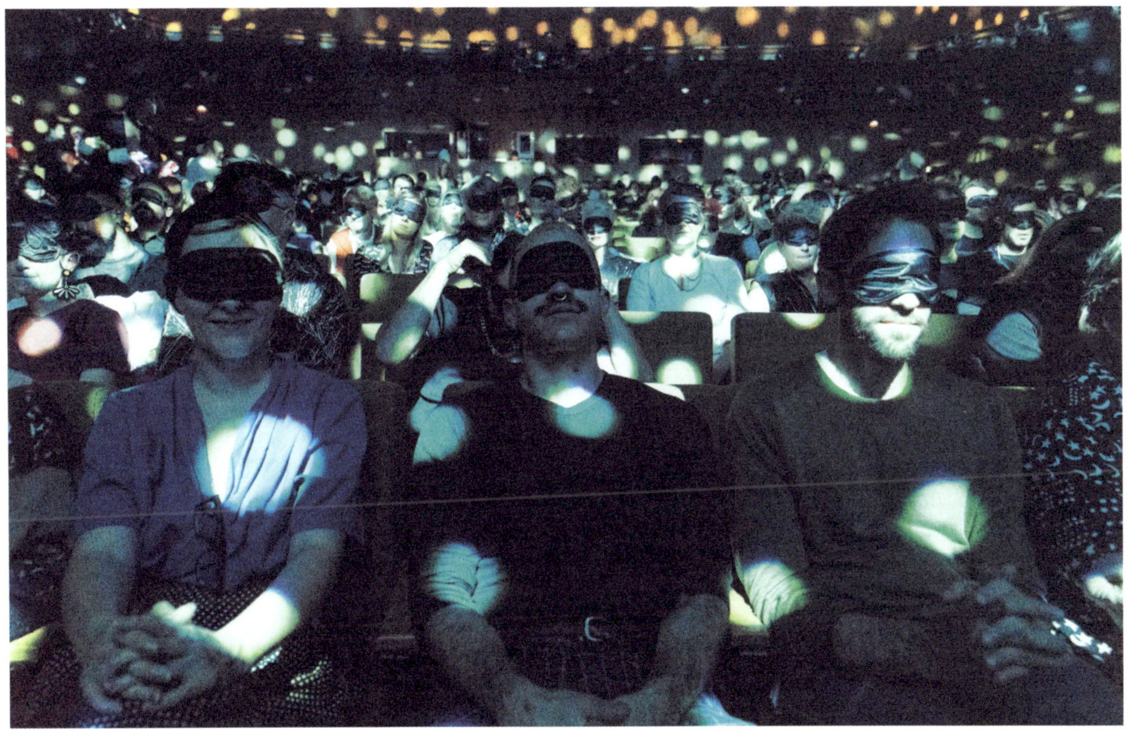

The audience blindfolded before the reveal (Berlin).

MD: And then it's just all balloons. I wanted you to look like you were in a cloud, the dandy in the cloud.
AM: *And this getup was all just built on top of the dandy jacket and top hat you started with?*
MD: Right. When we were at the Curran Theatre, in San Francisco, there was an amazing craft store, a discount place. I still had the jacket and top hat, but I knew I needed more. [To Taylor] I think I might have had you in fishnet, with lace gloves. And then I found great flowers, and I built the hat with those flowers. I spent like hundreds of dollars in that store! Oh my God, it was so pretty. With all those silklike scarves and weird salmon-colored dressing. And I added this big pussy bow.
TM: He loves the pussy bow.
MD: We would dress you up onstage, and then you would travel, and most of your costume wouldn't even show, like you were peeking out, saying, *I'm up here. . . .*
TM: And then you had the balloons. The balloon was like a boa.
MD: I probably had twenty, maybe forty, balloons. I started covering them in tulle-like poufs. And it started to become a cloud.
AM: *And that was that?*
MD: Not quite, he was still on the ground. In Philadelphia, I realized he was going to be up in the air, flying. So I'm like, *Finally, a real cloud!* I blew up as many balloons as I could. And I wanted to *move* Taylor like a cloud. And so *that* was it. Finally, after so many cities, we flew. Taylor became the dandy floating in a huge cloud of pastel balloons. Full-on huge cloud dandy fantasy.[6]
AM: *I know you say you're never going to do the full twenty-four hours again, but are there things in the show you would want to keep futzing with?*
TM: No.
MD: Always.

41
DAVID SIMON
Arguing

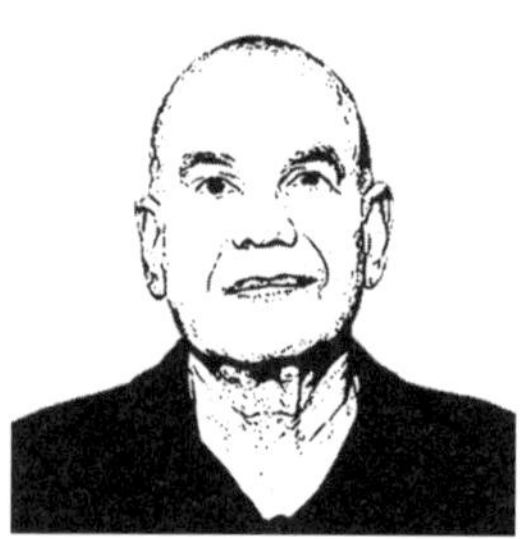

OCCUPATION: Television Creator

WORK DISCUSSED: *The Wire*, Season 2 (2003)

BORN: 1960

THE TELEVISION SERIES *The Wire* began as a (very good) cops and robbers show, and evolved into an (even better) critique of the American city and of capitalism generally. This it did very deliberately in season 2, when the creator, David Simon, made the crucial decision, amid much disagreement, to shift the show away from the dramatic world it had painstakingly built in its first season, to another—seemingly tangential—setting, in order to turn the series into a bigger, more blistering argument.

Simon uses the word *argument* often, in many contexts. He is far more interested in argument than art, in spite of the fact that he happens to be an unusually artful storyteller. He seems to take the art for granted, which is a little maddening for the envious. But his success as an artist is less about the free flow of associations you see a lot in these pages and more about what looks like the opposite: a dogged, polemical mindset that took hold very early and hardly budged. In our conversation, we traced the evolution of that mindset and of his unusual career, which was surprising to me because he didn't start out with any interest in television at all—in fact, it seemed closer, as he recounts it, to disdain. Most of the subjects of this book panted for the medium they were trying to master; Simon tolerated it.

Simon was a newspaperman, even a newspaper *type*—he resembled many of the men (this is mostly a male archetype) I met during my years as a newspaper journalist: gruff, smart, deeply class conscious, and quick to outrage. He entered television accidentally, and mainly, he said, as a way to sell his books. But he's quick to deflect suggestions that he was any kind of auteur; he frequently emphasized the collaborative nature of his work (and particularly the way *he* works), and indeed you will see that much of his day-to-day consists of wearing down collaborators and higher-ups. By all evidence, Simon is a brutally effective arguer—it may be his core talent. Still, he is clearly the main driver of his work: everything about *The Wire*, or the two books he wrote and

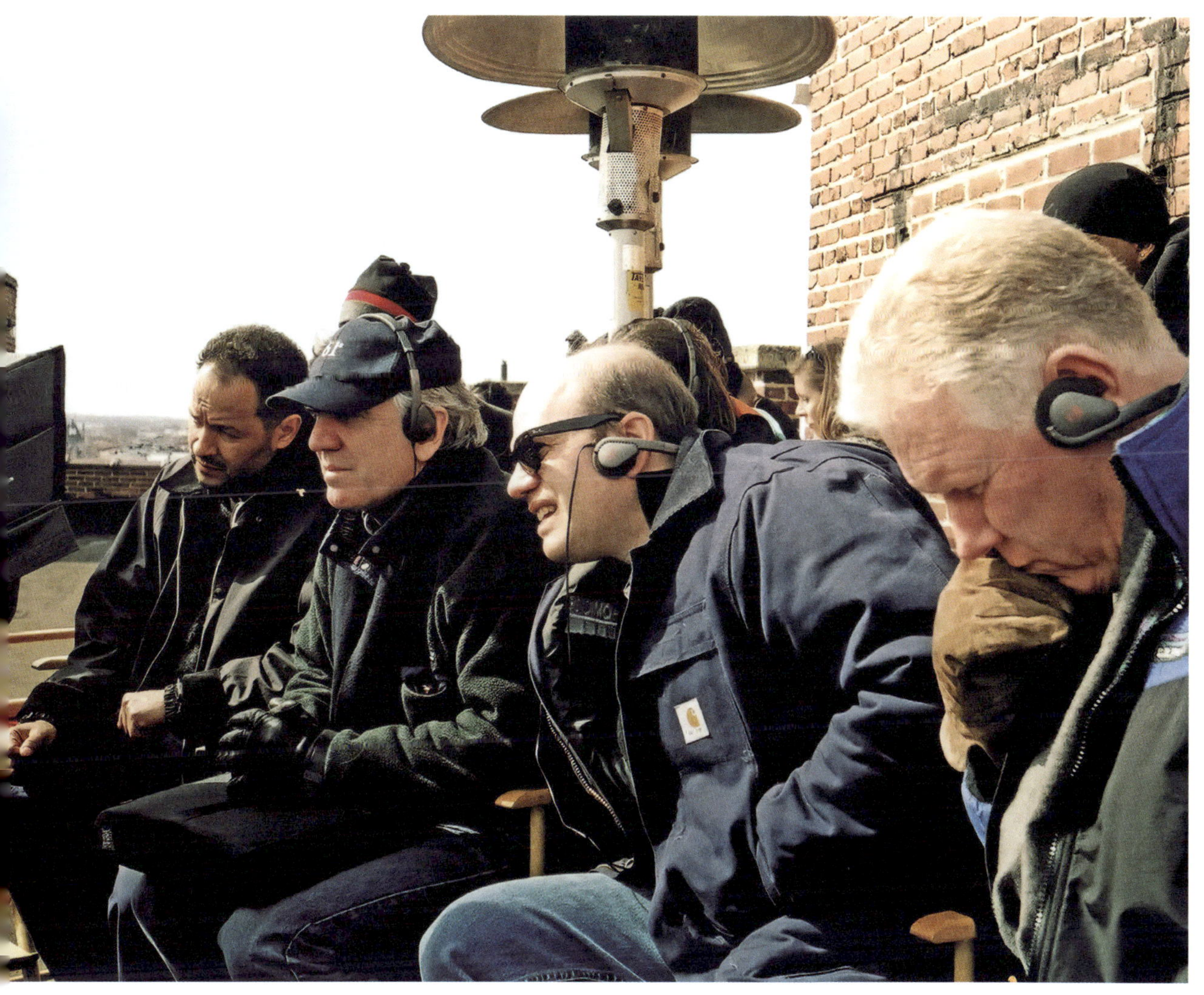

David Simon (in sunglasses) on the set of *The Wire*.

co-wrote, *Homicide* and *The Corner*, or the many series that followed *The Wire*—*Treme*, *The Deuce*, *Generation Kill*, and others—seem very much a product of a sensibility rooted in urban realism and a specific, nineteenth-century-style talent for telling detail- and character-rich stories as vehicles for political and moral critique.

A Hard-Boiled Childhood Like for so many others, his sensibility was largely inherited, in this case from a father who had romantic (and frustrated) ideas about journalism. "My dad wanted to be a newspaperman," Simon said. Instead, "he got hired to do PR in the Brill Building.[1] Brill was music. Good steady job. But he had friends who were newspapermen. The guy he really cultivated was the religion reporter of *The New York Times*, a man they called Pat but whose real name was Irving Spiegel. Pat could recite Shakespeare in Yiddish—on a table if people weren't paying enough attention

1. The Brill Building was the legendary home of a crush of Tin Pan Alley songwriters.

to him. He was a fucking character. My mom could barely tolerate him." But Simon was entranced, and inhaled all the usual hard-boiled texts—"Dashiell Hammett, Damon Runyon. It was in the ether of my house. We would parse this shit around the table." Simon's voice—the way he talks, the way he writes—seems almost lifted from these books.

When he got a job at his local paper, *The Baltimore Sun*, he was assigned to the police beat, where he got to cover, as he called it, "the mass production of murder. So now I had a canvas. In Baltimore they had, I guess it was 250 murders a year. I was always calling at ten at night, trying to get those angry Irish bastards to put up with me, and tell me if there had been a couple of murders, like give me some details. You know, motherfucker, just give me enough to write three paragraphs? I'm trying to cover my ass here. I had the four to twelve shift on the morning paper, you don't want to get beat by the afternoon paper. I started going to the unit and just hanging out.

"Christmas Eve, after I'd gotten to know a few of them, I walked up with a bottle, about nine, after the bosses had gone. I'm Jewish, I don't care it's Christmas Eve. So I had some good whiskey and paper cups. And we sat around bullshitting and they started telling good stories of . . . you know, Christmas murders. Which is like a whole subgenre of degeneracy. It was funny, absurd. I wrote it up as a column, 'Christmas Eve in the Homicide Unit,' which is almost its own punch line.

"When I sat down to write the column—well, first let me explain that the *Sun*, like most papers, had an honorific policy. Everybody was Mr. or Detective or Sergeant.

"But you're talking about a unit where the guys know each other by their last names at best. You didn't want to stumble over your newspaper's ornate style."

Simon was reflexively a finger-flipping guy, but leaving out the honorifics, this simple act of subversion, was enormously productive: it opened up a creative world to him. "By starting to say fuck it to quotes, shedding all its newspaper conventions, it really started to read like good fiction—that was a revelation.[2] After the column had already run, the paper's management figured out that I had taken out the honorifics. An editor comes back to me mad, says, 'You pulled a fast one on us.' "

Simon took a leave to write a book in that style. The book was *Homicide: A Year on the Killing Streets*, which, to his surprise, sold to television and became the NBC show *Homicide*. Simon himself didn't watch much television—old movies and sports mostly—but the book had been sent to Barry Levinson, the Baltimore director. "I think NBC had turned Levinson down for a show based on *Diner*," Simon told me. "They said, 'You got anything else?' Levinson [and his people] had gotten my book over the transom and read it and showed it to the network, and boom."

They asked Simon to write the pilot for *Homicide*, which he declined. He was already writing (co-writing, with one of his police sources named Ed Burns) another book, *The Corner*, this one set on a drug-infested block in Baltimore, which was much more important to him. He only wanted the series to work so he could sell more books. At least this is the way he describes it—television meant pretty much nothing to him. I asked him whether the prospect of writing for a new medium intimidated him. He paused. He was impatient with any talk of craft as especially relevant to his trajectory, but I kept pressing.[3]

"I looked at a couple of scripts. One thing I sensed was pacing. Every line has to justify itself. You don't start at the beginning of scenes, you don't end at the end, you come in late and leave early—all the things you could intuit if you were writing and saying, *How does this work?* People go to school for this shit.

"And I was thinking, *If this show runs for a couple of years, I'll sell some books. But if I fuck up the pilot* . . . I didn't know a guy could come up behind me and fix it, which is what I now know is how you do it. I said, 'Never mind me writing TV. Get somebody who knows what they're doing.' I said, 'You know, when you have five or six scripts and I can see what you've done with the characters, come back and maybe I'll try my hand at one.' So they did."

Tom Fontana, who was the showrunner of *Homicide*, told him to write an episode following, said Simon, "a case all the way from murder to death row. And being a police reporter, I said, 'Well, that's nineteen years of litigation.' But I didn't say no."

Simon and David Mills, a college friend, wrote the script for the episode in three weeks. "They [Fontana and the *Homicide* brass] showed it to NBC and NBC said, 'This is too depressing, we're not going to make this.' " But they gave the script to Robin Williams, whom Levinson had worked with before,[4] and asked him if he was interested in playing the father, as a guest star. Unexpectedly, he said yes. "So NBC said, 'Okay we'll shoot it now.' People like Robin Williams didn't do TV at the time. And the show pulled a thirty-four share."[5]

You hear enough of these stories, you realize how often fortune plays into success, at least as recounted by a teller humbly reconstructing his story from the top of the heap. But I wanted to know: Was he any good at this point?

Simon paused again. "Well, we were overwriting. I would write a paragraph that was too expositional. Tom would write *zzzz*'s next to it.

"I wasn't properly servicing the ensemble cast. This is the stuff you can never know until you're on the inside of a TV show. The script needed especially to service Robin Williams. When we wrote it, it didn't have Robin Williams. So it was more heavy with the detectives and the three kids who did the murder.

"David and I, being from newspapers, thought if 45 percent of your story went to rewrite, you're a fuckup. So we felt like, well, that sucked. David was sort of bummed about it. And then he talked to other people in LA who said, 'Run on that, man. Nobody gets that.' I can tell you now, being a showrunner, that if twenty of your sixty pages is filmed, you're getting another script. Because [it means] you can crackle, you know how to write a scene. Even if you might not be the interior voice of the show we're trying to make yet."

He got two thirds of his newspaper salary for one script. When they offered him a job, he took a buyout from the *Sun* and joined the *Homicide* staff. But—"I was still working on *The Corner*. I didn't think, *Oh well, now I'm in TV*. I thought I was going to go back to journalism. I'm making good TV penny working on a cop show based on a book in my town, I'm just nailing in boards. I'm happy to do it."

The Pivot One morning Tom Fontana gathered the staff of *Homicide* and showed them a test he had done—ten or so minutes—for a new cable channel called HBO. The show was *Oz*. "It's got a rape scene, a murder in the shower," said Simon. "And we said, 'They're gonna put that on television?' And Tom said, 'Yeah I think so.' "

You know what happened. Television was evolving in a way that completely altered the structure of the series form, and Simon was ready for it. "On HBO, it could be dark, profane; there are no advertisers to appease. We didn't have to write act-outs [the little cliff-hangers before a commercial break], you don't have to bring them back after the Lincolns"—he's talking about the car. "You just write an hour of TV."

Simon calls this moment, in TV-ese, "the pivot." You can't create anything unless your way of seeing is aligned with conditions on the ground, and now they were: there was suddenly a hunger for his noir-y groove and reportorial eye, which were perfectly matched with the morphing medium.[6] Things happened fast. Fontana helped him pitch a series based on *The Corner*. Simon told me he misunderstood what they were looking for and offered a fictional

2. See Gay Talese.

3. I was really fixated on Simon's artistic education because, as a journalist, I'd always had a fantasy about writing for television and didn't know if I'd be any good at it. Simon made the transition seem effortless, and maybe it was for him, or maybe at this point in his very successful career, it's just not as interesting to him as it was to me.

4. The movie was *Good Morning, Vietnam*.

5. Share refers to a percentage of the total audience watching TV at the time. The thirty-four in his memory was a little higher than the actual number, but the point was, the episode did really well.

6. This is as good a time as any to underline the fact that for work to be successful, it must match its moment in some way. Timing isn't everything, but it's a lot.

version of *The Corner*, which was, essentially, *The Wire*. They told him they wanted a docudrama-style series instead, with the material from his book, so that's what he gave them—"But again, all this to me is a way to sell books. [I think, *If they make* The Corner,] *I'm gonna sell a lot of copies of* The Corner *that I wouldn't otherwise sell to people. And I'll have a platform for a political argument I'm now trying to make.*" At this point, he was still, essentially, indifferent to television.

"The other thing that came out of the meeting was, 'We've noticed you're white, all the characters are Black. Do you have anybody you want to write with?' And I named some people. And I named Dave Mills, who was by this time on *LA Law* [and was African American]. And they jump out of their chair and say, 'You know Dave Mills?' So that kept me in TV."

And that's why when, on a panel one day, after *The Corner* had been aired, an executive at HBO asked him, "What else you got?" He already had an answer. "I just thought, *Well, I tried to sell you* The Wire *before. So now I'll really sell you* The Wire."

The Pitch "*The Wire* was half the opposition to what the underclass had built in America," said Simon. "And half what the underclass was building, which is the drug trade. The drug trade being a parable for people on the outs and how American institutions were now cracking under the strain of having to service two different realities: what was happening in the police department or the courthouse, and what was happening on the streets. We wanted to make things parallel."

Simon wrote a pitch for *The Wire* that is one of the great documents of the medium, a rich display of his persuasive power. It defined the show he wanted to make in brimstone rhetoric and laid out in a detailed nine-episode bible how he planned to get there, which is remarkably close to the show he ended up making. He brought in Ed Burns, his co-writer on *The Corner*—who Simon felt, from his reporting

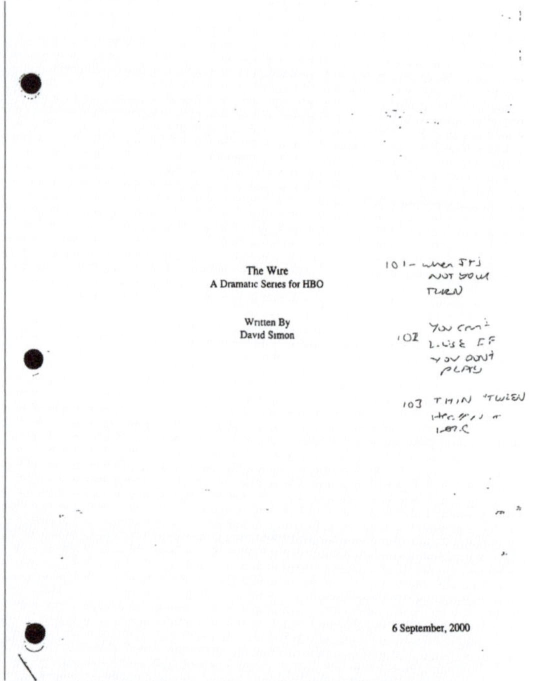

The Wire
A Dramatic Series for HBO

Written By
David Simon

6 September, 2000

Pitches for shows already commissioned, as this was, tend to be blueprints, but Simon's proposal is grander, a swing for the fences. It goes, "The great theme here is nothing less than a national existentialism: it is a police story set amid the dysfunction and indifference of an urban department, one that has failed to come to terms with the permanent nature of urban drug culture." And, "*The Wire* should be judged not merely as a descendent of *Homicide* or *NYPD Blue* but as a vehicle for making statements about the American city, and the American experiment."

The proposal lays out nine episodes and introduces characters. Some names are different—McNulty started out as McCardle, Stringer Bell was Stringy—and surveillance in the pitch's description was more front and center than it became—but what you most notice is how precisely Simon saw the show before he made it. If you're interested in *The Wire*, or in making television, it's illuminating and easily found online.

work, understood both cops and robbers as well as anyone—as his partner. He also felt that with Burns, he would be well served by having a "bounce"[7]—that is, he'd work better through ricochet than a solo effort and be a more effective creator if he had someone to tussle with.

He'd had to shaft Burns on the television iteration of *The Corner.* "I needed to bring David in on *The Corner*, so I basically had to deal Ed out in order to get it made. Ed wasn't too happy about that. For *The Corner* we had these pre-interviews at the beginning and the end, which were the only place we could get these systemic critiques of the drug war in. They were filmed in video, grainy, different from the film. I don't think it played precisely as we wanted it to, because when Chris Albrecht [his boss at HBO] got a look at the cuts, and he saw the first three minutes of the film were in black and white, he was like, 'No, fuck that. You know, we're not gonna have much of an audience anyway, but now you're really killing us.' So I lost that argument.[8]

"But I said to Ed, the parts we weren't able to do in *The Corner*, that's *The Wire*. *The Wire* is the why of the piece. Here's why the world's not working. So the same things that happen to McNulty [the cop protagonist] happened to D'Angelo [the drug dealer protagonist]." They loosely built the show on the scaffolding of a Baltimore drug case of Burns's that Simon had covered as a reporter.

Like a Novel Eventually Simon and Burns brought in the novelist George Pelecanos to collaborate on *The Wire* as well. ("And that was the beginning of hiring novelists. We realized we were making more of a novel than we were television.")

And they made the show. It was set in a ravaged section of Baltimore. Drug dealer versus cop, with its own stubbornly hard-to-understand patois, rich, complex characters, and a vividly imagined, wholly original street world. For those who stuck with it, the rewards were immense. The ratings weren't great, but HBO was patient. "Something funny happened," said Simon. "I wrote three scripts. And Carolyn Strauss [an HBO executive] said, 'I get it, I see what you're doing. It's getting better. It was a little slow, but it's getting better with every episode.'

"I thought, *Well, that's kind of how I read books.* The first three chapters of *Moby-Dick,* you know he goes to the town, there's a maritime sermon, he shares a bed with this guy with a lot of tattoos, you don't get to see the white whale. But that's not American television. So, like, I don't give a shit. This is how I know how to tell a story."

Bait and Switch Then before viewers had even made it to the end of that first season, Simon pulled a switch. He yanked the show away from the setting he and his collaborators had so carefully created and shifted its focus. He'd had this upending in mind the whole time, but he hadn't told HBO and he hadn't told his collaborators. They weren't happy. In a sense, they'd completed their storyline at the end of the first season, but Burns and other writers felt there was still plenty to mine and that the viewers (few as they were) would feel betrayed. But Simon was insistent.

"I knew if we got to a second season, we'd have to slice the city in a different way. Or we'd just become a cop show. I didn't say that to them until they gave the re-up for a second season. That's when I said, 'If we just keep chasing the drugs, the show is incremental. And we can run as long as we can interest people in the cops and robbers. But I don't want to spend five years of my life doing that. This is the time to start critiquing what's gone wrong in America.'

7. I came across the word *bounce* as a noun to describe a collaborator—a person to argue with, who makes you better—in the book *Difficult Men,* which describes the making of *The Wire, The Sopranos, Mad Men,* and other works of its era. It provided an excellent history of *The Wire* to read alongside Simon's version. I love this phrase, and recognize that bouncing, if I can turn it into a verb—with all its back and forth, push and pull—is really the only way I know how to do anything. But more of that later.

8. I had two very long conversations with Warren Beatty, trying to persuade him to be in this book (I hoped to talk about *Shampoo,* which I knew had a long and contentious history). He was amenable until he wasn't, but I listened to an only briefly interrupted, wild, charming, and combative two-and-a-half-hour, two-phone-call monologue—these days (and maybe always) his real art form is conversation. But per David Simon and this chapter, he talked about the advice Stanley Kubrick gave him, which was that the key creative act of movies was argument. And that you should have an argument every day. With at least three people. He thought this book should be about arguing—or, at least creative tension, which wasn't a terrible idea.

It was the first time the show was going to veer from being a straight war critique to be thematic about issues of urbanity. It was the bigger argument. And the next thing has to be the death of work . . . the idea that union-wage jobs, the things that used to propel a city toward middle-class sobriety and affluence, were dying. The corners are a factory because the factory is gone.

"And that coincided with reporting I had attempted to do, in a book that I had attempted to write, independent of the other stuff going on." Simon felt that that book would be a backup plan if *The Wire* were to fail. "I was looking for book number three, on the death of work. I had tried to get permission from the GM plant in Baltimore to let me in for a year and let me work the line. Then I asked Bethlehem Steel. GM wouldn't let me in, Beth Steel wouldn't let me in.

"Now I'm faced with season 2 of *The Wire*. I know GM won't let me in, so I think, *Let's do the port, longshoremen, and what happened to them*. I came into the writers' meeting. I had to sell George and Ed on the idea that we're walking away from the inner city. I told them, the inner city will still be there, we'll carry it as a B line. But the main storyline will be the port. And it laid there like a bagel. Ed thought there's so much more to say about the Barksdales [the main drug ring]. I said, 'Yeah, there's a lot. But if we don't expand the palate of the show now, people are always going to credit us for being a crime show and nothing more.' So basically I argued and argued with Ed. But then I went into HBO and pitched it." HBO agreed.

"At that point I'm also thinking I'll get to the school system, get to journalism. Basically, the decision to go to the port meant the show had moved in an irrevocable direction. Once you pivot once, you have to keep turning. The only one I knew we were going to do was city hall. We had to do that one pretty quick because we need to see decisions go up the ladder fast. So season 3 would have to be city hall. I didn't know if we were going to get more seasons.[9] But we were just always laying pipe for where we want to go. I knew the last season, if you told me it was the last season, was going to be a critique of media. What we pay attention to, that seemed like the last rational question. Like if the audience wants more bang bang, I could give a fuck. We tried to make the violence more abrupt. We didn't wound a lot of guys, unless we really needed the wounded. We didn't want violence to prevail as the currency. I've read interviews with David Chase[10] where he was saying the same thing."

Maybe Simon could take that risk because he was so uninvested in television's conventions. And because he was, at heart, a polemicist—that's what really drove him, and if there's anything that seems most true about creation, really successful creation, it's that it has to at least feel authentic to the creator. And then it was also true that he could root his story in an argument that in someone else's hands might have felt arid or haranguing because he happened also to be a master storyteller (perhaps that was what he'd gotten from Runyon and co.) with a beautifully trained eye (learned in journalism) and a deeply held moral bent (honed at family dinners). He also had good taste—he'd brought in collaborators who were literary masters. And, of course, his idea was smart and original, especially for television, and happened to lend itself perfectly to the shifting conventions of television drama. For all those reasons, it worked out. He made the show he wanted to make, and it turned out to be as good a show as anyone has ever made on TV.

Lessons from a Showrunner Meanwhile, back in the writers' room, here's how it works—

"It's democratic until it isn't. You try to win the room on the arguments. You try to have the room turn against a bad idea, a redundant idea, an idea that's not thematic to what you're trying to say.

9. Simon had to constantly plead for renewal, but at no time did he have to slug harder than when he went in to beg after the third season, when the HBO brass thought the show was finished. *Difficult Men* describes this as "the pitch of his life." Wrote Brett Martin, its author: "When Simon left, Albrecht turned to Strauss. 'He was like, "We've got to do this,"' [Strauss] said. 'And I was like "duh."'" Simon was impassioned and relentless. Albrecht: "Honestly, I think it was easier to do the fourth season than to have to call David up to have another meeting."

10. David Chase is the creator of *The Sopranos*.

11. The "vacants" were the abandoned buildings where the drug warlords had buried bodies.

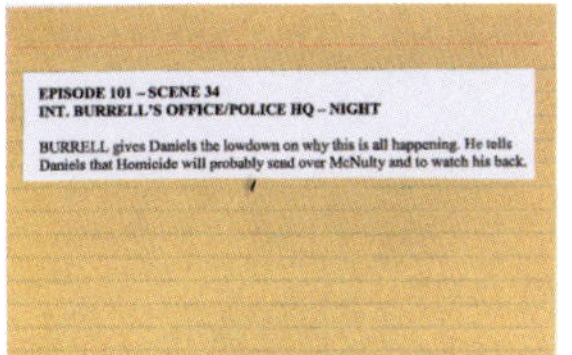

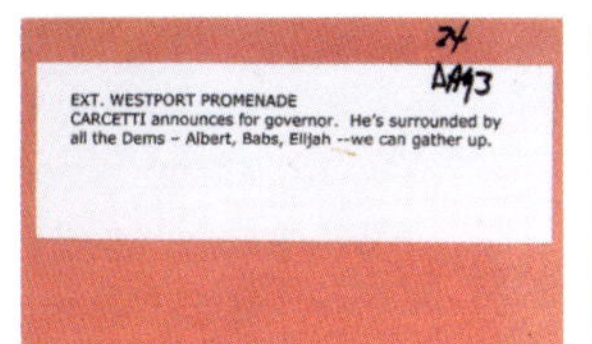

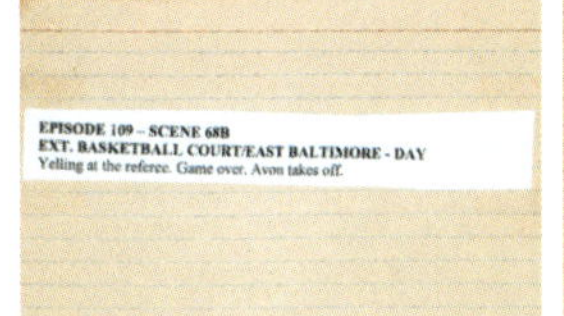

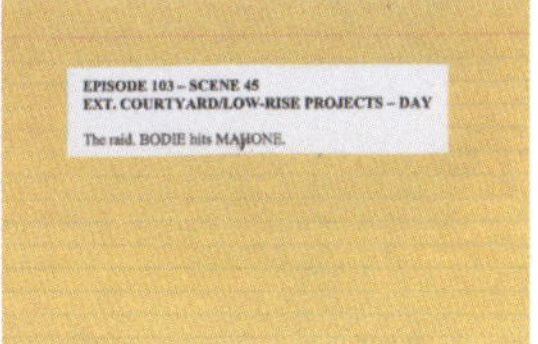

"Beat sheets" for *The Wire*. Basically, an outline in bits and pieces.

"Now if you've given it a day and a half and you're still arguing over whether Stringer [lieutenant drug kingpin] should be taking the SIM cards out of his phone, the showrunner has to say, 'We're going this way.' After which, that may solve the argument. Or you may get a six-page memo from Ed Burns explaining that you made the wrong decision.

"For instance, Ed did not want to soften Bodie [a key character in the drug mob]. Ed wanted Bodie to kill Wallace [a sympathetic boy], because Bodie was beyond redemption. He wanted Bodie to be as sociopathic as Marlo [a drug chief] throughout the run of the show. And I thought, *Wouldn't it be great to have the guy who killed the kid you cared about, if you are compelled over time to see him as as much a trapped animal as Wallace?* To this day Ed was like, 'You ruined that character.'

"The most difficult question in TV writing is, Why are you doing the show? And if you can answer that question, you usually answer what the show should be. Whether you have a hit or not, if they wheel a fucking semitruck of money up to your driveway and say, 'Please give us three more seasons of we don't care what, just keep it coming,' you have to be able to look at them and say, 'I don't have three seasons. I have other stories.'

"Could we have done one more season of *The Wire*? Yeah. But that was not the dynamic. We never pulled numbers.

"We could have done one on juvenile justice. There's a miniseries in that. But it was incremental to what *The Wire* was saying.

"There was one season I would have loved to have done. David Mills would go to the Broadway Market over in southeast. It used to be white working class. But now, Mills said, everyone was speaking Spanish. And he said, 'We should do immigration.' As soon as he said it, I was like, *He's right.* But we had to pull the bodies out of the vacants.[11] We couldn't go back. Plus, I would have had to return to HBO and go, 'Thank you for the last two seasons, I got one more.' I never brought it to HBO. We were prepping season 5. We couldn't put those scripts aside. But I realized that if we'd done a whole story within the culture of immigration, we'd have said something fresh about American dysfunction.

"There was one idea I did bring them. Once we did the city hall season, which I thought we did really well, I thought we could do a show around Carcetti [a politician who becomes mayor, then at the very end, governor], who was to me a completely viable political character. I wrote a pilot, and sent it to HBO. I said I would like to run a show concurrently with *The Wire*. Called *The Hall*, about city hall. After four years as mayor, of which two would have been the first two years of *The Hall*, [Carcetti] prepares to run for governor or senator. *The Hall* and *The Wire* would alternate. There would be different time frames going on at the same time, moving from Maryland to Washington. It was like, 'Man, what we'll be able to do by showing the interconnection. Oh man, this is fucking great.'

"And Chris said, 'You know, I can afford one show nobody's watching.' That was his answer."

42

GEORGE SAUNDERS

It's Your Book, You Can Do Whatever You Want

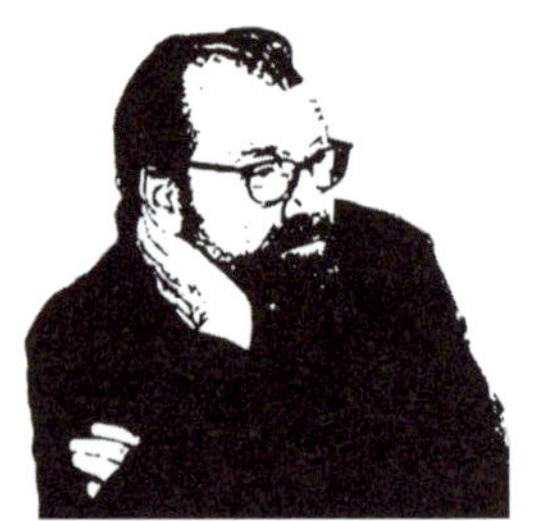

OCCUPATION: Writer

WORK DISCUSSED: *Lincoln in the Bardo* (2017)

BORN: 1958

I WAS A FAN of George Saunders's journalism before I knew he wrote fiction. I read a lot of journalism, and George was making some moves in his work that no one else was, mostly owing to the fantastic control he had in a voice that was always sharp, often caustic, and usually very funny. When I eventually found my way to his short stories, first collected in *CivilWarLand in Bad Decline* and then, later, in *Tenth of December*, I found they were even more inventive than his nonfiction—more biting and satiric, but also so giving that I became devoted. His technique was dazzling, but he also just seemed from his prose somehow to be a really good guy. Later I found out he was a writer other writers worship and want to imitate. I wasn't surprised.

But then it wasn't until I found myself reading *Lincoln in the Bardo*—a novel urgently passed around among people I trust—that I began to fully appreciate the extent of his creative powers, which are gargantuan. *Lincoln in the Bardo*, which won the Booker Prize, is a really weird book, even weirder than his stories. But it's a book that explodes with ambition, and it's worth saying at the outset that all of its odd and original fictional conceits—and they are many—are at the service of a straightforward and almost unbearable humanity. Some readers I know were exhausted by the book's reach, but for me its innovations are not just novel but entirely satisfying—emotionally, intellectually, all of it.

How did such a book come to be? George had never written a novel before. This one wandered a winding path over decades, some of it surfacing in a short story and then a play, neither of them published. All along, he kept pushing it aside, sometimes allowing it to just drift off, and sometimes as a forceful act of abnegation. Eventually the novel just seemed to will itself to happen, though that's not to say it wasn't also a battle to get there.

Here's what you ought to know about the book to understand our conversation: *Lincoln in the Bardo* is set in a graveyard, narrated by a chorus of people who don't quite know that

Notes, January 27, 2015:

I feel like everything is solid and good to page 140. L is back and V/B have just told W to go inside and see "what he wishes for you."

And now I have some choices. Here are the bits that seem to want to come soon (although I don't know in what order yet):

W goes into L. Some transition to either:

(a) The section(s) that begin "Blame and Guilt are the twin furies" – the stuff about what killed W and were the Lincolns somehow to blame.

(b) The history sections, starting with "Willie thrashed and screamed" and proceeding through to L leaving the coffin at the chapel and the line about him trying to go to Heaven. (Which Willie hears. This could be the spur to his decision to Go.)

The crowd has reassembled. The new testimonies, concluding with Mrs. Wright talking about Litzie, and then the short chapter that says L has heard none of this. | Good.

L has that self-argument that leads to him pronouncing W "meat." Imbedded in this is L's history section re the embalming. Coming out of this, W hears "meat" and is leveled by that, reduced to passivity.

Section where V/B urge everyone to come in and inhabit L, to persuade him of…what?

(a) To pick W up. Idea is, this is W's wish.

(b) (This is better, I think): V/B are desperately trying to get L to stick around long enough so that he will once again have the thought that initially inspired them – the idea that L's fondest wish for Willie is for him to be safe in some better place.

Tendrils suddenly speak, willing to negotiate. Rev bargains them into unbanding W, then grabs him and races off, to the chapel. Doesn't make it. He is taken. They all tear into the hive, get W free.

Willie goes. (When? Why?)

**

So what's the story?

Willie wants Lincoln to take him out of there. But inhabiting his father, he sees that he is dead, or meat. He is not going to go back home, ever. This renders him passive and despondent. Meanwhile L is about to leave the crypt. V urges everyone to go into L and try and delay him, just long enough for him to cycle through his thoughts and get back to that earlier one about Willie going somewhere safe and beautiful. They all go in. No dice. Great heartbreak for all. Lincoln leaves. Tendrils talk. Rev tricks them, races off, is taken. They rescue Willie. One more encounter with L, maybe at the gate. Whatever it is, it convinces W and he GOES. Which induces a crazy chain-reaction. Good stuff: Bevins decides to go, does one more uber-listing of the things of the world, which ends in: Goodbye. Devil/God comes to see what the heck has been going on. Levels with Vollman re his wife. Vollman refutes him. Devil drags off Stone and one more. Maybe ends with Vollman's speech again?

Note from George Saunders to George Saunders, a perfect illustration of the questions novelists ask as they trudge their way through their books.

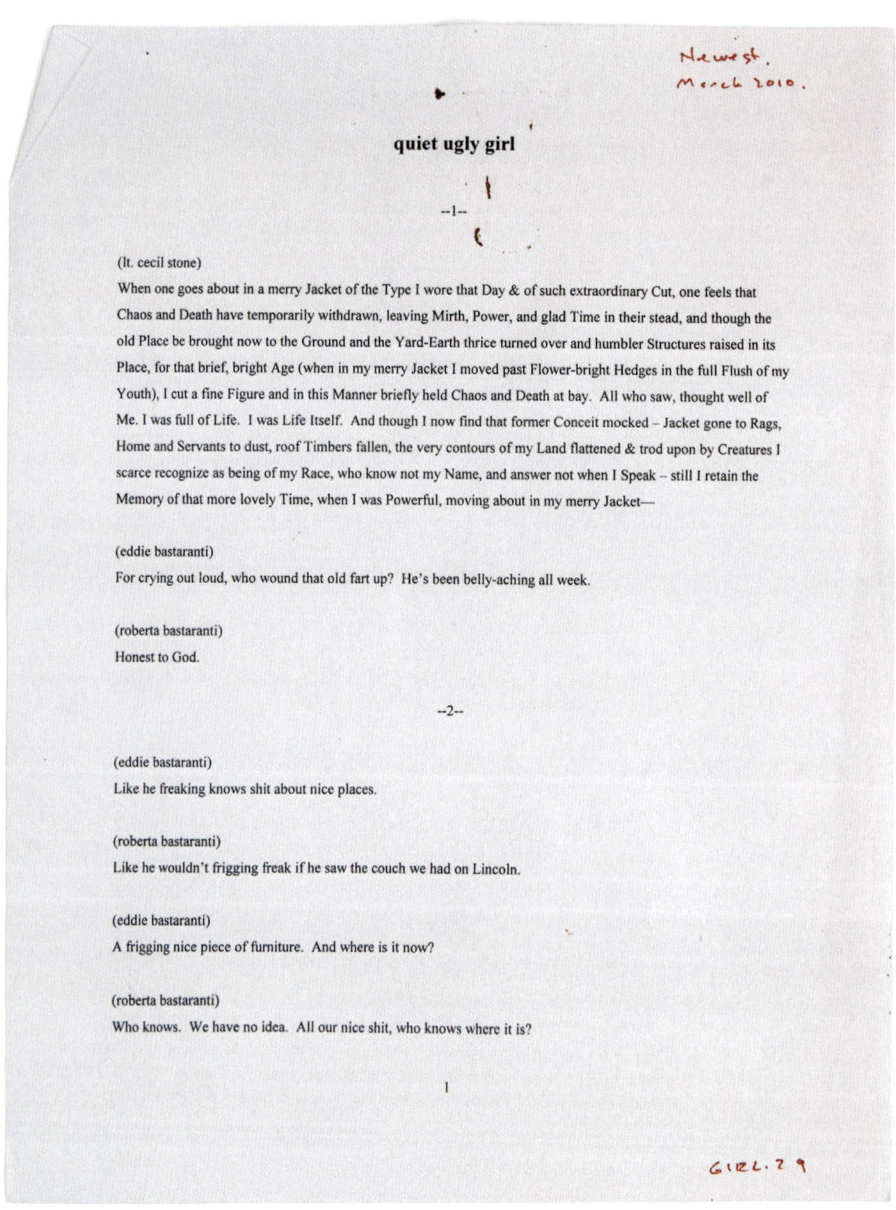

Newest.
March 2010.

quiet ugly girl

--1--

(lt. cecil stone)

When one goes about in a merry Jacket of the Type I wore that Day & of such extraordinary Cut, one feels that Chaos and Death have temporarily withdrawn, leaving Mirth, Power, and glad Time in their stead, and though the old Place be brought now to the Ground and the Yard-Earth thrice turned over and humbler Structures raised in its Place, for that brief, bright Age (when in my merry Jacket I moved past Flower-bright Hedges in the full Flush of my Youth), I cut a fine Figure and in this Manner briefly held Chaos and Death at bay. All who saw, thought well of Me. I was full of Life. I was Life Itself. And though I now find that former Conceit mocked – Jacket gone to Rags, Home and Servants to dust, roof Timbers fallen, the very contours of my Land flattened & trod upon by Creatures I scarce recognize as being of my Race, who know not my Name, and answer not when I Speak – still I retain the Memory of that more lovely Time, when I was Powerful, moving about in my merry Jacket—

(eddie bastaranti)

For crying out loud, who wound that old fart up? He's been belly-aching all week.

(roberta bastaranti)

Honest to God.

--2--

(eddie bastaranti)

Like he freaking knows shit about nice places.

(roberta bastaranti)

Like he wouldn't frigging freak if he saw the couch we had on Lincoln.

(eddie bastaranti)

A frigging nice piece of furniture. And where is it now?

(roberta bastaranti)

Who knows. We have no idea. All our nice shit, who knows where it is?

1

GIRL.29

Lincoln in the Bardo began, in a sense, as a short story . . .

they're dead and refuse to surrender to the beyond. Abraham Lincoln's son Willie has just died, and during the course of the book is visited—and held—by his grieving father. The plot involves the chorus, led by three dead men who speak in their own odd version of period dialect and set off visually and theatrically, trying to coax Willie out of the Bardo (the liminal place where all the characters have congregated) and into heaven,

4808659C4220

A Lincoln in the Bardo
George Saunders

play in play: to be ready 1 "CIRK".

ACT ONE

Graveyard.

Day.

Evidence of a brutal winter storm: snowdrifts, fallen branches, snapped-off trees.

Two crypts on the side of a steep wooded hill: one (stage-left) labeled BOWERS, the other (stage-right) labeled CARROLL.

Offstage: the sound of children singing a hymn.

A child-sized coffin on a cart is wheeled onstage by a GRAVEDIGGER and two ASSISTANTS.

The children's TEACHER follows behind the cart, on the arm of a tall, gaunt man, who looks as if he has accidentally attached himself to the group. This is ABRAHAM LINCOLN. He does not look like "our" Abraham Lincoln – just an awkward, unkempt older man, distracted and undone by grief.

Offstage, the children end their song.

The TEACHER turns nervously to LINCOLN.

TEACHER
Sir. If I may. He was…the most loveable boy…bright, sensible, sweet-tempered, gentle-mannered. So bravely and beautifully *himself* in all situations and circumstances. His leading trait was—several of us were discussing this, sir—a fearless and kindly frankness, as willing that everything should be as different as it pleased…but resting unmoved in his own conscious single-heartedness. I found myself studying him irresistibly, as one of the sweet problems of childhood that the world is blessed with in rare places.
(beat)
There was a greatness in him. We all felt it.

LINCOLN
Yes.

TEACHER
Please know that you are in our prayers, sir.

The TEACHER exits.

ASSISTANT #1 unlocks the Carroll crypt and opens the door. The GRAVEDIGGER steps over for a word.

GRAVEDIGGER
As a father myself – well, the thought of it. Nothing worse than the loss of a child, sir. The greatest blow. How does one bear up? Their little bodies, and so forth—so precious! I honestly don't think I could—

This visibly pains LINCOLN but the GRAVEDIGGER blunders on.

1

. . . and then took form as a play . . .

where he needs to go for his own everlasting good. Meanwhile, since some of the story is true (Willie's death, and the ambience of the Civil War, and Abraham Lincoln's deliberations at the time about what to do about it), large parts of the book are given over to snippets of historical accounts, most real but some made up. It takes many pages to understand what's going on—it's not even immediately clear who's speaking. But eventually

LINCOLN IN THE BARDO, CHAPTER XVI. (A FRAGMENT)

An exceedingly tall and unkempt fellow was making his way toward us through the darkness.

hans vollman

The boy had been delivered only that day...

roger beavins iii

The gentleman seemed lost. Several times he stopped, looked about, retraced his steps, reversed course.

hans vollman

...

Bursting out of the doorway, the lad took off running toward the man, look of joy on his face.

roger beavins iii

Which turned to consternation, when the man failed to sweep him up in his arms as, one gathered, must have been their custom.

the reverend everly thomas

The boy instead passed through the man, as the man continued to walk toward the white stone home...

roger beavins iii

He was fifteen yards away now, headed directly toward us.

roger beavins iii

The Reverend suggested we yield the path.

hans vollman

The Reverend having strong feelings about the impropriety of allowing oneself to be passed through.

roger beavins iii

The man reached the white stone home and let himself in with a key, the lad then following him in.

hans vollman

...

The man slid the box out of the slot in the wall, and set it down upon the floor.

roger beavins iii

And opened it. . . He emitted a single, heartrending sob.

hans vollman

Or gasp. I heard it as more of a gasp. A gasp of recognition. . . . as if to say: Here he is again, my child, just as he was. I have found him again, he was so dear to me.

the reverend everly thomas

Who was still so dear.

hans vollman

Yes.

roger beavins iii

The loss having been quite recent.

. . . until it finally became a novel. This is a tiny slice of a chapter (with minor internal cuts) in which Lincoln visits the cemetery to view his dead son. Vollman, Beavins, and Thomas are the book's chorus, speaking from the graveyard.

you figure it out.

George and I talked during the period around the publication of *A Swim in a Pond in the Rain*, a book that arose out of classes he taught at Syracuse University about how to write and read a short story. As such (or maybe he's like this all the time), he was very interested in trying to interrogate his own method and state of mind as the book evolved, which were still vivid in his recollection.

GEORGE SAUNDERS: I was visiting Washington and driving in a car with my kids and wife and her cousin Courtney. We passed the Oak Hill Cemetery, and Courtney offhandedly mentioned that Lincoln had gone in there after Willie's death and held him—like, you know, the pietà—and the Lincoln Memorial kind of cross fired in my mind. I thought that was beautiful, but you have an idea that's one circle, and then you have the way you're working at the moment. I couldn't imagine any intersection between those two. I was writing the stories in *CivilWarLand* at that time. I could see maybe doing a sarcastic version of the Lincoln story, but that didn't really appeal to me. So I let it sit, but also I found myself casually researching it. That was it.

And then some years later, I was living in a sweet little town called Pittsford, up on the Erie Canal. And there was a little pioneer cemetery and library we could walk to, and it was just heaven. Somebody in the town had self-published a book of historical photos of people, like playing croquet on the lawn, so you had the really cool experience of being able to walk by these old houses and know who built them. You'd go by the graveyard, and you'd see the names of the people who were playing croquet on the lawn. And then I started to think I'd want to write something that captures the feeling of being in one village for two hundred years, because that was new to me. I grew up in a suburb. One day we went to hear the Kronos Quartet, and listening to the music, I just started this kind of mental fantasy of a book set in that graveyard. I had the idea that all the people who ever lived in that town who were buried there were still around and they had a job, which was, whenever somebody new died in town, they had to do a sort of collective group monologue on his or her life, just summing it up. And that there would be a young woman who was not very pretty and had some weird mannerisms, had a rough life, never married, she went through life as a local joke, and it was she who died. So the idea was, okay, all these people who knew her at different stages of her life were going to be cross talking. I had this notion at the time—it was the days of the early internet, when they had those chat rooms and I thought they looked cool—you had a fragment of a line,

HOW HE FOUND HIS VOICE

GEORGE SAUNDERS: It was a little existential, you know? I was thirty-two years old and basically I thought, *Why does my prose not excite me?* And then: *Okay, what do you want not to sound like?* Anything that was normal or banal, like normal English sentences that anybody can write, I didn't like those. If a sentence sounded mundane, I would freakify it or cut it. I was saying to myself, *Go ahead and be a little weird*. I goofed around with some poems, just writing little Seussian things—doggerel. And the poems had more life in them than anything I was writing.

Compression was key for me. I found you could make yourself sound more like yourself by making really hard choices where you eliminate everyday phrases. Like, "On the way to work, I ate an apple." Well, maybe if the next sentence is at work, you can cut the first phrase. Small things like that—just a series of moves that got internalized. I had a certain sound in my head; I could just hear it. So I started fucking with that. And one of the ways I did it was I put those stories in theme parks, and then even if I was doing some sort of version of Hemingway, it was kind of funny. The clouds hung low over the Virgin Mary theme park!

I never really had a plan about those stories. I just wanted them not to suck. So if they started to become too familiar, I would just disrupt them. And that disruption became the driver. It was a long process and it paid off great, so that's why it was hard to move away from it with this book. You know, like, leave the party with he who brung you?

then somebody would interrupt.

I started goofing around with that. There are ghosts who had lowercase names, and they were chatting about this girl who had just died that night. So I had about a hundred pages of this story I called "Quiet Ugly Girl."

I worked a lot on it, and I really liked it. But it basically didn't work. It had nice riffs and nice tonalities—the interrupting I really liked—but I couldn't figure out the driver. So what, you know, she died? We're watching *Doctor Zhivago* now, and that has some great forward storytelling. This didn't. I couldn't get any purchase on who she was, or why I would want to tell this story. I finally just let it fade away.

And by the way, I was not thinking at all of Lincoln at this time. In fact, when I was writing the book, I never made the connection back to this story. I look back on it now, and it seems like it's kind of all laid out in front of me, but all those years, I never thought to put Lincoln into that graveyard until really late in the game.

So, wait, no, I'm getting ahead of myself.

A Decade Passes About ten years later, I was thinking about Lincoln again, and I was still stuck on the nonintersection of those sets—the material and my own voice. If you look at *CivilWarLand*, part of the charm is that you and I are on the same page and I'm winking at you in every sentence, ready to tell you how to regard the fictive world, which is a little below us and a little askew, and we can have fun making that world, and then quickly, instantaneously comparing it to the real world. But the Lincoln book would have to be much less ironic, more traditional, and you know, novelistic, and I just couldn't do it. So I thought, *Well, maybe I can do it some other way. Maybe in a play I could do it.* I was trying to give myself permission to use a different kind of language that was a little less edgy.

[I never wrote a play before.] I went through it many times, and I could never get it into fighting shape. But every time I went away from it, I thought, *Oh, I know there's something there.* I did hundreds of drafts, I have boxes of them.

I mean, you know, one of the things about revising is that I'm never a hundred percent sure something is good. Once you send it and someone approves of it, then maybe it goes to 87 percent.

And though I really didn't like a lot of it—my version of theatricalized language—I thought maybe if it had good actors? And nice sets, you know?

But the other thing I was thinking—I actually wrote this across one of the drafts of this play: "RUN AWAY." On New Year's Day I look back to see what I worked on during the year. And one New Year's I wrote: "RUN AWAY, DON'T TOUCH IT."

When I wrote those words, I was as close to pissed off at myself as I've ever been in writing. Like no, just, fuck, why are you doing this?

The one thing I'm pretty good at is being really honest with myself about my moment-to-moment excitement. And with both these projects, what happened is I got to a certain point and the big narrative ball wasn't rolling anymore. You know, it starts feeling just like typing. I always picture it like a river that's really tight and fast and then it gets wide and slow. And at some point it gets so wide and slow that it's a pond, and then a marsh. And then bleh.

When it comes to time wasters, I've got a thick skin. I had a teacher who said once, "If a young writer could know the difference between the stories he thinks he should write and the stories he should write, he'd save himself about twenty years." I'm still trying to save myself those twenty years. I'm pretty ruthless about that. You put the time in, you earn the right to tell it to piss off.

So I just wrote those words across it, and it felt really good.

1. The contract he makes with himself grants him permission to fuck up. So many of these artists employ similar means to psych themselves out—working in longhand so they can write freer, making a version of a painting they know they will paint over—building failure, or the possibility of failure, into the process. The mind seems pretty easy to trick. Also, fear of commitment is clearly as real in art as it is in love.

2. "How does the place work?" is such a fundamental question and applies to every medium in its own way—a novel, a portrait, a poem.

3. So many times George wrestles with sacrificing a part for the sake of a whole. It's one of the more wrenching struggles, as I know from my experience as a painter who screws up so many paintings by lacking the discipline to kill what needs to be killed for the painting to live.

Like, *Ugh, fuck, gosh, shoot. That was a close one.*

But I was still reading about Lincoln because the idea still interested me.

And Seven or Eight Years More Okay, so more time passes. *Tenth of December* was coming out. I'd finished it. And I had some version of, *All right, look, man, you're over fifty, you had a really good run.* You know how when you finish something in a certain mode, it begs you to come up with another mode? The *Tenth of December* mode was fully played out of me. Whenever I tried to start another story, I had the feeling like, *Now you're doing the same thing again.*

And you *do* want to do that Lincoln thing. You *don't* want to do that play. God, no. So why can't you do this? What's the problem? Oh, it's too vast. It's too beautiful. It's about love. These were actually not good answers for why I shouldn't do it. It felt like it could be the moment where I as an artist chickened out, and that was sad.

And then my mind went the other way. This is me talking to myself: *You were forty when your first book came out, it was a very hard-won victory that you got by going through a narrow doorway of a very weird voice that you've now perfected, why would you want to fuck that up?* This tone I was anticipating was a real departure. *You could become a laughingstock.*

A Pre-approved Waste of Time So I just said to myself, take the six months I was waiting to see *Tenth of December* published, a time when you're usually only worrying about the book that's coming out, and just goof around. If it's ridiculous, throw it away and nobody has to know you even started it. It was really important to make that kind of contract, where I could pre-approve the waste of time.[1]

And still, I thought, this was going to be just like the play. You're gonna throw it away. That kicked something open in my head—suddenly I was more play-full.

I looked back at the play. I plucked out a first monologue by a guy who had died, had had a bad marriage, his wife was a nymphomaniac. It felt a little misogynistic. I just flipped it in my mind and it went, *Okay, boom.* And I came up with the idea of the truncated consummation. [In *Lincoln*, the wife who had been a nymphomaniac in the play is instead a virgin.]

I didn't have a lot of thoughts about the book. I just grabbed a chunk of text, called it the start of the book, and began messing with it—very mechanical. I didn't think about the rules of the world I was creating, but a lot of the rules turned out to come from the play. The idea that somebody was trying to get Willie to leave was already worked out, I guess. I never thought of this before, but I think I had to use language I didn't like to work out some structures, and by the time I got around to using better language, the structures were in my memory to fill in. The angelic chorus in the book—that was in the play first. Lots of elements.

In the simplest essence, the story is, Lincoln was grieving. He comes to the graveyard, he interacts with the body. And Willie either goes to the right place or he doesn't. In an early draft, Lincoln comes three days in a row. But the material in the middle was boring. So one of the great simplifiers was no, he's just there one night, and he's gonna pick up the body like that early pietà image. In an early draft, I thought Willie could just stay. Or he could hang around for a while and for no particular reason leave. Which is no good. I had to put some risk in there, but I had to ask myself, *How does the place work?*[2] It always amounts to some almost sci-fi imposition that I make. And it's just trial and error, trial and error. I sometimes think structure is just finding a way to answer the question the flawed nature of your narrative causes the reader to ask. I'm trying to do a good job of imagining what the reader will stomach.

One of the first things I wrote was a monologue that never made it in.[3] It was Lincoln and two senators from Illinois who were taking the coffin from the chapel to the crypt. And it was funny—almost Gogolian in the way that these senators were kind of counterpoints. One was strict and the other was verbose. And

I finally just plucked it out because it was in a nineteenth-century guise and it just didn't fit. It took all the wind out of the sails and made it pretend. I didn't want this to be a pretend book, or a satire. I liked the section. It's a funny, funny section, but I had to say, *Okay, we're now in a different world where you, George, Mr. Proud of Being a Stylist, is going to have to stand down a bit.*

There was one draft that was a little sad and maudlin and straight. I had these barons—they were actually in "Quiet Ugly Girl," as a sort of dead 1950s Dean Martin kind of couple—and I loved them as comic relief because the draft was getting so self-important.

History, Made Up But maybe the biggest thing was that in these early drafts, the book was really heavy on ghosts, and something was missing. I realized it was just that all of the historical stuff that made it so compelling to me when I first heard about it had no way to get into the book. At some point I did three or four pages of very straight third-person Gore Vidal–esque Lincoln—basically Lincoln walked into the cemetery on a gloomy February night. But I looked at that, and thought, *Just no fucking way. That's not going to happen.* So I shut down that whole avenue, like in one day.

But it became clear I needed to get the historical stuff in there. I tried having the characters say it, which doesn't really make sense, like why would Lincoln be talking aloud about this party [an important scene in the book—a flashback to a party in the White House, while Willie lies sick upstairs in his bed]? I thought, *Well how did I know about that party?* Well, from those books. And a light came on: I'm like, *Can I quote directly from the books?*

And I remember just having a thought: *Well, it's your book. You can do whatever the fuck you want.*

So I put some of the historical accounts in, about the party, and it was really coming alive. Suddenly I could write about physical things and food and all that. And I was just curating it, excerpting from real sources. Then there were places where I'd been imagining a thing all these years and the excerpts didn't really do justice to the thing in my head. So I thought, *Well, can I make these up?* And I'm like, *Yeah, sure you can. That's what you're doing anyway, you know.*

And then it became, *Don't do that too much.* There was an important stage where I went through a big section of the book, toning down the made-up ones because they were sticking out like sore thumbs.

And a big moment for me—in one of the intermediate drafts I had the characters'

SO WHY CAN'T HE WRITE MUSIC THE WAY HE WRITES BOOKS?

GEORGE SAUNDERS: It's interesting. I play music and I cannot get to the point in music that I have in writing, I can't break away from the stuff I'm imitating. I just can't do it. I'm a good guitar player. And I'm not a bad lyricist. But the result isn't very interesting.

But—Random House let me record some music for my audiobook intros. I worked with this kid. And that was interesting because that music is actually original. There was a moment when it felt like I felt when I was first writing those *CivilWarLand* stories. It was kind of like, *Ach, fuck it.* You just give up trying to do anything in particular and just make a bunch of moment-to-moment decisions that seem edgy. Me and this guy—I'd play a riff and he'd cut it up, recycle it, add something to it. And it had energy that is a little similar to what I've done in writing. The situation meant that there could be no planning. Whatever I planned, he would mess with. That disrupted the conservative, cautious, controlling part of my mind. I had no pride whatsoever or possessiveness in what I put down.

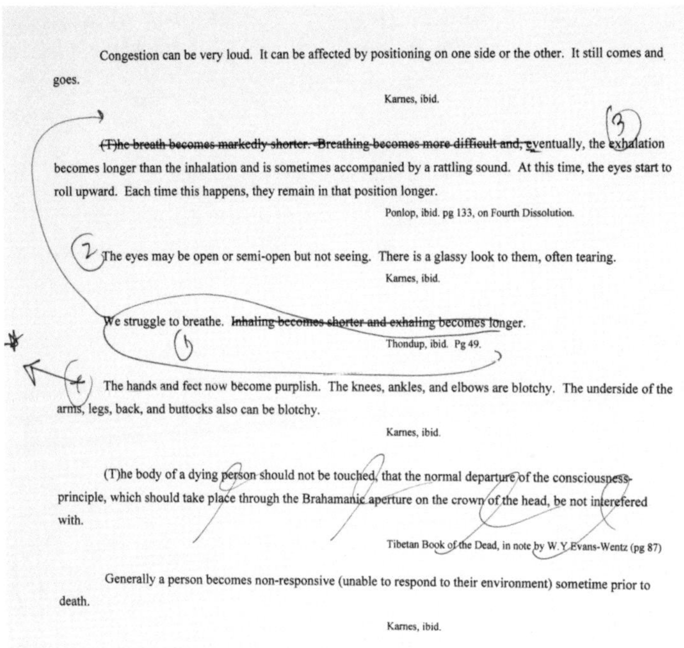

Congestion can be very loud. It can be affected by positioning on one side or the other. It still comes and goes.

Karnes, ibid.

~~(T)he breath becomes markedly shorter. Breathing becomes more difficult and, e~~ventually, the exhalation becomes longer than the inhalation and is sometimes accompanied by a rattling sound. At this time, the eyes start to roll upward. Each time this happens, they remain in that position longer.

Ponlop, ibid. pg 133, on Fourth Dissolution.

The eyes may be open or semi-open but not seeing. There is a glassy look to them, often tearing.

Karnes, ibid.

We struggle to breathe. ~~Inhaling becomes shorter and exhaling becomes longer.~~

Thondup, ibid. Pg 49.

The hands and feet now become purplish. The knees, ankles, and elbows are blotchy. The underside of the arms, legs, back, and buttocks also can be blotchy.

Karnes, ibid.

(T)he body of a dying person should not be touched, that the normal departure of the consciousness-principle, which should take place through the Brahamanic aperture on the crown of the head, be not interefered with.

Tibetan Book of the Dead, in note by W.Y.Evans-Wentz (pg 87)

Generally a person becomes non-responsive (unable to respond to their environment) sometime prior to death.

Karnes, ibid.

Playing around with historical accounts, which he would then mix with fictional ones.

identifiers at the top, as I'd done in "Quiet Ugly Girl," or in a screenplay. And I flipped it, putting the attributions on the bottom, and it was, *Oh wow, I can go anywhere with this*. As long as somebody said it, I could now accommodate it. And it just looked cool. I was moving at speed now, goofing around and playing.

I had written about a third of it. I was excited and knew it was working on some level, but with this one book more than anything I've ever written, I was aware that knowing it was working might not actually mean it was working. And I knew if I went out with it too early, and it was stupid and nobody could understand it, I would go back to my play mind and just run away from it. I sent it to Paula Redick [his wife], and she wrote me a note about it that I've always kept private, but was very nice. And then I realized, okay, I have a book to do. I'm gonna cash in on that six-month contract and go ahead.

A Long Sprint It took about four years. If you ran it in fast-forward, I think what you see is a series of six or seven page blocks being *spit out, refine, refine, refine*—all the way to the end. It was all very Rubik's cube-y, not thinking too much, just everyday going in and polishing what I can polish and waiting for handles to show up, each part written a hill at a time. Like, for example, let's get to the party scene. Then: What happens after the party scene? There would be stopping points where I'm like, *Oh God, I really don't know*. Lincoln comes in and leaves. What—what's the natural reaction to that? I was out one night, and I just thought, *Oh, they [the narrating chorus] are like superfans of Willie now, you know. Like a king has come to visit Willie, so he must be somebody special*. So, that's it, that's the next beat, and I could go ahead.

Generally I let myself do exactly what I felt like doing in the first draft. I don't even worry about it. I just put it down. And then when I really start to destabilize is in revision. But with this Lincoln book, I had to lower my standards a bit on the prose. Instead of trying to hit a home run with every phrase, I had to say, *Well no, this is just a normal person talking here—a Civil War soldier—it's got a certain diction*. I realized that what was going to do the work of originality was the structure.

I had that reverend-in-hell scene. [A horrifying and funny sequence I brought up to him, in which one of the narrators actually leaves his liminal state, approaches the judgment gate, realizes he's going to hell, and then hightails it back to the graveyard.] I don't really know why I wrote it—I was reading some books about death—but I wrote it quickly and it was really easy. And I thought, *Oh no, no, no, that's one too many, that's going to be a goiter on the book. If I put it in there, it's going to fuck it all up, just leave it out.* And sometimes those sections you eject just keep coming back in. It kept coming. Until I finally said, *Okay, if you want to be in the book so much, I'm going to put you there.* It was like some monster comes in and sits on your couch: "Okay, well, you've been here for a month, so you have to stay." And then of course the book starts reacting to it. Subconsciously, I think that scene had to be there because it basically answered the question of what happens next in this world. I always use the word *undeniable*. I don't know what it is, but it means it has earned its way into the story. That's the thing that's going to establish the structure. And the audacity of the sequence—I've come to recognize that feeling as something to go towards.

You ask how conscious I was of how much to frustrate the reader at the beginning, and the answer is I was thinking about it 100 percent of the time, and I did a whole lot of fine-tuning. In fact, I was surprised that people found it so difficult, because I really thought I had pitched it just right. I can even walk you through it. There were two or three hints during the initial Vollman-Bevin [two of the three chief narrators] conversation, where as soon as I mentioned the kid and as soon as I mentioned the sick box, I wrote a whole anecdote about Vollman's sort-of funeral. I think in my mind, any alert reader is going to know, *Okay, this guy is dead*, right? And then when you see the words Willie Lincoln, I'm like, *They've all got it now*, you know? But some people told me they had no idea of what was going on. The theatrical style really befuddled some really good readers who needed more—I was going to say *verbs*, but that's not it—*physical grounding*. Certain reading imaginations don't really take to it. I didn't know that at the time. I didn't want to be any more obtuse than I needed to be, but the reason we're doing it this way is so that later it will pay off. The reader's going to be well trained, and you're going to be able to do some cool things. It's almost like in music, where you do a motif early. I kept trying to find the optimum place that would be a little telegraphic but not too telegraphic.

I think I may have taken a trip to Fresno for a reporting trip for a magazine story during this time. I lived in a homeless camp. I only realized it later, but that was really important to the book. People would come up to me and tell me their story about how they wound up in the camp, and in those stories, they were always the only sane person there. And then the next day, they might come up and tell me the same story. I carried that over unconsciously into the Bardo, where people establish and maintain their identity through repetitive storytelling.

<u>Endgame</u> Towards the end, you have a certain ground secured behind you. I knew that up ahead of me, three of four things had to happen. I didn't know what sequence they had to happen in. [I pointed to a big white sheet of paper on which he'd written "Endgame." I asked him what it was.] I bought that big piece of paper on purpose just for that. Let me write out the possibilities, and then I'll reorder them a little bit. I'll know if one ordering seems more sensible than another. When there's a logical decision that has to be made, it helps me to write that out longhand. I was close enough to the end where I could see that the endgame is Willie has to go. Okay, if that's the centerpiece, what has to happen around it. So it's outlining but not theoretical outlining. The end product would be a list of the order of operations, something like that.

And then there was a burst. We had moved to California, but I was still here, teaching but not doing anything much else. And I just cranked. Twelve, fourteen, sixteen hours a day. And that part was magical. All these bowling pins just came down. Things that I didn't know the book was going to do, it started doing. I've never been in that mode before.[4] That was incredible.[5]

4. The flow state, experienced and described.

5. That contract? How George proceeds voice first? How he establishes rules in order to break them? Spits out, then refines? Refers to the book as if it were animate, and talking to him? Is ruthless with his work—but generous with himself? Is ultimately at the service of an overwhelming drive he can't really understand? It occurs to me that this chapter is kind of a summary of many of the themes that keep worming their way through this book.

Endgame

L demurs, leaves.

W goes.

Chain rxn.

Rev leaves = L.

Rev doubles back to save W.

Rev tells W truth.

Willie about to go, goes back to TC.

Rev goes out again — we con.

END.

[Rev stays? Goes?]

Endgame, plotted out. A little deciphering: L(incoln) demurs, leaves. W(illie) goes. Chain reaction. Last remark: [Rev(erend) stays? Goes?]

43

SUZAN-LORI PARKS

How Great Thou Art

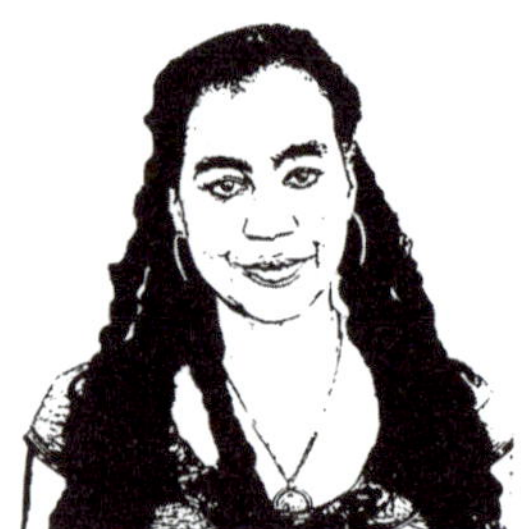

OCCUPATION: Playwright

WORK DISCUSSED: *Plays for the Plague Year* (2022)

BORN: 1963

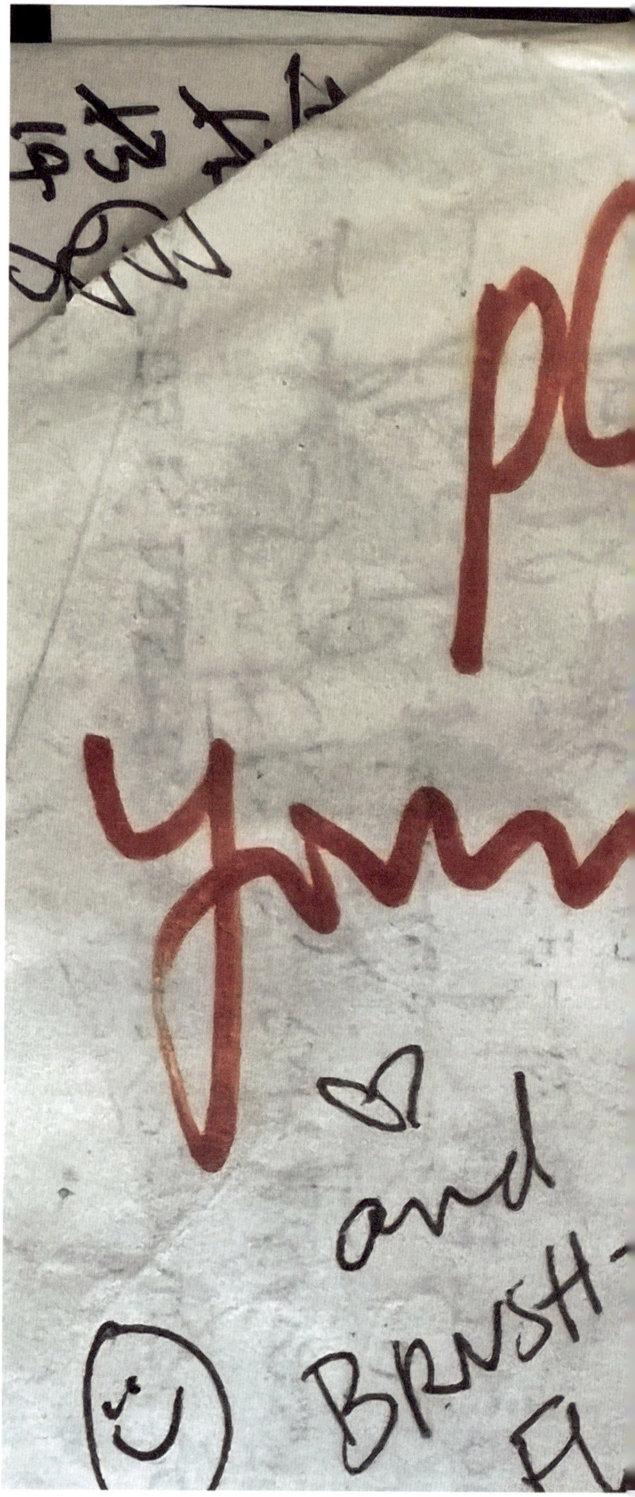

Suzan-Lori Parks: Do you have writer friends?
Adam Moss: *Some.*
SLP: I hate you.
AM: *You don't have that?*
SLP: I'm trying to make—no.
AM: *Maybe you don't want writer friends. Maybe you just like to be in your own writer world.*
SLP: Just a musician. He's my friend. I had to marry him.[1]
AM: *Do you have childhood friends?*
SLP: I moved around so much, I have no childhood friends. So now I think outside my immediate family, my most intimate relations are with my characters.

SUZAN-LORI PARKS is a playwright, winner of the Pulitzer Prize for *Topdog/Underdog*, among other plays and prizes,

1. Her husband is Christian Konopka, a composer, guitarist, and bassist.

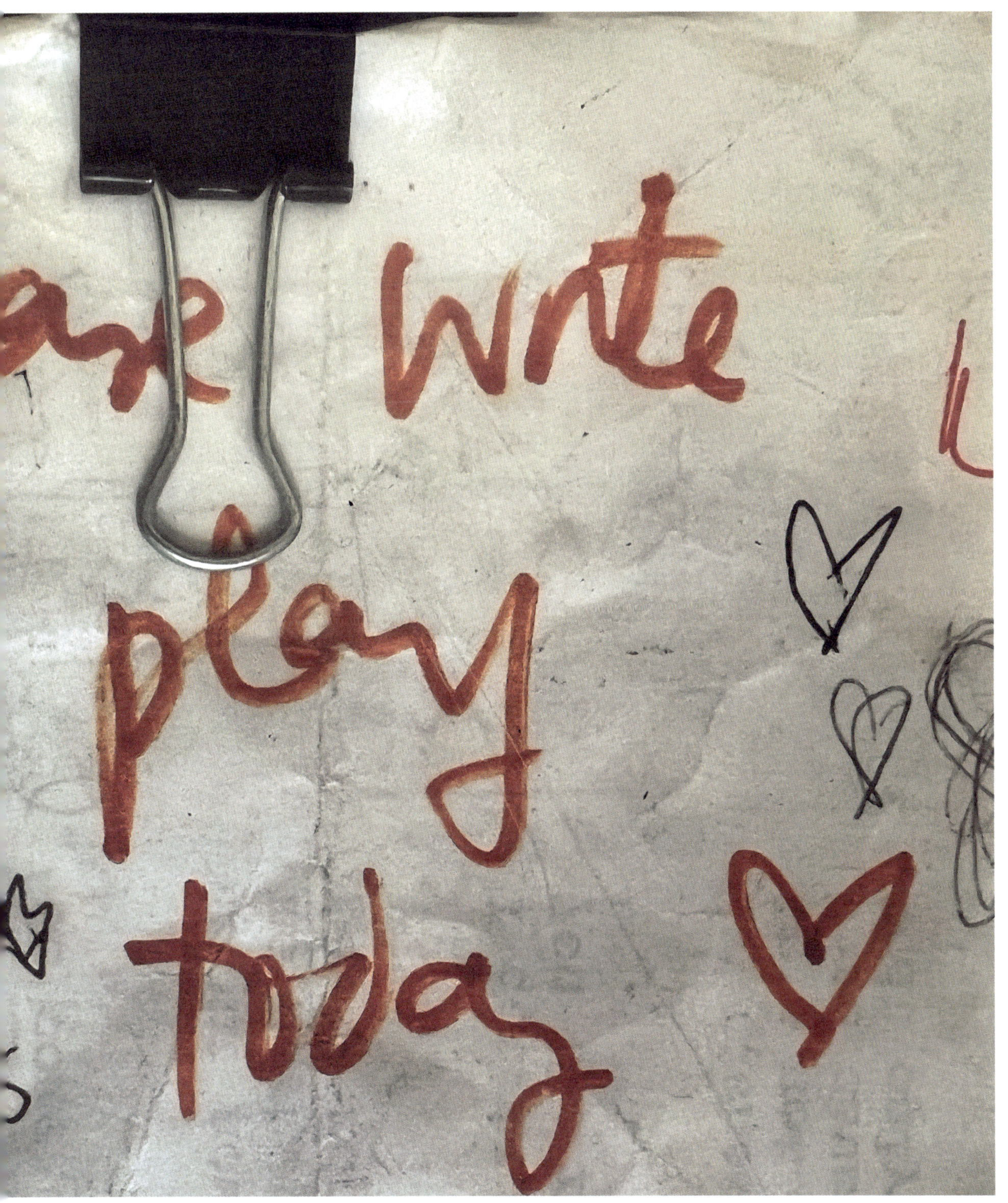

Suzan-Lori Parks's reminder to herself (while keeping herself amused).

but she also writes songs and novels and movies and TV shows, and hosts a performance piece/tutorial online and in real life called *Watch Me Work,* which is true to its title as well as being an audience-participation/creativity group therapy session. That's one of the reasons Tony Kushner told me I had to talk to her; the other is that he just thinks she's all around brilliant and he knows she thinks a lot about the kinds of questions I was asking him and everybody else. I had seen *Topdog/Underdog* years ago and found it remarkable, so I got in touch with her.

Suzan-Lori has a broad, gorgeous smile that can disappear quickly under cloud cover. When we first connected, she said she recently had begun an unusual project, called *Plays for the Plague Year.* It was set in the first year of COVID, but COVID was also a metaphor for pain, and the play was a test of art's capacity to heal, though it didn't start out that way. It began as an exercise to keep herself sane. She wrote a play a day about wherever her mind happened to wander during that first bizarre pandemic year. Eventually, she decided to knit them all together into one coherent work—or at least that was the plan.

For my purposes, it was as vivid an illustration as I might ever be able to devise of how an artist transfigures the real into the imagined, how, as she put it, "life becomes life," which is why hers is the final chapter of this book. I spent a year tracking the play's progress. During that same period, she was hyperproductive, wrapping up a TV show, writing a play about Thomas Jefferson and Sally Hemings and a Jimmy Cliff musical, trying to finish a novel, preparing *Topdog* for a revival, writing songs, raising a kid, all the while enduring wild fluctuations of elation and despondency. If you wanted to make some sense of how an artist works it all out, you didn't have to look any further than Suzan-Lori Parks.

Plays for the Plague Year—the Beginning

SLP: I am working on a TV show, *Genius: Aretha*. It's nine in the morning. I'm on a set in Atlanta. We're shooting episode six; we have five in the can. I'm the showrunner, first time I've ever done that. My headset's on. And on that March day [2020, moments before lockdown], I get a phone call from the big cheese, who says, "We're gonna shut your show down." And I fall on my knees, crying, because it's taken so much to get the show this far, and we're almost done. They say, "Don't worry, the hiatus will only be a few weeks." And as I come up struggling to my feet in the parking lot where we are shooting, I think, *Okay, I'm going to write a play a day*. And it happened like that.

AM: *To keep yourself occupied?*

SLP: Occupied, watching, awake, witnessing. One hundred plays for the first hundred days, witnessing.

AM: *So it was part therapy.*

SLP: The way everything I've ever made is part therapy.

AM: *Was it also opportunism—like you saw an artistic opportunity in it?*

SLP: See, opportunity, it wasn't—I'm one of the least opportunistic types of—

AM: *I didn't mean from a career point of view. Like, just, this COVID period is potentially great dramatic material.*

SLP: No, it wasn't like that. Say you're on the *Titanic*. And the *Titanic* goes down, and a cheap piece of wood floats by. You say, *I gotta hold on to this*. That's what it was. And I start writing that day.

AM: *In your hotel room? How long does that first play take?*

SLP: I don't know, thirty minutes. The phone was ringing, the sky was falling, it was just a mess. But I'm thinking, *Just hold on to this little piece of wood*. And remember, the plays are all kind of like just what happened. So I'm not really inventing everything, I'm just writing.

A Theatrical Mind We were talking after I'd watched several days of rehearsals for a workshop she was doing for the show, in

2. Technically she was playing a character called First Writer. That was when there were more than one of them. In the final draft, there's just one: the Writer, played by Suzan-Lori Parks.

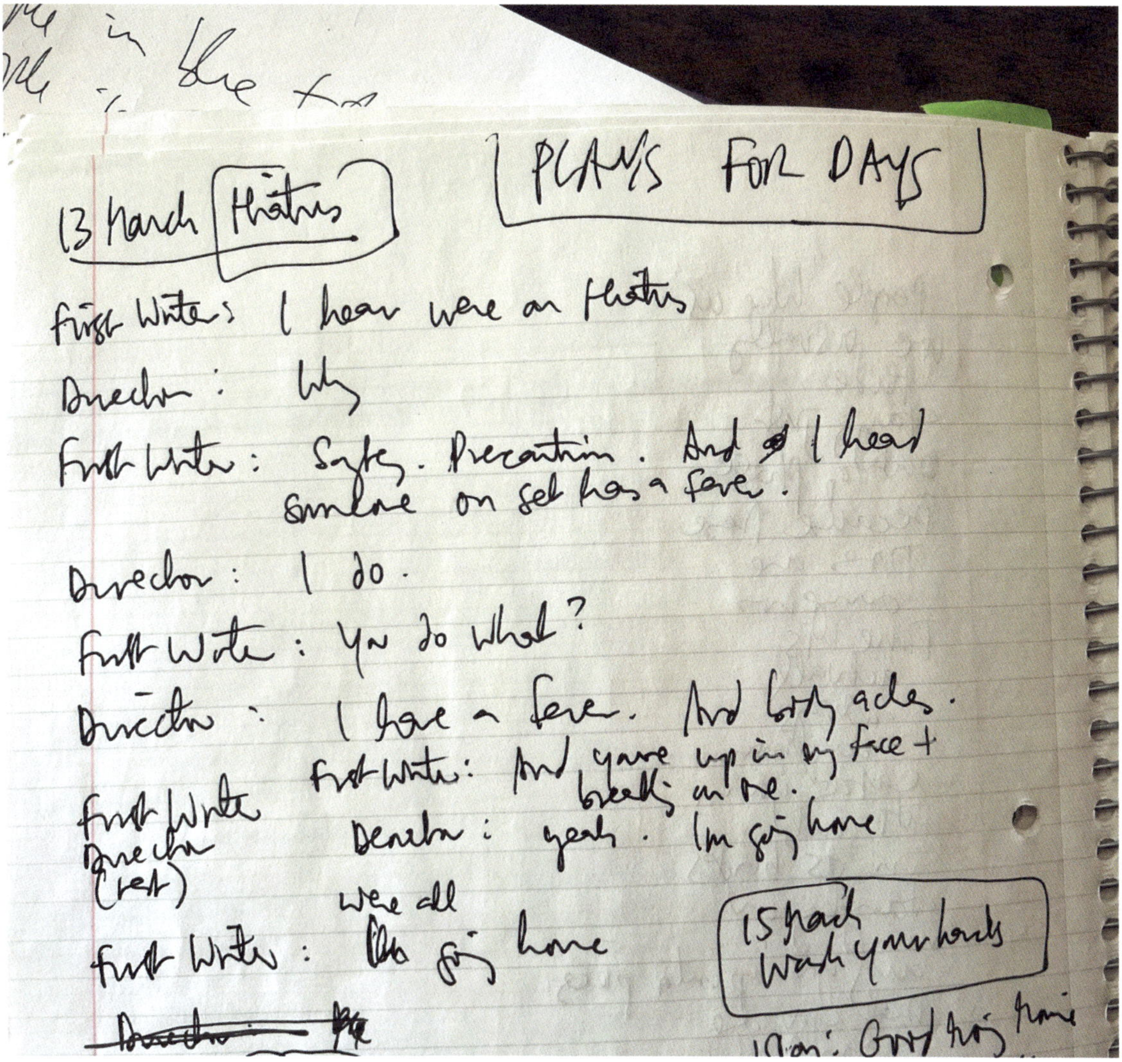

Plays for the Plague Year, originally called *Plays for Days*: first day.

which she starred as the main character, the Writer—which was meant to be herself, more or less.[2] This was unusual in itself because she does not generally act—in her own work or others. She'd never written anything so autobiographical before. She wrote songs for the play, too, for her and the cast to sing. She was all in.

Plays for the Plague Year follows the Writer and her husband and child through the pandemic, but after that first day the plays (that's what they were—tiny plays, short bursts, typically a page a piece, or a few minutes performed) became as concerned with the larger parade of what happened during that first year of COVID—Wuhan, washed hands, Donald Trump, George Floyd—as they were with the family. As Suzan-Lori was writing, she found herself employing various conceits, each getting their own series of plays—in some the just-dead (famous and unfamous who'd died that year) appear as ghosts; in others, she returns to an insipid television rom-com her character is watching, with a version of her in it, complete with laugh track; throughout, every once in a while, she and others break into song. It was musical but wasn't really a musical. It was a succession of sketches, but they added up (to what, was the overriding question). And though she was writing quickly, what was emerging was quite theatrical. She'd been writing plays for so long, that's just how she thought—theatrically. But still, I found myself pressing her to explain how it went from a therapy exercise to a piece of theater, because that seemed to me to be the central question I've been circling in this book: What is the *work* of art? How did her lived experience become a dramatic experience?

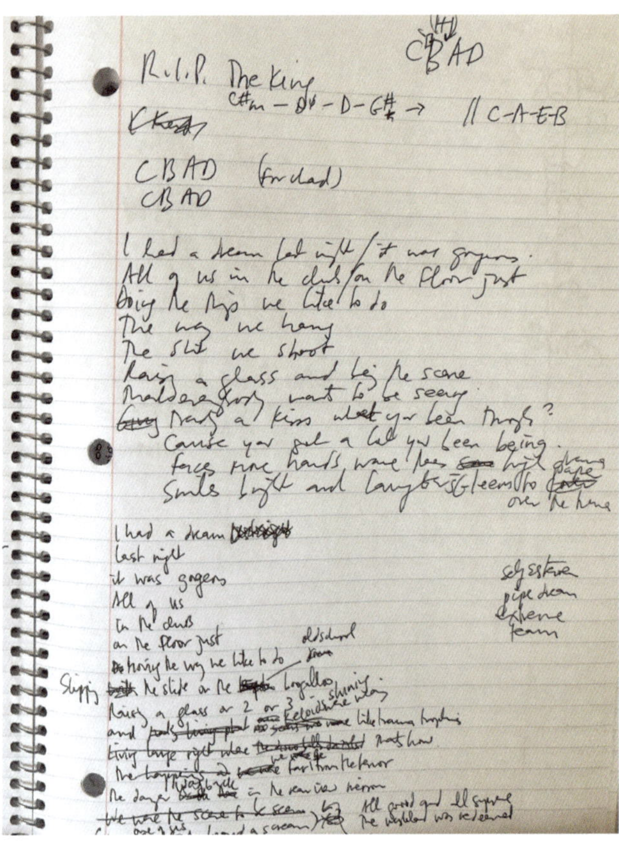

Writing "R.I.P. the King," a key song in *Plays for the Plague Year.*

Turning Life into Art

AM: *But you're also making choices, right? Editing your experience in terms of what you think might be dramatic material?*

SLP: I wasn't thinking that way—it was that wood to me—but yes, already in those first few days, I suppose I'm spooling it into theater. It wasn't a diary. Very consciously, I said, *I'm writing* Plays for the Plague Year.[3] *I'm writing plays. Which maybe, someday, will be performed.*

AM: *So you had the foresight to think through a title, and begin to imagine its eventual life.*

SLP: I didn't call it *Journals for the Pandemic Year*, which I could have. It was *Plays for the Plague Year*. The clang, the sound, the alliteration. It just caught my ear, bouncing off the Defoe.[4] And the process of seeing the title engendered, conceived the thing.

AM: *One element that appears in that first play is you. The plays revolve around this character you call the Writer. And this character has a defined personality, which is you but not entirely you. So you were already making yourself into a fiction.*

SLP: Yes, I guess that was important. The skin on my feet is crawling right now, because I'm realizing how weird that was. We're always performing ourselves. I'm aware that I'm always playing a part of the writer, in some play. But having a Writer character, I'd never done that. And it was me, yes, but it was also not me.

AM: *The character is very amusing.*

SLP: Like me!

AM: *She's a naïf, but she's also knowing. And cynical and innocent at the same time.*

SLP: That's part of me. In some ways I feel it's the real me. In life I am constrained, but I get to be the real me in a play.

AM: *When you headed back to New York, did you tell anyone you were writing these plays?*

SLP: I told my husband, but probably not until day three. At that point, I was thinking of the play mostly as a safety valve. Because I'm worried—about COVID, of course, but also about the TV project that just got shut down.

We were almost done shooting. I could have been done with the job. And I was ready.[5] While I was doing the show, I couldn't write anything else. It took everything. And I had plays to go back and write. I had musicals that I was working on. I had a novel. And so maybe I also saw the plays—maybe not as a piece of wood, but a tunnel. A tunnel out.

AM: *You're really astonishingly prolific.*

SLP: I'm in despair a lot, artistic despair. But I have a wonderful person in my husband Christian, who is there for me. That's very important for creative people, especially if you're working at a higher level, where the air is rare, friends are few, and knives are always out.

AM: *I didn't know you wrote music too. Was there a moment you decided,* This thing needs songs?

SLP: It was more like, I want to learn a song today. I was a songwriter before I was a writer-writer. So the songs came first. I think a lot of people have general talent, and we end up in the spaces where we feel most welcome. This is my theory based on my own experience. When I was a kid, I loved to make up songs. But songwriting wasn't a welcoming place.

AM: *Was it that you weren't welcomed by others? Or are you referring to your comfort with writing?*

SLP: Well, maybe one thing fed the other? In high school I loved to play the guitar. But Black people don't play the guitar. I heard this from Black people and from white people. I mean, there's Jimi Hendrix, and then a great falling off. It was the feeling I got from my friends. I watched my kid in front of the mirror this morning, and he's the only kid in his school with an Afro. So he's asking himself, *How do I fit in?* And I said to him, "You're such a handsome kid." And he said, "Yeah, that's my mom talking." My parents encouraged me, but your peer group is more influential, so I kind of went underground. Years later, I'm just like, *Well, I'm writing songs, this is a song, I'm gonna have a song there.*

AM: *How do you write a song?*

SLP: I sometimes sit at the piano, or play the guitar, and try to find a groove, find some chords I like. And I'm always trying to push my chord neighborhood, my chord vocabulary. And then the chord changes. And then I sing nonsense words usually. It was a comfort to hear that Paul McCartney wrote "Yesterday" singing the phrase *scrambled eggs*.[6] It's how children learn to speak.[7] Gradually the right words come into focus. It's the same thing, by the way, when I write a play without music. The rhythm is down, I just have to find the right words. Sometimes a rewrite is just finding the right words.

AM: *And over time, you're building the songs in, you're returning to these blocks or motifs—the visitations of the dead, recurring characters, the parallel universe rom-com. It's starting to take on the dimensions of a sophisticated theater piece. I'm sorry to keep pressing on this, but was there a transition?*

SLP: A transition between the therapeutic and the artistic?

AM: *Yes.*

SLP: What's the difference?

AM: *Well, starting to think structurally, building it.*

SLP: Is it also the sense that it might be of interest or service to others?

AM: *Yes. I have to make this part funny because otherwise it would be too bleak, that kind of thing.*

SLP: Very little of that happened in the daily writing of it. That really happened in the rehearsal. All these five plays in a row are about dead people. Do I really need them? In rewrite, I'm envisioning the audience. But where's the leap? When do you move from complete absorption into the recognition of an audience? When do I begin to recognize you? That's when it's art. That feeling—that there are actually people who I might want to share this with, when that happens, then you

3. Actually, as she discovered when she looked at the documents, the play was originally called *Plays for Days*. It wasn't the first time a subject (see Louise Glück) misremembered something she had thought was pivotal.

4. Daniel Defoe's novel *A Journal of the Plague Year*.

5. Her play includes a character, the Muse, who berates the Writer for doing hack work running the TV show. In our conversations, we talked often about the jobs she had to take for the money, and how much she wrestles with it. Most of the subjects of this book have similar torment. Have I given how artists pay for their lives short shrift? That struggle is as present in their heads as their artistic struggles.

6. "Yesterday" was called "Scrambled Eggs" until Paul McCartney found the words for it.

7. When you think about it, how children first intuit words that then develop (shape, harden, clarify) into language isn't a bad metaphor for this whole business.

might look at it in an architectural way. And that is fucking cool. But when did that happen here? I really don't know.

AM: *Until then, your subconscious and your years of practice are doing the work for you?*

SLP: Right. My active mind is getting me to the page every day. My active mind is pretty useful! I have a little note, like an index card, saying something like "Write your play today." And I carried it around, slapped it wherever I was to remind me to write.

AM: *So let's talk about the rom-com. Several of the plays are written as if they take place in a TV show the Writer is watching—offering a fun house mirror to what she is experiencing in real life. It's a kind of daring theatrical move. Can you explain it?*

SLP: Well, I'd been making a TV show . . . I guess I was just thinking about it. It was kind of to have a laugh—there are little things you do just to amuse yourself. Some days I'd say, *I don't know what to write today. So let's turn on the TV in my head.*

AM: *And what about the plays with ghosts? The dead people.*

SLP: Well, I mean, I see dead people! And I have a history of writing plays about dead people. Or with dead people. Or on dead people. Or for dead people. George Floyd and Breonna Taylor and Larry Kramer and John Prine . . .[8]

AM: *And all the dead anonymous people. The teacher, the principal.*

SLP: I just read the news. And there they were.

Write, Write, Write At Mount Holyoke, where Suzan-Lori went to college, she took a class with James Baldwin. Listening to the way she performed her stories in his fiction class, he steered her into writing plays. ("God bless him. To see something about me that I couldn't see.") He called her "an utterly astounding and beautiful creature who may become one of the most valuable artists of our time." His prophesy bore fruit pretty quickly. She became consumed with writing theater and won early success. Her work was inventive, irreverent, scorching, historical, literary: *Father Comes Home from the Wars (Parts 1, 2 & 3)*, Civil War plays—inspired by *The Odyssey*; *The Red Letter Plays*; *Fucking A* and *In the Blood*, playing off *The Scarlet Letter*; and *365 Days/365 Plays*, a project similar in structure to *Plays for the Plague Year*, except they're not meant to play as one play.[9] In 2001, she won a MacArthur "Genius Grant." There was no formula for her. Some plays took years. *Fucking A* was "a real slog," she said. She wrote *Topdog/Underdog* in three astonishing days (see page 399).

Plays for the Plague Year was proceeding along its own strange path. COVID was dragging on. The year 2020 became 2021. She kept writing, a half hour a day, while she tried to keep *Genius: Aretha* afloat first on Zoom, then back on location, while her son did his remote schooling, while her husband got COVID and long COVID, and she got pneumonia. "I had no time to read the plays all over. I mean it was nonstop: write, write, write."

Then a year and a month after she began, her ex-husband Paul died of COVID. It was April 2021. She stopped writing.

The previous November, she had taken a walk with Oskar Eustis, head of the Public Theater, where she is writer in residence.[10] "He says, 'Whatcha working on?'" said Suzan-Lori. "I say, 'Well I did a TV show.' He says, 'No, what else?' I say, 'This play-a-day thing.' I sent him the first half, six months' work. He says, 'Let me find you a director.'"

The first workshop, or reading, I saw was in late December 2021, for part 1; there was another a few months later for part 2. They'd assembled a small cast. Niegel Smith, a noted theater director who had worked with Taylor Mac (see page 358) and many other, often experimental, projects, was directing. They met for days in a rehearsal space across from the Public. At one read-through, Suzan-Lori's son sat in the back, listening to an adult play him, largely for comedy, which must have been strange, but he seemed unfazed, staring into his computer. He was used to his mother.

What I was seeing in these sessions was pretty much all the plays Suzan-Lori had written during this COVID period, bound in a black loose-leaf notebook. She writes in longhand, so she'd altered some language as she typed the pages up, but not much. Over the course of the rehearsals, she'd alter some more, they'd move some of the plays around, and cut plays simply by folding the pages over. They'd have to cut a lot. She'd organized it to play in parts over separate nights because it was so long—maybe six hours at this point.

"Niegel would say, 'I don't get what this one's about.' And I'd say, 'Eh, I don't know either,'" Suzan-Lori explained. "I was basically just trying to answer basic questions: Is it interesting? Is it watchable? Am I supposed to be up there playing the Writer? Is it okay to have songs in it? All that shit. No idea."

Acting was new to her, but she was good—one of the joys of watching her perform in these workshops was witnessing her own joy playing with this new muscle. The play—I'll start calling it a play, not plays, because the whole project at this point was to fuse it together into one coherent piece—wasn't entirely working, but large chunks of it were, and parts worked beautifully. And the songs—they were a revelation. As she sang her own material, she beamed, visibly lit from within.

Screwing with the Real Months passed. We met up a couple of weeks before they were going to do it again, at a higher-stakes workshop in June before an invited audience at Joe's Pub. She'd been hard at work at the revisions.

"I finished the rewrite of part I today," Suzan-Lori said. We were sitting on a bench in Washington Square Park. "I was under the fucking wheel the day before yesterday. I could not see how to untangle myself from the reality and the need to make a show. I was in a very bad place, I don't know how to do this. Can I go home now? The answer was 'No, you walked down that road, little girl!'"

As she was molding the plays a day into a complete work, she was confronting the problem we had been discussing all along: how or when to liberate herself from the very element that had shaped the project from the beginning: real life. She had written the plays as things happened, more or less (she had allowed herself a little fudging, but not much), which meant that she as a character didn't have any idea of things that she as the writer now knew in retrospect. But if she now knew where she was going, wouldn't she want control of how she (or we) got there? Wasn't that what would make this a play, not a diary?

In particular, as I understood it from her, what she had realized was that the play was missing a core dramatic element. There was no arc, as the jargon goes, to the core characters, the family. And she hadn't really dealt with the death of her ex-husband Paul, the very severe illness of her husband Christian, even her own COVID-panicked pneumonia. She had written a play of history, where there was a great deal of power gained from watching public events unfold that weren't very distant from your memory. As she put it, "We all get to experience that moment again"—the audience gets spritzed with hand sanitizer, the rise of Black Lives Matter is told in short plays in which Breonna Taylor and Ahmaud Arbery show up—it has a to-the-gut effect. The immediate flashback feature was powerful, and it's what I had responded to most as I'd seen it. But she wanted the play to work intimately as well: the tragedy of the play had to be personal. How had she missed that? She had stopped writing the plays after Paul's death. There was a reason. Paul's death would have to be the play's emotional crescendo. The stakes of Christian's illness would have to be raised as a through line.

One explanation for how she had missed this key dramatic need, of course, was that she hadn't known Paul would die, so he was hardly a character in her play as she was writing it. They'd talk on the phone,

8. All of whom had their own "ghost plays" within *Plays for the Plague Year* at some stage in the process.

9. Writing a play a day is almost a genre for her. In addition to the *365 Days/365 Plays* project and this one, she also wrote *100 Plays for the First Hundred Days,* chronicling the beginnings of the Trump administration. They are really alike only in form, however.

10. The Public—and Oskar Eustis—figures in a disproportionate number of these entries. It is—mostly—a coincidence, but the Public does play an invaluable role as an incubator of creative work.

but he wasn't a regular presence in her life. And maybe she hadn't really dealt with Christian's illness because it was too traumatic at the time—at some level, the plays were designed as a personal escape, the way to cope with pain by diverting it to her imagination, not necessarily to dwell in it.

But if she were to make the most effective piece of theater, she would have to approach this project as an artist, not only as a witness. So she said that was what she was doing now, carefully weaving Paul in earlier, so his death, as awful as it is to describe it in these terms, would pay off dramatically. Lingering on Christian's pain; also her own. It was not without risks: Would she upset the careful equilibrium between private and public that made the thing so original? But she was feeling that it was all a matter of balance, and maybe now it was working.

And one thing Suzan-Lori realized along the way (I hadn't seen it, but she was right) was that, even though she hadn't invited me in for this reason, the play was maybe about creativity itself. Suzan-Lori's imagination had transfigured her into the character "Writer" and then again into its rom-com doppelgänger—all, by her account, without conscious effort. The plays, if they had any real plot at all, were about the writing of plays. "My promise to myself was, I'll show up every day." That's what she thinks is most important about creating too—"showing up," no matter what, and being vulnerable and taking in, and then making some invented sense out of what you experience.

Being Vulnerable The Plague Year was the play's subject, so inevitably it was sad. But it was also sad because its main character was Suzan-Lori Parks, and it was impossible not to notice over time that there is a lot of sorrow in her, and that she writes so ferociously in order to do battle with what plagues her—not only during this year, but all the time.

"To be honest," she said. "I'm in despair. Pretty much every day." She brought despair up over and over: "We all need to have more conversations about frustration, upset," and over the course of our time spent together, we did. She talked about not being understood ("There's the artistic despair that happens when I create something that I think is beautiful and it's dismissed, in ways that I personally feel are less than fair"). She was in despair about politics, the rise of the far right, of course, but also the way the prevailing political climate had infected art—she was still raw about a white director who, early on, had been approached about this project and said he loved it, but felt it was a "Black play" (which wasn't at all true) and demurred, adding that Suzan-Lori wasn't the kind of young Black activist who could make it possible for him to do it, which was outrageous on many levels, but an especial affront to a playwright of such principle. ("Broke my little artist heart," said Suzan-Lori. "It's ugly and it's fucked up and I hate it.") She despaired about the way she felt constrained as a Black woman to contain her emotions—this was what she was getting at when she said the persona she had created for herself in the play was freer to be her than the her who was talking to me. ("I felt like I got to be me. I didn't have to be guarded.")

I don't mean to suggest she was consumed by sadness. She was warm, often buoyant, and always kind, and I loved being with her. But her joy was clearly fragile. Being open to hurt very much came with her territory; it's what allowed her to do what she does. "It's a constant—you know, battle," she said. "Because I'm aware of people's feelings. I look at people."[11]

And mostly what she despaired at were the very consequences of being an artist. She needed art, like oxygen. She was terrified of shutting down. It was like death to her.

SLP: If the creative act builds a bit of wood in the ocean one can hold on to, then the inability to do that creative act just feels like drowning. I feel despair when I can't seem to bring it forth. I feel the constricting of the throat. It's just the physical pain that I experience when I

have difficulty writing, like someone's strangling me. I can't breathe. I can't speak.
AM: *So you don't feel the fear of failure really? It's just the fear of not being able to create at all?*
SLP: Well, that's failure.
AM: *And if it's mediocre?*
SLP: Doesn't bother me. It might be mediocre. I'm so happy to have a piece of wood. I don't care if it's not oak. Wood laminate, good. If it floats, okay.
AM: *I remain amazed by how hard you work. During the time I've been watching you, you've been reworking this show, writing songs for it, acting in it; writing other shows, also a novel; doing production rewrites for Hollywood, teaching . . . And yet, no matter how busy you are, you still take time, which you clearly have so little of, to play creative therapist for struggling, wayward artist types in your Watch Me Work seminars.*[12] *Why? It seems so generous to me.*
SLP: Because I know what it's like to be lonely.[13]
AM: *Is there a question you feel the budding artists who come to these seminars are asking over and over?*
SLP: Am I allowed to be here? Am I okay? That's actually it: Am I okay?

Is She Okay? In June, I went to see the new version of *Plays for the Plague Year*. There was a great deal more about Christian's illness, but she'd worked in less about Paul than what she said she had been planning. You could see her calibration if you were looking for it. And she'd implied that she (or her character; it was always hard to untangle the difference), too, had COVID, though she hadn't. There were more songs, and they were working really well. But the play still wasn't entirely cohering. It wasn't clear to see what she would have to do to pull the whole thing together, but it was only another stage in a long process. She had five more months.

And then, five more months.

Finally It was November. That process was complete. The play was done and performed, this time for a paying audience, also at Joe's Pub at the Public. I went.

The final sweep of changes were subtle, but were all, to my eyes, just right. The play was now a single three-hour event—the parts had been collapsed. The cuts helped, as they almost always do. She had junked the rom-com, so the show felt less surreal and a bit more straightforward, but kept many of the visitations of the dead, which were its strongest dramatic element. They were now more pronounced, and even more chilling. The audience members I spoke to were most drawn to the COVID newsreel aspect, the reliving of recent history that I'd always found terrifically effective. It still was, though I wondered how it would wear as the events receded over time—maybe time would strengthen the work, or diminish it, it was hard to tell. It was scheduled to be mounted again in another six months.

As for the domestic drama, Suzan-Lori had indeed played up the illnesses. Now there was a little more Paul, and especially more Christian ("Hubby" in the play)—his long COVID was now really long, stretching over the play. But the most telling difference in the family story, enhanced through subtle interventions, was that the play was now much more of a love story between Suzan-Lori and Christian, or the Writer and Hubby. During our time together, I kept registering how tender she was in talking about her love for her husband. In this final push, she'd laced that love into the play itself.

And the biggest formal change was that the play now really *was* a musical—or at least much more so. It had an opening number, some dancing, even more songs. Throughout our conversations, she came most alive when talking about her songwriting; it seemed to give her the most happiness.[14] And now that

11. Attention.

12. *Watch Me Work* is an ongoing (free) session, live sometimes and online sometimes, where aspiring artists can ask Suzan-Lori questions about their struggles, both particular to things they are working on, and more generally.

13. She continued, "But I was just thinking of people out there . . . who are desirous of artistic community, but maybe haven't achieved the level to get . . . entrance into writers' rooms, and conversations . . . I want to be there for them." She has a big heart.

14. In addition to these songs, she also wrote some wonderful songs for the Jimmy Cliff musical, which was mounted some months later. I mentioned earlier how I listened for what most excited the subjects in the telling. For architect Liz Diller, it was conceptual art; for playwright Suzan-Lori Parks, it was songwriting. We all have our roads not taken.

spirit infused the work. She also added more gags, more bits, more sweeteners. She'd turned her terrible COVID year into something like an entertainment. But it was also still sad. I watched her onstage face beam and then fall, and beam and fall again, trying so hard to find good in the awful.

I'm not a critic, so I'll leave it there. It was clearly not going to be one of her major works, but out of the ashes of the pandemic she'd made something from nothing, which was, in the way art always is, amazing. And in this last performance, I noticed how much of what we'd been talking about for a year was actually in the play, not even as subtext, but as the dramatic material of the show itself. The play ended with her questioning the entire premise of the project—could writing the play actually help her work through her pain? Could art—not the experience of it but the making of it—really heal?

In the penultimate version of the play she says this:

This is America and so I'm looking for a happy ending. Can't seem to find it. Funny, writing these. First, you're telling the truth. Then you're obscuring the truth. Because, as you start anticipating the audience, when your mind's eye starts seeing other "I's" and "eyes" on it, you change it, or—it changes—becoming more digestible. Wow. Trippy, right?

And then in the final version, these words: "Maybe when I started I had this belief that theater would save us. But it won't. Not in the way I thought it would. But it does preserve us somehow." So no, and yes. Talking to Suzan-Lori, there was little doubt whether it had been worth it to her.

"I mean, I'm on fucking stage at fucking Joe's Pub," Suzan-Lori had said to me earlier. "What the fuck am I doing? I don't know. But I'm being true to the thing that called me, and that's my primary allegiance. I could have an allegiance to the Bank of America or Chase Bank or something. You know, we're all made differently. But for me it's a debt of gratitude. Like, I know how big, how great thou art."

She paused. "Creating, for me personally, it revolves around my love of work—or maybe my desperation to have that wood in the water.

"The intense desire. And also the joy. There is nothing better. This novel I've been working on? It's been fifteen years, on, off. I have like five drafts. And yesterday I slumped on the bed, I'm flopped on the bed going, 'Aaaaah, I can't figure it out.' And suddenly I saw the first beat of the first chapter, I could see it. I just looked at my husband and said, 'Ooh, you're sitting on the steps in the dark.' And he said, 'What time is it?' I said, 'I don't know.' He said, 'Is it midnight?' I said, 'Yes.' And for the first time I saw it."

Making art, she'd said, *requires* "despair. And a lot of hard work. There's a lot of flopping around, it's horrible. The subconscious cannot be rushed.[15] But we are lucky enough to do what we enjoy, right? Even if it's hard."

After the show, I biked home from the Public through the same now busy streets that had been emptied by the pandemic when I first began talking to her. And as I rode, I thought of the last minutes of the performance I'd just seen. I'd planned to come the previous week, but the show had been canceled. Lo and behold, after giving herself imagined COVID for dramatic purposes, she had caught the real thing. "Funny," she said in a text to me when I asked whether the show had been shut down because she'd gotten ill herself. "I have a show uptown and downtown running at the same time. And also the new play premiering in Minneapolis.[16] So I'm like, I'm totally at the edges of my Self. So what would SLP do? She would fully participate in the cycle of the creative process—life becomes art becomes life again. So, yes, I got COVID!"

That night, she'd come out for an encore. She had one more number to share. Sitting home, feeling sick, she told the audience, she had picked up her guitar.

"I had a fever," she sang—

"So I wrote this song."

15. Like Louise Glück, she waits. But never rests.

16. *Topdog* uptown, *Plays for the Plague Year* downtown, and in Minneapolis the "world premiere" of her play about Jefferson and Hemings, *Sally & Tom*.

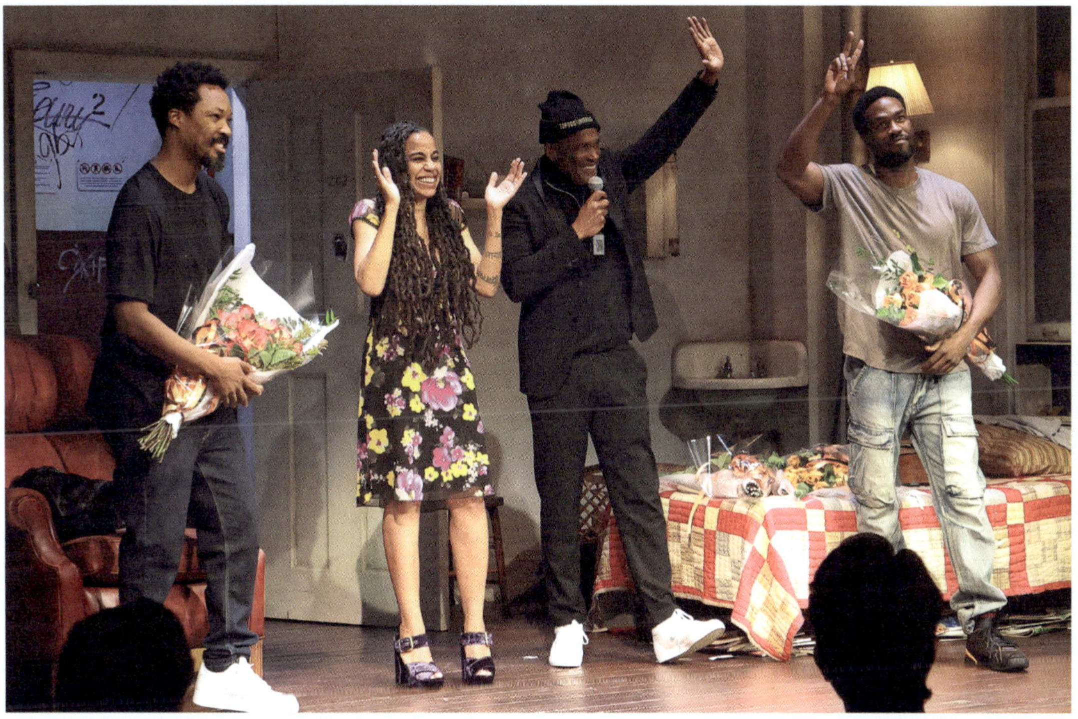

Suzan-Lori Parks, curtain call opening night, at the revival of *Topdog/Underdog*, which went on to win a Tony Award.

Topdog/Underdog *is about two brothers, Booth and Lincoln, once a three-card monte dealer. Booth, as you can guess, eventually kills Lincoln, at the end of a deep and marvelous play.*

SUZAN-LORI PARKS: "I remember this is the weirdest thing. Paul [her then-husband] and I were walking around on Canal Street, and there were these guys playing three-card monte. I had never stopped to watch, I don't know why I was watching that day. When they took the game down, I followed at a respectable distance. Where were they going? And Paul said, "Hey, let's go home and I'll show you how it's done."

Several months later I had a residency at a theater and it just came to me. I said to someone there, "Oh, two brothers, Lincoln and Booth," badump bump. And she said, "You'd better go home and write."

So I went back to the apartment and I could see the whole thing—they reminded me so much of various kooky menfolk in my family. And it was like, I didn't want them to be just talking, they had to do things. So I thought, *Wouldn't it be cool if they did that card trick?* I called Paul and I said, "I've got this cool idea for a play," and I read him the beats, scene 1, scene 2, scene 3. He said, "Oh, I think you're gonna write that real quick." I said, "I think so too." So I hung up the phone and started to write, and I just did, three days from beginning to end. And it was like, if someone were standing behind you with a gravy boat, and they were pouring silver liquid down the back of your hair. I'm taking dictation. I'm hearing it. I know it's strange. And then I finished. And it was euphoria, gratitude. I put a quote in the front. Was it Emerson? "I am God in nature, I am a weed by the wall." That's what it was. I am colossal. I am all-powerful. I am a small little delicate piece of garbage. It was all true.

THERE IS A PHRASE, variations of which many of the subjects of this book ended up uttering at some point. As they were describing why they did this or that, they would say they "listened" to the work, or the work would "tell" them what to do; the work would "speak" to them, as if a character in a book or a color on a canvas could issue orders. Tony Kushner asked his *Angels* alter ego, Louis, to explain the play to him; Cheryl Pope waited for the mother in her picture with no face to tell her whether she wanted a face. For a long while, I dismissed this phrasing as cliché—more of the empty language people often employ to describe how they work because creation is so hard to describe. Eventually, however, I began to think that no, maybe *listening* was the whole deal.

Listening to what the poem or song was telling them was another way of describing how they listened to themselves, taking whatever their imagination spewed forth, recognizing it and translating it back—simplifying it, usually—so their conscious self could go about manipulating it. And this attending ("I was just taking dictation," said Kushner, a common sentiment) was really, I realized, at the heart of the project of this book. That's what the exhibits they shared are about. The studies, notes, doodles—they are all ways the artists have of talking to themselves.

As I was rounding the bend of these encounters I found myself asking what these artists had in common. After all, with the conversations, I had assembled what added up to a (not particularly rigorous but pretty voluminous) dataset. And there were some things I noticed.

Art has a before and an after. The before is the training—the acquisition of skills, the assumption of habits. The after is the practical activity of putting finger to key, palm to clay, and going to town.

But there is also an in-between. It's the mysterious part. Some describe that mystery as magical, otherworldly. Others view it as their subconscious churning. It doesn't matter. All artists are mystics at heart, and they're talking about the same thing—and that thing is what they *can't* really talk about, because it cannot be put into language. So the artists discussed with me their childhoods and the first intimations of the idea for the work we were dissecting and then the practical steps of building a structure and fine-tuning a voice and refining that idea—all crucial. And though the obstinately romantic part of me couldn't help wondering, *Where is the "art" (the transcendence, the revelation, the bolt of lightning—that kind of thing)*, I also began to understand that was the wrong way to think about it. These artists tended to black out at the moment when, as Kara Walker put it, the switch turned on. They couldn't recall it for the most part, so they couldn't describe it. In a sense—a conscious sense—it didn't exist. The "art"—the magic—was the space in the middle, the hole in the doughnut, what happened when they got the before and after right.

So that's what we talked about, the before and the after. And as I was listening to them, what I was thinking about was that we—all of us—get hit by lightning all the time, but the bolts are rarely remembered and seldom understood. Our brains are always in the process of putting stuff together in illogical combinations—juxtapositions that are thought to be at the core of creation. We all make associations. We all dream. Artists don't have more interesting dreams than the rest of us (I'm pretty sure). They don't own imagination.

What they do seem to have is an unusual ability to cross over—to get entrance to that inarticulable place, and then to capture what they can make use of. Maybe it's a disassociation, but a particularly productive kind. All that listening, scrawling, sketching is their turning what they are grasping at, inchoately, into something they can act on.

Creativity occurs, Freud said, when people cease to police their imagination, or at least when their conscious selves don't put too serious a kibosh on it. Critical judgment is the next step: the making original, vivid sense of what you see. But it starts with the seeing. The painter Agnes Martin said, "we all have the same inner life. The difference lies in the recognition." "I don't think I'm gifted," said Francis Bacon. "I just think I'm receptive."

I came to understand the artists I talked to as occupying some version of George Saunders's Bardo—they had found a way to a liminal place, a place in between what they could dimly perceive and what they could control. But unlike George's characters, who were stuck, they had easy trespass across the border, with the help of all sorts of navigation tools they'd developed over the years. So many superstitions and games and hacks, deals with themselves, deliberate (and successful) acts of self-delusion—it was impossible to ignore. They play catch with their id; they trick their superego. "Nothing really begins to happen in a painting until you reach the point where conscious intention breaks up and ceases to be the thing that's driving you," said the painter Leon Kossoff. Jenny Saville talks often about "trapping" impulses. Cecily Brown said all art is just a matter of manipulating chance. Artists instigate and rely on accidents. And the really successful artist seems able to not just get the accident going properly but also, more important, know how to harness the result. Rembrandt, said Bacon, knew just what "irrational mark" to keep.

The process of making is about following what Tony Kushner called bread crumbs. I kept noticing how the subjects often talked of themselves as if they were two people, one laying the crumbs, the other picking them up. In many instances, these artists berated themselves—"Kara, where are you?"—until they could make their own meaning visible, with the free spirit in their head waiting impatiently for the plodder in the studio to get it and move on. At some point, they could.

In my more frustrated moments, I saw this ability to glide back and forth as a superpower they have. Which it is, in its way. But it is also just how they are built. After talking to these artists about the development of their work, I found it impossible to separate creativity from other aspects of personality. Artists have certain traits, both inborn and nurtured—and that flexibility of movement between their inner and outer selves is key. But it isn't all.

In my conversation with Sheila Heti, she put this into words that made simple sense to me. We were talking about what it might mean to be gifted:

Sheila Heti: I think [an artist] has to think that they have a gift, like a special gift.

I think you have to feel a little chosen. But everyone's chosen for something,

right? Somebody might be chosen to be a great husband and father. Somebody's chosen to write novels. I mean, it feels mystical, but I think it's actually just your brain is structured in such a way that it makes imagination easy.
AM: *So a personality matrix that makes it possible to create? Including what—access to your imagination?*
SH: Well, I don't even think it's access to imagination. I think it's just, I don't like—I don't like doing anything. Like I like sitting—I like being in bed. You know? And so, I can do my work, I have patience. I can sit for eight hours. I don't need to move around. That's harder to be a fiction writer, when you're moving around. You know, it's laziness. But, like, laziness helps, it's effective.
AM: *Well, it doesn't appear as if you're lazy. But I understand what you're saying.*
SH: I just don't think it's all virtues. I think it's flaws and virtues in this magical combination.

As I was going along, I tried to catalog what this magical combination might be. Natural ability—a good ear or eye or hand that could be trained? That was real—and a big advantage. Like in all kinds of development, the first years were crucial—the subjects I talked to had sensibilities (Chast), tastes (Derian), senses of humor (West) that got formed and crystallized as children, and that their work spun around. They were observant, sensitive, attentive (Howe). Some kids are like that, and they usually are as adults too—all really necessary artistic attributes. They were impressionable, but not too much: they absorbed (Crewdson), adapted (Coppola), and threw over (Morris) influences. They described their early years, often as lonely; they spent a lot of time by themselves. They drew pictures, built forts, wrote songs. They found vehicles (Hobbs) to express themselves (Quinn) when ordinary means failed. They turned to art for all sorts of reasons: to work out their pain (Pope) or identity (Lovell) or grief (Ndzube) or outrage (Kruger), or, most often, just because they couldn't see themselves doing anything else. Art gave them the most pleasure; or it was the way they escaped from hard things; or it was what they were good at, so they just kept doing it. They were encouraged (Machine Dazzle), or at least not discouraged (Mac), in their artistic work. They had a need to find others like them (Muhly, Bartlett) who shared similar characteristics that separated them from their peers, and those new communities spurred them on. They were all very smart—intelligence being an underrated feature of creative work, in my view—and developed crucial problem-solving skills (Sondheim). I was surprised to realize how much of art making is fundamentally intellectual—surprised because, even while knowing better, I found it very hard to let go of the naive notion that it is all feeling. But there's logic to it, organization, discernment. Maybe more important than feeling.

From what I could make out, this cohort I had assembled had other unusual capacities as well. They were spectacularly disciplined, with an impressive ability to focus. Curiosity, check. They were keenly aware of rules, but unafraid (eager—Simon) to break them. They had patience (Glück). They were perfectionist, up to a point, but, crucially, they were also able to tolerate imperfection (Cunningham). They were decisive, even if sometimes it took a long while to get there: when they needed to commit (Meiselas), they could. And endurance (Baldwin's word)! This they had in droves. Art requires stamina. Each of the subjects was a dog with a bone: relentless (De Los Angeles), relentless (Nosrat), relentless (Tharp), with the power to tolerate tedium (Glass) and chaos (Sillman) and doubt (Jacobs) and rejection (Heti) and despair (Parks), because they had faith (Sumney), a product of their experience but also, I am certain, of their temperament.

I had trouble appreciating the importance of faith because it seemed too nebulous (was my secularism, or cynicism, getting in the way?), but I came to see the hard truth of it. Faith—the bedrock confidence that you can actually do what you are trying to do—is what makes stamina possible. The photographer Walker Evans has a nice quote about its necessity: "It's logical to say that what I do is an act of faith. Other people may call it conceit, but I have to have faith and conviction. It came to me. And I worked it out. I used to suffer from a lack of it, and now that I've got it I suppose it seems self-centered. I have to have faith or I can't act." And the conceit he mentions? Pretty necessary too. As Joan Didion said, "In many ways writing [insert any other creative field here] is the act of saying *I*, of imposing oneself upon other people, of saying *listen to me, see it my way, change your mind*." If artists aren't necessarily narcissists, they at least have a conviction that they have something important to say and can find a way to say it.

So that's a long list. The point is, who's like that? And to borrow from Stephen Sondheim once again, the answer is: damn few. As Sheila Heti suggested, these artists have a particular set of characteristics that line up. It's possible they are also kind or loyal or good to their mothers, but those are not the traits relevant to their art making.

As I've pointed out, many got started early. At this stage they all take their craft for granted, but their ability to make anything is enabled by skills honed through a lifetime of practice. Craft is like language for them, formed when their brains were more plastic. If you read a lot of creativity self-help (and I do), you'll notice that the main focus is on how to unleash imaginations and give yourself permission to make art—which is fine as far as that goes. People who try to encourage creativity don't much dwell on skills or stress how years of training are integral to the making of art, maybe because to say so seems undemocratic. But skills for these artists is like an athlete's body memory integrated early, making the rest possible. Most of the time, before making anything, you have to know how. Craft matters. Studying the masters matters. Experience matters. There are no shortcuts.

Above all, the subjects seemed to have opposing forces working in pretty much equal measure: they were open and closed, free and disciplined, playful and ruthless—in some sense, child and adult. (I kept flashing to images of them as children, playacting with dolls and trains and forts, talking to—and listening to—themselves, as little kids do when they play alone. It just seemed a continuous line from the child they were to the person I was talking to.)

The point is, some of us are dreamy, some veer toward the anal, but few sit so perfectly in the middle. I couldn't help thinking about my subject pool as freaks—which I mean as a compliment. What began as a project fueled by envy, if I'm going to be honest with myself, turned into one closer to awe.

Well, *awe*'s not quite right. I am aware that in trying to remove the mystical from the equation, I ended up replacing the gods with (false) idols. But seeing this bunch up front only showed me how human they all were—screwed up, full of doubt, with a typical ratio of happiness to un. So maybe what I really ended up with is respect.

And where that left me, to close the loop I began in the introduction, was a realization that I don't necessarily have the traits they have, not many of them. But I'm also not six foot two, even though I would really like to be. I'm right handed. I have an insane number of moles. I like salty more than sweet. My handwriting's tiny. That's who I am. Perhaps my disposition is more suited to the collective work I spent my career doing, and less so to the solitary act of art making. I'm empathetic, I play well with others, I can usually get people to do what I want (not the most attractive quality, but a useful one). I seem to need what came up in the David Simon chapter as the "bounce," someone, something, to play off. The great editor Robert Gottlieb described editing as reacting, most of all—and that seems to describe the thing I do best. I was lucky enough to discover what fit me and then to spend much of my life doing it. I'm grateful for that. But, I don't focus very well. (That's why I became an editor, a dilettante.) I'm pretty inhibited—I have a fairly punishing relationship with my subconscious (a subject best left to me and my shrink). I started late and didn't bake in my skills when I was young.

So does that mean I can't make art? Far from it. Anybody can make art, though not everybody can be a great artist. The cartoonist Lynda Barry, who teaches creativity, has spoken about why we think differently about art than about riding a bicycle. When we hop on a bicycle, no part of us thinks that we'll be able to win the Tour de France, but with art, we think if we're not really good at it, we can't, or shouldn't, do it. That stuck with me.

In my zeal to be good, I had forgotten all the reasons I had taken up painting in the first place. There were so many: paint (oil in my case) is just an amazing substance to play with—a creamy, protean mess; I feel like God every time I create something from nothing; one satisfying mark is enough to make me feel really good for a whole minute; when I paint, my anxiety disappears; painting even, on a good day, gives me a body high. In short, I enjoy it! If I am sometimes bored with my work, I am never bored with making it. Isn't that enough?

It would be disingenuous to say I don't hope also to be good. But I have come around to the view (wishful perhaps, but also real) that it isn't necessary. I am not letting myself off the hook here; in one conversation with Amy Sillman, when I asked about what traits she noticed her most promising students all shared, she thought for a moment and said plainly, "They're not wimps. They may present as mild-mannered, but underneath, there's a clear and fundamental resolve." I do think maybe, as far as painting is concerned, that I *am* a wimp. But I also know from experience that wimpdom is something you can work through. Courage can be built up, summoned. And I can certainly get more skilled. If anything seems universally true in this survey, it is that no matter how hard it gets, real artists do not give up. So I won't give up either.

And maybe good will come. And maybe it won't. I just have to keep trying.

When I thought back on my conversations for this project, I realized how often my efforts at getting the subjects to express satisfaction at the completion of that novel or sculpture or song I so admired were met with a shrug. I kept looking for emotional closure, the declaration of accomplishment; I never got it. As they would describe the finishing of their project, the subjects expressed relief—exhaustion maybe. About its reception, maybe a brief rush. I know they also felt a pride in their work they were reluctant to acknowledge out loud, but that was not, it was very clear, what got them out of bed. They are artists because they are consumed with the making of art. Art is hard, and that is exactly what is so satisfying about it. Victories are fleeting. The struggle is every day.

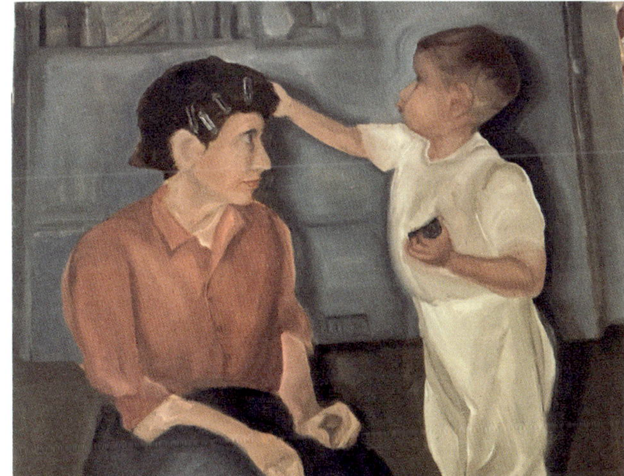

It's the work, they kept saying. Eventually I believed them.

And anyway, the project had given me a thought. I dug through my phone and found some iterative artifacts of my own painting. I kind of liked the way they looked, unfinished like that. Here's an old painting of my mother and me—I was digging out some emotional crud in it, and the picture reminded me of the way Cheryl Pope was working through her own mother and child issues in her chapter.

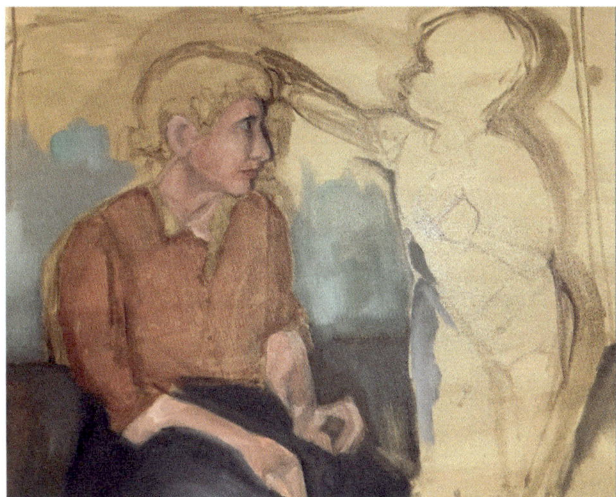

Anyway, I liked the crude ghosty version a whole lot better than the painting I finished.

So maybe I should make a series of pictures I deliberately interrupt. Too contrived? Maybe. Unoriginal? Definitely. But why not? It'd be fun.

ARTIST ARTIFACTS, AN HISTORICAL SAMPLING

Some outlines, sketches, and doodles you can find if you poke around.

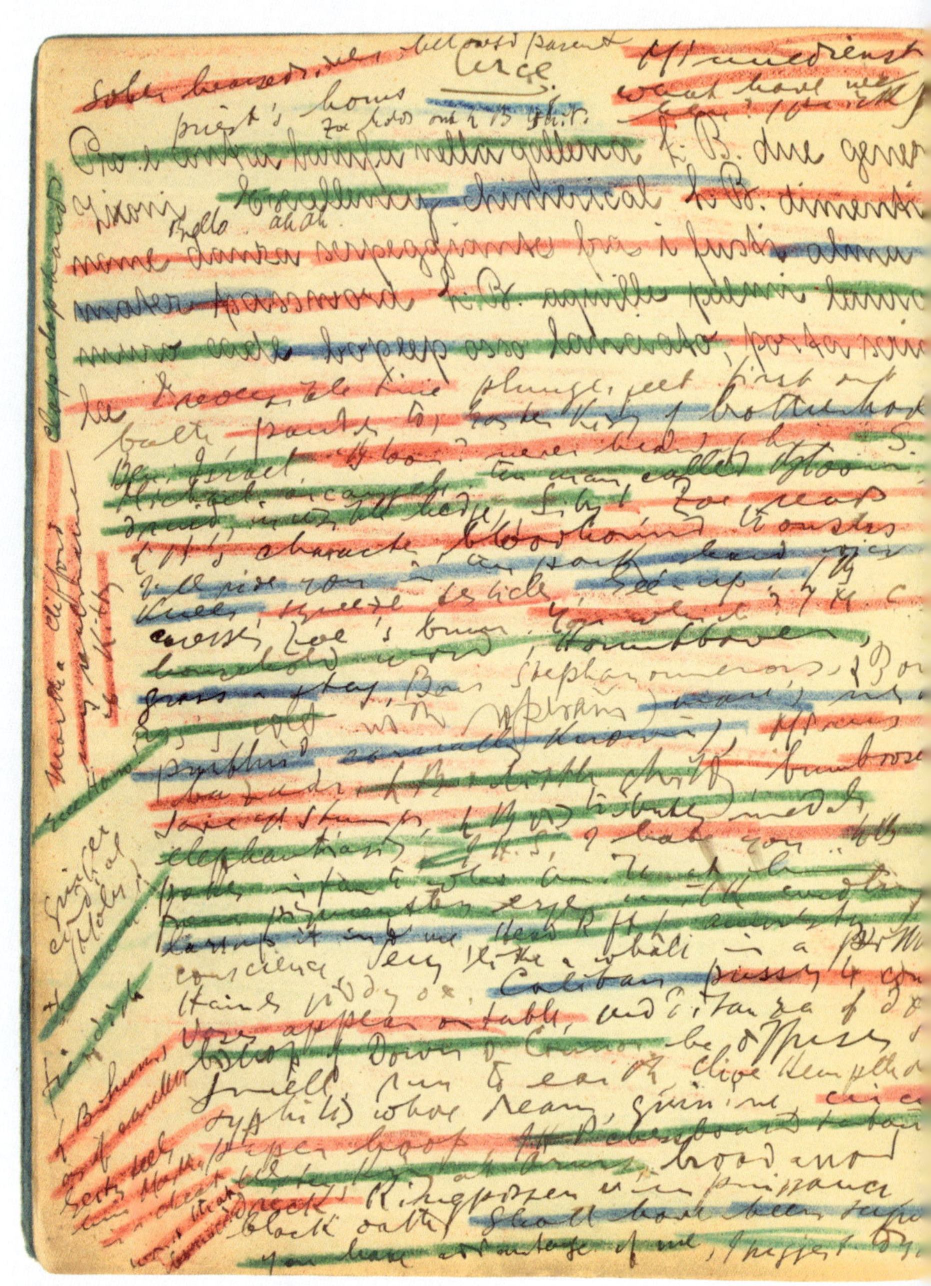

MARKINGS James Joyce crayons through *Ulysses*.

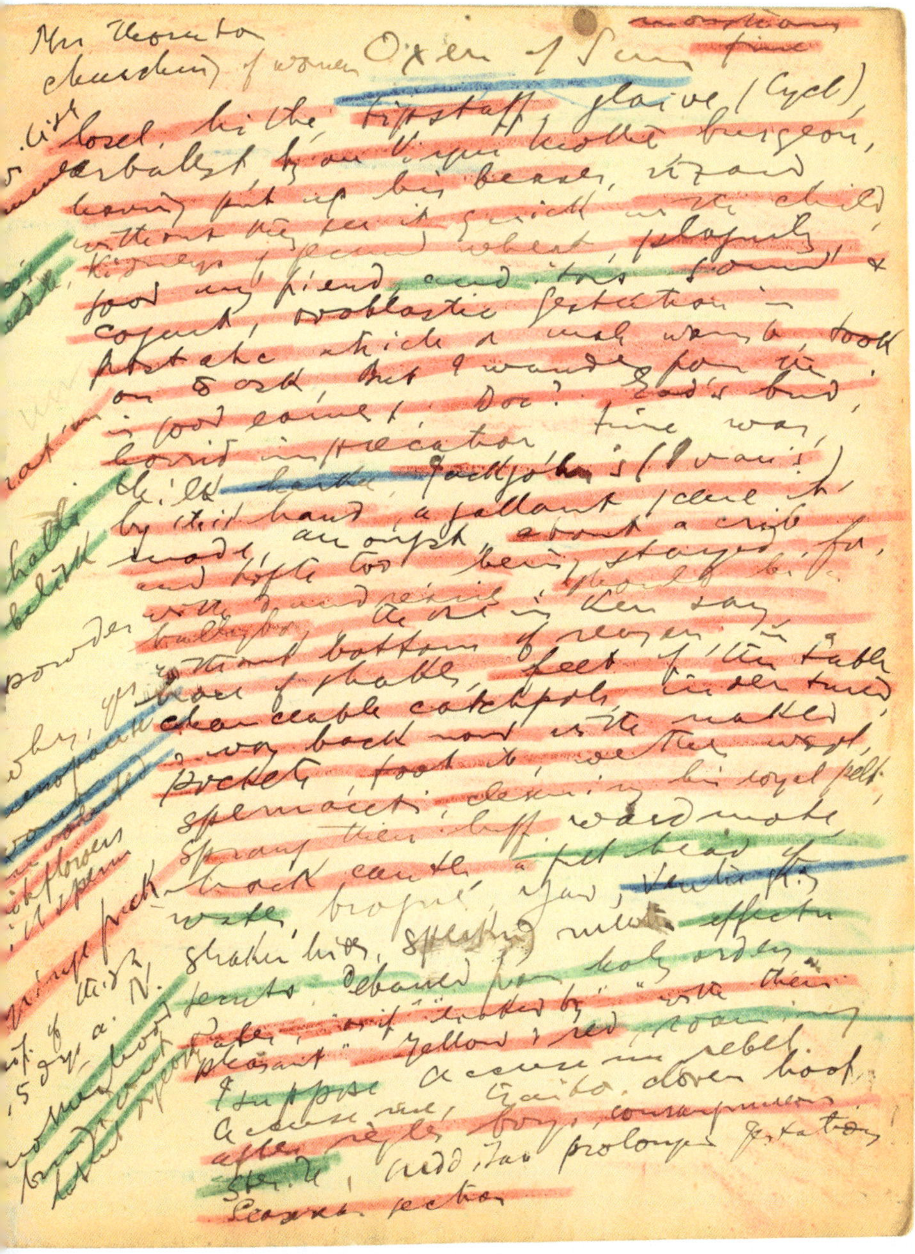

Mr Thornton

churching of women Oxen of Sun

fine

(Cycl)

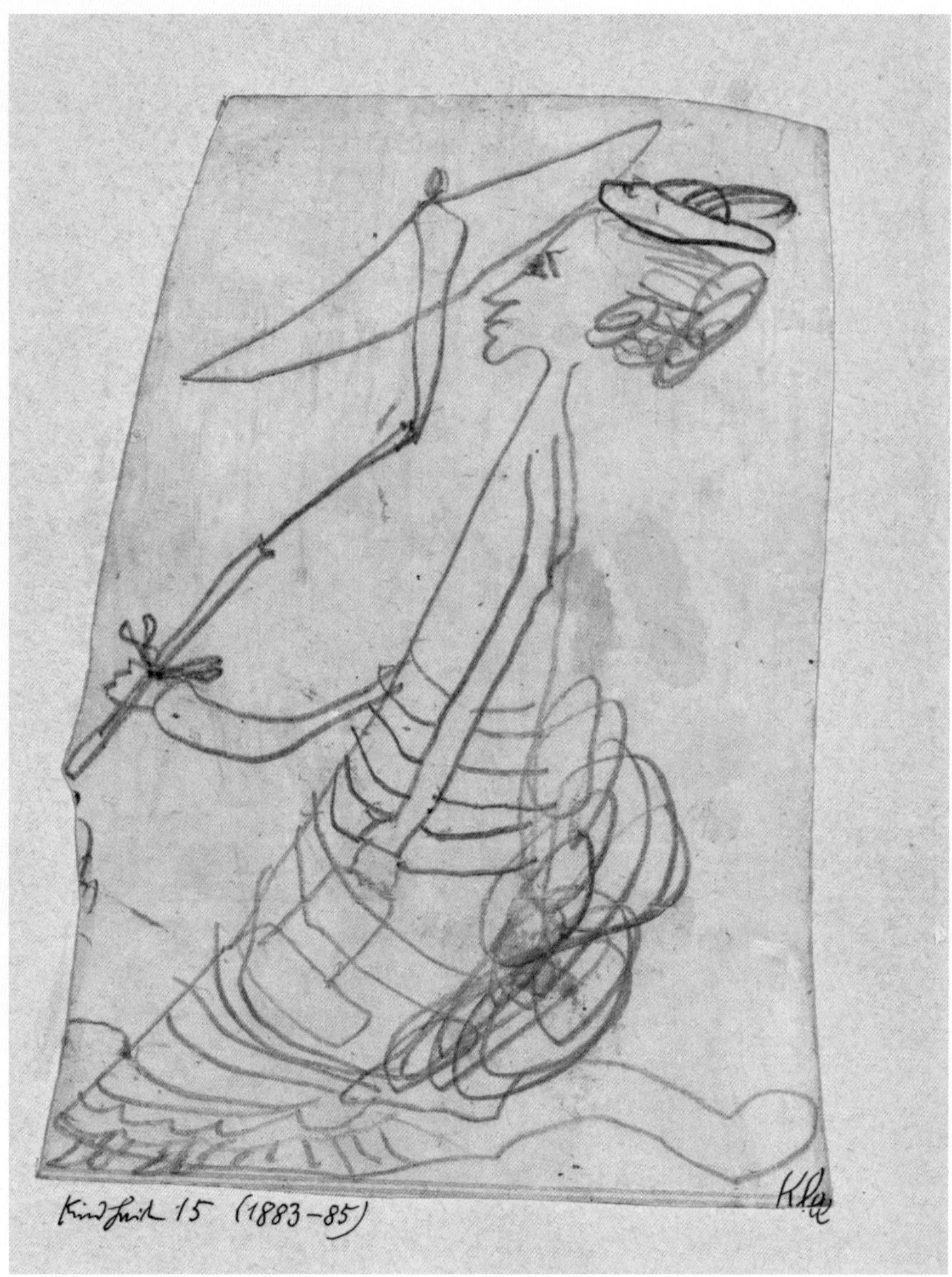

BEGINNINGS

Styles and interests visible from an artist's childhood works.

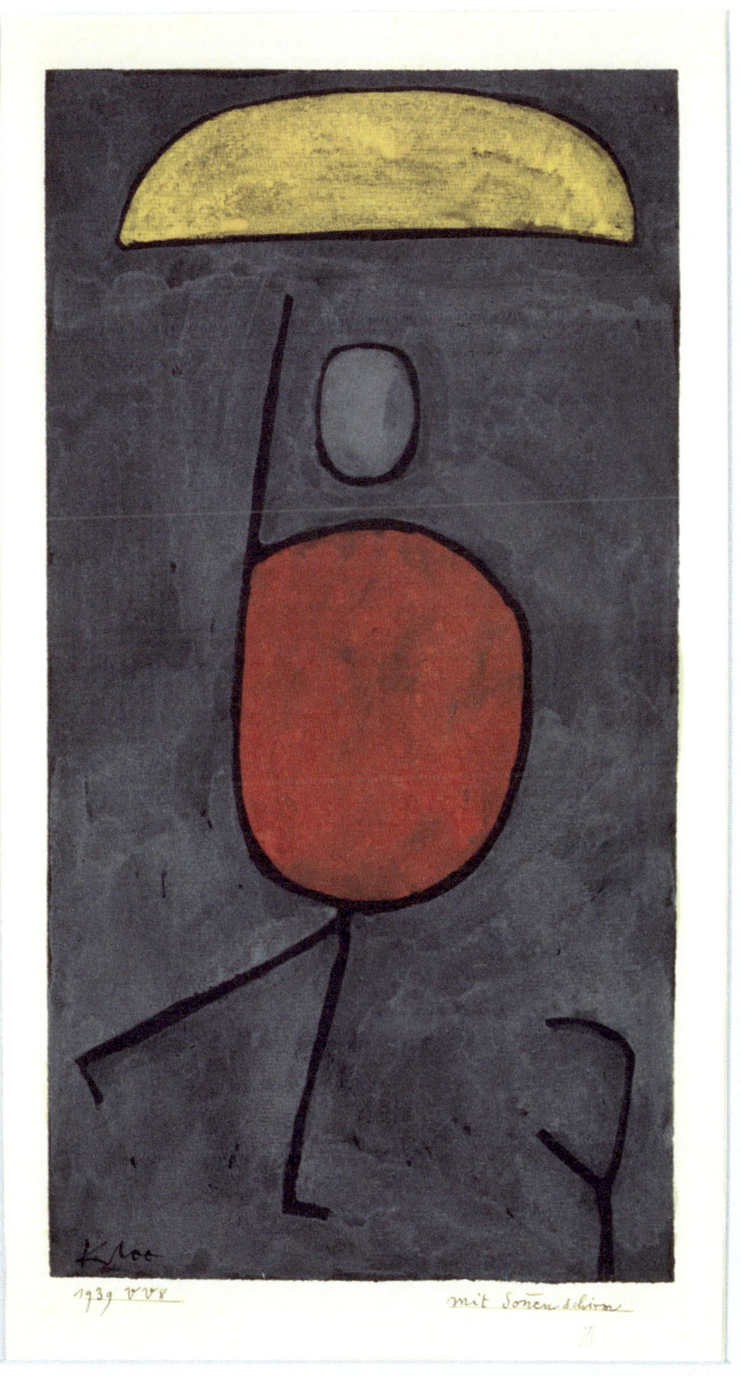

PAUL KLEE (B. 1879)

Lady With Parasol, between 1883 and 1885, left. Pencil on paper on cardboard, 4.5 × 3.5 in. Klee was between four and six years old.

With Parasol, 1939, above. Watercolor and pencil on paper, 14.4 × 7.7 in. Klee was sixty years old.

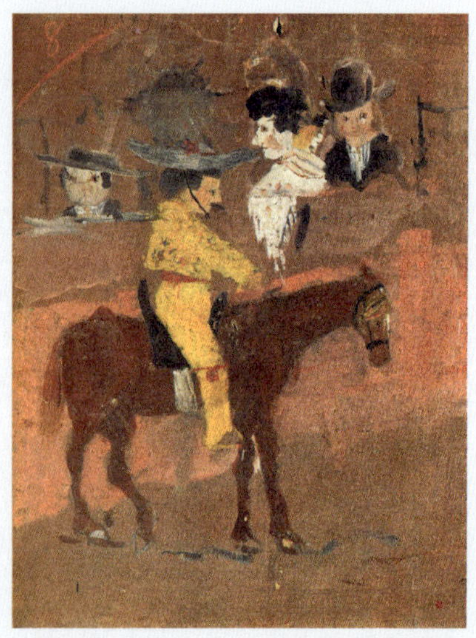

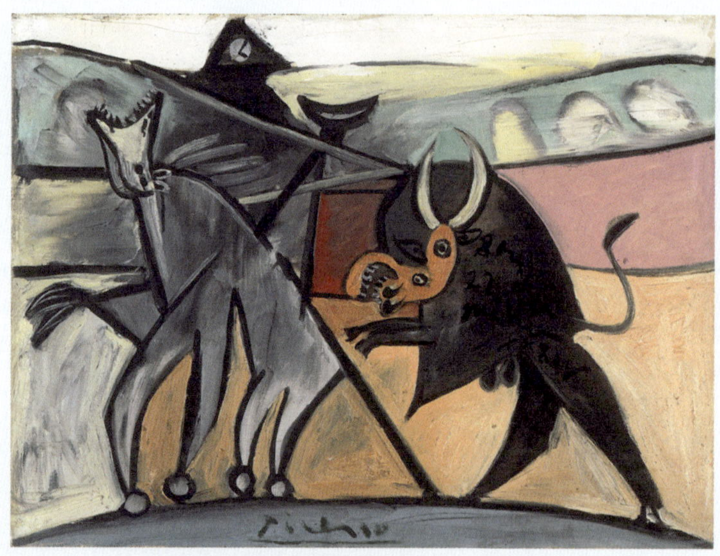

PABLO PICASSO (B. 1881)

Le Petit Picador Jaune, 1889. Oil on wood, 9.45 × 7.48 in. Picasso was eight years old.

Bullfight, 1934. Oil on canvas. 21.26 × 28.74 in. Picasso was fifty-three years old.

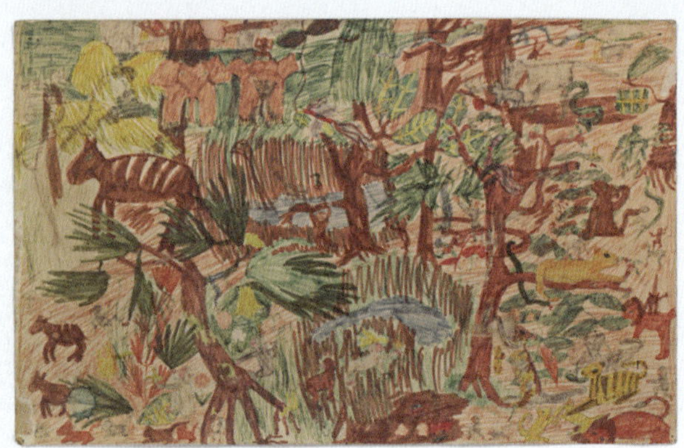

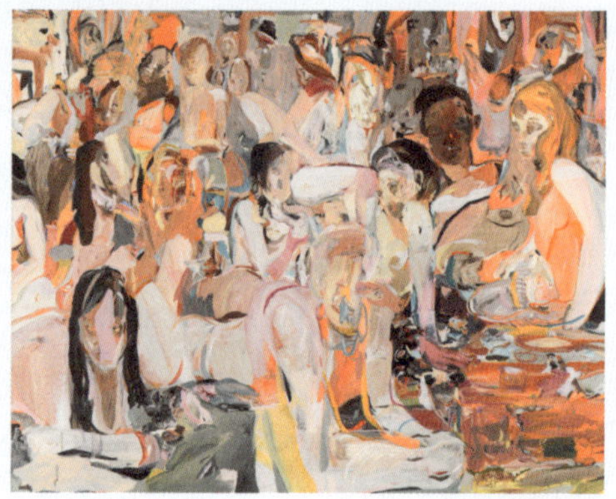

CECILY BROWN (B. 1969)

Jungle, 1977. Marker on paper, 8 × 12.5 in. Brown was seven or eight years old.

Untitled, 2013. Oil on linen, 77 × 97 in. Brown was forty-four.

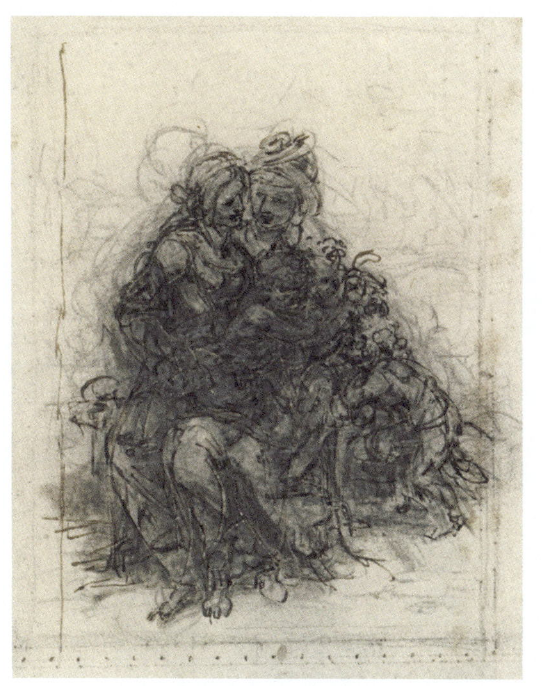

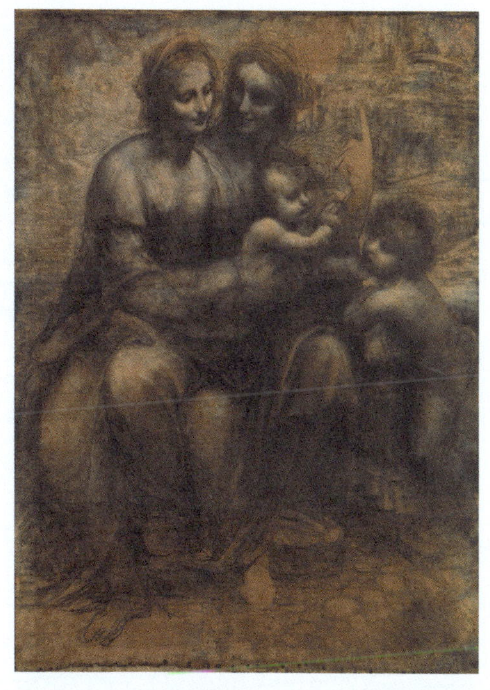

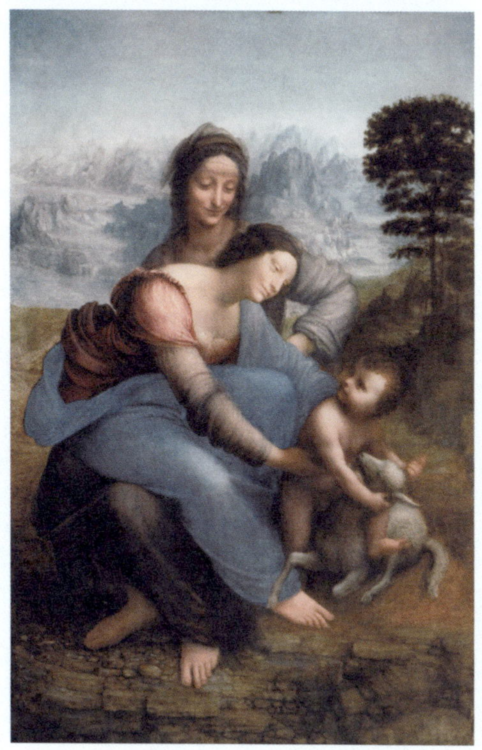

DOINGS AND REDOINGS
Leonardo da Vinci, developing the same theme from a drawing (detail above left); to an early work (above right), *The Virgin and Child with Saint Anne and Infant Saint John the Baptist*—also called *The Burlington House Cartoon*; to a painting (right), *The Virgin, the Child Jesus and Saint Anne*, itself probably unfinished when he died.

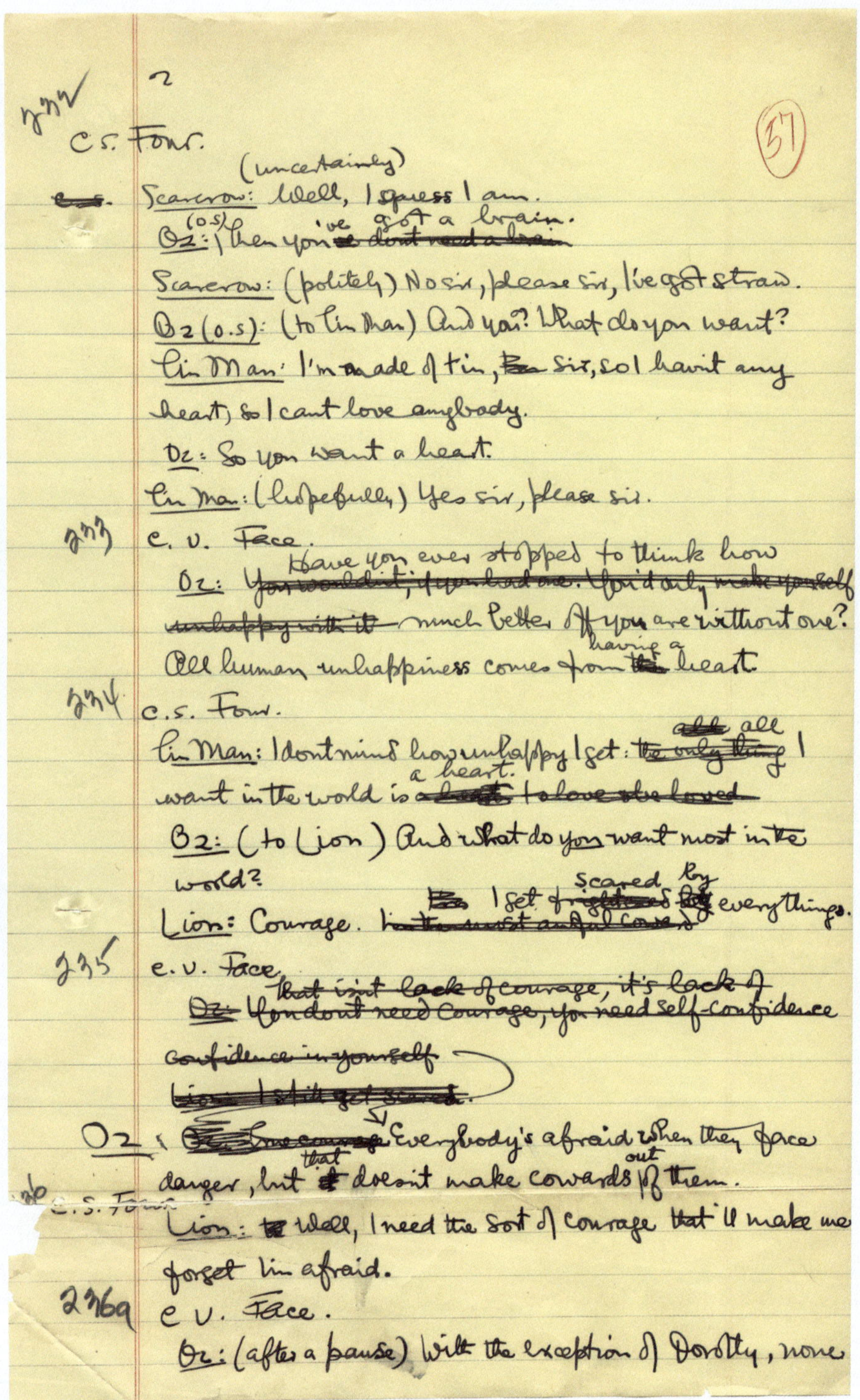
232 2

C.S. Four. (37)

Scarecrow: (uncertainly) Well, I guess I am.

Oz: (O.S.) Then you've got a brain.

Scarecrow: (politely) No sir, please sir, I've got straw.

Oz (O.S.): (to Tin Man) And you? What do you want?

Tin Man: I'm made of tin, sir, so I haven't any heart, so I can't love anybody.

Oz: So you want a heart.

Tin Man: (hopefully) Yes sir, please sir.

233 C.U. Face.

Oz: Have you ever stopped to think how much better off you are without one? All human unhappiness comes from having a heart.

234 C.S. Four.

Tin Man: I don't mind how unhappy I get: all I want in the world is a heart.

Oz: (to Lion) And what do you want most in the world?

Lion: Courage. I get scared by everythings.

235 C.U. Face.

Oz: Everybody's afraid when they face danger, but that doesn't make cowards out of them.

C.S. Four

Lion: Well, I need the sort of courage that'll make me forget I'm afraid.

236a C.U. Face.

Oz: (after a pause) With the exception of Dorothy, none

DRAFTS An early stab at the script for *The Wizard of Oz*, in longhand.

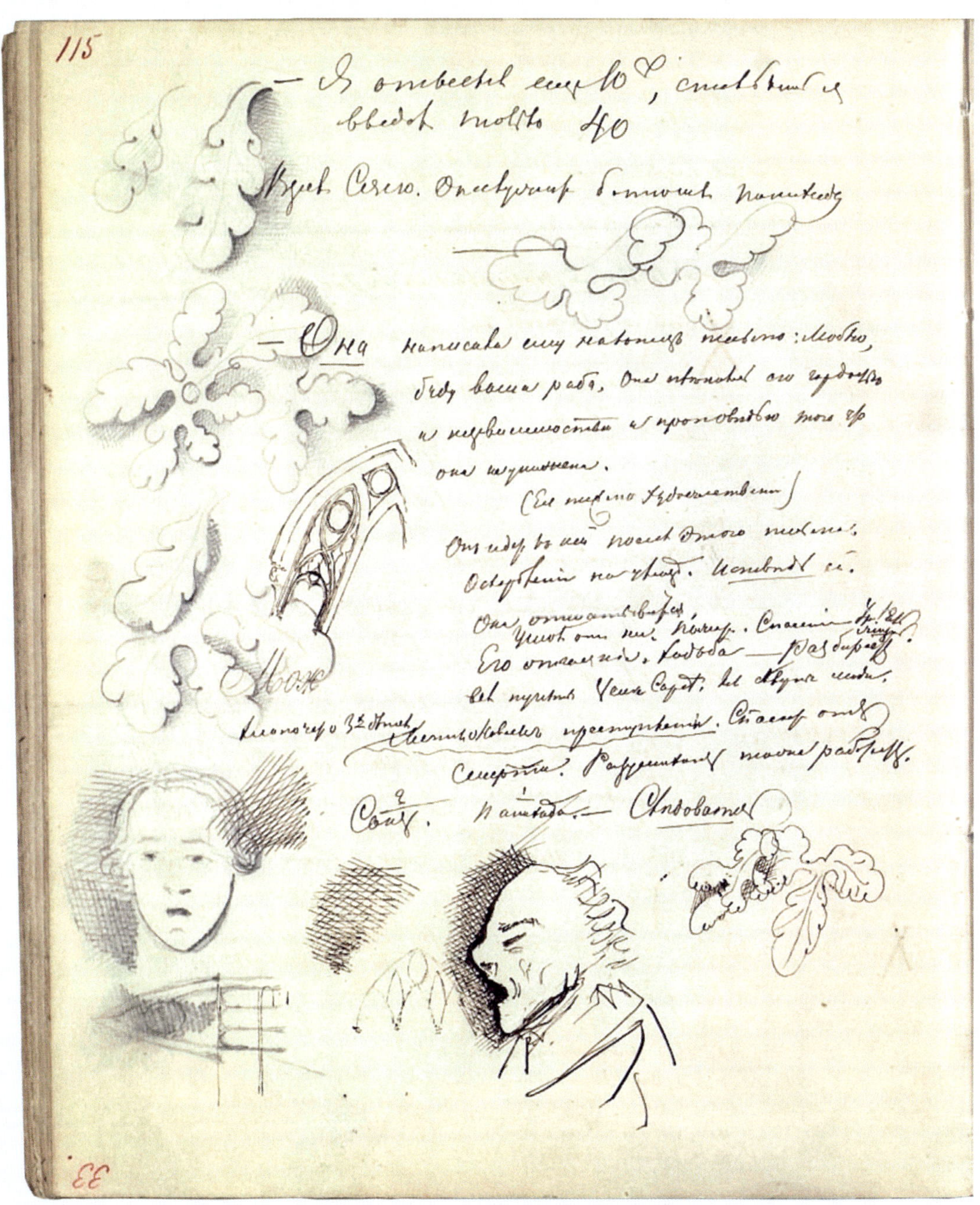

DOODLES Voluminous doodler Fyodor Dostoevsky working out *Crime and Punishment* and, apparently (it's not clear), playing around with what Raskolnikov and Svidrigailov might have looked like.

(Coda)

(1) college-from hunter — Independence grows bit by
dostoevsky
boys
bleached hair

(19) Loss of vir
✓ Jane's plac
✓ Hospital
✓ Jane's Su
(20) Jane's dea
✓ Buddy's
✓ Final inte

(2) Summer school:
DRA .
EDWIN loss of virginity
going to Europe - voyage on
"You'll never say you're not ha

Knopf books
Mother
A. Kazin
Yaddo
M. Moore?

(18) End of treatments
✓ dream about father
✓ Jane - lesbian
✓ contraceptives
(19) letter from Buddy
Jane's suicide
(20) loss of virginity
Buddy's visit
Back to school
Interview

Sect 2
16
13
14
17
17
77
+4 @ 15 = 60
137
119
256

Sections
280

✓ JANE
(16) ✓ Insu
VOT -
✓ Broken gl
✓ Roses
✓ "I [illegible]

(17) Move
Yanni
✓ Church Shock
✓ lips w

(18) Fina
✓ Bud
✓ Jane
Inte

Dream father
Edwin
Looses virginity
✓ Nurse-walks at [illegible] hospital
Lesbians
Jane + Dee Dee
Father
Buddy's letter

OUTLINES Sylvia Plath's
for The Bell Jar.

10 ✓ No writing course
✓ Dead stop
✓ Neighbours - Mrs A.
✓ Sleeplessness
✓ Increasing pills
✓ Visit to psychiatrist

✓ No luck on thesis - Confusion about what to do ✓ can't read ✓ Big freeze

In re JODY MOTHER MRS A.

✓ walks on common with sailors
Oswald (a) ghosts
Summer in suburbs
✓ BUDDY'S letters

11 2nd visit to psychiatrist
✓ Shorthand
Shock treatment at
✓ private mental hospital
✓ Windows barred
✓ Vow to kill self

12 Suicide attempts
✓ razor
✓ hanging
13 ✓ Egg rock - Jody - happy vignettes
drowning
✓ sleeping pills
✓ Volunteer work at hospital
- Oswald ✓
- hanging ✓
- drowning ✓
shadows
Father's grave

14 ✓ First hospital - anxious med students -
✓ eye care "blind man"
✓ steak
✓ 2nd hospital - city - mental ward
✓ Broken thermometers - padded cell
✓ Occupational therapy
✓ Crowd of med students
✓ visit of mother - mocking of other patients

Brother home

15 Drive in chauffeured car with Mrs P.
✓ to 3rd hospital
✓ Codman - end of hell JANE ✓
✓ Head doctor - god - history of hospital
16 ✓ suspicions
✓ Move - room
✓ Insulin & Dr. B.
Movies
Roses: birthday - I hate my mother
✓ Greenhouse
✓ walk hours
✓ lobotomy girl

broken glass
embroidered chicken
weaving
✓ woman in purple
church
walks

16 Move to Belknap
Laurel & Co.
'I don't deserve to be here'
18 No breakfast - shock treatment
inability to remember fatal predicament
18 CHARACTERS - others like me - college girls
Change - visitors
They'll take you back to college

BUDDY'S VISIT

JAY'S story

315
$\frac{}{105}$

213
$\frac{}{117}$

SMITH COLLEGE
MEMORANDUM
To
From
In re
Date

Oh Sumptuous
moment
Slower go
that I
may gloat on
thee.
'Twill never
be the same
to starve
Now I abundance
see.
Which was to
famish, then or
now.
the difference
of Day
Ask him
unto the Gallows
led - called
With morning
in the sky

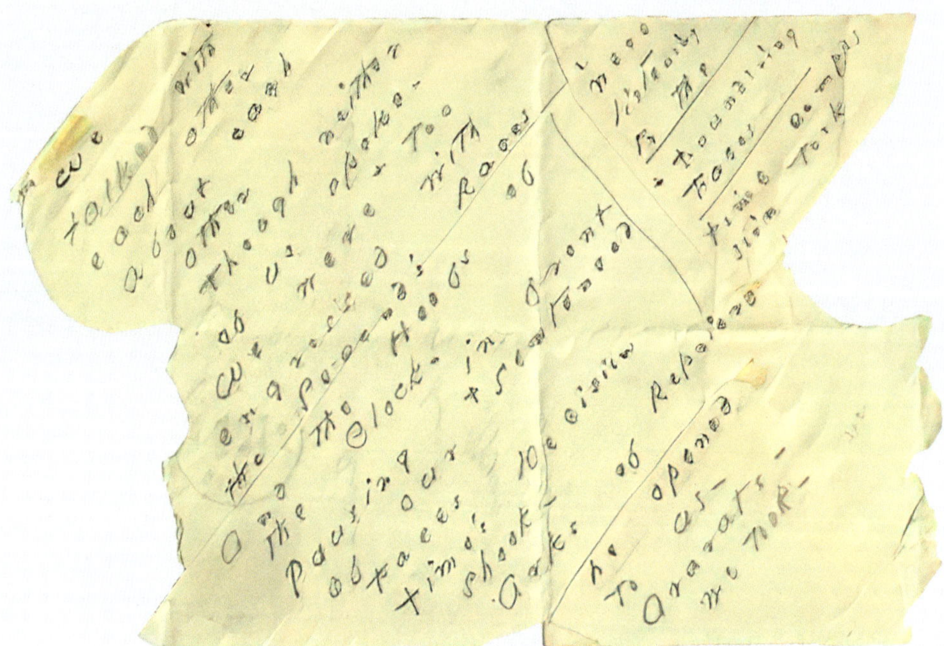

ENVELOPES

This very famous example of all the genres, the poems Emily Dickinson wrote in her hand on envelopes (which also include varieties of lines and stanzas she was trying out).

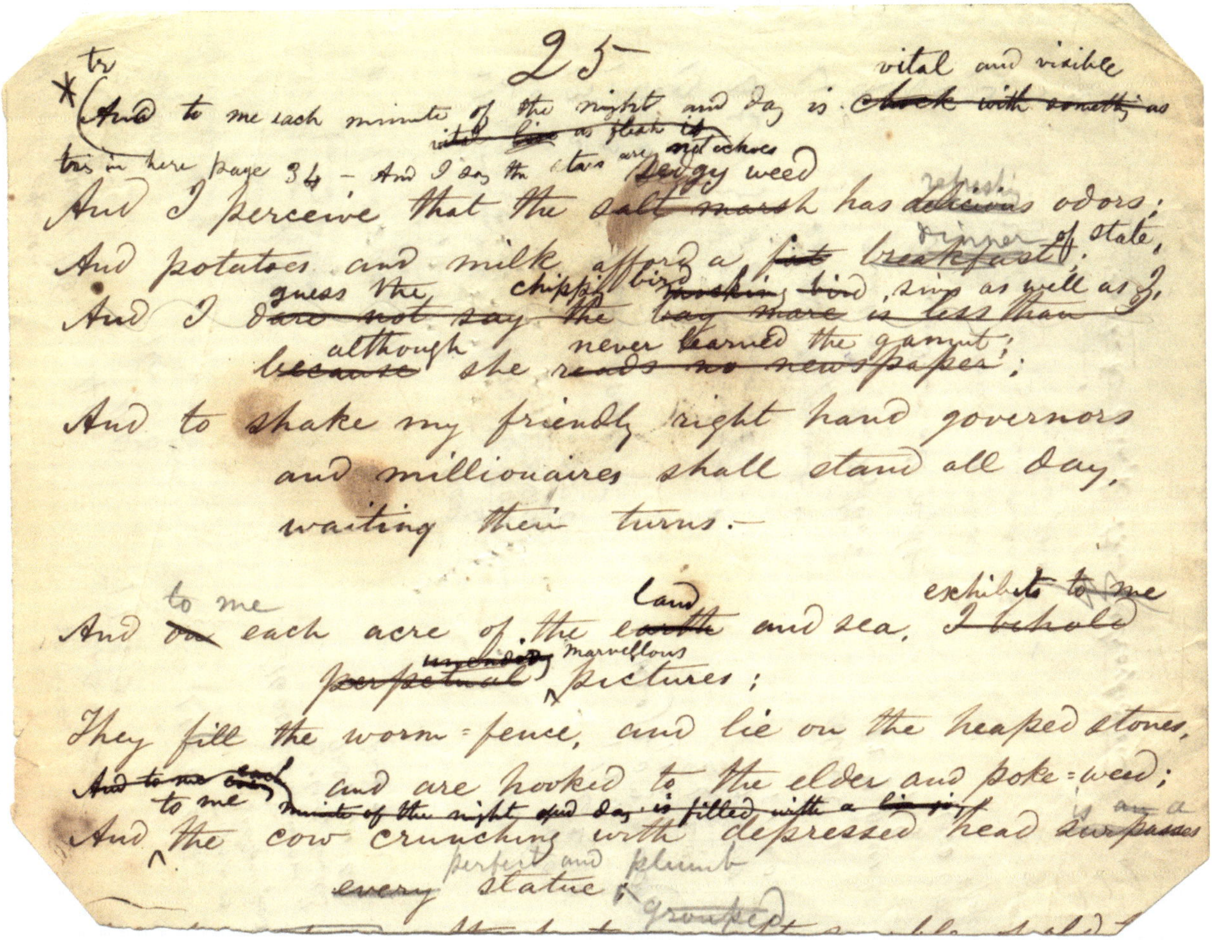

FORENSICS

One of the pleasures of artifacts—for academics or obsessive fans—is the way they reveal a chronology of intent. Walt Whitman wrote nine versions of *Leaves of Grass*, above. In fact, he kept revising the poems up to his death. The poet Robert Hass talked about how changes Whitman made to "Song of Myself" reflected his state at the time of each alteration, shifting the line "I come again and again" in the first edition to read "I come and I depart" as he moved closer to his death. Sometimes the shifts (parentheses added and subtracted, commas becoming periods, ellipses turning into dashes) are more subtle but no less resonant for scholars who feast on calibrations like these.

79

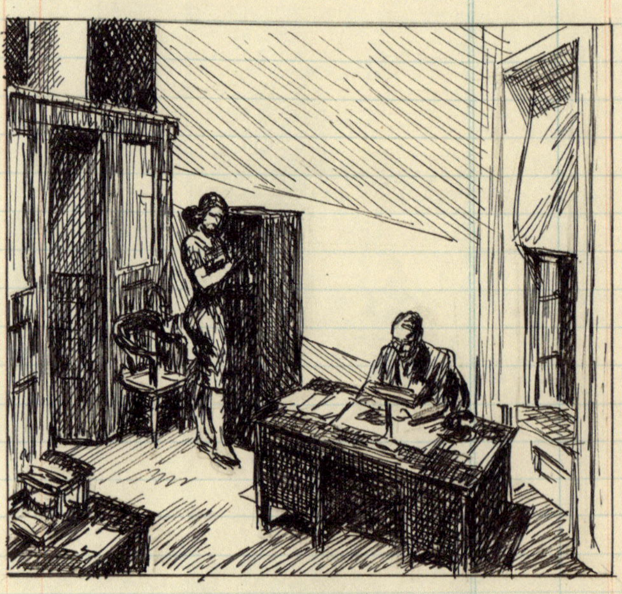

<u>Office at Night</u> 22×25. "Confidentially Yours" "Room 1005"
Feb. 22, 1940.

White walls, electric light from ceiling, from desk lamp (green cover) + from light outside window. Green floor (dark green), mahogany furniture, blue blotter on desk, green metal filing cabinet. Brown wood partitions with pebbled glass panes. Pale green window shade. Outside window ~~strip~~ edge of masonry putty color. Man in grey coat, blond hair. "Shirley" in blue dress, white collar, flesh stockings black pumps + black hair + plenty of lip stick. Figures stand out in space, not fastened to background.

Belgium canvas, double prime smooth. Blockx + Winsor Newton Colors
Poppy oil. Blockx Silver White (lead white)

75th Anniversary Exhib. of Salmagundi Club prize — $1000 May 4, 1945
invited as guest exhibitor.

~~Bought by Butler Art Institute, Youngstown, Ohio Spring 1948. 1500 - 1/3 = 1000.~~ Paid July 27, 49
Walker Art Center, Minneapolis, Min. 15~~00~~ - 1/3 = ~~1000~~ 1000 June 27, 49.
John Clancy cited value for insurance $15000 – 1964.

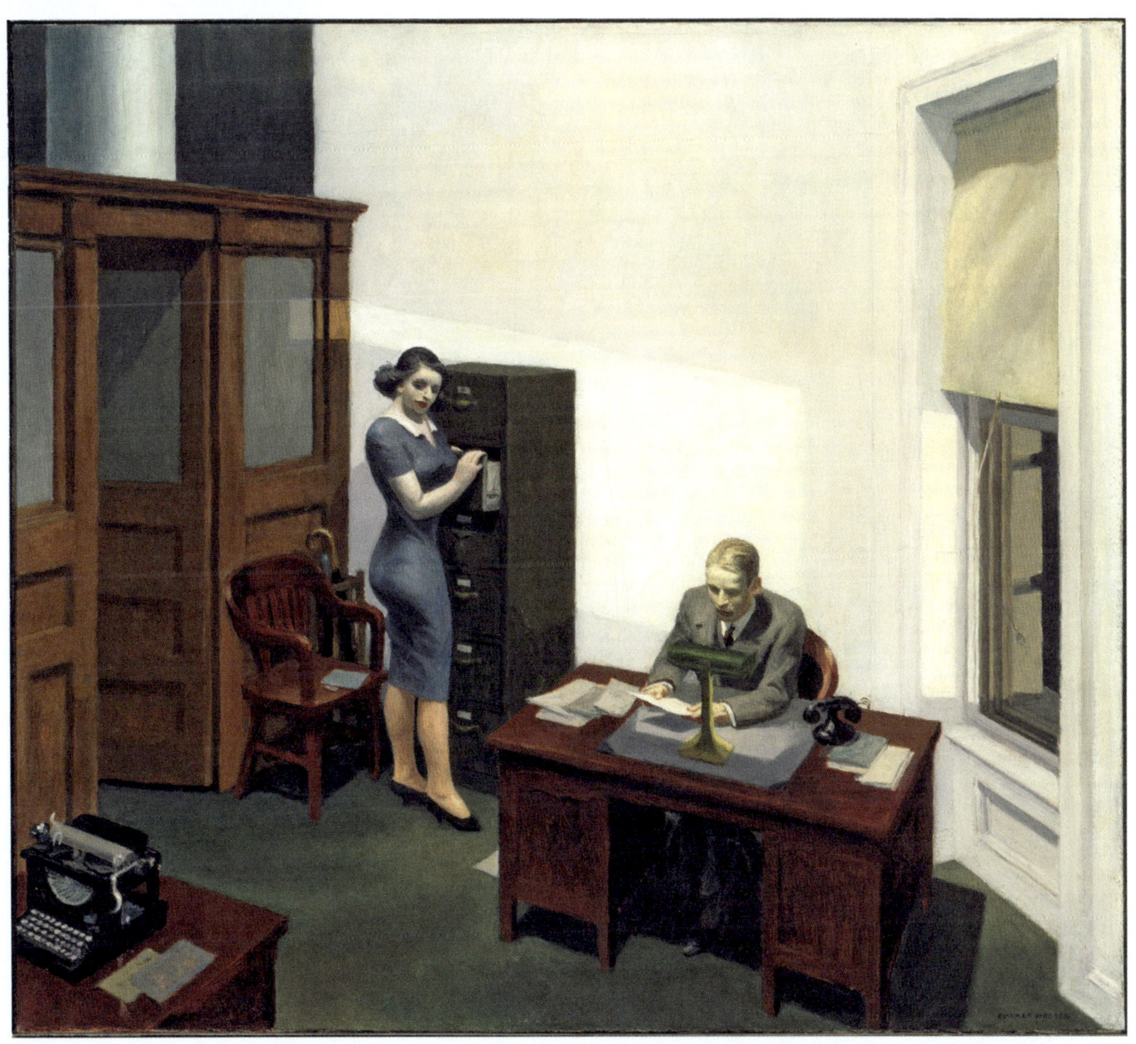

STUDIES

Many artists think through their plan for a work in sketches but few are as meticulous as Edward Hopper was in this diagram I came across in the museum show *Edward Hopper's New York*. It's a journal description and drawing for his painting *Office at Night*, which anticipates the painting down to every last detail. It even gives "Shirley" a name.

Acknowledgments

I OFTEN SAY that the best thing about magazines is that they are collective efforts, and sometimes—the happiest times—this book felt that way too. Foremost among my partners in this project were the artists who so generously answered my incessant and often ignorant questions—some again and again over a long period of time—and also rummaged through dead files and trash bins to help build these accounts. Several suggested others to join in and made introductions. I came to view them less as the subjects of this book than as its collaborators, and my conversations with them were the project's joy. I am beyond grateful to each of them.

Over the period I was writing it, this book had three different project managers: Caroline Wolff, Barrett Hellmann, and, for most of it, Mardee Goff. My thanks to each, but especially to Mardee, who soldiered with me even through her pregnancy and new motherhood. *Project manager* is an all-encompassing euphemism. Mardee was navigator, negotiator, scholar, counselor, and friend. I can't imagine how I could have written the book without her.

At different stages, two of the best editors I have ever worked with—Jared Hohlt and Susan Bolotin—read significant parts of the manuscript. Their general wisdom, excellent specific guidance, and overall soothing ways were invaluable. It was wonderful being edited by them after years watching enviously as others benefited from their care.

The book, with all of its many different and odd modes, was nearly impossible to design, but that didn't stop my *New York* magazine design partner Luke Hayman and his Pentagram colleagues Patrick Crowley, Rob Hewitt, and Anna LaGrone (also Matt Willey, in its earliest incarnation) from finding original (and exquisite) ways of marrying images and text, and of making this book and cover so handsome. The countless hours I spent moving red arrows around with the deft (and patient) Rob Hewitt were a particularly satisfying throwback to my magazine days. Every once in a while I would find myself explaining that I hoped the book would be a sort of interactive museum of creativity, with exhibits and wall text and talk wafting through its corridors. I had no idea what I was talking about, but Luke and his team met my half-brained hope with ingenuity and intelligence.

Matthew Sandager, who is a glorious animator, artist, and film editor, is also a very talented photographer who shot many of the images for this book and turned some of them into artworks of their own.

Jerry Saltz, the inspired art critic whom I was lucky enough to work with for years, is a real-life Yoda. My conversations with him about artists and creativity were crucial to my understanding of a subject I began by knowing very little about. He very delicately steered me away from some particularly bad ideas, and offered up excellent ones instead, many of which I've borrowed (stolen?). You should read his own sage words on what makes artists artists; he's the expert.

Isaac Shub and Hanna Park fact-checked the book. They did outstanding work; the mistakes that stubbornly remain are my fault.

Over the course of the research and writing of this book, I discussed it with many friends who read parts, argued with and encouraged me, offered suggestions, sent me relevant reading matter and connected me with others. Many of them happen to be artists themselves, who would have made excellent chapters in their own right. They include Matthew Burgess, David Cafiero, Marcelle Clements, Rachel Cline, Ken Corbett, Bill Goldstein, David Haskell, Judy Katz, Celeste Lecesne, Daniel Okrent, Elizabeth Povinelli, Jody Quon, Sal Randolph, Oren Rudavsky, Joseph Sheftel, David Shipley, Elazar Sontag, Patricia Towers, Pam Wasserstein, and Blake West.

The journalist Lynn Hirschberg was immensely helpful to me at the start of this book, but her contributions to it vastly preceded my even thinking of it, since our conversations about how artists work, her keen understanding of the territory, and a lifetime exploring these themes together as editor/writer (and as friends from our earliest days at *Esquire*, growing up together in journalism) are baked into the book. I am indebted to her.

Frank Rich first invited me to the *Veep* shoot, which, in a sense (though I didn't know it at the time), put this book in motion. He arranged a dinner for me to meet my hero Stephen Sondheim. He introduced me to Joe Lelyveld (an introduction that changed my life). That's not even to mention our cherished years of friend- and colleagueship.

Anna Wintour has been a crucial ally throughout my career and was a great friend to this book as well. I'm grateful, as always, for her generosity and insight.

I wrote a chunk of this book at Yaddo, the artists' retreat. My thanks to Elaina Richardson especially.

My agents David Kuhn and Nate Muscato at Aevitas were encouraging from the get-go, helped me imagine a much more ambitious book than I had originally considered, and then did their magic to make it possible. I'm glad I listened to them.

This book is not in a usual form, neither mostly words nor mostly pictures. It isn't exactly reportage or oral history or fanzine or memoir or theory, but a little of all of those things. It's just its own atypical god-knows-what, and when I first described what I was after I was afraid that would make some editors nervous. But at Penguin, Ann Godoff greeted its unorthodoxy with enthusiasm, offered just exactly the right words to get me moving in the right direction, and helped maneuver the book into the best realization of that idea I could manage. My deep thanks to her, to the terrific (wise, kind) Casey Denis, and to their Penguin colleagues Victoria Lopez, Megan Gerrity, Claire Vaccaro, and Darren Haggar.

Is it too strange to thank my psychotherapist? Sargam Mona Jain not only helped me work through whatever craziness comes with writing a book of this sort (and it was a kind of minefield for me, given some of its underpinnings), she also, more specifically, expressed an early interest in the aspects of this book that dealt with creativity and the mind, clarifying and enlarging my thinking. She also read parts—she'd make an excellent editor; I've come to see that shrink and editor are more aligned than I thought.

Finally, as I discovered over and over while writing this book, expression often fails to fully capture the feeling it's trying to convey. My husband, Daniel Kaizer, lived this book with me, read countless drafts, offered advice, criticism, reassurance. This is not the place to describe all the ways I love him, but it is, perhaps, to express my (inexpressible) gratitude.

Credits

COVER • Marcel Proust, Manuscript of *In Search of Lost Time*, Bibliothèque nationale de France

INTRODUCTION • Frank Gehry, Guggenheim Museum Bilbao, design sketch of the riverfront elevation, Bilbao, Spain, 1991 © Frank O. Gehry • Guggenheim Bilbao Museoa © FMGB Guggenheim Bilbao Museoa, photo by Erika Barahona Ede • Alice Neel, *Black Draftee (James Hunter)*, 1965, oil on canvas. 60 × 40 in, 152.4 x 101.6 cm © The Estate of Alice Neel. Courtesy of The Estate of Alice Neel and David Zwirner • Diego Rodríguez de Silva y Velázquez, *Philip IV*, 1623; 1628, oil on canvas, 198 × 101.5 cm, (P001182), Madrid, Museo Nacional del Prado. © Photographic Archive Museo Nacional del Prado • Marcel Proust, Manuscript of *In Search of Lost Time*, Bibliothèque nationale de France • "Blowin' In The Wind", Words and Music by Bob Dylan © Universal Tunes. Used by Permission - All Rights Reserved • Bob Dylan, "Blowin' In The Wind": autograph manuscript of three verses and chorus, [ca. 1962], The Morgan Library & Museum. MA 6202. Gift; George Hecksher; 1997. Photo: The Morgan Library & Museum, New York • Eric Fischl, *Bad Boy*, 1981, oil on canvas, 168 × 244 cm © 2023 Eric Fischl / Artists Rights Society (ARS), NY • All images of annotated script and score manuscripts from *Company* courtesy of the Estate of Stephen J. Sondheim © 2023. All rights reserved • Joanna Quinn, *Dreams and Desires - Family Ties*, Jesus Sequence Rough Keys, 2006 © Joanna Quinn/ Beryl Productions

1. KARA WALKER • Kara Walker, Rome, 2016. *Easter Parade in the Old Country*, graphite lumber marker and charcoal on paper. 73 ½ × 313 in, 2016 • Photo: Ari Marcopoulos • Stamp Photo: Paul Zimmerman / WireImage via Getty Images • Untitled sketches © Kara Walker • Powerpoint slides [found images] © Kara Walker • Kara Walker, *Untitled Sketch for Domino Materials*, 2013, molasses and graphite on paper, 8.5 × 11 in (21.6 × 27.9 cm) © Kara Walker • Untitled sketch © Kara Walker • Kara Walker, Detail of *Untitled*, 2013–14, charcoal and graphite on paper, 50.125 x 76 in (127.3 × 193 cm) © Kara Walker • Foreground: Kara Walker, *Sphinx sugar model/ study*, 2014, sugar on polystyrene, 31 × 63 × 22 in (78.7 × 160 × 55.9 cm) © Kara Walker • Kara Walker, Still from *An Audience*, 2014, digital video with sound, 27:18 min. © Kara Walker • Kara Walker, *A Subtlety, or the Marvelous Sugar Baby, an Homage to the unpaid and overworked Artisans who have refined our Sweet tastes from the cane fields to the Kitchens of the New World on the Occasion of the demolition of the Domino Sugar Refining Plant*, 2014. Polystyrene foam, sugar. Approximately 426 × 312 × 906 in (1,082 × 792.5 × 2,301.2 cm). Installation view: *At the behest of Creative Time Kara E. Walker has confected: A Subtlety, or the Marvelous Sugar Baby, an Homage to the unpaid and overworked Artisans who have refined our Sweet tastes from the cane fields to the Kitchens of the New World on the Occasion of the demolition of the Domino Sugar Refining Plant.* A project of Creative Time • Domino Sugar Refinery, Brooklyn, NY, May 10–July 6, 2014. Photo: Jason Wyche. Artwork © 2014 Kara Walker

2. TONY KUSHNER • Stamp Portrait: Everett Collection Inc / Alamy Stock Photo • Tony Kushner, Notebooks & Typescripts for *Angels in America*; Rare Book and Manuscript Library, Columbia University Library. Courtesy Tony Kushner

3. ROZ CHAST • Stamp Photo: Anna LaGrone • All images and materials courtesy of R. Chast

4. MICHAEL CUNNINGHAM • Stamp Portrait: Courtesy of Michael Cunningham • All materials and images copyright © 1998 by Michael Cunningham

5. MOSES SUMNEY • Photo: Spencer Kelly / spencerkelly.com • Stamp Photo: Christopher Lane / Contour via Getty Images • All materials and images courtesy of Moses Sumney

6. SOFIA COPPOLA • Photo: *Lost in Translation*, Director Sofia Coppola, Bill Murray on the set 2003 © Focus Features / courtesy Everett Collection • Stamp Photo: CelebrityArchaeology.com /Alamy Stock Photo • *Marie Antoinette*, Director Sofia Coppola, Kirsten Dunst on the set, 2006 © Entertainment Pictures/Alamy Stock Photo • Note for *Lost in Translation*, Courtesy of Sofia Coppola • Édouard Manet, *Luncheon on the Grass (Le Déjeuner sur l'herbe, 1863)*, oil on canvas, 208 × 264.5 cm (81.9 ×104.1 in). Musée d'Orsay, Paris • Bow Wow Wow, *See Jungle! See Jungle! Go Join Your Gang Yeah! City All Over, Go Ape Crazy*, released in October 1981 by RCA Records. Photo: Andy Earl • Movie still from *Marie Antoinette*, 2006, Sony Pictures Releasing. Courtesy of Sofia Coppola

7. SUSAN MEISELAS • Stamp Photo: Roger Cremers / laif / Redux • Contact frames of *Lulu and Debbie, Tunbridge, Vermont*, 1974 © Susan Meiselas, Magnum Photos • Contact sheet with *Lena's Third Season, Lehighton, Pennsylvania*, 1975 © Susan Meiselas, Magnum Photos • Contact frames of *Through the Dressing Room, Barton, Vermont*, 1974 © Susan Meiselas, Magnum Photos • *Susan Meiselas, field notebook*, 1973–75 © Susan Meiselas, Magnum Photos • Contact sheet with *Returning backstage, Essex Junction, Vermont*, 1973 © Susan Meiselas, Magnum Photos • Printer's proof of *Returning Backstage, Essex Junction, Vermont*, 1973 © Susan Meiselas, Magnum Photos

8. STEPHEN SONDHEIM • Photo: Michael Ochs Archives via Getty Image • Stamp Photo: Vera Anderson / WireImage via Getty Images • All images of annotated script and score manuscripts from *Company* courtesy of the Estate of Stephen J. Sondheim © 2023. All rights reserved • "Getting Married Today" from *Company*. Music and Lyrics by Stephen Sondheim. Copyright © 1970 Range Road Music Inc., Jerry Leiber Music, Silver Seahorse Music LLC and Rilting Music, Inc. Copyright Renewed. All Rights Administered by Round Hill Carlin. All Rights Reserved. Used by Permission. *Reprinted by Permission of Hal Leonard LLC* • "The Wedding Is Off" from *Company*. Music and Lyrics by Stephen Sondheim. Copyright © 2006, 2009 Range Road Music Inc., Jerry Leiber Music and Rilting Music, Inc. All Rights Administered by Round Hill Carlin. All Rights Reserved. Used by Permission. *Reprinted by Permission of Hal Leonard LLC* • Excerpt(s) from *Finishing the Hat: Collected Lyrics (1954–1981) with Attendant Comments, Principles, Heresies, Grudges, Whines and Anecdotes* by Stephen Sondheim, copyright © 2010 by Stephen Sondheim. Used by permission of Alfred A. Knopf, an imprint of the Knopf Doubleday Publishing Group, a division of Penguin Random House LLC. All rights reserved

9. LOUISE GLÜCK • Stamp Photo: Abaca Press/ Alamy Stock Photo • Materials and images courtesy Louise Glück • "Song," from *Winter Recipes from the Collective* by Louise Glück. Copyright © 2021 by Louise Glück. Reprinted by permission of Farrar, Straus and Giroux. All Rights Reserved

10. MARIA de LOS ANGELES • A drawing from *True North*, graphite and watercolor on paper, 18 × 24 in © Maria de Los Angeles. Photo: Matthew Sandager • Stamp Photo: Guadalupe Dress, mixed media on canvas, Bodega Bay, CA. Photo: Ryan Bonilla, 2019 • *Transcending Myths*, 2018, mixed media garments, 1500 works on paper. Schneider Museum of Art © Maria de Los Angeles. Photo: Raymond Sunwoo • *Guadalupe y Juan Diego*, 2015–2022, acrylic on canvas, 56 × 76 in © Maria de Los Angeles. Photo: Matthew Sandager • Maria de Los Angeles in front of *Valley of Dreams*, 2021, permanent mural, 12 × 12 ft, Glen Ellen, California © Maria de los Ángeles. Photo: Ryan Bonilla • *Untitled*, 2014–2023, acrylic on canvas, 68 × 80 in © Maria de Los Angeles. Photo: Matthew Sandager • *True North* (Mixed Media Fragments) © Maria de Los Angeles. Photo: Matthew Sandager • Series of drawings and small paintings from *True North* © Maria de Los Angeles. Photos: Matthew Sandager

11. NICO MUHLY • Stamp Photo: Ki Price / Camera Press / Redux • Notes © [2024] Nico Muhly. Photo: Matthew Sandager • Email correspondence between Nico Muhly & Michael Harley, 2014. © [2024] Nico Muhly

12. THOMAS BARTLETT • All materials and images courtesy of Thomas Bartlett

13. TWYLA THARP • Photos: Jack Mitchell / Archive Photos via Getty Images • Stamp Photo: Jamie McCarthy / WireImage via Getty Images • The Sperm Bank, Video Stills, courtesy of Twyla Tharp • Scroll and notes courtesy of Twyla Tharp. Photos: Heidi Bohnenkamp

14. JOHN DERIAN • Stamp Photo: Stephen Kent Johnson / OTTO • All materials and images courtesy of John Derian. Photos: Matthew Sandager

15. BARBARA KRUGER • Timeline: Mademoiselle Advert, 1960s. • *Peasant Uprisings in 17th Century France, Russia and China* by Roland Mousnier. First published in Great Britain in 1971 by George Allen & Unwin Ltd. © 1960 Harper & Row, Publishers, Inc. Used by permission of HarperCollins Publishers • Barbara Kruger, *Picture/Readings*, 1978, Black-and-white, color photographs and text, 40.6 × 101.6 cm, 16 × 40 in. Courtesy of the artist and Sprüth Magers • Barbara Kruger, *Untitled (Body)*, 1978, text/ photograph, 48.3 × 243.8 cm, 19 × 96 in. Courtesy of the artist and Sprüth Magers • Barbara Kruger, *Pictures and Promises: A Display of Advertisings, Slogans, and Interventions*, Gathered by Barbara Kruger, 1981. Exhibition poster, 8 ⅜ x 14 in. Courtesy of The Kitchen, NYC • Barbara Kruger,

Pictures and Promises: A Display of Advertisings, Slogans, and Interventions, Gathered by Barbara Kruger. The Kitchen, NYC, 1981. Installation view photo by Paula Court • Barbara Kruger, *Untitled (Your comfort is my silence)*, 1981 photograph and type on paper 10 ⅞ in x 7 ¾ in (28 cm x 20 cm). Glenstone Museum, Potomac, Maryland • Barbara Kruger, *Untitled (Your manias become science)*, 1982 gelatin silver print 42 5⁄16 x 50 15⁄16 x 2 ⅜ in (107 × 129 × 6 cm) framed. Glenstone Museum, Potomac, Maryland • Barbara Kruger, *Untitled (I shop therefore I am)*, 1987. Photographic silkscreen on vinyl. 283.5 × 287.6 × 6.3 cm, 111 ⅝ × 113 ¼ × 2 ½ in, Courtesy of the artist, Glenstone Museum, Potomac, Maryland and Sprüth Magers • Barbara Kruger, *Untitled (Your body is a battleground)*, 1989, Photographic silkscreen on vinyl, 284.5 × 284.5 cm, 112 × 112 in. Courtesy of the artist, The Broad Art Foundation and Sprüth Magers • Barbara Kruger, *Untitled (I hate myself)*, 1992, *Esquire* cover • Barbara Kruger, *Untitled (All violence is the illustration of a pathetic stereotype)*, 1991, Print on vinyl wallpaper, 488 × 584.2 cm, 192 × 230 in, Install view, Barbara Kruger, Mary Boone Gallery, New York, USA, January 5–January 26, 1991, Courtesy of the artist and Sprüth Magers • Barbara Kruger, *The Globe Shrinks*, 2010, 4-screen video installation, 13 min loop, Installation view, Sprüth Magers, Berlin, September 3–October 23, 2010, Courtesy of the artist and Sprüth Magers Photo: Jens Ziehe • Barbara Kruger, *School Bus*, 2012, Los Angeles, CA, LA Fund. Photo: Joshua White / JWPictures .com • Barbara Kruger, Still from the LED version of *Untitled (Your body is a battleground)*, 1989/2019 • Double page spread from: *THINKING OF ~~YOU~~. I MEAN ~~ME~~. I MEAN YOU.*, published by DelMonico Books/Art Institute of Chicago/ Los Angeles County Museum of Art/The Museum of Modern Art, 2021, pp. 126–127. Courtesy of the artist and Sprüth Magers • Barbara Kruger, *Untitled (Brain)*, 2008, *New York* magazine cover • Barbara Kruger, *Untitled (Loser)*, 2016, *New York* magazine cover, October 31 • Barbara Kruger, Still from the LED version of *Untitled (I shop therefore I am)*, 1987/2019. Double page spread from: *THINKING OF ~~YOU~~. I MEAN ~~ME~~. I MEAN YOU.*, published by DelMonico Books/ Art Institute of Chicago/Los Angeles County Museum of Art/The Museum of Modern Art, 2021, pp. 96–97. Courtesy of the artist and Sprüth Magers • Installation view, *Barbara Kruger*, David Zwirner, New York, June 30–August 12, 2022. Courtesy of David Zwirner. Photo: Kerry McFate

16. DAVID MANDEL • Stamp Photo: Paul Morigi/ Getty Images Entertainment via Getty Images • David Mandel and Julia Louis-Dreyfus on set of *Veep*. Photo credit: Justin M Lubin/HBO • All other materials and images courtesy of David Mandel

17. GREGORY CREWDSON • *Gregory Crewdson: Brief Encounters*, photographer Gregory Crewdson (on ladder) on set, 2012 © Zeitgeist Films/ courtesy of Everett Collection • Stamp Photo: Alberto Cristofari / Redux • Gregory Crewdson gazes at a billboard of *Redemption Center* (2018–2019), at the site where the picture was made. 2020, photo by Juliane Hiam © Crewdson Studio • Notes taken by Juliane Hiam while standing at location with the artist, while he was in the early stages of formulating the idea for the picture • Gregory Crewdson, *Untitled (2003–2008)*, digital pigment print, image size: 57 × 88 in © Gregory Crewdson • On the set of *Redemption Center*. 2018. Photo by Grace Clark © Crewdson Studio • On the set of *Redemption Center* during production, 2018. Photo by Grace Clark © Crewdson Studio • On the set of *Redemption Center*. 2018. Photo by Grace Clark © Crewdson Studio • Lisa Myers, production designer, making fog on the set of *Redemption Center*. 2018. Photo by Grace Clark © Crewdson Studio • Gregory Crewdson, *Redemption Center* (2018–2019), digital pigment print, image size: 50 × 88.9 in © Gregory Crewdson

18. MARIE HOWE • Stamp Photo: Colin McPherson / Corbis Entertainment via Getty Images • "The Singularity," from *New and Selected Poems* by Marie Howe. Copyright © 2024 by Marie Howe. Used by permission of W. W. Norton & Company, Inc. • House Doodle. Courtesy of Marie Howe • "Hurry," from *The Kingdom of Ordinary Time* by Marie Howe. Copyright © 2008 by Marie Howe. Used by permission of W. W. Norton & Company, Inc. • Journal Entry, March 16, 2018, courtesy of Marie Howe

19. GAY TALESE • Stamp Photo: Alberto Cristofari / Contrasto / Redux • All materials courtesy of Gay Talese. Photos: Matthew Sandager

20. CHERYL POPE • Stamp Photo: Courtesy of Cheryl Pope • Studies for *Mother and Child on Blue Mat*, Courtesy of the artist and Monique Meloche Gallery • Cheryl Pope, *Woman Bathing Child*, 2020, 47 × 70 in (119.4 × 177.8 cm), needle-punched wool roving on cashmere, painted wood frame. Courtesy of the artist and Monique Meloche Gallery • Studies for *Mother and Child on Blue Mat*, Courtesy of the artist and Monique Meloche Gallery • Detail of *Mother on a Blue Mat*. Courtesy of the artist and Monique Meloche Gallery. Private Collection of Halla Shami Sher • Cheryl Pope, *Mother and Child on Blue Mat*, 2021, 57 ½ x 63 ½ in (146.1 × 161.3 cm), needle-punched wool roving on cashmere, painted wood frame. Courtesy of the artist and Monique Meloche Gallery. Private Collection of Halla Shami Sher

21. SAMIN NOSRAT • Photo: San Francisco Chronicle / Hearst Newspapers via Getty Images • Stamp Photo: Emma McIntyre / Getty Images Entertainment via Getty Images • All materials and images Courtesy of Samin Nosrat & Wendy MacNaughton

22. JOANNA QUINN & LES MILLS • Joanna Quinn Stamp Photo: National Science and Media Museum • Les Mills Stamp Photo: Matthew Horwood / Getty Images Entertainment via Getty Images • All materials and images © Joanna Quinn / Beryl Productions

23. WESLEY MORRIS • Stamp Photo: Courtesy of Wesley Morris • All materials courtesy of Wesley Morris. Photos: Matthew Sandager

24. AMY SILLMAN • Stamp Photo: Courtesy of Amy Sillman • Amy Sillman, *Dub Stamp (1A)*, 2018, ink and acrylic on paper. One in a sequence of double-sided pieces. 60 ½ × 41 ¾ in (153.7 × 106 cm). Photo credit: John Berens. © Amy Sillman. Courtesy of the artist • Figures 1–38 © Amy Sillman. Courtesy of the artist • Amy Sillman, *Miss Gleason*, 2014, oil on canvas. 91 × 84 in. Collection of Los Angeles, MoCA. © Amy Sillman. Courtesy of the artist

25. ANDREW JARECKI • Stills from *Capturing the Friedmans*, 2003, HBO documentary film directed by Andrew Jarecki • Stamp Photo: Lucy Nicholson / Reuters / Redux • Pitch for The Children's Entertainment Project © Hit the Ground Running LLC • *Capturing the Friedmans* Moodboards © Hit the Ground Running LLC • Stills from *Capturing the Friedmans*, 2003, HBO documentary film directed by Andrew Jarecki • Jesse Friedman's yearbook page used with permission of Jesse Friedman

26. ROSTAM • Rostam Batmanglij pictured in Eames Walnut Stool © Eames Office LLC (eamesoffice.com). All rights reserved. Photo: Pippa Drummond for Herman Miller • Stamp Photo: Mike Coppola / Getty Images Entertainment via Getty Images • All materials and images © 2022 Matsor Projects

27. IRA GLASS • Stamp Photo: Larry Busacca / Contour via Getty Images • All materials and images courtesy of Ira Glass

28. SIMPHIWE NDZUBE • Stamp Photo: Courtesy of Simphiwe Nduzbe • Simphiwe Ndzube, *Inqawe*, 2021, acrylic on canvas, 40 × 30 in. Courtesy of the Artist and Nicodim Gallery • Studio image. Photo: Sarah Davis • Simphiwe Ndzube, *Goddess Nanana*, 2018, acrylic, spray paint, and collage on linen, 200 × 204 cm. © Simphiwe Ndzube. Courtesy Stevenson Amsterdam/Cape Town/Johannesburg. Photo: Mario Todeschini • Studio image. Photo: Sarah Davis • Dumile Feni, *Untitled (Horses and figures)*, 1987, from the exhibition catalog *Dumile Feni Retrospective* by Prince Mbusi Dube published by the Johannesburg Art Gallery, pp. 162–63. Courtesy of the Dumile Feni Estate • Process image of *Hunter* in the studio. Photo: Sarah Davis • Simphiwe Ndzube, *On the Shoulders of Giants*, 2018, mixed media, dimensions variable © Simphiwe Ndzube. Courtesy of Stevenson Amsterdam/Cape Town/Johannesburg. Photo: Karley Sullivan • Untitled sketch. Courtesy of Simphiwe Nduzbe • Process images of *Hunter* in the studio. Photo: Sarah Davis • Simphiwe Ndzube, *Hunter*, 2021, engraved with signature back left leg. Metal, fabric, resin, epoxy, chicken wire, glass eyes, false eyelashes, silicone. 80 × 39 ¾ × 28 ⅜ in © Simphiwe Ndzube, courtesy of Sadie Coles HQ, London. Photo: Robert Glowacki

29. DEAN BAQUET & TOM BODKIN • Dean Baquet Stamp Photo: Monica Schipper / Getty Images Entertainment via Getty Images • Tom Bodkin Stamp Photo: AP Images / Elaine Thompson • *The New York Times*, A1, May 24, 2020. From *The New York Times*. © 2020 The New York Times Company. All rights reserved. Used under license • *The New York Times*, A1, April 8, 2020. From *The New York Times*. © 2020 The New York Times Company. All rights reserved. Used under license • Tom Bodkin, "Covid Deaths" sketch 04/08/2020. Courtesy Tom Bodkin • *The New York Times*, A1, April 16, 2020. From *The New York Times*. © 2020 The New York Times Company. All rights reserved. Used under license • *The New York Times*, A1, May 9, 2020. From *The New York Times*. © 2020 The New York Times Company. All rights reserved. Used under license • Tom Bodkin–Dean Baquet memo, and 7/31/2020 A1 sketch: A) the text between Tom and Dean, B) the sketch of the 7/31/2020 A1 page. Courtesy Tom Bodkin • *The New York Times*, A1, July 31, 2020. From *The New York Times*. © 2020 The New York Times Company. All rights reserved. Used under license • *The New York Times*, A1, January 1, 2000. From *The New York Times*. © 2000 The New York Times Company. All rights reserved. Used under license

30. MAX PORTER • Stamp Photo: Courtesy of Max Porter. Photo: Francesca Jones • All materials and images courtesy of Max Porter

31. ELIZABETH DILLER • Blur Building, Concept Renderings, Courtesy of Diller Scofidio + Renfro • Stamp Photo: Geordie Wood • Blur Building, Napkin Sketch, Courtesy of Diller Scofidio + Renfro • Blur Building, Concept Sketch, Courtesy of Diller Scofidio + Renfro • Blur Building, Photo: Diller Scofidio + Renfro • Braincoat, Questionnaire, Courtesy of Diller Scofidio + Renfro • Braincoat, Rendering, Courtesy of Diller Scofidio + Renfro • Blur Building, Chocolate, Courtesy of Diller Scofidio + Renfro

32. IAN ADELMAN, CALVIN SEIBERT • Ian Adelman Stamp Photo: Courtesy of Ian Adelman • Calvin Seibert Stamp Photo: Courtesy of Calvin Seibert • Tulum, Mexico, December 30, 2016. Courtesy of Ian Adelman • Water Mill, New York, August 30, 2020. Courtesy of Ian Adelman • Water Mill, New York, September 11, 2020. Courtesy of Ian Adelman • Water Mill, New York, September 1, 2020. Courtesy of Ian Adelman • Brighton Beach, New York, September 20, 2020. Courtesy of Ian Adelman • Rockaway Beach, New York, June 21, 2017. Courtesy of Calvin Seibert • Rockaway Beach, New York, August 17, 2016. Courtesy of Calvin Seibert • Aulani Resort, Oahu, Hawaii, February 3, 2014. Courtesy of Calvin Seibert • Water Mill, New York, September 3, 2020. Courtesy of Ian Adelman • A sandcastle in eight stages, Todos Santos, Mexico, January 1, 2022. Courtesy of Ian Adelman

33. TYLER HOBBS • Stamp Portrait: Courtesy of Tyler Hobbs • *Untitled (pregnant woman)*, 2013, charcoal on paper, 17 × 14 in © Tyler Hobbs, all rights reserved • *Untitled and Unfinished (transitional drawing)*, 2013 or 2014, pen and ink on paper, 17 × 14 in © Tyler Hobbs, all rights reserved • *Untitled (Code Painting)*, 2013. © Tyler Hobbs, all rights reserved • *Finger Bib*, 2014, generative design, 1000 × 1875 px. © Tyler Hobbs, all rights reserved • *Ectogenesis 0.175*, 2019, generative design, series of unique digital prints, 10 iterations, 20 × 30 in © Tyler Hobbs, all rights reserved • *Fidenza*, first ever flow field output, 2016. © Tyler Hobbs, all rights reserved • *Fidenza*, early flow fields, raw, 2016 © Tyler Hobbs, all rights reserved • *Fidenza* sketchbook © Tyler Hobbs, all rights reserved • Early *Fidenza* flow fields, warming chord, 2016. © Tyler Hobbs, all rights reserved • *Fidenza* early sketch, 2020. © Tyler Hobbs, all rights reserved • *Fidenza* early sketch, 2020. © Tyler Hobbs, all rights reserved • *Anetta Mural*, 2020. © Tyler Hobbs, all rights reserved • *Fidenza #982*. © Tyler Hobbs, all rights reserved • *Fidenza # 410*. ©Tyler Hobbs, all rights reserved • *Fidenza #313*. © Tyler Hobbs, all rights reserved

34. MARC JACOBS • Photo: Designer Marc Jacobs in sample closet at Perry Ellis for Fall 1991 Ready To Wear Fit Session. Photo: David Turner / WWD / Penske Media via Getty Images • Stamp Photo: Everett Collection Inc / Alamy Stock Photo • Images and sketches courtesy Marc Jacobs. Photos: Matthew Sandager • Borna Sammak, *Not Yet Titled (Couch)*, 2018, cotton, wood, foam. 100h × 163w × 166d in 254h × 414.02w × 421.64d cm. Photo: Charles Benton. Courtesy of the artist, JTT, New York, and Sadie Coles HQ, London • Halston draping fabric on Carol Channing. Photo: Bettman / Contributor via Getty Images • Final Looks, Marc Jacobs Fall 2021 © Dan & Corina Lecca

35. GRADY WEST • Stamp Photo: Courtesy of Dina Martina • Photo: © David Belisle • Notebooks courtesy Dina Martina

36. WILL SHORTZ • Stamp Photo: Larry Busacca / Wireimage via Getty Images • All materials and images courtesy of Will Shortz

37. SHEILA HETI • Stamp Photo: TT News Agency / Alamy Stock Photo • All materials © Sheila Heti. Photos: Matthew Sandager

38. GERALD LOVELL • Photo: Jacob Consenstein • Stamp Photo: Courtesy of Gerald Lovell • Gerald Lovell, In Progress in Studio, 2021. Courtesy of Gerald Lovell and P·P·O·W, New York • Gerald Lovell, Instagram Post of *The Woman with The Eyes*, 2017, oil on wood panel, 36 × 49 in. Courtesy of Gerald Lovell and P·P·O·W, New York • Gerald Lovell, *Grace*, 2021. For Orange Barrel Media, at Friendship Tower, produced by Living Walls, The City Speaks Inc. Courtesy of Gerald Lovell and P·P·O·W, New York. Photo: William Feagins, Jr. © 2021, W. Feagins, Jr. • Gerald Lovell, In Progress in Studio, 2021. Courtesy of Gerald Lovell and P·P·O·W, New York • Gerald Lovell, *Chameleon*, 2021, oil on panel, 60 × 60 in. Courtesy of Gerald Lovell and P·P·O·W, New York • Gerald Lovell, Adam Moss portrait in progress in studio, 2021. Courtesy of Gerald Lovell and P·P·O·W, New York

39. JODY WILLIAMS & RITA SODI • Stamp Photo: Paul Quitoriano • Notebooks and sketches courtesy Jody Williams and Rita Sodi • Svizzerina, Melissa Hom Photography

40. TAYLOR MAC & MACHINE DAZZLE • Taylor Mac Stamp Photo: Jesse Dittmar / Redux • Machine Dazzle Stamp Photo: Patrick McMullan via Getty Images • Taylor Mac in performance, St. Ann's Warehouse (24-Hour Marathon), NY, 2016. Photo: © Teddy Wolff • Taylor Mac in performance, Joe's Pub at the Public, NY, July 23, 2012. Photo: © Kevin Yatarola • Taylor Mac in performance, St. Ann's Warehouse (24-Hour Marathon), NY, 2016. Photo: © Teddy Wolff • Taylor Mac in performance, Berliner Festpiele, Berlin, Germany, 2019. Photo: © Eike Walkenhorst • Audience during performance, Berliner Festpiele, Berlin, Germany, 2019. Photo: © Eike Walkenhorst

41. DAVID SIMON • Stamp Photo: Noam Galai / Getty Images Entertainment via Getty Images • David Simon on the set of *The Wire*. Photo: David Lee / HBO • All materials courtesy of David Simon

42. GEORGE SAUNDERS • Stamp Photo: Winni Wintermeyer / Redux • All materials courtesy of George Saunders. Photos: Matthew Sandager

43. SUZAN-LORI PARKS • Stamp Photo: Linda Nylind / eyevine / Redux • All materials courtesy Suzan-Lori Parks • Corey Hawkins, Suzan-Lori Parks, Kenny Leon, and Yahya Abdul-Mateen II attend curtain call during the opening night of *Topdog/Underdog* on Broadway for curtain call at Golden Theatre on October 20, 2022, in New York City. Photo: Arturo Holmes / Getty Images Entertainment via Getty Images

AFTERWORD • Adam Moss, painting in process and final painting © Adam Moss

APPENDIX • James Joyce, original manuscripts for *Ulysses*. Courtesy of the National Library of Ireland • Paul Klee, *Dame mit Sonnenschirm (Lady with Parasol)*, 1883–85, paper on cardboard, 4.5 × 3.5 in, Zentrum Paul Klee, Bern. Image credits: Zentrum Paul Klee, Bern • Paul Klee, *mit Sonnenschirm (with Parasol)*, 1939, 868 (VV 8). Wasserfarbe und Bleistift auf schwarzer Grundierung auf Papier, aufgezogen auf zweitem Papier, 36.6 × 19.5 cm. Kunstmuseum Basel, Kupferstichkabinett, Legat Richard Doetsch-Benziger. Photo Credit: Martin P. Bühler © Bilddaten gemeinfrei - Kunstmuseum Basel • Pablo Picasso, *Le Petit Picador Jaune*, 1889, oil on wood, 9.45 × 7.48 in, 24×19 cm, Collection Claude Picasso, Paris © Pablo Picasso • Pablo Picasso, *Bullfight*, 1934, oil on canvas. 54 × 73 cm. Image Credit: Museo Nacional Thyssen-Bornemisza / Scala / Art Resource, NY © 2023 Estate of Pablo Picasso / Artists Rights Society (ARS), New York • Cecily Brown, *Jungle*, 1977, marker on paper, 8 × 12.5 in © Cecily Brown, Courtesy of Paula Cooper Gallery, New York • Cecily Brown, *Untitled*, 2013, oil on linen, 77 × 97 in © Cecily Brown. Courtesy of Paula Cooper Gallery, New York • Leonardo da Vinci, *Sketches for the Virgin and Child with St Anne and the infant Saint John the Baptist, and some studies of machinery*, circa 1505–1508. Pen and ink and wash over black chalk heightened with white on paper, indented for transfer. 26.5 × 19.9 cm. The British Museum, London © The Trustees of the British Museum • Leonardo da Vinci (1452–1519), *The Virgin and Child with Saint Anne and the Infant Saint John the Baptist (The Burlington House Cartoon)*, about 1499–1500. Purchased with a special grant and contributions from the Art Fund, The Pilgrim Trust, and through a public appeal organized by the Art Fund, 1962 © The National Gallery, London • Leonardo da Vinci, *The Virgin, the Child Jesus and Saint Anne,* known as *Saint Anne,* 1503–1519, oil on wood (poplar), 1.68 × 1.13 m, Paris, Louvre • Handwritten first draft script for *Wizard of Oz* movie, Noel Langley. Photo Credit: Heritage Auctions, HA.com • Fyodor Dostoevsky's doodles on the pages of *Crime and Punishment* notebooks. Photo: Alexeyev Flippov/Alamy Stock Photo • Sylvia Plath, Holograph outline of *The Bell Jar* chapters, approximately spring 1961 © Estate of Sylvia Plath. Courtesy of Faber and Faber Ltd. • Emily Dickinson Collection, Manuscript #316, Archives and Special Collections, Amherst College • Emily Dickinson Collection, Manuscript #514, Archives and Special Collections, Amherst College • Walt Whitman's First Manuscript Drafts of "Song of Myself," *Leaves of Grass*, 1855. Harry Ransom Center, The University of Texas at Austin • Edward Hopper, Artist's ledger - Book II, page 79, 1907–1962. Ledger book with pen and ink and graphite pencil on paper. Overall (Closed): 11 13/16 × 7 1/2 × 1/2 in (30 × 19.1 × 1.3 cm). Overall (Open): 11 13/16 × 14 7/8 × 1/2 in (30 × 37.8 × 1.3 cm). Gift of Lloyd Goodrich. Inv.: 96.209. Image: Whitney Museum of American Art / Licensed by Scala / Art Resource, NY © 2023 Heirs of Josephine N. Hopper / Licensed by Artists Rights Society (ARS), NY • Edward Hopper, *Office at Night*, 1940, oil on canvas, 22 3/16 × 25 1/8 in, unframed; 30 5/16 × 33 15/16 × 2 3/4 in, framed. Gift of the T. B. Walker Foundation, Gilbert M. Walker Fund, 1948 Collection Walker Art Center, Minneapolis © 2023 Heirs of Josephine N. Hopper / Licensed by Artists Rights Society (ARS), NY

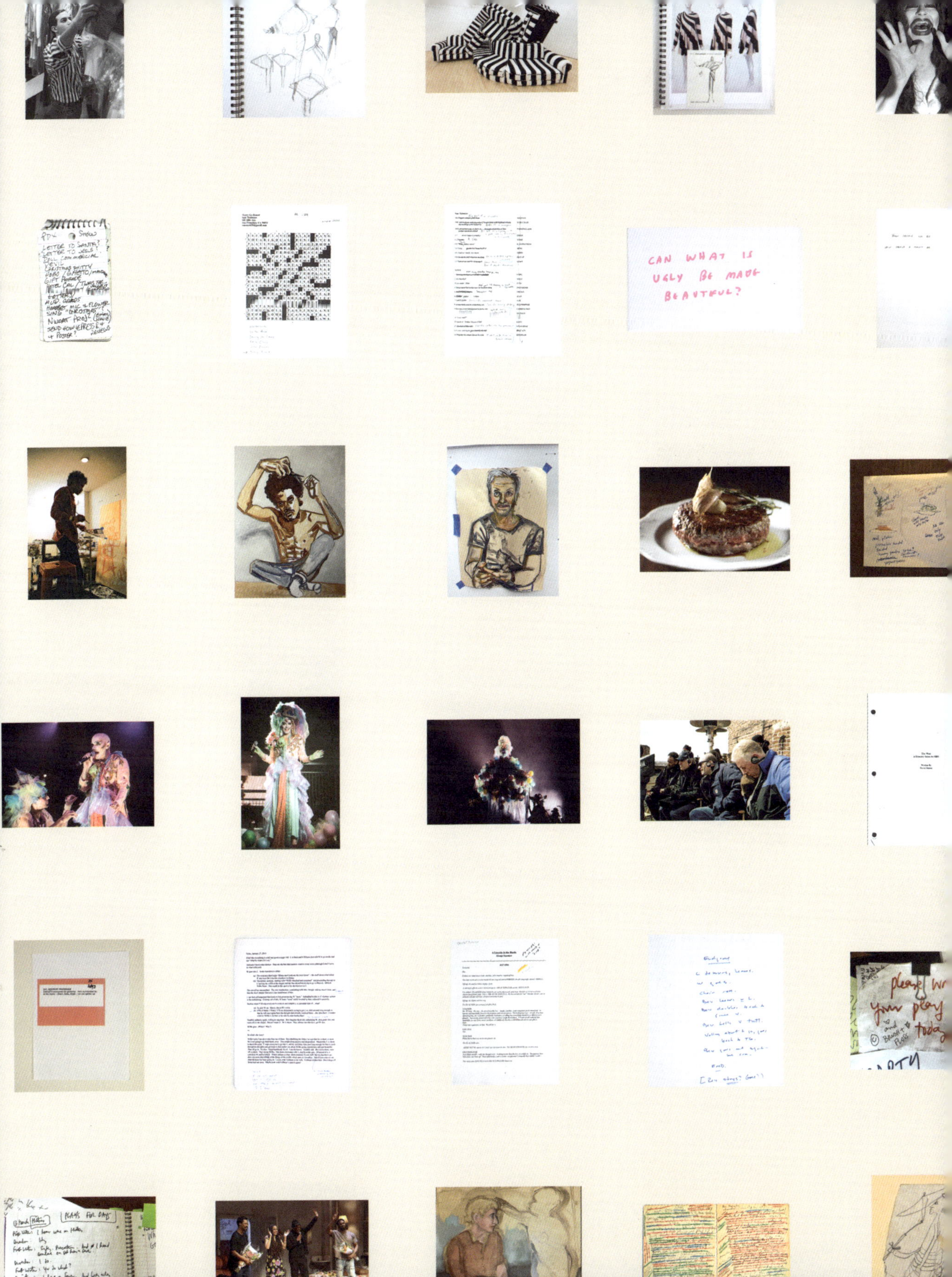
CAN WHAT IS
UGLY BE MADE
BEAUTIFUL?

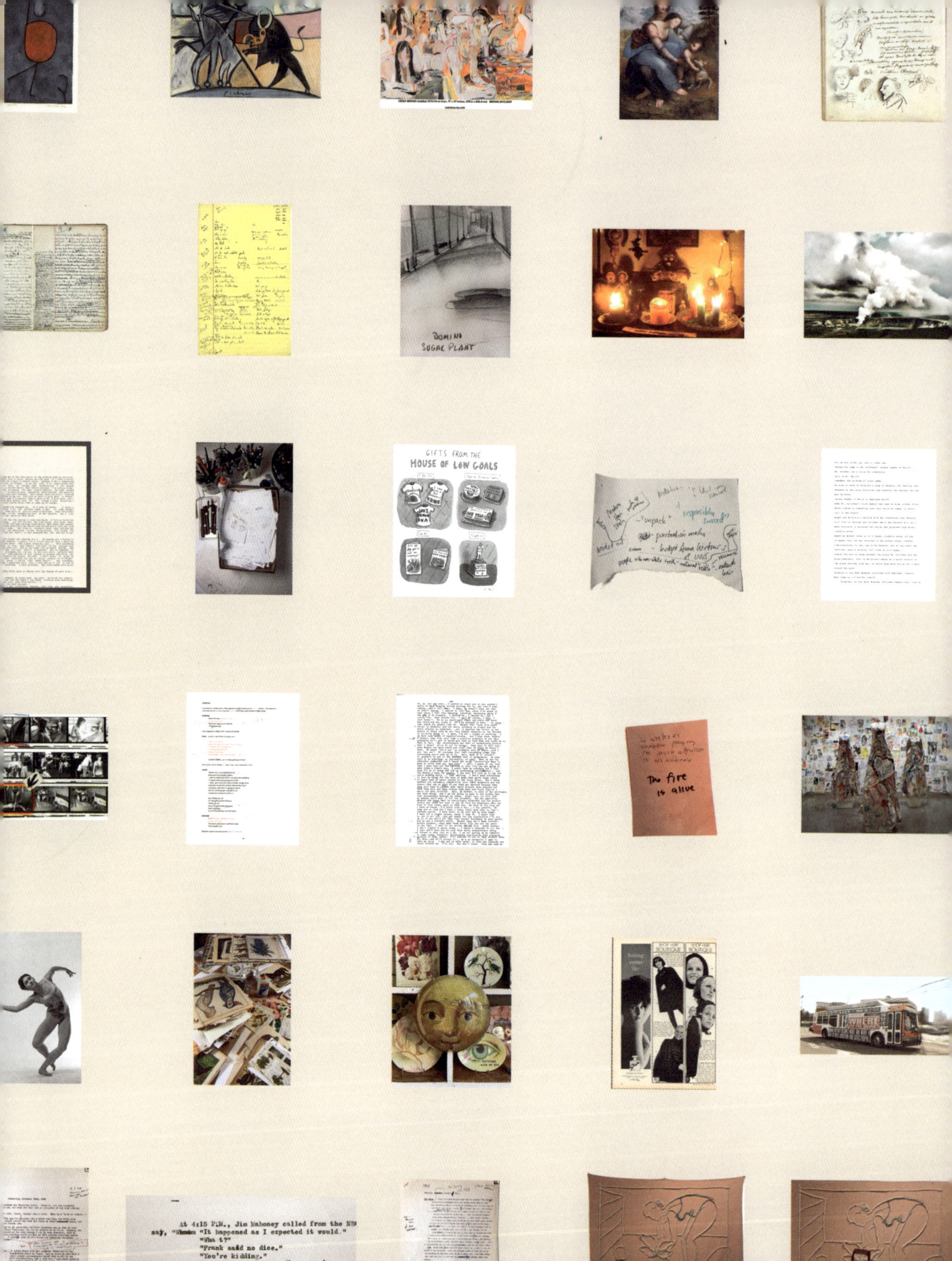

DOMINO
SUGAR PLANT
GIFTS FROM THE
HOUSE OF LOW GOALS
The fire
is alive
At 4:15 P.M., Jim Mahoney called from the
"It happened as I expected it would."
"Frank said no dice."
"You're kidding."
"No," Mahoney said.
live up to the deal."